THE POEMS

of

JOHN MILTON

Edited with Introduction and Notes

by

JAMES HOLLY HANFORD

SECOND EDITION

THE RONALD PRESS COMPANY , NEW YORK

11

Library of Congress Catalog Card Number: 53-5718

PRINTED IN THE UNITED STATES OF AMERICA

PREFACE

This volume contains all of Milton's original English verse, together with translations of representative Latin and Italian poems that are of biographical or literary interest. As in the previous edition, a chronological arrangement is followed in order to facilitate the study of Milton's poetical development. The translations used are those of William Cowper, chosen in preference to any other version because of their literary merit and their substantial fidelity to Milton.

In preparing this new edition, recent scholarship and continued occupation with the teaching of Milton, as well as the suggestions of other teachers, have led me to make certain changes. The life of Milton, treated in a separate introductory essay, has been expanded and rewritten. Explanatory and critical notes for the poems, including all of *Paradise Lost*, have been supplied throughout, and the section on Milton's development as a poet has been reorganized as a series of headnotes to the individual poems. In addition, each major phase of Milton's work has an explanatory introduction. And, of course, there is a new and fuller bibliography, and a further supplement of study questions.

I adhere in this edition to the textual principles first adopted many years ago. These principles have proved their validity. To modernize Milton's seventeenth-century spelling is to remove an obstacle to the understanding and enjoyment of his work. In spite of the interest of Milton's individual devices (e.g. the famous "mee"—"me" and "their"—"thir" in accented and unaccented positions in the verse, deliberately adopted but never carried through consistently), the gain in modernization is greater than the loss. A literal text has, for the reader who is more accustomed to twentieth- than to seventeenth-century printing, an antiquarian atmosphere which, since it was not intended by Milton or felt by his contemporaries, must be accounted misleading. Milton's contractions and elisions were probably largely a matter of theory. Robert Bridges, who worked out Milton's self-imposed rules and set great store by them, himself admits that the poet scanned the verses one way and read them another. It is unlikely that he pronounced "above th' Aonian Mount" as five syllables rather than seven, and whether we read his lines from a literal or a modified text, we should not struggle to frame our tongues to such eccentricity. It is not as if there were no natural compromise between entirely suppressing a syllable and giving it the weight it would have if sounded alone. The modern reader of Milton's lines should be left at liberty to engineer their rhythms according to his taste. If he is one of those who "scan with Midas ears," no typographical device will save him. I have therefore gone even further than W. A. Wright, whose standard text is the basis of my modernization, in spelling out in full almost all of Milton's contractions.

In the matter of punctuation also I have followed my original practice of keeping the old pointing wherever it could by any stretch of the imagination be justified as contributing to the rhythm or the meaning but feeling free to alter it when it seemed senseless or misleading, or merely archaic. Seventeenth-century sentence structure does not lend itself easily to logical punctuation, and the strict application of conventional rules invites the student to a staccato and prosaic reading of the verse. There are, moreover, many subtleties in the punctuation of the old texts which, even when they challenge attention as irregular, are too valuable to discard. In the following passage, for example, the insertion of commas in their orthodox places (i.e., after "Farewell," "fields," "hail," "thou," "Hell") badly breaks the phrasal units, which are clearly indicated in the original:

> Farewell happy fields
> Where joy forever dwells: Hail Horrors, hail
> Infernal world, and thou profoundest Hell
> Receive thy new possessor.

An even more striking instance of injurious change in the modernized texts is to be found in the lines,

> Natheless he so endured, till on the beach
> Of that inflamed sea, he stood and called
> His legions.

Wright puts the second comma in its grammatical position after "stood," but the pause belongs where it is, to prepare for the unified poetic phrase and image which follow. There are many instances of this sort of ambiguity of grammatical reference, which is preserved by a comma, destroyed by a semi-

colon or a period. See for another outstanding example the
first lines of the sonnet "Avenge, O Lord." These facts argue
for a respectful treatment of the original pointing. They do
not argue for its exact reproduction. Milton is doubtless responsible for some of it, but a great deal must have been the
work of others. There are many errors and eccentricities
which can only disturb the reader. The use of capitals by
Milton's printers is almost entirely eclectic, and it is in this
edition largely disregarded. There remains, however, a necessity of preserving the dignity of certain classes of words. The
editor quarrels with nobody's decision in this matter and prefers his own without defense.

The commentary is, of course, selective. There is no such
thing as a completely annotated Milton text and could not be.
On the other hand the simplest glossing of words and allusions
is bound to contain much that is unnecessary for any individual reader. Webster's dictionary and the *Encyclopaedia
Britannica* will adequately explain by far the largest number
of the difficulties ordinarily met with. Beyond that there are
the various special dictionaries, especially Lockwood's *Lexicon
of Milton's English Poetical Works* (The Macmillan Company), Osgood's *The Classical Mythology of Milton's Poems*
(Oxford University Press), and Gilbert's *A Geographical
Dictionary of Milton* (Yale University Press). Among the
most scholarly editions with notes are those of Verity (Cambridge University Press) and Hughes (Odyssey Press). A
mighty variorum edition is in preparation by members of the
Modern Language Association. It will be the first since that
of Todd in 1801. For textual purposes there is an elaborate
reproduction of the originals issued by the University of
Illinois under the editorship of Harris Fletcher. But the indis-
pensable aids to Miltonic study remain what they have always
been: a well-indexed English Bible, a Homer, a Virgil, a
Spenser, and a Shakespeare. The scriptural and other references in the notes will be valuable in proportion to the diligence with which they are employed. For the "good" student
of Milton may be defined as the one who reads, or at least
desires to read, the Bible, the ancients, and the greater mod-
erns as he read them.

JAMES HOLLY HANFORD

Princeton, N. J.
January, 1953

CONTENTS

THE POEMS OF THE SECOND PERIOD
(1642-1658)

PARADISE LOST

PARADISE REGAINED

SAMSON AGONISTES

APPENDIX

THE LIFE OF MILTON

THE LIFE OF MILTON

John Milton, eldest son of John Milton, a scrivener or law writer, was born in London on December 9, 1608. The elder Milton, disinherited by his father for transferring his allegiance from the Catholic to the Protestant church, had been an uncommonly successful business man and had made a considerable fortune. His incidental occupation was money lending, a practice not in those days held in high esteem. The mother is described by Milton himself as noted in the neighborhood for piety and good works. There were two other children, an elder sister, Anne, and a younger brother, Christopher. The family probably shared the Puritan sympathies of the London middle class, but this did not exclude them from the cultural refinements of the age. Shakespeare was still living when Milton was a boy. The city was the scene of civic ceremonial and royal splendors. Its buildings and monuments were themselves a book of history. Celebrated figures were familiar in the streets. Milton's father had perhaps been a professional musician and, as such, had associated with both artists and patrons. The society which Milton enjoyed from childhood must have included persons whose interests were not confined to practical affairs or to the immediate religious and political issues which were beginning to agitate the public mind. Comparative wealth had raised the family status and the elder Milton evidently sought a better education and a higher station for his children than his own. The younger son went to the Inns of Court and became a barrister and judge. Milton later thanked his father for not forcing him into this or any other gainful occupation. The intention was that he should enter the church.

Milton's intellectual precocity was early recognized and carefully cherished. Educational opportunity was provided for him, both by private tutors at home, and at St. Paul's School, which he entered in 1620 or earlier. He was, according to Aubrey, "a poet at the age of 10," and Milton himself refers

3

to the notice which his early writings attracted from his elders: "After I had for my first years, by the ceaseless diligence and care of my father (whom God recompense!), been exercised to the tongues and some sciences, as my age would suffer, by sundry masters and teachers, both at home and at the school, it was found that whether aught was imposed me by those that had the overlooking, or betaken to of my own choice in English, or other tongue, prosing or versing, but chiefly this latter, the style, by certain vital signs it had, was likely to live."

The young Milton throve at St. Paul's and always looked back to his years there with pleasure. He was much attached to one of the tutors, Alexander Gill, son of the distinguished headmaster of the school. The severe humanistic curriculum satisfied his instinct for genuine literary and scholarly cultivation. His personal environment was made happy by the presence in a more advanced class of Charles Diodati, son of a distinguished physician of Italian origin, with whom he formed a lasting friendship.

MILTON AT CAMBRIDGE

His life at Cambridge, whither he went as a Lesser Pensioner in 1625, was more uneven. The outstanding incident there was a quarrel with his first tutor, William Chappel, toward the end of his second year of residence. Legend says that Milton was whipped. He was certainly rusticated. The cause of the difficulty is unknown, but it is easy to believe that Milton, used as he was to adult praises, would have proved unable to endure discipline or correction from a person of narrow mould and insufficient sympathy.

On his return to Cambridge Milton was placed under another tutor, Mr. Tovey, and we hear no more of conflict with authority. He distinguished himself for his skill in composing the public orations and debates which constituted the goal of academic training, and he spoke with pride in later years of the honors which had been shown him by the University. That he had no enthusiasm for Cambridge is due in part to a failure to accept the ordinary student for what he was, in part to a disrelish of the dominant ideas and methods of the institution. The academic orations already alluded to contain abundant evidence of his point of view. As a humanist, he felt that the logic-chopping dissertations were a "feast of sow-thistles and brambles"; as a Platonist, he rebelled against the dominance of Aristotle; as a Baconian, he deplored the intellectual adherence of the University to the idea that the world was sinking further and further into stagnation and senility. His feeling about the main body of the students is vigorously expressed in a letter written in his third year to Alexander Gill: "Among us, as far as I know, there are only two or three, who without any acquaintance with criticism or philosophy do not instantly engage with raw and untutored judgments in the study of theology." It comes out even more significantly in the sixth Latin *Prolusion*, which belongs to about the same time. Here Milton asks in a half jesting, half angry way why they persist in calling him "The Lady." "Is it," he says, "because I have never been able to quaff huge tankards lustily . . . or, in short, because I have never proved my manhood in the same way as these debauched black-guards?" More and more his own ideas of behavior took an ascetic turn. The record of his emotional development, clearly written in the Latin poems, is also reviewed in a highly introspective way in a passage written after his Italian journey in reply to certain scandalous charges which had been brought against him by Bishop Hall. He notes as an important influence in his development the reading of fable and romance "from whence I learned what a noble virtue chastity must be, to the defense of which so many worthies, by such a dear adventure of themselves, had sworn," and of Plato, who taught him that "the first and chiefest office of love ends in the soul, producing those two happy twins of her divine generation, knowledge and virtue." Poetry in English rather than in Latin became his major literary interest after about 1628. The small group of lyrics written in his last years at the University includes the memorable ode, "On the Morning of Christ's Nativity."

LIFE AT HORTON

Milton took his A.B. degree March 26, 1629, his A.M. July 3, 1632. He then went to live with his parents on their country estate at Horton, whither his father had retired a short time before. His occupation in the five years of his residence there is thus described in an autobiographical statement in the *Second Defense of the English People*: "On my father's estate, where he had determined to pass the remainder of his days, I enjoyed an interval of uninterrupted leisure, which I entirely devoted to the perusal of Greek and Latin authors; though I occasionally visited the metropolis, either for the sake of purchasing books, or of learning something new in mathematics or in music, in which I at that time found a source of pleasure and amusement."

Milton thought of his Horton years as a time of preparation for some great enterprise. A prose letter written early in the period in response to the questionings of a friend gives evidence of much conscientious soul-searching. He convinces himself that it is not indolence or the desire to escape responsibility which has led him to postpone active life, but rather a sense of immaturity and unfitness. The "perusal of Greek and Latin authors" implied a steady course of study, chiefly in the history of the later Roman and the Greek Empires and in the Church Fathers. Just when Milton abandoned his intention of entering the church is not certain. It was evidently against his inclination as well as his convictions to be a minister under the tyranny of Archbishop Laud. The character of his studies and of the entries which he made at this time in his Commonplace Book shows clearly enough that his interests were political and ecclesiastical, as well as literary. He anticipated the great struggle in which his countrymen were to be engaged and was preparing himself to think soundly on public affairs, if not actually to play a part in them. There is, however, abundant evidence that he continued to enjoy and cultivate his aesthetic tastes even more freely than hitherto and that the ambition to be a poet remained dominant in his thought. "L'Allegro" and "Il Penseroso" are a complete record of his delights in nature, art, and music. The writing of *Arcades* and *Comus* suggests participation in the social life of the country gentry. "Lycidas" is an eloquent testimony to his capacity for surrender to the poetic mood.

The two sides of Milton's nature, the moral and the aesthetic, seem in the Horton period to be in balance. The charm and urbanity of his temper come out in the Latin epistle to his father (see below). There is more maturity here than in the earlier prose letter to a friend, but it was no doubt desirable for Milton to break away from the protection of his home environment. The death of his mother and the domiciling at Horton of Christopher and his new wife may have made home seem less attractive; it was shortly after these events that he undertook his Continental journey, leaving England in the spring of 1638.

THE GRAND TOUR

Milton's year abroad was in many ways the best and happiest of his life. He went with the usual cultural objectives of Renaissance travel, but he found something of far greater value to him, understanding and appreciation from foreigners of intellect and taste. The story of his experience may be given in his own language.

"I then became anxious to visit foreign parts, and particularly Italy. My father gave me his permission, and I left home with one servant. On my departure, the celebrated Henry Wotton, who had long been King James's ambassador at Venice, gave me a signal proof of his regard in an elegant letter which he wrote, breathing not only the warmest friendship, but containing some maxims of conduct which I found very useful in my travels. The noble Thomas Scudamore, King Charles's ambassador, to whom I carried letters of recommendation, received me most courteously at Paris. His lordship gave me a card of introduction to the learned Hugo Grotius, at that time ambassador from the Queen of Sweden to the French court, whose acquaintance I anxiously desired and to whose house I was accompanied by some of his lordship's friends. A few days later, when I set out for Italy, he gave me letters to the English merchants on my route, that they might show me any civilities in their power. Taking ship at Nice I arrived at Genoa and afterwards visited Leghorn, Pisa, and Florence. In the latter city, which I have always more particularly esteemed for the elegance of its dialect, its genius, and its taste, I stopped about two months; when I contracted an intimacy with many persons of rank and learning, and was a constant attendant at their literary parties, a practice which prevails there and tends so much to the diffusion of knowledge and the preservation of friendship. No time will ever abolish the agreeable recollections which I cherish of Jacob Gaddi, Carolo Dati, Frescobaldo, Cultellero, Bonomatthai, Clementillo, Francisco, and many others. From Florence I went to Siena, thence to Rome, where, after I had spent about two months viewing the antiquities of that renowned city, where I experienced the most friendly attentions from Lucas Holsten and other learned and ingenious men, I continued my route to Naples. There I was introduced by a certain recluse, with whom I had travelled from Rome, to John Baptista Manso, marquis of Villa, a nobleman of distinguished rank and authority, to whom Torquato Tasso, the illustrious poet, inscribed his book on friendship. During my stay he gave me singular proofs of his regard: he himself conducted me round the city and to the palace of the viceroy, and more than once paid me a visit at my lodgings. On my departure he gravely apologized for not having shown me more civility, which he said he had been restrained from doing because I had spoken with so little reserve on matters of religion. When I was preparing to pass over into Sicily and Greece, the melancholy intelligence which I received of the civil commotions in England made me alter my purpose; for I thought it base to be travelling for amusement abroad while my fellow-citizens were fighting for liberty at home. While I was on my way back to Rome, some merchants informed me that the English Jesuits had formed a plot against me if I returned to Rome, because I had spoken too freely on religion; for it was a rule which I laid down to myself in those places, never to be the first to begin any conversation on religion, but if any questions were put to me concerning my faith, to declare it without any reserve or fear. I nevertheless returned to Rome. I took no steps to conceal either my person or my character, and for about the space of two months I again openly defended, as I had done before, the reformed religion in the very metropolis of popery. By the favour of God I got safe back to Florence, where I was received with as much affection as if I had returned to my native country. There I stopped as many months as I had done before, except that I made an excursion for a few days to Lucca; and, crossing the Apennines, passed through Bologna and Ferrara to Venice. After I had spent a month in surveying the curiosities of this city and had put on board a ship the books which I had collected in Italy, I proceeded through Verona and Milan, and along the Leman lake to Geneva. The mention of this city brings to my recollection the slandering More, and makes me again call the Deity to witness, that in all those places in which vice meets with so little discouragement and is practised with so little shame, I never once deviated from the paths of integrity and virtue, and perpetually reflected that, though my conduct might escape the notice of men, it could

not elude the inspection of God. At Geneva I held daily con-
ferences with John Diodati, the learned professor of Theology.
Then pursuing my former route through France, I returned
to my native country, after an absence of one year and about
three months, at the time when Charles, having broken the
peace, was renewing what is called the Episcopal war with the
Scots, in which the royalists being routed in the first encounter,
and the English being universally and justly disaffected, the
necessity of his affairs at last obliged him to convene a Parliament."

The only important omissions in this statement are the visit
to Galileo, referred to in *Areopagitica*, and the fact that Milton
not only attended the meetings of the Florentine academies
but read Latin poems before them. The chronology of the
journey is fairly well established. Milton reached Florence
probably in August, 1638, spent October and November in
Rome, visited Naples, and was back at Florence before March,
1639. He probably spent a part of the following April and
May in Venice; he was in Geneva by July 10, 1639, and back
in England before the end of the month. The leisureliness of
his return seems inconsistent with his statement that he was
drawn back by the news of the civil commotions in England
but it is not really so. He means simply that he was interested
and concerned and preferred to be moving toward home rather
than away from it.

Pedagogue and Pamphleteer

By the time Milton reached Geneva he must have received
news of the death of his friend Diodati, but he did not fully
realize the significance of this event until he was back among
his old associations. His first task in England was the writing
of the *Epitaphium Damonis* in commemoration of his loss.
The world was evidently much changed for him, both emotionally and in outward circumstance. Instead of returning to
Horton he established himself independently in lodgings in
St. Bride's Churchyard, took his two nephews, Edward and
John Phillips, as pupils, and began at once to play the part in
life for which his long years of study and meditation had prepared him.

Among his earliest occupations was to set down in the manuscript book which he had hitherto reserved for the various

drafts of his minor poems a long list of subjects for dramas drawn from Scripture and from the chronicle histories of his native land. The plans for several of the Biblical subjects are developed into outlines, the various drafts of the plan for a drama on the fall of man being the most elaborate. That he was at last ready to venture on a serious literary work and hesitated only regarding the theme and mode of treatment is proved by a passage in *The Reason of Church Government* (1641). A year later, if Phillips is to be trusted, he actually began the composition of a dramatic *Paradise Lost*.

Meanwhile, however, events in public life had so shaped themselves as to invite him to employ his pen in political controversy. Between the summer of 1641 and the following spring he composed in quick succession five pamphlets on the burning issue of the hour, assailing the Episcopal system and advocating the Presbyterian form of church government. The first work, *Of Reformation Touching Church Discipline in England*, is a carefully reasoned historical discussion, showing close study of the progress of the English church from the time of Henry VIII. Writing later of the motives which impelled him to enter the conflict, Milton says that the general attack on the Episcopal system awakened all his attention and zeal. "I saw that a way was opening for the establishment of real liberty, that a foundation was laying for the deliverance of man from the yoke of slavery and superstition, . . . and as I had from my youth studied the distinctions between religious and civil rights, I perceived that if ever I wished to be of use, I ought at least not to be wanting to my country, to the Church, and to so many of my fellow Christians, in a crisis of so much danger; I therefore determined to relinquish the other pursuits in which I was engaged and to transfer the whole force of my talents and my industry to this one important object." The second pamphlet, *Of Prelatical Episcopacy*, which followed almost immediately, is specifically directed against a tract of James Ussher, Bishop of Armagh; the third, *Animadversions Upon the Remonstrants' Defence against Smectymnuus*, is a reply to Bishop Hall. The latter, writing like Ussher against the group of Puritan ministers represented by the composite pseudonym Smectymnuus, was, as Milton thought, getting rather the best of it. The cause invited, therefore, not only his patriotic but his chivalrous emotions, the fact that his old tutor, Young, was one of the Smectymnuuans doubtless adding a personal stimulus to his energy. In the fourth tract, *The Reason of Church Government*, where Milton's name appears for the first time on the title page, the subject is treated with greater breadth and eloquence. It is the longest of the ecclesiastical pamphlets and by its defense of freedom of worship points forward to *Areopagitica* and Milton's later individualism. Last of the series is the *Apology against a Pamphlet called "A Modest Confutation" of the Animadversions of the Remonstrant against Smectymnuus*. Here Milton is at last thoroughly aroused. Bishop Hall and his son have in their latest pamphlet launched scurrilous charges against him personally. He answers them savagely, returning abuse for abuse. The net result of the ecclesiastical controversy has been, so far as Milton is concerned, to change him temporarily from a man of letters to a partisan journalist. He will return to poetry only when he can no longer fight for causes, and the causes for which he fights will be largely determined by his personal experiences and desires.

FIRST MARRIAGE

In the spring of 1642 [1] Milton married Mary Powell, daughter of an Oxfordshire squire, who had chosen the king's side in the civil conflict. The story, as given by Edward Phillips, of Milton's sudden introduction of a seventeen-year-old bride into the studious atmosphere of his London school, of her dislike of the philosophical life and her early departure, of the poet's attempts to draw her back, and of his rising anger at her desertion, is one of the classic episodes of literary biography. It is not difficult to speculate as to the causes of the trouble. Milton idealized marriage and apparently expected too much of it. He already had a strong sense of his mission in life and he was absorbed in personal aspiration and in the immediacy of the public cause. It would have taken a mature and tactful woman to accommodate herself to his needs. The match had been made without realization of the differences between them in age, temperament, and upbringing. It might nevertheless have succeeded except for the accident of the outbreak of the war. Oxford, which the king had made his headquarters

---

[1] This date may now be regarded as established. See B. A. Wright, "Milton's First Marriage," *Modern Language Review*, XXVI (1931), 383–400.

shortly after Mary's return to her family, suddenly became an armed camp. We may guess that she was swept into the emotion of loyalty which surrounded her and found it easier to stay with her royalist friends than to return to a husband who had openly allied himself with the enemy. Milton was not the man to make allowances for her situation. He became hurt and indignant, and he attributed his unhappiness, first to his wife's individual shortcomings, then to the inferiority of woman generally, finally to the laws which made the marriage union indissoluble. Characteristically he converted his private grievance into a public issue and launched a campaign for free divorce. The writing of four pamphlets on the subject engaged his major energies for nearly two years. The first tract, *The Doctrine and Discipline of Divorce*, was composed hastily and published in the summer of 1643. Milton argues that, as the true bonds of marriage are spiritual rather than physical, incompatibility of temper is a sufficient ground for their dissolution. He takes the man's point of view throughout and it is difficult to avoid reading into his phrases—"mute and spiritless mate," "a living soul bound to a dead corpse"—a characterization of his own situation with Mary Powell.

THE DOCTRINE OF LIBERTY

The publication of this pamphlet brought hostile criticism from several sources and Milton was compelled to take to his defenses. A revised edition in 1644 added new authorities in support of the announced doctrines, and by March, 1645, he had published three further tracts on the subject: *The Judgment of Martin Bucer concerning Divorce*, *Tetrachordon*, and *Colasterion*. These later discussions have no such interest as the first. Milton's heart was no longer in the subject. The fruit of the marriage episode had been to leave him embittered against sex and angered at the Presbyterians, who had ungratefully opposed his great idea, but still hopeful and ardent in the abstract cause of liberty. Even before he published his last divorce tracts Milton had discovered for himself a new and nobler object of devotion. On July 14, 1643, Parliament, turning false to the principles which had made its own victories possible, passed an act restricting the freedom of the Press. Milton's *Areopagitica*, which appeared in November of the next year, besides attacking the specific law as retrogressive and menacing, sets forth in eloquent language the great doctrine of the autonomy of the individual soul. Men cannot be made good by external restraints. A faith which has never been challenged is no faith at all; adult human beings are capable of finding their own way to truth if they are left free to consider and to choose. The variety of contradictory doctrines which have sprung up among the sects is no cause for alarm but an evidence of life, portending nothing less than a reformation of reformation itself. England stands at the threshold of a new age, rejoicing like a strong man to run a race. To starch it into any kind of conformity would be to undo the work of revolution and to bring about a new bondage worse than that from which it has escaped. Milton is deeply distrustful of the Presbyterian party, but he still has faith in his countrymen. The lesson that they really prefer "bondage with ease" to "strenuous liberty" is one which he has still to learn.

With *Areopagitica* Milton for a time rested on his laurels. His conviction that "the laws of sound and virtuous education" were the "true bonds and ligaments of the commonwealth" led him to devote himself with eagerness to the theory and practice of teaching. The immediate result of his thought and experience was the wisely considered tract, *Of Education,* published in 1644. The composition of a *History of Britain* and of a digest of Christian theology occupied much of his attention for the next five years. Both were fundamental contributions to the cause which he had espoused, the one being designed to give a true picture of the evolution of the English state and church, the other to provide all Protestants with a rational body of doctrine based solely on the Bible. He also began in this interval to turn his thoughts again to poetry, though he apparently made no further attempt to undertake the epic. The first edition of his poems was published in 1645. He continued to teach school till 1647, after which he moved to a smaller house.

Meanwhile, in 1645, Mary Powell had returned to his bed and board. The fortunes of her family had suffered by their adherence to the royalist cause and they now stood under need of Milton's protection. The poet's biographer and nephew, Edward Phillips, tells a pretty story of how Milton was surprised into meeting his estranged wife at a friend's house, of how she begged on her knees before him and ultimately won forgiveness. "He might probably at first make some show of aversion and rejection, but partly his own generous nature, more inclinable to reconciliation than to perseverance in anger and revenge, and partly the strong intercession of friends on both sides, soon brought him to an act of oblivion, and a firm league of peace for the future." It is hard to see how much happiness could have resulted from their renewed union, but the birth of children (Anne in 1646, Mary in 1648) must have roused some new interests and hopes. The presence of the elder Powells in the household as refugees after the surrender of Oxford in 1646 may well have been distracting. A letter to Carlo Dati on April 21, 1647, remarks unpleasantly that his domestic establishment stuns him with noise and wastes him with vexation. Life under such conditions was hardly conducive to great achievement, but it was nevertheless more normal for him than solitude.

ENTRY INTO PUBLIC LIFE

In 1649 a new crisis in public affairs invited him again into the field of controversy. His old enemies, the Presbyterians, were opposing the judgment against Charles I. Before the trial was over, Milton had composed *The Tenure of Kings and Magistrates*, in which he argued, without specific application to the case in hand, for the legality of the deposition and execution of a monarch. The work was intended, Milton affirmed, "to reconcile the mind of the people to the event." It appeared shortly after the execution and by its bold timeliness entitled its author to favor and employment under the new government. He was accordingly appointed Latin Secretary to the Council of State at a salary of nearly £300 a year and took up official residence in Whitehall.

His whole personal and public status was now changed. Instead of being a mere volunteer champion of the cause of liberty he had become the official servant of a victorious party. The experience of working cooperatively with men who at least seemed to share his ideals was for Milton a new and happy one. He felt the invigoration of being partner in a great and dangerous enterprise and for four years toiled more purposefully and with fewer doubts and hesitations than he had perhaps ever done. His chief routine work was the drafting of foreign correspondence, but his pen was increasingly called upon to combat the menacing movement of public opinion against the regicide government. In October, 1649, he published *Eikonoklastes*, as an answer to the *Eikon Basilike*, "The True Portraiture of his Sacred Majesty in His Solitudes and Sufferings," a work purporting to be by the hand of the martyred king himself. "I did not insult over fallen majesty," he said later of this pamphlet; "I only preferred Queen Truth to King Charles." The task of damaging the royal image was an ungrateful one and Milton hardly appears at his best in its execution.

A year later he undertook a commission from the Council which must have seemed more worthy of his steel. The Dutch scholar Salmasius had been engaged by the exiled Charles II to draw up the case against the English regicides in such form as to set the mind of Europe firmly against the Commonwealth. He did so in the elaborately constructed Latin work, *Defensio Regia pro Carolo I*. The Council, alarmed at the influence of the work abroad, ordered Milton to answer it. His *Pro Populo Anglicano Defensio*, composed under the threat of loss of sight, appeared in March, 1651. This work was later to be regarded by Milton as his greatest achievement, one which entitled him to a place among the heroes and benefactors of mankind. It is hard for us now to accept his estimate. He answers all his opponent's arguments with an equal display of learning and ingenuity, but his best and worst efforts are expended in defaming the personality and intelligence of Salmasius himself. The actual effects of the pamphlet on European opinion are difficult to measure, but Milton himself believed that he had rendered the efforts of the "great kill-cow of Christendom" forever ridiculous; he received for his good services the thanks of the Council and a money present.

Already in this document Milton complains of failing health. Within the next few years he was to skirt perilously near the edge of catastrophe. His record becomes for a time one of continuous decline of efficiency in office. He was, by vote of the Council, relieved of a part of his duties. An anonymous reply to his *Defensio*, the *Regii Sanguinis Clamor*, in which he was personally attacked, remained for a long time unanswered. The obvious cause of Milton's trouble was, of course, his approaching blindness, which became complete in 1652. He also mentions as a contributory factor "the domestic grief of two funerals," i.e., those of his infant son, John, and of his wife, Mary, which occurred near together in the year 1652.

Milton's recovery of health and energy is a remarkable evidence both of his wisdom and his determination. He gave himself for a time to the poetic exercise of translating Psalms in a variety of unusual meters. He also cultivated the friendship of younger men—Marvell, Lawrence, Skinner—and employed their assistance in study and writing. Above all he sought the consolations of pride in his past achievements and the sense of the enjoyment of special favor from the Deity. God, to compensate him for the loss of physical sight, had illumined his mind with an inner radiance more precious and more pure. A group of sonnets, written in the years 1655–56, expressive, on the one hand, of resignation, courage, self-esteem, and, on the other, of genial affection for his friends, marks his return to emotional health and illustrates the means by which he lifted himself out of the depths. He could never again be as he had been in the first period of his secretaryship. He tended rather to fluctuate between brooding resignation and excited energy. He was to accomplish greater things than hitherto but only as the supernormal individual, separated from the possibility of participation on terms of equality in the enterprises of men.

Cromwell's Spokesman

The coup d'état of Cromwell in 1653 must have done much to stimulate Milton to renewed effort. It was easy for his imagination to portray himself as standing by the Protector's side, in his old capacity of inspirer and celebrator of great deeds. Cromwell, moreover, better than the Council, could use and value the special services which none but Milton could perform. Though in a subordinate position officially, for Phillip Meadows was now designated Latin Secretary, Milton was again ready to gird his loins for combat. He threw all his powers into the long delayed answer to Salmasius's successor and, spurred on to fury by the personal attack, wrote the most tremendous of his prose works, the *Pro Populo Anglicano Defensio Secunda*. This document, which appeared May 30, 1654, is, on the one hand, devoted to personal defense and self-aggrandizement, on the other, to the fulfilment of his early ambition to be the celebrator and interpreter of heroic deeds, a philosopher of true liberty, a wise and eloquent guide of men of action. Assured of divine guidance, Milton rises in wrath against the enemies of truth; he opens the whole story of his life as an evidence of his good faith and lofty purpose; he rejoices that he has been born in this day of his country's grandeur; he praises the great leaders of the Commonwealth, exhorting Cromwell to use his vast power wisely in the cause of truth. In a majestic peroration he bids the English nation preserve the state of liberty which they have arrived at and not sink back into the moral lethargy which invites new tyrannies. The *Second Defense* is an oration rather than a tract. It is John Milton's testimony that, however others may fail, he himself has fulfilled his function gloriously and left a monument to the singular and mighty achievements of his time.

The completion of the *Second Defense* marks the end of Milton's exclusive devotion to the public cause, and the beginning of a return to his own interrupted literary and poetic projects. Phillips says that he resumed work at this time on his *History of Britain* and on a Latin dictionary for which he had long since begun to make collections. In 1656, after having been for over five years a widower, he married Katharine Woodcock, and through her knew for the first time the normal satisfactions of domestic life. She lived only a year and four months after the marriage, giving birth to a daughter on October 19, 1657, and dying, together with the child, in the February following. The sonnet "On his Deceased Wife" bears witness to the poignancy of Milton's memory and regret. It is reasonable to connect these events with the beginning of work on the great epic. Aubrey says that the poet turned again to his dearest project "about two years before the king came in" (i.e., about May, 1658). We may conjecture that he had need of such an emotional outlet and also that some of the pressures which had delayed the undertaking were for a time relaxed. He was not, however, so deeply engaged that he could not turn again to the defense of liberty in the new crisis following the death of Cromwell. The *Ready and Easy Way to Establish a New Commonwealth* is a last desperate effort of his statesmanship to stay the rising tide of royalism by offering a workable program of Republican government. Before it was actually published, all rational expectation of the further pursuit of Miltonic policy was at an end. This he must, in spite of his continued effort, have realized, and the final paragraph, particularly as revised on the very eve of the Restoration, is a tragic and eloquent farewell to the great enterprise of liberty. Henceforth, except for a single pamphlet thirteen years later, Milton's pen no longer concerned itself with the issues of the day.

There has been much conjecture as to why Milton's life was spared amid the proscriptions which followed the setting up of the new government. Of his real danger there can be no doubt, for many men less conspicuous and who had less to answer for were named by Parliament among those to be excepted from the royal clemency. Phillips says that his friends interceded for him in the Council and the House and names Andrew Marvell as the chief of them. Aubrey declares that it was Sir William Davenant who secured his release, in return for a similar favor from Milton in 1650. In any case the government did well, even from its own point of view, to pardon him, for the execution of a blind old man who, whatever his political crimes, had brought honor to his country, could have done only harm to the Stuart cause. As it was, action was taken against him as the author of the *Defensio* and *Eikonoklastes*. The books were burned and Milton's arrest was ordered. He had, however, at the king's coming, gone into "abscondence and retirement" in a friend's house and was reported not to be found. He remained in hiding for a matter of months till the Act of Oblivion made him safe from a capital charge for treason. He was then taken into custody, we do not know for how long, but released on payment of a sizable fee or fine. After this he lived quietly but unforgotten, an object of occasional execration by royalist writers. It is hard to judge the precise degree of his notoriety, but no other person so conspicuously identified with the old regime appears to have been left unpunished.

Speculation is also in order as to what happened to the progress of *Paradise Lost* in this transition interval. Milton once described the mere removal from one residence to another as a cause of sickness. Perhaps he had found a remedy for perturbations arising from the disruption of his personal affairs. On the other hand, he may not have been able to go on with the poem till the excitement was over. If there was an interruption it presumably came before the seventh book, for at the beginning of the latter he plainly refers to his condition of life under the Restoration:

                          though fallen on evil days,
On evil days though fallen and evil tongues;
In darkness, and with dangers compassed round,
And solitude.

IN RETIREMENT

In this last period of his life, from 1660 till his death in
1674, Milton's material fortune suffered a great change, for
he had lost not only his salary as secretary, but the £2000
which he had invested in government securities and, according to Phillips, "another great sum by mismanagement and for
want of good advice." Milton's relative poverty is reflected in
his inability to buy books and engage skilled literary assistance
with the same freedom as in his days of affluence.

His mental and physical comfort were certainly not improved by anything in his relationship with the Powell family
or his own children. Phillips describes at length his attempt to
make his daughters serve him as readers and amanuenses. We
have documentary evidence of financial disagreements with
Mrs. Powell. There is finally the testimony of a maid servant
in the proceedings regarding his will to the effect that his
children combined "to cheat him in his marketings," and that
they "made away with some of his books and would have sold
the rest to the dunghill woman." That Milton managed to live
and work in a household of this temper must have been due
to the satisfaction he took in his third marriage, which took
place in February, 1663. His bride, Elizabeth Minshull, who
had been sought out for him by a friend, was but twenty-four
years old. Milton's days of romance were over but there is
every evidence that Elizabeth proved a good wife in practical
ways and supplied him with a much needed object of affection. She lived to cherish his memory and to report to John
Aubrey many details of his later years. The poet apparently
attempted by a verbal will to leave her all his property.

In the matter of residence Milton's life after his third marriage was more stable than it had been in earlier days. He
moved, perhaps as early as 1663, to an establishment in Artillery walk, away from the heart of London, with Bunhill fields
beyond. Here, as Phillips puts it, was his last stage in this
world. For a few months in 1665/6, however, he retreated to
a "pretty box" in the village of Chalfont St. Giles and it was

at this time that he showed the completed manuscript of *Paradise Lost* to his young Quaker friend Thomas Ellwood.

Last Days

Of Milton's personal and literary habits in his later years we have an abundant and interesting record. His health, except for attacks of gout, was apparently better, and his humor, in spite of domestic irritations, cheerful. He continued to sing and play the organ. He enjoyed exercise and sitting in the sun. He was regular in his habits, rising, according to Aubrey, at four in the morning, meditating till seven, and then dictating or having books read to him till dinner, after which he walked three or four hours in his garden. Elsewhere it is reported that he listened to the reading of good authors in the evening in order to "store his fancy against the morning." Poetry came to him when he was lying on his bed before daylight and only during the winter season. Friendship evidently continued to mean much to him, and he was surrounded by a considerable group of admirers. The younger men of his acquaintance often gave him literary assistance in return for instruction. The latest comer in his circle was Daniel Skinner, a rather unreliable young Trinity College graduate, later befriended by Samuel Pepys. Skinner inherited the manuscript of the theological work, *De Doctrina Christiana,* and would have published it had he not been warned that his chances of a public career would be ended if he did so. Milton's other literary heir was Edward Phillips, who had kept up his old association with his uncle and probably derived inspiration and assistance from him in his scholarly and literary publications. The other Phillips boy, John, had done much to offend Milton, but there is no evidence of a break in their relationship.

In addition to his more intimate associations Milton had enjoyed the acquaintance of distinguished foreigners both through correspondence and through personal contact. The travelers who, according to Aubrey, came in the earlier period to England "chiefly to see O. Protector & Mr. J. Milton" and "would see the house and chamber where he was born," doubtless continued their visits to some extent after his retirement. Toward the end of his life there were those who sought him out as a poet rather than as a great scholar and last survivor of the Commonwealth government. The most notable visit was that of Dryden, who asked permission to convert *Paradise Lost* into an opera and received the scornfully indulgent answer, "Yes, Mr. Dryden, you may tag my verses."

Paradise Lost was published in 1667. *Paradise Regained* and *Samson Agonistes* appeared in 1671. From them Milton derived neither great pecuniary profit nor great fame. There is a story of Sir John Denham's enthusiasm over *Paradise Lost,* "wet from the press," and Andrew Marvell commended the work to the public in a superb complimentary poem prefixed to the second edition. Milton received a total of ten pounds for the work, five on the delivery of the manuscript and five more in 1669, by which time some thirteen hundred copies had been sold. His widow finally sold the copyrights to a second edition for eight pounds. The other poems, so far as we know, made no impression on his contemporaries. But Milton cherished even his earliest compositions. He republished the 1645 volume, with additions, in the year before his death.

That Milton still retained much of the fervor of his old convictions and was still ready enough to guide England in a political and moral crisis is shown by the publication in 1673 of the tract *Of True Religion, Heresy, Toleration, and the Growth of Popery.* Charles II by his support of the Catholics had aroused increasing opposition in Parliament and among the main body of Protestant Englishmen. Milton in this belated pamphlet undertakes to lend a hand to those who were exhorting the public to "beware of this Roman weed." His argument is that if the Protestant sects do not forget their own differences and present a united front against the renewal of Catholic power, England will fall back into the religious condition from which it was saved by the Reformation. Milton says nothing for or against the principle of disenabling the Catholics from holding public office, which Parliament had just embodied in the Test Act. The constructive ways of "hindering the growth of Popery" are the ones which most appeal to him, as they have always done: to read duly and diligently the holy Scripture, to practice mutual forbearance and charity toward each other, and lastly to amend our lives. This is permanent Miltonic doctrine in both prose and poetry. But he is no longer immediately engaged, as he once was, in the great enterprise of liberty.

Milton's death occurred on November 8, 1674, as the result of an acute attack of gout or rheumatism, from which he had long suffered. His end came "with so little pain or emotion, that the time of his expiring was not perceived by those in the room." He was buried beside his father in the chancel of St. Giles Cripplegate.

"Life Beyond Life"

Milton's fame as a poet rose steadily from the moment of his death. Editions of the poems, particularly of *Paradise Lost,* increased in frequency after the Revolution of 1688. The criticisms of Addison in the *Spectator* placed Milton in the first rank of English authors. As the romantic currents of the eighteenth century became stronger the feeling that Milton represented the true ideal from which poetry had since declined became increasingly dominant. His versification was widely though servilely imitated in the eighteenth century; and the great romantics and Victorians felt his inspiration in more vital ways.

Both Milton's personality and his art have in all times been a theme of controversy. Samuel Johnson, in his *Lives of the Poets,* while admitting the greatness of *Paradise Lost,* denied all merit to "Lycidas" and the Sonnets, and disparaged the poet's personal character at every point. Macaulay, on the other hand, exalted him as among the noblest of men. He was admired as a great rebel by Blake, Byron, and Shelley, and as a great patriot and spiritual leader by Wordsworth. To Tennyson he was "the mighty organ voice of England." To his biographer, David Masson, he was very much a human being but a great man and a great poet none the less, a hero of the race, who for the best years of his life gave up for party what was meant for mankind but rose above the conflict and, when the causes which he fought for failed, had the resources within himself to embody his learning, his rich experience, and his religious faith in monumental works of art. The tradition, as the nineteenth century delivered it, made Milton's poetry a revelation of his personality and tended to pass judgment on the two as one. The early poems contained the record of a nature of peculiar charm, a sage and serious youthfulness happily in love with every form of excellence. The later works bore the marks of troubled passion, as well as high austerity, and a devotion to the Muse which had become indistinguishable from worship. In *Samson Agonistes* it seemed possible to find Milton's very soul. His tragedy and his faith were expressed in the fate and triumph of the Hebrew champion:

> O dark, dark, dark, amid the blaze of noon,

and

> Nothing is here for tears, nothing to wail
> Or knock the breast, no weakness, no contempt.

In the early twentieth century much attention was given to Milton's ideas and to his relationship to Puritanism on the one hand and to Humanism on the other. The distinction was drawn between his official theology and his dynamic beliefs. Emphasis was placed on the pantheistic element in his thinking. There was also an examination, notably by Denis Saurat, of the relationship of his special system to his experience of life and to basic conflicting drives of his personality. The present writer has contributed to this inquiry in a biographical study entitled *John Milton, Englishman.*

Recent criticism has been enlivened by controversy over Milton's established position as a poet. Some modernists have been led joyously to proclaim his downfall. On the other hand, a new kind of defense has been elicited which has seemed to many to put Milton for the first time among the poets of the past who are thoroughly acceptable to the present age. Such fluctuations of attitude and interest are in part an obvious reflection of mere literary fashion, but they represent also progressive exploration and discovery toward full understanding and ultimate consensus. It is clear in the whole course of Milton study that his fame both as a poet and a publicist has had vast recuperative power. He will in all probability go on being an English classic as long as the memory of the Anglo-Saxon or indeed of the Western European past is in any sort of honor. He may grow more remote with time, as all things do, but scholarship and informed authority will be at hand to explain, revive, define him, and to reassert his claims. As far as the world has any attention whatever to give to its monuments and heroes of the old tradition, Milton's life and work will have their share. And our estimate of his human value will be one of the ways we have of estimating ourselves.

THE POEMS OF THE FIRST PERIOD
1624–1642

INTRODUCTION TO
POEMS OF THE FIRST PERIOD
1624–1642

The fact that Milton dated many of his early poems invites the modern reader to interest himself in the order in which they were composed and in their author's development as an artist. In the collected volume which he published in 1645, he separated the Latin poems from the English and made a few changes in the chronological arrangement of the English poems according to form and subject,[1] but within the groups he let the poems stand largely as they were composed. His idea was partly, no doubt, to be sure that the reader would recognize very youthful compositions as such and make proper allowances, but we know from other evidence that he was given to watching his own growth, just as Wordsworth was, and regarded it as significant. We naturally follow him in this.

The periods into which his work falls correspond to the epochs in his personal life and to some extent to the great changes of national affairs which affected his career. The first big break comes with his return from Italy and his involvement in the civil war. When he wrote the Latin elegy on his youthful friend, Diodati, in 1640 he was full of plans for further poems. These, however, he set aside in the interest of his prose writing and in the years which followed produced only translations and a few memorable sonnets. The latter differ markedly from his early work and constitute a transition, albeit a slender one, to the great epic which he had regarded as the goal of his efforts and which he finally undertook in retirement after about eighteen years of intense concentration on other things.

The poems written at school and college, the Horton poems, and these few Latin compositions done in Italy, with the epitaph of Damon, written just after his return, constitute one

[1] In the 1645 edition of the poems serious and religious pieces in various meters come first; then a more secular group in couplets, then *Arcades*, "Lycidas," and *Comus*, all pastorals.

complete cycle of his youthful art. The first group culminates in the "Nativity Ode," in 1629, the second in "Lycidas," in 1637. These are great serious masterpieces, the equal in their way of *Paradise Lost* itself. The masque, *Comus,* is a composition of another inspiration but equally perfect in its artistry. Of the lesser lyrics "L'Allegro" and "Il Penseroso," of uncertain date, are the most delightful and the most universally popular.

The bulk of the earliest verse which Milton thought fit to preserve is in Latin.[2] His productiveness starts rather suddenly about the middle of his undergraduate career and continues with interruptions till his return from Italy. In the spring of 1628, when he was nineteen, he declared to himself and the world that his preferred medium was to be his mother tongue and from then till he left England on his foreign travels, a period of about ten years, he wrote the works above alluded to and about a dozen lesser lyrics—not a great output certainly and probably very marginal in his activity and effort but to us of fascinating interest for what they reveal. All this early work, even the unquestioned masterpieces, Milton regarded as merely preparatory to serious achievements later. It reflects a variety of literary enthusiasms and all the fluctuations of an adolescent experience. Yet it shows also a fairly consistent development of literary power and purpose. In English verse, Milton follows a variety of models—Sylvester, Spenser, Giles and Phineas Fletcher, Ben Jonson. His Latin poetry is at first Ovidian, then Virgilian, and his devotion to the classics and to Italian leaves a deep impress on his English poetry as well. The details of these relationships will best be given in connection with the individual works.

A corresponding development takes place in his attitudes and ideals. In the sixth Elegy and the poem on the Nativity he reacts sharply from the sensuous indulgence shown in the earlier Latin poems. In "L'Allegro" and "Il Penseroso" he excludes both love and morality from his consciousness in favor of a delighted enjoyment of art and nature. *Comus* and "Lycidas" represent a happy combination of the joyous and the exalted elements in the poetic consciousness.

Following the tradition of Virgil and Spenser, Milton consciously adopts the pastoral vein as an appropriate mode of

[2] The Latin originals are represented in this volume by Cowper's translations.

expression for his poetical immaturity. He bids farewell to it in *Epitaphium Damonis*, which, though composed after his return to England, is a record of the thoughts and experiences of the Italian journey and expresses a set of emotions which belong specifically to his youth.

Milton's style in this period varies with the sort of thing he is writing and with the immediate inspiration which possesses him. In general, he moves in the high tradition of Elizabethan poetry, but there is a subtle pervasion of a more modern and more individual quality which marks the early Milton as a new voice in English poetry. Only now and then does he exhibit anything but the most faultless artistic taste and tact. To many readers the subtle blending of elements of classic lucidity and the romantic intricacy of the baroque, the pastoral *genus humile* and Miltonic elevation, gives a result more satisfying as pure poetry than anything in his later work.

A Paraphrase on Psalm 114 and Psalm 136

Milton was, according to Aubrey, already a poet at the age of ten, but we have nothing from his pen at so early a date. His first work is represented by these two paraphrases from the Psalms. They may be school exercises, but one is tempted to believe that his father's interest had something to do with their composition, for the elder Milton had written some tunes for Ravenscroft's Psalter of 1621. The practice of versifying psalms in English goes back, however, to the beginnings of the Reformation and was an orthodox way for a pious poet to exercise his faculties. Milton's language, in such epithets as "froth-becurled" and "thunder-clasping," reflects not only his admiration for Homer, but for Joshua Sylvester as well, the English translator of Du Bartas, and suggests the ornate tradition of Renaissance expression which he was to develop into his own majestic idiom. Much is made in a recent commentary (Brooks and Hardy, *The Poems of Mr. John Milton*, p. 106) of the adjectives "glassy" and "fiery" in lines 17 and 18 of Psalm 114, as suggesting a picture of the rock being with one blow crushed, melted, and fused by its own fire into glass. Milton elsewhere, however, used "glassy" without any such metaphysical implication: "under the glassy, cool, translucent wave." The two last stanzas of Psalm 136 are a very

Miltonic amplification of the original text. We shall hear much of these Heavenly Mansions in his religious verse.

A PARAPHRASE ON PSALM 114

This and the following Psalm were done by the author at fifteen years old.

When the blest seed of Terah's faithful son,
After long toil their liberty had won,
And passed from Pharian fields to Canaan land,
Led by the strength of the Almighty's hand,
Jehovah's wonders were in Israel shown,
His praise and glory was in Israel known.
That saw the troubled sea, and shivering fled,
And sought to hide his froth-becurlèd head
Low in the earth; Jordan's clear streams recoil,
As a faint host that hath received the foil.   10
The high, huge-bellied mountains skip like rams
Amongst their ewes, the little hills like lambs.
Why fled the ocean? and why skipped the mountains?
Why turnèd Jordan toward his crystal fountains?
Shake Earth, and at the presence be aghast
Of Him that ever was, and aye shall last,
That glassy floods from rugged rocks can crush,
And make soft rills from fiery flint-stones gush.
                                        [1624]

PSALM 136

Let us with a gladsome mind
Praise the Lord, for he is kind;
        For his mercies aye endure,
        Ever faithful, ever sure.

Let us blaze his name abroad,
For of gods he is the God;
        For his, etc.

O let us his praises tell,
Who doth the wrathful tyrants quell;
        For his, etc.   10

1. **Terah's faithful son,** Abraham.
3. **Pharian,** Egyptian, from Pharaoh.

Who with his miracles doth make
Amazëd heaven and earth to shake;
For his, etc.

Who by his wisdom did create
The painted heavens so full of state;
For his, etc.

Who did the solid earth ordain
To rise above the watery plain;
For his, etc.

Who by his all-commanding might,   20
Did fill the new-made world with light;
For his, etc.

And caused the golden-tressëd sun
All the day long his course to run;
For his, etc.

The hornëd moon to shine by night,
Amongst her spangled sisters bright;
For his, etc.

He with his thunder-clasping hand,
Smote the first-born of Egypt land;   30
For his, etc.

And in despite of Pharao fell,
He brought from thence his Israel;
For his, etc.

The ruddy waves he cleft in twain,
Of the Erythræan main;
For his, etc.

The floods stood still like walls of glass,
While the Hebrew bands did pass;
For his, etc.   40

35–40. These stanzas are not in the Hebrew. Milton is recalling Sylvester, *The Divine Weeks*, I, 1, 171 ff., as Hughes points out:

> And on each side is flanked all along
> With walls of crystal, beautiful and strong . . .
> Two walls of glass built with a word alone.

The "walls of crystal" appear again when this episode is referred to in
Paradise Lost, XII, 197.

But full soon they did devour
The tawny king with all his power;
 For his, etc.

His chosen people he did bless
In the wasteful wilderness;
 For his, etc.

In bloody battle he brought down
Kings of prowess and renown;
 For his, etc.

He foiled bold Seon and his host,   50
That ruled the Amorrean coast;
 For his, etc.

And large-limbed Og he did subdue,
With all his over-hardy crew;
 For his, etc.

And to his servant Israel,
He gave their land therein to dwell;
 For his, etc.

He hath with a piteous eye
Beheld us in our misery;   60
 For his, etc.

And freed us from the slavery
Of the invading enemy;
 For his, etc.

All living creatures he doth feed,
And with full hand supplies their need;
 For his, etc.

Let us therefore warble forth
His mighty majesty and worth;
 For his, etc.   70

That his mansion hath on high
Above the reach of mortal eye;
 For his mercies aye endure.
 Ever faithful, ever sure.

[1624]

Elegy I

Milton divided his Latin poems into *Elegiae* and *Sylvae* (miscellaneous), referring rather to the meters in which they were written than to the subject matter. On the Latin title page he took pains to say that most of the pieces were composed "within his twentieth year," and to substantiate this he prefixed to eight of them an indication of the date, *anno aetatis* 16, 17, 18, 19, 20. A single poem among the *Sylvae* (not here reproduced) is headed "*anno aetatis* 16" and should, one would think, belong to the same year as the two psalms, written "at fifteen years old," but Milton's usage is peculiar. He means "at the age of sixteen" instead of "in his sixteenth year," and even so he is sometimes mistaken. The earliest dated Latin poem, one of a group of four formal laments on the deaths of academic dignitaries, was actually composed in the fall of 1626, Milton's third year at Cambridge, when he was seventeen.

Elegy I, which stands first in the Latin volume, without the usual indication of date, is thought to belong to the preceding spring, the end of Milton's second academic year, in which case it is his earliest original poem. The poetical awakening which it represents may well be the result of a dramatic incident which is alluded to in the opening lines. Milton had had a conflict with his college tutor and had been sent home to London in the middle of the term. The biographer Aubrey, well informed about Cambridge matters, says that he was whipped. The emotional reaction of a proud and sensitive boy like Milton, already convinced of the rightness of his ways, may well have been a powerful one. Whippings were common enough in school but not, apparently, in college. And if Milton needed discipline it was not because he was lazy or a dullard. The poem itself is written in a mood of well-controlled self-pity and defiance. Milton turns to his boyhood friend Diodati, now at Oxford, and expresses his satisfaction in the cultured delights with which he is consoling himself in London during his enforced vacation. These delights, except that Milton here admits an enthusiasm for the other sex, are substantially the same as those which he was later to record in "L'Allegro" and "Il Penseroso." The poem is, to employ Keats's phrase, the "pleasure thermometer" of a poet. In the closing lines Milton passes, though rather playfully, from his sensuously self-indulgent to his austere and moral mood.

In form and style the poem is an Ovidian imitation. Milton later confessed his youthful partiality for the soft allurements of Ovid's muse as something not praiseworthy but natural. He evidently feels that he is handling fire, and he avoids any approach to his master's looseness. On the other hand, he loads every rift of his verse with the ore of mythological allusion. The Latin style in this, as in all the poems, is excellent, the best, according to Macaulay, ever achieved by an Englishman. When, after the Horton period, Milton visited Italy it assured him an enthusiastic welcome in learned and artistic circles.

This first Elegy, and five other poems coming within two or three months of each other in the fall of 1626, constitute Milton's first creative moment, so far as we have record. One of the pieces is a little Latin epic on the Gunpowder plot. It contains motives later to be employed in glorified form in *Paradise Lost,* particularly the fiction of an infernal council plotting the destruction of mankind. Milton is here indebted to Phineas Fletcher's poem on the same subject, "The Apollyonists," with its Latin duplicate, *Locustae,* and also to Claudian's *In Rufinum.* The intense Protestant and anti-Jesuitical fervor of the work shows the poet responsive to the dominant form of religious patriotism of his day. In one of the memorial poems alluded to above, Milton expresses his share in the general sense of public calamity occasioned by the plague. It is interesting that he should identify himself at just this time with the larger world of England and with the fates of great personages in his university. He has grown up in an atmosphere of loyalty and he already balances personal with general concerns. This is, it seems to me, a not unnatural reaction from such an experience as is recorded in Elegy I.

The poems of 1626, whatever their specific motivation, must have marked Milton's entry into the forum of humanistic scholarship and taste. A high premium was set in academic circles on the ability to write excellently in the learned tongue. And so great was the proficiency of the best Latin poets of the Renaissance that a man of real genius might find satisfaction in this medium and never feel the need of expressing himself in his mother tongue at all. Milton, as we shall see, did this only for a time, if indeed he was not recreating himself with English all along.

It may be that with this first effort he had for the time being written himself out. At any rate we have only one recorded poem for the year 1627, Elegy IV. This again is personal, but larger issues are involved. Milton turns to his old tutor, Thomas Young, now far away in Germany, as he had turned in Elegy I to Diodati. He does not speak directly of himself but pours out sympathy and admiration for a great man injured by lack of appreciation at home, and in danger amid foreign wars. The counsel which he gives him strikes the note of spiritual exhortation frequently to be heard hereafter in Milton's verse, as it becomes also one of his main themes of eloquence in prose.

The original text of Milton's Latin poems is omitted in this edition. The translations, like those of the Italian sonnets, are by William Cowper.

ELEGY I

(Translation)

TO CHARLES DIODATI

At length, my friend, the far-sent letters come,
Charged with thy kindness, to their destined home;
They come, at length, from Deva's western side,
Where prone she seeks the salt Vergivian tide.
Trust me, my joy is great that thou shouldst be,
Though born of foreign race, yet born for me,
And that my sprightly friend, now free to roam,
Must seek again so soon his wonted home.
I well content, where Thames with influent tide
My native city laves, meantime reside,   10
Nor zeal nor duty now my steps impel
To reedy Cam, and my forbidden cell.
Nor aught of pleasure in those fields have I,
That, to the musing bard, all shade deny.
'Tis time that I a pedant's threats disdain,
And fly from wrongs my soul will ne'er sustain.
If peaceful days, in lettered leisure spent,
Beneath my father's roof, be banishment,
Then call me banished, I will ne'er refuse
A name expressive of the lot I choose.   20

3. **Deva,** the Dee. Milton's Latin adds "at Chester."
4. **Vergivian tide,** the Irish sea.
6. **of foreign race.** An inaccurate rendering. Milton says "It pleases me that a remote region nourishes a heart that loves me."

I would that, exiled to the Pontic shore,
Rome's hapless bard had suffered nothing more;
He then had equalled even Homer's lays,
And Virgil! thou hadst won but second praise.
For here I woo the Muse, with no control;
And here my books—my life—absorb me whole.
Here too I visit, or to smile, or weep,
The winding theatre's majestic sweep;
The grave or gay colloquial scene recruits
My spirits, spent in learning's long pursuits,   30
Whether some senior shrewd, or spendthrift heir,
Suitor, or soldier now unarmed, be there;
Or some coifed brooder o'er a ten years' cause
Thunder the Norman gibberish of the laws.
The lackey there oft dupes the wary sire,
And artful speeds the enamoured son's desire.
There, virgins oft, unconscious what they prove,
What love is know not, yet, unknowing, love.
Or if impassioned Tragedy wield high
The bloody sceptre, give her locks to fly   40
Wild as the winds, and roll her haggard eye,
I gaze, and grieve, still cherishing my grief,
At times even bitter tears yield sweet relief:
As when, from bliss untasted torn away,
Some youth dies, hapless, on his bridal day;—
Or when the ghost, sent back from shades below,
Fills the assassin's heart with vengeful woe,
When Troy, or Argos, the dire scene affords,
Or Creon's hall laments its guilty lords.
Nor always city-pent, or pent at home,   50
I dwell; but when spring calls me forth to roam,
Expatiate in our proud suburban shades
Of branching elm, that never sun pervades.
Here many a virgin troop I may descry,
Like stars of mildest influence, gliding by.
Oh forms divine! Oh looks that might inspire
Even Jove himself, grown old, with young desire!
Oft have I gazed on gem-surpassing eyes,
Outsparkling every star that gilds the skies,
Necks whiter than the ivory arm bestowed   60
By Jove on Pelops, or the Milky Road!
Bright locks, Love's golden snare; these falling low,

22. **Rome's hapless bard**, Ovid, exiled to the shore of the Black sea.
53. **branching elm**. The Latin reads "elms planted thick together."
Cowper has gracefully borrowed a phrase from *Arcades*.
60. **ivory arm**. Jove pieced out Pelops' missing shoulder with ivory.

Those playing wanton o'er the graceful brow!
Cheeks too, more winning sweet than after shower
Adonis turned to Flora's favourite flower!
Yield, heroines, yield, and ye who shared the embrace
Of Jupiter in ancient times, give place!
Give place, ye turbaned fair of Persia's coast!
And ye, not less renowned, Assyria's boast!
Submit, ye nymphs of Greece! ye, once the bloom   70
Of Ilion! and all ye of haughty Rome,
Who swept, of old, her theatres with trains
Redundant, and still live in classic strains!
To British damsels beauty's palm is due;
Aliens! to follow them is fame for you.
O city, founded by Dardanian hands,
Whose towering front the circling realms commands,
Too blest abode! no loveliness we see
In all the earth, but it abounds in thee.
The virgin multitude that daily meets,   80
Radiant with gold and beauty, in thy streets,
Outnumbers all her train of starry fires,
With which Diana gilds thy lofty spires.
Fame says, that wafted hither by her doves,
With all her host of quiver-bearing loves,
Venus, preferring Paphian scenes no more,
Has fixed her empire on thy nobler shore.
But lest the sightless boy enforce my stay,
I leave these happy walls, while yet I may.
Immortal Moly shall secure my heart   90
From all the sorcery of Circæan art,
And I will e'en repass Cam's reedy pools
To face once more the warfare of the schools.
Meantime accept this trifle! rhymes though few,
Yet such as prove thy Friend's remembrance true!

[1625-26]

ELEGY VII

Though printed last in the series of Milton's elegies this
poem, dated *anno aetatis 19*, is certainly earlier than Elegy V,
dated *anno aetatis 20*, and Elegy VI, which was demonstrably
written just after Milton's twenty-first birthday. In it Milton
acknowledges, lightly and in conventional language, the sway
of Cupid over his heart. In Elegy I Milton is allured by the

76. **city**, London, founded by the Trojan descendants of Dardanus.
90. **Moly.** See *Comus*, 636 and note.

beauty of English maidens generally but flees from the temptation of intimacy with them; here he makes at least a literary surrender, and is apparently rather proud of the fact. The English sonnet, "O Nightingale," prays for success in love. The Italian sonnets express a steady, contented, and self-satisfied devotion to some English beauty of foreign birth. In Elegy V we see Milton glorifying the amorous riot of earth and sky in springtime. Finally in Elegy VI we have him turning against the whole mood of sensuous indulgence. Such is the cycle of Milton's love poetry in the old Ovidian and courtly vein. Whether purely literary and imaginative or having some relationship to biographical fact, it tells us a good deal about the youthful poet. The excursion into the realm of passion is made with reservations and is later very deliberately discarded. As I have indicated in the biographical section (above, page 5), Milton interpreted his literary allegiances in an ascending scale of moral and spiritual value. It became a convention of the seventeenth century to reject the secular for the religious muse, but there is no parallel for the kind of progression which Milton observed in his own history as a poet.

ELEGY VII

(Translation)

As yet a stranger to the gentle fires
That Amathusia's smiling queen inspires,
Not seldom I derided Cupid's darts,
And scorned his claim to rule all human hearts.
"Go, child," I said, "transfix the timorous dove!
"An easy conquest suits an infant love;
"Enslave the sparrow, for such prize shall be
"Sufficient triumph to a chief like thee!
"Why aim thy idle arms at human kind?
"Thy shafts prevail not 'gainst the noble mind."   10
        The Cyprian heard, and, kindling into ire,
(None kindles sooner) burned with double fire.
        It was the spring, and newly-risen day
Peeped o'er the hamlets on the first of May;
My eyes, too tender for the blaze of light,
Still sought the shelter of retiring night,

2. **Amathusia**, Amathus, where Venus had a temple, but it is the goddess herself who was called **Amathusia**. This is Cowper's error, not Milton's.

When Love approached: in painted plumes arrayed
The insidious god his rattling darts betrayed,
Nor less his infant features, and the sly
Sweet intimations of his threatening eye.   20
  Such the Sigean boy is seen above,
Filling the goblet for imperial Jove;
Such he, on whom the nymphs bestowed their charms.
Hylas, who perished in a Naiad's arms.
Angry he seemed, yet graceful in his ire,
And added threats, not destitute of fire.
"My power," he said, "by others' pain alone
" 'Twere best to learn; now learn it by thy own!
"With those who feel my power that power attest,
"And in thy anguish be my sway confessed!   30
"I vanquished Phœbus, though returning vain
"From his new triumph o'er the Python slain,
"And when he thinks on Daphne, even he
"Will yield the prize of archery to me.
"A dart less true the Parthian horseman sped,
"Behind him killed, and conquered as he fled:
"Less true the expert Cydonian, and less true
"The youth whose shaft his latent Procris slew.
"Vanquished by me see huge Orion bend,
"By me Alcides, and Alcides' friend.   40
"At me should Jove himself a bolt design,
"His bosom first should bleed transfixed by mine.
"But all thy doubts this shaft will best explain,
"Nor shall it reach thee with a trivial pain.
"Thy muse, vain youth! shall not thy peace ensure,
"Nor Phœbus' serpent yield thy wound a cure."
  He spoke, and, waving a bright shaft in air
Sought the warm bosom of the Cyprian fair.
  That thus a child should bluster in my ear
Provoked my laughter, more than moved my fear.   50
I shunned not, therefore, public haunts, but strayed
Careless in city or suburban shade,
And passing, and repassing, nymphs that moved
With grace divine, beheld where'er I roved.
Bright shone the vernal day, with double blaze,
As beauty gave new force to Phœbus' rays.
By no grave scruples checked, I freely eyed
The dangerous show, rash youth my only guide,
And many a look of many a Fair unknown
Met full, unable to control my own.   60

21. **Sigean boy,** Ganymede, so called from Sigeius in the Troad.
37. **Cydonian,** native of Cydon in Crete, famous for archery.

But one I marked (then peace forsook my breast)—
One—oh how far superior to the rest!
What lovely features! such the Cyprian queen
Herself might wish, and Juno wish her mien.
The very nymph was she, whom, when I dared
His arrows, Love had even then prepared;
Nor was himself remote, nor unsupplied
With torch well-trimmed and quiver at his side;
Now to her lips he clung, her eyelids now,
Then settled on her cheeks, or on her brow;   70
And with a thousand wounds from every part
Pierced, and transpierced, my undefended heart.
A fever, new to me, of fierce desire
Now seized my soul, and I was all on fire;
But she, the while, whom only I adore,
Was gone, and vanished, to appear no more.
In silent sadness I pursue my way;
I pause, I turn, proceed, yet wish to stay,
And while I follow her in thought, bemoan,
With tears, my soul's delight so quickly flown.   80
When Jove had hurled him to the Lemnian coast,
So Vulcan sorrowed for Olympus lost,
And so Œclides, sinking into night,
From the deep gulf looked up to distant light.
    Wretch that I am, what hopes for me remain,
Who cannot cease to love, yet love in vain?
Oh could I once, once more behold the Fair,
Speak to her, tell her, of the pangs I bear,
Perhaps she is not adamant, would show
Perhaps some pity at my tale of woe.   90
O inauspicious flame!—'tis mine to prove
A matchless instance of disastrous love.
Ah spare me, gentle Power!—If such thou be,
Let not thy deeds and nature disagree.
Spare me, and I will worship at no shrine
With vow and sacrifice, save only thine.
Now I revere thy fires, thy bow, thy darts,
Now own thee sovereign of all human hearts.
Remove! no—grant me still this raging woe!
Sweet is the wretchedness that lovers know: 100
But pierce hereafter (should I chance to see
One destined mine) at once both her and me.

                                            [1628]

83. **Œclides,** Amphiarus, one of the seven against Thebes, thunder-struck by Jove.

ON THE DEATH OF A FAIR INFANT DYING OF A COUGH

Edward Phillips tells us that this poem was written on the occasion of the death of his own elder sister, Milton's niece. If this is so, Milton's date, *anno aetatis* 17, i.e., 1626, must be a mistake, for the vital records show that the first daughter of Edward and Anne Phillips was born January 12, 1626, and died January 22, 1628 (see W. R. Parker, *Times Literary Supplement*, December 17, 1938). A later child was born on the ninth of April following. In view of the last two lines of the poem, we may assume that event not yet to have taken place. There were no other children living at the time. Milton wrote the elegy, therefore, in the late winter or early spring of 1628, at the age of 19, toward the close of his fourth year at college.

This fact, so minutely determined against Milton's own statement, is of considerable interest, for we have only Latin poems written at college before this time. The "Vacation Exercise" (see page 43), declaring a preference for English, follows a few months later. It may be that the need of celebrating a family sorrow, interrupting the Latin versifying which had gone so merrily a little earlier, broke its spell if only for the moment. But this is, of course, pure conjecture. Milton resumed the Ovidian vein almost immediately and continued it, along with English, for the two fruitful years which followed.

The poem is a religious and didactic elegy in the seventeenth-century manner, full of mythological imagery, rather stilted and immature, but containing touches of sincere emotion. Both the verse and language suggest the school of Spenser, particularly the work of Phineas Fletcher, whose *Poetical Miscellanies*, though unpublished till 1633, may well have been available to Milton in manuscript at Cambridge. Milton still scatters compound epithets as freely as in the Psalm paraphrases. In stanza VIII he indulges in the use of the familiar types of allegorical abstraction perpetuated from the Middle Ages by the Spenserians. There is no trace of the influence of John Donne and his seventeenth-century imitators, though this has sometimes been affirmed. He is seeking elevation rather than forcefulness of expression, and he as yet knows of no way to attain it save by abounding in the aureate rhetoric of the age.

In tone this poem is characteristic of Milton's sage and serious attitude in youth. We may note particularly, in the last stanza, his schooling of the bereaved mother in self-control. Just so does the elder brother in *Comus* hold out to the younger strengthening assurances of philosophic faith.

ANNO AETATIS 17

ON THE DEATH OF A FAIR INFANT DYING OF A COUGH

I

O fairest flower no sooner blown but blasted,
Soft silken primrose fading timelessly,
Summer's chief honor if thou hadst outlasted
Bleak Winter's force that made thy blossom dry;
For he being amorous on that lovely dye
    That did thy cheek envermeil, thought to kiss
But killed alas, and then bewailed his fatal bliss.

II

For since grim Aquilo his charioteer,
By boisterous rape the Athenian damsel got,
He thought it touched his deity full near,   10
If likewise he some fair one wedded not,
Thereby to wipe away the infámous blot,
    Of long-uncoupled bed and childless eld,
Which 'mongst the wanton gods a foul reproach was held.

III

So mounting up in icy-pearlèd car,
Through middle empire of the freezing air
He wandered long, till thee he spied from far;
There ended was his quest, there ceased his care.
Down he descended from his snow-soft chair,
    But all unwares with his cold-kind embrace   20
Unhoused thy virgin soul from her fair biding-place.

IV

Yet art thou not inglorious in thy fate;
For so Apollo, with unweeting hand

9. **the Athenian damsel,** Orithyia. See Ovid *Metamorphoses* vi. 682 ff. Milton's elaboration of the mythological imagery is carried to a point which his later taste would reject.

Whilom did slay his dearly-lovëd mate,
Young Hyacinth born on Eurotas' strand,
Young Hyacinth the pride of Spartan land;
    But then transformed him to a purple flower:
Alack that so to change thee Winter had no power.

V

Yet can I not persuade me thou art dead
Or that thy corse corrupts in earth's dark womb,   30
Or that thy beauties lie in wormy bed,
Hid from the world in a low-delvëd tomb;
Could Heaven for pity thee so strictly doom?
    Oh no! for something in thy face did shine
Above mortality that showed thou wast divine.

VI

Resolve me then O Soul most surely blest
(If so it be that thou these plaints dost hear),
Tell me bright Spirit, where'er thou hoverest,
Whether above that high first-moving sphere
Or in the Elysian fields (if such there were),   40
    Oh say me true if thou wert mortal wight
And why from us so quickly thou didst take thy flight.

VII

Wert thou some star which from the ruined roof
Of shaked Olympus by mischance didst fall;
Which careful Jove in nature's true behoof
Took up, and in fit place did reinstall?
Or did of late Earth's sons besiege the wall
    Of sheeny Heaven, and thou some goddess fled
Amongst us here below to hide thy nectared head?

VIII

Or wert thou that just maid who once before   50
Forsook the hated earth, O tell me sooth,
And cam'st again to visit us once more?
Or wert thou [Mercy], that sweet smiling Youth?

    39. first moving sphere, the primum mobile or outer shell of the
visible universe, which was supposed to impart motion to the lower spheres
containing the heavenly bodies.
    47. Earth's sons, the Titans who once tried to scale Olympus in a
rebellion against the gods.
    50. Astraea, goddess of justice, who departed from the earth at the end
of the Golden Age.

Or that crowned Matron, sage white-robëd Truth?
 Or any other of that heavenly brood
Let down in cloudy throne to do the world some good.

IX

Or wert thou of the golden-wingëd host,
Who having clad thyself in human weed,
To earth from thy prefixëd seat didst post,
And after short abode fly back with speed,   60
As if to show what creatures Heaven doth breed,
 Thereby to set the hearts of men on fire
To scorn the sordid world, and unto Heaven aspire.

X

But oh why didst thou not stay here below
To bless us with thy heaven-loved innocence,
To slake his wrath whom sin hath made our foe,
To turn swift-rushing black perdition hence,
Or drive away the slaughtering pestilence,
 To stand 'twixt us and our deservëd smart;
But thou canst best perform that office where thou art.   70

XI

Then thou the mother of so sweet a child,
Her false-imagined loss cease to lament,
And wisely learn to curb thy sorrows wild;
Think what a present thou to God hast sent,
And render him with patience what he lent;
 This if thou do he will an offspring give,
That till the world's last end shall make thy name to live.
                                                    [1628]

AT A VACATION EXERCISE IN THE COLLEGE,

PART LATIN, PART ENGLISH

These English verses formed part of an elaborate student
exhibition which took place at the close of the Lent term in
1628, Milton's last year as an undergraduate. The poet had

---

56. cloudy throne. Throne was a technical term for the device by
which actors were lowered onto the stage from the "Heavens." The
imagery suggests that Milton was already familiar with the stage effects
in the elaborate contemporary masques.

57 ff. These are the angelic guardians of whom Milton is to make
much use in his later poetry.

been chosen as "Father" to lead the ceremonies. He first delivered a witty oration in Latin on the congenial theme, "That occasional indulgence in sportive exercises is not inconsistent with philosophical studies." There followed a burlesque address, also in Latin, to his ten "sons." Then comes the unexpected resort to English verse, with the invocation to his native language and the playful verses on two of the sons in their allegorical capacity as representatives of certain concepts in the philosophy of Aristotle. The introductory Latin orations are preserved among the *Prolusions*; the continuations in English prose are lost. Milton's use of English and his proud praising of his native tongue is an expression of his feeling that this after all was his true medium. It is characteristic of him that he should thus advertise his calling before his tutors and fellow students. The poem suggests his fastidious interest in words and style. He eschews "new-fangled toys and trimming slight," and declares his allegiance to the luxuriant Renaissance expression of poets like Spenser. His characterization of the type of subject which calls him points forward to his epic aspirations. The description would suit any mythological or religious subject and gives no indication that he has in mind either the wars of Arthur or the Fall of Man. Except for Psalm 114, this is Milton's first and only use of the heroic couplet.

ANNO AETATIS 19

AT A VACATION EXERCISE IN THE COLLEGE, PART LATIN, PART ENGLISH

The Latin Speeches ended, the English thus began:

Hail Native Language, that by sinews weak
Didst move my first endeavoring tongue to speak
And mad'st imperfect words with childish trips,
Half unpronounced, slide through my infant lips,
Driving dumb Silence from the portal door,
Where he had mutely sat two years before:
Here I salute thee and thy pardon ask,
That now I use thee in my latter task.
Small loss it is that thence can come unto thee,
I know my tongue but little grace can do thee;   10
Thou needst not be ambitious to be first,

Believe me I have thither packed the worst;
And, if it happen as I did forecast,
The daintiest dishes shall be served up last.
I pray thee then deny me not thy aid
For this same small neglect that I have made;
But haste thee straight to do me once a pleasure,
And from thy wardrobe bring thy chiefest treasure;
Not those new-fangled toys and trimming slight
Which takes our late fantastics with delight,   20
But cull those richest robes and gay'st attire
Which deepest spirits and choicest wits desire.
I have some naked thoughts that rove about
And loudly knock to have their passage out;
And weary of their place do only stay
Till thou has decked them in thy best array;
That so they may without suspect or fears
Fly swiftly to this fair assembly's ears;
Yet I had rather if I were to choose,
Thy service in some graver subject use,   30
Such as may make thee search thy coffers round,
Before thou clothe my fancy in fit sound:
Such where the deep transported mind may soar
Above the wheeling poles, and at Heaven's door
Look in, and see each blissful deity
How he before the thunderous throne doth lie,
Listening to what unshorn Apollo sings
To the touch of golden wires, while Hebe brings
Immortal nectar to her kingly sire;
Then passing through the spheres of watchful fire,   40
And misty regions of wide air next under,
And hills of snow and lofts of pilèd thunder,
May tell at length how green-eyed Neptune raves,
In Heaven's defiance mustering all his waves;
Then sing of secret things that came to pass
When beldam Nature in her cradle was;
And last of kings and queens and heroes old,
Such as the wise Demodocus once told
In solemn songs at king Alcinous' feast,
While sad Ulysses' soul and all the rest   50
Are held with his melodious harmony
In willing chains and sweet captivity.
But fie my wandering Muse how thou dost stray!
Expectance calls thee now another way;

20. **late fantastics.** Presumably some recent group of fancy writers
well known to the Cambridge audience.
48 ff. See *Odyssey* viii. 521 ff.

Thou know'st it must be now thy only bent
To keep in compass of thy Predicament:
Then quick about thy purposed business come,
That to the next I may resign my room.

Then ENS *is represented as Father of the Predicaments, his ten
sons, whereof the eldest stood for* SUBSTANCE *with his Canons,
which* ENS *thus speaking, explains:*

Good luck befriend thee Son; for at thy birth
The fairy ladies danced upon the hearth;   60
Thy drowsy nurse hath sworn she did them spy
Come tripping to the room where thou didst lie;
And sweetly singing round about thy bed,
Strew all their blessings on thy sleeping head.
She heard them give thee this, that thou should'st still
From eyes of mortals walk invisible;
Yet there is something that doth force my fear,
For once it was my dismal hap to hear
A sibyl old, bow-bent with crooked age,
That far events full wisely could presage,   70
And in time's long and dark prospective glass
Foresaw what future days should bring to pass:
'Your son,' said she, '(nor can you it prevent)
Shall subject be to many an *Accident.*
O'er all his brethren he shall reign as king,
Yet every one shall make him underling,
And those that cannot live from him asunder
Ungratefully shall strive to keep him under;
In worth and excellence he shall outgo them,
Yet being above them, he shall be below them;   80
From others he shall stand in need of nothing,
Yet on his brothers shall depend for clothing.
To find a foe it shall not be his hap,
And peace shall lull him in her flowery lap;
Yet shall he live in strife, and at his door

56. **in compass of thy Predicament**, within the logical boundaries of
the present assignment. Predicament is used in its technical sense of ultimate concepts or form of thought, category.
     Ens, absolute being, pure existence. Substance is the first of the ten
Aristotelian categories or predicaments. The other nine are quantity, quality, relation, place, time, position, possession, action, passivity. These are
the accidents or manifestations of substance. Milton plays on these ideas
in the following lines. Substance is the broader category, therefore king
over the others. Yet he is subject to them because he cannot be known
except by them. He is absolute but dependent on them for his clothing.
He gives order to them but they are perpetually at war. This is the scholas-
tic problem which the characters are invited to act out.

Devouring war shall never cease to roar;
Yea it shall be his natural property
To harbor those that are at enmity.'
What power, what force, what mighty spell, if not
Your learned hands, can loose this Gordian knot?   90

The next, QUANTITY *and* QUALITY, *spoke in prose, then* RELATION
    was called by his name.

Rivers arise; whether thou be the son
Of utmost Tweed, or Ouse, or gulfy Dun,
Or Trent, who like some earth-born giant spreads
His thirty arms along the indented meads,
Or sullen Mole, that runneth underneath,
Or Severn swift, guilty of maiden's death,
Or rocky Avon, or of sedgy Lea,
Or coaly Tyne, or ancient hallowed Dee,
Or Humber loud, that keeps the Scythian's name,
Or Medway smooth, or royal-towered Thame.   100

(The rest was prose.)

[1628]

ELEGY V

Elegy V, written in 1629, with its enthusiastic greeting of
the spring and its wealth of erotic imagery, represents an even
more complete surrender to the Pagan mood than Elegy VII.
The poet's experience of a renewed creative impulse in the
spring is at variance with Phillips's statement that his vein
flowed most freely from the autumnal to the vernal equinox
and we have another evidence of springtime inspiration in the
sonnet, "O Nightingale." Presumably Milton's habits of
composition changed in later years. With the abandonment
of love and wine as sources of poetry the poetic mood was less
likely to flourish in spring and summer. We may note that in
the Nativity ode Milton speaks of the dawn of Christmas day
as bringing him the theme. This is the first evidence of winter
inspiration.

91. **There were** two students named Rivers at Christ College and
Milton must be addressing one of them. Descriptions of the rivers of
England occur in both Spenser and Drayton.
96. **maiden's death.** The reference is to the Sabrina episode later used
in *Comus.*
99. Humber was a mythical Scythian king supposed to have been
drowned in this river.

ELEGY V

(Translation)

ON THE APPROACH OF SPRING

Time, never wandering from his annual round,
Bids Zephyr breathe the Spring, and thaw the ground;
Bleak Winter flies, new verdure clothes the plain,
And Earth assumes her transient youth again.
Dream I, or also to the Spring belong
Increase of genius, and new powers of song?
Spring gives them, and, how strange soe'er it seems,
Impels me now to some harmonious themes.
Castalia's fountain and the forkëd hill,
By day, by night, my raptured fancy fill;   10
My bosom burns and heaves, I hear within
A sacred sound that prompts me to begin.
Lo, Phœbus comes! with his bright hair he blends
The radiant laurel wreath; Phœbus descends:
I mount, and undepressed by cumbrous clay
Through cloudy regions win my easy way;
Rapt, through poetic shadowy haunts I fly;
The shrines all open to my dauntless eye,
My spirit searches all the realms of light,
And no Tartarean gulfs elude my sight.   20
But this ecstatic trance—this glorious storm
Of inspiration—what will it perform?
Spring claims the verse, that with his influence glows,
And shall be paid with what himself bestows.
   Thou, veiled with opening foliage, lead'st the throng
Of feathered minstrels, Philomel! in song;
Let us, in concert, to the season sing,
Civic and sylvan heralds of the Spring!
   With notes triumphant Spring's approach declare!
To Spring, ye Muses, annual tribute bear!   30
The Orient left and Æthiopia's plains,
The Sun now northward turns his golden reins;
Night creeps not now, yet rules with gentle sway,
And drives her dusky horrors swift away;
Now less fatigued, on this ethereal plain
Boötes follows his celestial wain;
And now the radiant sentinels above,

9. forkëd hill, Mount Parnassus, with its twin peaks.
   25-26. Milton himself translates these lines in the sonnet "O Nightingale."
   28. Civic and sylvan, literally "I in the city, you in the woods."

Less numerous, watch around the courts of Jove.
For, with the night, force, ambush, slaughter fly,
And no gigantic guilt alarms the sky.   40
Now haply says some shepherd, while he views,
Recumbent on a rock, the reddening dews,
"This night, this surely, Phœbus missed the Fair,
Who stops his chariot by her amorous care."
Cynthia, delighted by the morning's glow,
Speeds to the woodland, and resumes her bow;
Resigns her beams, and, glad to disappear,
Blesses his aid who shortens her career.
"Come"—Phœbus cries—"Aurora come—too late
Thou lingerest, slumbering, with thy withered mate!   50
Leave him, and to Hymettus' top repair!
Thy darling Cephalus expects thee there."
The goddess, with a blush, her love betrays,
But mounts, and, driving rapidly, obeys.
Earth now desires thee, Phœbus! and to engage
Thy warm embrace, casts off the guise of age;
Desires thee, and deserves; for who so sweet,
When her rich bosom courts thy genial heat?
Her breath imparts to every breeze that blows
Arabia's harvest, and the Paphian rose.   60
Her lofty front she diadems around
With sacred pines, like Ops on Ida crowned;
Her dewy locks with various flowers new-blown
She interweaves, various, and all her own,
For Proserpine, in such a wreath attired,
Tænarian Dis himself with love inspired.
Fear not, lest, cold and coy, the nymph refuse!
Herself, with all her sighing Zephyrs, sues;
Each courts thee, fanning soft his scented wing,
And all her groves with warbled wishes ring.   70
Nor, unendowed and indigent, aspires
The amorous Earth to engage thy warm desires,
But, rich in balmy drugs, assists thy claim,
Divine Physician! to that glorious name.
If splendid recompense, if gifts can move

43. Literally, "This night, this night surely, you lacked a woman
[puella] to hold back your fast horses." Modern prose translators share
Cowper's instinct for avoiding the shepherd's direct and pregnant speech:
"Surely this night, O Phœbus, thou hast lacked loving arms to hold thee
back, thee and thy swift horses."
    50. withered mate, Tithonus, who was granted immortality without
eternal youth.
    62. Ops, a goddess of fertility.
    66. Dis, Pluto, who had a temple on Mount Taenarus.

Desire in thee (gifts often purchase love),
She offers all the wealth her mountains hide,
And all that rests beneath the boundless tide.
How oft, when headlong from the heavenly steep
She sees thee playing in the western deep,   80
How oft she cries—"Ah Phœbus! why repair
Thy wasted force, why seek refreshment there?
Can Tethys win thee? wherefore shouldst thou lave
A face so fair in her unpleasant wave?
Come, seek my green retreats, and rather choose
To cool thy tresses in my crystal dews,
The grassy turf shall yield thee sweeter rest;
Come, lay thy evening glories on my breast,
And breathing fresh, through many a humid rose,
Soft whispering airs shall lull thee to repose!   90
No fears I feel like Semele to die,
Nor lest thy burning wheels approach too nigh,—
For thou canst govern them; here therefore rest,
And lay thy evening glories on my breast!"
     Thus breathes the wanton Earth her amorous flame,
And all her countless offspring feel the same;
For Cupid now through every region strays,
Brightening his faded fires with solar rays;
His new-strung bow sends forth a deadlier sound,
And his new-pointed shafts more deeply wound;   100
Nor Dian's self escapes him now untried,
Nor even Vesta at her altar-side;
His mother too repairs her beauty's wane,
And seems sprung newly from the deep again.
Exulting youths the Hymeneal sing,
With Hymen's name roofs, rocks, and valleys ring;
He, new-attired, and by the season drest,
Proceeds, all fragrant, in his saffron vest.
Now, many a golden-cinctured virgin roves
To taste the pleasures of the fields and groves;   110
All wish, and each alike, some favourite youth
Hers, in the bonds of Hymeneal truth.
Now pipes the shepherd through his reeds again,
Nor Phillis wants a song that suits the strain;
With songs the seaman hails the starry sphere,
And dolphins rise from the abyss to hear;

83. **Tethys,** wife of Oceanus.
91. **Semele,** who asked her lover, Jove, to appear in all his splendor and was destroyed by his brightness.
103. **His mother,** Venus, who was born of the sea-foam.

Jove feels himself the season, sports again
With his fair spouse, and banquets all his train.
Now too the Satyrs, in the dusk of eve,
Their mazy dance through flowery meadows weave,   120
And neither god nor goat, but both in kind,
Silvanus, wreathed with cypress, skips behind.
The Dryads leave their hollow sylvan cells
To roam the banks and solitary dells;
Pan riots now, and from his amorous chafe
Ceres and Cybele seem hardly safe;
And Faunus, all on fire to reach the prize,
In chase of some enticing Oread flies;
She bounds before, but fears too swift a bound,
And hidden lies, but wishes to be found.   130
Our shades entice the Immortals from above,
And some kind power presides o'er every grove;
And long, ye Powers, o'er every grove preside,
For all is safe and blest, where ye abide!
Return, O Jove! the age of gold restore—
Why choose to dwell where storms and thunder roar?
At least, thou, Phœbus! moderate thy speed!
Let not the vernal hours too swift proceed,
Command rough Winter back, nor yield the pole
Too soon to Night's encroaching, long control!   140
                                        [1629]

SONNET I

There is little to tell us when Milton wrote this first sonnet or
the Italian poems which follow it in the 1645 edition of the
Poems. They seem, however, to be closely associated with
Elegy V, two lines of which occur in exact English equivalent
in Sonnet I, and with Elegy VII, which like Sonnet III, confesses that Cupid has at last avenged himself on a scorner of
his power. In the English poem, Milton follows Chaucer in
writing himself humorously into the role of an unsuccessful
lover. The piece is reminiscent of Clanvowe's "The Cuckoo
and the Nightingale," which was included in the edition of
Chaucer which Milton used. The form, however, is Petrarchan.

    The idea that the Italian sonnets and the canzone were writ-
ten in Italy is based on a careless reading of them. The environment of youths and maidens who stand in a circle and
reproach Milton for using a foreign tongue is evidently English. The conceit of the second sonnet, that the poet is trying

to raise a southern flower in a northern climate, also points to
composition in England. Finally, it is unlikely that Milton
would have indulged in conventional sonneteering after his
deliberate change to serious themes in 1629. The first sonnet
gives us the lady's name in the riddling fashion of the
Petrarchan tradition. She must, if she is real, have been some
girl of Italian extraction in London. The solemn way in which
Milton speaks of his own personality in the last sonnet is characteristic. He is later to describe Adam as weak only in his
susceptibility to "female charm."

SONNET I

O nightingale, that on yon bloomy spray
    Warblest at eve, when all the woods are still,
    Thou with fresh hope the lover's heart dost fill,
    While the jolly hours lead on propitious May;
Thy liquid notes that close the eye of day,
    First heard before the shallow cuckoo's bill,
    Portend success in love; O if Jove's will
Have linked that amorous power to thy soft lay,
Now timely sing, ere the rude bird of hate
    Foretell my hopeless doom in some grove nigh,   10
    As thou from year to year hast sung too late
For my relief, yet hadst no reason why:
    Whether the Muse or Love call thee his mate,
    Both them I serve, and of their train am I.
                                        [1628?]

SONNET II

Donna leggiadra il cui bel nome onora
    L' erbosa val di Reno e il nobil varco,
    Ben è colui d' ogni valore scarco
Qual tuo spirto gentil non innamora,
Che dolcemente mostrasi di fuora,
    De' suói atti soavi giammai parco,
    E i don', che son d' amor saette ed arco,
Là onde l' alta tua virtù s' infiora.
Quando tu vaga parli, o lieta canti,
    Che mover possa duro alpestre legno,   10
    Guardi ciascun agli occhi ed agli orecchi
L'entrata chi di te si trova indegno;
    Grazia sola di sù gli vaglia, innanti
    Che 'l disio amoroso al cuor s' invecchi.
                                        [1628?]

(Translation)

Fair Lady! whose harmonious name the Rhine,
   Through all his grassy vale, delights to hear,
   Base were indeed the wretch who could forbear
   To love a spirit elegant as thine,
That manifests a sweetness all divine,
   Nor knows a thousand winning acts to spare,
   And graces, which Love's bow and arrows are,
   Tempering thy virtues to a softer shine.
When gracefully thou speakest, or singest gay,
   Such strains as might the senseless forest move,   10
   Ah then—turn each his eyes and ears away,
Who feels himself unworthy of thy love!
   Grace can alone preserve him, ere the dart
   Of fond desire yet reach his inmost heart.

SONNET III

Qual in colle aspro, al imbrunir di sera,
   L' avvezza giovinetta pastorella
   Va bagnando l' erbetta strana e bella,
   Che mal si spande a disusata spera
Fuor di sua natia alma primavera,
   Così Amor meco insù la lingua snella
   Desta il fior novo di strania favella,
   Mentre io di te, vezzosamente altera,
Canto, dal mio buon popol non inteso,
   E 'l bel Tamigi cangio col bel Arno.   10
   Amor lo volse, ed io, a l' altrui peso,
Seppi ch' Amor cosa mai volse indarno.
   Deh! foss' il mio cuor lento e 'l duro seno
   A chi pianta dal ciel si buon terreno.

                       [1628?]

(Translation)

As on a hill-top rude, when closing day
   Imbrowns the scene, some pastoral maiden fair
   Waters a lovely foreign plant with care,
   Borne from its native genial airs away,

---

   2. delights to hear. Literally "whose fair name honors the flowery valley of the Reno and the famous ford." The lady's name is the same as that of the Italian district Emilia, through which flow the Reno and the Rubicon, with its famous ford which Caesar crossed. Such use of an allusion to reveal indirectly the name of the lady addressed is common with Italian sonnet writers.

That scarcely can its tender bud display;
So on my tongue these accents, new and rare,
Are flowers exotic, which Love waters there.
While thus, O sweetly scornful! I essay
Thy praise in verse to British ears unknown,
And Thames exchange for Arno's fair domain;   10
So Love has willed, and ofttimes Love has shown
That what he wills he never wills in vain.
Oh that this hard and sterile breast might be
To Him, who plants from heaven, a soil as free!

CANZONE

Ridonsi donne e giovani amorosi,
M' accostandosi attorno, e "Perchè scrivi,
Perchè tu scrivi in lingua ignota e strana,
Verseggiando d' amor, e com t' osi?
Dinne, se la tua speme sia mai vana,
E de' pensieri lo miglior t' arrivi!"
Così mi van burlando: "altri rivi,
Altri lidi t' aspettan, ed altre onde,
Nelle cui verdi sponde
Spuntati ad or ad or a la tua chioma   10
L' immortal guiderdon d' eterne frondi.
Perchè alle spalle tue soverchia soma?"
   Canzon, dirotti, e tu per me rispondi,
Dice mia Donna, e 'l suo dir è il mio cuore,
"Questa è lingua di cui si vanta Amore."
                      [1628?]

(Translation)

They mock my toil—the nymphs and amorous swains—
"And whence this fond attempt to write," they cry,
"Love-songs in language that thou little knowest?
"How darest thou risk to sing these foreign strains?
"Say truly,—findest not oft thy purpose crossed,
"And that thy fairest flowers here fade and die?"
Then, with pretence of admiration high—
"Thee other shores expect, and other tides;
"Rivers, on whose grassy sides
"Her deathless laurel leaf, with which to bind   10
"Thy flowing locks, already Fame provides;
"Why then this burthen, better far declined?"

9. Literally "not understood by my own good people."
  10. To exchange Thames for Arno is merely to write in Italian instead
of English. The line does not imply that the poem was written in Italy.

Speak Muse! for me.—The fair one said, who guides
My willing heart, and all my fancy's flights,
"This is the language in which Love delights."

SONNET IV

Diodati (e te 'l dirò con maraviglia),
    Quel ritroso io, ch' amor spreggiar solea
    E de' suoi lacci spesso mi ridea,
    Già caddi, ov' uom dabben talor s' impiglia.
Nè treccie d' oro, nè guancia vermiglia
    M' abbaglian sì, ma sotto nûova idea
    Pellegrina bellezza che 'l cuor bea,
    Portamenti alti onesti, e nelle ciglia
Quel sereno fulgor d' amabil nero,
    Parole adorne di lingua più d' una,   10
    E 'l cantar che di mezzo l' emisfero
Traviar ben può la faticosa Luna;
    E degli occhi suoi avventa sì gran fuoco
    Che l' incerar gli orecchi mi fia poco.

                                  [1628?]

(Translation)

Charles—and I say it wondering—thou must know
    That I, who once assumed a scornful air,
    And scoffed at Love, am fallen in his snare;
    (Full many an upright man has fallen so.)
Yet think me not thus dazzled by the flow
    Of golden locks, or damask cheek; more rare
    The heartfelt beauties of my foreign fair,
    A mien majestic, with dark brows that show
The tranquil lustre of a lofty mind;
    Words exquisite, of idioms more than one,   10
    And song, whose fascinating power might bind,
And from her sphere draw down, the labouring moon;
    With such fire-darting eyes, that I should fill
    My ears with wax, she would enchant me still.

    1. The nymphs and swains are English, not Italian, for the latter would
not call his language "ignota e strana."
    8. other shores, i.e., poetic achievements in other languages.
    1 ff. See Elegy VII where Milton also announces himself for the first
time in love, and Elegy I, addressed to Diodati, where he is heart free but
in danger.
    7. my foreign fair. See the Italian, "a foreign type of beauty under
a new idea." This and the mention of dark complexion and "words adorned
with more languages than one" are a kind of retraction of the praise of
English maidens in Elegy I. It is tempting to think of the glamorous
stranger, if she is real, as someone in the Diodati circle.

SONNET V

Per certo i bei vostr' occhi, Donna mia,
    Esser non può che non sian lo mio sole;
    Sì mi percuoton forte, come ei suole
    Per l' arene di Libia chi s' invia,
Mentre un caldo vapor (nè sentì pria)
    Da quel lato si spinge ove mi duole,
    Che forse amanti nelle lor parole
    Chiaman sospir; io non so che si sia.
Parte rinchiusa e turbida si cela
    Scosso mi il petto, e poi n' uscendo poco   10
    Quivi d' attorno o s' agghiaccia o s' ingiela;
Ma quanto agli occhi giunge a trovar loco
    Tutte le notti a me suol far piovose,
    Finchè mia alba rivien colma di rose.
                                                    [1628?]

(Translation)

Lady! it cannot be but that thine eyes
    Must be my sun, such radiance they display,
    And strike me even as Phœbus him whose way
    Through horrid Libya's sandy desert lies.
Meantime, on that side steamy vapours rise
    Where most I suffer. Of what kind are they,
    New as to me they are, I cannot say,
    But deem them, in the lover's language—sighs.
Some, though with pain, my bosom close conceals,
    Which, if in part escaping thence, they tend   10
    To soften thine, thy coldness soon congeals.
While others to my tearful eyes ascend,
    Whence my sad nights in showers are ever drowned,
    Till my Aurora comes, her brow with roses bound.

SONNET VI

Giovane, piano, e semplicetto amante
    Poichè fuggir me stesso in dubbio sono,
    Madonna, a voi del mio cuor l' umil dono
    Farò divoto; io certo a prove tante
L' ebbi fedele, intrepido, costante,
    Di pensieri leggiadro, accorto, e buono;
    Quando rugge il gran mondo, e scocca il tuono,
    S' arma di se, e d' intero diamante,

Sonnet V. The personal quality of the other sonnets is rendered more striking by the merely conventional character of this one.

Tanto del forse e d' invidia sicuro,
  Di timori, e speranze al popol use,   10
  Quanto d' ingegno e d' alto valor vago,
E di cetra sonora, e delle Muse.
  Sol troverete in tal parte men duro
  Ove Amor mise l' insanabil ago.

                                                [1628?]

                   (Translation)

Enamoured, artless, young, on foreign ground,
  Uncertain whither from myself to fly,
  To thee, dear Lady, with an humble sigh
  Let me devote my heart, which I have found
By certain proofs, not few, intrepid, sound,
  Good, and addicted to conceptions high:
  When tempests shake the world, and fire the sky,
  It rests in adamant self-wrapt around,
As safe from envy, and from outrage rude,
  From hopes and fears that vulgar minds abuse,   10
  As fond of genius and fixed fortitude,
Of the resounding lyre, and every muse.
  Weak you will find it in one only part,
  Now pierced by Love's immedicable dart.

LINES APPENDED TO THE BOOK OF ELEGIES

                   (Translation)

  Such were the trophies that, in earlier days,
  By vanity seduced, I toiled to raise,
  Studious, yet indolent, and urged by youth,
  That worst of teachers! from the ways of truth;
  Till learning taught me, in his shady bower,
  To quit Love's servile yoke, and spurn his power.

    1. on foreign ground. There is nothing in the Italian text to justify
this. Cowper is simply following the old assumption that, because the
sonnets were written in Italian, they must belong to the Italian period.
    5–6. This is surely an early bit of self-portraiture. The last lines, saying
that susceptibility to love is the only weakness, contain an idea embodied
in Adam's account of himself in *Paradise Lost*. It is quite possible to say
that both passages are Petrarchan tradition.
    5. Till learning taught. Literally, "till the shady Academy offered
me its Socratic streams." We know from other statements that Milton
thought of the study of Plato as emancipating his mind from lower loves
and fixing it on the divine idea. One may guess that these lines belong to
a time when he was arranging the Latin poems for publication, perhaps in
1645. But the Platonic fervor was high when *Comus* was written and continued so through the Horton period.

Then, on a sudden, the fierce flame suppressed,
A frost continual settled on my breast,
Whence Cupid fears his flames extinct to see,
And Venus dreads a Diomede in me.   10
                              [Before 1645]

ON THE MORNING OF CHRIST'S NATIVITY

The close of Elegy VI alludes to this "birthday gift for Christ" as begun at the first light of dawn on Christmas day. It is interesting that the two poems—the elegy, a declaration that his muse will henceforth be devoted to lofty themes, and the ode, a first fruit of this higher mood—should have followed so closely upon Milton's own birthday. He was twenty-one on December 8, 1629.

The sanctity and joy of the Christmas season have never been more beautifully expressed than in these verses. Milton speaks at last with his own authentic accent, hymning the spiritual significance of Christ's birth as the beginning of the reign of peace and truth on earth. The opening lines are in the full tradition of orthodox Christianity, showing Milton to be as yet unaffected by the rationalistic and unitarian point of view which he later came to adopt. The hymn of the shepherds owes its primary inspiration to the Scriptural narrative, but the simple theme is embellished in characteristic fashion with the treasures of Milton's erudition. His favorite poetic symbol of the music of the spheres is turned to happy account, and his interest in the monstrous variety of the pagan divinities furnishes him with a significant and picturesque background against which to throw the simple majesty of Christ. We may note that he touches only in cursory fashion and with no great tenderness the manger scene itself. There is nothing of the sweetness of Crashaw's parallel poem on the Nativity. Milton's religious feeling has the solemnity and elevation of a church anthem.

In verse-form and style the ode owes much to the poetry of the Spenserian school, particularly to the lyrics of Phineas Fletcher. The conceits in stanzas i and ii of the Hymn are of the Elizabethan tradition generally. The poet soon discards them as his inspiration rises, and in stanzas iv, xii, and xvi he strikes a note which preludes the great Miltonic music of *Paradise Lost*. Two passages, stanzas iii and xv, employ imagery suggestive of the masque.

ON THE MORNING OF CHRIST'S NATIVITY
(Composed 1629)

I

This is the month, and this the happy morn,
Wherein the Son of Heaven's eternal King,
Of wedded Maid and Virgin Mother born,
Our great redemption from above did bring;
For so the holy Sages once did sing,
    That he our deadly forfeit should release,
And with his Father work us a perpetual peace.

II

That glorious form, that light unsufferable,
And that far-beaming blaze of majesty,
Wherewith he wont at Heaven's high council-table   10
To sit the midst of Trinal Unity,
He laid aside; and here with us to be,
    Forsook the courts of everlasting day,
And chose with us a darksome house of mortal clay.

III

Say Heavenly Muse, shall not thy sacred vein
Afford a present to the Infant God?
Hast thou no verse, no hymn, or solemn strain,
To welcome him to this his new abode,
Now while the Heaven by the sun's team untrod,
    Hath took no print of the approaching light,   20
And all the spangled host keep watch in squadrons bright?

IV

See how from far upon the eastern road
The star-led Wizards haste with odors sweet!
O run, prevent them with thy humble ode,
And lay it lowly at his blessed feet;
Have thou the honor first thy Lord to greet,
    And join thy voice unto the angel choir,
From out his secret altar touched with hallowed fire.

    5. **the holy Sages,** the Old Testament prophets.
    6. **deadly forfeit,** the forfeit of mankind to death as a penalty for Adam's sin.
    11. **Trinal Unity.** Milton apparently accepts the orthodox conception of the Trinity. Later his theology moved in the direction of Unitarianism.
    24. **prevent,** come before, anticipate. Milton expresses his zeal by picturing himself as offering the first gift at the manger.
    28. The same fire of inspiration that touches the angels' lips touches Milton's.

militant poet - offer his song in praise of God

THE HYMN   *ode form, answers and refrains*

I

It was the winter wild,
While the Heaven-born child   30
All meanly wrapped in the rude manger lies;
Nature in awe to him
Had doffed her gaudy trim,   *nature stands back for Christ's splendor*
    With her great Master so to sympathize;
It was no season then for her
To wanton with the sun her lusty paramour.

II

Only with speeches fair   *calm winds*
She woos the gentle air
    To hide her guilty front with innocent snow,   *fall of man affected nature snow covers guilt*
And on her naked shame,   40
Pollute with sinful blame,
    The saintly veil of maiden white to throw,
Confounded, that her Maker's eyes
Should look so near upon her foul deformities.

III

But he her fears to cease,
Sent down the meek-eyed Peace;
    She crowned with olive green, came softly sliding
Down through the turning sphere,
His ready harbinger,
    With turtle wing the amorous clouds dividing,   50
And waving wide her myrtle wand,
She strikes a universal peace through sea and land.

IV

No war or battle's sound
Was heard the world around:
    The idle spear and shield were high uphung,

34. sympathize, literally suffer with, in the sense of being no better clad than the child. Milton describes Nature wantoning with her paramour, the Sun, in Elegy V.
39. front, forehead. Nature, like man, bears the guilt of Adam.
45–52. The image of Peace descending through the clouds suggests the pageantry of the court masques. So also does the picture of the angelic hosts in stanza xi and that of Truth, Justice, and Mercy in stanza xv.
53 ff. The historical fact that the Roman Empire enjoyed peace at the time of Christ's birth was mentioned by the Church Fathers as fulfilling Isaiah's prophecy: "Nation shall not lift up the sword against nation, neither shall they learn war any more." Like the heavenly music this phenomenon was momentary and symbolic.

The hookèd chariot stood
Unstained with hostile blood,
   The trumpet spake not to the armèd throng,
And kings sat still with awful eye,
As if they surely knew their sovran Lord was by.   60

V

But peaceful was the night
Wherein the Prince of Light
   His reign of peace upon the earth began:
The winds with wonder whist,
Smoothly the waters kissed,
   Whispering new joys to the mild ocean,
Who now hath quite forgot to rave,
While birds of calm sit brooding on the charmèd wave.

VI

The stars with deep amaze
Stand fixed in steadfast gaze,   70
   Bending one way their precious influence,
And will not take their flight,
For all the morning light,
   Or Lucifer that often warned them thence;
But in their glimmering orbs did glow,
Until their Lord himself bespake, and bid them go.

VII

And though the shady gloom
Had given day her room,
   The sun himself withheld his wonted speed,
And hid his head for shame,   80
As his inferior flame
   The new-enlightened world no more should need;
He saw a greater sun appear
Than his bright throne or burning axletree could bear.

VIII

The shepherds on the lawn,
Or ere the point of dawn,
   Sat simply chatting in a rustic row;

    68. **birds of calm,** the halcyons, who brooded on the sea in calm weather.
    71. Ordinarily the stars exert a varied influence. At this time it was all favorable.
    85–92. The episode of the shepherds constitutes a slight link with pastoral poetry and justifies designating Christ as Pan, the god of shepherds and of nature, with allusion to the Greek meaning of the name, all, the universe.
    86. **Or ere,** before.

Full little thought they then
That the mighty Pan
  Was kindly come to live with them below;   90
Perhaps their loves, or else their sheep,
Was all that did their silly thoughts so busy keep.

Christ - shepherd
flood

IX

When such music sweet
Their hearts and ears did greet,
  As never was by mortal finger strook,
Divinely-warbled voice
Answering the stringèd noise,
  As all their souls in blissful rapture took;
The air such pleasure loth to lose,
With thousand echoes still prolongs each heavenly close.   100

X

Nature that heard such sound
Beneath the hollow round
  Of Cynthia's seat, the airy region thrilling, *moon -*
Now was almost won *anything below moon is sin*
To think her part was done,
  And that her reign had here its last fulfilling;
She knew such harmony alone
Could hold all Heaven and Earth in happier union. *union between universe and earth.*

XI   *chaos & disorder of earth to be set straight—*

At last surrounds their sight
A globe of circular light,   110
  That with long beams the shame-faced Night arrayed; *Felix culpa fortunate fall brought Christ to earth*
The helmèd Cherubim
And swordèd Seraphim,
  Are seen in glittering ranks with wings displayed,
Harping in loud and solemn choir,
With unexpressive notes to Heaven's new-born Heir.

XII

Such music (as 'tis said)
Before was never made,
  But when of old the Sons of Morning sung,
While the Creator great   120
His constellations set,

    97. **stringèd noise,** instrumental music.
    99. The pathetic fallacy abounds in this poem as it does in "Lycidas."
Cf. stanza ii of "The Hymn."
    100. **close,** cadence.
    117–32. Milton identifies the song the angels sang with that heard at

And the well-balanced world on hinges hung,
And cast the dark foundations deep,
And bid the weltering waves their oozy channel keep.

XIII

Ring out ye crystal spheres,
Once bless our human ears
    (If ye have power to touch our senses so),
And let your silver chime
Move in melodious time,
    And let the bass of Heaven's deep organ blow;   130
And with your ninefold harmony
Make up full consort to the angelic symphony.

XIV

For if such holy song
Enwrap our fancy long,
    Time will run back and fetch the Age of Gold,
And speckled Vanity
Will sicken soon and die,
    And leprous Sin will melt from earthly mould,
And Hell itself will pass away,
And leave her dolorous mansions to the peering day.   140

XV

Yea, Truth and Justice then
Will down return to men,
    Orbed in a rainbow; and like glories wearing,

the creation of the world, "when the morning stars sang together and the
sons of God shouted for joy" (Job 38:7); and this in turn with the Platonic
harmony poured forth by the celestial spheres in their motion around the
earth (*The Republic* x). Shakespeare phrases the latter idea in its Christian conception.

> There's not the smallest orb that thou behold'st
> But in his motion like an angel sings,
> Still quiring to the young-eyed cherubims;
> But whilst this muddy vesture of decay
> Doth grossly hem us in, we cannot hear it.
>   (*Merchant of Venice*, V, i, 61–65.)

Though this music in its fullness is unheard on earth the pure soul may
aspire to it. To Milton it symbolizes the source of his own higher poetic
inspiration.
    132. consort, instrumental harmony.
    133 ff. Milton's lines suggest the prophecy of a return of the golden
age in Virgil's fourth eclogue, a poem which was interpreted as Messianic
and may actually have been influenced by Hebrew ideas as embodied in
Isaiah.
    141–48. See note on lines 45–52. The opening up of a celestial scene
with allegorical figures enthroned is a characteristic effect in masques.

[margin handwritten note: Pythagorean around earth tended by angels (songs harmony of universe)]

Mercy will sit between,
Throned in celestial sheen,
  With radiant feet the tissued clouds down steering,
And Heaven as at some festival,
Will open wide the gates of her high palace-hall.

XVI

But wisest Fate says No,
This must not yet be so,   150
  The Babe lies yet in smiling infancy,
That on the bitter cross
Must redeem our loss,
  So both himself and us to glorify;
Yet first to those ychained in sleep,
The wakeful trump of doom must thunder through the deep,

XVII

With such a horrid clang
As on Mount Sinai rang
  While the red fire and smouldering clouds out brake.
The agèd Earth aghast   160
With terror of that blast,
  Shall from the surface to the center shake;
When at the world's last session,
The dreadful Judge in middle air shall spread his throne.

XVIII

And then at last our bliss
Full and perfect is,
  But now begins; for from this happy day
The old Dragon under ground
In straiter limits bound,
  Not half so far casts his usurpèd sway,   170

155. The "y" is grammatically a survival of the Old English prefix "ge." See note on *star-ypointing*, p. 74. Milton follows Spenser in the use of this and a few other archaic forms. They provide a poetic heightening, and serve to remove the language from the commonplace and to pay a kind of tribute to tradition. Milton had bidden his Native Language supply him with its richest robes and gayest attire. Spenser was one of the choice spirits who wove these robes, and *ychained, yclept, ypointing* are small stitches in the embroidery. Moreover, Spenser himself was an avowed disciple of Chaucer. Milton counted himself the lineal heir of both. In the context of this passage the Spenserian touch is particularly suggestive. Those who lie waiting for the resurrection are like persons who have been enchanted. Their senses have been miraculously "bound up." The idea carries with it something of the atmosphere of the fairy world, the world of the *Faerie Queene*.
157–60. When Moses received the tablets of the law, Exod. 19.

And wroth to see his kingdom fail,
Swinges the scaly horror of his folded tail.

XIX

The oracles are dumb;
No voice or hideous hum
   Runs through the archéd roof in words deceiving.
Apollo from his shrine
Can no more divine,
   With hollow shriek the steep of Delphos leaving.
No nightly trance or breathéd spell,
Inspires the pale-eyed priest from the prophetic cell.   180

XX

The lonely mountains o'er,
And the resounding shore,
   A voice of weeping heard, and loud lament;
From haunted spring and dale
Edged with poplar pale,
   The parting Genius is with sighing sent;
With flower-inwoven tresses torn
The Nymphs in twilight shade of tangled thickets mourn.

XXI

In consecrated earth,
And on the holy hearth,   190
   The Lars and Lemures moan with midnight plaint;
In urns and altars round,
A drear and dying sound
   Affrights the Flamens at their service quaint;
And the chill marble seems to sweat,
While each peculiar power forgoes his wonted seat.

   182-84. According to legend the pilot of a ship sailing from Cyprus heard a voice from shore bidding him announce that Pan was dead. When he did so there was a great noise of lamentation and from that time forth the oracles ceased to give responses. The whole idea of the succeeding stanzas is that the demon followers of Satan, who had imposed their worship on men in innumerable forms, are no longer able to deceive them and flee in terror from their shrines.

   191. The Lares and Lemures were the household spirits of Roman religion.

   194. Flamens, Roman priests.

   196-220. Having spoken of Greek and Roman superstition Milton now calls the roll of the hideous deities of Palestine and Egypt. The passage has a parallel in *Paradise Lost*, II, 376 ff. The twice-battered god is Dagon in I Sam. 5. Astoroth is Astarte, a moon goddess whose lover, Thammuz, was mourned annually in Syria. The Greek counterpart of the myth is that of Endymion and Artemis. Osiris, his sister and wife Isis, and her son Horus were the chief Egyptian divinities. The sacred chest containing the image of Osiris and carried by his priests is described in Herodotus.

XXII

Peor and Baälim
Forsake their temples dim,
  With that twice-battered god of Palestine,
And mooned Ashtaroth,   200
Heaven's queen and mother both,
  Now sits not girt with tapers' holy shine,
The Libyc Hammon shrinks his horn,
In vain the Tyrian maids their wounded Thammuz mourn.

XXIII

And sullen Moloch, fled,
Hath left in shadows dread
  His burning idol all of blackest hue;
In vain with cymbals' ring
They call the grisly king,
  In dismal dance about the furnace blue;   210
The brutish gods of Nile as fast,
Isis and Orus, and the dog Anubis haste.

XXIV

Nor is Osiris seen
In Memphian grove or green,
  Trampling the unshowered grass with lowings loud;
Nor can he be at rest
Within his sacred chest,
  Nought but profoundest Hell can be his shroud,
In vain with timbreled anthems dark
The sable-stoléd sorcerers bear his worshipped ark.   220

XXV

He feels from Juda's land
The dreaded Infant's hand,
  The rays of Bethlehem blind his dusky eyn;
Nor all the gods beside,
Longer dare abide,
  Not Typhon huge ending in snaky twine:
Our Babe, to show his Godhead true,
Can in his swaddling bands control the damnéd crew.

221 ff. The mood of the poem has wandered far from the ordinary
associations of the Nativity and Milton does not recall it easily. The suggestion of Christ's Herculean might in the cradle and the image of the sun
in bed have not been liked by some readers. The citation of a similar conceit from Marvell ("Upon Appleton House," 661-64) serves to emphasize
the inappropriateness of Milton's.

XXVI

So when the sun in bed,
Curtained with cloudy red,   230
    Pillows his chin upon an orient wave,
The flocking shadows pale
Troop to the infernal jail;
    Each fettered ghost slips to his several grave,
And the yellow-skirted fays
Fly after the night-steeds, leaving their moon-loved maze.

XXVII

But see, the Virgin blest
Hath laid her Babe to rest.
    Time is our tedious song should here have ending;
Heaven's youngest-teeméd star   240
Hath fixed her polished car,
    Her sleeping Lord with handmaid lamp attending,
And all about the courtly stable
Bright-harnessed angels sit in order serviceable.

                              [December 25, 1629]

ELEGY VI

This elegy, written shortly after December 25, 1629, is of
great importance biographically, expressing as it does a definite resolution on Milton's part to adopt henceforth a way of
life and thought more strictly in accord with the higher aspirations of his muse. Hitherto he has not hesitated to join
Diodati in his relaxed view of life and art. Now the Puritan
in him asserts itself. He does not care to continue the friendly
rivalry on Diodati's terms. He will rather henceforth follow
the guiding star of his own individuality, setting himself apart
from the kindly race of men, though viewing with indulgence
their easier way of life. A passage in the *Apology for Smectymnuus* illuminates this change of front. He had, he tells us, in
describing his youthful literary enthusiasms and the development of his ideals, been devoted to the "smooth elegiac poets,"
but with maturing years he had come to regret their looseness
and to prefer "the two famous renowners of Beatrice and

236. **moon-loved maze,** their dance by moonlight.
    240. **youngest-teemed,** latest born. The star of Bethlehem "came and
stood over where the young child was."
    243. The stable is a royal court.

Laura, who never write but honour of them to whom they devote their verse." He was thus led to the more firm persuasion that "he who would not be frustrate of his hope to write well hereafter in laudable things, ought himself to be a true poem; that is, a composition and pattern of the best and honourablest things; not presuming to sing praises of heroic men, or famous cities, unless he have in himself the experience and practice of all that is praiseworthy." The period to which he here refers is obviously the one which we have reached in this survey of the early poems, and the sixth elegy is the heightened expression of Milton's new view of himself as one committed by his profession as a poet to the ascetic way of life. We need not, of course, look for an unwavering adherence to this program, but Milton certainly never again allowed himself to fall into the erotic vein of Elegy V.

ELEGY VI

(Translation)

TO CHARLES DIODATI

Who, while he spent his Christmas in the country, sent the Author a poetical Epistle, in which he requested that his verses, if not so good as usual, might he excused on account of the many feasts to which his friends had invited him, and which would not allow him leisure to finish them as he wished.

With no rich viands overcharged, I send
Health, which perchance you want, my pampered friend;
But wherefore should thy muse tempt mine away
From what she loves, from darkness into day?
Art thou desirous to be told how well
I love thee, and in verse? verse cannot tell,
For verse has bounds, and must in measure move
But neither bounds nor measure knows my love.
How pleasant, in thy lines described, appear
December's harmless sports, and rural cheer!   10
French spirits kindling with cærulean fires,
And all such gambols as the time inspires!
   Think not that wine against good verse offends;
The Muse and Bacchus have been always friends,
Nor Phœbus blushes sometimes to be found
With ivy, rather than with laurel, crowned.
The Nine themselves ofttimes have joined the song

And revels of the Bacchanalian throng;
Not even Ovid could in Scythian air
Sing sweetly—why? no vine would flourish there,   20
What in brief numbers sung Anacreon's muse?
Wine, and the rose, that sparkling wine bedews.
Pindar with Bacchus glows—his every line
Breathes the rich fragrance of inspiring wine,
While, with loud crash o'erturned, the chariot lies
And brown with dust the fiery courser flies.
The Roman lyrist steeped in wine his lays,
So sweet in Glycera's and Chloe's praise.
Now too the plenteous feast and mantling bowl
Nourish the vigour of thy sprightly soul;   30
The flowing goblet makes thy numbers flow,
And casks not wine alone, but verse bestow.
Thus Phœbus favours, and the arts attend,
Whom Bacchus, and whom Ceres, both befriend:
What wonder, then, thy verses are so sweet,
In which these triple powers so kindly meet?
The lute now also sounds, with gold inwrought,
And touched with flying fingers, nicely taught;
In tapestried halls, high-roofed, the sprightly lyre
Directs the dancers of the virgin choir.   40
If dull repletion fright the muse away,
Sights, gay as these, may more invite her stay:
And, trust me, while the ivory keys resound,
Fair damsels sport, and perfumes steam around,
Apollo's influence, like ethereal flame,
Shall animate, at once, thy glowing frame,
And all the Muse shall rush into thy breast,
By love and music's blended powers possest.
For numerous powers light Elegy befriend,
Hear her sweet voice, and at her call attend;   50
Her Bacchus, Ceres, Venus, all approve,
And, with his blushing mother, gentle Love.
Hence to such bards we grant the copious use
Of banquets, and the vine's delicious juice.
But they, who demi-gods and heroes praise,
And feats performed in Jove's more youthful days,
Who now the counsels of high heaven explore,

49. **light Elegy.** "Elegy" is poetry written in elegiac couplets, alternat-
ing hexameter and pentameter. The theme of love predominates in the
Latin elegiac poets. The idea of a love lament passes over into that of a
lament for the dead and this has become the prevailing usage. Milton has,
in the "Vacation Exercise," already announced himself as an epic poet.
Contrasting his Christmas with Diodati's he also contrasts the sources of
inspiration of the two kinds of poetry.

Now shades, that echo the Cerberean roar,
Simply let these, like him of Samos, live;
Let herbs to them a bloodless banquet give;   60
In beechen goblets let their beverage shine,
Cool from the crystal spring, their sober wine!
Their youth should pass in innocence, secure
From stain licentious, and in manners pure,
Pure as the priest, when robed in white he stands,
The fresh lustration ready in his hands.
Thus Linus lived, and thus, as poets write,
Tiresias, wiser for his loss of sight;
Thus exiled Chalcas, thus the bard of Thrace,
Melodious tamer of the savage race;   70
Thus, trained by temperance, Homer led, of yore,
His chief of Ithaca from shore to shore,
Through magic Circe's monster-peopled reign,
And shoals insidious with the Siren train;
And through the realms where grizly spectres dwell,
Whose tribes he fettered in a gory spell:
For these are sacred bards, and, from above,
Drink large infusions from the mind of Jove.
   Wouldst thou, (perhaps 'tis hardly worth thine ear)
Wouldst thou be told my occupation here?   80
The promised King of peace employs my pen,
The eternal covenant made for guilty men,
The new-born Deity with infant cries
Filling the sordid hovel, where he lies;
The hymning Angels, and the herald star,
That led the Wise, who sought him from afar,
And idols on their own unhallowed shore
Dashed, at his birth, to be revered no more!
   This theme on reeds of Albion I rehearse:
The dawn of that blest day inspired the verse;   90
Verse that, reserved in secret, shall attend
Thy candid voice, my critic, and my friend!
                                   [December, 1629]

The Passion

This fragment is linked by the opening stanza to the poem
"On the Morning of Christ's Nativity" and must have been
written for the succeeding Easter (i.e., 1630). Milton had
perhaps designed a series of religious poems on the events of
the Christian year. But the Passion offers no such congenial

79 ff.   The allusion must be to the writing of the poem "On the
Morning of Christ's Nativity" in 1629.

theme as the Nativity, and the poem is a conspicuous failure. It is not so much Milton's years as his temperament which makes it impossible for him to rise to the mood of Christ's death and resurrection. Deprived of inspiration, he resorts to conceit and poetic ornament and gives up the effort before he is well started.

THE PASSION

I

Erewhile of music and ethereal mirth,
Wherewith the stage of Air and Earth did ring,
And joyous news of Heavenly Infant's birth,
My muse with Angels did divide to sing;
But headlong joy is ever on the wing,
    In wintry solstice like the shortened light
Soon swallowed up in dark and long outliving night.

II

For now to sorrow must I tune my song,
And set my harp to notes of saddest woe,
Which on our dearest Lord did seize ere long,   10
Dangers, and snares, and wrongs, and worse than so, ●
Which he for us did freely undergo.
    Most perfect Hero, tried in heaviest plight
Of labors huge and hard, too hard for human wight.

III

He sovran Priest, stooping his regal head,
That dropped with odorous oil down his fair eyes,
Poor fleshly tabernacle enterèd,
His starry front low-roofed beneath the skies;
Oh what a mask was there, what a disguise!
    Yet more: the stroke of death he must abide,   20
Then lies him meekly down fast by his brethren's side.

IV

These latest scenes confine my roving verse,
To this horizon is my Phœbus bound;
His godlike acts, and his temptations fierce,
And former sufferings, otherwhere are found;

    13. **Most perfect Hero.** Christ was likened to Hercules in the "Nativity Ode."

Loud o'er the rest Cremona's trump doth sound;
  Me softer airs befit and softer strings
Of lute or viol still, more apt for mournful things.

v

Befriend me Night, best patroness of grief,
Over the pole thy thickest mantle throw,   30
And work my flattered fancy to belief
That heaven and earth are colored with my woe;
My sorrows are too dark for day to know.
  The leaves should all be black whereon I write,
And letters where my tears have washed, a wannish white.

VI

See, see the chariot, and those rushing wheels
That whirled the prophet up at Chebar flood;
My spirit some transporting Cherub feels,
To bear me where the towers of Salem stood,
Once glorious towers, now sunk in guiltless blood;   40
  There doth my soul in holy vision sit,
In pensive trance, and anguish, and ecstatic fit.

VII

Mine eye hath found that sad sepulchral rock
That was the casket of Heaven's richest store,
And here though grief my feeble hands uplock,
Yet on the softened quarry would I score
My plaining verse as lively as before;
  For sure so well instructed are my tears,
That they would fitly fall in ordered characters.

VIII

Or should I thence hurried on viewless wing,   50
Take up a weeping on the mountains wild,
The gentle neighborhood of grove and spring
Would soon unbosom all their echoes mild,
And I (for grief is easily beguiled)
  Might think the infection of my sorrows loud
Had got a race of mourners on some pregnant cloud.

    26. Cremona's trump, the voice of Vida of Cremona, who had written an epic on the life of Christ.
    31. Make me think that the darkness is a reflection of my woe.
    45. His hands are locked up, i.e., clasped in grief at the thought of the sepulcher of Christ, so that he cannot write. His tears inscribe the poem on the rock.
    55–56. The poem has survived two outrageous conceits. This last one is too much for it.

This subject the author finding to be above the years he had when
  he wrote it, and nothing satisfied with what was begun, left it
  unfinished.

[1630]

ON SHAKESPEARE

The poem on Shakespeare was printed in the folio of 1632
and is therefore Milton's first publication. He himself dates
its composition in 1630, perhaps erroneously. Milton's attitude
toward his greatest English predecessor is one of unfeigned
but not uncritical enthusiasm. Shakespeare is for him, as he
was for Jonson, nature's poet, but here, as in the later allusion
in "L'Allegro," his want of art is regarded as no derogation
from his genius. The central conceit in the lines was perhaps
suggested by the second stanza of Browne's elegy on the
Countess of Pembroke:

> Marble piles let no man raise
> To her name; for after days
> Some kind woman, born as she,
> Reading this, like Niobe,
> Shall turn marble, and become,
> Both her mourner and her tomb.

ON SHAKESPEARE

1630

What needs my Shakespeare for his honored bones
The labor of an age in pilëd stones,
Or that his hallowed reliques should be hid
Under a star-ypointing pyramid?
Dear son of memory, great heir of fame,
What need'st thou such weak witness of thy name?
Thou in our wonder and astonishment
Hast built thyself a livelong monument.
For whilst to the shame of slow-endeavoring art,
Thy easy numbers flow, and that each heart   10

1 ff. The lines suggest Jonson's "Thou art a monument without a
tomb" in his epitaph on Shakespeare in the folio of 1623.
  3. star-ypointing. Cf. "Nativity" 155 and "L'Allegro" 12, but the
archaic usage is more striking here. Milton is perhaps echoing an "Epitaph
on Sir Edward Stanley," once attributed to Shakespeare, which has the
phrase "sky-aspiring Piramides."
  5. son of memory. The Muses were the daughters of Memory.

Hath from the leaves of thy unvalued book
Those Delphic lines with deep impression took,
Then thou our fancy of itself bereaving,
Dost make us marble with too much conceiving,
And so sepúlchred in such pomp dost lie,
That kings for such a tomb would wish to die.

[1630]

ON THE UNIVERSITY CARRIER

The date of the two pieces on the University Carrier is fixed
by the death of Old Hobson, their subject, on January 1, 1631,
at the age of 87. They are characteristic of the seventeenth-
century punning and conceited epigram. Milton's humor is
grim enough, but the mood is not unkindly.

ON THE UNIVERSITY CARRIER

*who sickened in the time of his vacancy, being forbid to go to
London by reason of the Plague.*

Here lies old Hobson, Death has broke his girt,
And here alas, hath laid him in the dirt;
Or else the ways being foul, twenty to one
He's here stuck in a slough, and overthrown.
'Twas such a shifter, that if truth were known,
Death was half glad when he had got him down;
For he had any time this ten years full,
Dodged with him, betwixt Cambridge and *The Bull.*
And surely, Death could never have prevailed,
Had not his weekly course of carriage failed;   10
But lately finding him so long at home,
And thinking now his journey's end was come,
And that he had ta'en up his latest inn,
In the kind of office of a chamberlin
Showed him his room where he must lodge that night,
Pulled off his boots, and took away the light.
If any ask for him, it shall be said,
'Hobson has supped, and's newly gone to bed.'

[1631]

11. **unvalued,** invaluable.
13 ff. By calling excessively on our imaginations we deprive ourselves of
consciousness and become his marble monument. So the Grecian urn in
Keats's poem "teases us out of thought as doth eternity."
Carrier, bearer of letters and parcels.
8. **The Bull,** an inn in London.
10. His trips were interrupted by the plague.

ANOTHER ON THE SAME

Here lieth one who did most truly prove
That he could never die while he could move;
So hung his destiny never to rot
While he might still jog on and keep his trot,
Made of sphere-metal, never to decay
Until his revolution was at stay.
Time numbers motion, yet (without a crime
'Gainst old truth) motion numbered out his time;
And like an engine moved with wheel and weight,
His principles being ceased, he ended straight.   10
Rest that gives all men life, gave him his death,
And too much breathing put him out of breath;
Nor were it contradiction to affirm
Too long vacation hastened on his term.
Merely to drive the time away he sickened,
Fainted, and died, nor would with ale be quickened;
'Nay,' quoth he, on his swooning bed outstretched,
'If I may not carry, sure I'll ne'er be fetched,
But vow, though the cross doctors all stood hearers,
For one carrier put down to make six bearers.'   20
Ease was his chief disease, and to judge right,
He died for heaviness that his cart went light.
His leisure told him that his time was come,
And lack of load made his life burdensome,
That even to his last breath (there be that say't)
As he were pressed to death, he cried, 'More weight!'
But had his doings lasted as they were,
He had been an immortal carrier.
Obedient to the moon he spent his date
In course reciprocal, and had his fate   30
Linked to the mutual flowing of the seas,
Yet (strange to think) his wain was his increase.
His letters are delivered all and gone,
Only remains this superscription.

[1631]

---

5. **sphere-metal**, the indestructible substance of the heavenly spheres.
10. **principles**, the source of its power to move, as in a clock run down.
18–20. The doctors are cross because Hobson, unable to carry, will not be carried except to his grave.
32. **wain**, wagon, with a pun on wane, decrease.

An Epitaph on the Marchioness of Winchester

The subject of this elegy is Lady Jane, wife of John Paulet, fifth Marquis of Winchester, a celebrated Catholic peer who later made a heroic defense of his house against the forces of Oliver Cromwell. She died on April 15, 1631. The composition shows Milton entering into a new discipleship in the matter of poetic expression. The verse-form and the classic simplicity of the style are Jonsonian, and offer a striking contrast to Milton's earlier and less happy manner in the elegy "On the Death of a Fair Infant." The same tenderness, however, is present in both poems; and the apparent recollection of the earlier piece in the line, "So have I seen some tender slip," suggests that Milton associated the two experiences. Whether Milton had any personal contact with this family is a question. His poem is more intimate in tone and shows greater knowledge of the facts than the elegies which were written on her by Ben Jonson and Sir William Davenant. The traveler, James Howell, says in a letter of 1626 that he is returning a sonnet to her with a Spanish translation which will go to the same music as the original. Another elegist who celebrated her death was the martyred English priest, Walter Colman. Milton's verses appear in a manuscript anthology which gives the exact date of her death, and designates the poet as "of Christ College, Cambridge."

AN EPITAPH ON THE MARCHIONESS
OF WINCHESTER

This rich marble doth inter
The honored wife of Winchester,
A Viscount's daughter, an Earl's heir,
Besides what her virtues fair
Added to her noble birth,
More than she could own from Earth.
Summers three times eight save one
She had told; alas too soon,
And so short time of breath,
To house with darkness and with death. 10

3. The Marchioness was daughter of Thomas, Viscount of Rock-Savage in Cheshire; she was heir on her mother's side, to the Earl of Rivers. The family later intermarried with Milton's patrons, the Egertons, who originated in Cheshire and held property there.

Yet had the number of her days
Been as complete as was her praise,
Nature and Fate had had no strife
In giving limit to her life.
Her high birth and her graces sweet
Quickly found a lover meet;
The virgin choir for her request
The god that sits at marriage feast;
He at their invoking came
But with a scarce well-lighted flame;   20
And in his garland as he stood,
Ye might discern a cypress bud.
Once had the early matrons run
To greet her of a lovely son,
And now with second hope she goes,
And calls Lucina to her throes;
But whether by mischance or blame,
Atropos for Lucina came,
And with remorseless cruelty
Spoiled at once both fruit and tree: 30
The hapless babe before his birth
Had burial, yet not laid in earth,
And the languished mother's womb
Was not long a living tomb.
So have I seen some tender slip,
Saved with care from winter's nip,
The pride of her carnation train,
Plucked up by some unheedy swain,
Who only thought to crop the flower
New shot up from vernal shower;   40
But the fair blossom hangs the head
Sideways as on a dying bed,
And those pearls of dew she wears,
Prove to be presaging tears
Which the sad morn had let fall
On her hastening funeral.
Gentle Lady may thy grave
Peace and quiet ever have;
After this thy travail sore
Sweet rest seize thee evermore,   50
That to give the world increase,
Shortened hast thy own life's lease;

11–14. I.e., she would then have died old and nature would not have contended against fate in limiting her days. An ellipsis is suggested by the adversative "yet." She died prematurely but her praise was complete.

28. **Atropos**, Fate, came instead of the goddess of childbirth.

Here, besides the sorrowing
That thy noble house doth bring,
Here be tears of perfect moan
Wept for thee in Helicon,
And some flowers and some bays
For thy hearse to strew the ways,
Sent thee from the banks of Came,
Devoted to thy virtuous name;   60
Whilst thou bright Saint high sitt'st in glory,
Next her much like to thee in story,
That fair Syrian shepherdess,
Who after years of barrenness,
The highly-favored Joseph bore
To him that served for her before,
And at her next birth much like thee,
Through pangs fled to felicity,
Far within the bosom bright
Of blazing Majesty and Light,   70
There with thee, new-welcome Saint,
Like fortunes may her soul acquaint,
With thee there clad in radiant sheen,
No Marchioness, but now a Queen.

                                        [1631]

SONG

The fact that this lyric does not appear in the Trinity manuscript suggests a date before *Arcades.* The lilt of lines 5–9
associates it with "L'Allegro." Very likely it was composed for
music.

ON MAY MORNING

Now the bright morning star, Day's harbinger,
Comes dancing from the east, and leads with her
The flowery May, who from her green lap throws
The yellow cowslip, and the pale primrose.

55 ff. **Here be tears,** etc. Milton, literally or metaphorically, sends the
poem together with flowers. Elegies, sometimes called "tears," were often
buried with the dead. *of perfect moan,* of an ideal grief born in Heaven.
63. Rachel, wife of Jacob, who died at the birth of Benjamin. Milton
is thinking of her as described by Dante (*Paradiso,* XXXII, 7-10). She
sits beside Beatrice in the third rank of the Celestial Rose. It is there that
the Marchioness will join her. This is the first clear reference to Dante
in Milton's poetry.

Hail bounteous May that dost inspire
Mirth and youth and warm desire,
Woods and groves are of thy dressing,
Hill and dale doth boast thy blessing.
Thus we salute thee with our early song,
And welcome thee, and wish thee long.　　　10

[1631?]

L'ALLEGRO

The date of this and its companion poem, "Il Penseroso," is uncertain. Their artistic perfection and their mood of relaxed enjoyment, together with the allusions in them to the sights and sounds of the English countryside, have made it natural to assign them to Milton's period of residence at Horton. They may equally well have been written in some vacation interval in his last years at the University. They do not occur in the Trinity manuscript, in which Milton set down almost all his lesser English poems as he wrote them, beginning with *Arcades*. There is a relationship in subject between "L'Allegro" and "Il Penseroso" on the one hand and Elegy I on the other, but we have no reason to suppose that Milton could write such finished English verse at the age of seventeen. The style and versification associate them rather with the "Epitaph on the Marchioness of Winchester."

Interpretations of the companion pieces have been various, but the need of any deeper explanation disappears if we regard the idea of two persons, the cheerful and the pensive man, as a mere poetic fiction and take the pieces together as an enthusiastic description of all the delights which a cultivated and responsive spirit can derive from nature, society, books, theatre, music, meditation. They are two moods rather than two individuals, and Milton knew them both, for even L'Allegro is more contemplative than he is social. He does not himself join the country dancers, and his smile, as he views the stoutly strutting cock or listens to the huntsman's horn, comes short of hearty laughter. It is to be noted, on the other hand, that Milton keeps his more serious and earnest thoughts out of both poems. Il Penseroso reads Spenser and Greek tragedy but not Scripture, history, or the Church Fathers. If he turns to Plato, it is not the *Republic* but the more fanciful *Timaeus* that he chooses, and he passes from that to the fascinating but irresponsible speculations of Hermes Trismegistus.

The question has been raised as to how the sets of experiences recorded in these poems can be fitted into the scheme of two single days. L'Allegro rises at dawn and walks abroad at sunrise. He watches the activity of ploughman and shepherd till afternoon; then he witnesses the country revels, hears the twilight stories in some upland hamlet, and finally spends a social evening in the towered city. No explanation is vouchsafed of the speedy change of scene and we are driven to the conclusion that Milton is piecing together parts of specimen days rather than describing an actual one. In "Il Penseroso" this is even clearer. The poet listens for the nightingale's even-song and missing it he walks unseen

> To behold the wandering Moon
> Riding near her highest noon.

A few lines later he describes himself as hearing the far-off curfew, the mention of which suggests an earlier hour. If the weather is bad, he burns his lamp at midnight and oft outwatches the Bear, while the drowsy bellman cries the hours of night. When the sun is hot, he goes abroad and finds noontide repose in some close covert. So far the sequence is fairly consistent. But the church service which follows in the description can hardly belong in even a rough, chronological scheme, and the "hairy gown and mossy cell" of the closing lines point forward to the poet's old age. The technique of this is characteristic of Milton, who throughout his poetry prefers the ideal and the typical to the realistic.

The parallels and contrasts in the occupations of L'Allegro and Il Penseroso are subtly worked out. We may observe that the injurious melancholy which is banished in the opening of the first poem is not the pleasing pensiveness which is invoked in the second, and that Euphrosyne is neither by ancestry nor by character the patroness of these vain deluding joys which are the fruit of idleness. Nature in different guises is a source of happiness in both poems, but Il Penseroso substitutes dreams and slumber for social merriment, the speculations of the mystics for oral folklore, and the reading of dramas for attendance at the theatre.

In style and inspiration these poems derive from the Elizabethans. They have the simplicity, the classic grace, the firm technique of Jonson. The idea was apparently suggested by a poem entitled "A Dialogue between Pleasure and Pain,"

prefixed to Burton's *Anatomy of Melancholy*, and there are
verbal reminiscences of John Fletcher and Nicolas Breton.

L'ALLEGRO

Hence loathèd Melancholy
   Of Cerberus and blackest Midnight born,
In Stygian cave forlorn
   'Mongst horrid shapes, and shrieks, and sights unholy,
Find out some uncouth cell,
   Where brooding Darkness spreads his jealous wings,
   And the night-raven sings;
There under ebon shades and low-browed rocks,
   As ragged as thy locks,
   In dark Cimmerian desert ever dwell.   10
But come thou Goddess fair and free,
In Heaven yclept Euphrosyne,
And by men, heart-easing Mirth,
Whom lovely Venus at a birth
With two sister Graces more
To ivy-crownèd Bacchus bore;
Or whether (as some sager sing)

Allegro, gay, joyful. Usage in music has made the word familiar in a
closely related sense.

1 ff. The specific genealogy of **Melancholy** is Milton's own invention,
although Night had often been represented as the mother of such personi-
fied abstractions as Death and Sleep. The general use of personification is
in line with classical and Renaissance tradition.

2. Cerberus, the three-headed dog who guarded the gate of Hades. By
substituting the beast Cerberus for Erebus, who was the legitimate spouse
of Night, Milton emphasizes the unnaturalness of Melancholy's parentage.

3. Stygian, belonging in general to the infernal regions. But here the
reference is probably more definite: Virgil's cave of Cerberus (*Aeneid* vi.
418 ff.) is located near the bank of the river Styx.

5. uncouth, unknown. There is also the implication of "weird" and
"dreadful."

7. night-raven, a bird of evil omen. Cf. Spenser, *Faerie Queene,* II,
xii, 36: "The hoarse Night-raven, trump of dolefull drere." *The Raven* of
Poe is based on this traditional conception.

8. ebon, black.

10. Cimmerian desert, a land of perpetual gloom and mist, described
by Homer. Cf. *Odyssey* xi. 13 ff.

11 ff. Note the sudden change in meter. The body of the poem is as
suggestive of light and movement as the introduction is of gloom and
lethargy.

12. yclept, called (from the past participle of O. E. *clipian*). See note
to "On Shakespeare" for the archaism. **Euphrosyne,** one of the three
Graces. The other two were Aglaia and Thalia.

The frolic wind that breathes the spring,
Zephyr with Aurora playing,
As he met her once a-Maying,   20
There on beds of violets blue,
And fresh-blown roses washed in dew,
Filled her with thee, a daughter fair,
So buxom, blithe, and debonair.
Haste thee Nymph, and bring with thee
Jest and youthful Jollity,
Quips and Cranks, and wanton Wiles,
Nods, and Becks, and wreathëd Smiles,
Such as hang on Hebe's cheek,
And love to live in dimple sleek;   30
Sport that wrinkled Care derides,
And Laughter holding both his sides.
Come, and trip it as ye go
On the light fantastic toe,
And in thy right hand lead with thee,
The mountain nymph, sweet Liberty;
And if I give thee honor due,
Mirth, admit me of thy crew,
To live with her, and live with thee,
In unreprovëd pleasures free;   40
To hear the lark begin his flight,
And singing startle the dull night,
From his watch-tower in the skies,

18 ff. For the second account of Mirth's parentage Milton is his own authority; for the first he has the authority of Servius, a fourth-century commentator on the *Aeneid*. While not repudiating the idea that Mirth may be born of Love and Wine, Milton prefers to think of her as the child of the West Wind and the Dawn.

24. buxom, lively. debonair, affable (from O. F. *de bon aire*, of good disposition).

27. quips, witty sayings. cranks, fantastic turns of speech. wanton wiles, playful tricks.

29. Hebe, the goddess of youth.

31. Note that *that* is the subject of *derides*.

34. On the light fantastic toe, i.e., making grotesque or whimsical patterns.

36. Milton is associating Liberty with the Oreads of Greek mythology, whose haunts were the uncultivated mountains and hills.

40. unreprovëd, unreprovable. In contrast to the "vain deluding Joys" banished in the opening line of "Il Penseroso," the pleasures set forth in "L'Allegro" are wholly innocent.

41 ff. To hear the lark, etc. This passage has been variously interpreted, both *lark* (41) and *dawn* (44) being taken as the subject of *to come*. Logically, however, the subject is *me* (38): i.e., the poet, awakened by the lark, comes to his window and greets the dawn, or whoever happens to be passing by. The construction of *to come* parallels that of *to live* (39) and *to hear* (41).

Till the dappled dawn doth rise;
Then to come in spite of sorrow,
And at my window bid good-morrow,
Through the sweet-briar, or the vine,
Or the twisted eglantine.
While the cock with lively din,
Scatters the rear of darkness thin,   50
And to the stack or the barn door,
Stoutly struts his dames before;
Oft listening how the hounds and horn
Cheerly rouse the slumbering Morn,
From the side of some hoar hill,
Through the high wood echoing shrill.
Sometime walking not unseen
By hedgerow elms, on hillocks green,
Right against the eastern gate,
Where the great sun begins his state,   60
Robed in flames and amber light,
The clouds in thousand liveries dight;
While the ploughman near at hand,
Whistles o'er the furrowed land,
And the milkmaid singeth blithe,
And the mower whets his scythe,
And every shepherd tells his tale
Under the hawthorn in the dale.
   Straight mine eye hath caught new pleasures
Whilst the landscape round it measures: 70
Russet lawns and fallows gray,
Where the nibbling flocks do stray,
Mountains on whose barren breast
The laboring clouds do often rest,
Meadows trim with daisies pied,
Shallow brooks and rivers wide.
Towers and battlements it sees

45. **in spite of sorrow,** in order to spite sorrow.
55. **hoar,** white with frost or perhaps with dew. The season is doubtful.
57. **not unseen.** Cf. "Il Penseroso," 65. In one mood, pleasure is associated with society; in the other, with solitude.
60. **state,** i.e., stately progress. The journey of the sun is compared to that of a monarch through his dominions.
62. **dight,** arrayed.
67. **tells his tale,** either (1) counts the number of his sheep, or (2) relates his story of love. Although the majority of commentators seem to favor the first interpretation, the second is at least equally sound. Milton probably has in mind the pastoral tradition of Theocritus, Virgil, and Spenser.
75. **pied,** variegated. As applied to flowers the epithet was more or less conventional. Cf. Shakespeare, *Love's Labour's Lost*, V, ii, 904: "When daisies pied and violets blue," etc.

Bosomed high in tufted trees,
Where perhaps some beauty lies,
The cynosure of neighboring eyes.   80
Hard by, a cottage chimney smokes,
From betwixt two aged oaks,
Where Corydon and Thyrsis met,
Are at their savory dinner set
Of herbs and other country messes,
Which the neat-handed Phillis dresses;
And then in haste her bower she leaves,
With Thestylis to bind the sheaves;
Or if the earlier season lead,
To the tanned haycock in the mead.   90
  Sometimes with secure delight
The upland hamlets will invite,
When the merry bells ring round,
And the jocund rebecks sound
To many a youth and many a maid,
Dancing in the chequered shade;
And young and old come forth to play
On a sunshine holiday,
Till the livelong daylight fail;
Then to the spicy nut-brown ale,   100
With stories told of many a feat,
How fairy Mab the junkets eat;
She was pinched and pulled she said,
And he by friar's lantern led
Tells how the drudging goblin sweat,
To earn his cream-bowl duly set,
When in one night, ere glimpse of morn,
His shadowy flail hath threshed the corn
That ten day-laborers could not end;

80. cynosure, center of attraction. The word, meaning literally "dog's tail," was originally a Greek name for the constellation Ursa Minor, which contains the Pole Star. The modern meaning is derived from the fact that the Pole Star was used as an object to steer by.
  83. Corydon and Thyrsis, names reminiscent of pastoral tradition, as are also Phillis and Thestylis (86 and 88).
  91. secure, carefree (Latin se + cura).
  94. rebecks, musical instruments of three strings, from which have developed the modern viola and violin.
  102. Mab, queen of the Fairies. See Romeo and Juliet, I, iv, 54–95 for a detailed poetic description of her.
  103, 104. she . . . he, i.e., individuals in the storytelling group. friar's lantern, the will-o'-the-wisp, or ignis fatuus, of popular superstition. The term probably originated from the confusion of some legend of a ghostly, lantern-bearing friar with earlier folklore.
  105. drudging goblin, Robin Goodfellow, whose domestic services are recorded in many folk tales.

Then lies him down the lubber fiend, 110
And stretched out all the chimney's length,
Basks at the fire his hairy strength;
And crop-full out of doors he flings,
Ere the first cock his matin rings.
Thus done the tales, to bed they creep,
By whispering winds soon lulled asleep.
 Towerèd cities please us then,
And the busy hum of men,
Where throngs of knights and barons bold
In weeds of peace high triumphs hold, 120
With store of ladies, whose bright eyes
Rain influence, and judge the prize
Of wit or arms, while both contend
To win her grace whom all commend.
There let Hymen oft appear
In saffron robe, with taper clear,
And pomp, and feast, and revelry,
With masque and antique pageantry;
Such sights as youthful poets dream
On summer eves by haunted stream. 130
Then to the well-trod stage anon,
If Jonson's learnèd sock be on,
Or sweetest Shakespeare, Fancy's child,
Warble his native wood-notes wild;
And ever against eating cares,
Lap me in soft Lydian airs,
Married to immortal verse,

119 ff. These lines may be taken as descriptive of L'Allegro's evening reading. But more likely they are meant to set forth actual experiences in the city, just as the preceding lines have set forth actual experiences in the country. Throughout the poem, Milton is dealing with typical activities congenial to a man in a social frame of mind; there is no reason for limiting these activities to the scope of a single day.

120. weeds, garments.

125. Hymen, the god of marriage, a familiar figure of the masque. The whole passage is descriptive of court festivities, such as frequently accompanied the celebration of a marriage.

132. sock, the *soccus* or low-heeled slipper worn by actors in classical comedy, in contrast to the *cothurnus* or buskin worn in tragedy. Cf. "Il Penseroso," 102.

133-34. Milton's picture of Shakespeare as the natural but unlettered genius reflects the conventional attitude of classical criticism. The contrast with Jonson became a commonplace.

136. Lydian airs, one of the three "modes" of ancient Greek music, the other two being the Dorian and the Phrygian. Lydian music was soft and sweet.

137. Married to immortal verse. Milton always set a high value on the perfect union of words and music. Cf. "At a Solemn Music" and the sonnet "To Mr. H. Lawes on His Airs."

Such as the meeting soul may pierce
In notes with many a winding bout
Of linkèd sweetness long drawn out,   140
With wanton heed and giddy cunning,
The melting voice through mazes running,
Untwisting all the chains that tie
The hidden soul of harmony;
That Orpheus' self may heave his head
From golden slumber on a bed
Of heaped Elysian flowers, and hear
Such strains as would have won the ear
Of Pluto, to have quite set free
His half-regained Eurydice.   150
  These delights if thou canst give,
Mirth with thee I mean to live.

                               [1631?]

IL PENSEROSO

Hence vain deluding Joys,
The brood of Folly without father bred,
How little you bested,
Or fill the fixèd mind with all your toys;
Dwell in some idle brain,
And fancies fond with gaudy shapes possess,

139. bout, turn or involution. Milton is referring to the complexities of Italian and English madrigals.
145 ff. Orpheus . . . Eurydice. Orpheus was the unparalleled musician of Greek mythology. On the death of his wife Eurydice, he descended to the infernal regions and so charmed Pluto with his harmonies that the god permitted him to take his wife back to earth. But there was one condition: as he left the underworld, he must not look behind him. Orpheus violated the condition, and Eurydice was snatched from his sight forever.
147. Elysian, belonging to Elysium, the abode of the blessed after death.
151–52. Cf. the closing lines of Marlowe's "The Passionate Shepherd to His Love":

> "If these delights thy mind may move
> Then live with me and be my love."

Penseroso (Italian), contemplative, pensive. The modern forms *pensieroso* and *pensoso* are occasionally used in music.
1 ff. Cf. the opening lines of "L'Allegro." Just as Milton there banishes a morbid, inhibiting kind of melancholy, he here banishes an immoderate, irresponsible levity. In each case he is dealing with the extreme rather than the normal. The two introductions are perfectly consistent.
2. without father bred. The Melancholy of "L'Allegro" is the issue of an unnatural union; the children of Folly are born in complete defiance of nature.
3. bested, avail, profit.
6. fond, foolish (the original meaning).

As thick and numberless
  As the gay motes that people the sunbeams,
Or likest hovering dreams,
    The fickle pensioners of Morpheus' train.   10
But hail thou Goddess, sage and holy,
Hail divinest Melancholy,
Whose saintly visage is too bright
To hit the sense of human sight,
And therefore to our weaker view
O'erlaid with black, staid Wisdom's hue;
Black, but such as in esteem
Prince Memnon's sister might beseem,
Or that starred Ethiop queen that strove
To set her beauty's praise above   20
The sea nymphs, and their powers offended;
Yet thou art higher far descended:
Thee bright-haired Vesta long of yore
To solitary Saturn bore;
His daughter she (in Saturn's reign
Such mixture was not held a stain).
Oft in glimmering bowers and glades
He met her, and in secret shades
Of woody Ida's inmost grove,
Whilst yet there was no fear of Jove.   30
  Come pensive Nun, devout and pure,
Sober, stedfast, and demure,
All in a robe of darkest grain,
Flowing with majestic train,
And sable stole of cypress lawn,
Over thy decent shoulders drawn.
Come, but keep thy wonted state,
With even step and musing gait,
And looks commercing with the skies,
Thy rapt soul sitting in thine eyes;   40
There held in holy passion still,

10. **Morpheus,** the god of dreams.

18. **Memnon's sister,** Hemera. Memnon was a mythical king of the Ethiopians. Although dark of skin, he was of splendid beauty; the same quality is assumed to be his sister's also.

19. **starred Ethiop queen,** Cassiopeia, who after death was placed in the constellation which bears her name.

23 ff. Saturn, beneficent patron of agriculture, was sole ruler of the gods during the Golden Age; his daughter Vesta was the chaste goddess of the hearth. Note that Milton particularly emphasizes the purity of their union. Melancholy's heritage is rich in allegorical suggestiveness.

29. **Ida,** a mountain in Crete, where the infant Jove was nurtured.

33. **grain,** color (from O. F. *graine,* a crimson dye). The shade indicated here is probably a dark purple.

Forget thyself to marble, till
With a sad leaden downward cast,
Thou fix them on the earth as fast.
And join with thee calm Peace and Quiet,
Spare Fast, that oft with gods doth diet,
And hears the Muses in a ring
Aye round about Jove's altar sing.
And add to these retirèd Leisure,
That in trim gardens takes his pleasure;   50
But first and chiefest, with thee bring
Him that yon soars on golden wing,
Guiding the fiery-wheelèd throne,
The Cherub Contemplation;
And the mute Silence hist along,
'Less Philomel will deign a song,
In her sweetest saddest plight,
Smoothing the rugged brow of Night,
While Cynthia checks her dragon yoke,
Gently o'er the accustomed oak;   60
Sweet bird that shunn'st the noise of folly,
Most musical, most melancholy!
Thee chauntress oft the woods among,
I woo to hear thy even-song;
And missing thee, I walk unseen
On the dry smooth-shaven green,
To behold the wandering moon,
Riding near her highest noon,
Like one that had been led astray
Through the Heaven's wide pathless way;   70
And oft, as if her head she bowed,
Stooping through a fleecy cloud.
Oft on a plat of rising ground
I hear the far-off curfew sound,

pleasure in solitude

42. **Forget thyself to marble**, i.e., become as silent and motionless as
a statue. Cf. the lines "On Shakespeare."
43. **sad**, sober, serious (with no implication of grief).
46. Cf. Elegy VI, 55 ff. The idea is both classical and Christian.
52–54. Ezek. 1:4 ff. and *Paradise Lost*, VI, 749–59. In taking a cherub
to symbolize Contemplation, Milton is apparently following a tradition of
Christian mysticism. According to the *Celestial Hierarchy* of Dionysius, the
cherubim, who constitute the second order of angels, have the faculty of
immediately contemplating Deity.
55. **hist**, summon quietly (imperative).
56. **Philomel**, the nightingale.
59. **Cynthia**, the moon. The association of a **dragon yoke** with her is
rather unusual, but not unprecedented. Cf. *A Midsummer Night's Dream*,
III, ii, 379: "For night's swift dragons cut the clouds full fast."
65. **I walk unseen**. Cf. "L'Allegro," 57 and note.

Over some wide-watered shore,
Swinging slow with sullen roar;
Or if the air will not permit,
Some still removèd place will fit,
Where glowing embers through the room
Teach light to counterfeit a gloom,   80
Far from all resort of mirth,
Save the cricket on the hearth,
Or the bellman's drowsy charm,
To bless the doors from nightly harm.
Or let my lamp at midnight hour
Be seen in some high lonely tower,
Where I may oft outwatch the Bear,
With thrice great Hermes, or unsphere
The spirit of Plato to unfold
What worlds or what vast regions hold   90
The immortal mind that hath forsook
Her mansion in this fleshly nook;
And of those dæmons that are found
In fire, air, flood, or under ground,
Whose power hath a true consent
With planet or with element.
Sometime let gorgeous Tragedy
In sceptred pall come sweeping by,
Presenting Thebes, or Pelops' line,
Or the tale of Troy divine,   100
Or what (though rare) of later age
Ennobled hath the buskined stage.

83. the bellman's drowsy charm. Cf. Herrick's lyric, "The Bellman":
"From noise of scare-fires rest ye free,
From murders Benedicite," etc.

87. outwatch the Bear, i.e., stay awake the entire night. The constellation of Ursa Major does not set in northern latitudes.

88. thrice great Hermes, Hermes Trismegistus. Originally the name was identified with the Egyptian god Thoth, the patron of magic and alchemy, who was the reputed source of all mystical doctrines. From about the third century, it was applied to the author (or authors) of various Neoplatonic writings emanating from Alexandria. Milton undoubtedly has in mind these so-called Hermetic books, some of which are extant.

88–89. or unsphere the spirit of Plato, i.e., call back the soul of Plato from its celestial dwelling place—perhaps through some Neoplatonic formula. The doctrine of the demons (93–96) is Hermetic. The passage as a whole is intended to suggest that vast realm of philosophical and pseudophilosophical speculation which delighted the mind of the Renaissance scholar.

97 ff. Milton is of course alluding to the works of Aeschylus, Sophocles, and Euripides. The royal houses of *Thebes* and *Troy,* and especially the descendants of *Pelops* (Agamemnon, Iphigenia, etc.) were the chief subjects of Greek tragedy.

98. pall, cloak, mantle (Latin *palla*).

    But, O sad Virgin, that thy power
Might raise Musæus from his bower,
Or bid the soul of Orpheus sing
Such notes as, warbled to the string,
Drew iron tears down Pluto's cheek,
And made Hell grant what Love did seek;
Or call up him that left half told
The story of Cambuscan bold,   110
Of Camball, and of Algarsife,
And who had Canace to wife,
That owned the virtuous ring and glass,
And of the wondrous horse of brass,
On which the Tartar king did ride;
And if aught else great bards beside
In sage and solemn tunes have sung,
Of tourneys and of trophies hung,
Of forests and enchantments drear,
Where more is meant than meets the ear.   120
    Thus Night oft see me in thy pale career,
Till civil-suited Morn appear,
Not tricked and frounced as she was wont
With the Attic boy to hunt,
But kerchieft in a comely cloud,
While rocking winds are piping loud,
Or ushered with a shower still,
When the gust hath blown his fill,
Ending on the rustling leaves,
With minute-drops from off the eaves.   130
And when the sun begins to fling
His flaring beams, me Goddess bring
To archèd walks of twilight groves,

102. **buskined stage.** See note on "L'Allegro," 132.

104. **Musaeus,** a mythical Greek poet, to whom were attributed various poems connected with the mysteries of Demeter at Eleusis.

105 ff. Cf. "L'Allegro," 145–50 and note. The Orpheus story seems to have made a particularly strong appeal to Milton's imagination.

109. **him that left half told,** etc., i.e., Chaucer, who left unfinished *The Squire's Tale* of Cambuscan, king of Tartary, and his three children, Camball, Algarsife, and Canace. The tale was continued by Spenser (*Faerie Queene*, IV, iii).

116 ff. These lines evidently refer to the epic-romances of Ariosto, Tasso, and Spenser. **Where more is meant than meets the ear** seems to be a definite allusion to the allegorical element in the *Faerie Queene.*

122. **civil-suited,** dressed in plain civilian attire. Note the quiet subdued tone of all the daytime images which follow. Milton preserves a twilight atmosphere to the very end of the poem.

124. **Attic boy.** Cephalus, grandson of Cecrops, king of Attica. Cephalus was beloved of Eos, goddess of the dawn.

130. **minute-drops,** drops falling at intervals of a minute.

And shadows brown that Silvan loves,
Of pine or monumental oak,
Where the rude axe with heavëd stroke
Was never heard the nymphs to daunt,
Or fright them from their hallowed haunt.
There in close covert by some brook,
Where no profaner eye may look,   140
Hide me from Day's garish eye,
While the bee with honied thigh,
That at her flowery work doth sing,
And the waters murmuring,
With such consort as they keep,
Entice the dewy-feathered Sleep;
And let some strange mysterious dream
Wave at his wings in airy stream
Of lively portraiture displayed,
Softly on my eyelids laid.   150
And as I wake, sweet music breathe
Above, about, or underneath,
Sent by some spirit to mortals good,
Or the unseen Genius of the wood.
But let my due feet never fail
To walk the studious cloister's pale,
And love the high embowëd roof,
With antic pillars massy proof,
And storied windows richly dight,
Casting a dim religious light.   160
There let the pealing organ blow
To the full-voiced choir below,
In service high and anthems clear,
As may with sweetness, through mine ear,
Dissolve me into ecstasies,
And bring all Heaven before mine eyes.
And may at last my weary age

134. **Silvan,** Silvanus, god of the woods and fields.

147 ff. The meaning seems to be this: Let some strange mysterious dream, unfolded in an airy stream of vivid pictures, come floating at the wings of Sleep as they are softly laid on my eyelids.

154. **Genius,** guardian deity.

156 ff. These lines probably reflect Milton's boyhood impression of St. Paul's cloisters and the solemn cathedral service. Although he later became suspicious of ecclesiastical ritual and ornament, he never ignored the aesthetic element in the religious experience. In one of his most Puritan utterances (*Of Reformation in England*), he still speaks of "the beauty of inward sanctity." **pale,** enclosure.

157. **And love,** i.e., let *me* never fail to love. Logic requires the substitution of a new subject. **embowëd,** vaulted.

158. **antic,** fantastically ornamented.

Find out the peaceful hermitage,
The hairy gown and mossy cell,
Where I may sit and rightly spell   170
Of every star that Heaven doth shew,
And every herb that sips the dew;
Till old experience do attain
To something like prophetic strain.
These pleasures Melancholy give,
And I with thee will choose to live.

[1631?]

SONNET VII

Milton made his twenty-fourth birthday (see note on line 2),
which took place six months after he left Cambridge, an
occasion for serious thought about his career and for the
poetic affirmation of a lofty resolution. His trouble at the slow
development of his powers is characteristic. Beneath his confidence in the ultimate attaining of his goal there was a deep
distrust. As he here expresses doubt of his maturity so in
Paradise Lost he fears that he is too old to fulfil his task. In
both cases his resort is to prayer and acquiescence. Who were
the more "timely-happy" spirits whose early ripening he envies
is uncertain. Thomas Randolph, who was at Cambridge with
Milton and whose verses were already famous, though unpublished, has been suggested, but Milton may have been thinking
of one of the ancients, for example, Statius.

SONNET VII

How soon hath Time, the subtle thief of youth,
    Stolen on his wing my three and twentieth year!
My hasting days fly on with full career,
    But my late spring no bud or blossom show'th.

169. **The hairy gown and mossy cell.** The suggestion of asceticism
noted in line 46 is here repeated. Observe, however, that Milton's emphasis is on the earthly satisfaction to be gained from the solitary, abstemious
life, rather than on its future spiritual benefits. The medieval ideal of
contemptus mundi is not what he has in mind.
    175-76. Cf. the closing lines of "L'Allegro."
    1 ff. The statements Milton makes about himself in this poem are to be
taken quite literally. He copied it out in a letter to an unknown friend as
evidence of the fact that he had taken note of a certain belatedness in himself. His "outward semblance" is certainly very youthful in his portrait at
the age of twenty-one and he was called "the lady" at Christ College.
    2. **three and twentieth.** In Milton's usage this seems to mean that he
was twenty-four years old. See Parker, "Some Problems in the Chronology
of Milton's Early Poems," *Rev. of English Studies*, XI (1935), p. 276.

Perhaps my semblance might deceive the truth,
That I to manhood am arrived so near,
And inward ripeness doth much less appear,
That some more timely-happy spirits endu'th.
Yet be it less or more, or soon or slow,
It shall be still in strictest measure even, 10
To that same lot, however mean or high,
Toward which Time leads me, and the will of Heaven;
All is, if I have grace to use it so,
As ever in my great Task-Master's eye.

[December, 1632]

ARCADES

It is interesting to find Milton, in spite of his declarations in favor of a grave heroic subject, indulging his muse in a form of literature so closely associated with secular enjoyments as the masque. Solitary study and high contemplation were evidently not so preoccupying that he could not gladly respond to an invitation to contribute his talent to an interesting social occasion. The composition of *Arcades* implies a relationship of the Milton family with the country gentry about Horton. The Countess Dowager of Derby was a great and distinguished lady. A daughter of Sir John Spenser of Allthorpe, she had married, first, Ferdinando Stanley, Lord Strange, then Sir Thomas Egerton, Lord Keeper of the Seal. To her Edmund Spenser, who counted himself one of the family, had dedicated *The Tears of the Muses*. The "noble persons" who presented themselves before the Countess as shepherds doubtless included the children of her son-in-law and stepson, Sir John Egerton, Earl of Bridgewater, in whose honor Milton was to compose *Comus*. Harry Lawes, the musician, was tutor in Sir John's and Lady Alice's households, and it was probably he who devised the masque and engaged Milton to write this portion of the text. The natural supposition is that Lawes performed the part of the Genius of the Wood, as he did the corresponding one of Thyrsis in *Comus*.

The poetry is of the same mintage as that of "L'Allegro" and "Il Penseroso," save that the address of the Genius strikes a

8. **timely-happy,** fortunate in the time of their maturing; **endu'th,** invests.

10. My development will be exactly even with my appointed lot; let it be as God wills.

11–12. My own part is to make the best use of what is given me as being ever under the eye of God.

deeper philosophic note. We observe the use of Milton's favorite image of the music of the spheres, already employed in the Nativity ode and in the *Prolusions*. The second lyric has a gemlike quality unrivalled in the tradition of the Jacobean masque. The date of *Arcades* is an interesting crux of Milton scholarship. A draft of the original in Milton's hand, with many alterations, occupies the first pages of the Trinity College Manuscript of the minor poems. It is followed by "At a Solemn Music," also apparently a first draft, then by two drafts of an undated letter to a friend containing the sonnet on his twenty-fourth birthday, presumably written shortly after December 9, 1632. The latter is described as "my nightly thoughts some while since." *Arcades* may possible precede that date but is more likely to have followed it in 1633 or even in 1634, the year of *Comus*. In 1631, a great tragedy had befallen the family of the Countess, her son-in-law, the Earl of Castlehaven, having been tried and executed for sodomy and the prostitution of his wife and daughter. The Countess's correspondence shows her to have been much disturbed by this event. Several of her widowed daughter's numerous offspring, both by this and by an earlier marriage, were domiciled with her and their social welfare became her great concern. We find one of them taking part, together with their cousins, the Egertons, in a masque at Court in 1634, by which time the mother had remarried. Lady Alice's account book of that year shows an elaborate visit to Harefield by the Earl of Bridgewater and other relatives before his departure for Wales. There had been also a family wedding there in the preceding April. These occasions and the particular entertainment of which *Arcades* was a part may have been incidents in the moral recovery of the Countess's household after its public disgrace; 1633 or 1634 is the likeliest year.

ARCADES

Part of an entertainment presented to the Countess Dowager of Derby at Harefield by some noble persons of her family, who appear on the scene in pastoral habit, moving toward the seat of state, with this song.

Countess Dowager of Derby. Third wife of Thomas Egerton, Lord Ellesmere, and mother-in-law as well as stepmother of his son, John, First

1. *Song*

Look Nymphs, and Shepherds look,
What sudden blaze of majesty
Is that which we from hence descry,
Too divine to be mistook.
This, this is she
To whom our vows and wishes bend,
Here our solemn search hath end.

Fame that her high worth to raise
Seemed erst so lavish and profuse,
We may justly now accuse   10
Of detraction from her praise;
    Less than half we find expressed,
    Envy bid conceal the rest.

Mark what radiant state she spreads,
In circle round her shining throne,
Shooting her beams like silver threads.
This, this is she alone,
    Sitting like a goddess bright
    In the center of her light.

Might she the wise Latona be,   20
Or the towered Cybele
Mother of a hundred gods;
Juno dares not give her odds;
    Who had thought this clime had held
    A deity so unparalleled?

As they come forward, THE GENIUS OF THE WOOD *appears, and
turning toward them, speaks.*

Gen. Stay gentle Swains, for though in this disguise,
I see bright honor sparkle through your eyes;
Of famous Arcady ye are, and sprung
Of that renownèd flood, so often sung,

Earl of Bridgewater. Some of her children and grandchildren lived under
her care at Harefield, which is near Horton, and Bridgewater frequently
visited her there.
    20. Latona was the mother of Apollo by Jupiter; Cybele is Rhea, mother
of Jupiter, who was pictured as wearing a crown of towers.
    26-27. Though they are in the disguise of rustics their noble birth
shines in their eyes.

Divine Alpheus, who by secret sluice,   30
Stole under seas to meet his Arethuse;
And ye the breathing roses of the wood,
Fair silver-buskined Nymphs as great and good,
I know this quest of yours and free intent
Was all in honor and devotion meant
To the great mistress of yon princely shrine,
Whom with low reverence I adore as mine,
And with all helpful service will comply
To further this night's glad solemnity,
And lead ye where ye may more near behold   40
What shallow-searching Fame hath left untold,
Which I full oft, amidst these shades alone,
Have sat to wonder at, and gaze upon.
For know by lot from Jove I am the power
Of this fair wood, and live in oaken bower,
To nurse the saplings tall, and curl the grove
With ringlets quaint and wanton windings wove;
And all my plants I save from nightly ill,
Of noisome winds and blasting vapors chill;
And from the boughs brush off the evil dew,   50
And heal the harms of thwarting thunder blue,
Or what the cross dire-looking planet smites,
Or hurtful worm with cankered venom bites.
When evening grey doth rise, I fetch my round
Over the mount and all this hallowed ground,
And early ere the odorous breath of morn
Awakes the slumbering leaves, or tasselled horn
Shakes the high thicket, haste I all about,
Number my ranks, and visit every sprout
With puissant words and murmurs made to bless;   60
But else in deep of night, when drowsiness
Hath locked up mortal sense, then listen I
To the celestial sirens' harmony,
That sit upon the nine enfolded spheres
And sing to those that hold the vital shears
And turn the adamantine spindle round,
On which the fate of gods and men is found.
Such sweet compulsion doth in music lie,

56. Gray borrows this phrase in the "Elegy": The odorous breath of
incense breathing morn.
63 ff. the celestial sirens' harmony. In the tenth book of *The Republic* Plato describes the heavenly music as made by eight sirens sitting on
spheres and each singing a different note. The spheres turn on a spindle
resting on the knees of Necessity, whose daughters are the three fates.

To lull the daughters of Necessity,
And keep unsteady Nature to her law,   70
And the low world in measured motion draw
After the heavenly tune, which none can hear
Of human mould with gross unpurgèd ear;
And yet such music worthiest were to blaze
The peerless height of her immortal praise
Whose luster leads us, and for her most fit,
If my inferior hand or voice could hit
Inimitable sounds; yet as we go,
Whate'er the skill of lesser gods can show,
I will assay, her worth to celebrate,   80
And so attend ye toward her glittering state;
Where ye may all that are of noble stem
Approach, and kiss her sacred vesture's hem.

II. Song

O'er the smooth enamelled green
Where no print of step hath been,
    Follow me as I sing,
    And touch the warbled string.
Under the shady roof
Of branching elm star-proof,
    Follow me;   90
I will bring you where she sits
Clad in splendor as befits
    Her deity.
Such a rural Queen
All Arcadia hath not seen.

III. Song

Nymphs and Shepherds dance no more
    By sandy Ladon's lilied banks;
On old Lycæus or Cyllene hoar,
    Trip no more in twilight ranks;
Though Erymanth your loss deplore,   100
    A better soil shall give ye thanks.
From the stony Mænalus,
Bring your flocks and live with us;
Here ye shall have greater grace,
To serve the Lady of this place.

[1633-34]

97. Ladon, a river in Arcadia associated with Pan, the god of shepherds. *sandy* is Ovid's epithet, *lilied* Milton's.
98. Lycæus, Cyllene, mountains in Arcadia.

Though Syrinx your Pan's mistress were,
Yet Syrinx well might wait on her.
Such a rural Queen
All Arcadia hath not seen.

ON TIME

This and the two similar poems which follow occur after
Arcades in the Trinity Manuscript and, in spite of their different character, may be assumed to belong between it and
Comus. They represent a return of Milton's meditative and
religious vein. The first illustrates his preoccupation in youth
with a theme which concerned him little in maturity, that of
immortality. The second records the inspiration which music
always held for him and brings in again the symbolic concord
of the spheres. The third echoes the Nativity ode and "The
Passion" and was perhaps intended to stand with them as one
of a series of divine poems on the events of the life of Christ.
Lawes set a poem "The Circumcision" by Cartwright to music,
and Milton may have intended these as songs. They are his
last attempt in the common style of seventeenth-century sacred
verse. "At a Solemn Music" has moments of true inspiration.

ON TIME

Fly envious Time, till thou run out thy race,
Call on the lazy leaden-stepping Hours,
Whose speed is but the heavy plummet's pace;
And glut thyself with what thy womb devours,
Which is no more than what is false and vain,
And merely mortal dross;
So little is our loss,
So little is thy gain.
For when as each thing bad thou hast entombed,
And last of all, thy greedy self consumed,   10
Then long Eternity shall greet our bliss
With an individual kiss,
And Joy shall overtake us as a flood;

On Time. The original title in Milton's manuscript is "To be set on a
clock case."
   1. Time is envious of life. Milton bids it make haste till it has done its
work and time shall be no more.
   2–3. The hours are measured by the slow-moving leaden weights of an
old-fashioned clock.
   12. individual, indivisible, i.e., eternal.

When every thing that is sincerely good
And perfectly divine,
With Truth, and Peace, and Love shall ever shine
About the supreme throne
Of him to whose happy-making sight alone
When once our heavenly-guided soul shall climb,
Then all this earthy grossness quit,   20
Attired with stars, we shall for ever sit,
Triumphing over Death, and Chance, and thee O Time.

[1633–34]

UPON THE CIRCUMCISION

Ye flaming Powers, and wingèd Warriors bright,
That erst with music and triumphant song
First heard by happy watchful shepherds' ear,
So sweetly sung your joy the clouds along
Through the soft silence of the listening night;
Now mourn, and if sad share with us to bear
Your fiery essence can distil no tear,
Burn in your sighs, and borrow
Seas wept from our deep sorrow;
He who with all Heaven's heraldry whilere   10
Entered the world, now bleeds to give us ease;
Alas, how soon our sin
   Sore doth begin
     His infancy to seize!

O more exceeding love, or law more just?
Just law indeed, but more exceeding love!
For we by rightful doom remediless
Were lost in death, till he that dwelt above
High-throned in secret bliss, for us frail dust
Emptied his glory, even to nakedness;   20
And that great covenant which we still transgress
Entirely satisfied,

Upon the Circumcision. The feast of the circumcision, commemorating Christ's submission to the Jewish law, is on January 1.

2. **erst,** not long ago; i.e., at the nativity.

7. Being of fiery substance the angels cannot shed tears, but can share our grief. The conceit is of the order of those in "The Passion."

15. Is justice or love more manifested in this first suffering of Christ for our sins, Milton asks, and answers that love is greater, since justice would be satisfied with our death.

21–22. Christ satisfies the law of God by perfectly fulfilling the covenant. At the same time he appeases God's anger against us for continually breaking it.

And the full wrath beside
Of vengeful justice bore for our excess,
And seals obedience first with wounding smart
This day, but O ere long,
   Huge pangs and strong
   Will pierce more near his heart.

[1633–34]

AT A SOLEMN MUSIC

Blest pair of Sirens, pledges of Heaven's joy,
Sphere-born harmonious sisters, Voice and Verse,
Wed your divine sounds, and mixed power employ,
Dead things with inbreathed sense able to pierce,
And to our high-raised phantasy present
That undisturbëd song of pure concent,
Aye sung before the sapphire-colored throne
To him that sits thereon,
With saintly shout and solemn jubilee,
Where the bright Seraphim in burning row   10
Their loud uplifted angel-trumpets blow,
And the Cherubic host in thousand choirs
Touch their immortal harps of golden wires,
With those just spirits that wear victorious palms,
Hymns devout and holy psalms
Singing everlastingly;
That we on Earth with undiscording voice
May rightly answer that melodious noise;
As once we did, till disproportioned sin
Jarred against Nature's chime, and with harsh din   20
Broke the fair music that all creatures made
To their great Lord, whose love their motion swayed
In perfect diapason, whilst they stood
In first obedience and their state of good.
O may we soon again renew that song,
And keep in tune with Heaven, till God ere long
To his celestial consort us unite,
To live with him, and sing in endless morn of light.

[1633–34]

Solemn Music, a concert of sacred music.
3. mixed power, the combined power of poetry and music.
6. concent, harmony.
7 ff. The imagery is from Ezek. 1:26 and Rev. 7:9; 14:3–4.
27. consort, company of musicians.

Comus

The date of *Comus* is given in the Trinity College Manuscript and in the anonymous edition published by Harry Lawes. It was performed at Ludlow Castle in Wales on September 29, 1634. We have no information as to the circumstances of this production other than that given in the editions. Milton may or may not have been present. Lawes himself took the part of the attendant Spirit. The audience and other actors must have been made up of the personal entourage of the Earl of Bridgewater and of the surrounding gentry. Lawes altered the text for stage presentation, converting the Spirit's epilogue into a prologue and cutting some of the longer speeches. The stage copy is still extant, with stage directions in his hand. These stage directions were incorporated in the printed editions and some of them were copied by Milton into the Trinity Manuscript. It is obvious that he and Lawes must have cooperated in the anonymous publication of 1637 though the preface states that Lawes had been driven to make the work public by the frequent requests of his friends for copies. The motto on the title page,

Eheu quid volui misero mihi, floribus austrum Perditus,

(Alas, what have I done to my wretched self;
I have ruined myself by letting the south wind blow upon
my flowers,)

sounds like the poet's choice. There is something more in it than the ordinary novice's shrinking from publicity. Milton realizes his sensitiveness to criticism. The success of what was, except for the lines on Shakespeare, his first published work must have warmed and emboldened him. One letter like that which came from Sir Henry Wotton in response to the gift of a copy of the 1637 edition was enough to assure him of "fit audience though few" for the loftier poems which he had in prospect. The text of *Comus* in the 1645 edition was set, with a few alterations, from the edition of 1637.

The title does not derive from Milton, who calls it simply "A Maske." It was first employed in an eighteenth-century stage version.

There has never been any disagreement as to the merits of *Comus* as a work of literature or its significance in Milton's poetic development. Written four years after his retirement at Horton, before the zest of studious leisure had worn off but after his ideas and purposes had acquired a temporary stability, it embodies in happy union the delicacy and the sobriety of his nature and is perfectly representative of his youthful art. Evidence of Milton's acquaintance with and delight in the tradition of the Jacobean masque is to be found in the Nativity ode and in "L'Allegro." The experiment in *Arcades* shows him to have already transcended it in the importance given to the poet's function. He incorporates in *Comus*, to be sure, the grotesque and the stately dances which constitute the essence of a masque, and he gives plenty of opportunity for the talents of Lawes and the youthful actors. But he insists on bringing home to the audience the full weight of his message and, as a consequence, the moral speeches extend to an unprecedented length. His procedure may not have helped in the contemporary effect of the production, but it insured *Comus* a permanent status as literature and enabled Milton to express more completely than he had hitherto done his deeply felt convictions.

The theme of the masque is the unassailable security of the virtuous mind amid every circumstance of violence and wrong. For Milton in this period of his life the symbol of all virtue is chastity. It was not for nothing that he had been called "The Lady" at college. He now dramatizes the idea which he has so carefully cherished in his own life and throws it into contrast with the solicitations of an easier way of happiness. There is no real dramatic conflict. The Lady, her knightly brothers, the flushed reveler, his allegorical monsters, the approving and protective Thyrsis stand frozen in a tableau.

Platonic ideas invest the whole conception as with a garment. *Comus* represents the principle of passion in the soul, the Lady that of reason. Since "soul is form and doth the body make," the men who have surrendered to passion's dominance "imbody and imbrute" until they "quite lose the property of their first being," "unmoulding reason's mintage charactered in the face." Such are Comus's monsters. Thyrsis is a symbol which has intruded from another sphere of thought. He is the counterpart of Arthur in the *Faerie Queene*—grace divine, vouchsafed by Heaven to assist the virtuous with effort not their own. The elder and the younger brothers are little philosophers, who receive confirmation and support in their understanding of the laws of life by this lesson. The whole pageant exists, indeed, for their benefit. Lord Brackley, by way of compliment, is represented as already established in the truth. But Milton knows that he is not. To make him, secondly to Thyrsis, a mouthpiece of the moral purport of *Comus*, as in lines 118 ff., is to send him forth into the dangerous society of court life as firm against temptation as if he had held daily converse with Socrates.

Emotional mysticism, learned elsewhere than in the grove of Academe, pervades the poem, especially at the close. The mystic marriage of the soul with God will be brought about by Thyrsis. It gives meaning to a denial of nature otherwise intolerable and absurd, and wings of inspiration to a theme which in the hands of a mere moralist would be chill as death.

The vital sources of the masque are to be sought in Milton's personal experience. We might even find the materials for Comus himself in an exaggerated view of Diodati, as Milton saw him when he wrote his sixth Latin elegy. For the monsters he need not seek beyond his Cambridge acquaintances:

> Rough satyrs danced and fawns with cloven heel.

The thesis that the self-imposed restraints are no bondage, that license is hostile to true liberty, that the mind is its own place, are deep personal convictions, passionately held and firmly lived by. The literary germ of the story is the close of Book III of the *Faerie Queene*, where Amoret resists the solicitations of Busirane and is rescued by the pure Britomart. The unchaste herd of Circe comes from the *Odyssey* by way of the *Faerie Queene*, Book II. Milton's debt to Peele's crazy folklore drama, *The Old Wives' Tale*, to Puteanus's Latin play, *Comus*, to Jonson's masque, *Pleasure Reconciled to Virtue*, and to Fletcher's *The Faithful Shepherdess* is less certain and less important but worth inquiring into.

The style of *Comus* is made up of many simples. Euripides furnishes the pattern of the lengthy prologue and of the stichomythia in lines 276–90. The lyrics are in the purest Jonsonian manner. The blank verse is, on the whole, that of the Elizabethan dramatists, with Shakespearean echoes clearly audible, but Milton has touched it with his own later idiom, particularly in the passages which voice his ethical convictions. Such a passage is to be found in lines 582–98, for the tone of which earlier English literature affords no precedent.

COMUS

A Masque Presented at Ludlow Castle, 1634

THE PERSONS

THE ATTENDANT SPIRIT, afterwards in the habit
of THYRSIS.
COMUS, with his Crew.
THE LADY.
FIRST BROTHER.
SECOND BROTHER.
SABRINA, the Nymph.

The first Scene discovers a wild wood.

The ATTENDANT SPIRIT *descends or enters.*

Before the starry threshold of Jove's court
My mansion is, where those immortal shapes
Of bright aerial spirits live insphered
In regions mild of calm and serene air,
Above the smoke and stir of this dim spot
Which men call Earth, and with low-thoughted care,
Confined and pestered in this pinfold here,
Strive to keep up a frail and feverish being,
Unmindful of the crown that Virtue gives
After this mortal change, to her true servants   10
Amongst the enthroned gods on sainted seats.
Yet some there be that by due steps aspire
To lay their just hands on that golden key
That opes the palace of Eternity.
To such my errand is, and but for such,
I would not soil these pure ambrosial weeds

1. In the acting version, preserved at Bridgewater House, the masque
opens with a song of 20 lines transferred with slight alterations from the
epilogue, 976 ff.: *From the Heavens now I fly,* etc.
3. **aerial spirits,** i.e., spirits of the air, called Sylphs in the Rosicrucian
mythology. Thyrsis is really an angel but Milton is careful to keep the poem
externally pagan. **insphered,** dwelling in the sphere which encircles earth.
5. Milton is thinking of the serene abode of the gods as the ancients
imaged it, but the contrast is not only with the cares of earth but with its sin.
There is always a Christian meaning not far below the surface.
7. **pestered,** shackled, *empester.* **pinfold,** pound.
10. **mortal change,** change of death.
11. Note the mingling of pagan and Christian language.
16. **ambrosial,** immortal. Ambrosia was the food of the gods. **weeds,**
garments.

With the rank vapors of this sin-worn mould.
  But to my task. Neptune besides the sway
Of every salt flood and each ebbing stream,
Took in by lot 'twixt high and nether Jove   20
Imperial rule of all the sea-girt isles
That like to rich and various gems inlay
The unadornëd bosom of the deep,
Which he to grace his tributary gods
By course commits to several government,
And gives them leave to wear their sapphire crowns
And wield their little tridents; but this Isle,
The greatest and the best of all the main,
He quarters to his blue-haired deities;
And all this tract that fronts the falling sun   30
A noble Peer of mickle trust and power
Has in his charge, with tempered awe to guide
An old and haughty nation proud in arms;
Where his fair offspring nursed in princely lore,
Are coming to attend their father's state
And new-entrusted scepter, but their way
Lies through the perplexed paths of this drear wood,
The nodding horror of whose shady brows
Threats the forlorn and wandering passenger.
And here their tender age might suffer peril,   40
But that by quick command from sovran Jove
I was despatched for their defence and guard;
And listen why, for I will tell you now
What never yet was heard in tale or song

17. sin-worn mould, i.e., our earthly bodies worn with sin.
18 ff. The universe was divided by lot among Neptune, Pluto, and Jove. Cf. *Iliad*, xv, 190 ff. Milton elaborates the myth to make Neptune ruler also of Britain.
20. nether Jove. Pluto was called Zeus of the underworld.
23. unadornëd, otherwise unadorned.
29. quarters. He divides this island instead of giving it to one deity. From the stage directions in other masques it appears that the sea gods were represented with blue hair.
31. A noble Peer, the Earl of Bridgewater. Milton, following the practice of the Elizabethans, incorporates the nobleman he wishes to compliment into the scheme of ancient mythology. mickle, great.
32. tempered awe, temperate firmness.
33. An old . . . arms. The valor and pride of the Welsh were traditional.
35. Are coming. The fictitious situation of the masque is closely attached to reality. Indeed, it is said that Lady Alice Egerton actually had been lost in the woods, but this is mere tradition.
39. forlorn, lost.
44. What never yet, etc. Milton means that the story of Comus is a hitherto unrevealed piece of mythology. He attaches his invention, however, to the familiar stories of Bacchus and Circe.

From old or modern bard in hall or bower.
Bacchus that first from out the purple grape
Crushed the sweet poison of misusëd wine,
After the Tuscan mariners transformed,
Coasting the Tyrrhene shore, as the winds listed,
On Circe's island fell. (Who knows not Circe   50
The daughter of the Sun? whose charmëd cup
Whoever tasted, lost his upright shape,
And downward fell into a grovelling swine.)
This Nymph that gazed upon his clustering locks,
With ivy berries wreathed, and his blithe youth,
Had by him, ere he parted thence, a son
Much like his father, but his mother more,
Whom therefore she brought up and Comus named,
Who ripe and frolic of his full-grown age,
Roving the Celtic and Iberian fields,   60
At last betakes him to this ominous wood,
And in thick shelter of black shades imbowered,
Excels his mother at her mighty art,
Offering to every weary traveller
His orient liquor in a crystal glass,
To quench the drouth of Phœbus, which as they taste
(For most do taste through fond intemperate thirst),
Soon as the potion works, their human count'nance,
The express resemblance of the gods, is changed
Into some brutish form of wolf, or bear,   70
Or ounce, or tiger, hog, or bearded goat,
All other parts remaining as they were.
And they, so perfect is their misery,

45. **hall or bower,** the main room and the chambers of a medieval castle. Cf. Wordsworth: "the heroic wealth of hall and bower."
46. **Bacchus,** etc. For the story of Bacchus's revenge on the sailors who tried to sell him into slavery see Ovid, *Metamorphoses* iii. 583 ff.
48. **After the Tuscan mariners transformed:** a Latin construction, *post nautas mutatos.* The whole sentence is framed on the Latin model.
50 ff. **Who knows . . . swine.** See the tenth book of the *Odyssey* for the story of Circe.
57. He is an enchanter and lustful, like Circe. He wears, however, Bacchus's crown of ivy.
60. **Celtic and Iberian fields,** France and Spain.
61. **ominous,** full of omens, enchanted.
67. **fond,** foolish.
71. **ounce,** lynx.
73–77. The moral significance of the transformation wrought by Circe (and here by Comus) is not indicated in the *Odyssey,* but the myth was so interpreted by the later Greeks. It is central in Spenser's adaptation of the story, *Faerie Queene* II, xii. The idea expressed in these lines is Milton's individual touch in the moralization, for in Homer and elsewhere the swine know that they have been men.

Not once perceive their foul disfigurement,
But boast themselves more comely than before,
And all their friends and native home forget,
To roll with pleasure in a sensual sty.
Therefore when any favored of high Jove,
Chances to pass through this adventurous glade,
Swift as the sparkle of a glancing star   80
I shoot from heaven to give him safe convoy,
As now I do. But first I must put off
These my sky-robes spun out of Iris' woof,
And take the weeds and likeness of a swain
That to the service of this house belongs,
Who with his soft pipe and smooth-dittied song
Well knows to still the wild winds when they roar,
And hush the waving woods, nor of less faith,
And in this office of his mountain watch
Likeliest, and nearest to the present aid   90
Of this occasion. But I hear the tread
Of hateful steps, I must be viewless now.

Comus *enters, with a charming-rod in one hand, his glass in the*
other, with him a rout of monsters, headed like sundry sorts of wild
beasts, but otherwise like men and women, their apparel glistering.
They come in making a riotous and unruly noise, with torches in
their hands.

Comus. The star that bids the shepherd fold
Now the top of heaven doth hold,
And the gilded car of day
His glowing axle doth allay
In the steep Atlantic stream,
And the slope sun his upward beam
Shoots against the dusky pole,
Pacing toward the other goal   100

83. Iris' woof. Cf. "Nativity Ode," 143; the enamelled arras of the
rainbow wearing.
86. smooth-dittied. An adjective in –ed like "bearded."
87. knows to, knows how to.
Comus enters, etc. The rout of monsters, with their grotesque dance,
constitutes the antimasque. A similar group appears in Browne's *Inner*
Temple Masque and elsewhere.
93. The star, the evening star, sometimes called the folding star.
94. top of Heaven doth hold; the phrase is loosely used, and does not
mean that the star was at the zenith. The time is early evening and Hesperus is setting in the west.
96. allay, cool. Cf. to "allay thirst."
97. steep, probably referring to its appearance from shore.
98–99. The setting (slope) sun shoots his beams upward from the horizon toward the zenith, which is already growing dark.

Of his chamber in the east.
Meanwhile welcome joy and feast,
Midnight shout and revelry,
Tipsy dance and jollity.
Braid your locks with rosy twine,
Dropping odors, dropping wine.
Rigor now is gone to bed,
And Advice with scrupulous head,
Strict Age, and sour Severity,
With their grave saws in slumber lie.   110
We that are of purer fire
Imitate the starry choir,
Who in their nightly watchful spheres,
Lead in swift round the months and years.
The sounds and seas with all their finny drove
Now to the moon in wavering morrice move,
And on the tawny sands and shelves
Trip the pert fairies and the dapper elves;
By dimpled brook and fountain brim,
The wood-nymphs decked with daisies trim,   120
Their merry wakes and pastimes keep:
What hath night to do with sleep?
Night hath better sweets to prove,
Venus now wakes, and wakens Love.
Come let us our rites begin,
'Tis only daylight that makes sin
Which these dun shades will ne'er report.
Hail goddess of nocturnal sport,
Dark-veiled Cotytto, to whom the secret flame
Of midnight torches burns; mysterious dame   130
That ne'er art called but when the dragon womb
Of Stygian darkness spits her thickest gloom,

101. Cf. Psalms 9:5: "the sun . . . cometh forth as a bridegroom out of
his chamber."
110. **saws,** maxims.
111. **purer fire,** the purer element, fire.
112. **the starry choir,** the chorus of stars.
116. **morrice,** morris dance.
117. **Tawny sands.** Cf. *The Tempest*, I, ii, 376 ff.

> Come unto these yellow sands   10
> And then take hands.

Milton first wrote "yellow" in the Cambridge MS.
118. The inverted first foot, the very light third beat, and the snapping
"p's" and "t's" in this line are worth noticing as the mechanical elements of
its effectiveness.
129. **Cotytto,** Thracian goddess whose licentious rites were secretly celebrated at night. Note the effect of deepening darkness as the passage proceeds.

And makes one blot of all the air,
Stay thy cloudy ebon chair
Wherein thou ridest with Hecat', and befriend
Us thy vowed priests, till utmost end
Of all thy dues be done, and none left out,
Ere the blabbing eastern scout,
The nice Morn on the Indian steep,
From her cabined loop-hole peep,   140
And to the tell-tale Sun descry
Our concealed solemnity.
Come, knit hands, and beat the ground,
In a light fantastic round.

The Measure

Break off, break off, I feel the different pace,
Of some chaste footing near about this ground.
Run to your shrouds within these brakes and trees,
Our number may affright. Some virgin sure
(For so I can distinguish by mine art)
Benighted in these woods. Now to my charms,   150
And to my wily trains; I shall ere long
Be well stocked with as fair a herd as grazed
About my mother Circe. Thus I hurl
My dazzling spells into the spongy air,
Of power to cheat the eye with blear illusion,
And give it false presentments, lest the place
And my quaint habits breed astonishment,
And put the damsel to suspicious flight,
Which must not be, for that's against my course;
I under fair pretence of friendly ends,   160
And well-placed words of glozing courtesy
Baited with reasons not unplausible,
Wind me into the easy-hearted man,
And hug him into snares. When once her eye

135. **Hecate,** the underworld form of Diana, later patroness of witches.
139. **nice,** overfastidious. **Indian steep,** cf. *A Midsummer Night's Dream*, II, i, 69: "The farthest steep of India."
144. **round,** a country dance or dance tune.
The Measure. The term usually applies to a rather stately dance but apparently not so here.
147. **shrouds,** shelters.
151. **trains,** tricks, enticements.
154. **spongy,** i.e., absorbing.
155. **blear,** blearing or blurring the eyesight.
156. **presentments,** presentations, illusions.
157. **quaint,** a suggestion that Comus is fantastically costumed.
161. **glozing,** flattering and false.

Hath met the virtue of this magic dust,
I shall appear some harmless villager
Whom thrift keeps up about his country gear.
But here she comes, I fairly step aside,
And hearken, if I may, her business here.

The LADY *enters.*

Lady. This way the noise was, if mine ear be true,   170
My best guide now. Methought it was the sound
Of riot and ill-managed merriment,
Such as the jocund flute or gamesome pipe
Stirs up among the loose unlettered hinds,
When for their teeming flocks and granges full
In wanton dance they praise the bounteous Pan,
And thank the gods amiss. I should be loth
To meet the rudeness and swilled insolence
Of such late wassailers; yet O where else
Shall I inform my unacquainted feet   180
In the blind mazes of this tangled wood?
My brothers, when they saw me wearied out
With this long way, resolving here to lodge
Under the spreading favor of these pines,
Stepped as they said to the next thicket side
To bring me berries, or such cooling fruit
As the kind hospitable woods provide.
They left me then, when the grey-hooded Even
Like a sad votarist in palmer's weed
Rose from the hindmost wheels of Phœbus' wain.   190
But where they are, and why they came not back,
Is now the labor of my thoughts; 'tis likeliest
They had engaged their wandering steps too far,
And envious darkness, ere they could return,
Had stolen them from me, else O thievish Night,
Why shouldst thou, but for some felonious end,
In thy dark lantern thus close up the stars,
That Nature hung in heaven, and filled their lamps
With everlasting oil, to give due light

165. **virtue,** power.
169. **hearken,** learn by listening to.
175. **grange,** granary.
177. **amiss,** because riotously.
178. **swilled insolence,** insolence which results from swilling wine.
179. **wassailers,** revelers.
182 ff. Milton's device for having the lady left alone is weak enough,
but the masque cares little for plausibility.
189. **votarist in palmer's weeds,** a person under a religious vow, clad
in garments of a pilgrim.

To the misled and lonely traveller?   200
This is the place, as well as I may guess,
Whence even now the tumult of loud mirth
Was rife and perfect in my listening ear,
Yet nought but single darkness do I find.
What might this be? A thousand fantasies
Begin to throng into my memory,
Of calling shapes and beckoning shadows dire,
And airy tongues that syllable men's names
On sands and shores and desert wildernesses.
These thoughts may startle well, but not astound   210
The virtuous mind, that ever walks attended
By a strong siding champion Conscience.—
O welcome pure-eyed Faith, white-handed Hope,
Thou hovering angel girt with golden wings,
And thou unblemished form of Chastity,
I see ye visibly, and now believe
That He, the Supreme Good, to whom all things ill
Are but as slavish officers of vengeance,
Would send a glistering guardian if need were
To keep my life and honor unassailed.   220
Was I deceived, or did a sable cloud
Turn forth her silver lining on the night?
I did not err, there does a sable cloud
Turn forth her silver lining on the night,
And casts a gleam over this tufted grove.
I cannot hallo to my brothers, but
Such noise as I can make to be heard farthest
I'll venture, for my new-enlivened spirits
Prompt me; and they perhaps are not far off.

Song

Sweet Echo, sweetest nymph that livest unseen   230
            Within thy airy shell
        By slow Meander's margent green,
    And in the violet-embroidered vale
        Where the love-lorn nightingale
    Nightly to thee her sad song mourneth well.

204. **single darkness,** darkness alone.
212. **strong siding,** strongly siding with.
215 ff. Milton makes chastity the center and touchstone of virtue generally, as it was in his own imagination at this time. He was doubtless influenced in this by Spenser (cf. esp. *Faerie Queene* III and the close of Book II, to which *Comus* is closely attached).
230 ff. One of the many echo songs in Renaissance literature. Lawes's music to this and other *Comus* songs is preserved.
231. **airy shell,** the sphere of air around the earth.

Canst thou not tell me of a gentle pair
That likest thy Narcissus are?
O if thou have
Hid them in some flowery cave,
Tell me but where,   240
Sweet Queen of Parley, Daughter of the sphere;
So may'st thou be translated to the skies,
And give resounding grace to all heaven's harmonies.

Comus. Can any mortal mixture of earth's mould
Breathe such divine enchanting ravishment?
Sure something holy lodges in that breast,
And with these raptures moves the vocal air
To testify his hidden residence;
How sweetly did they float upon the wings
Of silence, through the empty-vaulted night,   250
At every fall smoothing the raven down
Of darkness till it smiled. I have oft heard
My mother Circe with the Sirens three,
Amidst the flowery-kirtled Naiades,
Culling their potent herbs and baleful drugs,
Who as they sung, would take the prisoned soul
And lap it in Elysium; Scylla wept,
And chid her barking waves into attention,
And fell Charybdis murmured soft applause.
Yet they in pleasing slumber lulled the sense,   260
And in sweet madness robbed it of itself,
But such a sacred and home-felt delight,
Such sober certainty of waking bliss,
I never heard till now. I'll speak to her,
And she shall be my queen. Hail foreign wonder,
Whom certain these rough shades did never breed,
Unless the goddess that in rural shrine
Dwell'st here with Pan or Silvan, by blest song
Forbidding every bleak unkindly fog
To touch the prosperous growth of this tall wood.   270

36–37. **a gentle pair . . . are.** For the story of Echo and Narcissus see Ovid *Metamorphoses* iii. 356 ff.

242. **translated,** transferred. The celestial music of the spheres would then have a new grace of resonance.

251. **fall,** cadence. Cf. *Twelfth Night,* I, i, 4: "That strain again! it had a dying fall."

253. **Sirens,** sea-nymphs, described in the *Odyssey* and elsewhere, who by the charm of their singing lured men to death.

257–59. **Scylla . . . Charybdis,** monsters identified with the rocks and whirlpool on opposite sides of the Straits of Messina. Cf. *Odyssey,* xii, 73–110. Scylla had dogs growing from her waist.

265 ff. These lines suggest the meeting of Ferdinand with Miranda (*The Tempest,* I, ii, 418 ff.).

Lady. Nay gentle shepherd, ill is lost that praise
That is addressed to unattending ears.
Not any boast of skill, but éxtreme shift
How to regain my severed company
Compelled me to awake the courteous Echo
To give me answer from her mossy couch.
Comus. What chance good Lady hath bereft you thus?
Lady. Dim darkness and this leavy labyrinth.
Comus. Could that divide you from near-ushering guides?
Lady. They left me weary on a grassy turf.   280
Comus. By falsehood, or discourtesy, or why?
Lady. To seek in the valley some cool friendly spring.
Comus. And left your fair side all unguarded Lady?
Lady. They were but twain, and purposed quick return.
Comus. Perhaps forestalling night prevented them.
Lady. How easy my misfortune is to hit!
Comus. Imports their loss, beside the present need?
Lady. No less than if I should my brothers lose.
Comus. Were they of manly prime, or youthful bloom?
Lady. As smooth as Hebe's their unrazored lips.   290
Comus. Two such I saw, what time the labored ox
In his loose traces from the furrow came,
And the swinked hedger at his supper sat;
I saw them under a green mantling vine
That crawls along the side of yon small hill,
Plucking ripe clusters from the tender shoots,
Their port was more than human, as they stood;
I took it for a fairy vision
Of some gay creatures of the element,
That in the colors of the rainbow live,   300
And play in the plighted clouds. I was awe-struck,
And as I passed, I worshipped; if those you seek,
It were a journey like the path to Heaven
To help you find them.

277 ff. Note the classical *stichomythia* (i.e., dialogue in alternate single lines). This passage is a striking example of Milton's use of one of the characteristic devices of Greek tragedy. Another instance occurs in *Samson Agonistes,* line 1552 ff.

290. Hebe, goddess of youth and cup-bearer of the gods.

291–93. The method here used to denote time is frequently employed in pastoral poetry.

293. swinked, weary (from O. E. *swincan,* to labor).

297 ff. This compliment to the two brothers, apart from its dramatic significance, was probably intended by Milton to apply indirectly to Lord Brackley and Thomas Egerton. Flattering personal allusion was a common feature of the masque. Cf. note on line 31.

299. element, air, sky.

301. plighted, folded (from Latin *plicare*).

Lady.   Gentle villager
What readiest way would bring me to that place?
Comus. Due west it rises from this shrubby point.
Lady. To find out that, good shepherd, I suppose,
In such a scant allowance of star-light,
Would overtask the best land-pilot's art,
Without the sure guess of well-practised feet.   310
Comus. I know each lane and every alley green,
Dingle or bushy dell of this wild wood,
And every bosky bourn from side to side,
My daily walks and ancient neighborhood,
And if your stray attendance be yet lodged,
Or shroud within these limits, I shall know
Ere morrow wake or the low-roosted lark
From her thatched pallet rouse; if otherwise,
I can conduct you, Lady, to a low
But loyal cottage, where you may be safe   320
Till further quest.
Lady.   Shepherd I take thy word,
And trust thy honest-offered courtesy,
Which oft is sooner found in lowly sheds
With smoky rafters, than in tapestry halls
And courts of princes, where it first was named,
And yet is most pretended. In a place
Less warranted than this, or less secure,
I cannot be, that I should fear to change it.
Eye me blest Providence, and square my trial
To my proportioned strength. Shepherd lead on.—   330
                                        [*Exeunt.*

Enter the TWO BROTHERS.

Eld. Bro. Unmuffle ye faint stars, and thou fair moon
That wont'st to love the traveller's benison,
Stoop thy pale visage through an amber cloud,
And disinherit Chaos, that reigns here
In double night of darkness and of shades;
Or if your influence be quite dammed up
With black usurping mists, some gentle taper
Though a rush-candle from the wicker hole
Of some clay habitation visit us

313. **bosky bourn,** stream bordered with bushes.
323–26. Milton speaks the language of protest against the manners of
court society. He had probably not forgotten that the actors in *Comus* were
themselves courtiers.
327. **Less warranted,** giving less assurance of safety.
334. **disinherit,** dispossess.

With thy long levelled rule of streaming light,   340
And thou shalt be our star of Arcady
Or Tyrian Cynosure.
    Sec. Bro.   Or if our eyes
Be barred that happiness, might we but hear
The folded flocks penned in their wattled cotes,
Or sound of pastoral reed with oaten stops,
Or whistle from the lodge, or village cock
Count the night-watches to his feathery dames,
'Twould be some solace yet, some little cheering
In this close dungeon of innumerous boughs.
But O that hapless virgin our lost sister,   350
Where may she wander now, whither betake her
From the chill dew, amongst rude burs and thistles?
Perhaps some cold bank is her bolster now,
Or 'gainst the rugged bark of some broad elm
Leans her unpillowed head fraught with sad fears.
What if in wild amazement and affright,
Or while we speak, within the direful grasp
Of savage hunger or of savage heat?
    Eld. Bro. Peace brother, be not over-exquisite
To cast the fashion of uncertain evils;   360
For grant they be so, while they rest unknown,
What need a man forestall his date of grief,
And run to meet what he would most avoid?
Or if they be but false alarms of fear,
How bitter is such self-delusion?
I do not think my sister so to seek,
Or so unprincipled in virtue's book,
And the sweet peace that goodness bosoms ever,

340. Note how the sound suggests the idea of length.

341–42. star of Arcady or Tyrian Cynosure, i.e., a beacon by which they may direct their course as sailors do by the stars. The **star of Arcady** refers to the constellation Ursa Major, which mythology associated with the nymph Callisto, daughter of an Arcadian king. After being turned into a she-bear by Juno, she was given a place among the constellations by Jupiter. For **Cynosure,** see the note on "L'Allegro," line 80. The Greeks steered by Ursa Major, the Tyrians by Ursa Minor.

344. wattled cotes, sheepfolds made of interwoven branches. Arnold echoes the phrase in line 2 of "The Scholar-Gypsy": "Go, shepherd, and untie the wattled cotes."

345. pastoral reed, the shepherd's pipe.

349. innumerous, innumerable; so also in *Paradise Lost*, VII, 455, "innumerous living creatures."

358. hunger . . . heat, i.e., the hunger of savage beasts or the lust of savage men.

359. over-exquisite, too careful or exact.

360. cast, forecast, predict.

367. so to seek, so much at a loss.

As that the single want of light and noise
(Not being in danger, as I trust she is not)   370
Could stir the constant mood of her calm thoughts,
And put them into misbecoming plight.
Virtue could see to do what Virtue would
By her own radiant light, though sun and moon
Were in the flat sea sunk. And Wisdom's self
Oft seeks to sweet retired Solitude,
Where with her best nurse Contemplation
She plumes her feathers, and lets grow her wings,
That in the various bustle of resort
Were all to-ruffled, and sometimes impaired.   380
He that has light within his own clear breast
May sit in the center, and enjoy bright day,
But he that hides a dark soul and foul thoughts
Benighted walks under the mid-day sun;
Himself is his own dungeon.
    Sec. Bro.   'Tis most true
That musing Meditation most affects
The pensive secrecy of desert cell,
Far from the cheerful haunt of men and herds,
And sits as safe as in a senate-house,
For who would rob a hermit of his weeds,   390
His few books, or his beads, or maple dish,
Or do his grey hairs any violence?
But Beauty, like the fair Hesperian tree
Laden with blooming gold, had need the guard
Of dragon watch with unenchanted eye,
To save her blossoms, and defend her fruit
From the rash hand of bold Incontinence.
You may as well spread out the unsunned heaps

373–75. Cf. *Faerie Queene*, I, i, 12: "Virtue gives her selfe light
through darknesse for to wade." The self-sufficiency of virtue is one of
Milton's leading ideas.

375–80. Pattison and others have commented upon the autobiographical
significance of these lines. They clearly reflect the motive underlying Milton's retirement to Horton at the conclusion of his university days.

380. all to-ruffled, very much ruffled. The prefix to is an intensive
surviving from Middle English.

381. light within his own clear breast, the "inward light" of *Samson
Agonistes*, line 162. Cf. also *Paradise Lost*, III, 51–55. The doctrine of
inward illumination was much stressed by the seventeenth-century mystics.

382. in the center, i.e., of the earth.

385 ff. 'Tis most true, etc. Cf. "Il Penseroso," lines 167–74.

393. the fair Hesperian tree, the tree which bore the golden apples
given to Hera on the day of her marriage with Zeus. It grew in a garden
watched over by the daughters of Hesperus and by a dragon (line 395).
To obtain these apples was one of the labors of Hercules.

395. unenchanted, not capable of being enchanted.

Of miser's treasure by an outlaw's den,
And tell me it is safe, as bid me hope   400
Danger will wink on Opportunity,
And let a single helpless maiden pass
Uninjured in this wild surrounding waste.
Of night or loneliness it recks me not,
I fear the dread events that dog them both,
Lest some ill-greeting touch attempt the person
Of our unowned sister.
    Eld. Bro.   I do not, brother,
Infer as if I thought my sister's state
Secure without all doubt or controversy;
Yet where an equal poise of hope and fear   410
Does arbitrate the event, my nature is
That I incline to hope, rather than fear,
And gladly banish squint suspicion.
My sister is not so defenceless left
As you imagine, she has a hidden strength
Which you remember not.
    Sec. Bro.   What hidden strength,
Unless the strength of Heaven, if you mean that?
    Eld. Bro. I mean that too, but yet a hidden strength
Which if Heaven gave it, may be termed her own:
'Tis chastity, my brother, chastity.   420
She that has that, is clad in cómplete steel,
And like a quivered nymph with arrows keen,
May trace huge forests and unharbored heaths,
Infamous hills and sandy perilous wilds,
Where through the sacred rays of chastity,
No savage fierce, bandit or mountaineer,
Will dare to soil her virgin purity.
Yea there where very desolation dwells,
By grots and caverns shagged with horrid shades,
She may pass on with unblenched majesty,   430
Be it not done in pride or in presumption.
Some say no evil thing that walks by night,
In fog or fire, by lake or moorish fen,
Blue meager hag, or stubborn unlaid ghost,

418 ff. This speech of the Elder Brother gives a full exposition of the central doctrine of the poem.

423. unharbored, without shelter. The original meaning of harbor was simply "a place of refuge."

432. no evil thing that walks by night. Cf. "L'Allegro," line 104 and note.

434. blue, livid, cadaverous. Blue was the epithet traditionally applied to witches and hags; Shakespeare describes Sycorax as a *"blue*-eyed hag" (*The Tempest*, I, ii, 269).

That breaks his magic chains at curfew time,
No goblin or swart fairy of the mine,
Hath hurtful power o'er true virginity.
Do ye believe me yet, or shall I call
Antiquity from the old schools of Greece
To testify the arms of chastity?   440
Hence had the huntress Dian her dread bow,
Fair silver-shafted queen for ever chaste,
Wherewith she tamed the brinded lioness
And spotted mountain pard, but set at nought
The frivolous bolt of Cupid; gods and men
Feared her stern frown, and she was queen o' the woods.
What was that snaky-headed Gorgon shield
That wise Minerva wore, unconquered virgin,
Wherewith she freezed her foes to congealed stone,
But rigid looks of chaste austerity,   450
And noble grace that dashed brute violence
With sudden adoration and blank awe?
So dear to Heaven is saintly chastity,
That when a soul is found sincerely so,
A thousand liveried angels lackey her,
Driving far off each thing of sin and guilt,
And in clear dream and solemn vision
Tell her of things that no gross ear can hear,
Till oft converse with heavenly habitants
Begin to cast a beam on the outward shape,   460

435. According to popular superstition, ghosts were permitted to walk only between the hour of curfew (usually nine o'clock) and the first crowing of the cock.

436. **swart fairy of the mine,** a gnome or earth demon.

439. **schools of Greece,** i.e., the philosophical schools.

447-48. This moral interpretation of the significance of the Gorgon shield is Milton's own. As Verity points out, Milton is following the method of Plato in taking a seemingly outworn myth and investing it with a new meaning. For the story of how the Gorgon Medusa's head was cut off by Perseus and affixed to the shield of Minerva, see Ovid *Metamorphoses* iv. 772-803.

449. **freezed her foes.** Note the correspondence of sound to sense. Freezed was a fairly common preterit form in the seventeenth century.

451. **dashed,** confounded.

453 ff. Notice how Milton here turns completely from the language of mythology to that of a mingled Platonism and Christianity. Cf. the notes on lines 3, 4, and 11.

455-56. The Guardian Angel idea appealed to Milton strongly. In addition to the numerous references in his poems, there is an entire section in *The Christian Doctrine*, I, ix, dealing with "The Special Government of Angels."

459. **oft converse,** frequent intercourse.

The unpolluted temple of the mind,
And turns it by degrees to the soul's essence,
Till all be made immortal.   But when lust,
By unchaste looks, loose gestures, and foul talk,
But most by lewd and lavish act of sin,
Lets in defilement to the inward parts,
The soul grows clotted by contagion,
Imbodies and imbrutes, till she quite lose
The divine property of her first being.
Such are those thick and gloomy shadows damp   470
Oft seen in charnel vaults and sepulchres,
Lingering, and sitting by a new-made grave,
As loth to leave the body that it loved,
And linked itself by carnal sensualty
To a degenerate and degraded state.
　　Sec. Bro. How charming is divine Philosophy!
Not harsh and crabbëd as dull fools suppose,
But musical as is Apollo's lute,
And a perpetual feast of nectar'd sweets,
Where no crude surfeit reigns.
　　Eld. Bro.   List, list, I hear   480
Some far-off hallo break the silent air.
　　Sec. Bro. Methought so too; what should it be?
　　Eld. Bro.   For certain
Either some one like us night-foundered here,
Or else some neighbor woodman, or at worst,
Some roving robber calling to his fellows.
　　Sec. Bro. Heaven keep my sister! Again, again, and near!
Best draw, and stand upon our guard.
　　Eld. Bro.   I'll hallo;
If he be friendly he comes well, if not,
Defence is a good cause, and Heaven be for us.

461. The image here is Scriptural. Cf. John 2:26. "He spake of the
temple of his body." The basic concept is of course Platonic.
463–75. These lines are directly paraphrased from the Phaedo 81. "But
the soul which has been polluted, and is impure at the time of her departure, and is the companion and servant of the body always, . . . do you suppose that such a soul will depart pure and unalloyed? . . . She is held fast
by the corporeal, which the continual association and constant care of the
body have wrought into her nature . . . And this corporeal element, my
friend, is heavy, and weighty, and earthy, and is the element of sight by
which a soul is depressed and dragged down again into the visible world,
. . . prowling about tombs and sepulchres, near which, as they tell us, are
seen certain ghostly apparitions of souls which have not departed pure, but
are cloyed with sight and therefore visible." (Jowett's translation.)
476–80. The emotional fervor with which the Second Brother hails
"divine Philosophy" is indicative of Milton's own attitude. The association
of philosophy with music is also characteristically Miltonic.
479. nectar'd, heavenly. Nectar was the drink of the gods.

Enter the ATTENDANT SPIRIT, *habited like a shepherd.*

That hallo I should know; what are you? speak;   490
Come not too near, you fall on iron stakes else.
  Spir. What voice is that? my young Lord? speak again.
  Sec. Bro. O brother, 'tis my father's shepherd sure.
  Eld. Bro. Thyrsis, whose artful strains have oft delayed
The huddling brook to hear his madrigal,
And sweetened every musk-rose of the dale,
How camest thou here good swain? Hath any ram
Slipped from the fold, or young kid lost his dam,
Or straggling wether the pent flock forsook?
How couldst thou find this dark sequestered nook?   500
  Spir. O my loved master's heir and his next joy,
I came not here on such a trivial toy
As a strayed ewe, or to pursue the stealth
Of pilfering wolf; not all the fleecy wealth
That doth enrich these downs, is worth a thought
To this my errand, and the care it brought.
But oh my virgin Lady, where is she?
How chance she is not in your company?
  Eld. Bro. To tell thee sadly Shepherd, without blame,
Or our neglect, we lost her as we came.   510
  Spir. Ay me unhappy, then my fears are true.
  Eld. Bro. What fears good Thyrsis? Prithee briefly show.
  Spir. I'll tell ye, 'tis not vain or fabulous
(Though so esteemed by shallow ignorance),
What the sage poets, taught by the heavenly Muse,
Storied of old in high immortal verse
Of dire Chimeras and enchanted isles,
And rifted rocks whose entrance leads to Hell,
For such there be, but unbelief is blind.
Within the navel of this hideous wood,   520

habited like a shepherd. Cf. lines 82–85.
   491. iron stakes, i.e., their swords.
   494. Thyrsis, a traditional pastoral name used by Theocritus and Virgil.
In the *Epitaphium Damonis* Milton applies it to himself.
   495. huddling, hurrying, crowding. There is probably an implied allusion in this passage to the enchantment of nature by the lyre of Orpheus,
which "delayed even the swift-flowing streams" (Horace, Odes iii. 12.
9–10). The passage is intended as a compliment to Lawes, who played the
role of the Attendant Spirit.
   515. sage poets. Milton undoubtedly has Spenser in mind as well as
the epic poets of antiquity. In *Areopagitica* he refers to Spenser as "our
sage and serious poet."
   517. Chimeras, fire-breathing monsters, part lion, part serpent, and part
goat. Cf. *Iliad* vi. 81.
   520. navel, center.

Immured in cypress shades, a sorcerer dwells,
Of Bacchus and of Circe born, great Comus,
Deep skilled in all his mother's witcheries,
And here to every thirsty wanderer
By sly enticement gives his baneful cup,
With many murmurs mixed, whose pleasing poison
The visage quite transforms of him that drinks,
And the inglorious likeness of a beast
Fixes instead, unmoulding reason's mintage
Charactered in the face; this have I learnt   530
Tending my flocks hard by in the hilly crofts
That brow this bottom glade, whence night by night
He and his monstrous rout are heard to howl
Like stabled wolves, or tigers at their prey,
Doing abhorrëd rites to Hecate
In their obscurëd haunts of inmost bowers.
Yet have they many baits and guileful spells
To inveigle and invite the unwary sense
Of them that pass unweeting by the way.
This evening late, by then the chewing flocks   540
Had ta'en their supper on the savory herb
Of knot-grass dew besprent, and were in fold,
I sat me down to watch upon a bank
With ivy canopied, and interwove
With flaunting honeysuckle, and began,
Wrapt in a pleasing fit of melancholy,
To meditate my rural minstrelsy,
Till fancy had her fill; but ere a close
The wonted roar was up amidst the woods,
And filled the air with barbarous dissonance,   550
At which I ceased, and listened them a while,
Till an unusual stop of sudden silence
Gave respite to the drowsy-flighted steeds
That draw the litter of close-curtained Sleep.
At last a soft and solemn-breathing sound
Rose like a steam of rich distilled perfumes,

526. **murmurs,** incantations—such as those spoken by the witches in *Macbeth*, IV, i.
529. **reason's mintage,** the stamp or imprint of reason.
531. **crofts,** small enclosures used for pasture.
539. **unweeting,** unknowing.
547. **to meditate my rural minstrelsy,** i.e., to play on the shepherd's pipe. The use of meditate is a Latinism. Cf. "Lycidas," 66: "And strictly meditate the thankless Muse."
548. **ere a close,** i.e., before reaching the first cadence.
553. **drowsy-flighted.** This reading is adopted from Milton's manuscript. The early editions have *drowsie frighted*.

And stole upon the air, that even Silence
Was took ere she was ware, and wished she might
Deny her nature and be never more,
Still to be so displaced. I was all ear,   560
And took in strains that might create a soul
Under the ribs of Death, but oh ere long
Too well I did perceive it was the voice
Of my most honored Lady, your dear sister.
Amazed I stood, harrowed with grief and fear,
And 'O poor hapless nightingale' thought I,
'How sweet thou sing'st, how near the deadly snare!'
Then down the lawns I ran with headlong haste
Through paths and turnings often trod by day,
Till guided by mine ear I found the place   570
Where that damned wizard, hid in sly disguise
(For so by certain signs I knew), had met
Already, ere my best speed could prevent,
The aidless innocent lady his wished prey,
Who gently asked if he had seen such two,
Supposing him some neighbor villager;
Longer I durst not stay, but soon I guessed
Ye were the two she meant; with that I sprung
Into swift flight, till I had found you here;
But further know I not.
    Sec. Bro.   O night and shades,   580
How are ye joined with hell in triple knot
Against the unarmed weakness of one virgin,
Alone and helpless! Is this the confidence
You gave me brother?
    Eld. Bro.   Yes, and keep it still,
Lean on it safely, not a period
Shall be unsaid for me. Against the threats
Of malice or of sorcery, or that power
Which erring men call Chance, this I hold firm:
Virtue may be assailed, but never hurt,
Surprised by unjust force, but not enthralled,   590
Yea even that which Mischief meant most harm

558. **took,** charmed.
560. **still,** always.
565. **amazed,** utterly confounded. The word has a much stronger force
than in present usage.
568. **lawns,** open spaces in the forest.
589. **Virtue may be assailed, but never hurt.** Notice how Milton
keeps reiterating his central idea.
591-92. Cf. the famous passage in *Areopagitica:* "I cannot praise a
fugitive and cloistered virtue unexercised and unbreathed, that never sallies
out and seeks her adversary, but slinks out of the race, where that immortal

Shall in the happy trial prove most glory.
But evil on itself shall back recoil,
And mix no more with goodness, when at last
Gathered like scum, and settled to itself,
It shall be in eternal restless change
Self-fed and self-consumed; if this fail,
The pillared firmament is rottenness,
And earth's base built on stubble. But come let's on.
Against the opposing will and arm of Heaven   600
May never this just sword be lifted up,
But for that damned magician, let him be girt
With all the grisly legions that troop
Under the sooty flag of Acheron,
Harpies and Hydras, or all the monstrous forms
'Twixt Africa and Ind, I'll find him out,
And force him to return his purchase back,
Or drag him by the curls to a foul death,
Cursed as his life.
      Spir.   Alas good venturous youth,
I love thy courage yet, and bold emprise,   610
But here thy sword can do thee little stead;
Far other arms and other weapons must
Be those that quell the might of hellish charms.
He with his bare wand can unthread thy joints,
And crumble all thy sinews.
      Eld. Bro.   Why, prithee Shepherd,
How durst thou then thyself approach so near
As to make this relation?
      Spir.   Care and utmost shifts
How to secure the Lady from surprisal,
Brought to my mind a certain shepherd lad,

garland is to be run for, not without dust and heat. Assuredly we bring not
innocence into the world, we bring impurity much rather; *that which puri-
fies us is trial,* and trial is by what is contrary."
      597. **self-fed and self-consumed.** In *Paradise Lost,* II, 795–802, Sin
is represented as being perpetually fed upon by the monsters which come
forth hourly from her womb.
      604. **Acheron,** one of the four rivers of the lower world—here used for
the lower world itself.
      605. **Harpies,** ravenous monsters, half-woman and half-bird. Cf. *Aeneid*
iii. 225–28. **Hydras,** many-headed water serpents. The slaying of the
Lemean Hydra was one of the labors of Hercules.
      607. **purchase,** prey, booty (a common Elizabethan meaning).
      614–15. Cf. *The Tempest,* IV, i, 259–61.

> Go, charge my goblins that they grind their joints
> With dry convulsions, shorten up their sinews
> With aged cramps . . .

      619. **A certain shepherd lad,** etc. Probably the reference is to Milton

Of small regard to see to, yet well skilled 620
In every virtuous plant and healing herb
That spreads her verdant leaf to the morning ray.
He loved me well, and oft would beg me sing,
Which when I did, he on the tender grass
Would sit, and hearken even to ecstasy,
And in requital ope his leathern scrip,
And show me simples of a thousand names,
Telling their strange and vigorous faculties;
Amongst the rest a small unsightly root,
But of divine effect, he culled me out; 630
The leaf was darkish, and had prickles on it,
But in another country, as he said,
Bore a bright golden flower, but not in this soil;
Unknown and like esteemed, and the dull swain
Treads on it daily with his clouted shoon,
And yet more med'cinal is it than that Moly
That Hermes once to wise Ulysses gave;
He called it Hæmony, and gave it me,
And bade me keep it as of sovran use
'Gainst all enchantments, mildew blast, or damp, 640
Or ghastly Furies' apparition;
I pursed it up, but little reckoning made,
Till now that this extremity compelled,
But now I find it true; for by this means
I knew the foul enchanter though disguised,
Entered the very lime-twigs of his spells,

himself. If so, the passage may be taken as a memorial of his personal relationship to Henry Lawes, who is represented by the Spirit Thyrsis.

620-21. **of small regard to see to**, i.e., unimpressive in appearance
and achievement. Milton depicts himself as poor in outward semblance, but
possessing spiritual secrets of great value.

623 ff. If the above interpretation is correct, these lines reflect not only
Milton's keen delight in Lawes's music, but also a firm conviction that he
has been able to offer the musician something even better in return—the
mystical doctrine of chastity, as set forth in the poem.

631. **a small unsightly root**, i.e., the *Hæmony* of line 638, a term
which Milton apparently derived from the Greek *Hæmonia*, an old name
for Thessaly, the land of magic. Hæmony is obviously a symbol of some
saving moral principle (probably of the Platonic philosophy). In Milton's
own age and nation, the doctrine symbolized is unbeautified and of low
esteem: "but in another country" (i.e., in Greece), it "bore a bright golden
flower." If Milton is thinking specifically of Christian grace, as some critics
maintain, then the earlier and purer days of reformed religion would be the
soil on which it bore a flower.

636. **Moly**, the plant given to Odysseus by the god Hermes as a protection against the spells of Circe. Cf. *Odyssey* x. 281-306. Milton refers to it
in Elegy I and elsewhere as a symbol of the idea of chastity.

642. **pursed it up**, put it away in a purse.

And yet came off. If you have this about you
(As I will give you when we go), you may
Boldly assault the necromancer's hall;
Where if he be, with dauntless hardihood   650
And brandished blade rush on him, break his glass,
And shed the luscious liquor on the ground,
But seize his wand. Though he and his curst crew
Fierce sign of battle make, and menace high,
Or like the sons of Vulcan vomit smoke,
Yet will they soon retire, if he but shrink.
    Eld. Bro. Thyrsis lead on apace, I'll follow thee,
And some good angel bear a shield before us.

*The Scene changes to a stately palace, set out with all manner of de-
liciousness: soft music, tables spread with all dainties. COMUS
appears with his rabble, and THE LADY set in an enchanted chair,
to whom he offers his glass, which she puts by, and goes about to rise.*

    Comus. Nay Lady sit; if I but wave this wand,
Your nerves are all chained up in alabaster,   660
And you a statue, or as Daphne was,
Root-bound, that fled Apollo.
    Lady.   Fool do not boast,
Thou canst not touch the freedom of my mind
With all thy charms, although this corporal rind
Thou hast immanacled, while Heaven sees good.
    Comus. Why are you vexed Lady? why do you frown?
Here dwell no frowns, nor anger, from these gates
Sorrow flies far. See, here be all the pleasures
That fancy can beget on youthful thoughts,
When the fresh blood grows lively, and returns   670
Brisk as the April buds in primrose season.
And first behold this cordial julep here
That flames and dances in his crystal bounds
With spirits of balm and fragrant syrups mixed.

    652. Cf. *Faerie Queene,* II, xii, 57. When Acrasia offered her enchanted
cup to Guyon, he shattered it. "And with the liquor stained all the land."
    655. Vulcan, the god of fire.
    Stage direction. all manner of deliciousness, etc. Notice how through-
out this scene evil is set forth in its most alluring colors. The treatment
clearly foreshadows the temptations in *Paradise Lost* and *Paradise Regained.*
    661. Daphne, a Nymph who, fleeing from Apollo, was changed into a
laurel tree at her own request. The story is told by Ovid *Metamorphoses*
i. 660 ff.
    664. corporal rind, i.e., the body.
    672. julep, a drink flavored with aromatic herbs. The word originally
meant rose-water.

Not that Nepenthes which the wife of Thone,
In Egypt gave to Jove-born Helena
Is of such power to stir up joy as this,
To life so friendly, or so cool to thirst.
Why should you be so cruel to yourself,
And to those dainty limbs which Nature lent   680
For gentle usage and soft delicacy?
But you invert the covenants of her trust,
And harshly deal like an ill borrower
With that which you received on other terms,
Scorning the unexempt condition
By which all mortal frailty must subsist,
Refreshment after toil, ease after pain,
That have been tired all day without repast,
And timely rest have wanted; but fair virgin,
This will restore all soon.
    Lady.   'Twill not, false traitor,   690
'Twill not restore the truth and honesty
That thou hast banished from thy tongue with lies.
Was this the cottage and the safe abode
Thou told'st me of? What grim aspects are these,
These ugly-headed monsters? Mercy guard me!
Hence with thy brewed enchantments, foul deceiver;
Hast thou betrayed my credulous innocence
With vizored falsehood and base forgery,
And wouldst thou seek again to trap me here
With lickerish baits fit to ensnare a brute?   700
Were it a draught for Juno when she banquets,
I would not taste thy treasonous offer; none
But such as are good men can give good things,
And that which is not good, is not delicious
To a well-governed and wise appetite.
    Comus. O foolishness of men! that lend their ears
To those budge doctors of the Stoic fur,

675. **Nepenthes**, a drug having the power to drown pain and sorrow.
Cf. *Odyssey* iv. 219–29. At the entertainment given Telemachus at Sparta,
Helen placed this drug in the wine.
    685. **unexempt condition**, i.e., the condition from which no one is
exempt.
    688. **That.** The antecedent is **you** (line 682).
    700. **lickerish**, appetite-tempting.
    702 ff. These lines anticipate Christ's rejection of Satan's offer in
Paradise Regained, II, 320 ff. Asked if he will not eat, Christ replies,
"Thereafter as I like the giver." Cf. also Euripides *Medea* 618: "The gifts
of a bad man bring no advantage."
    707. **those budge doctors of the Stoic fur**, i.e., those teachers of
Stoicism whose fur-trimmed gowns denote their profession. **Budge** was a
kind of fur often used in the ornamentation of academic dress.

And fetch their precepts from the Cynic tub,
Praising the lean and sallow Abstinence.
Wherefore did Nature pour her bounties forth   710
With such a full and unwithdrawing hand,
Covering the earth with odors, fruits, and flocks,
Thronging the seas with spawn innumerable,
But all to please and sate the curious taste?
And set to work millions of spinning worms
That in their green shops weave the smooth-haired silk
To deck her sons; and that no corner might
Be vacant of her plenty, in her own loins
She hutched the all-worshipped ore and precious gems
To store her children with. If all the world   720
Should in a pet of temperance feed on pulse,
Drink the clear stream, and nothing wear but frieze,
The All-giver would be unthanked, would be unpraised,
Not half his riches known, and yet despised,
And we should serve him as a grudging master,
As a penurious niggard of his wealth,
And live like Nature's bastards, not her sons,
Who would be quite surcharged with her own weight,
And strangled with her waste fertility;
The earth cumbered, and the winged air darked with plumes,   730
The herds would over-multitude their lords,
The sea o'erfraught would swell, and the unsought diamonds
Would so emblaze the forehead of the deep,
And so bestud with stars, that they below
Would grow inured to light, and come at last
To gaze upon the sun with shameless brows.
List Lady, be not coy, and be not cozened

708. the Cynic tub. The reference is to the Cynic philosopher Diogenes, who is said to have lived in a tub.
719. hutched, enclosed.
722. frieze, a coarse woolen cloth, originally made in Friesland.
727. like Nature's bastards, i.e., like those who have no legitimate claim to inherit Nature's wealth.
733. forehead of the deep, the ceiling of Hell, here thought of as being within the earth as in Dante. The original reading of the passage makes this clear:

> Would so bestud the center with their starlight,
> Were they not taken thence, that they below . . .

In seventeenth-century scientific thought certain minerals were supposed to reproduce themselves like living creatures. See Robins, "The Key to a Problem in Milton's *Comus*," *Modern Language Quarterly*, XII (1951), 422 ff.
737–55. This passage is omitted in the Bridgewater MS. Apparently it was not spoken in the original performance.
737. cozened, cheated.

With that same vaunted name Virginity;
Beauty is Nature's coin, must not be hoarded,
But must be current, and the good thereof   740
Consists in mutual and partaken bliss,
Unsavory in the enjoyment of itself.
If you let slip time, like a neglected rose
It withers on the stalk with languished head.
Beauty is Nature's brag, and must be shown
In courts, at feasts, and high solemnities
Where most may wonder at the workmanship;
It is for homely features to keep home,
They had their name thence; coarse complexions
And cheeks of sorry grain will serve to ply   750
The sampler, and to tease the housewife's wool.
What need a vermeil-tinctured lip for that,
Love-darting eyes, or tresses like the morn?
There was another meaning in these gifts,
Think what, and be advised; you are but young yet.
    Lady. I had not thought to have unlocked my lips
In this unhallowed air, but that this juggler
Would think to charm my judgment, as mine eyes,
Obtruding false rules pranked in reason's garb.
I hate when Vice can bolt her arguments,   760
And Virtue has no tongue to check her pride.
Impostor, do not charge most innocent Nature,
As if she would her children should be riotous
With her abundance; she good cateress,
Means her provision only to the good,
That live according to her sober laws
And holy dictate of spare Temperance.
If every just man that now pines with want

739. **Beauty is Nature's,** etc. The sentiment is a commonplace **in** Renaissance literature. Cf. Shakespeare's Sonnets IV and VI.
743-44. Cf. *A Midsummer Night's Dream*, I, i, 76-78.

> But earthlier happy is the rose distilled,
> Than that which withering on the virgin thorn
> Grows, lives and dies in single blessedness.

750. **sorry grain,** unpleasing hue. Cf. note on "Il Penseroso," 33.
751. **tease,** to comb or card (the original meaning).
759. **pranked,** dressed up.
760. **bolt,** refine (a metaphor from flour making).
768 ff. The Lady's argument anticipates one of the leading contentions of modern socialism. Shakespeare has in mind the same idea when he puts into Gloucester's mouth a prayer that heaven deal quickly with "the superfluous and lust-dieted man":

> So distribution should undo excess,
> And each man have enough.
> (*King Lear*, IV, i, 73-74.)

Had but a moderate and beseeming share
Of that which lewdly-pampered Luxury   770
Now heaps upon some few with vast excess,
Nature's full blessings would be well dispensed
In unsuperfluous even proportion,
And she no whit encumbered with her store,
And then the Giver would be better thanked,
His praise due paid, for swinish gluttony
Ne'er looks to Heaven amidst his gorgeous feast,
But with besotted base ingratitude
Crams, and blasphemes his Feeder. Shall I go on?
Or have I said enough? To him that dares   780
Arm his profane tongue with contemptuous words
Against the sun-clad power of Chastity,
Fain would I something say, yet to what end?
Thou hast nor ear nor soul to apprehend
The sublime notion and high mystery
That must be uttered to unfold the sage
And serious doctrine of Virginity,
And thou art worthy that thou shouldst not know
More happiness than this thy present lot.
Enjoy your dear wit and gay rhetoric
That hath so well been taught her dazzling fence,   790
Thou art not fit to hear thyself convinced;
Yet should I try, the uncontrollèd worth
Of this pure cause would kindle my rapt spirits
To such a flame of sacred vehemence,
That dumb things would be moved to sympathize,
And the brute Earth would lend her nerves, and shake,
Till all thy magic structures reared so high,
Were shattered into heaps o'er thy false head.
     Comus. She fables not, I feel that I do fear   800
Her words set off by some superior power;

779–805. This passage does not occur in either the Cambridge or
Bridgewater MS., Milton seemingly having added it later to reinforce his
"sage and serious doctrine." The mystic quality of chastity is here given
special emphasis.
     785. **mystery,** a truth not humanly understandable except through
special revelation. The term is used in its Scriptural sense. Cf. *An Apology
for Smectymnuus* where Milton speaks of "having had the doctrine of Holy
Scripture unfolding those *chaste and high mysteries,* which timeliest care
infused, that 'the body is for the Lord, and the Lord for the body.'"
     790. **Enjoy your dear wit, and gay rhetoric.** Milton put a low value
on mere formal skill in language. His own poetic ideal, as stated in *The
Reason of Church Government,* was "not to make verbal curiosities the
end, (that were a toilsome vanity,) but to be an interpreter and relater of
the best and sagest things."
     797. **her nerves,** sinews, strength.
     801. **set off,** supported by.

And though not mortal, yet a cold shuddering dew
Dips me all o'er, as when the wrath of Jove
Speaks thunder and the chains of Erebus
To some of Saturn's crew. I must dissemble,
And try her yet more strongly. Come, no more,
This is mere moral babble, and direct
Against the canon laws of our foundation;
I must not suffer this, yet 'tis but the lees
And settlings of a melancholy blood;   810
But this will cure all straight; one sip of this
Will bathe the drooping spirits in delight
Beyond the bliss of dreams. Be wise, and taste.—

The BROTHERS *rush in with swords drawn, wrest his glass out of his
hand, and break it against the ground; his rout make sign of resistance but are all driven in; the* ATTENDANT SPIRIT *comes in.*

Spir. What, have you let the false enchanter scape?
O ye mistook, ye should have snatched his wand
And bound him fast; without his rod reversed,
And backward mutters of dissevering power,
We cannot free the Lady that sits here
In stony fetters fixed and motionless;
Yet stay, be not disturbed, now I bethink me,   820
Some other means I have which may be used,
Which once of Melibœus old I learnt,
The soothest shepherd that e'er piped on plains.

805. **Saturn's crew,** the Titans, who aided Saturn in his warfare
against Jove. The latter, having obtained thunder from the Cyclops,
hurled the Titans into the lower world, called Erebus.
808. **the canon laws of our foundation.** Canon laws are laws established by the Pope or by a church council; **foundation** is the term regularly
used to denote a monastery or similar religious institution. Milton's application is of course deliberately sarcastic.
809-10. The figure is based on the old physiology of the "humors,"
according to which a person's physical and mental state was determined by
the condition and proportion of the four bodily fluids—blood, phlegm,
choler (or yellow bile), and melancholy (or black bile). Cf. *Paradise Lost*,
XI, 543-46, and *Samson Agonistes*, 600.
813. **Be wise, and taste.** These words furnish the exact text of Satan's
exhortation to Eve, *Paradise Lost*, IX, 679-732.
816. **Without his rod reversed,** etc. Reversing the formula of enchantment was the traditional method of undoing its effects.
822. **Melibœus,** a classical pastoral name. Milton undoubtedly has
reference to Spenser, who in *The Shepheardes Calender* has paid a similar
tribute to Chaucer under the name of Tityrus. Spenser, following Geoffrey
of Monmouth, had also dealt with the Sabrina story (*Faerie Queene*, II,
x, 14-19).
823. **soothest,** truest.

There is a gentle Nymph not far from hence,
That with moist curb sways the smooth Severn stream,
Sabrina is her name, a virgin pure;
Whilom she was the daughter of Locrine,
That had the scepter from his father Brute.
She guiltless damsel flying the mad pursuit
Of her enragèd stepdame Guendolen,   830
Commended her fair innocence to the flood
That stayed her flight with his cross-flowing course;
The water-nymphs that in the bottom played,
Held up their pearlèd wrists and took her in,
Bearing her straight to agèd Nereus' hall,
Who piteous of her woes, reared her lank head,
And gave her to his daughters to imbathe
In nectared lavers strewed with asphodil,
And through the porch and inlet of each sense
Dropt in ambrosial oils, till she revived   840
And underwent a quick immortal change,
Made Goddess of the river; still she retains
Her maiden gentleness, and oft at eve
Visits the herds along the twilight meadows,
Helping all urchin blasts, and ill-luck signs
That the shrewd meddling elf delights to make,
Which she with precious vialed liquors heals.
For which the shepherds at their festivals
Carol her goodness loud in rustic lays,
And throw sweet garland wreaths into her stream   850
Of pansies, pinks, and gaudy daffodils.
And, as the old swain said, she can unlock
The clasping charm and thaw the numbing spell,
If she be right invoked in warbled song,
For maidenhood she loves, and will be swift
To aid a virgin such as was herself
In hard-besetting need; this will I try,
And add the power of some adjuring verse.

825. **Severn,** a river forming part of the ancient boundary between Wales and England.
828. **Brute,** Brutus, the legendary founder of Britain.
835. **Nereus,** father of the water-nymphs.
836. **lank,** drooping.
838. **In nectared lavers strewed with asphodil,** i.e., in baths of nectar (the drink of the gods), in which were floating asphodels (the flowers which covered the Elysian fields).
845. **Helping,** remedying. **urchin blasts,** diseases or blights sent by evil spirits.

Song

Sabrina fair
   Listen where thou art sitting   860
Under the glassy, cool, translucent wave,
   In twisted braids of lilies knitting
The loose train of thy amber-dropping hair
   Listen for dear honor's sake,
   Goddess of the silver lake,
     Listen and save.

Listen and appear to us
In name of great Oceanus,
By the earth-shaking Neptune's mace,
And Tethys' grave majestic pace,   870
By hoary Nereus' wrinkled look,
And the Carpathian wizard's hook,
By scaly Triton's winding shell,
And old soothsaying Glaucus' spell,
By Leucothea's lovely hands
And her son that rules the strands,

861. **glassy, cool, translucent.** These adjectives admirably describe
the quality of the song.

863. **amber-dropping,** i.e., wet with the amber-colored water—amber
being an epithet frequently applied to rivers. Possibly there is also an
allusion to the perfume ambergris, as in *Samson Agonistes*, 720.

866 ff. All of the proper names mentioned in this invocation refer to
classical water-deities. Cf. lines 18-29, where "this Isle" was placed under
the charge of Neptune and his "tributary gods."

868. **Oceanus,** "the father of all streams" (*Iliad*, xiv, 245). The river
Oceanus was supposed to encircle the earth.

869. **earth-shaking Neptune's mace,** the trident used as a scepter by
the god of the sea. Neptune is regularly described in classical literature as
"the earth-shaker."

870. **Tethys,** the wife of Oceanus. She is called by Hesiod (*Theogony*
368) "the venerable Tethys"—hence her **grave majestic pace.**

871. **Nereus.** Cf. line 835 and note. The epithets traditionally applied
to him emphasize his old age.

872. **Carpathian wizard's hook,** the shepherd's hook of Proteus, who
looked after the flocks (i.e. the seals) of Neptune. Proteus is described as
a wizard because of his power to foretell events and to change his shape;
his home was the island of Carpathos, near Crete.

873. **Triton's winding shell,** the trumpet used by the herald of
Neptune. Cf. Wordsworth's line: "Or hear old Triton blow his wreathèd
horn."

874. **Glaucus,** a fisherman of Boeotia who was changed into a sea-god
with the power of prophecy—hence soothsaying and spell.

875-76. **Leucothea . . . her son.** The reference is to Ino and her son
Melicertes who, in order to escape the madness of Athamas (Ino's husband),
plunged into the sea and were rescued by the dolphins. Both were deified,
Ino being known thereafter as *Leucothea* (i.e., "the white goddess") and
Melicertes as Palaemon.

By Thetis' tinsel-slippered feet,
And the songs of Sirens sweet,
By dead Parthenope's dear tomb,
And fair Ligea's golden comb,   880
Wherewith she sits on diamond rocks
Sleeking her soft alluring locks,
By all the nymphs that nightly dance
Upon thy streams with wily glance.
Rise, rise, and heave thy rosy head
From thy coral-paven bed,
And bridle in thy headlong wave,
Till thou our summons answered have.
                              Listen and save.

SABRINA *rises, attended by Water-nymphs, and sings.*

By the rushy-fringëd bank,   890
Where grows the willow and the osier dank,
    My sliding chariot stays,
Thick set with agate, and the azurn sheen
Of turquoise blue, and emerald green
    That in the channel strays,
Whilst from off the waters fleet
Thus I set my printless feet
O'er the cowslip's velvet head,
    That bends not as I tread,
Gentle swain, at thy request   900
    I am here.

Spir. Goddess dear
We implore thy powerful hand
To undo the charmëd band
Of true virgin here distressed,
Through the force and through the wile
Of unblest enchanter vile.

877. **Thetis,** a daughter of Nereus, and mother of Achilles. Homer regularly calls her "the silver-footed."
878. **Sirens.** Cf. note on line 253.
879. **Parthenope,** one of the Sirens, whose tomb was supposed to be located at Naples. Cf. Milton's third Latin epigram to Leonora: "Why credulous Naples, boast of your liquid-voiced Siren and the famous shrine of Achelous's daughter, Parthenope?"
880. **Ligea,** another of the Sirens. The reference to her **golden comb** and **soft alluring locks** (882) connects her with the mermaids of Northern mythology. Cf. Heine's *Die Lorelei.*
893. **azurn,** azure. The form does not occur elsewhere.
897. **printless feet,** cf. *The Tempest,* V, i, 34.

    And ye that on the sands with printless foot
    Do chase the ebbing Neptune.

Sabr. Shepherd 'tis my office best
To help ensnared chastity;
Brightest Lady look on me,   910
Thus I sprinkle on thy breast
Drops that from my fountain pure
I have kept of precious cure,
Thrice upon thy finger's tip,
Thrice upon thy rubied lip,
Next this marble venomed seat,
Smeared with gums of glutinous heat,
I touch with chaste palms moist and cold,
Now the spell hath lost his hold;
And I must haste ere morning hour   920
To wait in Amphitrite's bower.

SABRINA *descends and* THE LADY *rises out of her seat.*

Spir. Virgin, daughter of Locrine,
Sprung of old Anchises' line,
May thy brimmëd waves for this
Their full tribute never miss
From a thousand petty rills,
That tumble down the snowy hills;
Summer drouth or singëd air
Never scorch thy tresses fair,
Nor wet October's torrent flood   930
Thy molten crystal fill with mud;
May thy billows roll ashore
The beryl and the golden ore,
May thy lofty head be crowned
With many a tower and terrace round,
And here and there thy banks upon
With groves of myrrh and cinnamon.

Come Lady while Heaven lends us grace,
Let us fly this cursëd place,
Lest the sorcerer us entice   940
With some other new device.
Not a waste or needless sound
Till we come to holier ground;

917. **of glutinous heat,** i.e., glutinous when heated.
921. **Amphitrite,** the wife of Neptune and goddess of the sea.
922. **Locrine . . . Anchises' line.** Cf. lines 827–28. Anchises, father
of Aeneas, was the ancestor of Britain's legendary founder. Locrine belonged to the fifth generation of his descendants.
929. **tresses,** i.e., the foliage along the banks of the river.
934. **lofty head,** i.e., the river's source in the Welsh hills. Throughout
the passage note the double conception of Sabrina, as nymph and as river.

I shall be your faithful guide
Through this gloomy covert wide,
And not many furlongs thence
Is your Father's residence,
Where this night are met in state
Many a friend to gratulate
His wished presence, and beside   950
All the swains that there abide,
With jigs and rural dance resort.
We shall catch them at their sport,
And our sudden coming there
Will double all their mirth and cheer;
Come let us haste, the stars grow high,
But Night sits monarch yet in the mid sky.

*The Scene changes, presenting Ludlow Town, and the President's
Castle; then come in Country Dancers, after them the* ATTENDANT
SPIRIT, *with the two* BROTHERS *and* THE LADY.

Song

Spir. Back shepherds, back, enough your play
Till next sun-shine holiday;
Here be without duck or nod   960
Other trippings to be trod
Of lighter toes, and such court guise
As Mercury did first devise
With the mincing Dryades
On the lawns and on the leas.

This second Song presents them to their Father and Mother.

Noble Lord, and Lady bright,
I have brought ye new delight,
Here behold so goodly grown
Three fair branches of your own;
Heaven hath timely tried their youth,   970
Their faith, their patience, and their truth,
And sent them here through hard assays

960. The dances of the court, such as the pavane, are directly contrasted
with the less elegant "trippings" of the folk dancers. Both are indirectly
contrasted with the "measure" trod by the crew of Comus (line 92 ff.).

964. mincing, moving with dainty steps. The word does not imply
affectation, as it does in present usage.

966. Noble Lord and Lady, etc. This direct salutation of the Earl and
his Lady is quite in keeping with the traditions of the masque. At no time
is there any sharp distinction between the real and dramatic identity of the
actors.

972. assays, trials, tests.

With a crown of deathless praise,
To triumph in victorious dance
O'er sensual folly, and intemperance.

The dances ended, the SPIRIT *epiloguizes.*

Spir. To the ocean now I fly,
And those happy climes that lie
Where day never shuts his eye,
Up in the broad fields of the sky;
There I suck the liquid air   980
All amidst the gardens fair
Of Hesperus, and his daughters three
That sing about the golden tree.
Along the crispéd shades and bowers
Revels the spruce and jocund Spring,
The Graces and the rosy-bosomed Hours,
Thither all their bounties bring,
That there eternal Summer dwells,
And west winds with musky wing
About the cedarn alleys fling   990
Nard and cassia's balmy smells.
Iris there with humid bow
Waters the odorous banks that blow
Flowers of more mingled hue
Than her purfled scarf can show,
And drenches with Elysian dew
(List mortals, if your ears be true)
Beds of hyacinth and roses
Where young Adonis oft reposes,

976 ff. Cf. Ariel's song, *The Tempest*, V, i, 88–94.

> Where the bee sucks, there suck I,
> In a cowslip's bell I lie; etc.

980. **liquid**, clear (Latin *liquidus*).
981. **the gardens fair**, etc. See note on line 393.
984. **crispéd**, i.e., ruffled by the breeze.
985. **spruce**, well-attired.
992. **Iris**, the goddess of the rainbow.
995. **Purfled**, embroidered.
997. **if your ears be true**, i.e., sensitive to inner meanings. Milton's idea is that the myths commonly taken in a physical sense have a spiritual significance to those who read them rightly. The line instructs to look for allegory at this point. Lines 996–1012 were added in the 1637 edition.
999–1002. **Adonis . . . the Assyrian Queen.** Adonis, a beautiful youth beloved by Venus, while engaged in his favorite sport of hunting received a mortal wound from a wild boar. So great was the grief of Venus at his death that the gods of the lower world permitted him to return to earth for six months of every year. Venus is here called the Assyrian Queen because, under the names of Ashtaroth, Astarte, and Ishtar, she was first worshipped

Waxing well of his deep wound   1000
In slumber soft, and on the ground
Sadly sits the Assyrian queen;
But far above in spangled sheen
Celestial Cupid, her famed son, advanced,
Holds his dear Psyche, sweet entranced
After her wandering labors long,
Till free consent the gods among
Make her his eternal bride,
And from her fair unspotted side
Two blissful twins are to be born,   1010
Youth and Joy; so Jove hath sworn.
   But now my task is smoothly done,
I can fly, or I can run
Quickly to the green earth's end,
Where the bowed welkin slow doth bend,
And from thence can soar as soon
To the corners of the moon.
   Mortals that would follow me,
Love Virtue, she alone is free,
She can teach ye how to climb   1020

in the Orient; furthermore this particular story concerning her is of Eastern
origin. In making the myth symbolic of the immortality of love, Milton had
the example of Spenser. Cf. *Faerie Queene*, III, vi, 46–48.
   1004 ff. Cupid . . . Psyche. The love of Cupid for the mortal Psyche
was opposed by his mother, Venus. The latter subjected Psyche to many
wandering labors (1005), until rendered immortal by Jupiter she was at
last reunited with Cupid. Milton's application is again like Spenser's. Cf.
Faerie Queene, III, vi, 49–50. The obvious Christian parallel is the mystic
marriage of the soul with Christ. It would be inappropriate here to allude
to it explicitly, as he does at the close of "Lycidas" and the *Epitaphium
Damonis*. **advanced,** i.e., raised aloft. Plato in the *Symposium* distinguishes
between the earthly and the heavenly Venus. Thus celestial love is elevated
"far above" the Assyrian queen.
   1010. two blissful twins, etc. In Spenser's version of the story, Psyche
bears Cupid only one child—Pleasure. **Youth** is Milton's addition. Eight
years later, in the *Apology for Smectymnuus*, he refers to the same story—
this time in more strictly Platonic terms: "The first and chiefest office of
love begins and ends in the soul, producing those happy twins of her
divine generation, knowledge and virtue."
   1012. But now my task, etc. Cf. line 18.
   1015. bowed welkin, domed sky.
   1017. corners of the moon, i.e., the moon's horns, as they are more
generally called. Cf. *Macbeth*, III, v, 23–24.

> Upon the corner of the moon
> There hangs a vaporous drop profound.

   1018–19. Milton concludes with a final summary statement of the
poem's teaching. The principle here embodied is one that is fundamental
to all of his later thinking.

Higher than the sphery chime;
Or if Virtue feeble were,
Heaven itself would stoop to her.

[1634]

LYCIDAS

This elegy belongs to the last year of the Horton period, when Milton was already planning his Continental journey. It is dated November, 1637, in the Trinity Manuscript and was published in the next year, as the last poem in the Cambridge collection in memory of Edward King. The implication of the opening lines is that Milton intended to give no more time to minor verse but to hold his genius in reserve until he felt the power to carry forward his greater project. Even here he consciously allows the loftier music to break through the softer pastoral strains:

> Begin, and somewhat loudly sweep the string . . .
> That strain I heard was of a higher mood . . .
> Return Alpheus, the dread voice is past.

Milton inherited the theory that the epic poet naturally began with pastorals, and he must have counted the whole Horton group as belonging to that genre. In the *Epitaph of Damon*, written three years later, he confesses that his accustomed style is inadequate to his greater purposes:

And as for me,—'tis eleven nights and a day now since I—ah, I know not what large strains my pipe was trying to sound—I was accustoming my lips to new reeds, perhaps; the reeds flew asunder unable to endure longer the grave sounds to which i racked them.

We have, then, in "Lycidas" the pastoral becoming truly Miltonic. The poet controls the stops of the organ with perfect mastery, and the music rises and falls like the ebbing and flowing of the sea.

1021. **sphery chime,** i.e., the chiming spheres. The allusion is of course to the Platonic conception of the music of the spheres, as in the "Nativity Ode."

1023. **Heaven itself would stoop.** Again the Christian meaning of the poem is near the surface. Divine Grace reaches out to meet the weak endeavors of mankind. Thyrsis, the Attendant Spirit, the Guardian Angel, is a symbol of God's Grace. But in what sense is Virtue feeble? The Lady's Virtue is not feeble and she needs Heaven's protection only against outward harm. Milton, however, means more than this and elsewhere we shall find him becoming explicit.

The conventions of the pastoral elegy serve his purpose well. All the stock motives of Theocritus, Moschus, and Virgil are employed: the lament of nature, the question—"Where were ye, nymphs," the procession of mourners, the pastoral consolation. The ecclesiastical passage, which a modern reader might find intrusive, has precedent in Spenser's *Shepheardes Calender* and elsewhere. The poem is the last great monument of Italianate art. It was, in a sense, obsolete when it was written, yet it represents, as Mark Pattison has said, the high watermark of English poetry.

There is no evidence that Milton and King were intimates at Christ's. It was, however, not difficult for him to import a tone of authenticity into his expression of sorrow. Like Shelley writing of Keats he identifies himself with the lost poet and

> in another's fate now mourns his own.

The pattern of feeling in the lines descriptive of the association of the two shepherds in work and play may have come from his friendship with Diodati at St. Paul's. The tenderness with which he invests the circumstance of death goes back to the poem "On the Death of a Fair Infant," where the sorrow was wholly personal. So too does the faith in immortality expressed in the close. Both these notes are persistent in the poetry of Milton's youth. They rise to a climax in "Lycidas" and the *Epitaphium Damonis*; thereafter they are heard no more. The digressions on fame and the corrupt clergy embody the great emotions which came more and more to replace the elegiac mood as the motive forces of his poetry. It will be remembered that Milton himself had intended to enter the church but had been alienated from his purpose by dislike of the establishment and those individuals who were of it. His latent resentment perhaps animates St. Peter's great denunciation of his faithless church. But the passage has behind it a long tradition of Reformation and pre-Reformation literature expressive of indignation against clerical corruption.

Metrically "Lycidas" is uniquely adapted to Milton's poetic purpose. The verse is iambic pentameter, interspersed with iambic trimeter. The rhyme follows no fixed pattern and is sometimes absent. It is as if Milton surrendered himself completely to the fluctuating moods induced by grief and allowed them to dictate the poetic form. The last eight lines are the conventional *ottava rima*, suggestive of a renewed control of emotion and a return to regularity of life. The line "He touched the tender stops of various quills" may be interpreted as indicating Milton's awareness of the combination of widely different emotional materials in the song the uncouth swain has sung. It is worth while to compare the closing mood with that of Milton's other poems. *Comus* and the *Epitaphium Damonis* end in rapture; "Lycidas," *Paradise Lost, Paradise Regained,* and *Samson* with mature acceptance and a placid sense of freedom from disturbing feeling.

LYCIDAS

In this monody the author bewails a learned friend, unfortunately drowned in his passage from Chester on the Irish Seas, 1637. And by occasion foretells the ruin of our corrupted clergy then in their height.

Yet once more, O ye laurels, and once more
Ye myrtles brown, with ivy never sere,
I come to pluck your berries harsh and crude,
And with forced fingers rude,
Shatter your leaves before the mellowing year.
Bitter constraint, and sad occasion dear,
Compels me to disturb your season due;
For Lycidas is dead, dead ere his prime,
Young Lycidas, and hath not left his peer.

The name **Lycidas** occurs frequently in pastoral poetry. It is used, for example, by Theocritus (*Idyll* 7), and by Virgil (*Eclogue* 9).

1. **Yet once more,** *etc.* Milton had written no English poetry since *Comus* in 1634; instead he had been engaged in studious preparation for a future career. Now feeling that his preparation is still inadequate, he takes up his pen only because of the urgent demands of the occasion.

1-2. **laurels . . . myrtles . . . ivy,** evergreens traditionally used for crowns of honor. Laurel, sacred to Apollo, is symbolic of learning and poetic skill. Myrtle and ivy, sacred respectively to Venus and Bacchus, suggest such qualities as youth, beauty, joy, and friendship. **never sere,** never dry or withered.

3. **harsh and crude,** unripe, lacking the mellowness of maturity. The allusion in this and the two following lines is to Milton's sense of unreadiness for writing great poetry.

6. **dear,** grievous. In Milton's day, the word was applied to anything arousing strong emotion, unpleasant as well as pleasant. Cf. Shakespeare, *Henry V,* II, ii, 181: "all your dear offences."

7. **compels.** The verb is singular because constraint and occasion are regarded as forming one idea.

9-10. Note the repetition used to heighten the pathetic effect. Cf. Spenser's "Astrophel," 7-8.

> Young Astrophel, the pride of shepheards praise,
> Young Astrophel, the rusticke lasses love.

Who would not sing for Lycidas? he well knew   10
Himself to sing, and build the lofty rhyme.
He must not float upon his watery bier
Unwept, and welter to the parching wind,
Without the meed of some melodious tear.
  Begin then, Sisters of the sacred well,
That from beneath the seat of Jove doth spring,
Begin, and somewhat loudly sweep the string.
Hence with denial vain, and coy excuse;
So may some gentle muse
With lucky words favor my destined urn,   20
And as he passes turn,
And bid fair peace be to my sable shroud.
For we were nursed upon the self-same hill,
Fed the same flock, by fountain, shade, and rill.
  Together both, ere the high lawns appeared
Under the opening eyelids of the Morn,
We drove a-field, and both together heard
What time the gray-fly winds her sultry horn,
Battening our flocks with the fresh dews of night,

10. **Who would not sing,** etc. Cf. Virgil *Eclogue* 10.3. *Neget quis Carmina Gallo?* ("Who would refuse a song to Gallus?") **he well knew . . . to sing.** This is largely conventional, most pastoral elegies having been written for poets. King, however, was the author of at least a small amount of Latin verse.

14. **melodious tear,** i.e., a funeral elegy. The figure was more or less conventional; cf. Spenser's *Teares of the Muses.*

15. **Begin,** etc. This invocation follows a common pastoral formula. Cf. Theocritus, *Idyll* I, 64. "Begin, ye Muses dear, begin the pastoral song." **Sisters of the sacred well,** the nine muses. The **sacred well** probably refers to the Pierian spring at the foot of Mt. Olympus, although some editors connect it with the fountain of Aganippe, on Mt. Helicon. Olympus was the Homeric **seat of Jove** (line 16) and the birthplace of the muses. Their worship was later transferred to Helicon.

18. **coy,** offish, disdainful. This is a common seventeenth-century meaning.

19. **Muse,** i.e., poet. Note the **he** in line 21.

20. **lucky,** auspicious.

23 ff. **For we were nursed upon the self-same hill,** etc. In these pastoral terms, Milton is obviously recalling his life at the University in company with King. The allegory, however, is not to be interpreted too literally, as many details are introduced for their conventional propriety rather than for their correspondence to fact. For example, Cambridge is not located on a hill.

25. **high lawns,** spaces clear of trees, pastures.

28. **What time the gray-fly winds her sultry horn,** i.e., in the middle of the day. The allusion is obviously to the humming sound made by insects in the heat of noon, although the precise species of insect which Milton had in mind is an open question. **What time** was a common idiom; cf. Psalms 56:3, "What time I am afraid, I will trust in thee."

29. **Battening,** feeding.

Oft till the star that rose, at evening, bright   30
Toward Heaven's descent had sloped his westering wheel.
Meanwhile the rural ditties were not mute,
Tempered to the oaten flute;
Rough Satyrs danced, and Fauns with cloven heel
From the glad sound would not be absent long,
And old Damœtas loved to hear our song.
  But O the heavy change, now thou art gone,
Now thou art gone, and never must return!
Thee Shepherd, thee the woods and desert caves,
With wild thyme and the gadding vine o'ergrown,   40
And all their echoes mourn.
The willows and the hazel copses green
Shall now no more be seen
Fanning their joyous leaves to thy soft lays.
As killing as the canker to the rose,
Or taint-worn to the weanling herds that graze,
Or frost to flowers that their gay wardrobe wear,
When first the white-thorn blows,
Such, Lycidas, thy loss to shepherd's ear.
  Where were ye Nymphs when the remorseless deep   50
Closed o'er the head of your loved Lycidas?
For neither were ye playing on the steep,

30. the star that rose at evening, the evening star Hesperus, whose appearance was a signal for the shepherd to begin getting his flock into the fold, as in *Comus,* 93. **Rose** must be understood in the sense of "appeared," for the evening star is of course visible only in the west and for only a short time after sunset.

34. Satyrs . . . Fauns, sportive divinities of the fields and woods. The Satyrs belonged to Greek, the Fauns to Roman mythology; but by later writers they were commonly regarded as identical. Both were half-human, half-bestial in form. In introducing them here, Milton is following the example of Virgil, *Eclogue* 6.27.

36. Damœtas, a common pastoral name. Milton may have wished it to stand for some specific person, but the identification is uncertain.

45. canker, the canker-worm. Cf. Shakespeare, *Two Gentlemen of Verona,* I, i, 42–43.

As in the sweetest bud
The eating canker dwells, etc.

46. taint-worm, some sort of animal parasite, possibly the *tainct* mentioned by Sir Thomas Browne in *Vulgar Errors,* III, xvii, 2.

48. white-thorn, the hawthorn of "L'Allegro," 68.

50 ff. Where were ye, Nymphs, etc. This is closely imitated from Theocritus, *Idyll* 1:66–69, which had been imitated by Virgil also in *Eclogue* 10.9–12, and by many later pastoralists. The places mentioned are near the scene of King's shipwreck.

52. the steep, etc. The exact spot is in doubt, although the promontory of Holyhead, close to the western shore of Anglesey, seems to fit the description best. It is a region associated with the Druids, and was famous as a burial place.

Where your old bards, the famous Druids, lie,
Nor on the shaggy top of Mona high,
Nor yet where Deva spreads her wizard stream.
Ay me, I fondly dream!
Had ye been there—for what could that have done?
What could the Muse herself that Orpheus bore,
The Muse herself, for her enchanting son
Whom universal Nature did lament,   60
When by the rout that made the hideous roar,
His gory visage down the stream was sent,
Down the swift Hebrus to the Lesbian shore.
  Alas! what boots it with uncessant care
To tend the homely slighted shepherd's trade,
And strictly meditate the thankless Muse?
Were it not better done as others use,
To sport with Amaryllis in the shade,
Or with the tangles of Neæra's hair?

53. **your old bards, the famous Druids.** Cf. Milton's Latin epistle
Mansus, 42–43: "The Druids, an ancient folk occupied with the rites of
the gods, used to sing the praises of heroes and their deeds so worthy of
emulation."

54. **Mona**, the island of Anglesey, off the northwest coast of Wales.

55. **Deva**, the river Dee, on which Chester, the port from which King
sailed, is located. It is called a **wizard stream** because of its reputed powers of prophecy. Cf. Drayton, *Polyolbion*, X, 203–7.

A Brook, that was supposed much business to have seen,
Which had an ancient bound twixt Wales and England been,
And noted was by both to be an ominous Flood,
That changing of his fords, the future ill, or good,
Of either country told.

58. **Muse . . . that Orpheus bore**, Calliope. Even she, Milton says,
was powerless to save her son from a fatal end. What, then, could the
Nymphs have done for Lycidas?

59. **enchanting**, i.e., working enchantment by his music.

61 ff. Orpheus was torn in pieces by the frenzied Thracian women
when he refused to join them in the orgies of Bacchus which they were
celebrating. His head was thrown into the river Hebrus, and borne by the
current to the island of Lesbos. Cf. Ovid *Metamorphoses* xi. 1 ff. Milton
refers to the story again in *Paradise Lost*, VII, 32–38, identifying his own
lot with that of Orpheus.

65. **shepherd's trade**, i.e., the profession of poetry.

66. **meditate.** Cf. *Comus*, 547, and note.

67. **Were it not better done.** These lines are modeled on Virgil
Eclogue 2.14–15: "Were it not better to have endured the scorn of
haughty Amaryllis?" etc. The names Amaryllis and Neaera, both of which
occur frequently in pastoral verse, are mentioned together by Spenser in
Colin Clouts Come Home Againe. **as others use**, as others are accustomed to do. Milton is momentarily questioning the value of his own
high-minded poetic ideal in terms of the more earthy standards of his
contemporaries. Cf. Elegy VI.

Fame is the spur that the clear spirit doth raise 70
(That last infirmity of noble mind)
To scorn delights, and live laborious days;
But the fair guerdon when we hope to find,
And think to burst out into sudden blaze,
Comes the blind Fury with the abhorrèd shears,
And slits the thin-spun life. "But not the praise,"
Phœbus replied, and touched my trembling ears;
"Fame is no plant that grows on mortal soil,
Nor in the glistering foil
Set off to the world, nor in broad rumor lies, 80
But lives and spreads aloft by those pure eyes
And perfect witness of all-judging Jove;
As he pronounces lastly on each deed,
Of so much fame in Heaven expect thy meed."
O fountain Arethuse, and thou honored flood,
Smooth-sliding Mincius, crowned with vocal reeds,

70. **clear**, pure, unsullied.
71. **That last infirmity of noble mind.** Cf. Tacitus *Historiae* iv. 6: "Even in the case of wise men the desire for glory is last cut off." But Milton's line is an exact quotation from the play *Barnevelt* (1622).
73. **guerdon**, recompense.
74. **blaze**, i.e., of fame. Cf. *Paradise Regained*, III, 47: "For what is glory but the blaze of fame?"
75. **the blind Fury**, Atropos, one of the three fates of classical mythology. Her function was to cut the thread of life spun by Clotho and measured by Lachesis. Milton here calls her a **Fury** (thus associating her with the Erinyes) because he wishes to emphasize her vindictiveness; he adds the epithet *blind* to account for her mad unreason.
76. Cf. Spenser, *The Shepheardes Calender*, X, 19–20.
> "Cuddie, the prayse is better than the price
> The glory eke much greater than the gayne."
77. **Phoebus**, Apollo, god of poetry—here the voice of divine wisdom. **touched . . . ears.** The allusion is probably to the story of Midas, who, declaring that Pan was a better musician than Phoebus, had his ears changed by the offended god to those of an ass, to indicate his stupidity. Milton likens his own doubtful utterance to the foolishness of Midas, and his ears tremble in anticipation of Phoebus's reproof. Cf. the phrase "Midas ears" in the "Sonnet to Henry Lawes."
79–80. **glistering foil**, gold or silver leaf placed under gems to increase their brilliance—hence anything bright and showy. Milton means that true fame does not consist in brilliant appearances exhibited to the world, nor in popular approval (broad rumor).
81. **lives and spreads aloft.** The metaphor of the plant (line 78) is continued.
82. **all-judging Jove.** Milton of course means God, but he keeps the classical nomenclature for the sake of consistency.
85. **fountain Arethuse**, a spring located in the island of Ortygia, near the birthplace of Theocritus. It is used here as symbolic of the Sicilian pastoralists.
86. **Mincius**, an Italian river near which Virgil was born. Here it typifies Virgil's pastorals. **vocal reeds**, i.e., reeds used for shepherd's pipes.

That strain I heard was of a higher mood.
But now my oat proceeds,
And listens to the Herald of the Sea
That came in Neptune's plea.   90
He asked the waves, and asked the felon winds,
What hard mishap hath doomed this gentle swain?
And questioned every gust of rugged wings
That blows from off each beakëd promontory;
They knew not of his story,
And sage Hippotades their answer brings,
That not a blast was from his dungeon strayed,
The air was calm, and on the level brine,
Sleek Panope with all her sisters played.
It was that fatal and perfidious bark,   100
Built in the eclipse, and rigged with curses dark,
That sunk so low that sacred head of thine.
   Next Camus, reverend sire, went footing slow,
His mantle hairy, and his bonnet sedge,
Inwrought with figures dim, and on the edge
Like to that sanguine flower inscribed with woe.
"Ah, who hath reft" (quoth he) "my dearest pledge?"
Last came, and last did go,
The Pilot of the Galilean Lake;
Two massy keys he bore of metals twain   110

88. my oat proceeds, i.e., I resume my pastoral strain.
89. Herald of the Sea, Triton. Cf. note on *Comus,* 873.
90. came in Neptune's plea, came in Neptune's defense.
96. Hippotades, Aeolus, god of the winds.
98. The air was calm. The poem by Edward King's brother in the
Cambridge collection has a contrary implication. Cf. the lines

                        He, the fairest arm,
        Is torn away by an unluckie storm.

99. Panope, a sea-nymph, one of the fifty daughters of Nereus.
103. Camus, the god of the river Cam, which flows by Cambridge.
Here he stands for the University. **footing slow** appropriately describes
the sluggish movement of the current as well as the grief of the University.
104. bonnet sedge, i.e., the coarse grass growing along the banks.
Sedge is a conventional adornment of river deities. The terms **mantle** and
bonnet are undoubtedly meant to suggest academic dress.
106. that sanguine flower inscribed with woe, the hyacinth. Hya-
cinthus, a mythical Spartan youth, was killed by Zephyrus through
the unwitting agency of Apollo. Apollo thereupon caused a flower to spring
from the slain youth's blood, and incribed on its petals the words Αι, Αι
(Alas!). Cf. Ovid *Metamorphoses* x. 210 ff.
107. pledge, child. This use of pledge is based on the parallel use in
Latin of the word *pignus,* which often denotes a child (i.e., a pledge of
love).
109. the pilot of the Galilean Lake, St. Peter.
110. Two massy keys, etc. Cf. Matt. 16:19: "And I will give unto
thee the keys of the kingdom of heaven." The number of keys is tradi-

(The golden opes, the iron shuts amain).
He shook his mitred locks, and stern bespake,
"How well could I have spared for thee, young swain,
Enough of such as for their bellies' sake,
Creep and intrude and climb into the fold!
Of other care they little reckoning make,
Than how to scramble at the shearers' feast,
And shove away the worthy bidden guest;
Blind mouths! that scarce themselves know how to hold
A sheep-hook, or have learnt aught else the least   120
That to the faithful herdsman's art belongs!
What recks it them? What need they? They are sped;
And when they list, their lean and flashy songs
Grate on their scrannel pipes of wretched straw;
The hungry sheep look up, and are not fed,
But swoln with wind and the rank mist they draw,

tional but the distinction of metals and function is apparently Milton's
own idea.
    111. **amain**, with force.
    112. **mitred locks.** St. Peter appears in the garb of his office as first
Bishop of the Church.
    113 ff. This denunciation of the "corrupted clergy," one of the most
notable passages in the poem, gives us a forecast of Milton's later anti-
prelatical writings, as well as indicating clearly his ecclesiastical views in
1637. While not attacking the established church as an institution, he
condemns a large section of its ministers on three counts: (1) they are
guided by unworthy motives (lines 114-18), (2) they are ignorant (lines
119-22), (3) they are negligent in performing their duties (lines 123-29).
He concludes with a prophecy of speedy retribution (lines 130-31). The
literary antecedents of the passage are numerous, the most important in
English being the May Eclogue of Spenser's *Shepheardes Calender*. Ezek.
34:2-10 and John 10 furnish significant biblical parallels. The intensity
of the passage and its combination of details suggest the inspiration of
Dante, whose work Milton was studying about this time.
    115. **Creep, and intrude, and climb into the fold.** Cf. John 10:1:
"He that entereth not by the door into the sheepfold, but climbeth up
some other way, the same is a thief and a robber."
    118. **the worthy bidden guest.** Cf. Matt. 22:8: "they which were
bidden were not worthy."
    119. **Blind mouths**, i.e., blind and gluttonous men. The phrase is an
example of extraordinary compression of thought. Ruskin's comment
(*Sesame and Lilies*, 22) is illuminating: "A 'Bishop' means 'a person who
sees.' A 'Pastor' means 'a person who feeds.' The most unbishoply character a man can have is therefore to be Blind. The most unpastoral is, instead
of feeding, to want to be fed—to be a Mouth."
    122. **recks it them**, matters it to them. Cf. *Comus*, 404. **sped**, pro-
vided for. Cf. Shakespeare, *The Merchant of Venice*, II, ix, 71: "So be-
gone; you are sped."
    123. **lean and flashy songs**, i.e., meager, watery sermons, devoid of
spiritual substance.
    124. **scrannel**, thin, harsh. The sound of the word effectively suggests
its meaning.
    126. **wind . . . rank mist**, i.e., empty and false doctrines.

Rot inwardly, and foul contagion spread;
Besides what the grim wolf with privy paw
Daily devours apace, and nothing said;
But that two-handed engine at the door   130
Stands ready to smite once, and smite no more."
    Return Alpheus, the dread voice is past
That shrunk thy streams; return Sicilian Muse,
And call the vales, and bid them hither cast
Their bells and flowrets of a thousand hues.
Ye valleys low where the mild whispers use
Of shades and wanton winds and gushing brooks,
On whose fresh lap the swart star sparely looks,
Throw hither all your quaint enamelled eyes,
That on the green turf suck the honied showers,   140
And purple all the ground with vernal flowers.
Bring the rathe primrose that forsaken dies,
The tufted crow-toe, and pale jessamine,
The white pink, and the pansy freaked with jet,
The glowing violet,
The musk-rose, and the well-attired woodbine,
With cowslips wan that hang the pensive head,
And every flower that sad embroidery wears.

128. **the grim wolf with privy paw.** Probably this refers to the Church of Rome which at the time was secretly acquiring many converts in England. But it may simply mean the Devil.

130. **that two-handed engine,** etc. This is the most famous crux in Milton. Interpretations range from the axe "laid unto the root of the trees" (Matt. 3:20; Luke 3:9) to the two houses of Parliament. Perhaps the most likely allusion is to the sword of God's vengeance, the sword which Michael wielded "with huge two-handed sway" (*Paradise Lost*, VI, 251) and which went before the Cherubim in Eden (XII, 632–33). The menacing vagueness of the figure adds to its effectiveness.

132. **Return Alpheus.** Here, as after the digression on Fame, Milton announces his return to the pastoral mood. **Alpheus** is the name of an Arcadian river, which, after flowing in an underground channel for some distance, rises in Ortygia and mingles its waters with the "fountain Arethuse." The "dread voice" is the invective just uttered by St. Peter.

136. **use,** are accustomed to dwell.

138. **swart star,** i.e., Sirius, the dog-star, which was believed to have a blackening effect on vegetation. In fact the name Sirius is derived from a Greek word meaning "scorching." **sparely,** seldom.

142–50. This flower passage, which the MS. shows to have been omitted in the original draft, may owe something to the April Eclogue of Spenser's *Shepheardes Calender*. Cf. lines 136 ff.

> Bring better the pincke and purple cullambine,
>   With gelliflowres;
>   Bring coronations, and sops in wine,
>   Worne of paramoures, etc.

142. **rathe,** early. **that forsaken dies.** Milton first wrote "that unwedded dies." Cf. *The Winter's Tale*, IV, iv, 122–24.

144. **freaked,** variegated or spotted.

Bid amaranthus all his beauty shed,
And daffadillies fill their cups with tears,   150
To strew the laureate hearse where Lycid' lies.
For so to interpose a little ease,
Let our frail thoughts dally with false surmise;
Ay me! whilst thee the shores and sounding seas
Wash far away, where'er thy bones are hurled,
Whether beyond the stormy Hebrides,
Where thou perhaps under the whelming tide
Visit'st the bottom of the monstrous world;
Or whether thou to our moist vows denied,
Sleep'st by the fable of Bellerus old,   160
Where the great Vision of the guarded mount
Looks toward Namancos and Bayona's hold;
Look homeward Angel now, and melt with ruth;
And, O ye dolphins, waft the hapless youth.

149. amaranthus. The name comes from the Greek, meaning "not fading."

151. laureate hearse, i.e., the bier which has been decorated with memorial verse. Hearse might signify almost anything connected with a funeral; here it evidently refers to the frame on which the coffin rested or to the coffin itself. It was a common custom to affix to this the manuscripts of poetic eulogies.

153. Milton has been letting his fancy play with the notion that King's body is actually present for burial—a false surmise. Now by acknowledging that the supposition is a frail one (for the body is ultimately of no consequence), he prepares the way for the loftier thought to be developed in the next paragraph.

158. monstrous world, i.e., the world of monsters. Cf. *Comus*, 533, "monstrous rout."

159. moist vows, tearful rites.

160. fable of Bellerus old, i.e., the fabled abode of old Bellerus. The Roman name for Land's End, in the extreme southeast of Cornwall, was Bellerium; Milton connects the name with a mythical king or giant.

161. the great Vision of the guarded mount. The reference is to the archangel Michael, for whom St. Michael's Mount near Land's End, is named. According to tradition, the angel was occasionally visible on a craggy seat at the summit. Cf. *The Shepheardes Calender*, VII, 41–42.

> St. Michels mount who does not know,
> That wardes the Westerne coste?

162. Namancos and Bayona's hold, points on the coast of Spain, toward which Michael gazes in defiance. Hold of course means a stronghold or fortified castle.

163. Angel. St. Michael is bidden to turn his gaze from Spain to England and the cenotaph of Lycidas.

164. ye dolphins, etc. Milton undoubtedly has in mind the legend of Arion, a Greek poet and musician, who was borne ashore by dolphins after he had flung himself into the sea to escape being murdered by the sailors of a ship on which he was taking passage. Since the dolphins were supposed to be friendly to mankind and especially susceptible to the charms of music, they could properly be invoked to bring the body of Lycidas to shore.

Weep no more, woeful shepherds weep no more,
For Lycidas your sorrow is not dead,
Sunk though he be beneath the watery floor,
So sinks the day-star in the ocean bed,
And yet anon repairs his drooping head,
And tricks his beams, and with new-spangled ore,   170
Flames in the forehead of the morning sky:
So Lycidas, sunk low, but mounted high,
Through the dear might of Him that walked the waves,
Where other groves and other streams along,
With nectar pure his oozy locks he laves,
And hears the unexpressive nuptial song,
In the blest kingdoms meek of joy and love.
There entertain him all the saints above,
In solemn troops and sweet societies
That sing, and singing in their glory move,   180
And wipe the tears for ever from his eyes.
Now Lycidas, the shepherds weep no more;
Henceforth thou art the Genius of the shore,
In thy large recompense, and shalt be good
To all that wander in that perilous flood.
     Thus sang the úncouth swain to the oaks and rills,
While the still Morn went out with sandals gray;
He touched the tender stops of various quills,

165. **Weep no more**, etc. For a similar change in mood, cf. the November Eclogue of *The Shepheardes Calender*, 171 ff. But indeed the consolation had become traditional in pastoral elegy.
    168. **day-star**, the sun.
    170. **tricks**, decks, adorns. **with new-spangled ore**, i.e., with renewed radiance. Ore may possibly have been associated in Milton's mind with *aurum* (gold).
    173. **Him that walked the waves**. Cf. Matt. 14: 24–31.
    175. **With nectar pure**, etc. Cf. *Comus*, 838. Although the imagery of the passage is primarily Christian, Milton retains a connection with pagan mythology.
    176. **unexpressive**, inexpressible. **nuptial song**. Cf. Rev. 19:9: "Blessed are they which are called unto the marriage supper of the Lamb." Cf. also the closing lines of the *Epitaphium Damonis*.
    181. **And wipe the tears**, etc. Cf. Rev. 7:17 and 21:4: "And God shall wipe away all tears from their eyes."
    183. The idea may have been suggested by Virgil's fifth *Eclogue*, in which Daphnis, the subject of the elegy, is set forth as a deity and his favors invoked. Cf. lines 64–65: "A god is he, a god, Manalcas! O be thou good and gracious to thine own!"
    The concluding eight lines, which form a perfect stanza in ottava rima, are a narrative epilogue to the lament proper. The subdued ending is characteristic of the classic pastoral.
    186–90. **the uncouth swain**, the unknown rustic poet.
    188. **the tender stops of various quills**. The stops are the holes in a wind instrument—tender because responsive to the delicate touch of the

With eager thought warbling his Doric lay.
And now the sun had stretched out all the hills,   190
And now was dropped into the western bay;
At last he rose, and twitched his mantle blue:
To-morrow to fresh woods, and pastures new.

[November, 1637]

To His Father

The date of this poem is uncertain. Milton may, as Masson argues, have written it under the same anxiety and at the same time as the prose letter in which he defends himself to a friend for going on with studious preparation for his lifework instead of beginning it in a practical way. If so, the verses would belong to the beginning of the Horton period. Grierson and Tillyard, pointing out that the piece is an apology for the writing of poetry rather than for the continuance of study, believe that it would not have been appropriate until Milton had made clear his poetical purpose by writing *Comus*. The poem is more mature in feeling and expression than anything Milton had written hitherto. His attitude toward his parent is loving and appreciative but firm. Milton talks to his father as to a friend of his own age who has expressed doubts as to his wisdom in giving himself up to literature. He feels that he has proved his right to exercise his own judgment, and he wishes that judgment to be accepted and understood. He promises with confidence the fulfilment of an ambitious desire which his father has himself aroused, and he praises the art which he has chosen as his own in terms which imply an easy assurance that he is on solid ground. Belief in the superior function of the poet, inherited from the Renaissance tradition of literary

fingers; **quills** are reed pipes. The adjective **various** is used in allusion to the shifting moods of the poem.

189. Doric lay, pastoral song. The Greek pastoralists (Theocritus, Bion, and Moschus) all used the Doric dialect.

190. And now the sun had stretched out all the hills, i.e., the shadows cast by the hills had lengthened. The image is probably drawn from the concluding line of Virgil's first *Eclogue*: "And longer shadows fall from the high mountains."

192. twitched, i.e., gathered about him.

193. To-morrow to fresh woods and pastures new. Cf. Fletcher, *The Purple Island*, VI, 77: "To-morrow shall ye feast in pastures new." Milton is thinking of new poetic ventures and perhaps also of the journey to Italy which he was to undertake six months after he wrote this poem.

criticism and confirmed by his own feeling, was always strong in Milton. The suggested hostility toward the law and other gainful professions perhaps has as its basis a conflict of viewpoint in his own family, for his brother Christopher was preparing to follow his father's profession. The argument for the dignity and antiquity of the bard suggests Sidney's *Defense of Poesie*, a document which would have stirred Milton's heart as with a trumpet. The account of the elaborate education for which the poet is indebted to his father gives us the order in which he learned his languages. It also illustrates Milton's broad humanistic point of view. The tongues have been studied with due appreciation of their aesthetic and expressive value, but emphasis is placed, as in the tractate *Of Education*, on their use in the acquisition of universal knowledge.

TO HIS FATHER

(Translation)

Oh that Pieria's spring would through my breast
Pour its inspiring influence, and rush
No rill, but rather an o'erflowing flood!
That, for my venerable father's sake
All meaner themes renounced, my muse, on wings
Of duty borne, might reach a loftier strain.
For thee, my father! howsoe'er it please,
She frames this slender work; nor know I aught
That may thy gifts more suitably requite;
Though to requite them suitably would ask   10
Returns much nobler, and surpassing far
The meagre stores of verbal gratitude:
But, such as I possess, I send thee all.
This page presents thee in their full amount
With thy son's treasures, and the sum is nought;
Nought, save the riches that from airy dream
In secret grottoes, and in laurel bowers,
I have, by golden Clio's gift, acquired.
    Verse is a work divine; despise not thou
Verse therefore, which evinces (nothing more)   20
Man's heavenly source, and which, retaining still
Some scintillations of Promethean fire,
Bespeaks him animated from above.
The gods love verse; the infernal powers themselves
Confess the influence of verse, which stirs
The lowest deep, and binds in triple chains

Of adamant both Pluto and the Shades.
In verse the Delphic priestess, and the pale
Tremulous Sibyl, make the future known;
And he who sacrifices, on the shrine   30
Hangs verse, both when he smites the threatening bull,
And when he spreads his reeking entrails wide
To scrutinize the fates enveloped there.
We too, ourselves, what time we seek again
Our native skies, and one eternal now
Shall be the only measure of our being,
Crowned all with gold, and chanting to the lyre
Harmonious verse, shall range the courts above,
And make the starry firmament resound.
And, even now, the fiery spirit pure   40
That wheels yon circling orbs, directs, himself,
Their mazy dance with melody of verse
Unutterable, immortal, hearing which
Huge Ophiuchus holds his hiss suppressed;
Orion, softened, drops his ardent blade;
And Atlas stands unconscious of his load.
Verse graced of old the feasts of kings, ere yet
Luxurious dainties, destined to the gulf
Immense of gluttony, were known, and ere
Lycaeus deluged yet the temperate board.   50
Then sat the bard a customary guest
To share the banquet, and, his length of locks
With beechen honours bound, proposed in verse
The characters of heroes and their deeds
To imitation; sang of Chaos old,
Of Nature's birth, of gods that crept in search
Of acorns fallen, and of the thunder-bolt
Not yet produced from Aetna's fiery cave.
And what avails, at last, tune without voice,
Devoid of matter? Such may suit perhaps   60
The rural dance, but such was ne'er the song
Of Orpheus, whom the streams stood still to hear,
And the oaks followed. Not by chords alone
Well touched, but by resistless accents more,
To sympathetic tears the ghosts themselves
He moved: these praises to his verse he owes.

42. **melody of verse**, etc. Literally "immortal melody and inexpressible
song."
44. **Ophiuchus.** Milton says "the Serpent." Ophiuchus is the adjoining constellation, figured as a man holding the serpent in his mouth.
46. **Atlas,** whose shoulders upheld the heavens.
50. **Lycaeus,** Bacchus.

Nor thou persist, I pray thee, still to slight
The sacred Nine, and to imagine vain
And useless, powers, by whom inspired, thyself
Art skilful to associate verse with airs   70
Harmonious, and to give the human voice
A thousand modulations, heir by right
Indisputable of Arion's fame.
Now say, what wonder is it if a son
Of thine delight in verse, if, so conjoined
In close affinity, we sympathise
In social arts, and kindred studies sweet?
Such distribution of himself to us
Was Phœbus' choice; thou hast thy gift, and I
Mine also, and between us we receive,   80
Father and son, the whole inspiring god.
    No! howsoe'er the semblance thou assume
Of hate, thou hatest not the gentle Muse,
My father! for thou never bad'st me tread
The beaten path, and broad, that leads right on
To opulence, nor didst condemn thy son
To the insipid clamours of the bar,
To laws voluminous, and ill observed;
But, wishing to enrich me more, to fill
My mind with treasure, led'st me far away   90
From city din to deep retreats, to banks
And streams Aonian, and, with free consent,
Didst place me happy at Apollo's side.
I speak not now, on more important themes
Intent, of common benefits, and such
As nature bids, but of thy larger gifts,
My father! who, when I had opened once
The stores of Roman rhetoric, and learned
The full-toned language of the eloquent Greeks,
Whose lofty music graced the lips of Jove,   100
Thyself didst counsel me to add the flowers
That Gallia boasts; those too with which the smooth
Italian his degenerate speech adorns,
That witnesses his mixture with the Goth;
And Palestine's prophetic songs divine.
To sum the whole, whate'er the heaven contains,

70. The elder Milton's musical compositions are all settings of verse.
73. The poet Arion charmed the dolphins with his song and was rescued by them from drowning.
103. degenerate, in comparison with Latin from which it was derived.
Milton really admired the Italian tongue, as he did not admire the French.
105. Hebrew was taught in the highest class at St. Paul's School. Milton was presented with a Hebrew bible when he went to college.

The earth beneath it, and the air between,
The rivers and the restless deep, may all
Prove intellectual gain to me, my wish
Concurring with thy will; Science herself,   110
All cloud removed, inclines her beauteous head,
And offers me the lip, if, dull of heart,
I shrink not, and decline her gracious boon.
  Go now and gather dross, ye sordid minds
That covet it; what could my father more?
What more could Jove himself, unless he gave
His own abode, the heaven in which he reigns?
More eligible gifts than these were not
Apollo's to his son, had they been safe
As they were insecure, who made the boy   120
The world's vice-luminary, bade him rule
The radiant chariot of the day, and bind
To his young brows his own all-dazzling wreath.
I therefore, although last and least, my place
Among the learned in the laurel grove
Will hold, and where the conqueror's ivy twines,
Henceforth exempt from the unlettered throng
Profane, nor even to be seen by such.
Away, then, sleepless Care; Complaint, away;
And, Envy, with thy "jealous leer malign!"   130
Nor let the monster Calumny shoot forth
Her venomed tongue at me. Detested foes!
Ye all are impotent against my peace,
For I am privileged, and bear my breast
Safe, and too high for your viperean wound.
  But thou, my father! since to render thanks
Equivalent, and to requite by deeds
Thy liberality, exceeds my power,
Suffice it that I thus record thy gifts,
And bear them treasured in a grateful mind!   140
Ye too, the favourite pastime of my youth,
My voluntary numbers, if ye dare
To hope longevity, and to survive
Your master's funeral, not soon absorbed
In the oblivious Lethæan gulf,
Shall to futurity perhaps convey
This theme, and by these praises of my sire
Improve the fathers of a distant age!

                                        [1637?]

110. **Science,** knowledge in general, to which languages are the key.
131. **Calumny.** Hostile criticism is deprecated in the quotations prefixed to the first edition of *Comus* and to the *Poems* of 1645.

To Giovanni Battista Manso

This is the one important poetic fruit of Milton's Italian journey. It must have been written in December, 1638, the month of his stay in Naples. Manso, to whom he had been introduced by a certain friar with whom he had traveled from Rome, had treated him with great courtesy and been his guide to the sights of his native city. The acquaintance was for Milton the crowning experience of his trip to the continent, for it brought him into contact, not only with what was most excellent in the culture of contemporary Italy, but with the memories of the greater age which had just passed. Milton was very susceptible to appreciation from such a source as Manso. It brings out all his affability and charm. Under it his pride in his country and his confidence in himself expand, and he becomes glowingly enthusiastic as to his poetic plans. Milton needed precisely such a friendship for his best development and could thrive even on the memory of it. This incident is alluded to in the *Epitaphium Damonis,* where there is a description of two cups (actually books) given him by Manso as keepsakes.

TO GIOVANNI BATTISTA MANSO

MARQUIS OF VILLA

(*Translation*)

Giovanni Battista Manso, Marquis of Villa, is an Italian nobleman of the highest estimation among his countrymen, for genius, literature, and military accomplishments. To him Torquato Tasso addressed his "Dialogues on Friendship," for he was much the friend of Tasso, who has also celebrated him among the other princes of his country, in his poem entitled "Gerusalemme Conquistata," book xx.

> *Fra cavalier magnanimi, e cortesi,*
> *Risplende il Manso.*

During the Author's stay at Naples, he received at the hands of the Marquis a thousand kind offices and civilities, and, desirous not to appear ungrateful, sent him this poem a short time before his departure from that city.

These verses also to thy praise the Nine—
O Manso! happy in that theme—design,
For, Gallus and Mæcenas gone, they see

3. Two of the most famous tributes in Latin literature to patron friends are Horace's first ode, to Mæcenas, and Virgil's tenth eclogue, to Gallus.

None such besides, or whom they love as thee;
And if my verse may give the meed of fame,
Thine too shall prove an everlasting name.
Already such, it shines in Tasso's page
(For thou wast Tasso's friend) from age to age,
And, next, the Muse consigned (not unaware
How high the charge) Marino to thy care,   10
Who, singing to the nymphs Adonis' praise,
Boasts thee the patron of his copious lays.
To thee alone the poet would entrust
His latest vows, to thee alone his dust;
And thou with punctual piety hast paid,
In laboured brass, thy tribute to his shade.
Nor this contented thee,—but lest the grave
Should aught absorb of theirs which thou couldst save,
All future ages thou hast deigned to teach
The life, lot, genius, character of each,   20
Eloquent as the Carian sage, who, true
To his great theme, the life of Homer drew.
    I, therefore, though a stranger youth, who come
Chilled by rude blasts that freeze my northern home,
Thee dear to Clio, confident proclaim,
And thine, for Phœbus' sake, a deathless name.
Nor thou, so kind, wilt view with scornful eye
A Muse scarce reared beneath our sullen sky,
Who fears not, indiscreet as she is young,
To seek in Latium hearers of her song.   30
We too, where Thames with his unsullied waves
The tresses of the blue-haired Ocean laves,
Hear oft by night, or slumbering seem to hear,
O'er his wide stream, the swan's voice warbling clear,
And we could boast a Tityrus of yore,
Who trod, a welcome guest, your happy shore.

This opening allusion is precisely parallel to that in the *Epitaph of Damon*,
lines 1–2, where Theocritus and Moschus are recalled by mention of
Daphnis and Bion, poets whom they had lamented as Milton was lamenting
Diodati.

    10. **Marino**, a native of Naples who had died there as recently as 1625,
was in high esteem for his romantic epic, *Adone*, his *Slaughter of the Inno-*
cents, and other poems in the Baroque manner imitated by Crashaw.

    21. **Carian sage**, Herodotus to whom an extant life of Homer was
attributed. In thus complimenting Manso on the excellence of his biographical writing Milton speaks as though he had done a life of Marini as
well as one of Tasso, but no such work is known.

    34. **the swan's voice.** The swan was supposed to sing at the moment
of its approaching death and only then.

    35. **Tityrus**, Chaucer, so called in Spenser, after Virgil's use of this
pastoral name for himself. Chaucer's two visits to Italy took place in 1372
and 1378.

Yes, dreary as we own our northern clime,
Even we to Phœbus raise the polished rhyme.
We too serve Phœbus; Phœbus has received
(If legends old may claim to be believed)   40
No sordid gifts from us, the golden ear,
The burnished apple, ruddiest of the year,
The fragrant crocus, and, to grace his fane,
Fair damsels chosen from the Druid train;
Druids, our native bards in ancient time,
Who gods and heroes praised in hallowed rhyme.
Hence, often as the maids of Greece surround
Apollo's shrine with hymns of festive sound,
They name the virgins, who arrived of yore,
With British offerings, on the Delian shore;   50
Loxo, from giant Corineus sprung,
Upis, on whose blest lips the future hung,
And Hecærge, with the golden hair,
All decked with Pictish hues, and all with bosoms bare.
    Thou, therefore, happy sage, whatever clime
Shall ring with Tasso's praise in after time,
Or with Marino's, shalt be known their friend,
And with an equal flight to fame ascend.
The world shall hear how Phœbus and the Nine
Were inmates once, and willing guests of thine.   60
Yet Phœbus, when of old constrained to roam
The earth, an exile from his heavenly home,
Entered, no willing guest, Admetus' door,
Though Hercules had ventured there before.
But gentle Chiron's cave was near, a scene
Of rural peace, clothed with perpetual green,
And thither, oft as respite he required
From rustic clamours loud, the god retired.
There, many a time, on Peneus' bank reclined
At some oak's root, with ivy thick entwined,   70
Won by his hospitable friend's desire,
He soothed his pains of exile with the lyre.
Then shook the hills, then trembled Peneus' shore,
Nor Œta felt his load of forests more;
The upland elms descended to the plain,
And softened lynxes wondered at the strain.
    Well may we think, O dear to all above!
Thy birth distinguished by the smile of Jove,
And that Apollo shed his kindliest power,
And Maia's son, on that propitious hour,   80

50–55. The coming of these maidens from the north to Apollo's shrine
in Delos is alluded to by Callimachus, *Hymn to Delos*.

Since only minds so born can comprehend
A poet's worth, or yield that worth a friend.
Hence on thy yet unfaded cheek appears
The lingering freshness of thy greener years;
Hence, in thy front and features we admire
Nature unwithered and a mind entire.
Oh might so true a friend to me belong,
So skilled to grace the votaries of song,
Should I recall hereafter into rhyme
The kings and heroes of my native clime,   90
Arthur the chief, who even now prepares,
In subterraneous being, future wars,
With all his martial knights, to be restored
Each to his seat around the federal board;
And oh, if spirit fail me not, disperse
Our Saxon plunderers, in triumphant verse:
Then, after all, when, with the past content,
A life I finish, not in silence spent,
Should he, kind mourner, o'er my death-bed bend,
I shall but need to say—"Be yet my friend!"   100
He, too, perhaps, shall bid the marble breathe
To honour me, and with the graceful wreath,
Or of Parnassus or the Paphian isle,
Shall bind my brows,—but I shall rest the while.
Then also, if the fruits of faith endure,
And virtue's promised recompense be sure,
Borne to those seats to which the blest aspire
By purity of soul and virtuous fire,
These rites, as fate permits, I shall survey
With eyes illumined by celestial day,   110
And, every cloud from my pure spirit driven,
Joy in the bright beatitude of heaven!

[1639]

ON THE DEATH OF DAMON

Milton's friendship with Diodati had undergone a long development since the time of their association at St. Paul's and had
entwined itself with his most intimate ideals and aspirations.
A prose letter written on the eve of his departure had hailed
his friend as an embodiment of the highest wisdom, the earthly
representative of the idea of the beautiful and good which was
the object of his search. His death must have been a great

90 ff. See "On the Death of Damon," 216 ff. and note.

blow, though Milton had by his idealization of the relationship, which had long since ceased to be a matter of frequent
personal contact or even communication, in a sense prepared
himself for it. In this poem, written probably in 1640 and
printed separately for private circulation, he combines his early
tenderness toward the beloved object with a half religious
devotion to the spiritual values which this object had come to
represent. Diodati is in the concluding passage Milton's *alter
ego*, the virgin soul rewarded by an immortal ecstasy for its
uncompromising loyalty to the ideal. The poem lacks the
variety, the philosophic breadth, the elevation, and the serenity
of "Lycidas," but surpasses it in intensity of personal emotion.
The use of Latin and the stricter adherence to the conventions
of the pastoral are significant. Milton wants the restraints
which an artificial medium imposes. If he is to lay bare his
soul, it will not be for the crude, untutored populace to gaze on.

Milton's references to the events and emotions of his Italian
journey are particularly interesting. In lines 129 ff. he well
describes the joyous sense of power which he felt in his association with the Florentine literati. His satisfaction in the
experience implied the anticipation of a proud rehearsal of it
to his friend. The key to their relationship is certainly Milton's
desire for approval. So long as Diodati was alive there was
reservation in the poet's attitude. Now that he is dead he can
express himself with freedom. The expansive and enthusiastic description of his literary plans is paralleled by a more hesi-
tating account in the prose letter of 1637.

ON THE DEATH OF DAMON

(*Translation*)

THE ARGUMENT

Thyrsis and Damon, shepherds and neighbours, had always
pursued the same studies, and had, from their earliest days, been
united in the closest friendship. Thyrsis, while travelling for improvement, received intelligence of the death of Damon, and,
after a time, returning and finding it true, deplores himself, and
his solitary condition, in this poem.

By Damon is to be understood Charles Diodati, connected with
the Italian city of Lucca by his father's side, in other respects an
Englishman; a youth of uncommon genius, erudition, and virtue.

Ye nymphs of Himera (for ye have shed
Erewhile for Daphnis, and for Hylas dead,
And over Bion's long-lamented bier,
The fruitless meed of many a sacred tear),
Now through the villas laved by Thames rehearse
The woes of Thyrsis in Sicilian verse,
What sighs he heaved, and how with groans profound
He made the woods and hollow rocks resound
Young Damon dead; nor even ceased to pour
His lonely sorrows at the midnight hour.   10
   The green wheat twice had nodded in the ear,
And golden harvest twice enriched the year,
Since Damon's lips had gasped for vital air
The last, last time, nor Thyrsis yet was there;
For he, enamoured of the Muse, remained
In Tuscan Fiorenza long detained,
But, stored at length with all he wished to learn,
For his flock's sake now hasted to return;
And when the shepherd had resumed his seat
At the elm's root, within his own retreat,   20
Then 'twas his lot, then, all his loss to know,
And, from his burthened heart, he vented thus his woe:
   "Go, seek your home, my lambs; my thoughts are due
"To other cares than those of feeding you.
"Alas! what deities shall I suppose
"In heaven, or earth, concerned for human woes,
"Since, O my Damon! their severe decree
"So soon condemns me to regret of thee!
"Departest thou thus, thy virtues unrepaid
"With fame and honour, like a vulgar shade?   30
"Let him forbid it whose bright rod controls
"And separates sordid from illustrious souls,
"Drive far the rabble, and to thee assign
"A happier lot, with spirits worthy thine!
   "Go, seek your home, my lambs; my thoughts are due
"To other cares than those of feeding you.

   1. **Himera,** a river in Sicily, referred to by Theocritus and therefore thought of as a source of inspiration for pastoral poetry. Daphnis is lamented in the first Idyl of Theocritus, Bion in the third of Moschus. These two poems were the basic models for pastoral elegy. Hylas was a youth seized by water nymphs.
   11–14. Milton says that two springs and two harvests had passed since Diodati's death in August, 1638 (buried Aug. 27). He must then have written the poem over a year after his return to England in late July or early August, 1639.
   23–24. This refrain is an echo of that used by Virgil in *Eclogue* 7.
   31. Mercury, who conducted souls to the other world with his wand.

"Whate'er befall, unless by cruel chance
"The wolf first give me a forbidding glance,
"Thou shalt not moulder undeplored, but long
"Thy praise shall dwell on every shepherd's tongue;   40
"To Daphnis first they shall delight to pay,
"And, after him, to thee, the votive lay,
"While Pales shall the flocks and pastures love,
"Or Faunus to frequent the field or grove,
"At least, if ancient piety and truth,
"With all the learned labours of thy youth,
"May serve thee aught, or to have left behind
"A sorrowing friend, and of the tuneful kind.
　　"Go, seek your home, my lambs; my thoughts are due
"To other cares than those of feeding you.   50
"Yes, Damon! such thy sure reward shall be;
"But ah, what doom awaits unhappy me?
"Who now my pains and perils shall divide,
"As thou wast wont, for ever at my side,
"Both when the rugged frost annoyed our feet,
"And when the herbage all was parched with heat;
"Whether the grim wolf's ravage to prevent,
"Or the huge lion's, armed with darts we went?
"Whose converse, now, shall calm my stormy day,
"With charming song who now beguile my way?   60
　　"Go, seek your home, my lambs; my thoughts are due
"To other cares than those of feeding you.
"In whom shall I confide? whose counsel find
"A balmy medicine for my troubled mind?
"Or whose discourse with innocent delight
"Shall fill me now, and cheat the wintry night,
"While hisses on my hearth the pulpy pear,
"And blackening chestnuts start and crackle there,
"While storms abroad the dreary meadows whelm,
"And the wind thunders through the neighbouring elm?   70
　　"Go, seek your home, my lambs; my thoughts are due
"To other cares than those of feeding you.
"Or who, when summer suns their summit reach,
"And Pan sleeps hidden by the sheltering beech,

　　38. Alluding to the superstition that to be seen first by a wolf robs a man of speech.
　　43-44. Pales and **Faunus** were deities of the fields and flocks.
　　55-58. These lines well illustrate the way Milton preserves pastoral decorum even in so personal a poem as this. Samuel Johnson objected to the description of the association of Milton and King in "Lycidas," saying that "they had no flocks to feed." Still less did he and Diodati have lions and wolves to hunt. But most of the detail applies either literally or with a minimum of alteration to real persons.

"When shepherds disappear, nymphs seek the sedge,
"And the stretched rustic snores beneath the hedge,
"Who then shall render me thy pleasant vein
"Of Attic wit, thy jests, thy smiles, again?
    "Go, seek your home, my lambs; my thoughts are due
"To other cares than those of feeding you.   80
"Where glens and vales are thickest overgrown
"With tangled boughs, I wander now alone,
"Till night descend, while blustering wind and shower
"Beat on my temples through the shattered bower.
    "Go, seek your home, my lambs; my thoughts are due
"To other cares than those of feeding you.
"Alas! what rampant weeds now shame my fields,
"And what a mildewed crop the furrow yields!
"My rambling vines, unwedded to the trees,
"Bear shrivelled grapes; my myrtles fail to please;   90
"Nor please me more my flocks; they, slighted, turn
"Their unavailing looks on me, and mourn.
    "Go, seek your home, my lambs; my thoughts are due
"To other cares than those of feeding you.
"Ægon invites me to the hazel grove,
"Amyntas, on the river's bank to rove,
"And young Alphesibœus to a seat
"Where branching elms exclude the mid-day heat.
" 'Here fountains spring,—here mossy hillocks rise;
" 'Here Zephyr whispers, and the stream replies.'   100
"Thus each persuades, but, deaf to every call,
"I gain the thickets, and escape them all.
    "Go, seek your home, my lambs; my thoughts are due
"To other cares than those of feeding you.
"Then Mopsus said, (the same who reads so well
"The voice of birds, and what the stars foretell,
"For he by chance had noticed my return,)
" 'What means thy sullen mood, this deep concern?
" 'Ah, Thyrsis! thou art either crazed with love,
" 'Or some sinister influence from above;   110
" 'Dull Saturn's influence oft the shepherds rue;
" 'His leaden shaft oblique has pierced thee through,'
    "Go, go, my lambs, unpastured as ye are,
"My thoughts are all now due to other care.

87–93. The images suggest in a general way Milton's neglect of his work, or specifically of poetry. Actually he composed little for many years.
    95 ff. Milton is likely to be thinking of real acquaintances in some of the profusion of pastoral names which follows. Why otherwise, for example, should he say that Chloris lives beside the mouth of the Blackwater (lines 127-8, below)? He is not unlikely to be literal in saying he avoided their invitations.

"The nymphs, amazed, my melancholy see,
"And 'Thyrsis!' cry, 'what will become of thee?
" 'What wouldst thou, Thyrsis? such should not appear
" 'The brow of youth, stern, gloomy, and severe;
" 'Brisk youth should laugh and love,—ah, shun the fate
" 'Of those twice wretched mopes who love too late!'   120
  "Go, go my lambs, unpastured as ye are;
"My thoughts are all now due to other care.
"Ægle with Hyas came, to soothe my pain,
"And Baucis' daughter, Dryope the vain,
"Fair Dryope, for voice and finger neat
"Known far and near, and for her self-conceit;
"Chloris too came, whose cottage on the lands
"That skirt the Idumanian current stands;
"But all in vain they came, and but to see
"Kind words, and comfortable, lost on me.   130
  "Go, go, my lambs, unpastured as ye are;
"My thoughts are all now due to other care.
"Ah, blest indifference of the playful herd,
"None by his fellow chosen, or preferred!
"No bonds of amity the flocks enthral,
"But each associates and is pleased with all;
"So graze the dappled deer in numerous droves,
"And all his kind alike the zebra loves;
"The same law governs where the billows roar,
"And Proteus' shoals o'erspread the desert shore;   140
"The sparrow, meanest of the feathered race,
"His fit companion finds in every place,
"With whom he picks the grain that suits him best,
"Flirts here and there, and late returns to rest,
"And whom, if chance the falcon make his prey,
"Or hedger with his well-aimed arrow slay,
"For no such loss the gay survivor grieves,
"New love he seeks, and new delight receives.
"We only, an obdurate kind, rejoice,
"Scorning all others, in a single choice.   150
"We scarce in thousands meet one kindred mind;
"And if the long-sought good at last we find,
"When least we fear it, Death our treasure steals,
"And gives our heart a wound that nothing heals.
  "Go, go, my lambs, unpastured as ye are;
"My thoughts are all now due to other care.
"Ah, what delusion lured me from my flocks,
"To traverse Alpine snows and rugged rocks!
"What need so great had I to visit Rome,
"Now sunk in ruins, and herself a tomb?   160

"Or, had she flourished still as when of old
"For her sake Tityrus forsook his fold,
"What need so great had I to incur a pause
"Of thy sweet intercourse for such a cause,
"For such a cause to place the roaring sea,
"Rocks, mountains, woods, between my friend and me?
"Else, had I grasped thy feeble hand, composed
"Thy decent limbs, thy drooping eyelids closed,
"And, at the last, had said—'Farewell,—ascend,—
" 'Nor even in the skies forget thy friend!'   170
    "Go, go, my lambs, untended homeward fare;
"My thoughts are all now due to other care.
"Although well pleased, ye tuneful Tuscan swains!
"My mind the memory of your worth retains,
"Yet not your worth can teach me less to mourn
"My Damon lost;—he too was Tuscan born,
"Born in your Lucca, city of renown!
"And wit possessed, and genius, like your own.
"Oh, how elate was I, when stretched beside
"The murmuring course of Arno's breezy tide,   180
"Beneath the poplar grove I passed my hours,
"Now cropping myrtles, and now vernal flowers,
"And hearing, as I lay at ease along,
"Your swains contending for the prize of song!
"I also dared attempt (and, as it seems,
"Not much displeased attempting) various themes,
"For even I can presents boast from you,
"The shepherd's pipe, and osier basket too;
"And Dati, and Francini, both have made
"My name familiar to the beechen shade,   190
"And they are learned, and each in every place
"Renowned for song, and both of Lydian race.
    "Go, go, my lambs, untended homeward fare;
"My thoughts are all now due to other care.
"While bright the dewy grass with moonbeams shone,
"And I stood hurdling in my kids alone,
"How often have I said (but thou hadst found
"Ere then thy dark cold lodgment under ground),
"Now Damon sings, or springes sets for hares,
"Or wickerwork for various use prepares!   200

162. **Tityrus**, Chaucer, so called by Spenser. Milton refers to his two
journeys to Italy.

177. Diodati's grandfather came from Lucca, near Florence.

185–92. Milton refers to his performances in the academy at Florence
and to the complimentary poems written to him by various Italians. See
introduction, p. 7.

"How oft, indulging fancy, have I planned
"New scenes of pleasure that I hoped at hand,
"Called thee abroad as I was wont, and cried,
" 'What, hoa! my friend,—come lay thy task aside,
" 'Haste, let us forth together, and beguile
" 'The heat beneath yon whispering shades awhile,
" 'Or on the margin stray of Colne's clear flood,
" 'Or where Cassibelan's grey turrets stood!
" 'There thou shalt cull me simples, and shalt teach
" 'Thy friend the name and healing powers of each,   210
" 'From the tall bluebell to the dwarfish weed,
" 'What the dry land and what the marshes breed,
" 'For all their kinds alike to thee are known,
" 'And the whole art of Galen is thy own.'
"Ah, perish Galen's art, and withered be
"The useless herbs that gave not health to thee!
"Twelve evenings since, as in poetic dream
"I meditating sat some statelier theme,
"The reeds no sooner touched my lip, though new
"And unessayed before, than wide they flew,   220
"Bursting their waxen bands, nor could sustain
"The deep-toned music of the solemn strain;
"And I am vain perhaps, but I will tell
"How proud a theme I chose,—ye groves, farewell!
    "Go, go, my lambs, untended homeward fare;
"My thoughts are all now due to other care.
"Of Brutus, Dardan chief, my song shall be,
"How with his barks he ploughed the British sea,
"First from Rutupia's towering headland seen,
"And of his consort's reign, fair Imogen;   230
"Of Brennus and Belinus, brothers bold,
"And of Arviragus, and how of old
"Our hardy sires the Armorican controlled,
"And of the wife of Gorloïs, who, surprised
"By Uther, in her husband's form disguised
"(Such was the force of Merlin's art), became
"Pregnant with Arthur of heroic fame.
"These themes I now revolve,—and oh, if Fate
"Proportion to these themes my lengthened date,

    207-8. The river Colne flows near Horton; Cassibelaunus was a British leader against Julius Cæsar, who held the country north of the Thames.
    216 ff. Milton had already announced his intention to write an epic on British history. (See *Mansus*, 88 ff.) He now speaks of having begun it. The scope was to have been much that of Geoffrey of Monmouth's chronicle, from Brutus to King Arthur and the Roman conquest. The bursting of his shepherd pipe symbolizes the inadequacy of his youthful style to this new theme.

"Adieu my shepherd's reed! yon pine-tree bough   240
"Shall be thy future home; there dangle thou
"Forgotten and disused, unless ere long
"Thou change thy Latian for a British song;
"A British?—even so,—the powers of man
"Are bounded; little is the most he can:
"And it shall well suffice me, and shall be
"Fame, and proud recompense enough for me,
"If Usa, golden-haired, my verse may learn.
"If Alain bending o'er his crystal urn,
"Swift-whirling Abra, Trent's o'ershadowed stream,   250
"Thames, lovelier far than all in my esteem,
"Tamar's ore-tinctured flood, and, after these,
"The wave-worn shores of utmost Orcades.
    "Go, go, my lambs, untended homeward fare;
"My thoughts are all now due to other care.
"All this I kept in leaves of laurel-rind
"Enfolded safe, and for thy view designed
"This, and a gift from Manso's hand beside
"(Manso, not least his native city's pride),
"Two cups that radiant as their giver shone,   260
"Adorned by sculpture with a double zone.
"The spring was graven there; here slowly wind
"The Red-sea shores, with groves of spices lined;
"Her plumes of various hues amid the boughs
"The sacred, solitary Phœnix shows,
"And, watchful of the dawn, reverts her head
"To see Aurora leave her watery bed.—
"In other part, the expansive vault above,
"And there too, even there, the god of love;
"With quiver armed he mounts, his torch displays   270
"A vivid light, his gem-tipt arrows blaze,
"Around his bright and fiery eyes he rolls,
"Nor aims at vulgar minds or little souls,
"Nor deigns one look below, but aiming high
"Sends every arrow to the lofty sky;

    240–43. Milton says he will give up pastoral poetry, unless he writes
something in English. He cannot be a poet in both languages and will be
contented with an English audience.
    248–51. The English rivers mentioned are the Ouse, the Alne, the
Tamar, and the Humber.
    260 ff. Two cups, etc. Milton probably means that Manso gave him
books. He had published poems, including a translation of Lactantius on
the Phœnix, and a dialogue of Platonic love. These may have suggested
the two designs Milton describes. The symbolism of the celestial Cupid is
that of the close of Comus. The idea of virginity is still important to
Milton. Here and in the "unexpressive nuptial song" of "Lycidas" he has
in mind Rev. 14:1–3.

"Hence forms divine, and minds immortal, learn
"The power of Cupid, and enamoured burn.
  "Thou, also, Damon (neither need I fear
"That hope delusive), thou art also there;
"For whither should simplicity like thine   280
"Retire? where else such spotless virtue shine?
"Thou dwellest not (thought profane) in shades below,
"Nor tears suit thee;—cease then my tears to flow!
"Away with grief, on Damon ill bestowed!
"Who, pure himself, has found a pure abode,
"Has passed the showery arch, henceforth resides
"With saints and heroes, and from flowing tides
"Quaffs copious immortality and joy,
"With hallowed lips!—Oh! blest without alloy,
"And now enriched with all that faith can claim,   290
"Look down, entreated by whatever name,
"If Damon please thee most (that rural sound
"Shall oft with echoes fill the groves around)
"Or if Deodatus, by which alone
"In those ethereal mansions thou art known.
"Thy blush was maiden, and thy youth the taste
"Of wedded bliss knew never, pure and chaste:
"The honours, therefore, by divine decree
"The lot of virgin worth, are given to thee;
"Thy brows encircled with a radiant band,   300
"And the green palm-branch waving in thy hand,
"Thou in immortal nuptials shalt rejoice,
"And join with seraphs thy according voice.
"Where rapture reigns, and the ecstatic lyre
"Guides the blest orgies of the blazing quire."

THE POEMS OF THE SECOND PERIOD
1642–1658

INTRODUCTION TO
POEMS OF THE SECOND PERIOD
1642–1658

Milton's concern with poetry during the period of his devotion to public life was far less than he had hoped or intended that it should be. It is nevertheless evident that he continued to cherish his youthful talent, looking forward to an ultimate release of his creative energies for this more congenial task. Some critics believe that Milton was actually at work on the major poems during this epoch. It seems more likely that, having written the first lines of the projected drama on the Fall of Man, as his nephew Phillips says he did about 1642, he gave over further work on this large project until his duties as a publicist were largely at an end. In the meanwhile he occupied himself with poetry in a minor way, returning to it again and again as mood and occasion dictated. The record of his activity is almost a continuous one. There is, as we shall see, one sonnet in 1642 and two more by 1645. In that year, Milton published the first collected volume of his verse, *Poems of Mr. John Milton, both English and Latin, Composed at Several Times,* the three new sonnets being added to the seven previously written. The appearance of this volume perhaps quickened his interest, and in the three years following it he wrote six more sonnets, verse translations of nine psalms, and a Latin ode to the librarian of Oxford University accompanying a presentation copy of the 1645 Poems.

At this point, there is a gap, but in 1652, when he had become blind, Milton again turned to poetry, writing two memorable sonnets. A year later, he did eight more psalms on almost successive days in August, again, in 1655, four sonnets, and finally, not long after his second wife's death in February, 1658, the last great composition of this kind, commemorating her. Except for a few translated verses in the prose works this, so far as we know, is all. There is evidence that Milton intended a new edition of the Poems before this later sonnet series was quite complete. Why he gave it up at this time we do not know. The fact suggests that, amid whatever dramatic incidents of his public and his private life, he was still deeply interested in this phase of his career, and it prepares us to see him taking up work on the epic, even before the Restoration sent him into retirement, deprived of expectation regarding the future of the cause for which he had mainly toiled.

Setting aside the psalm translations of 1648 and 1653 and the "Ode to Rous," the interest of this body of poems, both artistic and biographical, far outweighs its volume or its pretensions. In the sonnet on his twenty-fourth birthday, Milton had already deserted the love theme of the Petrarchan tradition in favor of a "soul animating strain" derived from his ethical and religious experience. He had some precedent for this in both Italian and English literature. A whole section of the sonnets of one of his admired authors, Giovanni della Casa, was entitled "heroic sonnets," and we recall such poems as Raleigh's tribute to the author of the *Faerie Queene,* and Sidney's last sonnet in *Astrophel and Stella,* "Leave me, O love that reachest but to dust," and many others in which the form is made to do service for a variety of subject matter. But Milton's sonnets are highly individual. They range from graceful, yet serious, expressions of friendship to profound soul-searching, prophetic warning, and thunderous denunciation. "In his hands the thing became a trumpet." The language is often remarkably plain, but there is an energy of meaning, especially in the later sonnets, unparalleled in Milton's style till now. Particularly noteworthy is the use of simile and literary allusion. The sonnet to Lawes, for example, is glorified by a concluding reference to a memorable episode in Dante; the return of his deceased wife in vision is given high significance by being likened to that of Alcestis in Euripidean drama. The sonnets, in general, represent a spontaneous overflow of the emotions aroused by occasional experience, whether of common or of extraordinary sort. They are direct biographical records, sublimated to be sure, but deriving their power from an intense and sensitive nature, capable of the most delicate as well as the most passionate responses. There is no stranger judgment in literature than that of Samuel Johnson on the sonnets: "of the best it can only be said that they are not bad." Whatever, in the cold light of reason, we may think of Milton's politics or personality we cannot fail to accept the self-portraiture of these poems at its face value.

They commend Milton to us in his maturity, both as an individual and as a representative of his age, and they direct our expectation to corresponding qualities in the artistic masterpieces which he is about to write.

SONNETS

SONNET VIII

Milton entitled this sonnet in the Cambridge Manuscript as follows: "When the assault was intended to the City." A cancelled heading reads "On his dore when the City expected an assault." The occasion was the advance of the Royalist cavalry toward London in November, 1642, after the battle of Edgehill. Milton did not, of course, intend to pin the poem on his door to save his house from sack, but he enjoys thinking of himself as entitled to such consideration as was accorded Pindar on a similar occasion. That he should have allowed himself such a mood is no reflection on his courage in the crisis. We must remember that the issue between King and Parliament was not yet drawn in such a way for him as to inflame his intenser partisanship. Within a year he was to marry the daughter of a Cavalier.

SONNET VIII

Captain or Colonel, or Knight in arms,
    Whose chance on these defenceless doors may seize,
    If deed of honor did thee ever please,
    Guard them, and him within protect from harms;
He can requite thee, for he knows the charms
    That call fame on such gentle acts as these,
    And he can spread thy name o'er lands and seas,
    Whatever clime the sun's bright circle warms.
Lift not thy spear against the Muses' bower:
    The great Emathian conqueror bid spare   10
    The house of Pindarus, when temple and tower

1. **Colonel.** The older English pronunciation of this word was kur-o-nel.

9. It is poetry that Milton is pleading for. If it seems odd that such practical uses are suggested we may consider Sidney's wish at the end of the *Defense* that the despiser of poetry may "live in love and never get favor for lack of skill in a sonnet" and when he dies have his memory die from the earth for want of an epitaph.

10. **Emathian,** Macedonian. Alexander was said to have spared only the house of the poet Pindar when he destroyed Thebes in 335 B.C.

Went to the ground; and the repeated air
Of sad Electra's poet had the power
To save the Athenian walls from ruin bare.

[1642]

SONNET IX

This poem follows the preceding one in the Manuscript and is therefore to be dated between 1642 and 1645, when it appeared among his collected poems. Milton's sympathy has been drawn to some young girl who has been reproved. He speaks as an understanding elder friend, "deep-principled in virtue's book."

SONNET IX

Lady that in the prime of earliest youth,
    Wisely hast shunned the broad way and the green,
    And with those few art eminently seen
    That labor up the hill of heavenly Truth,
The better part with Mary and with Ruth
    Chosen thou hast; and they that overween,
    And at thy growing virtues fret their spleen,
    No anger find in thee, but pity and ruth.
Thy care is fixed and zealously attends
    To fill thy odorous lamp with deeds of light,   10
    And Hope that reaps not shame. Therefore be sure
Thou, when the Bridegroom with his feastful friends
    Passes to bliss at the mid-hour of night,
    Hast gained thy entrance, Virgin wise and pure.

[1642–1645]

SONNET X

This sonnet also belongs to the period 1642–45. The person addressed, as we learn from the manuscript heading, is Lady Margaret Ley, whose father James Ley, Earl of Marlborough,

13. After the capture of Athens in 404 B.C. one of the Spartans induced the others not to destroy the city by singing the first chorus of Euripides' *Electra*.
5. **The better part** is humility and gentleness, in contrast to the overweeningness of others, as well as devotion to the contemplative rather than the active life. See Luke 10:42 and Ruth 1:14.
9–14. The lady is like one of the wise virgins in the parable, Matt. 25:1–13.
11. **be sure,** be assured.

had presided over the House of Lords as Lord Chief Justice
and had died in 1629, shortly after the dissolution of Charles's
third Parliament. Milton's biographer, Edward Phillips, thus
commemorates the friendship between the poet and Lady
Margaret: "This lady, being a woman of great wit and ingenuity, had a particular honor for him, and took much delight in
his company, as likewise Captain Hobson, her husband, a very
accomplished gentleman." The combination of warmth and
respect with which Milton greets her is in striking contrast to
the usual sonneteering vein.

SONNET X

Daughter to that good Earl, once President
    Of England's Council and her Treasury,
    Who lived in both unstained with gold or fee,
    And left them both, more in himself content,
Till the sad breaking of that Parliament
    Broke him, as that dishonest victory
    At Chæronea, fatal to liberty,
    Killed with report that old man eloquent;
Though later born than to have known the days
    Wherein your father flourished, yet by you,   10
    Madam, methinks I see him living yet:
So well your words his noble virtues praise
    That all both judge you to relate them true
    And to possess them, honored Margaret.
                   [1642–1645]

SONNET XI

TO MR. H. LAWES ON HIS AIRS

Milton dates this sonnet February 9, 1645/6. It was first
published among other poetic tributes prefixed to Lawes's
Choice Psalms in 1648. Milton's devotion to the musician had
evidently survived their adherence to opposite sides in the
Rebellion, for Lawes, who had been a member of the King's

5. Charles I's third parliament dissolved in 1629.
6. **dishonest,** shameful because it ended the independence of the
Grecian cities.
8. **old man eloquent,** Isocrates, said to have starved himself after the
victory of Philip of Macedon whose aggressions he had roused Greece to
resist.

music and had traveled with Charles I to Scotland in 1633, had become an avowed Royalist. The specific compliment which Milton here pays him was a standard one. It is echoed by other poets, and Lawes himself has much to say in his preface of the stupid composers and singers who cared only for the music and rode roughshod over the words. In order to show them up he had used as the text for one of his own madrigals a series of titles drawn from the index to an Italian music book and pointed with amusement to the fact that many had accepted and sung it as a serious composition, without observing that the words were meaningless. It was hardly true to say that Lawes was the first musician to honor the poet's function, for the Elizabethan composers were skilled adapters of words to music.

SONNET XI

Harry whose tuneful and well-measured song
    First taught our English music how to span
    Words with just note and accent, not to scan
    With Midas' ears, committing short and long,
Thy worth and skill exempts thee from the throng,
    With praise enough for Envy to look wan;
    To after age thou shalt be writ the man
    That with smooth air couldst humor best our tongue.
Thou honor'st verse, and verse must lend her wing
    To honor thee, the priest of Phœbus' choir,   10
    That tun'st their happiest lines in hymn or story.
Dante shall give Fame leave to set thee higher
    Than his Casella, whom he wooed to sing,
    Met in the milder shades of Purgatory.
                                        [February 9, 1646]

2. **span,** measure.
4. Midas showed the badness of his ear in preferring the music of Pan to that of Apollo. Presumably his ears were no more discriminating after their transformation. **committing,** uniting, i.e., setting a short syllable to a long note.
11. **story.** A marginal note refers this to Lawes's setting of Cartwright's *Ariadne.*
13–14. Dante met his friend Casella at the beginning of his ascent of Purgatory, *Purgatorio* II, 76–117. He sings one of Dante's own canzone so sweetly that the spirits round about pause in their great business of purifying themselves for Heaven as if spellbound. Thus does the poet establish the musician's fame.
14. **milder shades,** milder than the other parts of Purgatory. Milton originally wrote "mildest."

SONNET XII

This sonnet is sometimes dated as early as 1644, but it follows the Lawes sonnet in the Cambridge Manuscript and was probably composed shortly after it, i.e., in 1646. It expresses Milton's deepening resentment as he realizes the character of the Presbyterian tyranny. As usual, his passionate convictions are the result of his inability to win acceptance for his own ideas among those who were in control of public policy. His first divorce tract had been preached against before Parliament by Herbert Palmer, and Milton turns against the regime which had earlier seemed to promise so much for freedom, becoming, first, an independent in his political sympathies and, later, a complete individualist.

SONNET XII

I did but prompt the age to quit their clogs
    By the known rules of ancient liberty,
    When straight a barbarous noise environs me
    Of owls and cuckoos, asses, apes, and dogs;
As when those hinds that were transformed to frogs
    Railed at Latona's twin-born progeny
    Which after held the sun and moon in fee.
    But this is got by casting pearl to hogs,
That bawl for freedom in their senseless mood,
    And still revolt when Truth would set them free.   10
    Licence they mean when they cry Liberty;
For who loves that, must first be wise and good:
    But from that mark how far they rove we see,
    For all this waste of wealth and loss of blood.
                             [1646?]

On the New Forcers of Conscience Under the Long Parliament

The note of indignant denunciation of those who would restrict true liberty is struck again in this poem, written on the occasion of the controversy between the Presbyterians and the Independents concerning toleration. The Westminster Assem-

2. **ancient liberty,** i.e., the liberty which Milton believed Scripture accorded in the matter of divorce.

5. **those hinds,** the Lycian peasants who refused a drink from their lake to Latona, bearing in her arms the infants Apollo and Diana.

by and its supporters, including Adam Stuart ("mere A. S."),
Samuel Rutherford, Thomas Edwards, and the Scot, Robert
Baillie ("Scotch what d'ye call"), were undertaking to enforce
conformity to the Presbyterian form of worship. Certain Independent ministers were crying for toleration. Milton had
already enrolled himself among the latter in *Areopagitica,* and
he here contributes to their cause a concentrated invective
against the party which had overthrown the ecclesiastical
tyranny only to establish an equally obnoxious one of their
own. The poem belongs to the form entitled *sonetto caudato*
or sonnet with a coda or tail. The tail in such a sonnet consisted of a half line and a couplet in addition to the regular
fourteen lines in sonnet form and might be repeated, as here.
"On the New Forcers of Conscience" lacks the elevation of
Milton's greater outbursts of righteous wrath, as for example
the passage on the clergy in "Lycidas" or the sonnet on the
Piedmont Massacre. His anger is too personal to call forth
that quality of emotion which elsewhere makes him, like the
Hebrew prophets and like Dante, the spokesman of God's
indignation against those who injure or oppress his people.

ON THE NEW FORCERS OF CONSCIENCE
UNDER THE LONG PARLIAMENT

Because you have thrown off your Prelate Lord,
    And with stiff vows renounced his Liturgy
    To seize the widowed whore Plurality
    From them whose sin ye envied, not abhorred;
Dare ye for this adjure the civil sword
    To force our consciences that Christ set free,
    And ride us with a classic hierarchy,
    Taught ye by mere A. S. and Rutherford?
Men whose life, learning, faith, and pure intent
    Would have been held in high esteem with Paul,   10
    Must now be named and printed heretics

    3. **Plurality,** pluralism, the practice of holding more than one church
benefice. Plurality has passed through many hands in the history of the
Christian church.
    7. **classic hierarchy.** A "classis" is a Presbytery. Milton is advocating
congregational autonomy and protesting against this governing body as the
equivalent of the old hierarchy.
    8. The individuals mentioned or alluded to in this poem were pamphlet
writers on the Presbyterian side.

By shallow Edwards and Scotch What-d'ye-call!
   But we do hope to find out all your tricks,
   Your plots and packings, worse than those of Trent,
      That so the Parliament
May with their wholesome and preventive shears
Clip your phylacteries, though baulk your ears,
      And succor our just fears,
When they shall read this clearly in your charge:
New Presbyter is but old Priest writ large.

                                   [1646?]

Sonnet XIII

This sonnet is headed in the Cambridge Manuscript as follows: "On the religious memory of Mrs. Catharine Thomason, my Christian friend, deceased, December 16, 1646." The lady thus commemorated was the wife of George Thomason, the bookseller, whose name has come down to posterity as the collector of an immense body of pamphlets written during the civil war. The Thomason Tracts, now in the British Museum, contain several of Milton's treatises, bearing on the title page the words, *Ex Dono Authoris*. We have no other evidence of Milton's intimacy with the family.

SONNET XIII

When Faith and Love which parted from thee never,
   Had ripened thy just soul to dwell with God,
   Meekly thou didst resign this earthy load
Of death, called life, which us from life doth sever.
Thy works and alms and all thy good endeavor
   Stayed not behind, nor in the grave were trod;
   But as Faith pointed with her golden rod,
   Followed thee up to joy and bliss for ever.

14. **Trent**, the council called by the Pope to combat the Reformation.
17. **Phylacteries**, boxes containing Scriptural passages worn by pious Jews. See Matt. 23:5. **baulk**, leave, skip. Milton first wrote "clip ye as close as marginal P—'s ears," referring to the Presbyterian pamphleteer William Prynne whose ears were cut off for attacking the bishops in 1633. Milton hated his later activities, including the "marginal stuffings" of his works.
20. **Priest** derives from Greek *presbyter* by way of the Anglo-Saxon *preost*. Elsewhere Milton says that priest and presbyter are the same name and thing.

Love led them on, and Faith who knew them best
    Thy handmaids, clad them o'er with purple beams   10
    And azure wings, that up they flew so drest,
And spake the truth of thee in glorious themes
    Before the Judge, who thenceforth bid thee rest
    And drink thy fill of pure immortal streams.

                           [1646]

Sonnet XIV

This sonnet belongs in subject matter and tone with "I did but prompt the age" and "On the New Forcers of Conscience." Its position in the Cambridge Manuscript seems to indicate that it was written later, perhaps in 1647 or 1648, though Milton makes it precede the other divorce sonnet in the 1673 edition. The poet can now look back on the public reception of his divorce tracts with an attitude of philosophic cynicism. Nothing more is to be expected from an ignorant and misguided generation which cannot even interpret his Greek title. His hatred of the Presbyterian Scots who are meddling in English affairs extends even to their uneuphonious names. Disgust with the present drives him back in mind to the early age of humanism in England, when honest classical learning and liberalism of thought went hand in hand.

SONNET XIV

A book was writ of late called *Tetrachordon*,
    And woven close, both matter, form, and style;
    The subject new: it walked the town a while,
    Numbering good intellects; now seldom pored on.
Cries the stall-reader, "Bless us! what a word on
    A title-page is this!"; and some in file
    Stand spelling false, while one might walk to Mile-
End Green. Why, is it harder sirs than *Gordon*,

    1. **Tetrachordon,** Milton's third divorce tract. A tetrachord is a series of four notes in a diatonic scale, used by Milton of the four chief passages in Scripture dealing with divorce.
    7. **spelling false,** interpreting wrongly.
    8–9. **Colkitto** is a real Scottish name, **Galasp** a happy Miltonic coinage. Why Gordon and Macdonnel should be jaw-breakers is hard to say. They are Scottish and presumably Presbyterian, which is enough. Milton is making a highly entertaining display of the pedagogue temperament in a state of heat. Matthew Arnold is similarly distressed by **Wragg and** Higgenbottom. There were no Wraggs by the Ilyssus.

Colkitto, or *Macdonnel,* or *Galasp?*
 Those rugged names to our like mouths grow sleek 10
 That would have made Quintilian stare and gasp.
Thy age, like ours, O soul of Sir John Cheek,
 Hated not learning worse than toad or asp,
 When thou taught'st Cambridge and King Edward Greek.

          [1647?]

SONNET XV

TO THE LORD GENERAL FAIRFAX, AT THE SIEGE OF COLCHESTER

This sonnet, with those on Cromwell and Vane, and the second sonnet on his blindness, were omitted from the edition of 1673 for political reasons. It was written in August, 1648. Milton is not merely expressing his admiration for a military victor but endeavoring to guide him toward the constructive tasks of peace. His heart is in the great struggle, and he thinks of himself as playing the role of inspirer and adviser to leaders for whom the true issues are likely to be obscured by the heat of action. Earnest convictions animate these political sonnets. They are no mere poetical exercises.

TO THE LORD GENERAL FAIRFAX,
AT THE SIEGE OF COLCHESTER

Fairfax, whose name in arms through Europe rings,
 Filling each mouth with envy or with praise,
 And all her jealous monarchs with amaze,
 And rumors loud that daunt remotest kings,
Thy firm unshaken virtue ever brings
 Victory home, though new rebellions raise
 Their Hydra heads, and the false North displays
 Her broken league to imp their serpent wings.
O yet a nobler task awaits thy hand,
 For what can war but endless war still breed, 10
 Till truth and right from violence be freed,

 12. Thy age did not, as ours does, hate, etc. Milton is right in thinking that reverence for the new learning was high in court circles in those early days. It had suffered the fate of comparative democratization in his own.
 7. false North, Scotland, where royalist risings had broken out, in spite of the Solemn League and Covenant.
 8. imp, to insert new feathers in a falcon's wing. The Hydra whose many heads grew again as fast as they were cut off is thought of as a dragon.

And public faith cleared from the shameful brand
Of public fraud. In vain doth Valor bleed
While Avarice and Rapine share the land.

[1648]

Sonnet XVI

When Milton wrote this poem in 1652, he had been for three years employed as Latin Secretary to the Commonwealth and must have felt himself a partner in the enterprises of state. His admiration of Cromwell was tempered by fear lest he should not employ his power to carry out the Miltonic policy of toleration. The "proposals" were for the regulation of religious teaching outside the ranks of the clergy. The particular clause which offended Milton was probably that which required certification of public speakers by two or more godly and orthodox ministers. Cromwell had thus far opposed measures of this kind, and Milton was to continue to support him to the end, but the great tribute which he pays him in the *Second Defense* in 1654 contains an earnest warning not to disappoint the hopes of those who are devoted to the cause of true liberty.

SONNET XVI

TO THE LORD GENERAL CROMWELL
ON THE PROPOSALS OF CERTAIN MINISTERS AT THE
COMMITTEE FOR PROPAGATION OF THE GOSPEL

Cromwell, our chief of men, who through a cloud
    Not of war only, but detractions rude,
    Guided by faith and matchless fortitude,
    To peace and truth thy glorious way hast ploughed,
And on the neck of crownèd Fortune proud
    Hast reared God's trophies and his work pursued,
    While Darwen stream with blood of Scots imbrued,
    And Dunbar field resounds thy praises loud,
And Worcester's laureate wreath; yet much remains
    To conquer still; Peace hath her victories   10
    No less renowned than War, new foes arise

7. **Darwen stream,** scene of Cromwell's decisive victory over the Scots at Preston, August 17, 1648. Dunbar and Worcester were later battles in the second civil war.

Threatening to bind our souls with secular chains.
Help us to save free conscience from the paw
Of hireling wolves whose Gospel is their maw.
[May, 1652]

SONNET XVII

Milton sent a copy of this sonnet to Sir Henry, July 3, 1652. The date is significant as marking the moment of the beginning of the war with Holland. Negotiations with the Dutch ambassadors, in which Vane had taken part, were terminated on June 30. Milton recognizes in Vane, more certainly than in Cromwell, a statesman according to his own ideas. He praises rather than counsels him, and justly, for Vane was an uncompromising defender of toleration and of the separation of church and state.

SONNET XVII

TO SIR HENRY VANE THE YOUNGER

Vane, young in years, but in sage counsel old,
    Than whom a better senator ne'er held
    The helm of Rome, when gowns not arms repelled
    The fierce Epirot and the African bold;
Whether to settle peace, or to unfold
    The drift of hollow states hard to be spelled;
    Then to advise how war may best, upheld,
    Move by her two main nerves, iron and gold,
In all her equipage; besides to know
    Both spiritual power and civil, what each means,   10
    What severs each, thou hast learned, which few have done.
The bounds of either sword to thee we owe.
    Therefore on thy firm hand Religion leans
    In peace, and reckons thee her eldest son.
[July, 1652]

    1. **young in years.** Vane was thirty-six. He had been a member of the Council of State since 1649.
    4. Pyrrhus, King of Epirus, and Hannibal.
    6. **hollow,** deceitful, with a pun on Holland. Vane had been dealing with the Dutch ambassadors in London who had remained talking peace when hostilities had already begun.
    13. **either sword,** spiritual and civil authority.

Sonnet XVIII

Milton must have penned this outburst while England was in the heat of its indignation at the brutal event which it celebrates. The Duke of Savoy's soldiers had attacked the Protestant sect of the Waldensians in April, 1655. Cromwell was roused and Milton drafted in his name a series of eloquent protests to Louis XIV, dated May 25. The poet's emotion was deep, and, for once, impersonal. None of his sonnets rises to a nobler height. It voices the passionate conviction of a nation.

SONNET XVIII

ON THE LATE MASSACRE IN PIEMONT

Avenge O Lord thy slaughtered saints, whose bones
   Lie scattered on the Alpine mountains cold,
   Even them who kept thy truth so pure of old
   When all our fathers worshipped stocks and stones,
Forget not; in thy book record their groans
   Who were thy sheep, and in their ancient fold
   Slain by the bloody Piemontese, that rolled
   Mother with infant down the rocks. Their moans
The vales redoubled to the hills, and they
   To heaven. Their martyred blood and ashes sow   10
   O'er all the Italian fields, where still doth sway
The triple Tyrant; that from these may grow
   A hundredfold, who having learnt thy way,
   Early may fly the Babylonian woe.

                                   [1655]

Sonnet XIX

Because of the tone of this sonnet in contrast to Sonnet XXII, also because the expression "Ere half my days," fits better with an earlier date, recent editors have inclined to think it written soon after Milton's blindness became complete, i.e., in 1652. I now believe this to be unjustifiable in view of its position in

---

3. **The Waldenses,** a sect founded in the twelfth century and excommunicated in the thirteenth, were looked on as the earliest Protestants.

12. **triple Tyrant,** the Pope, wearer of the tiara or triple crown.

14. **Babylonian woe,** the destruction announced in the Apocalypse. Following Protestant tradition Milton identified Babylon with Rome.

the 1673 Poems following Sonnet XVIII, on the Piedmont
massacre. The two blindness sonnets represent complementary
attitudes: the one, religious resignation, the other, pride and
firm resolve. It is worth while to compare this expression with
the sonnet "On His being Arrived to the Age of Twenty-
three," where blindness is not a complicating factor, and with
the great personal utterances in the *Second Defense* and
Paradise Lost (III, 1 ff. and IX, 1 ff.).

SONNET XIX

When I consider how my light is spent,
    Ere half my days, in this dark world and wide,
    And that one talent which is death to hide
    Lodged with me useless, though my soul more bent
To serve therewith my Maker, and present
    My true account, lest He returning chide,
    "Doth God exact day-labor, light denied,"
    I fondly ask. But Patience to prevent
That murmur, soon replies, "God doth not need
    Either man's works or his own gifts. Who best   10
    Bear his mild yoke, they serve him best. His state
Is kingly: thousands at his bidding speed
    And post o'er land and ocean without rest;
    They also serve who only stand and wait."
                          [1652?]

SONNET XX

Edward Lawrence, eldest son of Henry Lawrence, who had
been Lord President of the Council under the Commonwealth,
is mentioned among Milton's intimates by Phillips. He was
one of those younger men whom the poet cherished and loved
to instruct, especially after his blindness. The youthful promise of Lawrence is spoken of by his contemporaries in terms
which show that he well deserved the loving attention and
concern with which he is here greeted. It is interesting to find
the strenuous poet, who had taken hard labor to be his portion
in this life, advising relaxation. We may note, however, that

---

    1. though clear, Milton's blindness was diagnosed in his time as
amaurosis, an affection of the optic nerve which left the eye unchanged in
outward appearance.
    3. talent. The word is used in the double sense of gift and talent, a
sum of money, with allusion to the parable, Matt. 25:14-30.

the self-indulgence which he recommends is temperate and refined. Only the man of discriminating taste is entitled to "waste a sullen day" with wine and song.

SONNET XX

Lawrence of virtuous father virtuous son,
 Now that the fields are dank and ways are mire,
 Where shall we sometimes meet, and by the fire
 Help waste a sullen day, what may be won
From the hard season gaining? Time will run
 On smoother, till Favonius reinspire
 The frozen earth, and clothe in fresh attire
 The lily and rose, that neither sowed nor spun.
What neat repast shall feast us, light and choice,
 Of Attic taste, with wine, whence we may rise 10
 To hear the lute well touched, or artful voice
Warble immortal notes and Tuscan air?
 He who of those delights can judge, and spare
 To interpose them oft, is not unwise.

         [1655]

SONNET XXI

Cyriack Skinner was perhaps the most intimate friend of Milton's maturity. Little is known about him, save that his grandfather was the famous jurist, Sir Edward Coke, that he was nineteen years younger than Milton and had been his pupil, and that he practiced law and was deeply interested in political speculation. Again the poet counsels a less earnest preoccupation with serious things and invites his protégé to indulge in an hour of harmless mirth.

SONNET XXI

Cyriack, whose grandsire on the royal bench
 Of British Themis, with no mean applause
 Pronounced and in his volumes taught our laws,
 Which others at their bar so often wrench;

8. Matt. 6:28.

13. spare, forbear. The other meaning—spare time—is hardly defensible, though "oft" is not necessarily too often, and the subject of the poem is indulgence with discrimination, rather than self-restraint. In any case Milton is leaning on the Greek motto "nothing too much." Compare the doctrine of the next sonnet.

To-day deep thoughts resolve with me to drench
  In mirth that after no repenting draws;
  Let Euclid rest and Archimedes pause,
  And what the Swede intend, and what the French.
To measure life learn thou betimes, and know
  Toward solid good what leads the nearest way;   10
  For other things mild Heaven a time ordains,
And disapproves that care, though wise in show,
  That with superfluous burden loads the day,
  And when God sends a cheerful hour, refrains.

                                        [1655]

SONNET XXII

The third anniversary of Milton's blindness fell in the year
1655. His tone in speaking of it is in interesting contrast to
that of the other sonnet on the subject. While recognizing
the immense deprivation of the loss of sight he no longer feels
frustrated in his life purposes, and he can recall with pride the
cause to which he made the sacrifice. "My noble task" is, of
course, the *Defense of the English People,* the merits and
effects of which Milton was bound for his pride's sake to
magnify.

SONNET XXII

Cyriack, this three years' day these eyes, though clear
  To outward view, of blemish or of spot,
  Bereft of light their seeing have forgot;
  Nor to their idle orbs doth sight appear
Of sun or moon or star throughout the year,
  Or man or woman. Yet I argue not
  Against Heaven's hand or will, nor bate a jot
  Of heart or hope, but still bear up and steer
Right onward. What supports me dost thou ask?
  The conscience, friend, to have lost them overplied   10
  In Liberty's defence, my noble task,
Of which all Europe talks from side to side.
  This thought might lead me through the world's vain mask
  Content though blind, had I no better guide.

                                        [1655]

3. **his volumes.** The most famous is *The First Part of the Institutes of
the Laws of England,* called "Coke upon Littleton," and still in use.
  10. **conscience,** consciousness.
  14. The inner light, coming from God, is a better guide than any
merely human sense of rectitude.

Sonnet XXIII

Milton's second wife, Katharine Woodcock, died in February, 1658, after giving birth to a son three months before. The child survived her but a few weeks. The two years of their life together had been a period of new energy and hopefulness for Milton, and its termination left memories poignant but not unhappy. The bitter cynicism which had been generated by his long quarrel with Mary Powell was not dead, and it receives expression in his later work, but for the time being Milton evidently knew the joy of love satisfied.

SONNET XXIII

Methought I saw my late espousèd saint
    Brought to me like Alcestis from the grave,
    Whom Jove's great son to her glad husband gave,
    Rescued from death by force, though pale and faint.
Mine, as whom washed from spot of child-bed taint,
    Purification in the Old Law did save,
    And such as yet once more I trust to have
    Full sight of her in Heaven without restraint,
Came vested all in white, pure as her mind.
    Her face was veiled, yet to my fancied sight   10
    Love, sweetness, goodness, in her person shined
So clear as in no face with more delight.
    But oh as to embrace me she inclined,
    I waked, she fled, and day brought back my night.

                      [1658]

2. **Alcestis,** who had offered herself as a victim of Death in place of her husband, was brought back from the other world by Hercules. In the *Alcestis* of Euripides she is unrecognized by her husband until her veil is lifted. Milton wakes before the face is revealed to him, a consummation which must wait till he sees her once more in Heaven, where there will be no restraint of mortal sense.

6. Lev. 12. After a certain period following childbirth the woman brings an offering to the temple and the priest "shall make atonement for her and she shall be clean." This is the origin of the Churching of Women, now a ceremonial merely of blessing and thanksgiving. Milton here recalls its basic symbolism as a type of atonement for sin through the sacrifice of Christ. It is to be noted that this ritual was discarded by most of the reformed churches. It had been in the English Prayer Book but was not in the Commonwealth *Directory of Worship.* Milton is the last person in the world to have been concerned whether his wife had or had not fulfilled the days of her purgation. She came back to him a saved soul, a saint, having perhaps herself given life for life.

PARADISE LOST

A Poem
in Twelve Books

INTRODUCTION TO *PARADISE LOST*

COMPOSITION AND SOURCES

*P*aradise Lost is the fulfilment of Milton's ambition, nour-
ished from boyhood, to leave something so written to after-
times that they would not willingly let it die. We have already
noted some of the tentative steps in the development of his
plan. The "Vacation Exercise" (1628) indicated vaguely that
his leaning was toward some cosmic subject. Elegy VI (1629)
declares for the epic form. In *Mansus* (1639) and the *Epitaphium Damonis* (1640) he specifies the wars of Arthur as his
already chosen material, but in the *Reason of Church Government* (1641) he appears to be in doubt both as to the subject
and the form. The first indication of an interest in the Fall is
to be found in the list of subjects and plans drawn up by Milton within a few years after his return to England from Italy
and preserved in the Trinity College Manuscript. These plans
are all for dramatic compositions, but a similar one for epics
may have existed. The subjects are biblical and historical.
The scheme of a drama on the Fall is presented in four drafts,
of which only the final one need here be given:

Adam Unparadised. I The Angel Gabriel, either descending or
entering—showing, since this globe was created, his frequency as
much on Earth as in Heaven—describes Paradise. Next the
Chorus, showing the reason of his coming—to keep his watch in
Paradise, after Lucifer's rebellion, by command from God—and
withal expressing his desire to see and know more concerning
this excellent and new creature, Man.—II The Angel Gabriel, as
by his name signifying a Prince of Power, tracing Paradise with
a more free office, passes by the station of the Chorus, and, desired
by them, relates what he knew of Man, as the creation of Eve,
with their love and marriage.—III After this, Lucifer appears,
after his overthrow; bemoans himself; seeks revenge upon Man.
The Chorus prepare resistance at his first approach. At last, after
discourse of enmity on either side, he departs; whereat the Chorus
sings of the battle and victory in Heaven against him and his
accomplices, as before, after the first Act was sung a hymn of the

Creation.—IV Here again may appear Lucifer, relating and insulting in what he had done to the destruction of Man. Man next and Eve, having been by this time seduced by the Serpent, appears confusedly, covered with leaves. Conscience, in a shape, accuses him; Justice cites him to the place whither Jehovah called for him. In the meantime the Chorus entertains the stage and is informed by some Angel of the manner of the Fall. Here the Chorus bewails Adam's fall.—V Adam then and Eve return and accuse one another; but especially Adam lays the blame to his wife—is stubborn in his offence. Justice appears, reasons with him, convinces him. The Chorus admonisheth Adam, and bids him beware Lucifer's example of impenitence.—The Angel is sent to banish them out of Paradise; but, before, causes to pass before his eyes, in shapes, a masque of all the evils of this life and world. He is humbled, relents, despairs. At last appears Mercy, comforts him, promises him the Messiah; then calls in Faith, Hope, Charity; instructs him. He repents, gives God the glory, submits to his penalty. The Chorus briefly concludes.—Compare this with the former Draft.

Edward Phillips says that Milton actually began the composition of this drama about 1642 and that Satan's speech in *Paradise Lost,* Book IV, lines 33–41, formed a part of it. When and why he decided to throw the material into epic form is a matter of conjecture. It must have become evident to him, as he meditated the significance of his theme, that it involved too much to be confined within the "two hours traffic of the stage." His purpose came to embrace all his thinking on the destiny of man, all the wisdom he had derived from men, events, and books, all the passions which had been generated in him by a life of public and domestic conflict.

He began the poem after blindness had partly incapacitated him for public service, and philosophy had reconciled him to a life of solitary meditation—perhaps as early as 1655, certainly before the Restoration in 1660. It was published in ten books in 1667, revised and redivided into twelve for a second edition in 1674.

The materials for the story of *Paradise Lost* are derived from a wide variety of literary sources. The basis is, of course, the biblical narrative of the Fall in Genesis 1 and 2 and the prophetic account of the war in Heaven in Revelation 12. Milton has incorporated almost every detail of these passages in one place or another of the epic. He has also laid the Bible as a whole heavily under contribution, particularly in Michael's résumé of human history in Books XI and XII. For the elaboration of these basic materials Milton is indebted, first, perhaps, to biblical commentary, Jewish as well as Christian, then to the various imaginative treatments of the theme which had come to his attention. He may or may not have known the Anglo-Saxon paraphrase of Genesis or Vondel's brilliant Dutch drama, *Lucifer,* the two works which in imaginative quality come nearest to the level of the poem; he certainly knew and used Grotius's Latin play, *Adamus Exul.* Andreini's *Adamo,* a *sacra rappresentazione,* was reported by Voltaire to have been seen by Milton in Italy and to have given him the idea of writing on this subject. The dramatic plans, with their allegorical elements, lend some force to this suggestion. In the treatment of individual episodes the influence of many works of literature, English, Italian, and Classical, is more or less clearly discernible. Both Shakespeare and Spenser, among Elizabethan authors, played their part. So also did Giles and Phineas Fletcher, Milton's immediate predecessors in religious poetry of the Spenserian tradition. Homer, Virgil, Tasso were Milton's epic models. He borrowed more than one incident from Ariosto. Du Bartas, his earliest enthusiasm in serious poetry, remains a strong influence, particularly in the account of creation in Book VIII.

Philosophic Purport

The theme of *Paradise Lost* is, as its title tells us, the Fall of Man. Its doctrinal object is "to assert eternal Providence and justify the ways of God to man," meaning thereby to demonstrate the workings in human life of a purposeful and beneficent will and to show that the sufferings of humanity are due not to God but to man. Milton states the case explicitly in *Areopagitica.* "Many there be," he says, "that complain of divine Providence for suffering Adam to transgress. Foolish tongues! When God gave him reason, he gave him freedom to choose, for reason is but choosing; he had else been a mere artificial [mechanical] Adam, such an Adam as he is in the motions [puppet shows]."

The justification of God's ways, then, lies in Adam's freedom of will, and this is a central idea in the poem. It lies also in the liberation of mankind from the inherited consequences of Adam's sin by the sacrifice of Christ. The story itself involves the origin of sin in Satan's revolt through pride against the will of God, his fall from Heaven, his plot against Adam and Eve, their ruin and exile, the prophecy of redemption. We have, then, a smaller action enveloped in a larger. Milton begins at the logical point, namely, the moment when Satan lifts his head from the burning lake. The matter of the first two books involves the reorganization of Satan's forces and his setting out on the mission of seducing Adam and Eve from their obedience. Book III expounds the divine plan and brings Satan through Chaos to the newly created world. Books IV to VIII set the stage in Paradise for the temptation. Adam and Eve in their state of innocence are enlightened by a celestial visitor. They learn in detail of the war in Heaven, of the World's creation, of the danger which besets them. Books IX–X deal with the Fall and its immediate consequences. Adam and Eve sin, receive judgment, repent, and sue for pardon. Books XI–XII exhibit in Michael's prophetic narrative of the history of the race the remoter consequences of Adam's deed and recount the banishment of the unhappy pair from Eden.

In thus ordering his cosmic materials Milton has followed the principles of epic unity laid down by Aristotle and Horace and has employed the devices suggested by Homer and Virgil —episodic narrative and prophecy. Such inclusiveness could not easily have been achieved in drama.

There is, however, a more vital unity in *Paradise Lost* than is accounted for either by its coherence of plot or by its complete embodiment of the traditional scheme of man's salvation. Milton has grappled emotionally and philosophically, as well as theologically, with the problem of good and evil, and he has made the protagonists of his story symbols of two great forces which he sees and feels to be operative in human life. We can best understand his meaning if we consider first his idea of God and his creation.

God himself exists from all eternity. The Son and the angels were his first created work, the first extension of his being. Matter is a part of his substance and is from everlasting to everlasting. Creation, then, is not from nothing and even "spirits" are material. Primordial matter fills all space but, though a part of God, it does not feel his "virtue" until he elects to exercise over it his creative power, making it thereby rational and orderly. When in some unexplained way disorder intrudes on God's creation and Satan rebels against his will,

Ptolemic

he establishes the mundane universe and creates a lower order
of being to compensate the loss. The newly ordered world
consists of the earth as center, with a system of concentric
spheres revolving about it carrying the heavenly bodies. He
also creates Hell as a dungeon and place of punishment.

Had Satan remained docilely within his prison this scheme
of things might have continued so to all eternity, though not
without a certain progress. For Adam and Eve there would
have been no death. Their sinless offspring would have replenished the earth and turned it all to Eden. "Oft converse with
heavenly habitants" would have improved their knowledge
and insight; their bodies would have responded to the form
and pressure of their minds, until they themselves should
become all spirit and their dwelling Paradise indeed. Such a
program Adam envisages and communicates to Eve. It is suggested that God might some day reduce the remaining part of
Chaos to created order, and this would have been the logic of
his being.

The fact that Satan is left free to renew his attack on God
alters everything. Adam's happiness, like that of the angels,
depends on his obedience. The divine order, which "jars not
with liberty but well consists," must be preserved. When
Satan succeeds in communicating rebellion first to Eve, then
to Adam, evil has entered God's new order and a problem is
created. Not Chaos, which is neither good nor bad, but a per-
version of what was wrought out of it threatens to make head-
way. Had no remedy been provided, an active and eternal
dualism would have been established, with God continuously
losing ground as more and more of his weaker creatures were
brought to Satan's side. The method of this new attack, seduction instead of force, was infinitely more dangerous and required opposing measures, developed from God's wisdom and
mercy rather than from his power. In the new contest, as in
the old, Christ is the protagonist. As God had delegated him
to put an end to the war in Heaven by going forth with ease
in his flaming chariot, so now he elects him to be a propitia-
tory sacrifice for sinful man. His humility becomes, therefore,
the counterpart and opposite of Satan's pride. The two meet
on the spiritual plane, as before they had met on the physical,
and Christ is again the victor. Instead of extending his power
Satan will find it more restricted. The strife will go on through
human history, for men, having free choice, will often reject

salvation offered, until, at Christ's second coming, the account
is closed and Satan and his followers are finally confined to
Hell.

The contradiction in Milton's scheme of things is obvious.
His philosophic idealism must admit evil as a fact of experience, and Satan is as everlasting as God himself. The plan of
salvation will, however, when completed, reduce evil to a
passive instead of an active principle. Save for the excluded
portion, God will be supreme, with a supremacy no longer
containing within itself the seeds of strife.

The sources of Milton's thinking are to be found, first of
all, in the Christian system itself. He holds his conviction of
human freedom with Arminius against St. Augustine, Martin
Luther, and Calvin. His unitarian conception of God allies
him with a long heretical tradition which was anathema to
Puritan and Anglican alike. But his Christian thought was
deeply affected by two philosophic strains, Stoicism and Platonism. The first both supports and perturbs his ethics. Milton's temperament was stoical; his life is the record of an
almost superhuman effort of the will; his conception of duty
led him to crush the softer and more seductive emotions in the
interests of private ambition and the public welfare; it was his
boast that he was able to endure misfortune without swerving
from his march "right onward." He was therefore naturally
drawn to the philosophic system which made a virtue of these
traits, and he embodies them dramatically in Satan. On the
other hand, his Christian ethics teaches him that pride in
human power, unsupported by God, is false and sinful. He
must, therefore, officially condemn the stoical ideal. He does
so more than once, particularly through the mouth of Christ
in *Paradise Regained*:

> The Stoic last in philosophic pride
> By him called virtue; and his virtuous man,
> Wise, perfect in himself, and all possessing
> Equal to God, oft shames not to prefer,
> As fearing God nor man, contemning all,
> Wealth, pleasure, pain or torment, death and life,
> Which when he lists he leaves, or boasts he can,
> For all his tedious talk is but vain boast.

Stoical traits appear in Eve, when she proposes to Adam suicide or a childless life and is commended for her courage; in
Adam after the Fall; in Samson, and even in Christ himself,

but here they are accompanied by conscious submission to a higher will.

Platonic thought fuses more easily with Milton's Christian ideas and is an element of great importance in his poetry. The dualism of reason and passion is Platonic; so too is the conception of the correspondence between earthly and heavenly things which enables Milton to render in human terms the spiritual conflicts which are his theme. Platonism underlies his doctrine of a graded scale of being and his distinction between worthy and unworthy love. It also supports him with his philosophy of progress and development in the individual soul and in the race.

THE CHARACTERS

The philosophic significance of the leading personages in Milton's epic has already been discussed. We may consider them now as imaginative creations and as reflections of Milton's own experience of life. Satan is the most gloriously conceived of epic heroes, for he *is* the hero of *Paradise Lost,* as Dryden affirmed, if we mean by that the most active and the most memorable character in the poem. He appears in Books I and II as the type of unconquerable rebel. One feels that Milton has put into him the pride, the will to power, the intellectual and spiritual force which were a part of his own nature.[1] That he officially condemns him as one who has taken evil for his good is neither here nor there. Satan's wickedness does not obscure his moral force, nor did Milton intend that it should do so. The theory by which he justified his presentation of the prince of Hell in so admirable a light was that he was a fallen

[1] I have let stand as they were originally written this and various other statements implying the identification of Milton personally with the creatures of his imagination. They will be easily recognized for what they are, and it seems unnecessary to modify or refine on them in this place. It should, however, be remembered, in considering the reaction which has taken place against such biographical evaluations, that Milton himself invited them. He intended his work to be the witness of what he was, and this is why students persist in interpreting and passing judgment on his poems and his prose works as part of the total pattern of his life. The "Satan problem," which has always tended to dominate discussion, is, of course, a moral and religious as well as an aesthetic one, involving questions as to the integrity, meaningfulness, and acceptability of Milton's Christian thought. A gulf divides such an attitude as Shelley's from that of a believer like C. S. Lewis. To the former Milton's Satan is morally superior to his God. To the latter those who admire Satan in such terms are adoring the image of their own rebellious pride.

angel, ruined, indeed, but not yet degenerated, save in a single point, from his original brightness. The adventurous boldness of Satan receives new illustration in his flight through Chaos in Book III. With Book IV there is a change. Satan is committed by his adoption of the method of fraud and seduction in place of violence to a course of action which must inevitably impair his inner excellence. He exhibits envy and cruelty in his attack on Eve and becomes more and more conspicuously the father of lies. The deterioration of his outward form keeps pace with the base uses to which he puts himself, until he comes to assume symbolically the form of a serpent. His ingenuity in the temptation of Eve in Book IX is a last survival of the superior gifts with which he was endowed.

Adam, to whom interest shifts in Book IV, is, compared with Satan, a passive figure. He is intended to be the prototype of the human race, but since he has so few relationships and so little to do, the portrait is necessarily drawn on simple lines. We see him first dwelling in idyllic happiness amid the delights of Eden. He is tenderly but not weakly affectionate, humbly eager for the companionship of his superiors, avid of knowledge and a bit oracular in imparting it, soberly concerned about Eve's moral welfare and not unregardful of his own. When in Book VIII he recounts to Raphael his first conscious experience, he exhibits the fundamental instincts of mankind: curiosity about himself and the world, desire for communion with his creator, and passionate longing for a mate. Milton has drawn Adam as lover and husband in his own idealized image, with due recognition of the force of passion as a motive in human life. He confesses to the angel his sense of weakness in this respect and is warned not to allow his judgment to be swayed by the powerful emotion which draws him to Eve. When Eve offers him the apple his superior intellect recognizes immediately the work of Satan, and he clearly foresees the disastrous consequences of her act. He knows that the part of wisdom bids him refuse to join her in her sin, yet he deliberately resolves to share her fate. Again, Milton's feeling and imagination are all on the side of a decision which his mind condemns. The reader therefore finds it difficult to see Adam's deed as anything else than the thing Eve calls it: a "glorious trial of exceeding love." The effects of sin on Adam are parallel to its effects on Satan. He begins to reason falsely; his love of Eve degenerates into lust; he becomes harsh and cynical; he is alienated from his instinctive allegiance to God. But the depth of his nature is first clearly revealed by his experience of sin and suffering. His meditations as he gropes again toward God are like those of Job. He receives the judgment with a cry of inward agony, but after Michael's prophecy he turns with sober hopefulness toward the difficult pathway of recovery. The maturing Adam of the last books is a different person from the idyllic figure of the garden. Milton has developed his theme with depth and pathos and has won from his readers an emotional response which fully justifies his immense elaboration of the biblical narrative.

The study of eternal woman in Eve is even more subtle and provocative than that of man in Adam. An equal sympathy is hardly to be expected from Milton, yet there is a measure of understanding and admiration in the portrait, which critics have not adequately recognized. Eve in innocence is everything that Milton would have in a wife. She is gracious, loving, modest, studious of household good, wholly convinced of Adam's superior wisdom, and happily acquiescent in his authority. Even her weakness is engaging. There is no malice in the account of her momentary fixation on her own image reflected in a pool before she sees masculine reality in the person of Adam. This incident and the exhibition of curiosity which leads her to listen secretly to a part of the discourse of Adam and Raphael motivates her fall, as the emphasis on Adam's passion had motivated his. Milton's account of the development of trouble between the pair is based on broad experience of women's ways, and here he becomes for the first time critical. Eve's desire to work alone, though it takes the form first of solicitous regard for efficiency in work, then of an instinct toward moral maturity, is perverse. Eve does not lack intelligence, but she lacks self-knowledge and is stubborn. In Satan's hands she becomes like wax; Milton is remorseless in his exhibition of the play of emotion which finally makes her yield to what is, essentially, a seduction. Curiosity, vanity, jealousy, and pure sensual appetite combine to work her ruin. Her approach to Adam is hypocritical and selfish. She outdoes him in her abandoned surrender to the intoxication of sin, and her guilty reaction is of a lower type. Yet Milton allows goodness to triumph in her. Her plea to Adam for forgiveness, her bold but irrational suggestions for defeating the penalty imposed on their future offspring, her outburst of feminine grief at the thought of exile, her acceptance of the angelic revelation, and her final expression of obedience and undying love combine to show how deeply Milton has been drawn to his heroine and how richly he has conceived her. She is the one complete portrait of feminine humanity in all his poetry, but she stands worthily beside Satan and Adam as a work of passionate inspiration and consummate art.

Of the remaining figures, the great leaders of Satan's host— Beëlzebub, Moloch, Belial, Mammon—are the most interesting. The first is as convenient to the purposes of his master as greatness could desire. Roused from his stupor by Satan's fiery courage, he becomes the skilled manipulator of the infernal council in his master's interests. Milton has drawn in him the pattern of a statesman-politician. The others furnish more specialized cases of perverted excellence. Their several proposals and their types of eloquence illustrate their characters. Thus Moloch is the brutal warrior, Belial the corrupt and slothful trimmer, Mammon the coarse builder of a material empire. The hellish debate in Book II of *Paradise Lost* has a grandeur and significance which renders it superior to any of the similar episodes in epic tradition.

The divine personages are less dramatically impressive. God the father, as Pope declared, talks like a school divine. His majesty we have to take for granted; we do not feel it. Christ also is a mere theological entity, save in the spectacular account of his going forth to battle armed with thunderbolts and in the moment of his announced sacrifice. The two announcing angels, Raphael and Michael, have a certain amount of personality. The first is companionable and gracious, the second didactic and severe. Abdiel, who deserts the apostate band and returns to receive God's approval, embodies Milton's conception of himself as the isolated righteous man, unswayed by bad example and unterrified by force. Milton is here of the angels' party, as he had in Books I and II been of the devil's. In both instances he has given form and substance to his own most deeply felt emotions. If we miss in *Paradise Lost* such objective representation of human life as we find in Homer or Shakespeare, we have, by way of compensation, the most complete display that any poet has ever given of the elements and forces which make war on each other within the limits of a single, titanic personality.

STYLE

iambic

Milton is, according to Matthew Arnold, the outstanding representative of the grand manner in English poetry. His style in *Paradise Lost* is answerable to the greatness of his theme, yet not without variety and even charm. The measure, as he says simply in his preface, is English heroic verse without rhyme, as that of Homer in Greek and Virgil in Latin. The phrase suggests that his object was to rival the ancients in the medium of expression, as he felt that he had surpassed them in his choice of subject. Compared with his English predecessors in the use of unrhymed iambic pentameter, he is at once more orderly and more irregular. Formally, his lines are strictly decasyllabic, with occasional light endings. Robert Bridges has shown that Milton counted his syllables and explained to himself the apparent freedoms by a system of elisions and contractions. Thus in the line,

> Above the Aonian mount, while it pursues,

Milton did not reckon "the" as a syllable and, indeed, printed it "th'" as a guide to the mind if not to the voice of the reader. In the line,

> Of man's first disobedience, and the fruit,

the fourth syllable in "disobedience" is not counted, though there is no typographical indication that the word is to be spoken in any but the usual way. Milton scanned his verse one way and read it another, says Bridges. The effect on the modern reader, who can scarcely be expected to be aware of the poet's "rules," is that of an exceptionally free and an exceptionally harmonious versification. It is, however, in the placing of accents, and in the management of pause that Milton most shows his metrical individuality. Inversions are so frequent and so bold, heavy-light and light-heavy syllables are employed with such freedom, that the iambic pattern is often obscured, though never lost. Lines like the following, accented naturally, illustrate the lengths to which Milton goes in letting the rhythms of prose intrude upon those of verse:

> Which of us who beholds the bright surface . . .

> To the garden of bliss: It was a hill . . .

> Rocks, caves, lakes, fens, bogs, dens, and shades of death.

The matter of pause in Milton's verse is too complicated to examine in detail. It has often been pointed out that the line is only formally the unit, and the term "verse paragraphs" has been used to denote the long sweeps of rhythm through several complicated sentences. The first sixteen lines of *Paradise Lost* are such a unit. Milton's pauses within the line are exceptionally heavy; they sometimes occur, moreover, at unexpected places, for example in the first foot, as in the following:

> Thus with the year
> Seasons return, but not to me returns
> Day, or the sweet approach of Even or Morn.

In vocabulary, sentence form, and imagery Milton is no less individual than he is in metrical technique. His language is always elevated and generally far removed from that of common speech, though its basis is perhaps simpler than the usual critical descriptions would imply. Milton is fond of long words of literary character, of compounds, of Latinisms, of biblical phraseology, and of terms archaic even in his own time. These, woven on the fabric of vigorous and direct Anglo-Saxon, impart dignity to his style and give scope to his mastery of rhythm. Thus in the first 125 lines of *Paradise Lost* we find the following: "mortal taste," "secret (Lat. *secretus*) top," "chosen seed," "fast by the oracle of God," "chaos," "abyss," "illumine," "ethereal," "combustion," "perdition," "adamantine," "penal," "omnipotent," "affliction," "obdurate," "urges" (Lat. *urgere*), "deluge," "ever-burning," "unconsumed," "eternal," "ordained," "tempestuous," "transcendent," "myriads," "potent," "luster," "dubious," "unconquerable," "immortal," "extort," "suppliant," "ignominy," "empyreal," "irreconcilable," "apostate." The profusion of biblical, classical, and geographical names adds to the effect: for example, Eden, Oreb, Sinai, Aonian, in the opening paragraph. The simplest passages (e.g., Book II, lines 635–58 or Book XII, lines 610–23) are never ordinary. The most elaborate (e.g., Book XI, lines 385–411) are amazing in their linguistic virtuosity.

But Milton's uniqueness in expression is as much a matter of syntax as it is of vocabulary. There is a studied departure from the ordinary construction of prose, extending from mere inversion of the natural order in a phrase like "a dungeon horrible," to elaborately suspended sentences like the one with which the poem opens.

In the richness of his imagery Milton ranks with the most poetic of poets—Spenser, Shakespeare, Keats. Homely and minute observation is lacking. Milton prefers the great phenomena of nature to its detail. But when he is really inspired he writes with unsurpassed vividness:

> A dungeon horrible, on all sides round,
> As one great furnace flamed.

> this fair Moon,
> And these the gems of heaven, her starry train.

The appeals to the sense of smell are particularly striking:

> fragrant the fertil earth
> After soft shours. . . .

> The smell of grain, or tedded grass, or kine.

Milton's style, finally, is heavily embroidered with allusion. His materials are those of the scholar, but they are employed with an imaginative fervor which converts them to the stuff of poetry. He lays under contribution the whole treasury of human experience as found in books, and revels in his knowledge of history, geography, mythology, and the physical sciences. He uses the expanded simile freely as his epic predecessors from Homer to Shakespeare had done, but with a greater richness in the associations and with more precision and completeness in the application. The use of poetic ornament of this sort comes and goes in *Paradise Lost* as the mood and subject matter change. Milton's imagination is not always active. There are long stretches of plain narrative, and of exposition. The pictorial element is at its height in Books I, II (line 629 to end), III (line 416 to end), IV, VI. The infernal council in Book II, the dialogues of Adam and Eve and of Eve and Satan in Book IX, best illustrate Milton's mastery of dramatic eloquence.

There has in modern criticism been some disagreement as to the merits of Milton's poetic style. Ezra Pound, for example, was given to making statements like the following: "Milton ruined his work by not understanding that the genius of English is not the genius of Latin and that one can *not* write an uninflected language in the same way, using the same word order, that serves an inflected language." "It [a passage in the *Odyssey*] is a raw cut of concrete reality, combined with tremendous energy. The reality that becomes mere pompous rhetoric in Milton." The discriminating analysis which followed such challenges and was partly prompted by them has brought out many subtleties of artistic effect unmentioned in earlier literature on the subject. One consequence of these discussions has been to make Milton again an object of interest to writers and readers of contemporary poetry. The concern with Milton of acute and sensitive minds like Eliot and Empson has not resulted in "his glory's diminution" but the reverse.

PARADISE LOST

THE VERSE

The measure is English heroic verse without rime, as that of Homer in Greek, and of Virgil in Latin; rime being no necessary adjunct or true ornament of poem or good verse, in longer works especially, but the invention of a barbarous age, to set off wretched matter and lame metre; graced indeed since by the use of some famous modern poets, carried away by custom, but much to their own vexation, hindrance, and constraint to express many things otherwise, and for the most part worse than else they would have expressed them. Not without cause, therefore, some both Italian and Spanish poets of prime note have rejected rime both in longer and shorter works, as have also, long since, our best English tragedies, as a thing of itself, to all judicious ears, trivial and of no true musical delight; which consists only in apt numbers, fit quantity of syllables, and the sense variously drawn out from one verse into another, not in the jingling sound of like endings, a fault avoided by the learned ancients both in poetry and all good oratory. This neglect then of rime so little is to be taken for a defect, though it may seem so perhaps to vulgar readers, that it rather is to be esteemed an example set, the first in English, of ancient liberty recovered to heroic poem from the troublesome and modern bondage of riming.

PARADISE LOST

BOOK I

THE ARGUMENT

This first book proposes first in brief the whole subject, Man's disobedience, and the loss thereupon of Paradise wherein he was placed: then touches the prime cause of his fall, the Serpent, or

rather Satan in the Serpent; who revolting from God, and drawing
to his side many legions of angels, was by the command of God
driven out of Heaven with all his crew into the great Deep. Which
action passed over, the poem hastes into the midst of things, presenting Satan with his angels now fallen into Hell, described here,
not in the center (for Heaven and Earth may be supposed as yet
not made, certainly not yet accursed) but in a place of utter darkness, fitliest called Chaos. Here Satan with his angels lying on
the burning lake, thunderstruck and astonished, after a certain
space recovers, as from confusion, calls up him who next in order
and dignity lay by him; they confer of their miserable fall. Satan
awakens all his legions, who lay till then in the same manner
confounded; they rise: their numbers, array of battle, their chief
leaders named, according to the idols known afterwards in Canaan
and the countries adjoining. To these Satan directs his speech,
comforts them with hope yet of regaining Heaven, but tells them
lastly of a new world and new kind of creature to be created, according to an ancient prophecy or report in Heaven; for that angels
were long before this visible creation, was the opinion of many
ancient Fathers. To find out the truth of this prophecy, and what
to determine thereon, he refers to a full council. What his associates thence attempt. Pandemonium the palace of Satan rises,
suddenly built out of the Deep; the infernal peers there sit in
council.

exposition

Of Man's first disobedience, and the fruit
Of that forbidden tree, whose mortal taste
Brought death into the world, and all our woe,
With loss of Eden, till one greater Man
Restore us, and regain the blissful seat,
Sing Heavenly Muse, that on the secret top
Of Oreb, or of Sinai, didst inspire
That shepherd, who first taught the chosen seed,
In the beginning how the Heavens and Earth
Rose out of Chaos; or if Sion hill   10

1 ff. Milton follows the conventional epic procedure in his opening. For
the various elements or steps in this procedure, cf. *Iliad* i. 1 ff., *Aeneid* i. 1 ff.
   2. mortal, deadly.
   6. Heavenly Muse. The Christian poets adopted the classical muse of
Astronomy, whose name (Urania, the Heavenly) qualified her for the new
office, as the patroness of their divine inspiration. Milton identifies her with
the Holy Spirit of Scripture and so turns his invocation into a prayer. Cf.
the opening lines of Book VII.
   7. of Oreb or of Sinai. Cf. Exod. 19:20 and Deut. 4:10. Milton
carefully follows Scripture even in its apparent contradiction.
   8. That shepherd, Moses.
   10. Sion hill, Mount Zion, one of the hills on which the city of Jerusalem is built.

Delight thee more, and Siloa's brook that flowed
Fast by the oracle of God, I thence
Invoke thy aid to my adventurous song, *song of*
That with no middle flight intends to soar *epic style exalted —*
Above the Aonian mount; while it pursues
Things unattempted yet in prose or rhyme.
And chiefly thou O Spirit, that dost prefer
Before all temples the upright heart and pure,
Instruct me, for thou knowest; thou from the first
Wast present, and with mighty wings outspread   20
Dove-like sat'st brooding on the vast Abyss
And madest it pregnant: what in me is dark
Illumine, what is low raise and support;
That to the height of this great argument
I may assert Eternal Providence,
And justify the ways of God to men.
      Say first, for Heaven hides nothing from thy view,
Nor the deep tract of Hell, say first what cause
Moved our grand parents in that happy state,
Favored of Heaven so highly, to fall off   30
From their Creator, and transgress his will
For one restraint, lords of the world besides?
Who first seduced them to that foul revolt?
The infernal Serpent; he it was, whose guile,
Stirred up with envy and revenge, deceived
The Mother of Mankind; what time his pride
Had cast him out from Heaven, with all his host
Of rebel angels, by whose aid aspiring
To set himself in glory above his peers,

purpose — show how God has ordered & was just — to person. as true cause

11. **Siloa's brook**, "the waters of Shiloah that go softly" (Isa. 8:6).
12. **Fast by the oracle of God**, i.e., close to the Temple of Jerusalem.
15. **Above the Aonian mount.** Milton means that his theme is loftier than any that the Pagan poets could sing. The **Aonian mount** is Helicon, sacred to the muses.
21. Gen. 1:1, 2. The Hebrew word translated in the Authorized Version "moved" can also be rendered "brooded." The Holy Spirit takes the form of a dove in Luke 3:22.
24. **argument**, subject.
25. **assert**, maintain the cause of.
26. **justify**, make apparent the justice of. The real issue in Milton's mind is whether an intelligent and righteous will rules man's destiny, or a blind or capricious or malicious one. The justification hinges on (1) the affirmation of man's freedom and responsibility, and (2) the scheme of salvation through Christ which is set forth in the poem as a whole.
29. **our grand parents**, i.e., our original ancestors, Adam and Eve.
32. **for**, because of.
34. **The infernal Serpent**, etc. The chief Scriptural source for the revolt and fall of Satan is Rev. 12:9 ff. But cf. also Luke 10:18; II Pet. 2:4; Jude 6; Rev. 20:1, 2.

He trusted to have equalled the Most High,   40
If he opposed; and with ambitious aim
Against the throne and monarchy of God,
Raised impious war in Heaven and battle proud
With vain attempt. Him the Almighty Power
Hurled headlong flaming from the ethereal sky
With hideous ruin and combustion down
To bottomless perdition, there to dwell
In adamantine chains and penal fire,
Who durst defy the Omnipotent to arms.
Nine times the space that measures day and night   50
To mortal men, he with his horrid crew
Lay vanquished, rolling in the fiery gulf
Confounded though immortal. But his doom
Reserved him to more wrath; for now the thought
Both of lost happiness and lasting pain
Torments him; round he throws his baleful eyes,
That witnessed huge affliction and dismay
Mixed with obdurate pride and steadfast hate.
At once as far as angel's ken he views
The dismal situation waste and wild: 60
A dungeon horrible, on all sides round
As one great furnace flamed, yet from those flames
No light, but rather darkness visible
Served only to discover sights of woe,
Regions of sorrow, doleful shades, where peace
And rest can never dwell, hope never comes
That comes to all; but torture without end
Still urges, and a fiery deluge, fed
With ever-burning sulphur unconsumed:
Such place Eternal Justice had prepared   70
For those rebellious, here their prison ordained
In utter darkness, and their portion set

53. **Confounded**, defeated and ruined.
57. **witnessed**, bore witness to, expressed.
59. **angel's ken**, an angel's range of vision. Because there is no apostrophe in the original text editors have been led to take **ken** as a verb, meaning see. This, however, is not decisive, for the apostrophe is omitted generally in the old editions. Milton does not elsewhere use "ken" as a verb intransitively. In III, 622, we have "saw within ken a glorious angel stand."
63. **darkness visible**, darkness not quite absolute. The words perhaps express also the idea of the darkness having a positive quality. Cf. "the palpable obscure," II, 406; also Job 10:22, whence the first suggestion of this famous phrase.
64. **discover**, reveal.
65. Cf. Dante, *Inferno*, III, 9: "All hope abandon, ye who enter here."
68. **urges**, afflicts.
72. **utter**, outer—as in Scripture. But there is also a suggestion of the modern sense.

Reconcile ways of God to Man.

As far removed from God and light of Heaven
As from the center thrice to the utmost pole.
Oh how unlike the place from whence they fell!
There the companions of his fall, o'erwhelmed
With floods and whirlwinds of tempestuous fire,
He soon discerns, and weltering by his side
One next himself in power, and next in crime,
Long after known in Palestine, and named   80
Beëlzebub. To whom the Arch-Enemy,
And thence in Heaven called Satan, with bold words
Breaking the horrid silence thus began.
    "If thou beest he; but Oh how fallen! how changed
From him, who in the happy realms of light
Clothed with transcendent brightness didst outshine
Myriads, though bright: if he whom mutual league,
United thoughts and counsels, equal hope
And hazard in the glorious enterprise,
Joined with me once, now misery hath joined   90
In equal ruin: into what pit thou seest
From what height fallen, so much the stronger proved
He with his thunder, and till then who knew
The force of those dire arms? Yet not for those,
Nor what the potent victor in his rage
Can else inflict, do I repent or change,
Though changed in outward luster, that fixed mind
And high disdain, from sense of injured merit,
That with the Mightiest raised me to contend,
And to the fierce contention brought along   100
Innumerable force of spirits armed
That durst dislike his reign, and, me preferring,
His utmost power with adverse power opposed
In dubious battle on the plains of Heaven,
And shook his throne. What though the field be lost?
All is not lost; the unconquerable will,
And study of revenge, immortal hate,
And courage never to submit or yield:

    74. from the center thrice to the utmost pole. The center is the
center of the earth; the utmost pole is the pole of the outermost sphere of
the visible heavens. The distance from hell to the empyrean (the supreme
heaven) is ordinarily felt by Milton to be much greater than this exact calculation makes it.
    81. Beëlzebub. Cf. Matt. 12:24. Arch-Enemy. Satan in Hebrew
means "adversary."
    84 ff. If thou beest he, etc. The sentence is not completed. The entire
speech is made disjointed to indicate Satan's emotional stress. but Oh how
fallen, etc. Cf. Isa. 14:12, and Aeneid ii, 274, 275.
    105 ff. What though the field, etc. For a similar expression of de-
fiance, cf. Aeschylus Prometheus 1013-16.

And what is else not to be overcome?
That glory never shall his wrath or might 110
Extort from me. To bow and sue for grace
With suppliant knee, and deify his power
Who from the terror of this arm so late
Doubted his empire, that were low indeed,
That were an ignominy and shame beneath
This downfall; since by fate the strength of gods
And this empyreal substance cannot fail,
Since through experience of this great event,
In arms not worse, in foresight much advanced,
We may with more successful hope resolve 120
To wage by force or guile eternal war,
Irreconcilable to our grand foe,
Who now triumphs, and in the excess of joy
Sole reigning holds the tyranny of Heaven."
    So spake the apostate Angel, though in pain,
Vaunting aloud, but racked with deep despair;
And him thus answered soon his bold compeer.
    "O Prince, O Chief of many thronëd Powers,
That led the embattled Seraphim to war
Under thy conduct, and in dreadful deeds 130
Fearless, endangered Heaven's perpetual King,
And put to proof his high supremacy,
Whether upheld by strength, or chance, or fate;
Too well I see and rue the dire event,
That with sad overthrow and foul defeat
Hath lost us Heaven, and all this mighty host
In horrible destruction laid thus low,
As far as gods and heavenly essences
Can perish: for the mind and spirit remains
Invincible, and vigor soon returns, 140
Though all our glory extinct, and happy state
Here swallowed up in endless misery.
But what if he our conqueror (whom I now
Of force believe almighty, since no less
Than such could have o'erpowered such force as ours)

110. **That glory,** i.e., the glory of subduing Satan's will.
114. **Doubted,** feared for.
116 ff. **since by fate,** etc. Satan denies that he was created by and is therefore subordinate to God. His egotism makes him a polytheist or more specifically a Manichee. Cf. V, 854 ff.
120. **successful hope,** hope of success.
128–29. **thronëd Powers, Seraphim.** The angelic orders in Dante and the Catholic theologians are, from lowest to highest, as follows: Angels, Archangels, Principalities, Powers, Virtues, Dominions, Thrones, Cherubim, Seraphim. Milton uses many of these names interchangeably.

Have left us this our spirit and strength entire,
Strongly to suffer and support our pains,
That we may so suffice his vengeful ire,
Or do him mightier service as his thralls
By right of war, whate'er his business be,   150
Here in the heart of Hell to work in fire,
Or do his errands in the gloomy deep;
What can it then avail, though yet we feel
Strength undiminished, or eternal being
To undergo eternal punishment?"
    Whereto with speedy words the Arch-Fiend replied.
"Fallen Cherub, to be weak is miserable,
Doing or suffering: but of this be sure,
To do aught good never will be our task,
But ever to do ill our sole delight,   160
As being the contrary to his high will
Whom we resist. If then his providence
Out of our evil seek to bring forth good,
Our labor must be to pervert that end,
And out of good still to find means of evil;
Which oft-times may succeed, so as perhaps
Shall grieve him, if I fail not, and disturb
His inmost counsels from their destined aim.
But see the angry victor hath recalled
His ministers of vengeance and pursuit   170
Back to the gates of Heaven; the sulphurous hail
Shot after us in storm, o'erblown hath laid
The fiery surge, that from the precipice
Of Heaven received us falling, and the thunder,
Winged with red lightning and impetuous rage,
Perhaps hath spent his shafts, and ceases now
To bellow through the vast and boundless deep.
Let us not slip the occasion, whether scorn,
Or satiate fury yield it from our foe.
Seest thou yon dreary plain, forlorn and wild,   180
The seat of desolation, void of light,
Save what the glimmering of these livid flames
Casts pale and dreadful? Thither let us tend
From off the tossing of these fiery waves,
There rest, if any rest can harbor there,

148. suffice, satisfy.
167. if I fail not, unless I mistake (Latin ni fallor).
178. Let us not slip, Let us not let slip.
185. There rest, etc. Cf. Richard II, V, i. 5, 6:
      "Here let us rest, if this rebellious earth
      Have any resting for her true king's queen."

And re-assembling our afflicted powers,
Consult how we may henceforth most offend
Our enemy, our own loss how repair,
How overcome this dire calamity,
What reinforcement we may gain from hope;   190
If not, what resolution from despair."
    Thus Satan talking to his nearest mate
With head uplift above the wave, and eyes
That sparkling blazed; his other parts besides,
Prone on the flood, extended long and large,
Lay floating many a rood, in bulk as huge
As whom the fables name of monstrous size,
Titanian or Earth-born, that warred on Jove,
Briareos or Typhon, whom the den
By ancient Tarsus held, or that sea-beast   200
Leviathan, which God of all his works
Created hugest that swim the ocean stream:
Him haply slumbering on the Norway foam,
The pilot of some small night-foundered skiff,
Deeming some island, oft, as seamen tell,
With fixèd anchor in his scaly rind,
Moors by his side under the lee, while night
Invests the sea, and wishèd morn delays:
So stretched out huge in length the Arch-Fiend lay
Chained on the burning lake; nor ever thence   210
Had risen or heaved his head, but that the will
And high permission of all-ruling Heaven
Left him at large to his own dark designs,
That with reiterated crimes he might

186. afflicted powers, routed forces. Latin *afflictus* means "beaten down."
    194–95. eyes That sparkling blazed. Cf. Spenser, *Faerie Queene*, I, xi, 14.
    197. as whom, as those whom.
    198. Titanian, or Earth-born. The Titans and Giants in classical mythology were sons of Heaven (Uranus) and Earth (Ge). For the Giants' war on Jove, cf. Hesiod *Theogony*.
    199. Briareos or Typhon. The former was a Titan, the latter a Giant. Cf. *Aeneid* x. 565–68; Aeschylus, *Prometheus*, 351–72.
    201. Leviathan. Cf. Psalms 104:26, and Job 41. The monster was often associated with the whale or the crocodile. Milton does not specifically identify it with either, although he suggests characteristics of both.
    203 ff. This is an old traveller's story, the most familiar version being in the *Arabian Nights*. night-foundered, i.e., lost in the darkness as completely as a sunken ship is lost in the ocean.
    208. invests, covers as with a garment.
    210. Chained on the burning lake. Cf. II Pet. 2:4; Jude 6; Rev. 20:1, 2. Milton does not ask himself whether the chains are real or metaphorical.

Heap on himself damnation, while he sought
Evil to others, and enraged might see
How all his malice served but to bring forth
Infinite goodness, grace and mercy shown
On Man by him seduced, but on himself
Treble confusion, wrath and vengeance poured.   220
    Forthwith upright he rears from off the pool
His mighty stature; on each hand the flames
Driven backward slope their pointing spires, and rolled
In billows, leave in the midst a horrid vale.
Then with expanded wings he steers his flight
Aloft, incumbent on the dusky air
That felt unusual weight till on dry land
He lights, if it were land that ever burned
With solid, as the lake with liquid fire,
And such appeared in hue; as when the force   230
Of subterranean wind transports a hill
Torn from Pelorus, or the shattered side
Of thundering Ætna, whose combustible
And fuellëd entrails thence conceiving fire,
Sublimed with mineral fury, aid the winds,
And leave a singëd bottom all involved
With stench and smoke: such resting found the sole
Of unblest feet. Him followed his next mate,
Both glorying to have scaped the Stygian flood
As gods, and by their own recovered strength,   240
Not by the sufferance of supernal power.
    "Is this the region, this the soil, the clime,"
Said then the lost Archangel, "this the seat
That we must change for Heaven, this mournful gloom

226. **incumbent,** leaning on (Latin *incumbens*).
232. **Pelorus,** Cape Faro in Sicily, near Mt. Aetna. Cf. *Aeneid* iii.
571–82.
235. **sublimed,** sublimated, converted to gaseous form, but also with the
original sense of lifted up; **the winds,** i.e., the winds or gases within the
earth which were supposed to be the cause of earthquakes. Cf. I *Henry IV,*
III, 1, 28–30:

> oft the teeming earth
> Is with a kind of colic pinched and vex'd
> By the imprisoning of unruly wind
> Within her womb.

Milton's complete formula for a volcanic explosion seems to be this: The
subterranean wind blows off part of the mountain. The friction generates
heat and sets fire to the combustible materials, including the explosive
matter. The force of the latter is added to that of the winds.
236. **involved,** wrapped in.
239. **Both glorying . . . power.** Cf. *Odyssey* iv. 502–4.
244. **change for,** take in exchange for.

For that celestial light? Be it so, since he
Who now is sovran can dispose and bid
What shall be right. Farthest from him is best,
Whom reason hath equalled, force hath made supreme
Above his equals. Farewell happy fields
Where joy for ever dwells: Hail horrors, hail   250
Infernal world, and thou profoundest Hell
Receive thy new possessor: one who brings
A mind not to be changed by place or time.
The mind is its own place, and in itself
Can make a Heaven of Hell, a Hell of Heaven.
What matter where, if I be still the same,
And what I should be, all but less than he
Whom thunder hath made greater? Here at least
We shall be free; the Almighty hath not built
Here for his envy, will not drive us hence: 260
Here we may reign secure, and in my choice
To reign is worth ambition, though in Hell:
Better to reign in Hell than serve in Heaven.
But wherefore let we then our faithful friends,
The associates and co-partners of our loss,
Lie thus astonished on the oblivious pool,
And call them not to share with us their part
In this unhappy mansion; or once more
With rallied arms to try what may be yet
Regained in Heaven, or what more lost in Hell?"   270
  So Satan spake, and him Beëlzebub
Thus answered. "Leader of those armies bright,
Which but the Omnipotent none could have foiled,
If once they hear that voice, their liveliest pledge
Of hope in fears and dangers, heard so oft
In worst extremes, and on the perilous edge

246. **sovran**, sovereign, supreme in power.
254-55. Cf. Horace *Epistles* i. xi. 27; also *Comus*, 381-85. The supremacy of the mind is one of Milton's favorite ideas. The corollary of this utterance of Satan's is to be found in IV, 20-23.
256-58. **all but less than**, etc. Usually interpreted as "all but equal to" or "less only than," but other or additional meanings are possible. "What I should be" is, in Satan's mind, God's equal. He would rather be anything but inferior and, since the mind is its own place, he *can* be equal in everything but power. The confusion of grammar is no greater than the confusion of frustrated human emotion.
263. Cf. the remark of Caesar recorded by Plutarch: "I had rather be the first man here than the second man in Rome." Cf. also Ps. 84:10 and *Odyssey* xi. 488.
266. **oblivious**, causing forgetfulness. Milton is thinking of the classical Lethe.
276. **edge**. Latin *acies*, edge, means also battle line.

Of battle when it raged, in all assaults
Their surest signal, they will soon resume
New courage and revive, though now they lie
Grovelling and prostrate on yon lake of fire,   280
As we erewhile, astounded and amazed;
No wonder, fallen such a pernicious height!"
    He scarce had ceased when the superior Fiend
Was moving toward the shore; his ponderous shield,
Ethereal temper, massy, large, and round,
Behind him cast; the broad circumference
Hung on his shoulders like the moon, whose orb
Through optic glass the Tuscan artist views
At evening from the top of Fesolë,
Or in Valdarno, to descry new lands,   290
Rivers or mountains in her spotty globe.
His spear, to equal which the tallest pine
Hewn on Norwegian hills, to be the mast
Of some great ammiral, were but a wand,
He walked with, to support uneasy steps
Over the burning marle, not like those steps
On Heaven's azure; and the torrid clime
Smote on him sore besides, vaulted with fire.
Nathless he so endured, till on the beach
Of that inflamëd sea, he stood and called   300
His legions, angel forms, who lay entranced,
Thick as autumnal leaves that strew the brooks
In Vallombrosa, where the Etrurian shades
High over-arched embower; or scattered sedge
Afloat, when with fierce winds Orion armed

    288. the Tuscan artist, Galileo, whom Milton had visited during his
stay in Italy. Cf. V, 262 for another reference to Galileo's telescope.
    289. Fesolë, Fiesole, a small town located on a hill just outside
Florence.
    290. Valdarno, the valley of the Arno, in which Florence is located.
Galileo's last residence was at Arcetri, west of the main part of the city. He
was blind or almost so when Milton visited him and lamented that he could
no longer look at the universe which his discoveries had made more wonderful. He died in 1641. Yet Milton uses the present tense in speaking of
him. There is inexactness also in the place references. Milton is writing
poetry, not history.
    294. ammiral, admiral, flagship.
    296. marle, soil.   **299. Nathless,** nevertheless.
    302 ff. Note the series of brilliant Homeric similes used to emphasize the
numbers of the fallen angels. They are compared (1) when lying on the
lake, to fallen leaves and floating sea-weed; (2) when flying, to a cloud of
locusts; (3) when alighted, to a huge invading army.
    303. Vallombrosa, a district about eighteen miles from Florence, con-
taining a famous monastery which Milton is said to have visited. The name
is Italian for "shady valley."

Hath vexed the Red-Sea coast, whose waves o'erthrew
Busiris and his Memphian chivalry
While with perfidious hatred they pursued
The sojourners of Goshen, who beheld
From the safe shore their floating carcasses   310
And broken chariot wheels; so thick bestrewn
Abject and lost lay these, covering the flood,
Under amazement of their hideous change.
He called so loud, that all the hollow deep
Of Hell resounded. "Princes, Potentates,
Warriors, the flower of Heaven, once yours, now lost,
If such astonishment as this can seize
Eternal spirits; or have ye chosen this place
After the toil of battle to repose
Your wearied virtue, for the ease you find   320
To slumber here, as in the vales of Heaven?
Or in this abject posture have ye sworn
To adore the conqueror, who now beholds
Cherub and Seraph rolling in the flood
With scattered arms and ensigns, till anon
His swift pursuers from Heaven gates discern
The advantage, and descending tread us down
Thus drooping, or with linkèd thunderbolts
Transfix us to the bottom of this gulf.
Awake, arise, or be for ever fallen!"   330
    They heard and were abashed, and up they sprung
Upon the wing, as when men wont to watch
On duty, sleeping found by whom they dread,
Rouse and bestir themselves ere well awake.
Nor did they not perceive the evil plight
In which they were, or the fierce pains not feel;
Yet to their general's voice they soon obeyed
Innumerable. As when the potent rod

305. **Orion, a** constellation proverbially associated with storms, *nimbosus Orion.*
307 ff. Cf. Exod. 14. **Busiris** was an ancient Egyptian king, whom Milton for some reason identifies with the Pharaoh whose hosts were drowned in the Red Sea. **Memphian** is here equivalent to Egyptian, Memphis being the ancient capital of Egypt. **The sojourners of Goshen** are of course the Israelites.
312. **Abject,** cast down (Latin *abjectus*).
320. **virtue,** valor, strength (Latin *virtus*).
327. **linkèd thunderbolts.** The thunderbolts are compared to linked cannon balls.
335. **Nor did they not, i.e.,** they did. The idiom is based on the Latin *neque non.*
338 ff. **As when the potent rod,** etc. Cf. Exod. 10:12-15. Moses was Amram's son.

Of Amram's son in Egypt's evil day,
Waved round the coast, up called a pitchy cloud   340
Of locusts, warping on the eastern wind,
That o'er the realm of impious Pharaoh hung
Like night, and darkened all the land of Nile:
So numberless were those bad angels seen
Hovering on wing under the cope of Hell
'Twixt upper, nether, and surrounding fires;
Till, as a signal given, the uplifted spear
Of their great Sultan waving to direct
Their course, in even balance down they light
On the firm brimstone, and fill all the plain;   350
A multitude, like which the populous North
Poured never from her frozen loins, to pass
Rhene or the Danaw, when her barbarous sons
Came like a deluge on the South, and spread
Beneath Gibraltar to the Libyan sands.
Forthwith from every squadron and each band
The heads and leaders thither haste where stood
Their great commander; godlike shapes and forms
Excelling human, Princely Dignities,
And Powers that erst in Heaven sat on thrones;   360
Though of their names in heavenly records now
Be no memorial, blotted out and rased
By their rebellion from the Books of Life.
Nor had they yet among the sons of Eve
Got them new names, till wandering o'er the Earth,
Through God's high sufferance for the trial of Man,
By falsities and lies the greatest part
Of mankind they corrupted to forsake
God their Creator, and the invisible
Glory of him that made them to transform   370
Oft to the image of a brute, adorned

340. **pitchy,** dark as pitch.
341. **warping,** working slowly forward with a bending or swerving motion. The term is primarily nautical.
345. **cope,** vault or canopy. The word originally denoted a kind of garment (cape), but the metaphorical use was common before Milton's time.
351. **A multitude,** etc. Milton concentrates in a simile the history of the barbarian invasions of the Roman Empire. Successive inroads were made by the Goths, the Vandals, and the Huns.
353. **Rhene,** the Rhine (from Latin Rhenus). **Danaw,** the Danube (from German *Donau*).
355. **Beneath Gibraltar,** i.e., south of Gibraltar. The Vandals crossed from Spain into North Africa.
364 ff. **Nor had they yet,** etc. The idea that the fallen angels become the pagan divinities goes back to early Patristic sources. The identification furnishes Milton with abundant biblical and mythological data regarding the inhabitants of hell. Cf. "Nativity Ode," 168 ff.

apologize to reader
for using known
deities

With gay religions full of pomp and gold,
And devils to adore for deities:
Then were they known to men by various names,
And various idols through the heathen world.
    Say, Muse, their names then known, who first, who last,
Roused from the slumber on that fiery couch,   *Followers of*
At their great Emperor's call, as next in worth   *Satan*
Came singly where he stood on the bare strand,
While the promiscuous crowd stood yet aloof.   380
    The chief were those who from the pit of Hell
Roaming to seek their prey on Earth, durst fix   *idols*
Their seats long after next the seat of God,
Their altars by his altar, gods adored
Among the nations round, and durst abide
Jehovah thundering out of Sion, throned
Between the Cherubim; yea, often placed
Within his sanctuary itself their shrines,
Abominations; and with cursèd things
His holy rites and solemn feasts profaned,   390 *most fierce*
And with their darkness durst affront his light.   *moloch*
First Moloch, horrid king besmeared with blood   *all of these deities*
Of human sacrifice, and parents' tears,   *are in hell*
Though for the noise of drums and timbrels loud   *militant puritan*
Their children's cries unheard, that passed through fire *as later. & Gods*
To his grim idol. Him the Ammonite   *of past.*
Worshipped in Rabba and her watery plain,
In Argob and in Basan, to the stream
Of utmost Arnon. Nor content with such   *ass. self w/*
Audacious neighborhood, the wisest heart   *conquest old* 400
Of Solomon he led by fraud to build   *gods -*
His temple right against the temple of God
On that opprobrious hill, and made his grove
The pleasant valley of Hinnom, Tophet thence

    386–87. throned Between the Cherubim. Cf. Ps. 80:1. The refer-
ence is to the golden figures placed over the Ark of the Covenant.
    392 ff. First, Moloch, etc. The list of the principal demons is parallel
to Homer's catalogue of the ships (*Iliad* ii. 484 ff.) and Virgil's of the
Trojan warriors (*Aeneid* vii. 641 ff.). A new appeal to the Muse is made
by both ancient authors at this point.
    392. Moloch. Cf. II Kings 23:10, etc.
    398–99. Argob, Basan, Arnon, all on the east side of the Jordan.
These, like many of the other names in the passage, are used more for their
suggestive sound than for their precise signification. The usual form of
Basan is Bashan, but Milton regularly avoids *sh.*
    403. that opprobrious hill, the Mount of Olives, called after Solo-
mon's offense "the mount of corruption." Cf. II Kings 23:13.
    404. Hinnom, a ravine southwest of Jerusalem. **Tophet,** cf. II Kings
23:10; Jer. 7:31.

And black Gehenna called, the type of Hell.
Next Chemos, the óbscene dread of Moab's sons,
From Aroar to Nebo, and the wild
Of southmost Abarim; in Hesebon
And Horonaim, Seon's realm, beyond
The flowery dale of Sibma clad with vines,   410
And Elealè to the Asphaltic pool.
Peor his other name, when he enticed
Israel in Sittim on their march from Nile
To do him wanton rites, which cost them woe.
Yet thence his lustful orgies he enlarged
Even to that hill of scandal, by the grove
Of Moloch homicide, lust hard by hate;
Till good Josiah drove them thence to Hell.
With these came they, who from the bordering flood
Of old Euphrates to the brook that parts   420
Egypt from Syrian ground, had general names
Of Baalim and Ashtaroth, those male,
These feminine. For spirits when they please
Can either sex assume, or both; so soft
And uncompounded is their essence pure,
Not tied or manacled with joint or limb,
Nor founded on the brittle strength of bones,
Like cumbrous flesh; but in what shape they choose,
Dilated or condensed, bright or obscure,
Can execute their airy purposes,   430
And works of love or enmity fulfil.
For those the race of Israel oft forsook
Their living Strength, and unfrequented left
His righteous altar, bowing lowly down
To bestial gods; for which their heads as low
Bowed down in battle, sunk before the spear
Of despicable foes. With these in troop

406. **Chemos,** the god of the Moabites, practically identical with Moloch.

407 ff. **Aroar,** etc., i.e. from the southern boundary of the Moabites to Mt. Nebo (Pisgah) on the north.

411. **Asphaltic pool,** the Dead Sea, so called from the asphalt or bitumen which it contains.

413–14. Cf. Num. 25:1–5.

419. Cf. II Kings 23.

421. **Baalim and Ashtaroth.** The Phoenician and Canaanitish people worshiped Baal and Astoreth (Astarte) under various manifestations, collectively designated by the plurals ending in -*im* (masculine) and -*oth* (feminine).

425. **uncompounded,** simple, not mixed. Milton's idea is that the angelic substance belongs to the realm of the abstract and general rather than of the concrete and particular. This Platonic notion underlies his whole representation of heaven.

Came Astoreth, whom the Phœnicians called
Astarte, Queen of Heaven, with crescent horns;
To whose bright image nightly by the moon   440
Sidonian virgins paid their vows and songs;
In Sion also not unsung, where stood
Her temple on the offensive mountain, built
By that uxorious king, whose heart though large,
Beguiled by fair idolatresses, fell
To idols foul. Thammuz came next behind,
Whose annual wound in Lebanon allured
The Syrian damsels to lament his fate
In amorous ditties all a summer's day,
While smooth Adonis from his native rock   450
Ran purple to the sea, supposed with blood
Of Thammuz yearly wounded: the love-tale
Infected Sion's daughters with like heat,
Whose wanton passions in the sacred porch
Ezekiel saw, when by the vision led
His eye surveyed the dark idolatries
Of alienated Judah. Next came one
Who mourned in earnest, when the captive ark
Maimed his brute image, head and hands lopt off
In his own temple, on the grunsel edge,   460
Where he fell flat, and shamed his worshippers:
Dagon his name, sea monster, upward man
And downward fish; yet had his temple high
Reared in Azotus, dreaded through the coast
Of Palestine, in Gath and Ascalon,
And Accaron and Gaza's frontier bounds.
Him followed Rimmon, whose delightful seat

439. **Astarte**, a moon goddess, also symbolized by the planet Venus.
She was the counterpart of the Greek Aphrodite.
444. **That uxorious king**, Solomon. Cf. I Kings 11:1-5.
446. **Thammuz**, identical with the Greek Adonis, was god of the solar
year and symbol of fertility. Mourning for his death in the autumn and
rejoicing at his revival in the spring were important Pagan ceremonials in
Babylonia and Phoenicia, and later in Egypt and Greece. Cf. Ezek. 8:13-
14; also Theocritus *Idyll* 14.
450. **Adonis.** The reference here is not to the god himself but to a
small river rising in the Lebanon mountains. Its discoloration by red sedi-
ment occasioned the belief to which Milton alludes.
456. **dark**, secret.
457 ff. Cf. I Sam. 5:1-5. Dagon was the national god of the Philistines.
460. **grunsel**, ground-sill, threshold.
464 ff. **Azotus, Gath, Ascalon, Accaron, Gaza**, the five chief cities
of the Philistines. Ashdod and Ekron are used for *Azotus* and *Accaron* in
the Authorized Version. The forms of Milton's proper names are frequently
based on the Vulgate or the Septuagint.
467. **Rimmon**, a Syrian deity.

Was fair Damascus, on the fertile banks
Of Abbana and Pharphar, lucid streams.
He also against the house of God was bold;   470
A leper once he lost and gained a king,
Ahaz his sottish conqueror, whom he drew
God's altar to disparage and displace
For one of Syrian mode, whereon to burn
His odious offerings, and adore the gods
Whom he had vanquished. After these appeared
A crew who under names of old renown,
Osiris, Isis, Orus, and their train,
With monstrous shapes and sorceries abused
Fanatic Egypt and her priests, to seek   480
Their wandering gods disguised in brutish forms
Rather than human. Nor did Israel scape
The infection, when their borrowed gold composed
The calf in Oreb; and the rebel king
Doubled that sin in Bethel and in Dan,
Likening his Maker to the grazèd ox,
Jehovah, who in one night when he passed
From Egypt marching, equalled with one stroke
Both her first-born and all her bleating gods.
Belial came last, than whom a spirit more lewd   490
Fell not from Heaven, or more gross to love
Vice for itself. To him no temple stood
Or altar smoked; yet who more oft than he
In temples and at altars, when the priest
Turns atheist, as did Eli's sons, who filled
With lust and violence the house of God.

471. a leper, Naaman. Cf. II Kings 5.
472. Ahaz, a king of Judah. Cf. II Kings 16.
478. Osiris, the chief male deity of the Egyptians, was worshiped
under the form of a sacred bull. Isis, the sister and wife of Osiris, was represented with the head or horns of a cow. Orus, or Horus, son of Osiris and
Isis, was generally represented with the head of a hawk. Cf. "Nativity
Ode" 211–15.
479. abused, deceived.
482 ff. Cf. Exod. 32. The borrowed gold was that taken from the
Egyptians (Exod. 12:35).
484. the rebel king, Jeroboam. Cf. I Kings 12:28, 29.
487 ff. Cf. Exod. 12:29.
490 ff. Belial was not originally a proper name, but an abstract noun
meaning "wickedness." In the New Testament it is sometimes used as synonymous with Satan: e.g., in II Cor. 6:15. Milton makes Belial the embodiment of effeminacy and lust, far more depraved than Satan.
493–505. These famous lines suggest conditions under Charles II but
could apply more generally. The biblical term "sons of Belial" was common
in the mouth of Puritans.
496. Eli's sons. Cf. I Sam. 2:12 ff.

In courts and palaces he also reigns
And in luxurious cities, where the noise
Of riot ascends above their loftiest towers,
And injury and outrage; and when night   500
Darkens the streets, then wander forth the sons
Of Belial, flown with insolence and wine.
Witness the streets of Sodom, and that night
In Gibeah, when the hospitable door
Exposed a matron, to avoid worse rape.
    These were the prime in order and in might;
The rest were long to tell, though far renowned,
The Ionian gods, of Javan's issue held
Gods, yet confessed later than Heaven and Earth,
Their boasted parents; Titan, Heaven's first-born,   510
With his enormous brood, and birthright seized
By younger Saturn; he from mightier Jove,
His own and Rhea's son, like measure found;
So Jove usurping reigned. These, first in Crete
And Ida known, thence on the snowy top
Of cold Olympus ruled the middle air,
Their highest Heaven; or on the Delphian cliff,
Or in Dodona, and through all the bounds
Of Doric land; or who with Saturn old
Fled over Adria to the Hesperian fields,   520
And o'er the Celtic roamed the utmost isles.
    All these and more came flocking; but with looks
Downcast and damp, yet such wherein appeared
Obscure some glimpse of joy, to have found their Chief
Not in despair, to have found themselves not lost
In loss itself; which on his countenance cast
Like doubtful hue. But he, his wonted pride
Soon recollecting, with high words that bore

502. **flown**, flushed (literally), and swollen (metaphorically).
505. Cf. Gen. 19:4–8; Judg. 19:22–24.
508. **Ionian**, Greek (the word being used generically). **Javan's issue**, the offspring of Javan, son of Japheth (cf. Gen. 10:2); i.e., the Greeks. The name Javan is etymologically identical with Ion, whence Ionia and Ionian.
509. **confessed later**, i.e., admitted to be of later origin. The Greeks themselves made Heaven and Earth the ancestors of their deities.
510. **Titan**, here specifically Oceanus, eldest of the Titans. For the genealogy of Jove and the overthrow of Saturn, cf. Hesiod *Theogony* 133 ff.
515. **Ida**, the reputed birthplace of Jove.
516. **middle air**. The older physics divided the air into three regions.
517. **Delphian cliff**. Mount Parnassus above Delphi, seat of the famous oracle of Apollo.
520. **Adria**, the Adriatic sea. **Hesperian fields**, Italy.
521. **Celtic**. The noun "fields" is understood from the preceding line. **the utmost isles**, Britain.

Semblance of worth, not substance, gently raised
Their fainting courage, and dispelled their fears.   530
Then straight commands that, at the warlike sound
Of trumpets loud and clarions, be upreared
His mighty standard; that proud honor claimed
Azazel as his right, a Cherub tall;
Who forthwith from the glittering staff unfurled
The imperial ensign, which full high advanced
Shone like a meteor streaming to the wind,
With gems and golden luster rich emblazed,
Seraphic arms and trophies; all the while
Sonorous metal blowing martial sounds;   540
At which the universal host up sent
A shout that tore Hell's concave, and beyond
Frighted the reign of Chaos and old Night.
All in a moment through the gloom were seen
Ten thousand banners rise into the air
With orient colors waving; with them rose
A forest huge of spears; and thronging helms
Appeared, and serried shields in thick array
Of depth immeasurable. Anon they move
In perfect phalanx to the Dorian mood   550
Of flutes and soft recorders; such as raised
To height of noblest temper heroes old
Arming to battle, and instead of rage
Deliberate valor breathed, firm and unmoved
With dread of death to flight or foul retreat;
Nor wanting power to mitigate and swage
With solemn touches troubled thoughts, and chase

531 ff. **Then straight commands,** etc. Milton represents the host of
Satan as an army disciplined according to the military science of the ancients. **Phalanx** (l. 550 ff.) is the Greek term for battalion. The **Dorian
mood** is one of three modes or scales of ancient Greek music; it is represented by Plato (*Republic* iii. 399) as fittest to inspire valor. **Flutes** (of which
the **recorder** is a variety) are mentioned by Thucydides as the instruments
to the sound of which the Spartans marched to battle. **Soft** seems like an
inappropriate adjective, but Milton's idea is that the highest courage is not
a furor of the blood but a temperate resolution of the soul inspired by
thoughtfulness. The music also helps to reconcile the fallen angels to their
lot. A whole philosophy of art in its relation to action is implied in these
lines.

534. **Azazel,** Satan's standard bearer in the apocryphal Book of Enoch.
The name also occurs in Lev. 16:8, 10, 26, where the Authorized Version
renders it "scapegoat."

536. **advanced,** uplifted. Cf. *The Tempest,* I, ii, 405: "the fringed
curtains of thine eyes advance."

543. **reign,** kingdom (Latin *regnum*).

546. **orient,** bright, lustrous.

548. **serried,** locked together.

Anguish and doubt and fear and sorrow and pain
From mortal or immortal minds. Thus they,
Breathing united force with fixëd thought,   560
Moved on in silence to soft pipes that charmed
Their painful steps o'er the burnt soil; and now
Advanced in view they stand, a horrid front
Of dreadful length and dazzling arms, in guise
Of warriors old, with ordered spear and shield,
Awaiting what command their mighty Chief
Had to impose. He through the armëd files
Darts his experienced eye, and soon traverse
The whole battalion views, their order due,
Their visages and stature as of gods;   570
Their number last he sums. And now his heart
Distends with pride, and hardening in his strength
Glories; for never since created Man,
Met such embodied force, as named with these
Could merit more than that small infantry
Warred on by cranes: though all the giant brood
Of Phlegra with the heroic race were joined
That fought at Thebes and Ilium, on each side
Mixed with auxiliar gods; and what resounds
In fable or romance of Uther's son   580
Begirt with British and Armoric knights;
And all who since, baptized or infidel,
Jousted in Aspramont, or Montalban,

563. **horrid,** bristling (Latin *horridus*).
567 ff. Satan glances first along the files from front to rear, then along
the ranks from right to left.
573. **since created man,** i.e., since man's creation. The construction is
a Latinism: *post hominem creatum.*
575. **that small infantry,** the Pigmies, whose unsuccessful struggle
with the cranes is mentioned by Homer (*Iliad* iii. 3–6). Milton says that
compared to Satan's host all the famous hosts of legend joined together
would be as insignificant as a Pigmy army. **Infantry** may be a pun.
577. **Phlegra,** the scene of the battle between the giants and the gods.
Cf. Pindar *Nemean Odes* i. 67; Ovid *Metamorphoses* x. 150, 151.
579. **on each . . . gods.** In the *Iliad* and elsewhere, the gods are represented as joining with the Greeks and Trojans in battle.
580. **Uther's son,** King Arthur.
581. **British and Armoric knights.** Some of Arthur's knights came
from the island of Britain, some from the peninsula of Armorica, modern
Brittany. Milton's classification shows a precise reading of Malory and
Geoffrey of Monmouth.
583 ff. The references here are to places celebrated in the wars of the
Christians and Saracens as narrated in the Italian romances, notably in
Ariosto's *Orlando Furioso*. **Aspramont** and **Montalban** were in France,
Trebisond in Asia Minor. Charlemagne was not killed at Fontarabbia as
these lines seem to imply. But the rear-guard of his army was cut to pieces

Damasco, or Marocco, or Trebisond,
Or whom Biserta sent from Afric shore
When Charlemain with all his peerage fell
By Fontarabbia. Thus far these beyond
Compare of mortal prowess, yet observed
Their dread commander. He above the rest
In shape and gesture proudly eminent   590
Stood like a tower; his form had yet not lost
All her original brightness, nor appeared
Less than Archangel ruined, and the excess
Of glory obscured: as when the sun new-risen
Looks through the horizontal misty air
Shorn of his beams, or from behind the moon
In dim eclipse disastrous twilight sheds
On half the nations, and with fear of change
Perplexes monarchs. Darkened so, yet shone
Above them all the Archangel; but his face   600
Deep scars of thunder had intrenched, and care
Sat on his faded cheek, but under brows,
Of dauntless courage, and considerate pride
Waiting revenge. Cruel his eye, but cast
Signs of remorse and passion to behold
The fellows of his crime, the followers rather
(Far other once beheld in bliss), condemned
For ever now to have their lot in pain,
Millions of spirits for his fault amerced
Of Heaven, and from eternal splendors flung   610
For his revolt, yet faithful how they stood,
Their glory withered: as when Heaven's fire
Hath scathed the forest oaks or mountain pines,
With singèd top their stately growth though bare
Stands on the blasted heath. He now prepared
To speak; whereat their doubled ranks they bend
From wing to wing, and half enclose him round
With all his peers: attention held them mute.
Thrice he assayed, and thrice in spite of scorn,

in the pass of Roncesvalles (about forty miles from Fontarabbia), and
among those slain was Roland (Orlando), the most famous of his twelve
"peers."
    594–99. **as when the sun . . . monarchs.** According to John Toland,
these lines were objected to by the censor as suggesting a prophecy of the
downfall of Charles II.
    597. **disastrous,** ill-starred, portentous (Latin *dis* + *astrum*, star).
    603. **considerate,** well-considered, thoughtful.
    605. **remorse and passion,** pity and intense sorrow.
    609. **amerced of,** deprived of as if by a fine.
    616–17. **whereat . . . wing.** Note the exact use of military terms.

Tears such as angels weep, burst forth; at last   620
Words interwove with sighs found out their way.
"O myriads of immortal spirits, O Powers
Matchless, but with the Almighty, and that strife
Was not inglorious, though the event was dire,
As this place testifies, and this dire change
Hateful to utter. But what power of mind
Foreseeing or presaging, from the depth
Of knowledge past or present, could have feared
How such united force of gods, how such
As stood like these, could ever know repulse?   630
For who can yet believe, though after loss,
That all these puissant legions, whose exile
Hath emptied Heaven, shall fail to re-ascend
Self-raised, and re-possess their native seat.
For me, be witness all the host of Heaven,
If counsels different, or danger shunned
By me, have lost our hopes. But he who reigns
Monarch in Heaven, till then as one secure
Sat on his throne, upheld by old repute,
Consent or custom, and his regal state   640
Put forth at full, but still his strength concealed,
Which tempted our attempt, and wrought our fall.
Henceforth his might we know, and know our own,
So as not either to provoke, or dread *Beelzebub & Satan*
New war provoked; our better part remains
To work in close design, by fraud or guile *to overcome God*
What force effected not; that he no less *not power or #*
At length from us may find, who overcomes
By force, hath overcome but half his foe.
Space may produce new worlds; whereof so rife   650
There went a fame in Heaven that he ere long *what couldn't use*
Intended to create, and therein plant *in heaven now use fraud & guile*

624. **event**, outcome (Latin *eventus*).
637–40. Satan is misapplying Milton's own theory of kingship: i.e.,
rulers hold their thrones by **consent or custom** rather than by divine right.
Cf. *The Tenure of Kings and Magistrates*.
646 ff. In turning from **force** to **close design**, Satan shows his familiar-
ity with the two well-recognized Machiavellian methods of gaining power.
651. **fame**, rumor (Latin *fama*). Milton would have known interpretations of the story which made the creation of the world precede the revolt
of Satan. In Vondel's *Lucifer* it is jealousy of the creation of man rather
than of the promotion of Christ which motivates Satan's attempt. God, of
course, foreknew that man would be created to take the place of the fallen
angels but he revealed only a part of the truth. Satan's later statement (II,
350) that God had declared he would favor man above the angels may be
simply a lie. At least, there is no sugestion that Satan was jealous of man
before he saw him in Paradise (IV, 358–60).

A generation, whom his choice regard
Should favor equal to the sons of Heaven.
Thither, if but to pry, shall be perhaps
Our first eruption, thither or elsewhere;
For this infernal pit shall never hold
Celestial spirits in bondage, nor the Abyss
Long under darkness cover. But these thoughts
Full counsel must mature. Peace is despaired,   660
For who can think submission! War then, war
Open or understood, must be resolved."
    He spake; and to confirm his words, out flew
Millions of flaming swords, drawn from the thighs
Of mighty Cherubim; the sudden blaze
Far round illumined Hell. Highly they raged
Against the Highest, and fierce with graspëd arms
Clashed on their sounding shields the din of war,
Hurling defiance toward the vault of Heaven.
    There stood a hill not far, whose grisly top   670
Belched fire and rolling smoke; the rest entire
Shone with a glossy scurf, undoubted sign
That in his womb was hid metallic ore,
The work of sulphur. Thither winged with speed
A numerous brigad hastened: as when bands
Of pioneers with spade and pickaxe armed
Forerun the royal camp, to trench a field,
Or cast a rampart. Mammon led them on,
Mammon, the least erected spirit that fell
From Heaven, for even in Heaven his looks and thoughts   680
Were always downward bent, admiring more
The riches of Heaven's pavement, trodden gold,
Than aught divine or holy else enjoyed
In vision beatific. By him first
Men also, and by his suggestion taught,
Ransacked the center, and with impious hands
Rifled the bowels of their mother Earth
For treasures better hid. Soon had his crew
Opened into the hill a spacious wound

660. despaired, i.e., despaired of (Latin *desperatur*).
674. The work of sulphur. Sulphur and quicksilver were held by the alchemists to be the "parents" of the metals.
676. pioneers, engineers.
678. Mammon. The word was originally a common noun, meaning "riches." Cf. Matt. 6:24; Luke 16:9–13. Cf. also Spenser's use of it to denote the god of wealth (*Faerie Queene*, II, vii, 8 ff.).
679. erected, high-souled, noble.
684. vision beatific. *Visio beatifica* was the phrase regularly used by medieval theologians to describe the experience of "seeing" God.

And digged out ribs of gold. Let none admire   690
That riches grow in Hell; that soil may best
Deserve the precious bane. And here let those
Who boast in mortal things, and wondering tell
Of Babel, and the works of Memphian kings,
Learn how their greatest monuments of fame,
And strength, and art, are easily outdone
By spirits reprobate, and in an hour
What in an age they with incessant toil
And hands innumerable scarce perform.
Nigh on the plain, in many cells prepared,   700
That underneath had veins of liquid fire
Sluiced from the lake, a second multitude
With wondrous art founded the massy ore,
Severing each kind, and scummed the bullion dross.
A third as soon had formed within the ground
A various mould, and from the boiling cells
By strange conveyance filled each hollow nook,
As in an organ from one blast of wind
To many a row of pipes the sound-board breathes.
Anon out of the earth a fabric huge   710
Rose like an exhalation, with the sound
Of dulcet symphonies and voices sweet,
Built like a temple, where pilasters round
Were set, and Doric pillars overlaid
With golden architrave; nor did there want
Cornice or frieze with bossy sculptures graven;
The roof was fretted gold. Not Babylon,
Nor great Alcairo such magnificence
Equalled in all their glories, to enshrine

690. admire, wonder (Latin *admirari*).
691–92. That riches . . . bane. Cf. Horace *Odes* iii. 3–49.
694. Babel. Cf. Gen. 11:1–9. the works of Memphian kings, i.e., the Pyramids of the Pharaohs. Memphian is equivalent to Egyptian, as in 307 above.
703. founded, fused, melted.
708–10. As in . . . breathes. Milton evidently understands the construction of the organ, an instrument on which he himself was a performer. There is another reference to it in XI, 558–63. Sound-board is the top board of the wind chest.
713 ff. Built like . . . gold. Note Milton's careful use of architectural terms to suggest the style of an ancient Greek temple. It has been plausibly suggested that he had also in mind Saint Peter's Church in Rome. Pilasters are square columns supporting the master beam or architrave, on which are placed the frieze and cornice. By bossy sculptures are meant figures or ornaments projected in relief. The roof of fretted gold is one adorned with inwrought patterns.
718. Alcairo, the ancient city of Memphis, near the site of modern Cairo.

Belus or Serapis their gods, or seat   720
Their kings, when Egypt with Assyria strove
In wealth and luxury. The ascending pile
Stood fixed her stately height, and straight the doors
Opening their brazen folds discover wide
Within, her ample spaces, o'er the smooth
And level pavement; from the archëd roof
Pendent by the subtle magic many a row
Of starry lamps and blazing cressets fed
With naphtha and asphaltus yielded light
As from a sky. The hasty multitude   730
Admiring entered, and the work some praise,
And some the architect: his hand was known
In Heaven by many a towered structure high,
Where sceptred angels held their residence,
And sat as princes, whom the supreme King
Exalted to such power, and gave to rule,
Each in his Hierarchy, the Orders bright.
Nor was his name unheard or unadored
In ancient Greece; and in Ausonian land
Men called him Mulciber; and how he fell   740
From Heaven, they fabled, thrown by angry Jove
Sheer o'er the crystal battlements: from morn
To noon he fell, from noon to dewy eve,
A summer's day; and with the setting sun
Dropped from the zenith like a falling star,
On Lemnos the Ægæan isle. Thus they relate,
Erring; for he with this rebellious rout
Fell long before; nor aught availed him now
To have built in Heaven high towers; nor did he scape
By all his engines, but was headlong sent   750
With his industrious crew to build in Hell.
  Meanwhile the wingëd heralds by command
Of sovran power, with awful ceremony

720. **Belus,** the god Bel or Baal, whose great temple at Babylon is mentioned by Herodotus (*History* i. 181–83). **Serapis,** an Egyptian deity practically identified with Osiris. The most famous of his temples was at Alexandria, but there was also one at Memphis.
  726–30. Cf. *Aeneid* i. 726–27.
  732 ff. **the architect.** Milton is alluding to the Greek god Hephaestus (the Roman Vulcan or Mulciber), who built the palaces on Olympus. Possibly he means to identify Hephaestus with Mammon, as some editors believe; the text, however, hardly justifies that inference.
  737. Milton accepts the medieval idea of the angelic hierarchies without going into detail about it. Cf. 127, 128 and note.
  739. **Ausonian land,** Italy.
  742–43. **from morn to noon he fell.** Cf. *Iliad* i. 591 ff.
  750. **engines,** devices, inventions.
  753. **awful,** awe inspiring.

And trumpet's sound, throughout the host proclaim
A solemn council forthwith to be held
At Pandemonium, the high capitol
Of Satan and his peers; their summons called
From every band and squarèd regiment
By place or choice the worthiest; they anon
With hundreds and with thousands trooping came   760
Attended. All access was thronged, the gates
And porches wide, but chief the spacious hall
(Though like a covered field, where champions bold
Wont ride in armed, and at the Soldan's chair
Defied the best of Panim chivalry
To mortal combat or career with lance)
Thick swarmed, both on the ground and in the air,
Brushed with the hiss of rustling wings. As bees
In spring time, when the sun with Taurus rides,
Pour forth their populous youth about the hive   770
In clusters; they among fresh dews and flowers
Fly to and fro, or on the smoothèd plank,
The suburb of their straw-built citadel,
New rubbed with balm, expatiate and confer
Their state affairs. So thick the airy crowd
Swarmed and were straitened; till the signal given,
Behold a wonder! they but now who seemed
In bigness to surpass Earth's giant sons,
Now less than smallest dwarfs, in narrow room
Throng numberless, like that Pygmean race   780
Beyond the Indian mount, or fairy elves,
Whose midnight revels, by a forest side
Or fountain, some belated peasant sees,

756. **Pandemonium,** the abode of all the demons (from Greek παν, all and δαίμον, demon). The name, which is a Miltonic coinage, may have been suggested by *Pantheon,* the abode of all the gods.
757 ff. **their summons,** etc. The council is in reality a sort of military Parliament.
763–66. The allusion is to the single combats between Pagans and Crusaders described in the Italian romances of chivalry. **Soldan** is a variant of Sultan.
768 ff. **As bees,** etc. Cf. *Iliad* ii. 87 ff.; also *Aeneid* i. 430 ff. and vi. 707 ff.
769. **when the Sun with Taurus rides,** i.e., when the sun is in the zodiacal sign of the Bull (between April 19 and May 20).
774. **expatiate and confer,** walk abroad (Latin *spatiari*) and discuss. For the idea of the beehive as a commonwealth, cf. *Henry V,* I, ii, 188 ff.
776. **straitened,** crowded.
780 ff. See note on 575 above. The **Indian mount** is probably Imaus in the Himalayas. Cf. Pliny *Natural History* vii. 2.
781 ff. Milton is here drawing on the traditions of English fairy poetry. Cf. *A Midsummer Night's Dream,* II, i, 141.

Or dreams he sees, while overhead the Moon
Sits arbitress, and nearer to the Earth
Wheels her pale course; they on their mirth and dance
Intent, with jocund music charm his ear;
At once with joy and fear his heart rebounds.
Thus incorporeal spirits to smallest forms
Reduced their shapes immense, and were at large,   790
Though without number still, amidst the hall
Of that infernal court. But far within,
And in their own dimensions like themselves,
The great Seraphic Lords and Cherubim
In close recess and secret conclave sat,
A thousand demi-gods on golden seats,
Frequent and full. After short silence then
And summons read, the great consult began.

BOOK II

THE ARGUMENT

The consultation begun, Satan debates whether another battle
is to be hazarded for the recovery of Heaven: some advise it, others
dissuade. A third proposal is preferred, mentioned before by Satan,
to search the truth of that prophecy or tradition in Heaven concerning another world, and another kind of creature, equal, or not
much inferior, to themselves, about this time to be created. Their
doubt who shall be sent on this difficult search; Satan, their chief,
undertakes alone the voyage; is honoured and applauded. The
council thus ended, the rest betake them several ways and to several employments, as their inclinations lead them, to entertain the
time till Satan return. He passes on his journey to Hell gates,
finds them shut, and who sat there to guard them; by whom at
length they are opened, and discover to him the great gulf between
Hell and Heaven; with what difficulty he passes through, directed
by Chaos, the Power of that place, to the sight of this new world
which he sought.

785. **arbitress**, spectator.
790. **were at large**, had ample room.
793. **like themselves**, i.e., in their own shapes. Much has been said of
the poetic suggestiveness of this whole passage and of the multiplicity of
meaning and allusion in its detail. The latter, however, seems to be prin-
cipally evocative and ornamental and the net impression that of the multi-
tudinousness of the host and of the contrasting dignity of the great leaders
whose forms remain unchanged. This is about where representative democracy stood in Milton's mind by the time he wrote these lines.
795. **recess**, retirement.
797. **frequent**, crowded. Cf. Latin *frequens*, as in *frequens senatus*, a
full senate.

High on a throne of royal state, which far
Outshone the wealth of Ormus and of Ind,
Or where the gorgeous East with richest hand
Showers on her kings barbaric pearl and gold,
Satan exalted sat, by merit raised
To that bad eminence; and from despair
Thus high uplifted beyond hope, aspires
Beyond thus high, insatiate to pursue
Vain war with Heaven, and by success untaught,
His proud imaginations thus displayed.   10
    "Powers and Dominions, Deities of Heaven,
For since no deep within her gulf can hold
Immortal vigor, though oppressed and fallen,
I give not Heaven for lost. From this descent
Celestial Virtues rising, will appear
More glorious and more dread than from no fall,
And trust themselves to fear no second fate.
Me though just right, and the fixed laws of Heaven
Did first create your leader, next, free choice,
With what besides, in counsel or in fight,   20
Hath been achieved of merit, yet this loss
Thus far at least recovered, hath much more
Established in a safe unenvied throne
Yielded with full consent. The happier state
In Heaven, which follows dignity, might draw
Envy from each inferior; but who here
Will envy whom the highest place exposes
Foremost to stand against the Thunderer's aim
Your bulwark, and condemns to greatest share
Of endless pain? Where there is then no good   30
For which to strive, no strife can grow up there
From faction; for none sure will claim in Hell
Precedence, none whose portion is so small
Of present pain, that with ambitious mind
Will covet more. With this advantage then

1 ff. For an interesting parallel to Milton's infernal council, cf. Tasso,
Jerusalem Delivered, Canto IV.
    2. Ormus, a city on the Persian Gulf, famous as a market for precious
stones. It is often mentioned by Renaissance travelers. Ind, India.
    4. barbaric pearl and gold. Cf. *Aeneid* ii. 504: *barbarico auro*. The
sprinkling of powdered pearls and gold dust on a monarch at his coronation
was an Oriental custom. Shakespeare (*Antony and Cleopatra*, II, v, 45, 46)
makes a similar reference to it.
    9. success, i.e., ill-success, the outcome of his former attempt.
    17. trust themselves, etc., i.e., their experience has given them such
confidence that they will not fear to fall again.
    24 ff. Satan, like Belial (112 ff.), knows how to "make the worse ap-
pear the better reason."

To union, and firm faith, and firm accord,
More than can be in Heaven, we now return
To claim our just inheritance of old,
Surer to prosper than prosperity
Could have assured us; and by what best way,   40
Whether of open war or covert guile,
We now debate; who can advise, may speak."
   He ceased, and next him Moloch, sceptred king,
Stood up, the strongest and the fiercest spirit
That fought in Heaven; now fiercer by despair.
His trust was with the Eternal to be deemed
Equal in strength, and rather than be less
Cared not to be at all; with that care lost
Went all his fear: of God, or Hell, or worse
He recked not, and these words thereafter spake.   50
   "My sentence is for open war. Of wiles,
More unexpert, I boast not; them let those
Contrive who need, or when they need, not now.
For while they sit contriving, shall the rest,
Millions that stand in arms, and longing wait
The signal to ascend, sit lingering here
Heaven's fugitives, and for their dwelling-place
Accept this dark opprobrious den of shame,
The prison of his tyranny who reigns
By our delay? No, let us rather choose,   60
Armed with Hell flames and fury, all at once
O'er Heaven's high towers to force resistless way,
Turning our tortures into horrid arms
Against the Torturer; when to meet the noise
Of his almighty engine he shall hear
Infernal thunder, and for lightning see
Black fire and horror shot with equal rage
Among his angels, and his throne itself
Mixed with Tartarean sulphur and strange fire,
His own invented torments. But perhaps   70
The way seems difficult and steep to scale
With upright wing against a higher foe.
Let such bethink them, if the sleepy drench

50. **thereafter spake,** spoke accordingly.
   51. **sentence,** judgment, opinion (Latin *sententia*). Moloch is the type of blunt warrior who knows no other method of winning an object than to fight for it. Milton must have known such among the leaders of the Commonwealth.
   63. **tortures,** i.e., the flames which torture.
   65. **engine,** instrument—referring to the thunderbolt.
   69. **Tartarean,** infernal (from Tartarus, a classical name for hell).
   73. **such,** i.e., those who reason thus. **sleepy drench** sleep-producing

Of that forgetful lake benumb not still,
That in our proper motion we ascend
Up to our native seat; descent and fall
To us is adverse. Who but felt of late
When the fierce foe hung on our broken rear
Insulting, and pursued us through the deep,
With what compulsion and laborious flight   80
We sunk thus low? The ascent is easy then;
The event is feared; should we again provoke
Our stronger, some worse way his wrath may find
To our destruction; if there be in Hell
Fear to be worse destroyed; what can be worse
Than to dwell here, driven out from bliss, condemned
In this abhorrèd deep to utter woe;
Where pain of unextinguishable fire
Must exercise us without hope of end
The vassals of his anger, when the scourge   90
Inexorably, and the torturing hour
Calls us to penance? More destroyed than thus
We should be quite abolished and expire.
What fear we then? what doubt we to incense
His utmost ire? which to the height enraged,
Will either quite consume us, and reduce
To nothing this essential, happier far
Than miserable to have eternal being;
Or if our substance be indeed divine,
And cannot cease to be, we are at worst   100
On this side nothing; and by proof we feel
Our power sufficient to disturb his Heaven,
And with perpetual inroads to alarm,
Though inaccessible, his fatal throne;
Which if not victory is yet revenge."
He ended frowning, and his look denounced
Desperate revenge, and battle dangerous

drink. The word **drench** suggests contempt. Cf. *I Henry IV*, II, iv, 121:
"Give my roan horse a drench."
    74. **forgetful**, causing forgetfulness. Cf. I, 266 and note.
    75–77. The natural (**proper**) motion of Spirits, as of fire, is upward.
For them to fall is therefore unnatural (**adverse**).
    79. **Insulting.** The original Latin meaning (*insultans*, leaping upon)
is implied.
    82. **event**, outcome (as in I, 624).
    89. **exercise**, torment.
    94. **what doubt we**, i.e., why do we hesitate.
    97. **essential**, essence, spiritual being.
    104. **fatal**, upheld by fate. Admitting that the throne is so upheld,
Moloch is forced to grant its inaccessibility.
    106. **denounced**, proclaimed.

To less than gods. On the other side up rose
Belial, in act more graceful and humane;
A fairer person lost not Heaven; he seemed   110
For dignity composed and high exploit;
But all was false and hollow; though his tongue
Dropped manna, and could make the worse appear
The better reason, to perplex and dash
Maturest counsels: for his thoughts were low;
To vice industrious, but to nobler deeds
Timorous and slothful: yet he pleased the ear,
And with persuasive accent thus began.
    "I should be much for open war, O Peers,
As not behind in hate, if what was urged   120
Main reason to persuade immediate war,
Did not dissuade me most, and seem to cast
Ominous conjecture on the whole success:
When he who most excels in fact of arms,
In what he counsels and in what excels
Mistrustful, grounds his courage on despair
And utter dissolution, as the scope
Of all his aim, after some dire revenge.
First, what revenge? The towers of Heaven are filled
With armëd watch, that render all access   130
Impregnable; oft on the bordering deep
Encamp their legions, or with óbscure wing
Scout far and wide into the realm of Night,
Scorning surprise. Or could we break our way
By force, and at our heels all Hell should rise
With blackest insurrection, to confound
Heaven's purest light, yet our great enemy
All incorruptible would on his throne
Sit unpolluted, and the ethereal mould
Incapable of stain would soon expel   140
Her mischief, and purge off the baser fire,

109. act, bearing.
    113. manna. Cf. Exod. 16:31: "the taste of it was like wafers made
with honey."
    119 ff. Cf. with the abrupt beginning of Moloch's speech the insinuat-
ing oratory of Belial. Like a skilled debater, he turns his opponent's own
argument against him.
    124. fact of arms, feat of arms (Latin *factum*, deed).
    132. óbscure. In Milton, as in Shakespeare, two-syllable adjectives of
Latin derivation generally accent the first syllable when the next word begins
with an accent.
    136. blackest insurrection. Cf. 65–70. Belial answers Moloch point
by point.
    139. mould, substance.
    141. Her mischief, i.e., the damage or pollution caused by hell-fire.

Victorious. Thus repulsed, our final hope
Is flat despair; we must exasperate
The almighty victor to spend all his rage,
And that must end us, that must be our cure,
To be no more; sad cure; for who would lose,
Though full of pain, this intellectual being,
Those thoughts that wander through eternity,
To perish rather, swallowed up and lost
In the wide womb of uncreated Night,   150
Devoid of sense and motion? And who knows,
Let this be good, whether our angry foe
Can give it, or will ever? How he can
Is doubtful; that he never will is sure.
Will he, so wise, let loose at once his ire,
Belike through impotence, or unaware,
To give his enemies their wish, and end
Them in his anger, whom his anger saves
To punish endless? 'Wherefore cease we then?'
Say they who counsel war; 'we are decreed,   160
Reserved, and destined to eternal woe;
Whatever doing, what can we suffer more,
What can we suffer worse?' Is this then worst,
Thus sitting, thus consulting, thus in arms?
What when we fled amain, pursued and struck
With Heaven's afflicting thunder, and besought
The Deep to shelter us? this Hell then seemed
A refuge from those wounds. Or when we lay
Chained on the burning lake? that sure was worse.
What if the breath that kindled those grim fires   170
Awaked should blow them into sevenfold rage
And plunge us in the flames? or from above
Should intermitted vengeance arm again
His red right hand to plague us? What if all
Her stores were opened, and this firmament
Of Hell should spout her cataracts of fire,

149 ff. Cf. *Measure for Measure*, III, ii, 118-132. Both passages
superbly express the same instinctive shrinking before the thought of annihilation or of a future state of unknown suffering.
   152. Let this be good, i.e., granting that this (annihilation) is desirable.
   156. Belike, no doubt. As frequently in Shakespeare, the word implies
irony. impotence, lack of self-control (Latin *impotentia*).
   165. What when, i.e., how was it when. amain, with all haste, pre-
cipitately.
   170. Cf. Isa. 30:33.
   174. red right hand. Horace (*Odes* i. 2. 3, 4) uses the same phrase
with reference to Jove.

Impendent horrors, threatening hideous fall
One day upon our heads; while we perhaps
Designing or exhorting glorious war,
Caught in a fiery tempest shall be hurled   180
Each on his rock transfixed, the sport and prey
Of racking whirlwinds, or for ever sunk
Under yon boiling ocean, wrapped in chains;
There to converse with everlasting groans,
Unrespited, unpitied, unreprieved,
Ages of hopeless end; this would be worse.
War therefore, open or concealed, alike
My voice dissuades; for what can force or guile
With him, or who deceive his mind, whose eye
Views all things at one view? He from Heaven's height   190
All these our motions vain, sees and derides;
Not more almighty to resist our might
Than wise to frustrate all our plots and wiles.
Shall we then live thus vile, the race of Heaven
Thus trampled, thus expelled to suffer here
Chains and these torments? Better these than worse,
By my advice; since fate inevitable
Subdues us, and omnipotent decree,
The victor's will. To suffer, as to do,
Our strength is equal, nor the law unjust   200
That so ordains: this was at first resolved,
If we were wise, against so great a foe
Contending, and so doubtful what might fall.
I laugh when those who at the spear are bold
And venturous, if that fail them, shrink and fear
What yet they know must follow, to endure
Exile, or ignominy, or bonds, or pain,
The sentence of their conqueror: this is now
Our doom; which if we can sustain and bear,
Our supreme foe in time may much remit   210
His anger, and perhaps, thus far removed,
Not mind us not offending, satisfied
With what is punished; whence these raging fires
Will slacken, if his breath stir not their flames.
Our purer essence then will overcome

    177. impendent, overhanging.
    182. racking, twisting, torturing.
    185. Now how the repetition of the prefix intensifies the effect of utter
hopelessness. Cf. *Hamlet,* I, v, 77: "Unhouseled, disappointed, unaneled."
    186. of hopeless end, without hope of end.
    191. motions, proposals, plots.
    213. With what is punished, i.e., with the punishment already in-
flicted.

Their noxious vapor, or inured not feel,
Or changed at length, and to the place conformed
In temper and in nature, will receive
Familiar the fierce heat, and void of pain;
This horror will grow mild, this darkness light,   220
Besides what hope the never-ending flight
Of future days may bring, what chance, what change
Worth waiting, since our present lot appears
For happy though but ill, for ill not worst,
If we procure not to ourselves more woe."
    Thus Belial with words clothed in reason's garb,
Counselled ignoble ease, and peaceful sloth,
Not peace; and after him thus Mammon spake.
    "Either to disenthrone the King of Heaven
We war, if war be best, or to regain   230
Our own right lost. Him to unthrone we then
May hope, when everlasting Fate shall yield
To fickle Chance, and Chaos judge the strife:
The former, vain to hope, argues as vain
The latter; for what place can be for us
Within Heaven's bound, unless Heaven's Lord supreme
We overpower? Suppose he should relent
And publish grace to all, on promise made
Of new subjection; with what eyes could we
Stand in his presence humble, and receive   240
Strict laws imposed, to celebrate his throne
With warbled hymns, and to his Godhead sing
Forced halleluiahs; while he lordly sits
Our envied Sovran, and his altar breathes
Ambrosial odors and ambrosial flowers,
Our servile offerings. This must be our task
In Heaven, this our delight; how wearisome
Eternity so spent in worship paid
To whom we hate. Let us not then pursue,
By force impossible, by leave obtained   250
Unacceptable, though in Heaven, our state
Of splendid vassalage, but rather seek
Our own good from ourselves, and from our own
Live to ourselves, though in this vast recess,

    219. **Familiar the fierce heat,** etc., i.e., the fierce heat, by becoming
familiar, will be no longer painful. The considerations which move Belial
are in complete accordance with his character and philosophy.
    220. **light . . . flight.** Note the rhyme.
    224. **For happy,** etc., i.e., viewed as a happy situation the present one
is bad, but it is not so bad as it might be.
    234. **argues,** proves (Latin *arguere*).
    249. **pursue.** seek to regain.

Free, and to none accountable, preferring
Hard liberty before the easy yoke
Of servile pomp. Our greatness will appear
Then most conspicuous, when great things of small,
Useful of hurtful, prosperous of adverse
We can create, and in what place soe'er   260
Thrive under evil, and work ease out of pain
Through labor and endurance. This deep world
Of darkness do we dread? How oft amidst
Thick clouds and dark doth Heaven's all-ruling Sire
Choose to reside, his glory unobscured,
And with the majesty of darkness round
Covers his throne; from whence deep thunders roar,
Mustering their rage, and Heaven resembles Hell!
As he our darkness, cannot we his light
Imitate when we please? This desert soil   270
Wants not her hidden luster, gems and gold;
Nor want we skill or art, from whence to raise
Magnificence; and what can Heaven show more?
Our torments also may in length of time
Become our elements, these piercing fires
As soft as now severe, our temper changed
Into their temper; which must needs remove
The sensible of pain. All things invite
To peaceful counsels, and the settled state
Of order, how in safety best we may   280
Compose our present evils, with regard
Of what we are and where, dismissing quite
All thoughts of war: ye have what I advise."
    He scarce had finished, when such murmur filled
The assembly, as when hollow rocks retain
The sound of blustering winds, which all night long
Had roused the sea, now with hoarse cadence lull
Seafaring men o'erwatched, whose bark by chance
Or pinnace anchors in a craggy bay

---

256. **Hard liberty.** Cf. *Samson Agonistes*, 268-71. Milton puts his
own judgment of human indolence, which prefers "bondage with ease" to
"strenuous liberty," into the mouth of a demon. So Satan perverts to his
uses many of Milton's deepest personal convictions (e.g., cf. I, 639, 640
and note). Temperamentally the poet can better sympathize with those
who counsel action than with those who, like Belial, yield to mere inertia.
    264. **Thick clouds and dark.** Cf. Psalms 18:11-13; 97:2.
    271. **wants not,** is not without.
    278. **sensible,** sense. The use of an adjective for a noun is a Latinism
which Milton frequently adopts.
    281. **compose,** adjust.
    284 ff. Cf. *Iliad* ii. 144; *Aeneid* x. 9.

After the tempest: such applause was heard   290
As Mammon ended, and his sentence pleased,
Advising peace; for such another field
They dreaded worse than Hell: so much the fear
Of thunder and the sword of Michaël
Wrought still within them; and no less desire
To found this nether empire, which might rise
By policy and long process of time,
In emulation opposite to Heaven.
Which when Beëlzebub perceived, than whom,
Satan except, none higher sat, with grave   300
Aspéct he rose, and in his rising seemed
A pillar of state; deep on his front engraven
Deliberation sat and public care;
And princely counsel in his face yet shone,
Majestic though in ruin: sage he stood,
With Atlantean shoulders fit to bear
The weight of mightiest monarchies; his look
Drew audience and attention still as night
Or summer's noontide air, while thus he spake.
"Thrones and imperial Powers, Offspring of Heaven,   310
Ethereal Virtues; or these titles now
Must we renounce, and changing style, be called
Princes of Hell? for so the popular vote
Inclines, here to continue, and build up here
A growing empire; doubtless; while we dream,
And know not that the King of Heaven hath doomed
This place our dungeon, not our safe retreat
Beyond his potent arm, to live exempt
From Heaven's high jurisdiction, in new league
Banded against his throne, but to remain   320
In strictest bondage, though thus far removed,
Under the inevitable curb, reserved
His captive multitude. For he, be sure,

290 ff. **such applause,** etc. Mammon's proposal is an improvement on
Belial's in that it supplies an activity consistent with the abandonment of a
futile renewal of the attempt on Heaven. But the desire for revenge expressed by Moloch and felt by all the demons remains to be satisfied.
  294. **the sword of Michaël.** Cf. VI, 250 ff.
  299. **Beëlzebub.** Cf. I, 79–81 and note. In the Old Testament the
name is applied to the sun-god of the Philistines.
  302. **front,** forehead.
  306. **Atlantean shoulders,** shoulders like those of Atlas, who in Greek
mythology supported the heavens.
  313. **the popular vote,** i.e., the state of opinion indicated by the applause given Mammon.
  315. **doubtless.** The word is used sarcastically.

In height or depth, still first and last will reign
Sole king, and of his kingdom lose no part
By our revolt, but over Hell extend
His empire, and with iron scepter rule
Us here, as with his golden those in Heaven.
What sit we then projecting peace and war?
War hath determined us, and foiled with loss   330
Irreparable; terms of peace yet none
Vouchsafed or sought; for what peace will be given
To us enslaved, but custody severe,
And stripes, and arbitrary punishment
Inflicted? and what peace can we return,
But to our power hostility and hate,
Untamed reluctance, and revenge though slow,
Yet ever plotting how the conqueror least
May reap his conquest, and may least rejoice
In doing what we must in suffering feel?   340
Nor will occasion want, nor shall we need
With dangerous expedition to invade
Heaven, whose high walls fear no assault or siege
Or ambush from the Deep. What if we find
Some easier enterprise? There is a place
(If ancient and prophetic fame in Heaven
Err not), another world, the happy seat
Of some new race called Man, about this time
To be created like to us, though less
In power and excellence, but favored more   350
Of him who rules above; so was his will
Pronounced among the gods, and by an oath,
That shook Heaven's whole circumference, confirmed.
Thither let us bend all our thoughts, to learn
What creatures there inhabit, of what mould

324. **first and last.** Cf. Rev. 1:11: "I am Alpha and Omega, the first and the last."

327. **iron scepter.** Cf. Psalms 2:9: "Thou shalt break them with the rod of iron."

330. **determined us,** ended us or perhaps determined our future.

336. **to our power,** up to the limits of our power.

337. **Untamed reluctance,** untamable resistance.

346. **fame,** rumor. See I, 651 and note. Cf. VII, 140 ff.

353. Cf. *Iliad* i. 530; *Aeneid* ix. 106.

354. **Thither let us,** etc. Beëlzebub's proposal does not exclude Mammon's, which had itself appropriated Belial's; but it goes beyond both in supplying a rational project of revenge. The whole movement of the discussion has been constructively forward toward the formation of a policy satisfactory to all, and Beëlzebub, who is Satan's mouthpiece, has been simply waiting the opportune moment to introduce Satan's own scheme. His intelligence is far more comprehensive than that of the preceding

Or substance, how endued, and what their power,
And where their weakness, how attempted best,
By force or subtlety. Though Heaven be shut,
And Heaven's high Arbitrator sit secure
In his own strength, this place may lie exposed,   360
The utmost border of his kingdom, left
To their defence who hold it; here perhaps
Some advantageous act may be achieved
By sudden onset, either with Hell fire
To waste his whole creation, or possess
All as our own, and drive as we were driven,
The puny habitants; or if not drive,
Seduce them to our party, that their God
May prove their foe, and with repenting hand
Abolish his own works. This would surpass   370
Common revenge, and interrupt his joy
In our confusion, and our joy upraise
In his disturbance; when his darling sons
Hurled headlong to partake with us, shall curse
Their frail original, and faded bliss,
Faded so soon. Advise if this be worth
Attempting, or to sit in darkness here
Hatching vain empires." Thus Beëlzebub
Pleaded his devilish counsel, first devised
By Satan, and in part proposed; for whence,   380
But from the author of all ill, could spring
So deep a malice, to confound the race
Of Mankind in one root, and Earth with Hell
To mingle and involve, done all to spite
The great Creator? But their spite still serves
His glory to augment. The bold design
Pleased highly those infernal States, and joy
Sparkled in all their eyes; with full assent
They vote: whereat his speech he thus renews.
    "Well have ye judged, well ended long debate,   390
Synod of gods, and like to what ye are,
Great things resolved; which from the lowest deep
Will once more lift us up, in spite of Fate,

speakers. It is easy to believe that Milton had been present at deliberations
of the Council of State, and that he had noted with care the play of mind
in them.
    356. endued, equipped.
    375. original, originator, i.e., Adam.
    380. in part proposed, i.e., in his earlier speech, I, 645 ff.
    382. confound, destroy completely.
    387. States, princes or representatives.

Nearer our ancient seat; perhaps in view
Of those bright confines, whence with neighboring arms
And opportune excursion we may chance
Re-enter Heaven; or else in some mild zone
Dwell not unvisited of Heaven's fair light
Secure, and at the brightening orient beam
Purge off this gloom; the soft delicious air,   400
To heal the scar of these corrosive fires
Shall breathe her balm. But first whom shall we send
In search of this new world? whom shall we find
Sufficient? who shall tempt with wandering feet
The dark unbottomed infinite Abyss
And through the palpable obscure find out
His uncouth way, or spread his aîry flight
Upborne with indefatigable wings
Over the vast abrupt, ere he arrive
The happy isle; what strength, what art can then   410
Suffice, or what evasion bear him safe
Through the strict senteries and stations thick
Of angels watching round? Here he had need
All circumspection, and we now no less
Choice in our suffrage; for on whom we send,
The weight of all and our last hope relies."
     This said, he sat; and expectation held
His look suspense, awaiting who appeared
To second, or oppose, or undertake
The perilous attempt; but all sat mute,   420
Pondering the danger with deep thoughts; and each
In other's countenance read his own dismay
Astonished; none among the choice and prime
Of those Heaven-warring champions could be found
So hardy as to proffer or accept
Alone the dreadful voyage; till at last

none willing to volunteer

394. **Nearer our ancient seat.** Later the demons have access to "the middle air," where, for example, Satan assembles his council in *Paradise Regained*, I, 39 ff.

404. **tempt,** attempt, try (Latin *temptare*).

406. **palpable obscure,** tangible darkness. For the use of adjective for noun, cf. note on 278. The idea of darkness perceptible to the sense of touch was apparently suggested by Exod. 10:21, rendered in the Vulgate *tenebrae tam densae ut palpari queant.*

407. **uncouth,** unknown, strange.

409. **the vast abrupt,** the region of Chaos, which is a gulf or breach (Lat. *abruptum*), an emptiness.

412. **stations,** outposts, guards (Latin *stationes*).

415. **choice in our suffrage,** care in our selection.

418. **suspense,** suspended. The form is that of the Latin participle, *suspensum.*

Satan, whom now transcendent glory raised
Above his fellows, with monarchal pride
Conscious of highest worth, unmoved thus spake.
"O Progeny of Heaven, empyreal Thrones,   430
With reason hath deep silence and demur
Seized us, though undismayed. Long is the way
And hard, that out of Hell leads up to light;
Our prison strong, this huge convex of fire,
Outrageous to devour, immures us round
Ninefold, and gates of burning adamant
Barred over us prohibit all egress.
These passed, if any pass, the void profound
Of unessential Night receives him next
Wide gaping, and with utter loss of being   440
Threatens him, plunged in that abortive gulf.
If thence he scape into whatever world,
Or unknown region, what remains him less
Than unknown dangers and as hard escape.
But I should ill become this throne, O Peers,
And this imperial sovranty, adorned
With splendor, armed with power, if aught proposed
And judged of public moment, in the shape
Of difficulty or danger, could deter
Me from attempting. Wherefore do I assume   450
These royalties, and not refuse to reign,
Refusing to accept as great a share
Of hazard as of honor, due alike
To him who reigns, and so much to him due
Of hazard more, as he above the rest
High honored sits? Go therefore mighty Powers,
Terror of Heaven, though fallen; intend at home,
While here shall be our home, what best may ease
The present misery, and render Hell
More tolerable; if there be cure or charm   460
To respite or deceive, or slack the pain
Of this ill mansion; intermit no watch

431. **demur,** hesitation.
432. **Long is the way.** Cf. the famous lines in *Aeneid* vi. 126–29.
439. **unessential,** having no real being. Night and Chaos are thought of by Milton as merely negative, not really created.
441. **abortive,** prematurely brought forth and therefore unformed.
445 ff. **But I should ill,** etc. Satan's offer is parallel to that of Christ in III, 217 ff. Cf. also his own later assumption of the task of tempting Christ, *Paradise Regained*, I, 44–105.
450. **Me.** Note the emphasis given by the meter.
457. **intend,** plan, consider.
462. **deceive,** beguile.

Against a wakeful foe, while I abroad
Through all the coasts of dark destruction seek
Deliverance for us all: this enterprise
None shall partake with me." Thus saying rose
The Monarch, and prevented all reply;
Prudent, lest from his resolution raised
Others among the chief might offer now
(Certain to be refused) what erst they feared;   470
And so refused might in opinion stand
His rivals, winning cheap the high repute
Which he through hazard huge must earn. But they
Dreaded not more the adventure than his voice
Forbidding; and at once with him they rose;
Their rising all at once was as the sound
Of thunder heard remote. Towards him they bend
With awful reverence prone; and as a god
Extol him equal to the Highest in Heaven.
Nor failed they to express how much they praised,   480
That for the general safety he despised
His own: for neither do the spirits damned
Lose all their virtue; lest bad men should boast
Their specious deeds on Earth, which glory excites,
Or close ambition varnished o'er with zeal.
   Thus they their doubtful consultations dark
Ended rejoicing in their matchless chief:
As when from mountain tops the dusky clouds
Ascending, while the North wind sleeps, o'erspread
Heaven's cheerful face, the louring element   490
Scowls o'er the darkened landscape snow or shower;
If chance the radiant sun with farewell sweet
Extend his evening beam, the fields revive,
The birds their notes renew, and bleating herds

    467. prevented, anticipated (a good example of the transition from the
older, literal meaning of the word to the modern).
    468. from his resolution raised, encouraged by his bravery.
    477-79. This deification of Satan is a precedent for the idolatries of
men. The phrase with awful reverence may be taken with bend or with
prone.
    483. virtue, merit—but not moral goodness, for that, Milton would hold,
is inconsistent with disobedience to God.
    484. specious deeds, deeds which, though having all the appearance
of being public-spirited and self-sacrificing, are really the fruit of personal
ambition masquerading as zeal for the common good. Under Milton's
theory the demons can furnish a precedent for all that is great and magnanimous in men except the one essential of a righteous will. He never
forgets that Satan and the rest are angels fallen.
    490. element, sky.
    492. If chance, if it chances that.

Attest their joy, that hill and valley rings.
O shame to men! Devil with devil damned
Firm concord holds, men only disagree
Of creatures rational, though under hope
Of heavenly grace; and God proclaiming peace,
Yet live in hatred, enmity, and strife   500
Among themselves, and levy cruel wars,
Wasting the Earth, each other to destroy:
As if (which might induce us to accord)
Man had not hellish foes enow besides,
That day and night for his destruction wait!
　The Stygian council thus dissolved; and forth
In order came the grand infernal Peers;
Midst came their mighty Paramount, and seemed
Alone the antagonist of Heaven, nor less
Than Hell's dread Emperor, with pomp supreme,   510
And god-like imitated state; him round
A globe of fiery Seraphim enclosed
With bright emblazonry, and horrent arms.
Then of their session ended they bid cry
With trumpet's regal sound the great result.
Toward the four winds four speedy Cherubim
Put to their mouths the sounding alchemy
By herald's voice explained; the hollow Abyss
Heard far and wide, and all the host of Hell
With deafening shout, returned them loud acclaim.   520
　Thence more at ease their minds and somewhat raised
By false presumptuous hope, the rangèd powers
Disband, and wandering each his several way
Pursues, as inclination or sad choice
Leads him perplexed, where he may likeliest find
Truce to his restless thoughts, and entertain
The irksome hours, till his great chief return.
Part on the plain, or in the air sublime,
Upon the wing, or in swift race contend,
As at the Olympian games or Pythian fields;   530

509. **Alone the antagonist**, i.e., worthy in himself to be the antagonist.
512. **globe**, circle, as in the Roman military sense of *globus*.
513. **horrent**, bristling. Cf. I, 563 and note.
517. **sounding alchemy**, i.e., trumpets made of so-called "alchemy gold."
523 ff. **and wandering**, etc. Milton makes the recreations of the demons parallel to those of men, and equally expressive of their various temperaments. The milder spirits are the poets and philosophers.
528. **sublime**, aloft (Latin *sublimus*).
530. **The Olympian games**, held every four years at Olympia in honor of Zeus, and the **Pythian**, held at Delphi in honor of Apollo (slayer of the

Part curb their fiery steeds, or shun the goal
With rapid wheels, or fronted brigads form:
As when to warn proud cities war appears
Waged in the troubled sky, and armies rush
To battle in the clouds; before each van
Prick forth the airy knights, and couch their spears,
Till thickest legions close; with feats of arms
From either end of Heaven the welkin burns.
Others with vast Typhœan rage more fell
Rend up both rocks and hills, and ride the air   540
In whirlwind; Hell scarce holds the wild uproar:
As when Alcides from Œchalia crowned
With conquest, felt the envenomed robe, and tore
Through pain up by the roots Thessalian pines,
And Lichas from the top of Œta threw
Into the Euboic sea. Others more mild,
Retreated in a silent valley, sing
With notes angelical to many a harp
Their own heroic deeds and hapless fall
By doom of battle; and complain that Fate   550
Free Virtue should enthrall to Force or Chance.
Their song was partial, but the harmony
(What could it less when spirits immortal sing?)
Suspended Hell, and took with ravishment
The thronging audience. In discourse more sweet
(For eloquence the soul, song charms the sense)

Python), were the two great athletic festivals of ancient Greece. Milton
follows epic precedent in introducing a description of heroic games.
    531. Part curb, etc. This is poetic diction for "engage in horse or
chariot racing." The phrase **shun the goal** is from Horace *Odes* i. 1.4.
    532. fronted brigads form, i.e., to carry on a kind of mock combat or
tourney. Such sports were still practiced in Milton's boyhood, but here he
is no doubt drawing chiefly on his readings from romance.
    533 ff. Possibly this simile has reference to some specific portent re-
corded in history or literature. Cf., for example, *Julius Caesar*, II, ii, 19–24.
    539 ff. The hill-throwing activity of the demons imitates that of the
angels in the battle in Heaven (VI, 642 ff.). Riding the whirlwind became
a favorite occupation of the Devil's protégées, the witches.
    542. Alcides is another name for Hercules. Poisoned by a robe received
from his wife, he in his agony hurled into the sea his companion, Lichas,
who had brought the robe to him. Afterwards he ascended Mt. Œta in
Thessaly, where he burned himself to death. Cf. Sophocles, *Trachiniae*,
which opens with the news of Hercules' conquest of King Eurytus of
Œchalia.
    551. Free Virtue, i.e., the individualistic expansion of the soul.
    552. partial, imperfect, because they have lost their hold on the divine
source of poetic truth. There is a reflection here of Milton's verdict on
ancient pagan literature. To interpret **partial** in the sense of "biased in
their own favor" gives a less Miltonic meaning.

Others apart sat on a hill retired
In thoughts more elevate, and reasoned high   *debate*
Of providence, foreknowledge, will, and fate,
Fixed fate, free will, foreknowledge absolute,   560
And found no end, in wandering mazes lost.
Of good and evil much they argued then,   *intellectualism*
Of happiness and final misery,   *divorced fr*
Passion and apathy, and glory and shame,   *faith*
Vain wisdom all, and false philosophy;
Yet with a pleasing sorcery could charm
Pain for a while or anguish, and excite
Fallacious hope, or arm the obdurëd breast
With stubborn patience as with triple steel.
Another part, in squadrons and gross bands,   570
On bold adventure to discover wide
That dismal world, if any clime perhaps
Might yield them easier habitation, bend
Four ways their flying march, along the banks
Of four infernal rivers that disgorge
Into the burning lake their baleful streams;
Abhorrëd Styx, the flood of deadly hate;   *4 streams of Hell*
Sad Acheron of sorrow, black and deep;   *flow to center*
Cocytus, named of lamentation loud
Heard on the rueful stream; fierce Phlegethon,   580
Whose waves of torrent fire inflame with rage.
Far off from these a slow and silent stream,
Lethe, the river of oblivion, rolls *forgetfulness*
Her watery labyrinth, whereof who drinks
Forthwith his former state and being forgets,
Forgets both joy and grief, pleasure and pain.
Beyond this flood a frozen continent
Lies dark and wild, beat with perpetual storms
Of whirlwind and dire hail, which on firm land
Thaws not, but gathers heap, and ruin seems   590
Of ancient pile; all else deep snow and ice,
A gulf profound as that Serbonian bog

557 ff. **Others apart sat,** etc. Loss of true faith compels the invention
of philosophy. The Stoic is most popular, as affording the best remedy in
misfortune by its doctrine of **apathy** or insensibility to suffering.
568. obdurëd, hardened. Cf. Horace *Odes* i. III. 9.
570. gross, compact.
577 ff. Milton, like Dante, provides for the four rivers of the classical
Hades in his Christian hell. His description of them points to the etymological significance of their names, which are derived from Greek verb
stems meaning "to hate," "to sorrow," "to wail," and "to burn." Lethe
("forgetfulness") is usually thought of as separate from the others, and
Milton so represents it.
592–93. The **Serbonian bog** is Lake Serbonis in Lower Egypt. **Dami-**

Betwixt Damiata and Mount Casius old,
Where armies whole have sunk; the parching air
Burns frore, and cold performs the effect of fire.
Thither by harpy-footed Furies haled,
At certain revolutions all the damned
Are brought; and feel by turns the bitter change
Of fierce extremes, extremes by change more fierce,
From beds of raging fire to starve in ice   600
Their soft ethereal warmth, and there to pine
Immovable, infixed, and frozen round,
Periods of time; thence hurried back to fire.
They ferry over this Lethean sound
Both to and fro, their sorrow to augment,
And wish and struggle, as they pass, to reach
The tempting stream, with one small drop to lose
In sweet forgetfulness all pain and woe,
All in one moment, and so near the brink;
But Fate withstands, and to oppose the attempt   610
Medusa with Gorgonian terror guards
The ford, and of itself the water flies
All taste of living wight, as once it fled
The lip of Tantalus. Thus roving on
In cónfused march forlorn, the adventurous bands,
With shuddering horror pale, and eyes aghast,
Viewed first their lamentable lot, and found
No rest. Through many a dark and dreary vale
They passed, and many a region dolorous,
O'er many a frozen, many a fiery Alp,   620
Rocks, caves, lakes, fens, bogs, dens, and shades of death,
A universe of death, which God by curse

ata (mentioned by Ariosto, Tasso, and Dante) is a city at the mouth of the
Nile. Milton's phraseology regarding the region suggests that he had been
reading Sandys' *Relation*, where it is noted that Serbonis is close to Mt.
Cassius and that in it "whole armies have been devoured."

595. **frore,** frozen. Milton is fond of such contradictions as **burns
frore.** Cf. "darkness visible" (I, 63), "for evil only good" (II, 623), "dark
with excessive bright" (III, 380), etc.

600. **to starve in ice.** The meaning is clearer than the grammar. They
are moved from beds of fire to have their warmth perish (starve) in ice.

610 ff. Milton introduces into hell the monsters of classical mythology,
apparently regarding them as native inhabitants at the time of the fallen
angels' arrival.

611. **Medusa,** one of the three Gorgons, whose horrible countenances,
crowned with snakes for hair, turned all beholders to stone.

614. **Tantalus,** a mythical king of Lydia, whose punishment in the
lower world was to stand in a pool of water which receded whenever he
tried to drink.

621. Note that the line is made up entirely of monosyllables. The effect
is one of monotonous desolation.

Created evil, for evil only good,
Where all life dies, death lives, and Nature breeds,
Perverse, all monstrous, all prodigious things,
Abominable, inutterable, and worse
Than fables yet have feigned, or fear conceived,
Gorgons and Hydras, and Chimæras dire.
  Meanwhile the Adversary of God and Man,
Satan with thoughts inflamed of highest design,   630
Puts on swift wings, and toward the gates of Hell
Explores his solitary flight; sometimes
He scours the right-hand coast, sometimes the left;
Now shaves with level wing the deep, then soars
Up to the fiery concave towering high.
As when far off at sea a fleet descried
Hangs in the clouds, by equinoctial winds
Close sailing from Bengala, or the isles
Of Ternate and Tidore, whence merchants bring
Their spicy drugs: they on the trading flood   640
Through the wide Ethiopian to the Cape,
Ply stemming nightly toward the pole. So seemed
Far off the flying Fiend. At last appear
Hell bounds high reaching to the horrid roof,
And thrice threefold the gates; three folds were brass,
Three iron, three of adamantine rock,
Impenetrable, impaled with circling fire,
Yet unconsumed. Before the gates there sat
On either side a formidable shape;
The one seemed woman to the waist, and fair,   650
But ended foul in many a scaly fold
Voluminous and vast, a serpent armed

625. prodigious, unnatural.
628–29. The Hydra was a nine-headed serpent; the Chimæra a fire-
breathing monster, part lion, part goat, and part dragon. Cf. Aeneid vi.
287–89.
637. equinoctial winds, the trade winds which blow from the east at
the time of the equinoxes.
638. Close, i.e., in close formation or perhaps close-hauled. Bengala,
Bengal.
639. Ternate and Tidore, two of the so-called "spice islands" or
Moluccas.
641. the wide Ethiopian to the Cape, the Indian Ocean to the Cape
of Good Hope.
642. stemming, pressing forward.
647. impaled, surrounded.
648 ff. Before the gates, etc. The allegory of Sin and Death has its
basis in Jas. 1:15. Literary precedents for Milton's personifications are numerous: e.g., Faerie Queene, I, i, 14, 15; Fletcher, Purple Island, XII, 27.
Sin is imaged in terms of the classical Scylla; cf. Aeneid iii. 424 ff. Death
is a familiar figure in medieval literature and art.

With mortal sting. About her middle round
A cry of Hell-hounds never ceasing barked
With wide Cerberean mouths full loud, and rung
A hideous peal; yet, when they list, would creep,
If aught disturbed their noise, into her womb,
And kennel there, yet there still barked and howled
Within unseen. Far less abhorred than these
Vexed Scylla bathing in the sea that parts   660
Calabria from the hoarse Trinacrian shore;
Nor uglier follow the night-hag, when, called
In secret, riding through the air she comes,
Lured with the smell of infant blood, to dance
With Lapland witches, while the laboring moon
Eclipses at their charms. The other shape,
If shape it might be called that shape had none
Distinguishable in member, joint, or limb;
Or substance might be called that shadow seemed,
For each seemed either; black it stood as Night,   670
Fierce as ten Furies, terrible as Hell,
And shook a dreadful dart; what seemed his head
The likeness of a kingly crown had on.
Satan was now at hand, and from his seat
The monster moving onward came as fast,
With horrid strides; Hell trembled as he strode.
The undaunted Fiend what this might be admired,
Admired, not feared; God and his Son except,
Created thing nought valued he nor shunned;
And with disdainful look thus first began.   680
    "Whence and what art thou, execrable Shape,
That darest, though grim and terrible, advance
Thy miscreated front athwart my way
To yonder gates? Through them I mean to pass,

660. The rock Scylla is located in the Straits of Messina, between
southern Italy (**Calabria**) and Sicily (**the Trinacrian shore**). According
to classical myth, Scylla was originally a beautiful nymph, who flung herself into the sea after being hideously transformed by the magic herbs of
Circe.
    662–66. There is much genuine witch superstition in this passage. The
nighthag is Hecate, goddess of the underworld and of witchcraft. Cf.
Macbeth, III, v, and IV, i. For Lapland as a home of witchcraft, cf. Burton's "Digression of Spirits" in Book I of the *Anatomy of Melancholy*.
    665. **laboring moon.** The epithet is based on the Latin use of *laborare*
to mean "suffer eclipse." Cf. Virgil *Georgics* ii. 478.
    670. **each seemed either,** i.e., substance and shadow were indistin-
guishable.
    677. **admired,** wondered.
    678–79. **not feared . . . shunned.** Milton means that Satan feared *no*
created thing, but only God and his Son.

That be assured, without leave asked of thee.
Retire, or taste thy folly, and learn by proof,
Hell-born, not to contend with spirits of Heaven."
   To whom the goblin, full of wrath, replied:
"Art thou that traitor angel, art thou he,
Who first broke peace in Heaven and faith, till then   690
Unbroken, and in proud rebellious arms
Drew after him the third part of Heaven's sons
Conjured against the Highest, for which both thou
And they, outcast from God, are here condemned
To waste eternal days in woe and pain?
And reckon'st thou thyself with spirits of Heaven,
Hell-doomed, and breath'st defiance here and scorn
Where I reign king, and to enrage thee more,
Thy king and lord? Back to thy punishment,
False fugitive, and to thy speed add wings,   700
Lest with a whip of scorpions I pursue
Thy lingering, or with one stroke of this dart
Strange horror seize thee, and pangs unfelt before."
   So spake the grisly terror, and in shape,
So speaking and so threatening, grew tenfold
More dreadful and deform. On the other side,
Incensed with indignation, Satan stood
Unterrified, and like a comet burned,
That fires the length of Ophiuchus huge
In the arctic sky, and from his horrid hair   710
Shakes pestilence and war. Each at the head
Levelled his deadly aim; their fatal hands
No second stroke intend; and such a frown
Each cast at the other, as when two black clouds
With Heaven's artillery fraught, come rattling on
Over the Caspian, then stand front to front
Hovering a space, till winds the signal blow
To join their dark encounter in mid air:
So frowned the mighty combatants, that Hell
Grew darker at their frown, so matched they stood;   720

---

688. goblin, demon, fiend.
692. the third part of Heaven's sons. Cf. Rev. 12:4.
693. conjured, sworn together, banded by oath.
697. Hell-doomed. Death uses the term in direct retort to Satan's
"Hell-born" (687).
701. whip of scorpions. Cf. I Kings 12:11.
709. Ophiuchus, "the Serpent-bearer." Milton erroneously locates
this constellation in northern heavens because Satan is said in Scripture to
come from the "parts of the North."
716. The Caspian Sea is frequently mentioned in Renaissance literature
as a region of storms.

For never but once more was either like
To meet so great a foe. And now great deeds
Had been achieved, whereof all Hell had rung,
Had not the snaky sorceress that sat
Fast by Hell gate and kept the fatal key,
Risen, and with hideous outcry rushed between.
    "O father, what intends thy hand," she cried,
"Against thy only son? What fury O son,
Possesses thee to bend that mortal dart
Against thy father's head? and know'st for whom;   730
For him who sits above and laughs the while
At thee ordained his drudge, to execute
Whate'er his wrath, which he calls justice, bids,
His wrath which one day will destroy ye both!"
    She spake, and at her words the hellish pest
Forbore; then these to her Satan returned:
    "So strange thy outcry, and thy words so strange
Thou interposest, that my sudden hand
Prevented spares to tell thee yet by deeds
What it intends; till first I know of thee,   740
What thing thou art, thus double-formed, and why
In this infernal vale first met thou call'st
Me father, and that phantasm call'st my son.
I know thee not, nor ever saw till now
Sight more detestable than him and thee."
    To whom thus the portress of Hell gate replied:
"Hast thou forgot me then, and do I seem
Now in thine eye so foul? once deemed so fair
In Heaven, when at the assembly, and in sight
Of all the Seraphim with thee combined   750
In bold conspiracy against Heaven's King,
All on a sudden miserable pain
Surprised thee; dim thine eyes, and dizzy swum
In darkness, while thy head flames thick and fast
Threw forth, till on the left side opening wide,
Likest to thee in shape and countenance bright,
Then shining heavenly fair, a goddess armed
Out of thy head I sprung. Amazement seized
All the host of Heaven; back they recoiled afraid
At first, and called me *Sin*, and for a sign   760

---

722. **so great a foe**, i.e., Christ. Cf. *Paradise Regained*, IV, 562 ff.;
I Cor. 15:26.
    736. **these**, i.e., these words.
    749 ff. The birth of Sin from the head of Satan is like that of Minerva
from the head of Jove. The rebellious angels, though at first startled, found
her alluring. Now in hell she appears in her true ugliness.

Portentous held me; but familiar grown,
I pleased, and with attractive graces won
The most averse, thee chiefly, who full oft
Thyself in me thy perfect image viewing
Becam'st enamored; and such joy thou took'st
With me in secret, that my womb conceived
A growing burden. Meanwhile war arose,
And fields were fought in Heaven; wherein remained
(For what could else) to our almighty foe
Clear victory, to our part loss and rout   770
Through all the Empyrean! down they fell
Driven headlong from the pitch of Heaven, down
Into this Deep, and in the general fall
I also; at which time this powerful key
Into my hand was given, with charge to keep
These gates for ever shut, which none can pass
Without my opening. Pensive here I sat
Alone, but long I sat not, till my womb,
Pregnant by thee, and now excessive grown,
Prodigious motion felt and rueful throes.   780
At last this odious offspring whom thou seest
Thine own begotten, breaking violent way
Tore through my entrails, that with fear and pain
Distorted, all my nether shape thus grew
Transformed; but he my inbred enemy
Forth issued, brandishing his fatal dart
Made to destroy. I fled, and cried out *Death*;
Hell trembled at the hideous name, and sighed
From all her caves, and back resounded *Death*.
I fled; but he pursued (though more, it seems,   790
Inflamed with lust than rage) and swifter far,
Me overtook, his mother, all dismayed,
And in embraces forcible and foul
Engendering with me, of that rape begot
These yelling monsters that with ceaseless cry
Surround me, as thou saw'st, hourly conceived
And hourly born, with sorrow infinite
To me; for when they list, into the womb
That bred them they return, and howl and gnaw
My bowels, their repast; then bursting forth   800
Afresh, with conscious terrors vex me round,
That rest or intermission none I find.
Before mine eyes in opposition sits
Grim Death my son and foe, who sets them on,

772. pitch, height.

And me his parent would full soon devour
For want of other prey, but that he knows
His end with mine involved; and knows that I
Should prove a bitter morsel, and his bane,
Whenever that shall be; so Fate pronounced.
But thou O father, I forewarn thee, shun   810
His deadly arrow; neither vainly hope
To be invulnerable in those bright arms,
Though tempered heavenly; for that mortal dint,
Save he who reigns above, none can resist."
    She finished; and the subtle Fiend his lore
Soon learned, now milder, and thus answered smooth.
    "Dear daughter, since thou claim'st me for thy sire,
And my fair son here show'st me, the dear pledge
Of dalliance had with thee in Heaven, and joys
Then sweet, now sad to mention, through dire change   820
Befallen us unforeseen, unthought of, know
I come no enemy, but to set free
From out this dark and dismal house of pain,
Both him and thee, and all the heavenly host
Of spirits that in our just pretences armed,
Fell with us from on high. From them I go
This uncouth errand sole, and one for all
Myself expose, with lonely steps to tread
The unfounded deep, and through the void immense
To search with wandering quest a place foretold   830
Should be, and, by concurring signs, ere now
Created vast and round, a place of bliss
In the purlieus of Heaven, and therein placed
A race of upstart creatures, to supply
Perhaps our vacant room, though more removed,
Lest Heaven surcharged with potent multitude
Might hap to move new broils. Be this or aught
Than this more secret now designed, I haste
To know; and this once known, shall soon return,
And bring ye to the place where thou and Death   840

    809. so Fate pronounced. Like Satan, Sin recognizes Fate as the su-
preme power. Cf. I, 116.
    813. tempered heavenly, hardened by heavenly process. dint, blow.
    815. lore, lesson. Satan now proceeds to show himself as "the father
of lies."
    825. pretences, claims.
    827. This uncouth errand sole, alone on this uncertain errand.
    829. unfounded, without foundation, bottomless.
    833. purlieus, outskirts.
    835-37. Satan attributes fear and meanness to God in the creation of
man at a safe distance (more removed) from Heaven.

Sin, daughter & mate of Satan

Shall dwell at ease, and up and down unseen
Wing silently the buxom air, embalmed
With odors; there ye shall be fed and filled
Immeasurably, all things shall be your prey."
   He ceased, for both seemed highly pleased, and Death
Grinned horrible a ghastly smile, to hear
His famine should be filled, and blessed his maw
Destined to that good hour. No less rejoiced
His mother bad, and thus bespake her sire.
   "The key of this infernal pit, by due   850
And by command of Heaven's all-powerful King
I keep, by him forbidden to unlock
These adamantine gates; against all force
Death ready stands to interpose his dart,
Fearless to be o'ermatched by living might.
But what owe I to his commands above
Who hates me, and hath hither thrust me down
Into this gloom of Tartarus profound,
To sit in hateful office here confined,
Inhabitant of Heaven and heavenly-born,   860
Here in perpetual agony and pain,
With terrors and with clamors compassed round
Of mine own brood, that on my bowels feed?
Thou art my father, thou my author, thou
My being gavest me; whom should I obey
But thee, whom follow? Thou wilt bring me soon
To that new world of light and bliss, among
The gods who live at ease, where I shall reign
At thy right hand voluptuous, as beseems
Thy daughter and thy darling, without end."   870
   Thus saying, from her side the fatal key,
Sad instrument of all our woe, she took;
And towards the gate rolling her bestial train,
Forthwith the huge portcullis high up drew,
Which but herself not all the Stygian powers
Could once have moved; then in the key-hole turns
The intricate wards, and every bolt and bar
Of massy iron or solid rock with ease
Unfastens. On a sudden open fly
With impetuous recoil and jarring sound   880
The infernal doors, and on their hinges grate
Harsh thunder, that the lowest bottom shook

disobeys God

Gates of Hell are opened forever

842. **buxom,** yielding, buoyant.
865. **whom should I obey.** Sin disobeys God, as it is her nature to do.
868. **The gods who live at ease.** The phrase is echoed from *Iliad* vi.

138.

Of Erebus. She opened, but to shut
Excelled her power; the gates wide open stood,
That with extended wings a bannered host
Under spread ensigns marching might pass through
With horse and chariots ranked in loose array;
So wide they stood, and like a furnace mouth
Cast forth redounding smoke and ruddy flame.
Before their eyes in sudden view appear   890
The secrets of the hoary deep, a dark
Illimitable ocean without bound,
Without dimension; where length, breadth, and height,
And time, and place, are lost; where eldest Night
And Chaos, ancestors of Nature, hold
Eternal anarchy, amidst the noise
Of endless wars, and by confusion stand.
For Hot, Cold, Moist, and Dry, four champions fierce,
Strive here for mastery, and to battle bring
Their embryon atoms; they around the flag   900
Of each his faction, in their several clans,
Light-armed or heavy, sharp, smooth, swift, or slow,
Swarm populous, unnumbered as the sands
Of Barca or Cyrene's torrid soil,
Levied to side with warring winds, and poise
Their lighter wings. To whom these most adhere,
He rules a moment; Chaos umpire sits,
And by decision more embroils the fray
By which he reigns; next him high arbiter
Chance governs all. Into this wild Abyss,   910
The womb of Nature and perhaps her grave,

883. **Erebus,** one of the classical names for hell. In its strictest sense, it denoted the region between Hades and the upper world.

889. **redounding,** overflowing, surging (from Latin *redundare*).

890 ff. Cf. Ovid's description of Chaos, *Metamorphoses* i. 5–20.

895. **Nature,** the created universe.

898. **Hot, Cold, Moist, and Dry,** i.e., the attributes of the four elements (fire, earth, water, air), out of which, in the older Physics, all substances were composed.

900. **embryon atoms.** The atoms were the germinal units of matter in the Epicurean system as expounded by Lucretius, who calls them *semina rerum* and represents them as having different shapes.

903 ff. **as the sands . . . wings.** The figure implies that the sands are raised (**levied**) by the winds to serve as ballast (**poise their lighter wings**). **Levied** has its military connotation (i.e., the sands are **levied** like troops of soldiers) as well as its literal meaning. **Lighter** has the force of "too light" (a Latinism).

904. **Barca, Cyrene,** cities in northern Africa.

906. **To whom these most adhere,** i.e., the attribute (**Hot, Cold,** etc.) which attracts the most atoms.

911. **and perhaps her grave.** According to Lucretius, all things will

courtiers of chaos + concord
night all things leading to chaos
rumor-chance-up
tumult — *confusion*
discord
elements

BOOK II   257

Of neither sea, nor shore, nor air, nor fire,
But all these in their pregnant causes mixed
Confusedly, and which thus must ever fight,
Unless the Almighty Maker them ordain
His dark materials to create more worlds,
Into this wild Abyss the wary Fiend
Stood on the brink of Hell and looked a while,
Pondering his voyage; for no narrow frith
He had to cross. Nor was his ear less pealed   920
With noises loud and ruinous (to compare
Great things with small) than when Bellona storms,
With all her battering engines bent to raze
Some capital city; or less than if this frame
Of Heaven were falling, and these elements
In mutiny had from her axle torn
The steadfast Earth. At last his sail-broad vans
He spreads for flight, and in the surging smoke
Uplifted spurns the ground; thence many a league
As in a cloudy chair ascending rides   930
Audacious, but that seat soon failing, meets
A vast vacuity: all unawares
Fluttering his pennons vain plumb down he drops
Ten thousand fathom deep, and to this hour
Down had been falling, had not by ill chance
The strong rebuff of some tumultuous cloud
Instinct with fire and niter hurried him
As many miles aloft; that fury stayed,
Quenched in a boggy Syrtis, neither sea,
Nor good dry land, nigh foundered on he fares,   940
Treading the crude consistence, half on foot,

sometime return to the disordered state out of which they were brought by
the action of chance. To Milton, the creation of Nature or the orderly
universe was the work not of chance but of Providence, and its destruction
will be the same, namely, at the day of judgment. The **perhaps** introduces
a speculative element which is hardly consistent with Milton's inherited
theology.
    913. pregnant causes, potential elements. The differentiation of the
elements is not yet accomplished.
    919. frith, firth, channel.
    920. pealed, deafened.
    921–22. to compare, Great things with small. The phrase is from
Virgil *Georgics* iv. 176. **Bellona,** Roman goddess of war.
    927. vans, vanes, wings.
    933. pennons, pinions, wings.
    937. instinct, imbued, charged.
    939. Syrtis, quicksand. The Syrtes were two gulfs on the north coast
of Africa, much dreaded for their quicksands.
    941. crude consistence, unrefined mixture. **Crude** means literally
"uncooked."

Half flying; behoves him now both oar and sail.
As when a gryphon through the wilderness
With wingèd course o'er hill or moory dale,
Pursues the Arimaspian, who by stealth
Had from his wakeful custody purloined
The guarded gold: so eagerly the Fiend
O'er bog or steep, through strait, rough, dense, or rare,
With head, hands, wings, or feet pursues his way,
And swims or sinks, or wades, or creeps, or flies.   950
At length a universal hubbub wild
Of stunning sounds and voices all confused
Borne through the hollow dark assaults his ear
With loudest vehemence; thither he plies,
Undaunted to meet there whatever power
Or spirit of the nethermost Abyss
Might in that noise reside, of whom to ask
Which way the nearest coast of darkness lies
Bordering on light; when straight behold the throne
Of Chaos, and his dark pavilion spread   960
Wide on the wasteful Deep; with him enthroned
Sat sable-vested Night, eldest of things,
The consort of his reign; and by them stood
Orcus and Ades, and the dreaded name
Of Demogorgon; Rumor next and Chance,
And Tumult and Confusion all embroiled,
And Discord with a thousand various mouths.
    To whom Satan turning boldly, thus. "Ye Powers
And Spirits of this nethermost Abyss,
Chaos and ancient Night, I come no spy,   970
With purpose to explore or to disturb
The secrets of your realm, but by constraint
Wandering this darksome desert, as my way

943. gryphon, griffin, a mythical monster with the head and wings of
an eagle and the body of a lion. According to Pliny (*Natural History*
vii. 2) and others, the griffins had in their possession vast gold mines which
the Arimaspians, the one-eyed inhabitants of Scythia, were continually
trying to obtain.

948. dense or rare, matter condensed or rarefied. Cf. the phrase
"through thick and thin."

961 ff. Cf. the description of Pluto's palace in *Aeneid* vi. 273–81; also
in *Faerie Queene*, II, vii, 21–25.

964. Orcus and Ades, Latin and Greek names for Pluto, god of the
underworld.

964–65. dreaded name of Demogorgon, i.e., Demogorgon, whose
name is dreaded (a Latinism). The reference is to a mysterious deity mentioned by Spenser (*Faerie Queene*, IV, ii, 47). Perhaps the name is a
corruption of *demiourgos*, which was used by Neoplatonic writers to desig-
nate a creative agency inferior to God.

Lies through your spacious empire up to light,
Alone and without guide, half lost, I seek
What readiest path leads where your gloomy bounds
Confine with Heaven; or if some other place
From your dominion won, the Ethereal King
Possesses lately, thither to arrive
I travel this profound. Direct my course;   980
Directed no mean recompense it brings
To your behoof, if I that region lost,
All usurpation thence expelled, reduce
To her original darkness and your sway
(Which is my present journey) and once more
Erect the standard there of ancient Night;
Yours be the advantage all, mine the revenge."
Thus Satan; and him thus the Anarch old
With faltering speech and visage incomposed
Answered. "I know thee, stranger, who thou art,   990
That mighty leading angel, who of late
Made head against Heaven's King, though overthrown.
I saw and heard, for such a numerous host
Fled not in silence through the frighted deep
With ruin upon ruin, rout on rout,
Confusion worse confounded; and Heaven gates
Poured out by millions her victorious bands
Pursuing. I upon my frontiers here
Keep residence; if all I can will serve
That little which is left so to defend,   1000
Encroached on still through our intestine broils
Weakening the scepter of old Night: first Hell
Your dungeon stretching far and wide beneath;
Now lately Heaven and Earth, another world
Hung o'er my realm, linked in a golden chain
To that side Heaven from whence your legions fell.
If that way be your walk, you have not far;
So much the nearer danger; go and speed;
Havoc and spoil and ruin are my gain."
He ceased; and Satan stayed not to reply,   1010
But glad that now his sea should find a shore,
With fresh alacrity and force renewed

977. confine with, border on.
981 ff. Satan diplomatically gives the impression that his journey was undertaken in the special interest of Chaos.
989. incomposed, discomposed. Chaos is a symbol of spiritual as well as of material disorder. His features exhibit his tumultuous passions.
1001. still, constantly.
1004. Heaven here means the sky of the newly created world; in 1006 it means the Empyrean.

Springs upward like a pyramid of fire
Into the wild expanse, and through the shock
Of fighting elements, on all sides round
Environed, wins his way; harder beset
And more endangered, than when Argo passed
Through Bosporus betwixt the justling rocks;
Or when Ulysses on the larboard shunned
Charybdis, and by the other whirlpool steered.   1020
So he with difficulty and labor hard
Moved on, with difficulty and labor he;
But he once passed, soon after when Man fell,
Strange alteration! Sin and Death amain
Following his track, such was the will of Heaven,
Paved after him a broad and beaten way
Over the dark Abyss, whose boiling gulf
Tamely endured a bridge of wondrous length
From Hell continued reaching the utmost orb
Of this frail world; by which the spirits perverse   1030
With easy intercourse pass to and fro
To tempt or punish mortals, except whom
God and good angels guard by special grace.
    But now at last the sacred influence
Of light appears, and from the walls of Heaven
Shoots far into the bosom of dim Night
A glimmering dawn; here Nature first begins
Her farthest verge, and Chaos to retire
As from her outmost works a broken foe,
With tumult less and with less hostile din,   1040
That Satan with less toil, and now with ease
Wafts on the calmer wave by dubious light
And like a weather-beaten vessel holds
Gladly the port, though shrouds and tackle torn;
Or in the emptier waste, resembling air,

1016 ff. The reference is to the expedition of Jason in search of the Golden Fleece. The justling rocks are the Symplegades (from the Greek verb meaning "to strike together"), so called because they dashed against each other at intervals, crushing the vessels that attempted to sail between them. For the adventure of Ulysses with Charybdis and Scylla (the other Whirlpool), cf. Odyssey xii. 73 ff.

1024. amain, with haste.

1028. a bridge, etc. Cf. X, 293 ff.

1029. the utmost orb, i.e., the outermost of the nine spheres surrounding the earth.

1033–34. The guardian angel idea is a favorite with Milton; in his theology, however, the special grace falls only on those who merit it by their own efforts. Cf. Comus, 455 and note.

1039. her, Nature's.

1043. holds, i.e., holds his course toward.

Weighs his spread wings, at leisure to behold
Far off the empyreal Heaven, extended wide
In circuit, undetermined square or round,
With opal towers and battlements adorned
Of living sapphire, once his native seat;   1050
And fast by hanging in a golden chain,
This pendent world, in bigness as a star
Of smallest magnitude close by the moon.
Thither full fraught with mischievous revenge,
Accurst, and in a cursèd hour, he hies.

BOOK III

THE ARGUMENT

God, sitting on his throne, sees Satan flying towards this World,
then newly created; shows him to the Son, who sat at his right
hand; fortells the success of Satan in perverting mankind; clears
his own justice and wisdom from all imputation, having created
Man free and able enough to have withstood his tempter; yet
declares his purpose of grace towards him, in regard he fell not
of his own malice, as did Satan, but by him seduced. The Son
of God renders praises to his Father for the manifestation of his
gracious purpose towards Man; but God again declares that
grace cannot be extended towards Man without the satisfaction
of Divine Justice: Man hath offended the majesty of God by
aspiring to Godhead, and therefore, with all his progeny, devoted
to death, must die, unless some one can be found sufficient to
answer for his offence, and undergo his punishment. The Son of
God freely offers himself a ransom for Man: the Father accepts
him, ordains his incarnation, pronounces his exaltation above
all names in Heaven and Earth; commands all the angels to
adore him: they obey, and hymning to their harps in full choir,
celebrate the Father and the Son. Meanwhile Satan alights upon
the bare convex of this World's outermost orb; where wandering
he first finds a place since called the Limbo of Vanity; what persons and things fly up thither; thence comes to the gate of Heaven,
described ascending by stairs, and the waters above the firmament

1050. **living, vivid.** The two words are etymologically equivalent.
1051. **golden chain.** Milton appropriates the more or less symbolic
chain which has been famous among poets since Homer (*Iliad* viii. 18–27).
Cf. *Faerie Queene*, II, vii, 46, 47.
1052. **This pendent world,** i.e., the entire visible universe with its
encircling spheres. The impression of distance given here contradicts the
measurement in I, 73, 74.

that flow about it. His passage thence to the orb of the sun: he finds there Uriel, the regent of that orb, but first changes himself into the shape of a meaner angel, and pretending a zealous desire to behold the new creation, and Man whom God had placed here, inquires of him the place of his habitation, and is directed; alights first on Mount Niphates.

Hail holy Light, offspring of Heaven first-born,
Or of the Eternal coeternal beam
May I express thee unblamed? since God is light,
And never but in unapproachèd light,
Dwelt from eternity, dwelt then in thee,
Bright effluence of bright essence increate.
Or hear'st thou rather pure ethereal stream,
Whose fountain who shall tell? Before the sun,
Before the Heavens thou wert, and at the voice
Of God, as with a mantle didst invest   10
The rising world of waters dark and deep,
Won from the void and formless infinite.
Thee I revisit now with bolder wing,
Escaped the Stygian pool, though long detained
In that obscure sojourn, while in my flight
Through utter and through middle darkness borne
With other notes than to the Orphean lyre
I sung of Chaos and eternal Night,
Taught by the heavenly Muse to venture down
The dark descent, and up to re-ascend,   20
Though hard and rare: thee I revisit safe,
And feel thy sovran vital lamp; but thou
Revisit'st not these eyes, that roll in vain
To find thy piercing ray, and find no dawn;
So thick a drop serene hath quenched their orbs,
Or dim suffusion veiled. Yet not the more
Cease I to wander where the Muses haunt
Clear spring, or shady grove, or sunny hill,

2–3. May I, without blame, call thee coeternal with God?
6. Light is God's essence and as such is uncreated; but it is also what flows from him (effluence) and was the first created thing.
7–8. Or hear'st. Milton now says that the relation of the effluence to the essence is a mystery.
16. utter, outer, i.e., Hell.
17. Orphean lyre. There was an Orphic hymn to night. Milton means that his poem is of higher inspiration, being based on Scripture.
25. drop serene, a translation of the medical term *gutta serena*, used of blindness in which the eye is not clouded. The "clear drop" is a humor which blocks the optic nerve.
26. dim suffusion, translates *suffusio nigra*, a synonym of *gutta obscura* (dark drop), meaning cataract.

Smit with the love of sacred song; but chief
Thee Sion, and the flowery brooks beneath   30
That wash thy hallowed feet, and warbling flow,
Nightly I visit; nor sometimes forget
Those other two equalled with me in fate,
So were I equalled with them in renown,
Blind Thamyris and blind Mæonides,
And Tiresias and Phineus prophets old:
Then feed on thoughts, that voluntary move
Harmonious numbers; as the wakeful bird
Sings darkling, and in shadiest covert hid
Tunes her nocturnal note. Thus with the year   40
Seasons return; but not to me returns
Day, or the sweet approach of even or morn,
Or sight of vernal bloom, or summer's rose,
Or flocks, or herds, or human face divine;
But cloud instead, and ever-during dark
Surrounds me, from the cheerful ways of men
Cut off, and for the book of knowledge fair
Presented with a universal blank
Of Nature's works to me expunged and razed,
And wisdom at one entrance quite shut out.   50
So much the rather thou celestial Light
Shine inward, and the mind through all her powers
Irradiate, there plant eyes, all mist from thence
Purge and disperse, that I may see and tell
Of things invisible to mortal sight.
    Now had the Almighty Father from above,
From the pure Empyrean where he sits
High throned above all height, bent down his eye,
His own works and their works at once to view.
About him all the sanctities of Heaven   60
Stood thick as stars, and from his sight received
Beatitude past utterance; on his right
The radiant image of his glory sat,
His only Son; on Earth he first beheld
Our two first parents, yet the only two
Of mankind, in the happy garden placed,
Reaping immortal fruits of joy and love,
Uninterrupted joy, unrivalled love
In blissful solitude. He then surveyed
Hell and the gulf between, and Satan there   70
Coasting the wall of Heaven on this side Night

29. **sacred song**, poetry, which is divine as coming from the muses.
30. To visit the brooks by Sion is to read Scripture.
35. **Mæonides**, Homer.

In the dun air sublime, and ready now
To stoop with wearied wings and willing feet
On the bare outside of this World, that seemed
Firm land imbosomed without firmament,
Uncertain which, in ocean or in air.
Him God beholding from his prospect high,
Wherein past, present, future he beholds,
Thus to his only Son foreseeing spake.
   "Only begotten Son, seest thou what rage   80
Transports our Adversary, whom no bounds
Prescribed, no bars of Hell, nor all the chains
Heaped on him there, nor yet the main Abyss
Wide interrupt can hold; so bent he seems
On desperate revenge, that shall redound
Upon his own rebellious head. And now
Through all restraint broke loose he wings his way
Not far off Heaven, in the precincts of light,
Directly towards the new-created World,
And Man there placed, with purpose to assay   90
If him by force he can destroy, or worse,
By some false guile pervert; and shall pervert;
For Man will hearken to his glozing lies,
And easily transgress the sole command,
Sole pledge of his obedience; so will fall
He and his faithless progeny. Whose fault?
Whose but his own? Ingrate, he had of me
All he could have; I made him just and right,
Sufficient to have stood, though free to fall.
Such I created all the Ethereal Powers   100
And spirits, both them who stood and them who failed;
Freely they stood who stood, and fell who fell.
Not free, what proof could they have given sincere
Of true allegiance, constant faith, or love,

   72. sublime, elevated.
   74–76. Satan is ready to light on the *primum mobile*, the outer shell of
the created universe, not on the earth itself. The substance of this shell is
indeterminate. The "firmament" is the visible sky, which separates the
waters above from the waters beneath the earth. The shell is "without,"
i.e., outside of this firmament, or perhaps rather not composed of it, as the
other spheres must be. The "waters above" are described in III, 518, and
VII, 619. They constitute the crystalline sphere, inside the *primum mobile*, but also make a sea on top of it. Milton is not only adjusting the
biblical account of creation to the Ptolemaic idea of the spheres but making
the conception philosophic as well. The *primum mobile* is a link between
God and his universe.
   76. uncertain which, it being uncertain whether the shell hung in
water or in air. Milton suggests that the business about the firmament and
the waters is obscure, as indeed it is.

Where only what they needs must do, appeared,
Not what they would? what praise could they receive?
What pleasure I from such obedience paid,
When will and reason (reason also is choice)
Useless and vain, of freedom both despoiled,
Made passive both, had served necessity,   110
Not me. They therefore as to right belonged,
So were created, nor can justly accuse
Their Maker, or their making, or their fate,
As if predestination overruled
Their will, disposed by absolute decree
Or high foreknowledge; they themselves decreed
Their own revolt, not I. If I foreknew,
Foreknowledge had no influence on their fault,
Which had no less proved certain unforeknown.
So without least impulse or shadow of fate,   120
Or aught by me immutably foreseen,
They trespass, authors to themselves in all,
Both what they judge and what they choose; for so
I formed them free, and free they must remain,
Till they enthrall themselves: I else must change
Their nature, and revoke the high decree
Unchangeable, eternal, which ordained
Their freedom; they themselves ordained their fall.
The first sort by their own suggestion fell,
Self-tempted, self-depraved; Man falls, deceived   130
By the other first; Man therefore shall find grace,
The other none. In mercy and justice both,
Through Heaven and Earth, so shall my glory excel,
But mercy first and last shall brightest shine."
    Thus while God spake, ambrosial fragrance filled
All Heaven, and in the blessed spirits elect
Sense of new joy ineffable diffused.
Beyond compare the Son of God was seen
Most glorious; in him all his Father shone
Substantially expressed; and in his face   140
Divine compassion visibly appeared,
Love without end, and without measure grace,
Which uttering thus he to his Father spake.
    "O Father, gracious was that word which closed
Thy sovran sentence, that Man should find grace;

114 ff. Predestination, in Milton's theology, was a conditional decree
of God, not an absolute one, as in strict Calvinism. This Arminian principle was essential and is discussed at length in *Christian Doctrine*, I, iii.
Milton is not the first or the last thinker to maintain the paradox that God
foresees but not immutably.

For which both Heaven and Earth shall high extol
Thy praises with the innumerable sound
Of hymns and sacred songs, wherewith thy throne
Encompassed shall resound thee ever blest.
For should Man finally be lost, should Man   150
Thy creature late so loved, thy youngest son
Fall circumvented thus by fraud, though joined
With his own folly? that be from thee far,
That far be from thee, Father, who art judge
Of all things made, and judgest only right.
Or shall the Adversary thus obtain
His end, and frustrate thine, shall he fulfil
His malice, and thy goodness bring to nought,
Or proud return though to his heavier doom,
Yet with revenge accomplished, and to Hell   160
Draw after him the whole race of mankind,
By him corrupted? or wilt thou thyself
Abolish thy creation, and unmake,
For him, what for thy glory thou hast made?
So should thy goodness and thy greatness both
Be questioned and blasphemed without defence."
     To whom the great Creator thus replied.
"O Son, in whom my soul hath chief delight,
Son of my bosom, Son who art alone
My word, my wisdom, and effectual might,   170
All hast thou spoken as my thoughts are, all
As my eternal purpose hath decreed:
Man shall not quite be lost, but saved who will,
Yet not of will in him, but grace in me
Freely vouchsafed; once more I will renew
His lapsëd powers, though forfeit and enthralled
By sin to foul exorbitant desires;
Upheld by me, yet once more he shall stand
On even ground against his mortal foe,
By me upheld, that he may know how frail   180
His fallen condition is, and to me owe
All his deliverance, and to none but me.
Some I have chosen of peculiar grace
Elect above the rest; so is my will.

175–76. Man's free will, like Satan's, has lapsed with his disobedience.
Because his sin came from an outside suggestion his power to choose good is
renewed by an act of Grace, as Satan's is not.
     184. elect. In Calvinistic thought the elect include all who are to be
saved, in contrast to the "reprobate," who are predestined before their birth
to be damned; with Milton, on the other hand, the elect are only a special
group of saints to whom goodness and salvation come easily. The rest of
mankind are prone to sin but capable of repentance. If they persistently

God will save all those who accept his grace and show they want salvation

The rest shall hear me call, and oft be warned
Their sinful state, and to appease betimes
The incensèd Deity, while offered grace
Invites; for I will clear their senses dark,
What may suffice, and soften stony hearts
To pray, repent, and bring obedience due.   190
To prayer, repentance, and obedience due,
Though but endeavored with sincere intent,
Mine ear shall not be slow, mine eye not shut.
And I will place within them as a guide
My umpire Conscience, whom if they will hear,
Light after light well used they shall attain,
And to the end persisting, safe arrive.
This my long sufferance and my day of grace
They who neglect and scorn shall never taste;   *hardened*
But hard be hardened, blind be blinded more,   *sinners*   200
That they may stumble on, and deeper fall;   *no mercy*
And none but such from mercy I exclude.
But yet all is not done; Man disobeying,
Disloyal breaks his fealty, and sins
Against the high supremacy of Heaven,
Affecting Godhead, and so losing all,
To expiate his treason hath nought left,
But to destruction sacred and devote,
He with his whole posterity must die;
Die he or justice must; unless for him   210
Some other able, and as willing, pay
The rigid satisfaction, death for death.
Say Heavenly Powers, where shall we find such love?
Which of ye will be mortal to redeem
Man's mortal crime, and just the unjust to save?
Dwells in all Heaven charity so dear?"
    He asked, but all the heavenly choir stood mute,
And silence was in Heaven; on Man's behalf
Patron or intercessor none appeared,
Much less that durst upon his own head draw   220
The deadly forfeiture, and ransom set.
And now without redemption all mankind
Must have been lost, adjudged to Death and Hell

refuse to heed God's warning voice he hardens their hearts progressively,
as he did Satan's, so that they stumble blindly deeper and deeper into sin.
To the nontheological mind Milton's doctrine no more escapes irrationality
than Calvin's.
    204 ff. God's immutable decree cannot be evaded. If justice is to be
satisfied there must be death for sin. The solution is the sacrifice of Christ,
who, like Adam, is the representative of mankind.

By doom severe, had not the Son of God,
In whom the fulness dwells of love divine,
His dearest mediation thus renewed.

"Father, thy word is passed, Man shall find grace;
And shall grace not find means, that finds her way,
The speediest of thy wingèd messengers,
To visit all thy creatures, and to all   230
Comes unprevented, unimplored, unsought?
Happy for Man, so coming; he her aid
Can never seek, once dead in sins and lost;
Atonement for himself or offering meet,
Indebted and undone, hath none to bring.
Behold me then, me for him, life for life
I offer; on me let thine anger fall;
Account me Man; I for his sake will leave
Thy bosom, and this glory next to thee
Freely put off, and for him lastly die   240
Well pleased; on me let Death wreak all his rage;
Under his gloomy power I shall not long
Lie vanquished; thou hast given me to possess
Life in myself for ever; by thee I live;
Though now to Death I yield, and am his due
All that of me can die, yet that debt paid,
Thou wilt not leave me in the loathsome grave
His prey, nor suffer my unspotted soul
For ever with corruption there to dwell;
But I shall rise victorious, and subdue   250
My vanquisher, spoiled of his vaunted spoil;
Death his death's wound shall then receive, and stoop
Inglorious, of his mortal sting disarmed.
I through the ample air in triumph high
Shall lead Hell captive maugre Hell, and show
The powers of darkness bound. Thou at the sight
Pleased, out of Heaven shalt look down and smile,
While by thee raised I ruin all my foes,
Death last, and with his carcass glut the grave:
Then with the multitude of my redeemed,   260
Shall enter Heaven long absent, and return,
Father, to see thy face, wherein no cloud
Of anger shall remain, but peace assured

236 ff. Christ's highly dramatic offer, with its reception, is in studied
contrast to Satan's in Book II, 430 ff.
247. "Thou wilt not leave my soul in Hell; neither wilt thou suffer
thy Holy one to see corruption." Ps. 16:10.
253. "O death, where is thy sting?" I Cor. 15:55.
259. "The last enemy to be destroyed is death." I Cor. 15:26.

And reconcilement; wrath shall be no more
Thenceforth, but in thy presence joy entire."
　His words here ended, but his meek aspéct
Silent yet spake, and breathed immortal love
To mortal men, above which only shone
Filial obedience. As a sacrifice
Glad to be offered, he attends the will   270
Of his great Father. Admiration seized
All Heaven, what this might mean, and whither tend
Wondering; but soon the Almighty thus replied.
　"O thou in Heaven and Earth the only peace
Found out for mankind under wrath, O thou
My sole complacence! well thou know'st how dear
To me are all my works, nor Man the least
Though last created, that for him I spare
Thee from my bosom and right hand, to save,
By losing thee a while, the whole race lost!   280
Thou therefore, whom thou only canst redeem,
Their nature also to thy nature join;
And be thyself Man among men on Earth,
Made flesh, when time shall be, of virgin seed,
By wondrous birth; be thou in Adam's room
The head of all mankind, though Adam's son.
As in him perish all men, so in thee
As from a second root shall be restored,
As many as are restored; without thee, none.
His crime makes guilty all his sons; thy merit   290
Imputed shall absolve them who renounce
Their own both righteous and unrighteous deeds,
And live in thee transplanted, and from thee
Receive new life. So Man, as is most just,
Shall satisfy for Man, be judged and die,
And dying rise, and rising with him raise
His brethren, ransomed with his own dear life.
So heavenly love shall outdo hellish hate,
Giving to death, and dying to redeem,
So dearly to redeem what hellish hate   300
So easily destroyed, and still destroys
In those who, when they may, accept not grace.
Nor shalt thou by descending to assume
Man's nature, lessen or degrade thine own.
Because thou hast, though throned in highest bliss
Equal to God, and equally enjoying
God-like fruition, quitted all to save
A world from utter loss, and hast been found
By merit more than birthright Son of God,

Found worthiest to be so by being good,   310
Far more than great or high; because in thee
Love hath abounded more than glory abounds;
Therefore thy humiliation shall exalt
With thee thy manhood also to this throne;
Here shalt thou sit incarnate, here shalt reign
Both God and Man. Son both of God and Man,
Anointed universal King. All power
I give thee; reign for ever, and assume
Thy merits; under thee as Head supreme
Thrones, Princedoms, Powers, Dominions, I reduce.   320
All knees to thee shall bow, of them that bide
In Heaven, or Earth, or under Earth in Hell;
When thou attended gloriously from Heaven
Shalt in the sky appear, and from thee send
The summoning Archangels to proclaim
Thy dread tribunal, forthwith from all winds
The living, and forthwith the cited dead
Of all past ages to the general doom
Shall hasten, such a peal shall rouse their sleep.
Then all thy saints assembled, thou shalt judge   330
Bad men and angels; they arraigned shall sink
Beneath thy sentence; Hell, her numbers full,
Thenceforth shall be for ever shut. Meanwhile
The World shall burn, and from her ashes spring
New Heaven and Earth, wherein the just shall dwell,
And after all their tribulations long
See golden days, fruitful of golden deeds,
With Joy and Love triumphing, and fair Truth.
Then thou thy regal scepter shalt lay by,
For regal scepter then no more shall need;   340
God shall be all in all. But all ye gods,
Adore him, who to compass all this dies,
Adore the Son, and honor him as me."
    No sooner had the Almighty ceased, but all
The multitude of angels with a shout
Loud as from numbers without number, sweet
As from blest voices, uttering joy, Heaven rung
With jubilee, and loud hosannas filled
The eternal regions. Lowly reverent
Towards either throne they bow, and to the ground   350
With solemn adoration down they cast
Their crowns inwove with amarant and gold,
Immortal amarant, a flower which once
In Paradise, fast by the Tree of Life
Began to bloom, but soon for Man's offence

To Heaven removed where first it grew, there grows
And flowers aloft shading the Fount of Life,
And where the River of Bliss through midst of Heaven
Rolls o'er Elysian flowers her amber stream;   360
With these that never fade the spirits elect
Bind their resplendent locks inwreathed with beams;
Now in loose garlands thick thrown off, the bright
Pavement, that like a sea of jasper shone,
Impurpled with celestial roses smiled.
Then crowned again their golden harps they took,
Harps ever tuned, that glittering by their side
Like quivers hung, and with preamble sweet
Of charming symphony they introduce
Their sacred song, and waken raptures high;   370
No voice exempt, no voice but well could join
Melodious part, such concord is in Heaven.
    Thee Father first they sung Omnipotent,
Immutable, Immortal, Infinite,
Eternal King; thee Author of all being,
Fountain of light, thyself invisible
Amidst the glorious brightness where thou sitt'st
Throned inaccessible, but when thou shadest
The full blaze of thy beams, and through a cloud
Drawn round about thee like a radiant shrine,   380
Dark with excessive bright thy skirts appear,
Yet dazzle Heaven, that brightest Seraphim
Approach not, but with both wings veil their eyes.
Thee next they sang, of all creation first,
Begotten Son, Divine Similitude,
In whose conspicuous countenance, without cloud
Made visible, the Almighty Father shines,
Whom else no creature can behold; on thee
Impressed the effulgence of his glory abides,
Transfused on thee his ample Spirit rests.
He Heaven of Heavens and all the powers therein   390
By thee created, and by thee threw down
The aspiring Dominations. Thou that day
Thy Father's dreadful thunder didst not spare,
Nor stop thy flaming chariot wheels, that shook
Heaven's everlasting frame, while o'er the necks
Thou drovest of warring angels disarrayed.
Back from pursuit, thy powers with loud acclaim
Thee only extolled, Son of thy Father's might,

380.   There is in God—some say—
          A deep, but dazzling darkness.
                    Vaughan, *The Night.*

To execute fierce vengeance on his foes,
Not so on Man; him through their malice fallen,   400
Father of mercy and grace, thou didst not doom
So strictly, but much more to pity incline.
No sooner did thy dear and only Son
Perceive thee purposed not to doom frail Man
So strictly, but much more to pity inclined,
He to appease thy wrath, and end the strife
Of mercy and justice in thy face discerned,
Regardless of the bliss wherein he sat
Second to thee, offered himself to die
For Man's offence. O unexampled love,   410
Love nowhere to be found less than divine,
Hail, Son of God, Savior of men, thy name
Shall be the copious matter of my song
Henceforth, and never shall my harp thy praise
Forget, nor from thy Father's praise disjoin.
　　Thus they in Heaven, above the starry sphere,
Their happy hours in joy and hymning spent.
Meanwhile, upon the firm opacous globe
Of this round World, whose first convex divides
The luminous inferior orbs, enclosed   420
From Chaos and the inroad of Darkness old,
Satan alighted walks. A globe far off
It seemed, now seems a boundless continent
Dark, waste, and wild, under the frown of Night
Starless exposed, and ever-threatening storms
Of Chaos blustering round, inclement sky;
Save on that side which from the wall of Heaven,
Though distant far some small reflexion gains
Of glimmering air less vexed with tempest loud.
Here walked the Fiend at large in spacious field.   430
As when a vulture on Imaus bred,
Whose snowy ridge the roving Tartar bounds,
Dislodging from a region scarce of prey
To gorge the flesh of lambs or yeanling kids
On hills where flocks are fed, flies toward the springs
Of Ganges or Hydaspes, Indian streams;
But in his way lights on the barren plains
Of Sericana, where Chineses drive
With sails and wind their cany wagons light:

431. **As when a vulture.** The vulture flies southwest from a mountain
range in central Asia, across the western plains of China (called Sericana
in old maps), to the fertile plains of Northern India.
　　436. **Hydaspes,** classical name for the Jehlam River.
　　439. The sailing wagons are mentioned by the seventeenth-century
geographer, Heylin.

So on this windy sea of land, the Fiend   440
Walked up and down alone bent on his prey,
Alone, for other creature in this place,
Living or lifeless to be found was none,
None yet, but store hereafter from the Earth
Up hither like aerial vapors flew
Of all things transitory and vain, when sin
With vanity had filled the works of men.
Both all things vain, and all who in vain things
Built their fond hopes of glory or lasting fame,
Or happiness in this or the other life;   450
All who have their reward on earth, the fruits
Of painful superstition and blind zeal,
Nought seeking but the praise of men, here find
Fit retribution, empty as their deeds;
All the unaccomplished works of Nature's hand,
Abortive, monstrous, or unkindly mixed,
Dissolved on Earth, fleet hither, and in vain,
Till final dissolution, wander here,
Not in the neighboring moon, as some have dreamed;
Those argent fields more likely habitants,   460
Translated saints, or middle spirits hold
Betwixt the angelical and human kind.
Hither of ill-joined sons and daughters born,
First from the ancient world those giants came
With many a vain exploit, though then renowned;
The builders next of Babel on the plain
Of Sennaar, and still with vain design
New Babels, had they wherewithal, would build;
Others came single: he who to be deemed
A god, leaped fondly into Ætna flames,   470
Empedocles; and he who to enjoy
Plato's Elysium, leaped into the sea,
Cleombrotus, and many more too long,
Embryos and idiots, eremites and friars
White, black, and grey, with all their trumpery.
Here pilgrims roam, that strayed so far to seek
In Golgotha him dead who lives in Heaven;
And they who to be sure of Paradise,
Dying put on the weeds of Dominic,

444 ff. Milton adapts the satire of Ariosto, who describes a limbo of earthly follies in the moon. See line 459. The vanities which Milton lists are monuments of misguided, fanatical, or disproportioned effort.

471. Empedocles leaped into the crater of Mount Etna to make his name live forever.

472. Plato's Elysium, the after-world as described in the *Phaedo*.

479-80. Milton's fanatical hatred of the Roman church blinds him to

Or in Franciscan think to pass disguised;   480
They pass the planets seven, and pass the fixed,
And that crystalline sphere whose balance weighs
The trepidation talked, and that first moved;
And now Saint Peter at Heaven's wicket seems
To wait them with his keys, and now at foot
Of Heaven's ascent they lift their feet, when lo!
A violent cross wind from either coast
Blows them transverse, ten thousand leagues awry
Into the devious air; then might ye see
Cowls, hoods and habits with their wearers tossed   490
And fluttered into rags; then reliques, beads,
Indulgences, dispenses, pardons, bulls,
The sport of winds. All these upwhirled aloft
Fly o'er the backside of the World far off
Into a limbo large and broad, since called
The Paradise of Fools; to few unknown
Long after, now unpeopled and untrod.
   All this dark globe the Fiend found as he passed,
And long he wandered, till at last a gleam
Of dawning light turned thitherward in haste   500
His travelled steps; far distant he descries
Ascending by degrees magnificent
Up to the wall of Heaven a structure high,
At top whereof, but far more rich appeared
The work as of a kingly palace gate
With frontispiece of diamond and gold
Embellished; thick with sparkling orient gems
The portal shone, inimitable on Earth
By model, or by shading pencil drawn.
The stairs were such as whereon Jacob saw   510
Angels ascending and descending, bands

the beauty of everything in its tradition. He has read Dante's great tribute
to the Dominican and Franciscan orders, yet he thinks of them only as the
refuge for hypocrites who make haste to take the robe on their deathbed
to make sure of Heaven. Readers have been justly offended by this passage
on artistic as well as religious grounds. But Milton believed that the greatest
danger to true faith, as inculcated in the poem, lay in reliance on man-
made traditions and outward forms. The material is not inappropriate,
therefore, in this book, where the central doctrines of Christianity are set
forth.
   481. the fixed, the sphere of the fixed stars.
   483-84. The balance of the crystalline sphere determined the much
talked of swaying or libration, which in the Ptolemaic system belonged to
the celestial system, in the Copernican, of course, to the earth. See VIII,
130. First moved, the *primum mobile,* which imparted motion to the other
spheres.
   510. For Jacob's vision see Gen. 28:10–19.

Of guardians bright, when he from Esau fled
To Padan-Aram in the field of Luz,
Dreaming by night under the open sky,
And waking cried, "This is the gate of Heaven."
Each stair mysteriously was meant, nor stood
There always, but drawn up to Heaven sometimes
Viewless, and underneath a bright sea flowed
Of jasper, or of liquid pearl, whereon
Who after came from Earth, sailing arrived,   520
Wafted by angels, or flew o'er the lake
Rapt in a chariot drawn by fiery steeds.
The stairs were then let down, whether to dare
The Fiend by easy ascent, or aggravate
His sad exclusion from the doors of bliss.
Direct against which opened from beneath,
Just o'er the blissful seat of Paradise,
A passage down to the Earth, a passage wide,
Wider by far than that of after-times   530
Over Mount Sion, and, though that were large,
Over the Promised Land to God so dear,
By which, to visit oft those happy tribes,
On high behests his angels to and fro
Passed frequent, and his eye with choice regard
From Paneas the fount of Jordan's flood,
To Beërsaba, where the Holy Land
Borders on Egypt and the Arabian shore;
So wide the opening seemed, where bounds were set
To darkness, such as bound the ocean wave.
　　Satan from hence, now on the lower stair   540
That scaled by steps of gold to Heaven gate
Looks down with wonder at the sudden view
Of all this World at once. As when a scout
Through dark and desert ways with peril gone
All night, at last by break of cheerful dawn
Obtains the brow of some high-climbing hill,
Which to his eye discovers unaware
The goodly prospect of some foreign land
First seen, or some renowned metropolis
With glistering spires and pinnacles adorned,   550
Which now the rising sun gilds with his beams.
Such wonder seized, though after Heaven seen,
The spirit malign, but much more envy seized
At sight of all this World beheld so fair.

---

535. **Paneas,** Dan on the north boundary of the Holy Land. God surveyed all Palestine through the opening "from Dan to Beersheba."

Round he surveys, and well might, where he stood,
So high above the circling canopy
Of Night's extended shade; from eastern point
Of Libra to the fleecy star that bears
Andromeda far off Atlantic seas
Beyond the horizon; then from pole to pole 560
He views in breadth, and without longer pause
Down right into the World's first region throws
His flight precipitant, and winds with ease
Through the pure marble air his oblique way
Amongst innumerable stars, that shone
Stars distant, but nigh hand seemed other worlds,
Or other worlds they seemed, or happy isles,
Like those Hesperian Gardens famed of old,
Fortunate fields, and groves, and flowery vales,
Thrice happy isles, but who dwelt happy there 570
He stayed not to inquire. Above them all
The golden sun in splendor likest Heaven
Allured his eye. Thither his course he bends,
Through the calm firmament; but up or down,
By center, or eccentric, hard to tell,
Or longitude, where the great luminary
Aloof the vulgar constellations thick,
That from his lordly eye keep distance due,
Dispenses light from far; they as they move
Their starry dance in numbers that compute 580
Days, months, and years, towards his all-cheering lamp
Turn swift their various motions, or are turned
By his magnetic beam, that gently warms
The Universe, and to each inward part
With gentle penetration, though unseen,
Shoots invisible virtue even to the deep:
So wondrously was set his station bright.
    There lands the Fiend, a spot like which perhaps
Astronomer in the sun's lucent orb
Through his glazed optic tube yet never saw. 590
The place he found beyond expression bright,

    558. the fleecy star, the sign of Aries, the Ram, opposite Libra and just below the constellation of Andromeda.
    562. first region. The air was divided into upper, middle, and lower regions.
    564. marble, lucent and shining, like some marble.
    574. up or down, etc. Satan's course was devious and obscure, its ambiguity being perhaps heightened by the uncertainty whether one should call the earth or the sun the center.
    588–90. Galileo had discovered the sun spots with his telescope.
    591 ff. Milton revels in the picturesque terms of Alchemy. The sun is

Compared with aught on Earth, metal or stone;
Not all parts like, but all alike informed
With radiant light, as glowing iron with fire.
If metal, part seemed gold, part silver clear;
If stone, carbuncle most or chrysolite,
Ruby or topaz, to the twelve that shone
In Aaron's breast-plate, and a stone besides,
Imagined rather oft than elsewhere seen,
That stone, or like to that, which here below   600
Philosophers in vain so long have sought;
In vain, though by their powerful art they bind
Volatile Hermes, and call up unbound
In various shapes old Proteus from the sea,
Drained through a limbec to his native form.
What wonder then if fields and regions here
Breathe forth elixir pure, and rivers run
Potable gold, when with one virtuous touch
The arch-chemic sun, so far from us remote,
Produces, with terrestrial humor mixed,   610
Here in the dark so many precious things
Of color glorious and effect so rare?
Here matter new to gaze the Devil met
Undazzled; far and wide his eye commands,
For sight no obstacle found here, nor shade,
But all sunshine, as when his beams at noon
Culminate from the equator, as they now
Shot upward still direct, whence no way round
Shadow from body opaque can fall, and the air,
Nowhere so clear, sharpened his visual ray   620
To objects distant far, whereby he soon
Saw within ken a glorious angel stand,
The same whom John saw also in the sun.
His back was turned, but not his brightness hid;
Of beaming sunny rays, a golden tiar
Circled his head, nor less his locks behind
Illustrious on his shoulders fledge with wings
Lay waving round; on some great charge employed
He seemed, or fixed in cogitation deep.
    Glad was the spirit impure, as now in hope   630
To find who might direct his wandering flight

the arch-transmuter of metals and contains the philosopher's stone, which
the alchemists of earth seek in vain. To bind volatile Hermes is to fix
mercury; old Proteus's native form is water.
    608–9. One touch of the sun's power, mixed with the moisture of earth,
produces flowers, jewels, etc.
    623. Rev. 19:17.

To contemplate God's works—to discover new reasons for praising him

To Paradise the happy seat of Man,
His journey's end and our beginning woe.
But first he casts to change his proper shape,
Which else might work him danger or delay.
And now a stripling Cherub he appears,
Not of the prime, yet such as in his face
Youth smiled celestial, and to every limb
Suitable grace diffused, so well he feigned;
Under a coronet his flowing hair   640
In curls on either cheek played, wings he wore
Of many a colored plume sprinkled with gold,
His habit fit for speed succinct, and held
Before his decent steps a silver wand.
He drew not nigh unheard; the angel bright,
Ere he drew nigh, his radiant visage turned,
Admonished by his ear, and straight was known
The Archangel Uriel, one of the seven
Who in God's presence, nearest to his throne
Stand ready at command, and are his eyes   650
That run through all the Heavens, or down to the Earth
Bear his swift errands over moist and dry,
O'er sea and land. Him Satan thus accosts;
    "Uriel, for thou of those seven spirits that stand
In sight of God's high throne, gloriously bright,
The first art wont his great authentic will
Interpreter through highest Heaven to bring,
Where all his sons thy embassy attend;
And here art likeliest by supreme decree
Like honor to obtain, and as his eye   660
To visit oft this new creation round;
Unspeakable desire to see and know
All these his wondrous works, but chiefly Man,
His chief delight and favor, him for whom
All these his works so wondrous he ordained,
Hath brought me from the choirs of Cherubim
Alone thus wandering. Brightest Seraph tell
In which of all these shining orbs hath Man
His fixèd seat, or fixèd seat hath none,
But all these shining orbs his choice to dwell;   670
That I may find him, and with secret gaze,
Or open admiration him behold
On whom the great Creator hath bestowed

637. not of the prime, not yet in the prime of life.
648 ff. Uriel, named in Rabbinical literature as one of the seven angels
described in Zech. 4:10, as "the eyes of the Lord, which run to and fro
through the whole earth."

Worlds, and on whom hath all these graces poured;
That both in him and all things, as is meet,
The Universal Maker we may praise;
Who justly hath driven out his rebel foes
To deepest Hell, and to repair that loss
Created this new happy race of men
To serve him better: wise are all his ways."   680
    So spake the false dissembler unperceived;
For neither man nor angel can discern
Hypocrisy, the only evil that walks
Invisible, except to God alone,
By his permissive will, through Heaven and Earth;
And oft though Wisdom wake, Suspicion sleeps
At Wisdom's gate, and to Simplicity
Resigns her charge, while Goodness thinks no ill
Where no ill seems: which now for once beguiled
Uriel, though regent of the sun, and held   690
The sharpest-sighted spirit of all in Heaven;
Who to the fraudulent impostor foul,
In his uprightness answer thus returned.
    "Fair Angel, thy desire which tends to know
The works of God, thereby to glorify
The great Work-master, leads to no excess
That reaches blame, but rather merits praise
The more it seems excess, that led thee hither
From thy empyreal mansion thus alone,
To witness with thine eyes what some perhaps   700
Contented with report, hear only in Heaven:
For wonderful indeed are all his works,
Pleasant to know, and worthiest to be all
Had in remembrance always with delight;
But what created mind can comprehend
Their number, or the wisdom infinite
That brought them forth, but hid their causes deep?
I saw when at his word the formless mass,
This World's material mould, came to a heap.
Confusion heard his voice, and wild uproar   710
Stood ruled, stood vast infinitude confined;
Till at his second bidding Darkness fled,
Light shone, and order from disorder sprung.
Swift to their several quarters hasted then

    708 ff. This account of creation owes much to Plato's *Timaeus*, which
is the basic philosophical authority for the theory of one primordial matter
out of which God formed the universe, instead of by fiat out of nothing.
Acceptance of this starting point gives the special character of Miltonic
doctrine, as outlined above.

The cumbrous elements, earth, flood, air, fire,
And this ethereal quintessence of Heaven
Flew upward, spirited with various forms,
That rolled orbicular, and turned to stars
Numberless, as thou seest, and how they move;
Each had his place appointed, each his course;   720
The rest in circuit walls this Universe.
Look downward on that globe whose hither side
With light from hence, though but reflected, shines;
That place is Earth the seat of Man, that light
His day, which else as the other hemisphere,
Night would invade, but there the neighbouring moon
(So call that opposite fair star) her aid
Timely interposes, and her monthly round
Still ending, still renewing, through mid Heaven,
With borrowed light her countenance triform   730
Hence fills and empties to enlighten the Earth,
And in her pale dominion checks the night.
That spot to which I point is Paradise,
Adam's abode, those lofty shades his bower.
Thy way thou canst not miss, me mine requires."
    Thus said, he turned, and Satan bowing low,
As to superior spirits is wont in Heaven,
Where honor due and reverence none neglects,
Took leave, and toward the coast of Earth beneath,
Down from the ecliptic, sped with hoped success,   740
Throws his steep flight in many an airy wheel,
Nor stayed, till on Niphates' top he lights.

BOOK IV

THE ARGUMENT

Satan, now in prospect of Eden, and nigh the place where he
must now attempt the bold enterprise which he undertook alone
against God and Man, falls into many doubts with himself, and
many passions, fear, envy, and despair; but at length confirms
himself in evil, journeys on to Paradise, whose outward prospect
and situation is described, overleaps the bounds, sits in the shape
of a cormorant on the Tree of Life, as highest in the Garden, to

715 ff. The four elements form the earth. A fifth essence rises above
them and becomes the stars and the surrounding wall of the universe.
730. triform, Latin *triformis*, referring to the goddess's threefold incarnation as Luna in the sky, Diana on earth, and Hecate in the underworld.
742. Niphates, a mountain in the Taurus range in Armenia, named
in *Paradise Regained* as the place where Satan brought Christ to survey the
kingdoms of the earth.

look about him. The Garden described; Satan's first sight of Adam
and Eve; his wonder at their excellent form and happy state, but
with resolution to work their fall; overhears their discourse;
thence gathers that the Tree of Knowledge was forbidden them
to eat of under penalty of death, and thereon intends to found
his temptation by seducing them to transgress; then leaves them
a while, to know further of their state by some other means.
Meanwhile Uriel, descending on a sunbeam, warns Gabriel, who
had in charge the gate of Paradise, that some evil spirit had
escaped the Deep, and passed at noon by his sphere, in the shape
of a good angel, down to Paradise; discovered after by his furious
gestures in the mount. Gabriel promises to find him ere morning.
Night coming on, Adam and Eve discourse of going to their rest:
their bower described; their evening worship. Gabriel, drawing
forth his bands of night-watch to walk the round of Paradise,
appoints two strong angels to Adam's bower, lest the evil spirit
should be there doing some harm to Adam or Eve sleeping; there
they find him at the ear of Eve, tempting her in a dream, and
bring him, though unwilling, to Gabriel; by whom questioned, he
scornfully answers, prepares resistance, but hindered by a sign
from Heaven, flies out of Paradise.

O for that warning voice, which he who saw
The Apocalypse heard cry in Heaven aloud,
Then when the Dragon, put to second rout,
Came furious down to be revenged on men,
"Woe to the inhabitants on Earth!" that now,
While time was, our first parents had been warned
The coming of their secret foe, and scaped,
Haply so scaped, his mortal snare; for now
Satan, now first inflamed with rage, came down,
The tempter ere the accuser of mankind,   10
To wreak on innocent frail Man his loss
Of that first battle, and his flight to Hell.
Yet not rejoicing in his speed, though bold,
Far off and fearless, nor with cause to boast,
Begins his dire attempt, which nigh the birth
Now rolling, boils in his tumultuous breast,
And like a devilish engine back recoils

1 ff. This opening passage is based on the vision of St. John recorded in
Rev. 12. Cf. especially verse 12: "Woe to the inhabiters of the earth and
of the sea! for the devil is come down unto you, having great wrath."

10. The tempter ere the accuser. In St. John's vision, Satan, routed
from heaven for the second time, comes down to earth as "the accuser of
our brethren" (Rev. 12:10). But, as Milton points out, he first came to
earth in the role of tempter. The word "devil" is a corruption of the Greek
diabolos, meaning literally "slanderer" or "accuser."

11. wreak, avenge.

Upon himself; horror and doubt distract
His troubled thoughts, and from the bottom stir
The Hell within him, for within him Hell   20
He brings, and round about him, nor from Hell
One step no more than from himself can fly
By change of place. Now conscience wakes despair
That slumbered, wakes the bitter memory
Of what he was, what is, and what must be
Worse; of worse deeds worse sufferings must ensue.
Sometimes towards Eden which now in his view
Lay pleasant, his grievëd look he fixes sad,
Sometimes towards Heaven and the full-blazing sun,
Which now sat high in his meridian tower.   30
Then much revolving, thus in sighs began.
  "O thou that with surpassing glory crowned,
Look'st from thy sole dominion like the god
Of this new world; at whose sight all the stars
Hide their diminished heads; to thee I call,
But with no friendly voice, and add thy name
O Sun, to tell thee how I hate thy beams
That bring to my remembrance from what state
I fell, how glorious once above thy sphere;
Till pride and worse ambition threw me down   40
Warring in Heaven against Heaven's matchless King.
Ah wherefore! He deserved no such return
From me, whom he created what I was
In that bright eminence, and with his good
Upbraided none; nor was his service hard.
What could be less than to afford him praise,
The easiest recompense, and pay him thanks,
How due! Yet all his good proved ill in me,

18 ff. For this conception of hell as a mental state, cf. I, 254, 255; also
the utterance of Mephistophilis in Marlowe's *Dr. Faustus*, 94–96:

> Hell hath no limits, nor is circumscribed
> In one self place; for where we are is hell,
> And where hell is, there must we ever be.

27. The literal meaning of **Eden** is "delight."
31. **much revolving**, pondering many things. The phrase is a Latinism
(*multa volvens*).
32 ff. According to Edward Phillips, Milton wrote these lines as early
as 1642, intending them as the opening speech in his projected drama on
the Fall. The whole passage, indeed, has a dramatic quality somewhat
reminiscent of Shakespeare. Cf., for example, the soliloquies of Iago
(*Othello*, I, iii, 389–410; II, i, 295–321; II, iii, 342–68).
41. Cf. I, 116, 117 and note. The uncompromising egotism of Satan's
public utterances now gives way to a secret admission of God's supremacy.

And wrought but malice; lifted up so high
I 'sdeined subjection, and thought one step higher   50
Would set me highest, and in a moment quit
The debt immense of endless gratitude,
So burdensome still paying, still to owe;
Forgetful what from him I still received,
And understood not that a grateful mind
By owing owes not, but still pays, at once
Indebted and discharged; what burden then?
Oh had his powerful destiny ordained
Me some inferior angel, I had stood
Then happy; no unbounded hope had raised   60
Ambition. Yet why not? some other Power
As great might have aspired, and me though mean
Drawn to his part; but other Powers as great
Fell not, but stand unshaken, from within
Or from without, to all temptations armed.
Hadst thou the same free will and power to stand?
Thou hadst. Whom hast thou then or what to accuse,
But Heaven's free love dealt equally to all?
Be then his love accurst, since love or hate,
To me alike it deals eternal woe.   70
Nay cursed be thou; since against his thy will
Chose freely what it now so justly rues.
Me miserable! which way shall I fly
Infinite wrath and infinite despair?
Which way I fly is Hell; myself am Hell;
And in the lowest deep a lower deep
Still threatening to devour me opens wide,
To which the Hell I suffer seems a Heaven.
O then at last relent: is there no place
Left for repentance, none for pardon left?   80
None left but by submission; and that word
Disdain forbids me, and my dread of shame
Among the spirits beneath, whom I seduced
With other promises and other vaunts
Than to submit, boasting I could subdue
The Omnipotent. Ay me, they little know

50. 'sdeined, disdained (from Italian *sdegnare*).
51. quit, requite, pay.
52–57. Satan means that gratitude is in itself payment, whereas payment alone does not release from a debt of gratitude. Cicero *De officiis* ii. 20, expresses a similar sentiment.
66. the same free will and power to stand. Cf. III, 102: "Freely they stood who stood, and fell who fell." Milton reiterates this idea again and again.
73. Me miserable! a Latinism (*me miserum*).

How dearly I abide that boast so vain,
Under what torments inwardly I groan;
While they adore me on the throne of Hell,
With diadem and scepter high advanced   90
The lower still I fall, only supreme
In misery; such joy ambition finds.
But say I could repent, and could obtain
By act of grace my former state; how soon
Would height recall high thoughts, how soon unsay
What feigned submission swore: ease would recant
Vows made in pain, as violent and void.
For never can true reconcilement grow
Where wounds of deadly hate have pierced so deep;
Which would but lead me to a worse relapse   100
And heavier fall: so should I purchase dear
Short intermission bought with double smart.
This knows my Punisher; therefore as far
From granting he, as I from begging peace.
All hope excluded thus, behold instead
Of us, outcast, exiled, his new delight,
Mankind created, and for him this World.
So farewell hope, and with hope farewell fear,
Farewell remorse! All good to me is lost;
Evil be thou my good; by thee at least   110
Divided empire with Heaven's King I hold
By thee, and more than half perhaps will reign;
As Man ere long, and this new World shall know."
    Thus while he spake, each passion dimmed his face
Thrice changed with pale, ire, envy, and despair,
Which marred his borrowed visage, and betrayed
Him counterfeit, if any eye beheld.
For heavenly minds from such distempers foul
Are ever clear. Whereof he soon aware,
Each perturbation smoothed with outward calm,   120
Artificer of fraud; and was the first
That practised falsehood under saintly show,
Deep malice to conceal, couched with revenge.
Yet not enough had practised to deceive

87. abide, suffer for.
90. advanced, elevated. Me (89) is the word modified.
94. By act of grace, i.e., by asking pardon.
115. Thrice changed with pale, i.e., each of the passions (ire, envy,
and despair) dims the natural luster of his countenance. Pale is of course
used as a noun.
118. For heavenly minds, etc. Probably Milton is thinking of *Aeneid*
i. 11: *tantaene animis caelestibus irae.* Cf. VI, 788, and IX, 729.
123. couched with, lying hidden with.

Uriel once warned; whose eye pursued him down
The way he went, and on the Assyrian mount
Saw him disfigured, more than could befall
Spirit of happy sort. His gestures fierce
He marked and mad demeanor, then alone,
As he supposed, all unobserved, unseen.   130
    So on he fares, and to the border comes
Of Eden, where delicious Paradise,
Now nearer, crowns with her enclosure green,
As with a rural mound the champaign head
Of a steep wilderness, whose hairy sides
With thicket overgrown, grotesque and wild,
Access denied; and overhead up grew
Insuperable height of loftiest shade,
Cedar, and pine, and fir, and branching palm,
A sylvan scene, and as the ranks ascend   140
Shade above shade, a woody theater
Of stateliest view. Yet higher than their tops
The verdurous wall of Paradise up sprung;
Which to our general sire gave prospect large
Into his nether empire neighboring round.
And higher than that wall a circling row
Of goodliest trees loaden with fairest fruit,
Blossoms and fruits at once of golden hue
Appeared, with gay enamelled colors mixed;
On which the sun more glad impressed his beams   150
Than in fair evening cloud, or humid bow,
When God hath showered the earth; so lovely seemed
That landscape. And of pure now purer air
Meets his approach, and to the heart inspires
Vernal delight and joy, able to drive
All sadness but despair; now gentle gales
Fanning their odoriferous wings dispense
Native perfumes, and whisper whence they stole
Those balmy spoils. As when to them who sail

126. **the Assyrian mount,** Niphates.
132 ff. Eden is apparently thought of as embracing the greater part of
the Tigris and Euphrates region. Paradise is a garden in the east of Eden.
Cf. 208–10; also Gen. 2:8.
134. **champaign head,** level summit. In locating the Garden on a hill,
Milton follows Dante and Ariosto; the ultimate source of the idea is probably Ezek. 28:13, 14.
145. **nether empire,** i.e., the outlying territories of Eden.
149. **enamelled,** bright and variegated.
153. **of pure now purer.** This idiom is like O *miserable of happy,* i.e.,
miserable after happy, and Horace's *ex humili potens,* mighty after being
humble. We would say "purer and purer air."
159 ff. Renaissance travel literature contains numerous references to

Beyond the Cape of Hope, and now are past   160
Mozambic, off at sea north-east winds blow
Sabæan odors from the spicy shore
Of Araby the Blest, with such delay
Well pleased they slack their course, and many a league
Cheered with the grateful smell old Ocean smiles.
So entertained those odorous sweets the Fiend
Who came their bane, though with them better pleased
Than Asmodëus with the fishy fume,
That drove him, though enamored, from the spouse
Of Tobit's son, and with a vengeance sent   170
From Media post to Egypt, there fast bound.
  Now to the ascent of that steep savage hill
Satan had journeyed on, pensive and slow;
But further way found none, so thick entwined,
As one continued brake, the undergrowth
Of shrubs and tangling bushes had perplexed
All path of man or beast that passed that way.
One gate there only was, and that looked east
On the other side; which when the Arch-Felon saw,
Due entrance he disdained, and in contempt,   180
At one slight bound high overleaped all bound
Of hill or highest wall, and sheer within
Lights on his feet. As when a prowling wolf,
Whom hunger drives to seek new haunt for prey,
Watching where shepherds pen their flocks at eve
In hurdled cotes amid the field secure,
Leaps o'er the fence with ease into the fold;
Or as a thief bent to unhoard the cash
Of some rich burgher, whose substantial doors,
Cross-barred and bolted fast, fear no assault,   190
In at the window climbs, or o'er the tiles:
So clomb this first grand thief into God's fold;
So since into his Church lewd hirelings climb.

the phenomenon which forms the basis of this simile. **Mozambic,** described
at some length by Purchas, was a province on the east coast of Africa, opposite Madagascar. The famous spices of Sheba (whence the **Sabæan** odors)
are mentioned in II Chron. 9:9.
  167 ff. The allusion is to an episode related in the apocryphal Book of
Tobit, 8. Tobit's son is married to a maiden of Media, who is beloved by
the evil spirit Asmodeus; to get rid of this spirit he is instructed by the angel
Raphael to burn the heart and liver of a fish. The odor drives Asmodeus
into Egypt, where the angel binds him. Milton refers to the story again in
V, 221–23.
    172. savage, woody (from Latin *silvaticus*).
    176. perplexed, made difficult. Cf. *Comus,* 37.
    181. bound . . . bound. Note the play on words.
    193. Cf. "Lycidas," 113–31 and notes.

Thence up he flew, and on the Tree of Life,
The middle tree and highest there that grew,
Sat like a cormorant; yet not true life
Thereby regained, but sat devising death
To them who lived; nor on the virtue thought
Of that life-giving plant, but only used
For prospect, what well used had been the pledge   200
Of immortality. So little knows
Any, but God alone, to value right
The good before him, but perverts best things
To worst abuse, or to their meanest use.
   Beneath him with new wonder now he views
To all delight of human sense exposed
In narrow room Nature's whole wealth, yea more,
A Heaven on Earth, for blissful Paradise
Of God the garden was, by him in the east
Of Eden planted; Eden stretched her line   210
From Auran eastward to the royal towers
Of great Seleucia, built by Grecian kings,
Or where the sons of Eden long before
Dwelt in Telassar. In this pleasant soil
His far more pleasant garden God ordained;
Out of the fertile ground he caused to grow
All trees of noblest kind for sight, smell, taste;
And all amid them stood the Tree of Life,
High-eminent, blooming ambrosial fruit
Of vegetable gold; and next to life   220
Our death the Tree of Knowledge grew fast by,
Knowledge of good bought dear by knowing ill.
Southward through Eden went a river large,
Nor changed his course, but through the shaggy hill
Passed underneath ingulfed, for God had thrown
That mountain as his garden mould, high raised
Upon the rapid current, which through veins
Of porous earth with kindly thirst up drawn,
Rose a fresh fountain, and with many a rill
Watered the garden; thence united fell   230

194. **Tree of Life.** Cf. Gen. 2:9.
196. **like a cormorant,** i.e., in the shape of a ravenous bird of prey.
211. **Auran,** a district of Syria, about fifty miles south of Damascus.
212. **Seleucia,** a city on the Tigris, about twenty miles southeast of
modern Bagdad. It was built by Seleucus, one of Alexander's generals.
214. **Telassar,** an ancient site in Mesopotamia. Cf. II Kings 19:12;
Isa. 37:12.
219. **blooming,** bearing.
223 ff. **Southward . . . no account.** Cf. Gen. 2:10. In IX, 71–73
Milton identifies this river with the Tigris.

Down the steep glade, and met the nether flood,
Which from his darksome passage now appears,
And now divided into four main streams,
Runs diverse, wandering many a famous realm
And country whereof here needs no account;
But rather to tell how, if art could tell,
How from that sapphire fount the crispèd brooks,
Rolling on orient pearl and sands of gold,
With mazy error under pendent shades
Ran nectar, visiting each plant, and fed   240
Flowers worthy of Paradise, which not nice art
In beds and curious knots, but Nature boon
Poured forth profuse on hill and dale and plain,
Both where the morning sun first warmly smote
The open field, and where the unpierced shade
Imbrowned the noon-tide bowers. Thus was this place,
A happy rural seat of various view;
Groves whose rich trees wept odorous gums and balm,
Others whose fruit burnished with golden rind
Hung amiable, Hesperian fables true,   250
If true, here only, and of delicious taste.
Betwixt them lawns, or level downs, and flocks
Grazing the tender herb, were interposed,
Or palmy hillock, or the flowery lap
Of some irriguous valley spread her store,
Flowers of all hue, and without thorn the rose.
Another side, umbrageous grots and caves
Of cool recess, o'er which the mantling vine
Lays forth her purple grape, and gently creeps
Luxuriant; meanwhile murmuring waters fall   260
Down the slope hills, dispersed, or in a lake,
That to the fringèd bank with myrtle crowned
Her crystal mirror holds, unite their streams.
The birds their choir apply; airs, vernal airs,

233. **four main streams.** Cf. Gen. 2:10–14.
238. **orient**, lustrous, as in *orient colors, orient morning-light*, etc.
239. **error**, wandering (the literal meaning of Latin *error*).
241–42. The natural profusion of Paradise is contrasted with the artificial arrangement of an Italian garden. **nice**, fastidious. **boon**, bounteous. This passage played a part in supporting later preference for the so-called English garden and for the love of natural scenery generally.
247. **various view**, varied aspect.
250–51. Milton means that here, if anywhere, was to be found such fruit as classical myth attributed to the Garden of the Hesperides. Cf. *Comus*, 393, and note. **amiable**, lovely (Latin *amabilis*).
255. **irriguous**, well-watered (Latin *irriguus*).
256. **without thorn the rose.** On the basis of Gen. 3:18, the Church Fathers maintained that there were no thorns or thistles before Adam's sin.

Breathing the smell of field and grove, attune
The trembling leaves, while universal Pan,
Knit with the Graces and the Hours in dance,
Led on the eternal Spring.   Not that fair field
Of Enna, where Proserpine gathering flowers
Herself a fairer flower by gloomy Dis   270
Was gathered, which cost Ceres all that pain
To seek her through the world; nor that sweet grove
Of Daphne by Orontes, and the inspired
Castalian spring, might with this Paradise
Of Eden strive; nor that Nyseian isle,
Girt with the river Triton, where old Cham
Whom Gentiles Ammon call and Lybian Jove,
Hid Amalthea and her florid son
Young Bacchus from his stepdame Rhea's eye;
Nor where Abassin kings their issue guard,   280
Mount Amara, though this by some supposed
True Paradise, under the Ethiop line
By Nilus' head, enclosed with shining rock,
A whole day's journey high, but wide remote
From this Assyrian garden, where the Fiend
Saw undelighted all delight, all kind
Of living creatures new to sight and strange.
Two of far nobler shape erect and tall,

266 ff. Classical writers often made "the dance of the Hours" symbolic
of the orderly succession of the seasons. By having Pan and the Graces join
in the dance, Milton greatly enriches the symbolism. The idea of eternal
spring in Eden is suggested by some of the Church Fathers and by Dante.

268. Milton, in characteristic manner, romanticizes Paradise by introducing a far-flung series of comparisons. The whole passage is more suggestive of Baroque art and of seventeenth-century Italian poetry than it is
even of Spenser. It bears comparison also with English Ovidian narrative
like Marlowe's Hero and Leander.

269. Enna, a city in central Sicily. The neighboring fields are described
by Ovid (Metamorphoses v. 385 ff.) and by Diodorus Siculus (Bibliotheca
Historica v. 3) as the scene of Proserpine's rape.

273. Daphne, a town situated on the river Orontes, about five miles
from Antioch. It contained a grove and fountain sacred to Apollo, the
fountain being named after the more famous Castalian spring at Delphi.

275. that Nyseian isle, the island of Nysa, situated in the midst of the
river Triton in northern Africa. The associated myth is given by Diodorus
Siculus (Bibliotheca Historica iii. 67), together with a detailed description
of the locality. The identification of Jupiter Ammon wth Noah's son Ham
(Cham) is an interesting Miltonic touch.

281. Mount Amara, a high hill on the Abyssinian plateau. It is described at length by Purchas (Pilgrimage, 843-46) and by Heylin (Cos-
mography, IV, 64), both of whom connect it with the place of seclusion
where, according to tradition, the Abyssinian princes were sent to be
educated.

282. Ethiop line, the equator.

God-like erect, with native honor clad
In naked majesty seemed lords of all,   290
And worthy seemed, for in their looks divine
The image of their glorious Maker shone,
Truth, wisdom, sanctitude severe and pure,
Severe but in true filial freedom placed;
Whence true authority in men; though both
Not equal, as their sex not equal seemed;
For contemplation he and valor formed,
For softness she and sweet attractive grace;
He for God only, she for God in him.
His fair large front and eye sublime declared   300
Absolute rule; and hyacinthine locks
Round from his parted forelock manly hung
Clustering, but not beneath his shoulders broad:
She as a veil down to the slender waist
Her unadornèd golden tresses wore
Dishevelled, but in wanton ringlets waved
As the vine curls her tendrils, which implied
Subjection, but required with gentle sway,
And by her yielded, by him best received,
Yielded with coy submission, modest pride,   310
And sweet reluctant amorous delay.
Nor those mysterious parts were then concealed;
Then was not guilty shame, dishonest shame
Of Nature's works, honor dishonorable,
Sin-bred, how have ye troubled all mankind
With shows instead, mere shows of seeming pure,
And banished from man's life his happiest life,
Simplicity and spotless innocence.
So passed they naked on, nor shunned the sight
Of God or angel, for they thought no ill;   320
So hand in hand they passed, the loveliest pair
That ever since in love's embraces met:

289. **God-like erect.** Milton makes man's upright stature a symbol of his superiority to the brutes and of his instinctive aspiration.

295 ff. Throughout the poem Milton carefully distinguishes between the relative endowments and obligations of man and woman. The sexes are not equal, he insists, and authority quite properly belongs to the male. But the position which he accords woman, when considered in the light of theological tradition, is exceedingly high.

300. **front,** brow (Latin *frons*).

301. **hyacinthine,** i.e., dark in color. Cf. *Odyssey* vi. 231.

301–5. Cf. I Cor. 11:14, 15. But St. Paul says the woman's long hair was given her for a covering.

306. **wanton,** loose, unbound.

313. **dishonest,** unchaste.

Adam the goodliest man of men since born
His sons, the fairest of her daughters Eve.
Under a tuft of shade that on a green
Stood whispering soft, by a fresh fountain side
They sat them down; and after no more toil
Of their sweet gardening labor than sufficed   *West*
To recommend cool Zephyr, and made ease   *wind*
More easy, wholesome thirst and appetite   330
More grateful, to their supper-fruits they fell,
Nectarine fruits which the compliant boughs
Yielded them, sidelong as they sat recline
On the soft downy bank damasked with flowers.
The savory pulp they chew, and in the rind
Still as they thirsted scoop the brimming stream;
Nor gentle purpose, nor endearing smiles
Wanted, nor youthful dalliance, as beseems
Fair couple linked in happy nuptial league,
Alone as they. About them frisking played   340
All beasts of the earth, since wild, and of all chase
In wood or wilderness, forest or den;
Sporting the lion ramped, and in his paw
Dandled the kid; bears, tigers, ounces, pards,
Gambolled before them; the unwieldy elephant
To make them mirth used all his might, and wreathed
His lithe proboscis; close the serpent sly
Insinuating, wove with Gordian twine
His braided train, and of his fatal guile
Gave proof unheeded; others on the grass   350
Couched, and now filled with pasture gazing sat,
Or bedward ruminating; for the sun

   323. **the goodliest man of men since born**, etc. The idiom is obviously illogical, but it has ample precedent in Elizabethan English as well as in Greek and Latin. Cf. *A Midsummer Night's Dream*, V, i, 250.
   333. **recline**, i.e., reclining.
   334. **damasked**, ornamented with a variegated pattern.
   337. **purpose**, conversation.
   339 ff. Cf. Isa. 11:6–9. "The wolf shall also dwell with the lamb, and the leopard shall lie down with the kid," etc. The biblical millennium of innocence and peace and the classical golden age of innocence came together in Milton's mind and both are present in his idea of the Garden. Paul Elmer More very well says that the central theme of *Paradise Lost* is Paradise itself, the world without sin and conflict, the pastoral age, the utopia toward which the harassed mind of the struggling, competitive, wartorn world of modern Europe ever turned in its poetic dream.
   343. **ramped**, reared on his hind legs.
   348. **Gordian twine**, intricate tangle. The reference is to the famous Gordian knot, which no one could untie but which Alexander the Great finally cut with his sword.
   352. **ruminating**, chewing the cud (Latin *ruminantes*).

Declined was hasting now with prone career
To the Ocean Isles, and in the ascending scale
Of Heaven the stars that usher evening rose:
When Satan still in gaze, as first he stood,
Scarce thus at length failed speech recovered sad.
  "Oh Hell! what do mine eyes with grief behold!
Into our room of bliss thus high advanced
Creatures of other mould, earth-born perhaps,   360
Not spirits yet to heavenly spirits bright
Little inferior; whom my thoughts pursue
With wonder, and could love, so lively shines
In them divine resemblance, and such grace
The hand that formed them on their shape hath poured.
Ah gentle pair, ye little think how nigh
Your change approaches, when all these delights
Will vanish and deliver ye to woe,
More woe, the more your taste is now of joy;
Happy, but for so happy ill secured   370
Long to continue, and this high seat your Heaven
Ill fenced for Heaven to keep out such a foe
As now is entered; yet no purposed foe
To you whom I could pity thus forlorn
Though I unpitied. League with you I seek,
And mutual amity so strait, so close,
That I with you must dwell, or you with me
Henceforth; my dwelling haply may not please
Like this fair Paradise, your sense, yet such
Accept your Maker's work; he gave it me,   380
Which I as freely give; Hell shall unfold,
To entertain you two, her widest gates,
And send forth all her kings; there will be room,
Not like these narrow limits, to receive
Your numerous offspring; if no better place,
Thank him who puts me loath to this revenge
On you who wrong me not, for him who wronged.
And should I at your harmless innocence
Melt, as I do, yet public reason just,

    354. the Ocean Isles, i.e., the extreme west. Milton may here have in
mind the Azores, as in 592; but the figure is used by classical writers without definite geographical reference.
    362. little inferior. Cf. Ps. 8:5: "For Thou hast made him a little
lower than the angels."
    381 ff. Hell shall . . . kings. Cf. Isa. 14:9.
    389. By excusing his crime on the ground of political expediency, Satan
once more demonstrates his proficiency in Machiavellian statecraft. Cf.
I, 645–47, and note. That he can feel human pity is a survival of the divine
endowment which he has perverted. All this seems simple enough, but by

Honor and empire with revenge enlarged,   390
By conquering this new World, compels me now
To do what else though damned I should abhor."
    So spake the Fiend, and with necessity,
The tyrant's plea, excused his devilish deeds.
Then from his lofty stand on that high tree
Down he alights among the sportful herd
Of those four-footed kinds, himself now one,
Now other, as their shape served best his end
Nearer to view his prey, and unespied
To mark what of their state he more might learn   400
By word or action marked. About them round
A lion now he stalks with fiery glare;
Then as a tiger, who by chance hath spied
In some purlieu two gentle fawns at play,
Straight couches close, then rising, changes oft
His couchant watch, as one who chose his ground
Whence rushing he might surest seize them both
Griped in each paw; when Adam first of men
To first of women Eve thus moving speech,
Turned him all ear to hear new utterance flow.   410
    "Sole partner and sole part of all these joys,   _only — chief_
Dearer thyself than all, needs must the Power
That made us, and for us this ample World,
Be infinitely good, and of his good
As liberal and free as infinite,
That raised us from the dust and placed us here
In all this happiness, who at his hand
Have nothing merited, nor can perform
Aught whereof he hath need, he who requires
From us no other service than to keep   420
This one, this easy charge, of all the trees

the time critics, philosophers, and moralists have tried their wits in analysis
of the "Satan problem" there is much to bother about. Dante's sinners,
forever damned, exhibit many noble traits of mind and heart. His devils,
on the other hand, are symbols of pure evil.
    395 ff. Satan's assumption of animal forms is similarly described in
Sylvester's _Du Bartas._ The idea was perhaps originally suggested by I Pet.
5:8.
    404-5. To enable Satan to gain the information necessary for the carry-
ing out of his design, Milton makes use of an overheard conversation, an
essentially dramatic device. The conversation itself, however, is distinctly
epic in character.
    411. Note the double play on words: **partner . . . part; sole . . . sole.**
The first _sole_ is used in the ordinary sense of "only," the second in the
sense of "unrivaled," or "chief."
    419-20. Cf. Acts 17:25, and Milton's first sonnet on his blindness: God
doth not need either man's work or his own gifts.

In Paradise that bear delicious fruit
So various, not to taste that only Tree
Of Knowledge, planted by the Tree of Life,
So near grows death to life, whate'er death is,
Some dreadful thing no doubt; for well thou know'st
God hath pronounced it death to taste that Tree;
The only sign of our obedience left
Among so many signs of power and rule
Conferred upon us, and dominion given   430
Over all other creatures that possess
Earth, air, and sea. Then let us not think hard
One easy prohibition, who enjoy
Free leave so large to all things else, and choice
Unlimited of manifold delights;
But let us ever praise him, and extol
His bounty, following our delightful task
To prune these growing plants, and tend these flowers,
Which were it toilsome, yet with thee were sweet."
     To whom thus Eve replied. "O thou for whom   440
And from whom I was formed flesh of thy flesh,
And without whom am to no end, my guide
And head, what thou hast said is just and right.
For we to him indeed all praises owe,
And daily thanks, I chiefly who enjoy
So far the happier lot, enjoying thee
Pre-eminent by so much odds, while thou
Like consort to thyself canst nowhere find.
That day I oft remember, when from sleep
I first awaked, and found myself reposed   450
Under a shade on flowers, much wondering where
And what I was, whence thither brought, and how.
Not distant far from thence a murmuring sound
Of waters issued from a cave and spread
Into a liquid plain, then stood unmoved
Pure as the expanse of Heaven; I thither went
With unexperienced thought, and laid me down
On the green bank, to look into the clear
Smooth lake, that to me seemed another sky.
As I bent down to look, just opposite   460

     428. sign of our obedience. Milton says in *Of Christian Doctrine* that
the sin of Adam and Eve in eating the forbidden fruit included all the sins.
It does so, however, only symbolically, since the prohibition is a mere test of
obedience without specific content. Sin is a consequence of the will to sin.
     460 ff. Milton quite evidently has in mind the story of Narcissus. Cf.
Ovid *Metamorphoses* iii. 407 ff. **Whom fliest thou,** below, is a pastoral
formula. Eden is a kind of Arcady and Adam and Eve, with their unper-
verted instincts, belong to the idyllic world.

A shape within the watery gleam appeared
Bending to look on me: I started back,
It started back, but pleased I soon returned,
Pleased it returned as soon with answering looks
Of sympathy and love; there I had fixed
Mine eyes till now, and pined with vain desire,
Had not a voice thus warned me. 'What thou seest,
What there thou seest, fair creature, is thyself,
With thee it came and goes; but follow me,
And I will bring thee where no shadow stays   470
Thy coming, and thy soft embraces, he
Whose image thou art, him thou shalt enjoy
Inseparably thine; to him shalt bear
Multitudes like thyself, and thence be called
Mother of human race.' What could I do
But follow straight, invisibly thus led?
Till I espied thee, fair indeed and tall,
Under a platane; yet methought less fair,
Less winning soft, less amiably mild,
Than that smooth watery image; back I turned,   480
Thou following cried'st aloud, 'Return fair Eve,
Whom fliest thou? whom thou fliest, of him thou art,
His flesh, his bone; to give thee being I lent
Out of my side to thee, nearest my heart,
Substantial life, to have thee by my side
Henceforth an individual solace dear.
Part of my soul I seek thee, and thee claim
My other half.' With that thy gentle hand
Seized mine, I yielded, and from that time see
How beauty is excelled by manly grace   490
And wisdom, which alone is truly fair."
    So spake our general mother, and with eyes
Of conjugal attraction unreproved,
And meek surrender, half embracing leaned
On our first father; half her swelling breast
Naked met his under the flowing gold
Of her loose tresses hid. He in delight
Both of her beauty and submissive charms
Smiled with superior love, as Jupiter

470. **stays**, awaits.
479. **less amiably mild**, i.e., less fitted to inspire love.
486. **individual**, inseparable (Latin *individuus*).
487. **Part of my soul.** The same phrase occurs twice in Horace (*Odes*
I, iii, 8; II, xvii, 5). Cf. Elegy IV, 19–20.
491. **wisdom, which alone is truly fair.** Cf. Plato *Symposium* 210.
493. **unreproved**, unreprovable. Cf. "L'Allegro," 40.

On Juno smiles, when he impregns the clouds 500
That shed May flowers; and pressed her matron lip
With kisses pure. Aside the Devil turned
For envy, yet with jealous leer malign
Eyed them askance, and to himself thus plained.
  "Sight hateful, sight tormenting! thus these two
Imparadised in one another's arms,
The happier Eden, shall enjoy their fill
Of bliss on bliss, while I to Hell am thrust,
Where neither joy nor love, but fierce desire,
Among our other torments not the least, 510
Still unfulfilled with pain of longing pines;
Yet let me not forget what I have gained
From their own mouths. All is not theirs, it seems;
One fatal tree there stands, of Knowledge called,
Forbidden them to taste. Knowledge forbidden?
Suspicious, reasonless. Why should their Lord
Envy them that? can it be sin to know,
Can it be death? and do they only stand
By ignorance, is that their happy state,
The proof of their obedience and their faith? 520
O fair foundation laid whereon to build
Their ruin! Hence I will excite their minds
With more desire to know, and to reject
Envious commands, invented with design
To keep them low whom knowledge might exalt
Equal with gods. Aspiring to be such,
They taste and die; what likelier can ensue?
But first with narrow search I must walk round
This garden, and no corner leave unspied;
A chance but chance may lead where I may meet 530
Some wandering spirit of Heaven, by fountain side,
Or in thick shade retired, from him to draw
What further would be learned. Live while ye may,
Yet happy pair; enjoy, till I return,
Short pleasures, for long woes are to succeed."
  So saying, his proud step he scornful turned,

500. **impregns**, impregnates. There is an allusion here to *Iliad* xiv.
346-51 and to the interpretation of this passage by the ancient scholiast.
Hera typifies the lower air or haze which surrounds the earth, Zeus the
upper air (aether). The mingling of the two produces the spring with its
flowers (see Osgood, *Classical Mythology*, under Jove).
  504. **plained**, complained, murmured.
  521 ff. Satan's own experience has taught him the allurement of godlike
power, and the outcome of any attempt to gain it. He therefore has little
difficulty in determining the most effective temptation. Cf. IX, 705 ff.
  530. **A chance but**, there is a chance that.

But with sly circumspection, and began
Through wood, through waste, o'er hill, o'er dale, his roam.
Meanwhile in utmost longitude, where Heaven
With Earth and Ocean meets, the setting sun   540
Slowly descended, and with right aspect
Against the eastern gate of Paradise
Levelled his evening rays. It was a rock
Of alabaster, piled up to the clouds,
Conspicuous far, winding with one ascent
Accessible from Earth, one entrance high;
The rest was craggy cliff, that overhung
Still as it rose, impossible to climb.
Betwixt these rocky pillars Gabriel sat,
Chief of the angelic guards, awaiting night;   550
About him exercised heroic games
The unarmed youth of Heaven, but nigh at hand
Celestial armory, shields, helms, and spears,
Hung high, with diamond flaming and with gold.
Thither came Uriel, gliding through the even
On a sun beam, swift as a shooting star
In autumn thwarts the night, when vapors fired
Impress the air, and shows the mariner
From what point of his compass to beware
Impetuous winds. He thus began in haste.   560
    "Gabriel, to thee thy course by lot hath given
Charge and strict watch that to this happy place
No evil thing approach or enter in;
This day at height of noon came to my sphere
A spirit, zealous, as he seemed, to know
More of the Almighty's works, and chiefly Man
God's latest image. I described his way
Bent all on speed, and marked his airy gait;
But in the mount that lies from Eden north,
Where he first lighted, soon discerned his looks   570

    539. in utmost longitude, in the extreme west.
    541. with right aspect, i.e., directly opposite. The setting sun, now on
a level with the rock which forms the eastern gate of Paradise, throws its
beams horizontally against the inner side.
    551. heroic games. Cf. II, 528–32.
    555. Uriel. The name means literally "Light of God." Cf. III, 645 ff.
    557. thwarts, crosses.
    561. The Scriptural references to Gabriel (Dan. 8, 9; Luke 1) depict
him as a peaceful messenger of God. Milton makes him a great warrior,
second only to Michael. Cf. VI, 44–46. thy course by lot. The terms are
those used in Scripture to describe the assignment of the Temple offices.
Cf. Luke 1:8–9.
    567. God's latest image. Christ is of course the first, and after him are
the angels.
    568. his airy gait, i.e., the course which he took through the air.

Alien from Heaven, with passions foul obscured.
Mine eye pursued him still, but under shade
Lost sight of him; one of the banished crew
I fear, hath ventured from the Deep, to raise
New troubles; him thy care must be to find."
    To whom the wingèd warrior thus returned.
"Uriel, no wonder if thy perfect sight,
Amid the sun's bright circle where thou sitt'st,
See far and wide. In at this gate none pass
The vigilance here placed, but such as come   580
Well known from Heaven; and since meridian hour
No creature thence. If spirit of other sort,
So minded, have o'erleaped these earthy bounds
On purpose, hard thou know'st it to exclude
Spiritual substance with corporeal bar.
But if within the circuit of these walks,
In whatsoever shape he lurk, of whom
Thou tell'st, by morrow dawning I shall know."
    So promised he, and Uriel to his charge
Returned on that bright beam, whose point now raised   590
Bore him slope downward to the sun now fallen
Beneath the Azores; whether the prime orb,
Incredible how swift, had thither rolled
Diurnal, or this less volubil Earth
By shorter flight to the east, had left him there
Arraying with reflected purple and gold
The clouds that on his western throne attend.
    Now came still Evening on, and Twilight gray
Had in her sober livery all things clad;
Silence accompanied, for beast and bird,   600
They to their grassy couch, these to their nests
Were slunk, all but the wakeful nightingale;
She all night long her amorous descant sung;
Silence was pleased. Now glowed the firmament
With living sapphires; Hesperus that led

580. **vigilance,** guard. The abstract is used for the concrete.
590. **that bright beam, whose point now raised.** The sunbeam, which was horizontal when Uriel arrived at the gate of Paradise (555, 556), is now inclined upward.
592 ff. Milton shows his knowledge of both the Ptolemaic and the Copernican systems of astronomy, without committing himself as to which is right.
592. **the prime orb,** the sun.
594. **volubil,** swiftly rolling. The accent is on the second syllable, as in Latin *volubilis.*
603. **descant,** a song, or rather a soprano part.
605. **Hesperus,** the evening star. Cf. Spenser's description in *Epithalamium,* 288–90.

The starry host, rode brightest, till the Moon
Rising in clouded majesty, at length
Apparent queen unveiled her peerless light,
And o'er the dark her silver mantle threw.
When Adam thus to Eve. "Fair consort, the hour   610
Of night, and all things now retired to rest
Mind us of like repose, since God hath set
Labor and rest, as day and night to men
Successive, and the timely dew of sleep
Now falling with soft slumberous weight inclines
Our eye-lids; other creatures all day long
Rove idle, unemployed, and less need rest;
Man hath his daily work of body or mind
Appointed, which declares his dignity,
And the regard of Heaven on all his ways;   620
While other animals unactive range,
And of their doings God takes no account.
To-morrow ere fresh morning streak the east
With first approach of light, we must be risen,
And at our pleasant labor, to reform
Yon flowery arbors, yonder alleys green,
Our walks at noon, with branches overgrown,
That mock our scant manuring, and require
More hands than ours to lop their wanton growth.
Those blossoms also, and those dropping gums,   630
That lie bestrown unsightly and unsmooth,
Ask riddance, if we mean to tread with ease;
Meanwhile, as Nature wills, night bids us rest."
   To whom thus Eve with perfect beauty adorned.
"My author and disposer, what thou bidd'st
Unargued I obey; so God ordains.
God is thy law, thou mine; to know no more
Is woman's happiest knowledge and her praise.
With thee conversing I forget all time,
All seasons and their change, all please alike.   640
Sweet is the breath of Morn, her rising sweet,
With charm of earliest birds; pleasant the Sun
When first on this delightful land he spreads
His orient beams, on herb, tree, fruit, and flower,
Glistering with dew; fragrant the fertile Earth

608. **Apparent,** manifest. Cf. "heir apparent."
   614. **the timely dew of sleep.** Shakespeare (*Richard III*, IV, i, 84)
uses a similar phrase, "the golden dew of sleep."
   628. **manuring,** cultivating (from O. F. *manuvrer*).
   640. **all seasons,** i.e., all times of the day. Spring is the only season of
the year that Eve has yet experienced.
   642. **charm,** song.

After soft showers; and sweet the coming on
Of grateful Evening mild, then silent Night
With this her solemn bird and this fair Moon,
And these the gems of Heaven, her starry train:
But neither breath of Morn when she ascends   650
With charm of earliest birds, nor rising Sun
On this delightful land, nor herb, fruit, flower,
Glistering with dew, nor fragrance after showers,
Nor grateful Evening mild, nor silent Night,
With this her solemn bird, nor walk by moon,
Or glittering star-light, without thee is sweet.
But wherefore all night long shine these? for whom
This glorious sight, when sleep hath shut all eyes?"
    To whom our general ancestor replied.
"Daughter of God and Man, accomplished Eve,   660
Those have their course to finish, round the Earth
By morrow evening, and from land to land
In order, though to nations yet unborn,
Ministering light prepared, they set and rise;
Lest total Darkness should by night regain
Her old possession, and extinguish life
In nature and all things; which these soft fires
Not only enlighten, but with kindly heat
Of various influence foment and warm,
Temper or nourish, or in part shed down   670
Their stellar virtue on all kinds that grow
On Earth, made hereby apter to receive
Perfection from the sun's more potent ray.
These then, though unbeheld in deep of night,
Shine not in vain, nor think, though men were none,
That Heaven would want spectators, God want praise;
Millions of spiritual creatures walk the Earth
Unseen, both when we wake, and when we sleep.
All these with ceaseless praise his works behold
Both day and night. How often from the steep   680

650 ff. Note how the imagery of the preceding nine lines is repeated
with subtle variations in phrasing. Milton frequently makes effective use of
repetition (cf., e.g., VII, 25, 26) but nowhere else does he work it into so
elaborate a pattern. He is adorning or sophisticating a Homeric device, as
he does in his use of similes, and in his structural adaptation of the epic
throwback.
    665. total Darkness, i.e., the darkness of Chaos. Cf. II, 984.
    667 ff. The doctrine of stellar influence, which formed the basis of
astrology, was still widely current in the seventeenth century. Milton seems
to take its validity for granted.
    680 ff. Cf. VII, 252-60. Man, before his senses are deadened by sin, is
capable of hearing and appreciating the heavenly harmonies. The idea is

Of echoing hill or thicket have we heard
Celestial voices to the midnight air,
Sole, or responsive each to other's note,
Singing their great Creator; oft in bands
While they keep watch, or nightly rounding walk,
With heavenly touch of instrumental sounds
In full harmonic number joined, their songs
Divide the night, and lift our thoughts to Heaven."
  Thus talking, hand in hand alone they passed
On to their blissful bower; it was a place   690
Chosen by the sovran Planter, when he framed
All things to Man's delightful use; the roof
Of thickest covert was inwoven shade,
Laurel and myrtle, and what higher grew
Of firm and fragrant leaf; on either side
Acanthus, and each odorous bushy shrub
Fenced up the verdant wall; each beauteous flower,
Iris all hues, roses, and jessamine
Reared high their flourished heads between, and wrought
Mosaic; under-foot the violet,   700
Crocus, and hyacinth with rich inlay
Broidered the ground, more colored than with stone
Of costliest emblem. Other creature here,
Beast, bird, insect, or worm durst enter none;
Such was their awe of Man. In shadier bower
More sacred and sequestered, though but feigned,
Pan or Sylvanus never slept, nor Nymph
Nor Faunus haunted. Here in close recess
With flowers, garlands, and sweet-smelling herbs
Espousëd Eve decked first her nuptial bed,   710
And heavenly choirs the hymenæan sung,
What day the genial angel to our sire
Brought her in naked beauty more adorned,

closely bound up with the Pythagorean and Platonic doctrine of sphere-
music. Cf. Milton's discussion in his second academic prolusion, *On the
Harmony of the Spheres.*
    688. Divide the night, i.e., into watches. The phrase is a literal trans-
lation of the Roman *dividere noctem,* which in military usage meant to
mark by a trumpet signal the hours for changing the guard.
    694 ff. Cf. *Iliad* xiv. 347 ff.; also the famous flower passage in "Lycidas,"
142–51.
    703. emblem, embossed or inlaid ornamentation (Latin *emblema*).
    707. Pan, Sylvanus, and **Faunus** were classical deities of the fields and
woods. The qualifying **though but feigned** phrase, used with reference to
their haunts, implies a judgment on much of the subject matter of pagan
poetry. Milton frequently asserts the superior truth of his own materials.
Cf. 250, 251, and note.
    712. genial, nuptial (Latin *genialis*), instrumental to marriage.

Pandora

More lovely than Pandora, whom the gods
Endowed with all their gifts, and O too like
In sad event, when to the unwiser son
Of Japhet brought by Hermes, she ensnared
Mankind with her fair looks, to be avenged
On him who had stole Jove's authentic fire.
  Thus at their shady lodge arrived, both stood,   720
Both turned, and under open sky adored
The God that made both sky, air, Earth, and Heaven,
Which they beheld, the moon's resplendent globe
And starry pole: "Thou also mad'st the night,
Maker Omnipotent, and thou the day,
Which we in our appointed work employed
Have finished happy in our mutual help
And mutual love, the crown of all our bliss
Ordained by thee, and this delicious place
For us too large, where thy abundance wants   730
Partakers, and uncropped falls to the ground.
But thou hast promised from us two a race
To fill the Earth, who shall with us extol
Thy goodness infinite, both when we wake,
And when we seek, as now, thy gift of sleep."
  This said unanimous, and other rites
Observing none, but adoration pure
Which God likes best, into their inmost bower
Handed they went; and eased the putting off
These troublesome disguises which we wear,   740
Straight side by side were laid, nor turned, I ween,
Adam from his fair spouse, nor Eve the rites
Mysterious of connubial love refused;

---

714 ff. The allusion is to a myth related by Hesiod. To be avenged on Prometheus, who had stolen fire from heaven for the use of mortals, Jove sent to earth **Pandora** ("the all-gifted"), on whom each of the gods had bestowed some fatal charm. Hermes conducted her to Epimetheus, the unwiser son of Japhet, who married her, despite the warning of his brother. Thereupon all the ills which she had brought from heaven were released to afflict humanity. Milton makes a similar application of the story in the *Doctrine and Discipline of Divorce*, II, 3.

719. authentic, original.

722. both sky, air, Earth, and Heaven, etc. The use of **both** with reference to more than two objects is fairly common in Elizabethan English. Cf. *Venus and Adonis*, 747.

724. A similar abrupt transition to direct address occurs in *Aeneid* viii. 293.

735. thy gift of sleep. Cf. Psalms 127:2.

736 ff. Cf. *The Christian Doctrine*, II, 4, where Milton's attitude toward external worship is fully set forth.

739. Handed, hand in hand.

Whatever hypocrites austerely talk
Of purity and place and innocence,
Defaming as impure what God declares
Pure, and commands to some, leaves free to all.
Our Maker bids increase; who bids abstain
But our destroyer, foe to God and Man?
Hail wedded Love, mysterious law, true source   750
Of human offspring, sole propriety
In Paradise of all things common else.
By thee adulterous lust was driven from men
Among the bestial herds to range; by thee,
Founded in reason, loyal, just, and pure,
Relations dear, and all the charities
Of father, son, and brother first were known.
Far be it, that I should write thee sin or blame,
Or think thee unbefitting holiest place,
Perpetual fountain of domestic sweets,   760
Whose bed is undefiled and chaste pronounced,
Present or past, as saints and patriarchs used.
Here Love his golden shafts employs, here lights
His constant lamp, and waves his purple wings,
Reigns here and revels; not in the bought smile
Of harlots, loveless, joyless, unendeared,
Casual fruition; nor in court-amours,
Mixed dance, or wanton mask, or midnight ball,
Or serenate, which the starved lover sings
To his proud fair, best quitted with disdain.   770
These lulled by nightingales, embracing slept,
And on their naked limbs the flowery roof
Showered roses, which the morn repaired. Sleep on

744 ff. **Whatever hypocrites,** etc. Cf. I Tim. 4:1–3. Throughout this
passage, Milton is quite obviously taking issue with the advocates of monas-
ticism and celibacy. Cf. Augustine, *City of God,* XIV, 11 ff.
    750. **wedded love, mysterious law.** Cf. Eph. 4:31–32.
    751. **sole propriety,** sole property. Their love for each other is the one
thing in Paradise which Adam and Eve have as their exclusive possession.
    756. **charities,** affections (Latin *caritates*).
    761. **Whose bed is undefiled.** Cf. Heb. 13:4.
    764. The imagery is suddenly changed from Scriptural to classical. For
the reference to Cupid's **golden shafts** (which were used to inspire love,
while his leaden ones were used to repel it), cf. Ovid *Metamorphoses* i.
468–71.
    767. **nor in court-amours,** etc. Milton may be thinking specifically of
the court of Charles II; but he is also thinking of the general chivalric tradition, the artificial conventions of which he believes to be irreconcilable with
the ideal domestic relationship.
    769. **serenate,** serenade (Italian *serenata*). **starved,** i.e., suffering from
cold.

Blest pair; and O yet happiest if ye seek
No happier state, and know to know no more.
Now had night measured with her shadowy cone
Half way up hill this vast sublunar vault,
And from their ivory port the Cherubim
Forth issuing at the accustomed hour stood armed
To their night-watches in warlike parade,   780
When Gabriel to his next in power thus spake.
    "Uzziel, half these draw off, and coast the south
With strictest watch; these other wheel the north;
Our circuit meets full west." As flame they part,
Half wheeling to the shield, half to the spear.
From these, two strong and subtle spirits he called
That near him stood, and gave them thus in charge.
    "Ithuriel and Zephon, with winged speed
Search through this garden; leave unsearched no nook;
But chiefly where those two fair creatures lodge,   790
Now laid perhaps asleep secure of harm.
This evening from the sun's decline arrived
Who tells of some infernal spirit seen
Hitherward bent (who could have thought?) escaped
The bars of Hell, on errand bad no doubt:
Such where ye find, seize fast, and hither bring."
    So saying, on he led his radiant files,
Dazzling the moon; these to the bower direct
In search of whom they sought. Him there they found
Squat like a toad, close at the ear of Eve;   800

775. **know to know no more,** i.e., are wise enough not to seek further
knowledge.
776 ff. Night is the shadow of the earth cast by the sun. Since the sun
is the larger body, the shadow, if viewed in its totality, would be a cone; and
if the point of the cone had moved halfway from the horizon to the zenith
(**half way up hill**), one-fourth of the night would be past. In other words,
assuming the days and nights to be of equal length, the time would be nine
o'clock.
    778. **port,** gate (Latin *porta*). The Cherubim are appropriately assigned
to sentinel duty because of their superior power of vision.
    782. **Uzziel.** The name, which means "Strength of God," occurs in
Exod. 6:18.
    785. **Half wheeling to the shield, half to the spear,** i.e., half turning
to the left, half to the right. The terms "shield side" and "spear side" were
used by both the Greeks and the Romans.
    786. **subtle,** i.e., quick to observe.
    788. **Ithuriel and Zephon.** Both names are derived from Hebrew
words meaning "discover" or "search."
    791. **secure of,** without fear of.
    793. **Who,** i.e., one who. Latin *qui* is frequently used with the ante-
cedent omitted.
    798. **these,** i.e., Ithuriel and Zephon.

Assaying by his devilish art to reach
The organs of her fancy, and with them forge
Illusions as he list, phantasms and dreams;
Or if, inspiring venom, he might taint
The animal spirits that from pure blood arise
Like gentle breaths from rivers pure, thence raise
At least distempered, discontented thoughts,
Vain hopes, vain aims, inordinate desires
Blown up with high conceits engendering pride.
Him thus intent Ithuriel with his spear   810
Touched lightly; for no falsehood can endure
Touch of celestial temper, but returns
Of force to its own likeness. Up he starts
Discovered and surprised. As when a spark
Lights on a heap of nitrous powder, laid
Fit for the tun some magazine to store
Against a rumored war, the smutty grain
With sudden blaze diffused, inflames the air:
So started up in his own shape the Fiend.
Back stept those two fair angels half amazed   820
So sudden to behold the grisly king;
Yet thus, unmoved with fear, accost him soon.
    "Which of those rebel spirits adjudged to Hell
Com'st thou, escaped thy prison; and transformed,
Why sat'st thou like an enemy in wait
Here watching at the head of these that sleep?"
    "Know ye not then," said Satan, filled with scorn,
"Know ye not me? Ye knew me once no mate
For you, there sitting where ye durst not soar;
Not to know me argues yourselves unknown,   830
The lowest of your throng; or if ye know,
Why ask ye, and superfluous begin
Your message, like to end as much in vain?"
    To whom thus Zephon, answering scorn with scorn.
"Think not, revolted spirit, thy shape the same,
Or undiminished brightness, to be known
As when thou stood'st in Heaven upright and pure;

807. Cf. Eve's account of her dream, and Adam's philosophical discourse thereon, V, 30 ff.
813. Of force, of necessity, perforce.
829. there sitting where ye durst not soar, i.e., in the higher places of heaven. Ithuriel and Zephon had belonged to a lower order of angels than Satan.
830. argues, proves (Latin *arguere*).
835 ff. The degeneration in Satan's physical appearance is in keeping with the Platonic doctrine (stated in *Comus*, 459–75) that the soul transforms the body for better or worse to its own essence. Cf. *Phaedo* 81.

That glory then, when thou no more wast good,
Departed from thee, and thou resemblest now
Thy sin and place of doom obscure and foul.   840
But come, for thou, be sure, shalt give account
To him who sent us, whose charge is to keep
This place inviolable, and these from harm."
   So spake the Cherub, and his grave rebuke
Severe in youthful beauty, added grace
Invincible. Abashed the Devil stood,
And felt how awful goodness is, and saw
Virtue in her shape how lovely; saw, and pined
His loss; but chiefly to find here observed
His luster visibly impaired; yet seemed   850
Undaunted. "If I must contend," said he,
"Best with the best, the sender not the sent;
Or all at once; more glory will be won,
Or less be lost." "Thy fear," said Zephon bold,
"Will save us trial what the least can do
Single against thee wicked, and thence weak."
   The Fiend replied not, overcome with rage;
But like a proud steed reined, went haughty on,
Champing his iron curb. To strive or fly
He held it vain; awe from above had quelled   860
His heart, not else dismayed. Now drew they nigh
The western point, where those half-rounding guards
Just met, and closing stood in squadron joined
Awaiting next command. To whom their chief
Gabriel from the front thus called aloud.
   "O friends, I hear the tread of nimble feet
Hasting this way, and now by glimpse discern
Ithuriel and Zephon through the shade,
And with them comes a third, of regal port,
But faded splendor wan; who by his gait   870
And fierce demeanor seems the Prince of Hell,
Not likely to part hence without contest;
Stand firm, for in his look defiance lours."
   He scarce had ended, when those two approached
And brief related whom they brought, where found,

---

843. these, i.e., Adam and Eve.
   856. wicked, and thence weak. Cf. *Samson Agonistes*, 834: "All wickedness is weakness."
   861 ff. Note the military exactness of Milton's description. The maneuver ordered by Gabriel (782–84) has been executed, and the full angelic guard is now drawn up along the western extremity of Paradise.
   866 ff. Gabriel's words suggest those of Nestor as he hears the sound of Odysseus and Diomedes returning from the Trojan camp. Cf. *Iliad* x. 533 ff.
   869. port, bearing.

How busied, in what form and posture couched.
To whom with stern regard thus Gabriel spake.
"Why hast thou, Satan, broke the bounds prescribed
To thy transgressions, and disturbed the charge
Of others, who approve not to transgress   880
By thy example, but have power and right
To question thy bold entrance on this place;
Employed it seems to violate sleep, and those
Whose dwelling God hath planted here in bliss?"
    To whom thus Satan, with contemptuous brow.
"Gabriel, thou hadst in Heaven the esteem of wise,
And such I held thee; but this question asked
Puts me in doubt. Lives there who loves his pain?
Who would not, finding way, break loose from Hell,
Though thither doomed? Thou wouldst thyself, no doubt,   890
And boldly venture to whatever place
Farthest from pain, where thou mightst hope to change
Torment with ease, and soonest recompense
Dole with delight, which in this place I sought;
To thee no reason; who know'st only good,
But evil hast not tried. And wilt object
His will who bound us? let him surer bar
His iron gates, if he intends our stay
In that dark durance. Thus much what was asked.
The rest is true, they found me where they say;   900
But that implies not violence or harm."
    Thus he in scorn. The warlike angel moved,
Disdainfully half smiling thus replied.
"O loss of one in Heaven to judge of wise,
Since Satan fell, whom folly overthrew,
And now returns him from his prison scaped,
Gravely in doubt whether to hold them wise
Or not, who ask what boldness brought him hither
Unlicensed from his bounds in Hell prescribed;
So wise he judges it to fly from pain   910
However, and to scape his punishment.
So judge thou still, presumptuous, till the wrath,
Which thou incurr'st by flying, meet thy flight
Sevenfold, and scourge that wisdom back to Hell,
Which taught thee yet no better, that no pain
Can equal anger infinite provoked.

    886. the esteem of wise, the repute of being wise.
    904. O loss of one in Heaven to judge of wise, i.e., What a loss
Heaven has sustained in the loss of one so well qualified to judge of wisdom.
The line furnishes an extreme example of Milton's use of ellipsis.
    911. However, in whatever manner.

But wherefore thou alone? wherefore with thee
Came not all Hell broke loose? is pain to them
Less pain, less to be fled or thou than they
Less hardy to endure? Courageous chief,   920
The first in flight from pain, hadst thou alleged
To thy deserted host this cause of flight,
Thou surely hadst not come sole fugitive."
    To which the Fiend thus answered frowning stern.
"Not that I less endure, or shrink from pain,
Insulting angel, well thou know'st I stood
Thy fiercest, when in battle to thy aid
The blasting vollied thunder made all speed
And seconded thy else not dreaded spear.
But still thy words at random, as before,   930
Argue thy inexperience what behoves
From hard assays and ill successes past
A faithful leader, not to hazard all
Through ways of danger by himself untried.
I therefore, I alone first undertook
To wing the desolate Abyss, and spy
This new-created World, whereof in Hell
Fame is not silent, here in hope to find
Better abode, and my afflicted powers
To settle here on Earth, or in mid air;   940
Though for possession put to try once more
What thou and thy gay legions dare against;
Whose easier business were to serve their Lord
High up in Heaven, with songs to hymn his throne,
And practised distances to cringe, not fight."
    To whom the warrior angel soon replied.
"To say and straight unsay, pretending first
Wise to fly pain, professing next the spy,
Argues no leader but a liar traced,
Satan, and couldst thou 'faithful' add? O name,   950
O sacred name of faithfulness profaned!

---

921. **The first in flight,** etc. Satan has taken great pride in the courage
demanded by his journey of exploration (cf. II, 430–66; 826–31). Gabriel's
insistence that it was entered upon through cowardice is therefore peculiarly
fitted to exasperate him.
    926–27. **I stood Thy fiercest,** i.e., I withstood thy fiercest attack.
    928. **The blasting vollied thunder.** Cf. VI, 831 ff.
    938. **Fame,** report. Cf. I, 651; II, 346.
    942. **gay,** bright, shining. Having lost his own brilliance, Satan dispar-
ages the quality in those who have retained it.
    943. Cf. Aeschylus *Prometheus Bound* 937, 938.
    945. **practised distances to cringe,** i.e., to make the obeisances pre-
scribed by court etiquette.

Faithful to whom? to thy rebellious crew?
Army of fiends, fit body to fit head;
Was this your discipline and faith engaged,
Your military obedience, to dissolve
Allegiance to the acknowledged Power Supreme?
And thou sly hypocrite, who now wouldst seem
Patron of liberty, who more than thou
Once fawned, and cringed, and servilely adored
Heaven's awful Monarch? wherefore but in hope   960
To dispossess him, and thyself to reign?
But mark what I areed thee now: Avaunt;
Fly thither whence thou fledst. If from this hour
Within these hallowed limits thou appear,
Back to the infernal pit I drag thee chained,
And seal thee so, as henceforth not to scorn
The facile gates of Hell too slightly barred."
So threatened he, but Satan to no threats
Gave heed, but waxing more in rage replied.
"Then when I am thy captive talk of chains,   970
Proud limitary Cherub, but ere then
Far heavier load thyself expect to feel
From my prevailing arm, though Heaven's King
Ride on thy wings, and thou with thy compeers,
Used to the yoke, drawest his triumphant wheels
In progress through the road of Heaven star-paved."
While thus he spake, the angelic squadron bright
Turned fiery red, sharpening in mooned horns
Their phalanx, and began to hem him round
With ported spears, as thick as when a field   980
Of Ceres ripe for harvest waving bends
Her bearded grove of ears, which way the wind
Sways them; the careful ploughman doubting stands
Lest on the threshing-floor his hopeful sheaves

962. **areed**, advise, an archaism used by Milton only here.
966. **And seal thee**. Cf. Rev. 20:3.
971. **limitary**, i.e., set to guard the frontiers (Latin *limites*). Satan uses the word in sarcastic allusion to the "hallowed limits" spoken of by Gabriel (964).
974. **ride on thy wings**. Cf. VI, 771; also Ps. 18:10.
978. **in mooned horns**, in the form of a crescent.
980. **with ported spears**, i.e., with spears held slantwise against the body, points to the left, preparatory to leveling them for the charge. The command "Port arms" is still used in the modern manual.
980–81. **a field of Ceres**, i.e., a field of grain (Ceres being the ancient goddess of agriculture). The simile may have been suggested by *Iliad* ii. 147.
984. **hopeful sheaves**. The phrase seems to be a recollection of Virgil's *expectata seges* (*Georgics* i. 226).

Prove chaff. On the other side Satan alarmed
Collecting all his might dilated stood,
Like Teneriff or Atlas unremoved:
His stature reached the sky, and on his crest
Sat Horror plumed; nor wanted in his grasp
What seemed both spear and shield. Now dreadful deeds   990
Might have ensued, nor only Paradise
In this commotion, but the starry cope
Of Heaven perhaps, or all the elements
At least had gone to wrack, disturbed and torn
With violence of this conflict, had not soon
The Eternal to prevent such horrid fray
Hung forth in Heaven his golden scales, yet seen
Betwixt Astræa and the Scorpion sign,
Wherein all things created first he weighed,
The pendulous round Earth with balanced air   1000
In counterpoise, now ponders all events,
Battles and realms: in these he put two weights
The sequel each of parting and of fight;
The latter quick up flew, and kicked the beam;
Which Gabriel spying, thus bespake the Fiend.
    "Satan, I know thy strength, and thou know'st mine,
Neither our own, but given; what folly then
To boast what arms can do, since thine no more
Than Heaven permits, nor mine, though doubled now
To trample thee as mire: for proof look up,   1010
And read thy lot in yon celestial sign
Where thou art weighed, and shown how light, how weak,
If thou resist." The Fiend looked up, and knew
His mounted scale aloft: nor more; but fled
Murmuring; and with him fled the shades of Night.

985. alarmed, aroused, put on guard.
987. Teneriff, a high peak on one of the Canary Islands. Atlas, a
range of mountains in northern Africa. According to classical myth, the
heavens rested on its summit. unremoved, unremovable.
993. all the elements, i.e., the fabric of the terrestrial universe, as distinct from "the starry cope."
997 ff. The passage is based on the famous figure of the golden scales
in Iliad viii. 69–72. Milton, however, makes two significant additions: he
identifies the scales with the zodiacal constellation Libra, which is located
between Virgo (Astræa) and the Scorpion; and he further identifies them
with the scales mentioned in Isa. 40:12, as being used by God to weigh the
elements of the universe.
1001. ponders, weighs (the literal meaning of Latin ponderare).
1003. the sequel, i.e., the consequence to Satan.
1010. To trample thee as mire. Cf. Isa. 10:6.
1012. thou art weighed, etc. Cf. Dan. 5:27.
1014. nor more, i.e., made no further show of resistance.

BOOK V

THE ARGUMENT

Morning approached, Eve relates to Adam her troublesome dream; he likes it not, yet comforts her; they come forth to their day labors; their morning hymn at the door of their bower. God, to render Man inexcusable, sends Raphael to admonish him of his obedience, of his free estate, of his enemy near at hand—who he is, and why his enemy, and whatever else may avail Adam to know. Raphael comes down to Paradise; his appearance described; his coming discerned by Adam afar off, sitting at the door of his bower; he goes out to meet him, brings him to his lodge, entertains him with the choicest fruits of Paradise got together by Eve; their discourse at table. Raphael performs his message, minds Adam of his state and of his enemy; relates, at Adam's request, who that enemy is, and how he came to be so, beginning from his first revolt in Heaven, and the occasion thereof; how he drew his legions after him to the parts of the North, and there incited them to rebel with him, persuading all but only Abdiel, a Seraph, who in argument dissuades and opposes him, then forsakes him.

Now Morn her rosy steps in the eastern clime
Advancing, sowed the earth with orient pearl,
When Adam waked, so customed, for his sleep
Was airy light, from pure digestion bred,
And temperate vapors bland, which the only sound
Of leaves and fuming rills, Aurora's fan,
Lightly dispersed, and the shrill matin song
Of birds on every bough; so much the more
His wonder was to find unwakened Eve
With tresses discomposed, and glowing cheek,   10
As through unquiet rest. He on his side
Leaning half-raised, with looks of cordial love
Hung over her enamored, and beheld
Beauty, which whether waking or asleep,
Shot forth peculiar graces; then with voice
Mild, as when Zephyrus on Flora breathes,
Her hand soft touching, whispered thus. "Awake
My fairest, my espoused, my latest found,
Heaven's last best gift, my ever new delight,
Awake, the morning shines, and the fresh field   20
Calls us; we lose the prime, to mark how spring

5. temperate vapors, gases ascending from the stomach to the brain were the cause of sleep. Adam's diet being temperate, his sleep was soft.

Our tended plants, how blows the citron grove,
What drops the myrrh, and what the balmy reed,
How Nature paints her colors, how the bee
Sits on the bloom extracting liquid sweet."
 Such whispering waked her, but with startled eye
On Adam, whom embracing, thus she spake.
 "O sole in whom my thoughts find all repose,
My glory, my perfection, glad I see
Thy face, and morn returned, for I this night,   30
Such night till this I never passed, have dreamed,
If dreamed, not as I oft am wont, of thee,
Works of day past, or morrow's next design,
But of offence and trouble, which my mind
Knew never till this irksome night. Methought
Close at mine ear one called me forth to walk
With gentle voice, I thought it thine; it said,
'Why sleep'st thou Eve? now is the pleasant time,
The cool, the silent, save where silence yields
To the night-warbling bird, that now awake   40
Tunes sweetest his love-labored song; now reigns
Full-orbed the moon, and with more pleasing light
Shadowy sets off the face of things; in vain,
If none regard; Heaven wakes with all his eyes,
Whom to behold but thee, Nature's desire,
In whose sight all things joy, with ravishment
Attracted by thy beauty still to gaze.'
I rose as at thy call, but found thee not;
To find thee I directed then my walk;
And on, methought, alone I passed through ways   50
That brought me on a sudden to the tree
Of interdicted knowledge. Fair it seemed,
Much fairer to my fancy than by day;
And as I wondering looked, beside it stood
One shaped and winged like one of those from Heaven
By us oft seen; his dewy locks distilled
Ambrosia; on that tree he also gazed;
And 'O fair plant,' said he, 'with fruit surcharged,
Deigns none to ease thy load and taste thy sweet,
Nor god, nor man; is knowledge so despised?   60
Or envy, or what reserve forbids to taste?
Forbid who will, none shall from me withhold
Longer thy offered good, why else set here?'
This said he paused not, but with venturous arm
He plucked, he tasted; me damp horror chilled
At such bold words vouched with a deed so bold.
But he thus, overjoyed, 'O fruit divine,

Sweet of thyself, but much more sweet thus cropped,
Forbidden here, it seems, as only fit
For gods, yet able to make gods of men;   70
And why not gods of men, since good, the more
Communicated, more abundant grows,
The author not impaired, but honored more?
Here, happy creature, fair angelic Eve,
Partake thou also; happy though thou art,
Happier thou may'st be, worthier canst not be;
Taste this, and be henceforth among the gods
Thyself a goddess, not to Earth confined,
But sometimes in the air, as we; sometimes
Ascend to Heaven, by merit thine, and see   80
What life the gods live there, and such live thou.'
So saying, he drew nigh, and to me held,
Even to my mouth of that same fruit held part
Which he had plucked; the pleasant savory smell
So quickened appetite that I, methought,
Could not but taste. Forthwith up to the clouds
With him I flew, and underneath beheld
The Earth outstretched immense, a prospect wide
And various. Wondering at my flight and change
To this high exaltation, suddenly   90
My guide was gone, and I, methought, sunk down,
And fell asleep; but O how glad I waked
To find this but a dream!" Thus Eve her night
Related, and thus Adam answered sad.
    "Best image of myself and dearer half,
The trouble of thy thoughts this night in sleep
Affects me equally; nor can I like
This uncouth dream, of evil sprung I fear;
Yet evil whence? in thee can harbor none,
Created pure. But know that in the soul   100
Are many lesser faculties, that serve
Reason as chief; among these Fancy next
Her office holds; of all external things,
Which the five watchful senses represent,
She forms imaginations, airy shapes,
Which Reason joining or disjoining, frames
All what we affirm or what deny, and call

98. **uncouth**, strange.
100 ff. Fancy or imagination forms images from sense data. Reason
organizes them into knowledge and judges them good or bad. In dreams
and daydreams imagination acts unchecked by reason. Except by intuition
Milton's age knew nothing of the Freudian unconscious and the "dream
work." The hierarchy of the senses, imagination, and reason goes back to
antiquity.

Our knowledge or opinion; then retires
Into her private cell when Nature rests.
Oft in her absence mimic Fancy wakes   110
To imitate her; but misjoining shapes,
Wild work produces oft, and most in dreams,
Ill matching words and deeds long past or late.
Some such resemblances methinks I find
Of our last evening's talk in this thy dream,
But with addition strange; yet be not sad.
Evil into the mind of god or man
May come and go, so unapproved, and leave
No spot or blame behind; which gives me hope
That what in sleep thou didst abhor to dream,   120
Waking thou never wilt consent to do.
Be not disheartened then, nor cloud those looks
That wont to be more cheerful and serene
Than when fair Morning first smiles on the world,
And let us to our fresh employments rise
Among the groves, the fountains, and the flowers
That open now their choicest bosomed smells
Reserved from night, and kept for thee in store."
    So cheered he his fair spouse, and she was cheered,
But silently a gentle tear let fall   130
From either eye, and wiped them with her hair;
Two other precious drops that ready stood,
Each in their crystal sluice, he ere they fell
Kissed as the gracious signs of sweet remorse
And pious awe, that feared to have offended.
    So all was cleared, and to the field they haste.
But first from under shady arborous roof,
Soon as they forth were come to open sight
Of day-spring, and the sun, who scarce up risen
With wheels yet hovering o'er the ocean brim,   140
Shot parallel to the Earth his dewy ray,
Discovering in wide landscape all the east
Of Paradise and Eden's happy plains,
Lowly they bowed adoring, and began
Their orisons, each morning duly paid
In various style, for neither various style
Nor holy rapture wanted they to praise
Their Maker, in fit strains pronounced or sung

---

110. mimic Fancy, Fancy, the mimic of nature.
    118. so unapproved, thus (i.e., coming and going, as described above)
unapproved by reason.
    146. in various style, not according to a set ritual as in the Catholic
and Anglican churches.

Unmeditated, such prompt eloquence
Flowed from their lips, in prose or numerous verse,   150
More tuneable than needed lute or harp
To add more sweetness, and they thus began.
  "These are thy glorious works, Parent of good,
Almighty, thine this universal frame,
Thus wondrous fair; thyself how wondrous then!
Unspeakable, who sitt'st above these Heavens
To us invisible or dimly seen
In these thy lowest works, yet these declare
Thy goodness beyond thought, and power divine.
Speak ye who best can tell, ye Sons of Light,   160
Angels, for ye behold him, and with songs
And choral symphonies, day without night,
Circle his throne rejoicing, ye in Heaven;
On Earth join all ye creatures to extol
Him first, him last, him midst, and without end.
Fairest of stars, last in the train of night,
If better thou belong not to the dawn,
Sure pledge of day, that crown'st the smiling Morn
With thy bright circlet, praise him in thy sphere
While day arises, that sweet hour of prime.   170
Thou Sun, of this great world both eye and soul,
Acknowledge him thy greater; sound his praise
In thy eternal course, both when thou climb'st,
And when high noon hast gained, and when thou fall'st.
Moon, that now meet'st the orient sun, now fliest
With the fixed stars, fixed in their orb that flies,
And ye five other wandering Fires that move
In mystic dance not without song, resound
His praise, who out of darkness called up light.
Air, and ye Elements, the eldest birth   180
Of Nature's womb, that in quaternion run
Perpetual circle, multiform, and mix

  150. numerous, metrical.
  158 ff. "The Heavens declare the glory of God." Ps. 19:1; but Ps. 148
furnishes the main inspiration for the morning hymn.
  176. We still speak of the "fixed stars," though we do not think of them
as embedded in a swiftly turning sphere. The grandeurs of the universe
cease to be imaginable when the stars are scattered through space. For the
effects of the idea of the "universe in depth" on the seventeenth-century
mind see Marjorie Nicolson, "The Telescope and Imagination," *Modern
Philology* (1935), 233 ff.
  177. wandering fires. Planet means wanderer in Greek. The term
originally included the Sun and Moon, as well as Venus, Mercury, Mars,
Jupiter, and Saturn.
  181-83. quaternion, fourfold combination. The elements change from
one to another in perpetual cycle.

And nourish all things, let your ceaseless change
Vary to our great Maker still new praise.
Ye Mists and Exhalations that now rise
From hill or steaming lake, dusky or gray,
Till the sun paint your fleecy skirts with gold,
In honor to the world's great Author rise;
Whether to deck with clouds the uncolored sky,
Or wet the thirsty earth with falling showers,   190
Rising or falling still advance his praise.
His praise ye Winds, that from four quarters blow,
Breathe soft or loud; and wave your tops, ye Pines,
With every plant, in sign of worship wave.
Fountains, and ye that warble, as ye flow,
Melodious murmurs, warbling tune his praise.
Join voices all ye living Souls; ye Birds,
That singing up to Heaven gate ascend,
Bear on your wings and in your notes his praise;
Ye that in waters glide, and ye that walk   200
The earth, and stately tread, or lowly creep,
Witness if I be silent, morn or even,
To hill, or valley, fountain, or fresh shade,
Made vocal by my song, and taught his praise.
Hail universal Lord, be bounteous still
To give us only good; and if the night
Have gathered aught of evil or concealed,
Disperse it, as now light dispels the dark."
    So prayed they innocent, and to their thoughts
Firm peace recovered soon and wonted calm.   210
On to their morning's rural work they haste,
Among sweet dews and flowers; where any row
Of fruit-trees over-woody reached too far
Their pampered boughs, and needed hands to check
Fruitless embraces. Or they led the vine
To wed her elm; she spoused about him twines
Her marriageable arms, and with her brings
Her dower, the adopted clusters, to adorn
His barren leaves. Them thus employed beheld
With pity Heaven's high King, and to him called   220
Raphael, the sociable spirit, that deigned
To travel with Tobias, and secured
His marriage with the seven-times-wedded maid.

    198. A Shakespearean recollection:
                    Hark, hark! the lark
                    At Heaven's gate sings.
    221-22. The allusion is to the apocryphal Book of Tobit. Raphael's
quality of affability is in contrast to the severity of Michael.

"Raphael," said he, "thou hear's what stir on Earth
Satan from Hell scaped through the darksome gulf
Hath raised in Paradise, and how disturbed
This night the human pair, how he designs
In them at once to ruin all mankind.
Go therefore, half this day as friend with friend
Converse with Adam, in what bower or shade   230
Thou find'st him from the heat of noon retired,
To respite his day-labor with repast
Or with repose; and such discourse bring on,
As may advise him of his happy state,
Happiness in his power left free to will,
Left to his own free will, his will though free
Yet mutable; whence warn him to beware
He swerve not, too secure. Tell him withal
His danger, and from whom; what enemy,
Late fallen himself from Heaven, is plotting now   240
The fall of others from like state of bliss;
By violence, no, for that shall be withstood,
But by deceit and lies; this let him know,
Lest wilfully transgressing he pretend
Surprisal, unadmonished, unforewarned."
     So spake the Eternal Father, and fulfilled
All justice; nor delayed the wingèd saint
After his charge received; but from among
Thousand celestial Ardors, where he stood
Veiled with his gorgeous wings, up springing light   250
Flew through the midst of Heaven; the angelic choirs
On each hand parting, to his speed gave way
Through all the empyreal road; till at the gate
Of Heaven arrived, the gate self-opened wide
On golden hinges turning, as by work
Divine the sovran Architect had framed.
From hence, no cloud, or, to obstruct his sight,
Star interposed, however small he sees,
Not unconform to other shining globes,
Earth and the Garden of God, with cedars crowned   260
Above all hills. As when by night the glass
Of Galileo, less assured, observes
Imagined lands and regions in the moon;
Or pilot from amidst the Cyclades
Delos or Samos first appearing kens
A cloudy spot. Down thither prone in flight
He speeds, and through the vast ethereal sky
Sails between worlds and worlds, with steady wing

244. **pretend,** hold forth as an excuse.

Now on the polar winds, then with quick fan
Winnows the buxom air; till within soar   270
Of towering eagles, to all the fowls he seems
A phœnix, gazed by all, as that sole bird
When to enshrine his reliques in the sun's
Bright temple, to Egyptian Thebes he flies.
At once on the eastern cliff of Paradise
He lights, and to his proper shape returns,
A Seraph winged; six wings he wore, to shade
His lineaments divine; the pair that clad
Each shoulder broad, came mantling o'er his breast
With regal ornament; the middle pair   280
Girt like a starry zone his waist, and round
Skirted his loins and thighs with downy gold
And colors dipt in Heaven; the third his feet
Shadowed from either heel with feathered mail,
Sky-tinctured grain. Like Maia's son he stood,
And shook his plumes, that heavenly fragrance filled
The circuit wide. Straight knew him all the bands
Of angels under watch; and to his state
And to his message high in honor rise;
For on some message high they guessed him bound.   290
Their glittering tents he passed, and now is come
Into the blissful field, through groves of myrrh,
And flowering odors, cassia, nard, and balm;
A wilderness of sweets; for Nature here
Wantoned as in her prime, and played at will
Her virgin fancies, pouring forth more sweet,
Wild above rule or art, enormous bliss.
Him through the spicy forest onward come
Adam discerned, as in the door he sat
Of his cool bower, while now the mounted sun   300
Shot down direct his fervid rays to warm
Earth's inmost womb, more warmth than Adam needs;
And Eve within, due at her hour prepared
For dinner savory fruits, of taste to please
True appetite, and not disrelish thirst
Of nectarous draughts between, from milky stream,
Berry or grape: to whom thus Adam called.
   "Haste hither Eve, and worth thy sight behold

270. **buxom,** yielding.
   272. **phœnix.** This mythical bird, of which only one existed, built itself a funeral pyre once in five hundred years and renewed its youth in the
flames. It then carried its ashes to the temple of the Sun.
   285. **Maia's son,** Mercury, Jove's messenger.
   297. **enormous,** without norm or rule. The phrase is in apposition
with the preceding idea of wild profusion.

Eastward among those trees what glorious shape
Comes this way moving; seems another morn   310
Risen on mid-noon; some great behest from Heaven
To us perhaps he brings, and will vouchsafe
This day to be our guest. But go with speed,
And what thy stores contain, bring forth and pour
Abundance, fit to honor and receive
Our heavenly stranger; well we may afford
Our givers their own gifts, and large bestow
From large bestowed, where Nature multiplies
Her fertile growth, and by disburdening grows
More fruitful; which instructs us not to spare."   320
    To whom thus Eve. "Adam, Earth's hallowed mould,
Of God inspired, small store will serve, where store,   *Eve*
All seasons, ripe for use hangs on the stalk;
Save what by frugal storing firmness gains
To nourish, and superfluous moist consumes.
But I will haste and from each bough and brake,
Each plant and juiciest gourd, will pluck such choice
To entertain our angel guest, as he
Beholding shall confess that here on Earth
God hath dispensed his bounties as in Heaven."   330
    So saying, with dispatchful looks in haste
She turns, on hospitable thoughts intent   *domestic*
What choice to choose for delicacy best,
What order, so contrived as not to mix
Tastes, not well joined, inelegant, but bring
Taste after taste upheld with kindliest change,
Bestirs her then, and from each tender stalk
Whatever Earth, all-bearing mother, yields
In India East or West, or middle shore
In Pontus or the Punic coast, or where   340
Alcinöus reigned, fruit of all kinds, in coat
Rough, or smooth-rined, or bearded husk, or shell
She gathers, tribute large, and on the board
Heaps with unsparing hand; for drink the grape
She crushes, inoffensive must, and meaths
From many a berry, and from sweet kernels pressed
She tempers dulcet creams; nor these to hold
Wants her fit vessels pure; then strews the ground
With rose and odors from the shrub unfumed.
    Meanwhile our primitive great sire, to meet   350
His godlike guest, walks forth, without more train

341. The ever-blooming garden of Alcinous, king of the Phaeacians, is
described in *Odyssey* vii. 125–28.
  345. must, new wine; meaths, meads.

Accompanied than with his own complete
Perfections; in himself was all his state,
More solemn than the tedious pomp that waits
On princes, when their rich retinue long
Of horses led, and grooms besmeared with gold
Dazzles the crowd, and sets them all agape.
Nearer his presence Adam though not awed,
Yet with submiss approach and reverence meek,
As to a superior nature, bowing low,   360
Thus said. "Native of Heaven, for other place
None can than Heaven such glorious shape contain;
Since by descending from the Thrones above,
Those happy places thou hast deigned a while
To want, and honor these, vouchsafe with us
Two only, who yet by sovran gift possess
This spacious ground, in yonder shady bower
To rest, and what the garden choicest bears
To sit and taste, till this meridian heat
Be over, and the sun more cool decline."   370
Whom thus the angelic Virtue answered mild.
"Adam, I therefore came, nor art thou such
Created, or such place hast here to dwell,
As may not oft invite, though spirits of Heaven,
To visit thee; lead on then where thy bower
O'ershades; for these mid-hours, till evening rise
I have at will." So to the sylvan lodge
They came, that like Pomona's arbor smiled
With flowerets decked and fragrant smells; but Eve
Undecked save with herself, more lovely fair   380
Than wood-nymph, or the fairest goddess feigned
Of three that in Mount Ida naked strove,
Stood to entertain her guest from Heaven; no veil
She needed, virtue-proof; no thought infirm
Altered her cheek. On whom the Angel "Hail"
Bestowed, the holy salutation used
Long after to blest Mary, second Eve.
"Hail Mother of Mankind, whose fruitful womb
Shall fill the world more numerous with thy sons
Than with these various fruits the trees of God   390
Have heaped this table." Raised of grassy turf
Their table was, and mossy seats had round,
And on her ample square from side to side
All autumn piled, though spring and autumn here

378. Pomona, the orchard goddess.
381-82. the fairest goddess, Venus, who was awarded the prize of
beauty against Juno and Minerva by Paris on Mount Ida.

Danced hand in hand. A while discourse they hold;
No fear lest dinner cool; when thus began
Our Author. "Heavenly stranger, please to taste
These bounties which our Nourisher, from whom
All perfect good unmeasured out descends,
To us for food and for delight hath caused   400
The Earth to yield; unsavory food perhaps
To spiritual natures; only this I know,
That one celestial Father gives to all."
     To whom the Angel. "Therefore what he gives
(Whose praise be ever sung) to Man in part
Spiritual, may of purest spirits be found   *body*
No ingrateful food: and food alike those pure   *&*
Intelligential substances require   *soul*
As doth your rational; and both contain
Within them every lower faculty   410
Of sense, whereby they hear, see, smell, touch, taste,
Tasting concoct, digest, assimilate,
And corporeal to incorporeal turn.
For know, whatever was created needs
To be sustained and fed; of elements
The grosser feeds the purer: earth the sea,
Earth and the sea feed air, the air those fires
Ethereal, and as lowest first the moon;
Whence in her visage round those spots unpurgëd
Vapors not yet into her substance turned.   420
Nor doth the moon no nourishment exhale
From her moist continent to higher orbs.
The sun that light imparts to all, receives
From all his alimental recompense
In humid exhalations, and at even
Sups with the ocean. Though in Heaven the trees
Of life ambrosial fruitage bear, and vines
Yield nectar, though from off the boughs each morn
We brush mellifluous dews, and find the ground
Covered with pearly grain; yet God hath here   430
Varied his bounty so with new delights
As may compare with Heaven; and to taste
Think not I shall be nice." So down they sat,
And to their viands fell, nor seemingly

396. This reminder of the social convenience of an uncooked banquet
has excited laughter among the irreverent. But Milton wants to interest us
in all the speculations, literal and otherwise, about Eden, as he himself was
interested.
     404 ff. Raphael begins at once his exposition of the relations between
body and spirit. We shall have much of this as the conversation goes on.
     412. concoct, refine by heating.

The Angel, nor in mist, the common gloss
Of theologians, but with keen dispatch
Of real hunger, and concoctive heat
To transubstantiate; what redounds transpires
Through spirits with ease; nor wonder; if by fire
Of sooty coal the empiric alchemist   440
Can turn, or holds it possible to turn
Metals of drossiest ore to perfect gold,
As from the mine. Meanwhile at table Eve
Ministered naked, and their flowing cups
With pleasant liquors crowned. O innocence
Deserving Paradise! If ever, then,
Then had the Sons of God excuse to have been
Enamored at that sight; but in those hearts
Love unlibidinous reigned, nor jealousy
Was understood, the injured lover's hell.   450
    Thus when with meats and drinks they had sufficed,
Not burdened nature, sudden mind arose
In Adam, not to let the occasion pass
Given him by this great conference to know
Of things above this world, and of their being
Who dwell in Heaven, whose excellence he saw
Transcend his own so far, whose radiant forms,
Divine effulgence, whose high power so far
Exceeded human, and his wary speech
Thus to the empyreal minister he framed: 460
    "Inhabitant with God, now know I well
Thy favor, in this honor done to Man,
Under whose lowly roof thou hast vouchsafed
To enter, and these earthly fruits to taste,
Food not of angels, yet accepted so,
As that more willingly thou couldst not seem
At Heaven's high feasts to have fed; yet what compare?"
    To whom the wingèd Hierarch replied.
"O Adam, one Almighty is, from whom

438. **what redounds transpires;** the *reductio ad absurdum* of Milton's angelology.

469 ff. The elaborate account of the "scale of nature" gives the basic philosophical assumptions of Milton's cosmology and of his ethics. The parallel prose exposition in *Christian Doctrine* I, vii, is really no clearer or more explicit than this poetic one. Matter and spirit, man and angel, earth and heaven differ not in kind but in degree. They may, therefore, pass one into the other. There is greater order as we ascend, from chaos to the differentiated elements, from sensation to reason, from human understanding to intuition of the Divine. The doctrine is anti-ascetic, for all the stages of experience are good unless perverted. But the hierarchy must remain unbroken, the lower never aspiring to usurp the place or function of the higher, except as it tends naturally to transcend itself by moving toward the

All things proceed, and up to him return,   470
If not depraved from good, created all
Such to perfection, one first matter all,
Endued with various forms, various degrees
Of substance, and in things that live, of life;
But more refined, more spiritous and pure,
As nearer to him placed or nearer tending,
Each in their several active spheres assigned,
Till body up to spirit work, in bounds
Proportioned to each kind. So from the root
Springs lighter the green stalk, from thence the leaves   480
More airy, last the bright consummate flower
Spirits odorous breathes; flowers and their fruit,
Man's nourishment, by gradual scale sublimed,
To vital spirits aspire, to animal,
To intellectual; give both life and sense,
Fancy and understanding, whence the soul
Reason receives, and reason is her being,
Discursive, or intuitive; discourse
Is oftest yours, the latter most is ours,
Differing but in degree, of kind the same.   490
Wonder not then, what God for you saw good
If I refuse not, but convert, as you,
To proper substance. Time may come when men
With angels may participate, and find
No inconvenient diet, nor too light fare;
And from these corporal nutriments perhaps
Your bodies may at last turn all to spirit,
Improved by tract of time, and winged ascend
Ethereal, as we, or may at choice
Here or in heavenly Paradises dwell;   500
If ye be found obedient, and retain
Unalterably firm his love entire
Whose progeny you are. Meanwhile enjoy
Your fill what happiness this happy state
Can comprehend, incapable of more."
   To whom the Patriarch of Mankind replied.
"O favorable Spirit, propitious guest,
Well hast thou taught the way that might direct
Our knowledge, and the scale of Nature set

original source of all being. This is not pantheism in the ordinary sense, but
it is in express opposition to traditional Christian thought, as Milton understood it.
   483. sublimed, elevated, refined.
   488. Discursive, logical. Cf. Hamlet's "a beast that wants discourse of
reason."

From center to circumference, whereon   510
In contemplation of created things
By steps we may ascend to God. But say,
What meant that caution joined, *If ye be found
Obedient?* Can we want obedience then
To him, or possibly his love desert
Who formed us from the dust, and placed us here
Full to the utmost measure of what bliss
Human desires can seek or apprehend?"
    To whom the Angel. "Son of Heaven and Earth,
Attend: That thou art happy, owe to God;   520
That thou continuest such, owe to thyself,
That is, to thy obedience; therein stand.
This was that caution given thee; be advised.
God made thee perfect, not immutable;
And good he made thee, but to persevere
He left it in thy power, ordained thy will
By nature free, not over-ruled by fate
Inextricable, or strict necessity;
Our voluntary service he requires,
Not our necessitated; such with him   530
Finds no acceptance, nor can find, for how
Can hearts not free, be tried whether they serve
Willing or no, who will but what they must
By destiny, and can no other choose?
Myself, and all the angelic host that stand
In sight of God enthroned, our happy state
Hold, as you yours, while our obedience holds;
On other surety none; freely we serve,
Because we freely love, as in our will
To love or not; in this we stand or fall.   540
And some are fallen, to disobedience fallen,
And so from Heaven to deepest Hell; O fall
From what high state of bliss into what woe!"
    To whom our great Progenitor. "Thy words
Attentive, and with more delighted ear,
Divine instructor, I have heard, than when
Cherubic songs by night from neighboring hills
Aërial music send; nor knew I not
To be both will and deed created free;
Yet that we never shall forget to love   550
Our Maker, and obey him whose command
Single, is yet so just, my constant thoughts
Assured me and still assure; though what thou tell'st

544 ff. "How charming is divine philosophy," as the Younger Brother
says in *Comus*, 476.

Hath passed in Heaven, some doubt within me move,
But more desire to hear, if thou consent,
The full relation, which must needs be strange,
Worthy of sacred silence to be heard;
And we have yet large day, for scarce the sun
Hath finished half his journey, and scarce begins
His other half in the great zone of heaven."   560
   Thus Adam made request, and Raphael
After short pause assenting, thus began.
   "High matter thou enjoin'st me, O prime of men,
Sad task and hard, for how shall I relate
To human sense the invisible exploits
Of warring spirits; how without remorse
The ruin of so many glorious once
And perfect while they stood; how last unfold
The secrets of another world, perhaps
Not lawful to reveal? Yet for thy good   570
This is dispensed, and what surmounts the reach
Of human sense I shall delineate so,
By likening spiritual to corporal forms,
As may express them best, though what if Earth
Be but the shadow of Heaven, and things therein
Each to other like, more than on Earth is thought?
   "As yet this world was not, and Chaos wild
Reigned where these Heavens now roll, where Earth now rests
Upon her center poised, when on a day
(For time, though in eternity, applied   580
To motion, measures all things durable
By present, past, and future) on such day
As Heaven's great year brings forth, the empyreal host
Of angels by imperial summons called,
Innumerable before the Almighty's throne
Forthwith from all the ends of Heaven appeared
Under their Hierarchs in orders bright.
Ten thousand thousand ensigns high advanced,
Standards and gonfalons 'twixt van and rear
Stream in the air, and for distinction serve   590
Of Hierarchies, of orders, and degrees;

566. **remorse,** sorrow.
571. By dispensation for Adam's good he is permitted to reveal the secrets.
574–76. The Platonic doctrine that all the phenomena of earth have counterparts in a world of divine reality helps Milton at this point. There is an "idea" of war, which can be imperfectly perceived in the actualities of human conflict. The "great year" of Heaven and its cycle of day and night are the same conception. There is time in eternity!
588. **advanced,** raised. Cf. "The fringed curtain of thine eyes advance."

Or in their glittering tissues bear emblazed
Holy memorials, acts of zeal and love
Recorded eminent. Thus when in orbs
Of circuit inexpressible they stood,
Orb within orb, the Father Infinite,
By whom in bliss embosomed sat the Son,
Amidst as from a flaming mount, whose top
Brightness had made invisible, thus spake.
  "'Hear all ye Angels, progeny of light,   600
Thrones, Dominations, Princedoms, Virtues, Powers,
Hear my decree, which unrevoked shall stand.
This day I have begot whom I declare
My only Son, and on this holy hill
Him have anointed, whom ye now behold
At my right hand; your head I him appoint;
And by myself have sworn to him shall bow
All knees in Heaven, and shall confess him Lord.
Under his great vicegerent reign abide
United as one individual soul   610
For ever happy. Him who disobeys
Me disobeys, breaks union, and that day
Cast out from God and blessed vision, falls
Into utter darkness, deep ingulfed, his place
Ordained without redemption, without end.'
  "So spake the Omnipotent, and with his words
All seemed well pleased; all seemed, but were not all.
That day, as other solemn days, they spent
In song and dance about the sacred hill;
Mystical dance, which yonder starry sphere   620
Of planets and of fixed in all her wheels
Resembles nearest, mazes intricate,
Eccentric, intervolved, yet regular
Then most, when most irregular they seem;

    601. The names of the angelic orders include, besides those given here:
Angels, Archangels, Cherubim, and Seraphim. Milton does not assign them
an exact order, as Dante does. He assumes, however, that such a hierarchy
exists.

    603. This day I have begot. Milton is interpreting Ps. 2:6–7: "Yet
have I set my king upon my holy hill of Zion. I will declare the decree: the
Lord hath said unto me, Thou art my son; this day have I begotten thee."
Begot is used in the sense of proclaiming and anointing Christ as Messiah.
In Milton's theology Christ was not coeternal with God, but he was the first
created thing, and it was through his agency that the angels themselves
were created. This act of proclamation excites Satan's jealous ambition and
constitutes the motivation of the epic.

    618 ff. Dance and song are the essentially Miltonic satisfactions of the
Heavenly Host. The feasting which follows matches that of the Greek gods
on Mount Olympus, as described by Homer.

And in their motions harmony divine
So smooths her charming tones, that God's own ear
Listens delighted.   Evening now approached
(For we have also our evening and our morn,
We ours for change delectable, not need),
Forthwith from dance to sweet repast they turn   630
Desirous; all in circles as they stood,
Tables are set, and on a sudden piled
With angels' food, and rubied nectar flows
In pearl, in diamond, and massy gold,
Fruit of delicious vines, the growth of Heaven.
On flowers reposed, and with fresh flowerets crowned,
They eat, they drink, and in communion sweet
Quaff immortality and joy, secure
Of surfeit where full measure only bounds
Excess, before the all-bounteous King, who showered   640
With copious hand, rejoicing in their joy.
Now when ambrosial night, with clouds exhaled
From that high mount of God, whence light and shade
Spring both, the face of brightest Heaven had changed
To grateful twilight (for night comes not there
In darker veil) and roseate dews disposed
All but the unsleeping eyes of God to rest,
Wide over all the plain, and wider far
Than all this globous Earth in plain outspread
(Such are the courts of God), the angelic throng,   650
Dispersed in bands and files, their camp extend
By living streams among the trees of life,
Pavilions numberless and sudden reared,
Celestial tabernacles, where they slept
Fanned with cool winds, save those who in their course
Melodious hymns about the sovran throne
Alternate all night long.   But not so waked
Satan, so call him now, his former name
Is heard no more in Heaven; he of the first,
If not the first Archangel, great in power,   660
In favor, and pre-eminence, yet fraught

637–40. These lines are a revision made for the second edition. The
original reading was

> They eat, they drink, and with refection sweet
> Are filled, before the all bounteous King, who showered
> With copious hand, rejoicing in their joy.

There is no other instance of just this kind of inspired addition to the text.
     638–39. full measure. The meaning is that the angels could eat and
drink to fullness without the surfeit of excess. In men there is no such
boundary because their appetite is depraved.

With envy against the Son of God, that day
Honored by his great Father, and proclaimed
Messiah King anointed, could not bear
Through pride that sight, and thought himself impaired.
Deep malice thence conceiving and disdain,
Soon as midnight brought on the dusky hour
Friendliest to sleep and silence, he resolved
With all his legions to dislodge, and leave
Unworshipped, unobeyed, the throne supreme,   670
Contemptuous, and his next subordinate
Awakening, thus to him in secret spake.
    " 'Sleep'st thou companion dear, what sleep can close
Thy eyelids? and remember'st what decree
Of yesterday, so late hath passed the lips
Of Heaven's Almighty. Thou to me thy thoughts
Wast wont, I mine to thee was wont to impart;
Both waking we were one; how then can now
Thy sleep dissent? New laws thou seest imposed;
New laws from him who reigns, new minds may raise   680
In us who serve, new counsels, to debate
What doubtful may ensue. More in this place
To utter is not safe. Assemble thou
Of all those myriads which we lead the chief;
Tell them that by command, ere yet dim Night
Her shadowy cloud withdraws, I am to haste,
And all who under me their banners wave,
Homeward with flying march where we possess
The quarters of the North, there to prepare
Fit entertainment to receive our King,   690
The great Messiah, and his new commands,
Who speedily through all the Hierarchies
Intends to pass triumphant, and give laws.'
    "So spake the false Archangel, and infused
Bad influence nto the unwary breast
Of his associate; he together calls,
Or several one by one, the regent powers,
Under him regent, tells, as he was taught,
That the Most High commanding, now ere night,
Now ere dim night had disencumbered Heaven,   700
The great Hierarchal standard was to move;
Tells the suggested cause, and casts between
Ambiguous words and jealousies, to sound
Or taint integrity; but all obeyed

671. his next subordinate, Beelzebub.
    703-4. to sound Or taint. Sounding or exploring is, of course, the
first step in tainting or corrupting.

The wonted signal, and superior voice
Of their great Potentate; for great indeed
His name, and high was his degree in Heaven;
His countenance, as the morning star that guides
The starry flock, allured them, and with lies
Drew after him the third part of Heaven's host.   710
Meanwhile the Eternal eye, whose sight discerns
Abstrusest thoughts, from forth his holy mount
And from within the golden lamps that burn
Nightly before him, saw without their light
Rebellion rising, saw in whom, how spread
Among the Sons of Morn, what multitudes
Were banded to oppose his high decree;
And smiling, to his only Son thus said.
    " 'Son, thou in whom my glory I behold
In full resplendence, Heir of all my might,   720
Nearly it now concerns us to be sure
Of our omnipotence, and with what arms
We mean to hold what anciently we claim
Of deity or empire: such a foe
Is rising, who intends to erect his throne
Equal to ours, throughout the spacious North;
Nor so content, hath in his thought to try
In battle, what our power is or our right.
Let us advise, and to this hazard draw
With speed what force is left, and all employ   730
In our defence, lest unawares we lose
This our high place, our sanctuary, our hill.'
    "To whom the Son, with calm aspéct and clear,
Lightning divine, ineffable, serene,
Made answer. 'Mighty Father, thou thy foes
Justly hast in derision, and secure
Laught'st at their vain designs and tumults vain,
Matter to me of glory, whom their hate
Illustrates, when they see all regal power
Given me to quell their pride, and in event   740
Know whether I be dextrous to subdue
Thy rebels, or be found the worst in Heaven.'
    "So spake the Son, but Satan with his powers
Far was advanced on wingéd speed, an host
Innumerable as the stars of night,
Or stars of morning, dew-drops, which the sun

710. "And his tail drew the third part of the stars of heaven, and did
cast them to the earth." Rev. 12:4. This chapter contains the chief scriptural authority for the war in Heaven.
    739. **illustrates,** makes glorious.

Impearls on every leaf and every flower.
Regions they passed, the mighty regencies
Of Seraphim and Potentates and Thrones
In their triple degrees, regions to which   750
All thy dominion, Adam, is no more
Than what this garden is to all the earth
And all the sea, from one entire globose
Stretched into longitude; which having passed,
At length into the limits of the North
They came, and Satan to his royal seat
High on a hill, far blazing, as a mount
Raised on a mount, with pyramids and towers
From diamond quarries hewn, and rocks of gold,
The palace of great Lucifer (so call   760
That structure in the dialect of men
Interpreted), which not long after, he
Affecting all equality with God,
In imitation of that mount whereon
Messiah was declared in sight of Heaven,
The Mountain of the Congregation called;
For thither he assembled all his train,
Pretending so commanded to consult
About the great reception of their King,
Thither to come, and with calumnious art   770
Of counterfeited truth thus held their ears.
    "'Thrones, Dominations, Princedoms, Virtues, Powers,
If these magnific titles yet remain
Not merely titular, since by decree
Another now hath to himself engrossed
All power, and us eclipsed under the name
Of King anointed, for whom all this haste
Of midnight march and hurried meeting here,
This only to consult, how we may best
With what may be devised of honors new,   780
Receive him coming to receive from us
Knee-tribute yet unpaid, prostration vile,
Too much to one, but double how endured,
To one and to his image now proclaimed?
But what if better counsels might erect
Our minds and teach us to cast off this yoke?
Will ye submit your necks, and choose to bend
The supple knee? Ye will not, if I trust
To know ye right, or if ye know yourselves
Natives and Sons of Heaven possessed before   790

753-54. From a single, integrated spherical (globose) shape flattened
out into length, as in Mercator's projection.

By none, and if not equal all, yet free,
Equally free; for orders and degrees
Jar not with liberty, but well consist.
Who can in reason then or right assume
Monarchy over such as live by right
His equals, if in power and splendor less,
In freedom equal? or can introduce
Law and edict on us, who without law
Err not? much less for this to be our Lord,   800
And look for adoration, to the abuse
Of those imperial titles which assert
Our being ordained to govern, not to serve?'
    "Thus far his bold discourse without control
Had audience, when among the Seraphim
Abdiel, than whom none with more zeal adored
The Deity, and divine commands obeyed,
Stood up, and in a flame of zeal severe
The current of his fury thus opposed.
    " 'O argument blasphemous, false, and proud!   810
Words which no ear ever to hear in Heaven
Expected, least of all from thee, ingrate,
In place thyself so high above thy peers.
Canst thou with impious obloquy condemn
The just decree of God, pronounced and sworn,
That to his only Son by right endued
With regal scepter, every soul in Heaven
Shall bend the knee, and in that honor due
Confess him rightful King? Unjust thou say'st,
Flatly unjust, to bind with laws the free,
And equal over equals to let reign,   820
One over all with unsucceeded power.
Shalt thou give law to God, shalt thou dispute
With him the points of liberty, who made
Thee what thou art, and formed the powers of Heaven
Such as he pleased, and circumscribed their being?
Yet by experience taught we know how good,
And of our good and of our dignity
How provident he is, how far from thought
To make us less; bent rather to exalt
Our happy state under one head more near   830
United. But to grant it thee unjust,

792. The doctrine is true of the loyal angels, false of the disobedient
ones, who are slaves to their own passion.
    795. Monarchy. Milton believed that monarchy would be the best
form of government if the monarch were the best of men; he sees no analogy
between Satan's doctrine and his own present republicanism.

That equal over equals monarch reign:
Thyself though great and glorious dost thou count,
Or all angelic nature joined in one,
Equal to him, begotten Son, by whom
As by his Word the mighty Father made
All things, even thee, and all the spirits of Heaven
By him created in their bright degrees,
Crowned them with glory, and to their glory named
Thrones, Dominations, Princedoms, Virtues, Powers,   840
Essential Powers, nor by his reign obscured,
But more illustrious made, since he the head
One of our number thus reduced becomes,
His laws our laws, all honor to him done
Returns our own. Cease then this impious rage,
And tempt not these; but hasten to appease
The incensèd Father and the incensèd Son
While pardon may be found, in time besought.'
    "So spake the fervent Angel; but his zeal
None seconded, as out of season judged,   850
Or singular and rash, whereat rejoiced
The Apostate, and more haughty thus replied.
    " 'That we were formed then say'st thou? and the work
Of secondary hands, by task transferred
From Father to his Son? Strange point and new!
Doctrine which we would know whence learned. Who saw
When this creation was? Remember'st thou
Thy making, while the Maker gave thee being?
We know no time when we were not as now;
Know none before us, self-begot, self-raised   860
By our own quickening power, when fatal course
Had circled his full orb, the birth mature
Of this our native Heaven, Ethereal Sons.
Our puissance is our own; our own right hand
Shall teach us highest deeds, by proof to try
Who is our equal. Then thou shalt behold
Whether by supplication we intend
Address, and to begirt the Almighty throne
Beseeching or besieging. This report,
These tidings carry to the anointed King;   870
And fly, ere evil intercept thy flight.'
    "He said, and as the sound of waters deep
Hoarse murmur echoed to his words applause
Through the infinite host, nor less for that

860. **self-begot.** Satan holds or affects to hold the dualistic belief of
the Manichees. Cf. I, 116 ff. This is his great heresy, out of which all his
sins and errors flow.

The flaming Seraph fearless, though alone
Encompassed round with foes, thus answered bold.
  " 'O alienate from God, O Spirit accurst,   *abdiel*
Forsaken of all good; I see thy fall
Determined, and thy hapless crew involved
In this perfidious fraud, contagion spread   880
Both of thy crime and punishment. Henceforth
No more be troubled how to quit the yoke
Of God's Messiah; those indulgent laws
Will not be now vouchsafed; other decrees
Against thee are gone forth without recall;
That golden scepter which thou didst reject
Is now an iron rod to bruise and break
Thy disobedience. Well thou didst advise.
Yet not for thy advice or threats I fly
These wicked tents devoted, lest the wrath   890
Impendent, raging into sudden flame
Distinguish not: for soon expect to feel
His thunder on thy head, devouring fire.
Then who created thee lamenting learn,
When who can uncreate thee thou shalt know.'
  "So spake the Seraph Abdiel faithful found,
Among the faithless, faithful only he;   *faithful*
Among innumerable false, unmoved,
Unshaken, unseduced, unterrified
His loyalty he kept, his love, his zeal;   900
Nor number nor example with him wrought
To swerve from truth, or change his constant mind,
Though single. From amidst them forth he passed,
Long way through hostile scorn, which he sustained
Superior, nor of violence feared aught;
And with retorted scorn his back he turned
On those proud towers to swift destruction doomed."

BOOK VI

THE ARGUMENT

  Raphael continues to relate how Michael and Gabriel were sent
forth to battle against Satan and his angels. The first fight described; Satan and his Powers retire under night. He calls a
council; invents devilish engines, which, in the second day's fight,
put Michael and his angels to some disorder; but they at length,

---

  896 ff. Abdiel is the prototype of all who stand out in their own conviction against the opinions of the many. This image of the one just man
recurs frequently in Milton's imagination, and he interpreted his own
behavior in the light of innumerable examples, past and present.

pulling up mountains, overwhelmed both the force and machines
of Satan. Yet, the tumult not so ending, God, on the third day,
sends Messiah his Son, for whom he had reserved the glory of
that victory. He, in the power of his Father, coming to the place,
and causing all his legions to stand still on either side, with his
chariot and thunder driving into the midst of his enemies, pursues them, unable to resist, towards the wall of Heaven; which
opening, they leap down with horror and confusion into the
place of punishment prepared for them in the deep. Messiah
returns with triumph to his Father.

"All night the dreadless angel unpursued
Through Heaven's wide champaign held his way, till Morn,
Waked by the circling Hours, with rosy hand
Unbarred the gates of light. There is a cave
Within the mount of God, fast by his throne,
Where light and darkness in perpetual round
Lodge and dislodge by turns, which makes through Heaven
Grateful vicissitude, like day and night;
Light issues forth, and at the other door
Obsequious darkness enters, till her hour   10
To veil the Heaven, though darkness there might well
Seem twilight here; and now went forth the Morn
Such as in highest Heaven, arrayed in gold
Empyreal; from before her vanished Night,
Shot through with orient beams; when all the plain
Covered with thick embattled squadrons bright,
Chariots, and flaming arms, and fiery steeds,
Reflecting blaze on blaze, first met his view.
War he perceived, war in procinct, and found
Already known what he for news had thought   20
To have reported; gladly then he mixed
Among those friendly powers who him received
With joy and acclamations loud, that one,
That of so many myriads fallen, yet one
Returned not lost: on to the sacred hill
They led him high applauded, and present
Before the seat supreme; from whence a voice
From midst a golden cloud thus mild was heard.
    " 'Servant of God, well done, well hast thou fought

    10. obsequious, obedient, or, perhaps, following in duly appointed
round.
    19. in procinct, in readiness.
    29. Servant of God, a translation of the name Abdiel. There is a remi-
niscence of the parable of the talents (Matt. 25:14 ff.): "Well done, good
and faithful servant." Milton took this parable to himself. as we see in the
first sonnet on his blindness and elsewhere. Abdiel is receiving the reward
of heavenly approval which constitutes the only true fame.

The better fight, who single hast maintained   30
Against revolted multitudes the cause
Of truth, in word mightier than they in arms;
And for the testimony of truth hast borne
Universal reproach, far worse to bear
Than violence; for this was all thy care,
To stand approved in sight of God, though worlds   *reward*
Judged thee perverse. The easier conquest now
Remains thee, aided by this host of friends,
Back on thy foes more glorious to return
Than scorned thou didst depart, and to subdue   40
By force, who reason for their law refuse,
Right reason for their law, and for their King
Messiah, who by right of merit reigns.
Go Michael, of celestial armies prince,   *Michael*
And thou in military prowess next,   *Gabriel*
Gabriel, lead forth to battle these my sons
Invincible, lead forth my armèd saints
By thousands and by millions ranged for fight,
Equal in number to that godless crew
Rebellious; them with fire and hostile arms   50
Fearless assault, and to the brow of Heaven
Pursuing, drive them out from God and bliss,
Into their place of punishment, the gulf
Of Tartarus, which ready opens wide
His fiery chaos to receive their fall.'   *fall*
    "So spake the Sovran Voice, and clouds began
To darken all the hill, and smoke to roll
In dusky wreaths reluctant flames, the sign
Of wrath awaked; nor with less dread the loud   *nature*
Ethereal trumpet from on high gan blow;   *grace*
At which command the powers militant   60
That stood for Heaven, in mighty quadrate joined
Of union irresistible, moved on
In silence their bright legions, to the sound
Of instrumental harmony that breathed
Heroic ardor to adventurous deeds
Under their godlike leaders, in the cause
Of God and his Messiah. On they move
Indissolubly firm; nor obvious hill,
Nor straitening vale, nor wood, nor stream divides   70

35. Cf. "Lycidas," 83–84:
        As He pronounces lastly on each deed
        Of so much fame in Heaven expect thy meed.
58. reluctant, i.e., struggling through the smoke.
69. obvious, in the way.

Their perfect ranks; for high above the ground
Their march was, and the passive air upbore
Their nimble tread; as when the total kind
Of birds in orderly array on wing
Came summoned over Eden to receive
Their names of thee; so over many a tract
Of Heaven they marched, and many a province wide
Tenfold the length of this terrene. At last
Far in the horizon to the North appeared
From skirt to skirt a fiery region, stretched   80
In battailous aspéct, and nearer view
Bristled with upright beams innumerable
Of rigid spears, and helmets thronged, and shields
Various, with boastful argument portrayed,
The banded powers of Satan hasting on
With furious expedition; for they weened
That self-same day by fight or by surprise
To win the mount of God, and on his throne
To set the envier of his state, the proud
Aspirer, but their thoughts proved fond and vain   90
In the mid-way. Though strange to us it seemed
At first, that angel should with angel war,
And in fierce hosting meet, who wont to meet
So oft in festivals of joy and love
Unanimous, as sons of one great Sire,
Hymning the Eternal Father. But the shout
Of battle now began, and rushing sound
Of onset ended soon each milder thought.
High in the midst exalted as a god
The Apostate in his sun-bright chariot sat   100
Idol of majesty divine, enclosed
With flaming Cherubim and golden shields;
Then lighted from his gorgeous throne, for now
'Twixt host and host but narrow space was left,
A dreadful interval, and front to front
Presented stood in terrible array
Of hideous length. Before the cloudy van,
On the rough edge of battle ere it joined,
Satan, with vast and haughty strides advanced,
Came towering, armed in adamant and gold;   110
Abdiel that sight endured not, where he stood
Among the mightiest, bent on highest deeds,
And thus his own undaunted heart explores.

78. terrene, earth.
101. Idol, image, but with the suggestion also of an object of false
worship.

" 'O Heaven! that such resemblance of the Highest
Should yet remain, where faith and realty
Remain not; wherefore should not strength and might
There fail where virtue fails, or weakest prove
Where boldest, though to sight unconquerable?
His puissance, trusting in the Almighty's aid,
I mean to try, whose reason I have tried   120
Unsound and false; nor is it aught but just,
That he who in debate of truth hath won,
Should win in arms, in both disputes alike
Victor; though brutish that contest and foul,
When reason hath to deal with force, yet so
Most reason is that reason overcome.'
    "So pondering, and from his armèd peers
Forth stepping opposite, half-way he met
His daring foe, at this prevention more
Incensed, and thus securely him defied.   130
    " 'Proud, art thou met? Thy hope was to have reached
The height of thy aspiring unopposed,
The throne of God unguarded, and his side
Abandoned at the terror of thy power
Or potent tongue; fool, not to think how vain
Against the Omnipotent to rise in arms;
Who out of smallest things could without end
Have raised incessant armies to defeat
Thy folly; or with solitary hand
Reaching beyond all limit, at one blow   140
Unaided could have finished thee, and whelmed
Thy legions under darkness; but thou seest
All are not of thy train; there be who faith
Prefer, and piety to God, though then
To thee not visible, when I alone
Seemed in thy world erroneous to dissent
From all. My sect thou seest; now learn too late
How few sometimes may know, when thousands err.'
    "Whom the grand Foe with scornful eye askance
Thus answered. 'Ill for thee, but in wished hour   150
Of my revenge, first sought for thou return'st
From flight, seditious angel, to receive
Thy merited reward, the first assay
Of this right hand provoked, since first that tongue
Inspired with contradiction durst oppose
A third part of the gods, in synod met
Their deities to assert, who while they feel

    115. realty, reality. There is no true likeness between Satan and God.
    118. to sight, to all appearances.

Vigor divine within them, can allow
Omnipotence to none. But well thou com'st
Before thy fellows, ambitious to win   160
From me some plume, that thy success may show
Destruction to the rest. This pause between
(Unanswered lest thou boast) to let thee know:
At first I thought that liberty and Heaven
To heavenly souls had been all one; but now
I see that most through sloth had rather serve,
Ministering spirits, trained up in feast and song;
Such hast thou armed, the minstrelsy of Heaven,
Servility with freedom to contend,
As both their deeds compared this day shall prove.'   170
    "To whom in brief thus Abdiel stern replied.
'Apostate, still thou err'st, nor end wilt find
Of erring, from the path of truth remote:
Unjustly thou depravest it with the name
Of servitude to serve whom God ordains,
Or Nature; God and Nature bid the same,
When he who rules is worthiest, and excels
Them whom he governs. This is servitude,
To serve the unwise, or him who hath rebelled
Against his worthier, as thine now serve thee,   180
Thyself not free, but to thyself enthralled;
Yet lewdly darest our ministering upbraid.
Reign thou in Hell thy kingdom, let me serve
In Heaven God ever blest, and his divine
Behests obey, worthiest to be obeyed,
Yet chains in Hell, not realms expect. Meanwhile,
From me returned, as erst thou saidst, from flight,
This greeting on thy impious crest receive.'
    "So saying, a noble stroke he lifted high,
Which hung not, but so swift with tempest fell   190
On the proud crest of Satan, that no sight
Nor motion of swift thought, less could his shield
Such ruin intercept. Ten paces huge
He back recoiled; the tenth on bended knee
His massy spear upstayed; as if on Earth
Winds under ground or waters forcing way
Sidelong had pushed a mountain from his seat,
Half sunk with all his pines. Amazement seized
The rebel Thrones, but greater rage to see
Thus foiled their mightiest; ours joy filled, and shout,   200
Presage of victory and fierce desire

196. **Winds under ground.** Subterranean winds were held to be the
cause of earthquakes.

Of battle: whereat Michael bid sound
The Archangel trumpet; through the vast of Heaven
It sounded, and the faithful armies rung
Hosannah to the Highest; nor stood at gaze
The adverse legions, nor less hideous joined
The horrid shock. Now storming fury rose,
And clamor such as heard in Heaven till now
Was never; arms on armor clashing brayed
Horrible discord, and the madding wheels   210
Of brazen chariots raged; dire was the noise
Of conflict; overhead the dismal hiss
Of fiery darts in flaming volleys flew,
And flying vaulted either host with fire.
So under fiery cope together rushed
Both battles main, with ruinous assault
And inextinguishable rage; all Heaven
Resounded, and had Earth been then, all Earth
Had to her center shook. What wonder? when
Millions of fierce encountering angels fought   220
On either side, the least of whom could wield
These elements, and arm him with the force
Of all their regions: how much more of power
Army against army numberless to raise
Dreadful combustion warring, and disturb,
Though not destroy, their happy native seat;
Had not the Eternal King Omnipotent
From his strong hold of Heaven high overruled
And limited their might; though numbered such
As each divided legion might have seemed   230
A numerous host, in strength each armèd hand
A legion; led in fight, yet leader seemed
Each warrior single as in chief, expert
When to advance, or stand, or turn the sway
Of battle, open when, and when to close
The ridges of grim war; no thought of flight,
None of retreat, no unbecoming deed
That argued fear; each on himself relied,
As only in his arm the moment lay
Of victory; deeds of eternal fame   240
Were done, but infinite; for wide was spread
That war and various; sometimes on firm ground
A standing fight; then soaring on main wing

216. **Both battles main,** the main battle lines of both sides.
229. Johnson in his *Life of Milton* points out the poetic absurdity of the
war in Heaven, which rages so terrifically yet lies in the hollow of God's
hand.

Tormented all the air; all air seemed then
Conflicting fire. Long time in even scale
The battle hung; till Satan, who that day
Prodigious power had shown, and met in arms
No equal, ranging through the dire attack
Of fighting Seraphim confused, at length
Saw where the sword of Michael smote, and felled   250
Squadrons at once, with huge two-handed sway
Brandished aloft the horrid edge came down
Wide-wasting; such destruction to withstand
He hasted, and opposed the rocky orb
Of tenfold adamant, his ample shield,
A vast circumference. At his approach
The great Archangel from his warlike toil
Surceased, and glad as hoping here to end
Intestine war in Heaven, the Arch-foe subdued
Or captive dragged in chains, with hostile frown   260
And visage all inflamed first thus began.
    "'Author of evil, unknown till thy revolt,
Unnamed in Heaven, now plenteous as thou seest
These acts of hateful strife, hateful to all,
Though heaviest by just measure on thyself
And thy adherents: how hast thou disturbed
Heaven's blessèd peace, and into Nature brought
Misery, uncreated till the crime
Of thy rebellion! how hast thou instilled
Thy malice into thousands, once upright   270
And faithful, now proved false! But think not here
To trouble holy rest; Heaven casts thee out
From all her confines; Heaven, the seat of bliss,
Brooks not the works of violence and war.
Hence then, and evil go with thee along,
Thy offspring, to the place of evil, Hell,
Thou and thy wicked crew! there mingle broils,
Ere this avenging sword begin thy doom,
Or some more sudden vengeance winged from God
Precipitate thee with augmented pain.'   280
    "So spake the Prince of Angels; to whom thus
The Adversary. 'Nor think thou with wind
Of airy threats to awe whom yet with deeds
Thou canst not. Hast thou turned the least of these
To flight, or if to fall, but that they rise
Unvanquished, easier to transact with me,

286. Do you expect it to be easier to deal with me than with them?
The grammar is difficult but Miltonic. Milton starts to say: "Has your
experience with the others given you any reason to hope that you will find

That thou shouldst hope, imperious, and with threats
To chase me hence? Err not that so shall end
The strife which thou call'st evil, but we style
The strife of glory; which we mean to win,   290
Or turn this Heaven itself into the Hell
Thou fablest; here however to dwell free,
If not to reign. Meanwhile, thy utmost force
(And join him named Almighty to thy aid)
I fly not, but have sought thee far and nigh.'
    "They ended parle, and both addressed for fight
Unspeakable; for who, though with the tongue
Of angels, can relate, or to what things
Liken on Earth conspicuous, that may lift
Human imagination to such height   300
Of godlike power; for likest gods they seemed,
Stood they or moved, in stature, motion, arms,
Fit to decide the empire of great Heaven.
Now waved their fiery swords, and in the air
Made horrid circles; two broad suns their shields
Blazed opposite, while expectation stood
In horror; from each hand with speed retired,
Where erst was thickest fight, the angelic throng,
And left large field, unsafe within the wind
Of such commotion; such as (to set forth   310
Great things by small) if, Nature's concord broke,
Among the constellations war were sprung,
Two planets rushing from aspéct malign
Of fiercest opposition in mid sky,
Should combat, and their jarring spheres confound.
Together both with next to almighty arm
Uplifted imminent, one stroke they aimed
That might determine, and not need repeat,
As not of power, at once; nor odds appeared
In might or swift prevention. But the sword   320
Of Michael from the armory of God

it easier to transact with me?" But then, ignoring the fact that an object has
already been supplied for the phrase "that thou should'st hope," he goes on
to supply another: "to chase me hence." These changes in construction are
a feature of Milton's style and do not ordinarily give trouble, though this
one does.
    288. Err not, do not make the mistake of thinking.
    313–14. Planets opposite in the Zodiac were at an unfortunate angle
with reference to their influence on earth. This is their "malign aspect."
Milton imagines them as leaving their stations and running angrily against
each other.
    320. prevention, readiness to anticipate the stroke of the opponent by
striking first.

Was given him tempered so, that neither keen
Nor solid might resist that edge. It met
The sword of Satan, with steep force to smite
Descending, and in half cut sheer, nor stayed,
But with swift wheel reverse, deep entering sheared
All his right side; then Satan first knew pain,
And writhed him to and fro convolved; so sore
The griding sword with discontinuous wound
Passed through him; but the ethereal substance closed   330
Not long divisible, and from the gash
A stream of nectarous humor issuing flowed
Sanguine, such as celestial spirits may bleed,
And all his armor stained erewhile so bright.
Forthwith on all sides to his aid was run
By angels many and strong, who interposed
Defence, while others bore him on their shields
Back to his chariot, where it stood retired
From off the files of war; there they him laid
Gnashing for anguish and despite and shame   340
To find himself not matchless, and his pride
Humbled by such rebuke, so far beneath
His confidence to equal God in power.
Yet soon he healed; for spirits, that live throughout
Vital in every part, not as frail Man
In entrails, heart or head, liver or reins,
Cannot but by annihilating die;
Nor in their liquid texture mortal wound
Receive, no more than can the fluid air.
All heart they live, all head, all eye, all ear,   350
All intellect, all sense; and as they please
They limb themselves, and color, shape, or size
Assume, as likes them best, condense or rare.
"Meanwhile in other parts like deeds deserved
Memorial, where the might of Gabriel fought,
And with fierce ensigns pierced the deep array
Of Moloch furious king, who him defied,
And at his chariot wheels to drag him bound
Threatened, nor from the Holy One of Heaven
Refrained his tongue blasphemous; but anon   360
Down cloven to the waist, with shattered arms
And uncouth pain fled bellowing. On each wing
Uriel and Raphael his vaunting foe,
Though huge and in a rock of diamond armed,

329. **griding,** "cutting keenly and painfully through," N.E.D. **discontinuous,** separating the flesh so that it is not continuous.
335. **was run,** translating the Latin passive tense, used impersonally.

Vanquished, Adramelech and Asmadai,
Two potent Thrones, that to be less than gods
Disdained, but meaner thoughts learned in their flight,
Mangled with ghastly wounds through plate and mail;
Nor stood unmindful Abdiel to annoy
The atheist crew, but with redoubled blow,   370
Ariel and Arioch, and the violence
Of Ramiel, scorched and blasted, overthrew.
I might relate of thousands, and their names
Eternize here on Earth; but those elect
Angels, contented with their fame in Heaven,
Seek not the praise of men: the other sort
In might though wondrous and in acts of war,
Nor of renown less eager, yet by doom
Cancelled from Heaven and sacred memory,
Nameless in dark oblivion let them dwell.   380
For strength from truth divided and from just,
Illaudable, nought merits but dispraise
And ignominy, yet to glory aspires
Vain-glorious, and through infamy seeks fame.
Therefore eternal silence be their doom.
    "And now their mightiest quelled, the battle swerved,
With many an inroad gored; deformèd rout
Entered, and foul disorder; all the ground
With shivered armor strown, and on a heap
Chariot and charioter lay overturned   390
And fiery foaming steeds; what stood, recoiled
O'er-wearied, through the faint Satanic host,
Defensive scarce, or with pale fear surprised,
Then first with fear surprised and sense of pain,
Fled ignominious, to such evil brought
By sin of disobedience, till that hour
Not liable to fear or flight or pain.
Far otherwise the inviolable saints
In cubic phalanx firm advanced entire,
Invulnerable, impenetrably armed: 400
Such high advantages their innocence
Gave them above their foes, not to have sinned,
Not to have disobeyed; in fight they stood
Unwearied, unobnoxious to be pained
By wound, though from their place by violence moved.
    "Now Night her course began, and over Heaven
Inducing darkness, grateful truce imposed,
And silence on the odious din of war;

368. **plate and mail,** plate and chain armor.
404. **unobnoxious,** not liable to injury.

Under her cloudy covert both retired,
Victor and vanquished. On the foughten field   410
Michael and his angels prevalent
Encamping placed in guard their watches round,
Cherubic waving fires; on the other part
Satan with his rebellious disappeared,
Far in the dark dislodged, and void of rest,
His potentates to council called by night,
And in the midst thus undismayed began.
 "'O now in danger tried, now known in arms
Not to be overpowered, companions dear,
Found worthy not of liberty alone,   420
Too mean pretence, but what we more affect,
Honor, dominion, glory, and renown;
Who have sustained one day in doubtful fight
(And if one day, why not eternal days?)
What Heaven's Lord had powerfullest to send
Against us from about his throne, and judged
Sufficient to subdue us to his will,
But proves not so. Then fallible, it seems,
Of future we may deem him, though till now
Omniscient thought. True is, less firmly armed,   430
Some disadvantage we endured and pain,
Till now not known, but known, as soon contemned,
Since now we find this our empyreal form
Incapable of mortal injury,
Imperishable and though pierced with wound,
Soon closing, and by native vigor healed.
Of evil then so small, as easy think
The remedy: perhaps more valid arms,
Weapons more violent, when next we meet,
May serve to better us, and worse our foes,   440
Or equal what between us made the odds,
In nature none. If other hidden cause
Left them superior, while we can preserve
Unhurt our minds, and understanding sound,
Due search and consultation will disclose.'
 "He sat; and in the assembly next upstood
Nisroch, of Principalities the prime;
As one he stood escaped from cruel fight,
Sore toiled, his riven arms to havoc hewn,
And cloudy in aspéct thus answering spake.   450
 "'Deliverer from new Lords, leader to free
Enjoyment of our right as gods; yet hard

411. prevalent, prevailing, victorious.
421. pretence, pretension, object of aspiration.

For gods, and too unequal work we find
Against unequal arms to fight in pain,
Against unpained, impassive; from which evil
Ruin must needs ensue; for what avails
Valor or strength, though matchless, quelled with pain
Which all subdues, and makes remiss the hands
Of mightiest. Sense of pleasure we may well
Spare out of life perhaps, and not repine,   460
But live content, which is the calmest life;
But pain is perfect misery, the worst
Of evils, and, excessive, overturns
All patience. He who therefore can invent
With what more forcible we may offend
Our yet unwounded enemies, or arm
Ourselves with like defence, to me deserves
No less than for deliverance what we owe.'
   "Whereto with look composed Satan replied:
'Not uninvented that which thou aright   470
Believest so main to our success, I bring.
Which of us who beholds the bright surface
Of this ethereous mould whereon we stand,
This continent of spacious Heaven, adorned
With plant, fruit, flower ambrosial, gems and gold,
Whose eye so superficially surveys
These things, as not to mind from whence they grow
Deep under ground, materials dark and crude,
Of spiritous and fiery spume, till touched
With Heaven's ray, and tempered, they shoot forth   480
So beauteous, opening to the ambient light.
These in their dark nativity the Deep
Shall yield us pregnant with infernal flame;
Which into hollow engines long and round
Thick-rammed, at the other bore with touch of fire
Dilated and infuriate, shall send forth
From far with thundering noise among our foes
Such implements of mischief as shall dash
To pieces and o'erwhelm whatever stands
Adverse, that they shall fear we have disarmed   490
The Thunderer of his only dreaded bolt.

479. **spume**, froth, scum.
481. **ambient**, encompassing.
484 ff. The gunpowder episode has been objected to as inappropriate,
but it is in accordance with Milton's general idea that the war in Heaven is
a type of war on earth. Also, the infernal connotations of gunpowder were
still very strong in Milton's day. It was an "invention of the devil" in more
than a metaphorical sense. Englishmen never forgot the diabolical Gunpowder Plot, which Milton in a Latin poem traced to Satan himself.

Nor long shall be our labor; yet ere dawn
Effect shall end our wish. Meanwhile revive;
Abandon fear; to strength and counsel joined
Think nothing hard, much less to be despaired.'
    "He ended; and his words their drooping cheer
Enlightened, and their languished hope revived.
The invention all admired, and each how he
To be the inventor missed; so easy it seemed
Once found, which yet unfound most would have thought   500
Impossible. Yet haply of thy race
In future days, if malice should abound,
Some one intent on mischief, or inspired
With devilish machination, might devise
Like instrument to plague the sons of men
For sin, on war and mutual slaughter bent.
Forthwith from council to the work they flew,
None arguing stood, innumerable hands
Were ready, in a moment up they turned
Wide the celestial soil, and saw beneath   510
The originals of Nature in their crude
Conception; sulphurous and nitrous foam
They found, they mingled, and with subtle art,
Concocted and adusted, they reduced
To blackest grain, and into store conveyed.
Part hidden veins digged up (nor hath this Earth
Entrails unlike) of mineral and stone,
Whereof to found their engines and their balls
Of missive ruin; part incentive reed
Provide, pernicious with one touch to fire.   520
So all ere day-spring, under conscious night
Secret they finished, and in order set
With silent circumspection, unespied.
    "Now when fair Morn orient in Heaven appeared
Up rose the victor angels, and to arms
The matin trumpet sung; in arms they stood
Of golden panoply, refulgent host,
Soon banded; others from the dawning hills
Looked round, and scouts each coast light-armèd scour,
Each quarter, to descry the distant foe,   530
Where lodged, or whither fled, or if for fight,
In motion or in halt. Him soon they met

493. Our wish will be given effect.
494. When strength and wisdom are united nothing is hard or to be
despaired of.
514. adusted, reduced to ashes.
519. missive ruin, destruction sent as a missile; incentive, kindling.

Under spread ensigns moving nigh, in slow
But firm battalion; back with speediest sail
Zophiel, of Cherubim the swiftest wing,
Came flying, and in mid air aloud thus cried:
   " 'Arm, warriors, arm for fight; the foe at hand,
Whom fled we thought, will save us long pursuit
This day; fear not his flight; so thick a cloud
He comes, and settled in his face I see   540
Sad resolution and secure. Let each
His adamantine coat gird well, and each
Fit well his helm, gripe fast his orbèd shield,
Borne even or high; for this day will pour down,
If I conjecture aught, no drizzling shower,
But rattling storms of arrows barbed with fire.'
   "So warned he them, aware themselves, and soon
In order, quit of all impediment;
Instant without disturb they took alarm,
And onward move embattled; when behold   550
Not distant far, with heavy pace the foe
Approaching gross and huge; in hollow cube
Training his devilish enginry, impaled
On every side with shadowing squadrons deep,
To hide the fraud. At interview both stood
A while; but suddenly at head appeared
Satan; and thus was heard commanding loud.
   " 'Vanguard, to right and left the front unfold;
That all may see who hate us, how we seek
Peace and composure, and with open breast   560
Stand ready to receive them, if they like
Our overture, and turn not back perverse;
But that I doubt; however, witness Heaven,
Heaven witness thou anon, while we discharge
Freely our part. Ye who appointed stand,
Do as you have in charge, and briefly touch
What we propound, and loud that all may hear.'
   "So scoffing in ambiguous words, he scarce
Had ended, when to right and left the front
Divided, and to either flank retired;   570
Which to our eyes discovered, new and strange,

548. impediment, Latin *impedimenta,* baggage.
552 ff. Milton found a description of this formation, a hollow square masking artillery, in one of his military authorities. He had studied the technicalities of the art of war, as it was natural for a humanistic scholar to do, and he taught the subject in his school.
553. impaled, surrounded.
555. At interview, confronting each other.
560. composure, composition, agreement.

A triple-mounted row of pillars laid
On wheels (for like to pillars most they seemed
Or hollowed bodies made of oak or fir
With branches lopped, in wood or mountain felled),
Brass, iron, stony mould, had not their mouths
With hideous orifice gaped on us wide,
Portending hollow truce. At each behind
A Seraph stood, and in his hand a reed
Stood waving tipped with fire; while we suspense,   580
Collected stood within our thoughts amused;
Not long, for sudden all at once their reeds
Put forth, and to a narrow vent applied
With nicest touch. Immediate in a flame,
But soon obscured with smoke, all Heaven appeared,
From those deep-throated engines belched, whose roar
Embowelled with outrageous noise the air,
And all her entrails tore, disgorging foul
Their devilish glut, chained thunderbolts and hail
Of iron globes, which on the victor host   590
Levelled, with such impetuous fury smote,
That whom they hit none on their feet might stand,
Though standing else as rocks, but down they fell
By thousands, Angel on Archangel rolled;
The sooner for their arms; unarmed they might
Have easily as spirits evaded swift
By quick contraction or remove; but now
Foul dissipation followed and forced rout;
Nor served it to relax their serried files.
What should they do? If on they rushed, repulse   600
Repeated, and indecent overthrow
Doubled, would render them yet more despised,
And to their foes a laughter; for in view
Stood ranked of Seraphim another row
In posture to displode their second tire

576. **brass, iron, stony mould.** Milton does not decide what substance the cannon were made of. They are ideal, abstract cannon. Their earthly replicas must be made of one substance or the other.

581. **amused,** puzzled. The packing of the line with meaning is characteristic. The angels were in a state of suspense or uncertainty; they stood together and with composure of mind ("collected" apparently has this double force); they were confused as to what was going to happen (taking "within our thoughts" as going both with "stood collected" and "amused").

587. **embowelled,** disembowelled.

598. **dissipation,** dispersion.

605. **tire,** probably tier, the technical term for a row of guns, but the spelling suggests French *tirer,* to fire, and the sense is sometimes given as "volley."

Of thunder; back defeated to return
They worse abhorred. Satan beheld their plight,
And to his mates thus in derision called.
　"'O friends, why come not on these victors proud?   610
Erewhile they fierce were coming; and when we,
To entertain them fair with open front
And breast (what could we more?), propounded terms
Of composition, straight they changed their minds,
Flew off, and into strange vagaries fell,
As they would dance; yet for a dance they seemed
Somewhat extravagant and wild, perhaps
For joy of offered peace. But I suppose
If our proposals once again were heard,
We should compel them to a quick result.'
　"To whom thus Belial, in like gamesome mood.   620
'Leader, the terms we sent were terms of weight,
Of hard contents, and full of force urged home,
Such as we might perceive amused them all,
And stumbled many; who receives them right,
Had need from head to foot well understand;
Not understood, this gift they have besides,
They show us when our foes walk not upright.'
　"So they among themselves in pleasant vein
Stood scoffing, heightened in their thoughts beyond
All doubt of victory; Eternal Might   630
To match with their inventions they presumed
So easy, and of his thunder made a scorn,
And all his host derided, while they stood
A while in trouble. But they stood not long;
Rage prompted them at length, and found them arms
Against such hellish mischief fit to oppose.
Forthwith (behold the excellence, the power,
Which God hath in his mighty angels placed!)
Their arms away they threw, and to the hills
(For earth hath this variety from Heaven   640
Of pleasure situate in hill and dale)
Light as the lightning glimpse they ran, they flew;
From their foundations loosening to and fro
They plucked the seated hills with all their load,
Rocks, waters, woods, and by the shaggy tops

　　625. understand, in the double meaning of comprehend and be supported.
　　630. doubt, fear.
　　640–41. Earth derives from Heaven its pleasing variety of hill and dale.
Cf. the "grateful vicissitude" of day and night which exists in Heaven as on
Earth (VI, 8). In Book V, lines 574–76, the doctrine of the analogy
between heavenly and earthly forms is stated explicitly.

Uplifting bore them in their hands. Amaze,
Be sure, and terror seized the rebel host,
When coming towards them so dread they saw
The bottom of the mountains upward turned;
Till on those cursèd engines' triple-row   650
They saw them whelmed, and all their confidence
Under the weight of mountains buried deep,
Themselves invaded next, and on their heads
Main promontories flung, which in the air
Came shadowing, and oppressed whole legions armed;
Their armor helped their harm, crushed in and bruised
Into their substance pent, which wrought them pain
Implacable, and many a dolorous groan,
Long struggling underneath, ere they could wind
Out of such prison, though spirits of purest light,   660
Purest at first, now gross by sinning grown.
The rest in imitation to like arms
Betook them, and the neighboring hills uptore;
So hills amid the air encountered hills,
Hurled to and fro with jaculation dire,
That underground they fought in dismal shade;
Infernal noise; war seemed a civil game
To this uproar; horrid confusion heaped
Upon confusion rose. And now all Heaven
Had gone to wrack, with ruin overspread,   670
Had not the Almighty Father, where he sits
Shrined in his sanctuary of Heaven secure,
Consulting on the sum of things, foreseen
This tumult, and permitted all, advised;
That his great purpose he might so fulfil,
To honor his anointed Son avenged
Upon his enemies, and to declare
All power on him transferred; whence to his Son,
The assessor of his throne, he thus began.
    " 'Effulgence of my glory, Son beloved,   680
Son in whose face invisible is beheld
Visibly, what by Deity I am,
And in whose hand what by decree I do,
Second Omnipotence, two days are passed,
Two days, as we compute the days of Heaven,
Since Michael and his powers went forth to tame
These disobedient; sore hath been their fight,
As likeliest was when two such foes met armed;
For to themselves I left them; and thou know'st,

674. advised, advisedly.
679. assessor, one who sits beside another, fellow-occupant.

Equal in their creation they were formed,
Save what sin hath impaired, which yet hath wrought   690
Insensibly, for I suspend their doom;
Whence in perpetual fight they needs must last
Endless, and no solution will be found.
War wearied hath performed what war can do,
And to disordered rage let loose the reins,
With mountains as with weapons armed, which makes
Wild work in Heaven, and dangerous to the main.
Two days are therefore passed, the third is thine;
For thee I have ordained it, and thus far   700
Have suffered, that the glory may be thine
Of ending this great war, since none but thou
Can end it. Into thee such virtue and grace
Immense I have transfused, that all may know
In Heaven and Hell thy power above compare,
And this perverse commotion governed thus,
To manifest thee worthiest to be Heir
Of all things, to be Heir and to be King
By sacred unction, thy deservèd right.
Go then thou Mightiest in thy Father's might,   710
Ascend my chariot, guide the rapid wheels
That shake Heaven's basis, bring forth all my war,
My bow and thunder, my almighty arms
Gird on, and sword upon thy puissant thigh;
Pursue these sons of Darkness, drive them out
From all Heaven's bounds into the utter deep;
There let them learn, as likes them, to despise
God and Messiah his anointed King.'
    "He said, and on his Son with rays direct
Shone full; he all his Father full expressed   720
Ineffably into his face received
And thus the Filial Godhead answering spake.
    " 'O Father, O Supreme of Heavenly Thrones,
First, Highest, Holiest, Best, thou always seek'st
To glorify thy Son, I always thee,

692. Insensibly. Sin makes them unequal to the loyal angels, but its
effects are not yet apparent. Cf. Milton's idea of the gradual impairment
of Satan's beauty.
    695 ff. Cf. Sonnet to Fairfax: "For what can war but endless war still
breed." Milton's war in Heaven is the symbol and prototype of all war, in
its destructiveness and futility. It begins by having some of the trappings of
romance and qualities of heroism, moves on toward inhumanity, and ends
in chaos. This, however, is necessary, and Milton, unlike his Quaker
friends, recognizes such necessity in his discussion of war in *Of Christian
Doctrine*.
    698. main, mainland, i.e., the whole continent of Heaven. Cf. "Span-
ish main."

As is most just; this I my glory account,
My exaltation, and my whole delight,
That thou in me well pleased, declar'st thy will
Fulfilled, which to fulfil is all my bliss.
Scepter and power, thy giving, I assume,   730
And gladlier shall resign, when in the end
Thou shalt be All in All, and I in thee
For ever, and in me all whom thou lovest;
But whom thou hat'st, I hate, and can put on
Thy terrors, as I put thy mildness on,
Image of thee in all things; and shall soon,
Armed with thy might, rid Heaven of these rebelled,
To their prepared ill mansion driven down,
To chains of darkness, and the undying worm,
That from thy just obedience could revolt,   740
Whom to obey is happiness entire.
Then shall thy saints, unmixed, and from the impure
Far separate, circling thy holy mount,
Unfeigned halleluiahs to thee sing,
Hymns of high praise, and I among them chief.'
    "So said, he o'er his scepter bowing, rose
From the right hand of Glory where he sat
And the third sacred morn began to shine
Dawning through Heaven. Forth rushed with whirlwind sound
The chariot of Paternal Deity,   750
Flashing thick flames, wheel within wheel, undrawn,
Itself instinct with spirit, but convoyed
By four Cherubic shapes. Four faces each
Had wondrous; as with stars, their bodies all
And wings were set with eyes; with eyes the wheels
Of beryl, and careering fires between:
Over their heads a crystal firmament,
Whereon a sapphire throne, inlaid with pure
Amber, and colors of the showery arch.
He in celestial panoply all armed   760
Of radiant Urim, work divinely wrought,
Ascended, at his right hand Victory
Sat eagle-winged, beside him hung his bow

749 ff. The description is based on the first chapter of Ezekiel, where,
however, there are wheels but no chariot. Milton had earlier, in *Apology
for Smectymnuus,* transformed Ezekiel's vision into a symbol of his own.
See Hughes's note.
    752. instinct, animated and impelled.
    761. Urim, precious stones worn in the breastplate of the Jewish high
priest. Exod. 28:30.
    762 ff. Milton mingles classical and biblical imagery. Christ wields
thunderbolts like Jupiter, and Victory sits beside him.

And quiver with three-bolted thunder stored,
And from about him fierce effusion rolled
Of smoke, and bickering flame, and sparkles dire;
Attended with ten thousand thousand saints,
He onward came, far off his coming shone,
And twenty thousand (I their number heard)
Chariots of God, half on each hand, were seen.   770
He on the wings of Cherub rode sublime
On the crystalline sky, in sapphire throned,
Illustrious far and wide, but by his own
First seen; them unexpected joy surprised,
When the great ensign of Messiah blazed
Aloft by angels borne, his sign in Heaven;
Under whose conduct Michael soon reduced
His army, circumfused on either wing,
Under their Head embodied all in one.
Before him Power Divine his way prepared;   780
At his command the uprooted hills retired
Each to his place, they heard his voice and went
Obsequious, Heaven his wonted face renewed,
And with fresh flowerets hill and valley smiled.
   "This saw his hapless foes, but stood obdured,
And to rebellious fight rallied their powers
Insensate, hope conceiving from despair.
In heavenly spirits could such perverseness dwell?
But to convince the proud what signs avail,
Or wonders move the obdurate to relent?   790
They hardened more by what might most reclaim,
Grieving to see his glory, at the sight
Took envy, and aspiring to his height,   envy
Stood re-embattled fierce, by force or fraud
Weening to prosper, and at length prevail
Against God and Messiah, or to fall
In universal ruin last, and now
To final battle drew, disdaining flight,
Or faint retreat; when the great Son of God
To all his host on either hand thus spake.   800

   771-72. "And above the firmament that was over their heads was the
likeness of a throne, as the appearance of a sapphire stone." Ezek. 1:26.
   771. Cf. II Sam. 22:11: "And he rode upon a cherub, and did fly."
The total picture is elaborate in the highest degree and reminds us of the
ornate religious painting of the seventeenth century.
   777. reduced, led back.
   778. circumfused, spread out, deployed.
   783. Obsequious, obedient.
   791. what might most reclaim, i.e., the presence of Christ, the Redeemer.

" 'Stand still in bright array ye Saints, here stand
Ye angels armed, this day from battle rest;
Faithful hath been your warfare, and of God
Accepted, fearless in his righteous cause,
And as ye have received, so have ye done
Invincibly. But of this cursèd crew
The punishment to other hand belongs:
Vengeance is his, or whose he sole appoints;
Number to this day's work is not ordained
Nor multitude, stand only and behold   810
God's indignation on these godless poured
By me; not you but me they have despised,
Yet envied; against me is all their rage,
Because the Father, to whom in Heaven supreme
Kingdom and power and glory appertains,
Hath honored me according to his will.
Therefore to me their doom he hath assigned,
That they may have their wish, to try with me
In battle which the stronger proves, they all,
Or I alone against them, since by strength   820
They measure all, of other excellence
Not emulous, nor care who them excels;
Nor other strife with them do I vouchsafe.'
    "So spake the Son, and into terror changed
His countenance too severe to be beheld
And full of wrath bent on his enemies.
At once the Four spread out their starry wings
With dreadful shade contiguous, and the orbs
Of his fierce chariot rolled, as with the sound
Of torrent floods, or of a numerous host.   830
He on his impious foes right onward drove,
Gloomy as night; under his burning wheels
The steadfast Empyrean shook throughout,
All but the throne itself of God. Full soon
Among them he arrived; in his right hand
Grasping ten thousand thunders, which he sent
Before him, such as in their souls infixed
Plagues; they astonished all resistance lost,
All courage; down their idle weapons dropped;
O'er shields and helms and helmèd heads he rode   840
Of Thrones and mighty Seraphim prostrate,
That wished the mountains now might be again

832. gloomy as night, a Homeric phrase.
836. Like Zeus. Milton also has the image of Apollo in mind, as, advancing like the night, he shot the arrows of pestilence on the Greeks in
Iliad I.

Thrown on them as a shelter from his ire.
Nor less on either side tempestuous fell
His arrows, from the fourfold-visaged Four,
Distinct with eyes, and from the living wheels,
Distinct alike with multitude of eyes;
One spirit in them ruled, and every eye
Glared lightning, and shot forth pernicious fire
Among the accursed, that withered all their strength,   850
And of their wonted vigor left them drained,
Exhausted, spiritless, afflicted, fallen.
Yet half his strength he put not forth, but checked
His thunder in mid volley, for he meant
Not to destroy, but root them out of Heaven.
The overthrown he raised, and as a herd
Of goats or timorous flock together thronged,
Drove them before him thunder-struck, pursued
With terrors and with furies to the bounds
And crystal wall of Heaven, which opening wide,   860
Rolled inward, and a spacious gap disclosed
Into the wasteful deep; the monstrous sight
Strook them with horror backward, but far worse
Urged them behind; headlong themselves they threw
Down from the verge of Heaven, eternal wrath
Burned after them to the bottomless pit.
    "Hell heard the unsufferable noise, Hell saw
Heaven ruining from Heaven, and would have fled
Affrighted; but strict Fate had cast too deep
Her dark foundations, and too fast had bound.   870
Nine days they fell; confounded Chaos roared,
And felt tenfold confusion in their fall
Through his wild anarchy, so huge a rout
Encumbered him with ruin. Hell at last
Yawning received them whole, and on them closed,
Hell, their fit habitation, fraught with fire
Unquenchable, the house of woe and pain.
Disburdened Heaven rejoiced, and soon repaired
Her mural breach, returning whence it rolled.
Sole victor, from the expulsion of his foes   880
Messiah his triumphal chariot turned.
To meet him all his saints, who silent stood
Eye-witnesses of his almighty acts,
With jubilee advanced; and as they went,

846. **distinct,** marked, adorned.
866. This line is unique in its metrical irregularity and effectiveness.
881. Is the Messiah in the chariot or above, inspiring its motions? Cf.
line 889 below.

Shaded with branching palm, each order bright,
Sung triumph, and him sung victorious King,
Son, Heir, and Lord, to him dominion given,
Worthiest to reign. He celebrated rode
Triumphant through mid Heaven, into the courts
And temple of his mighty Father throned   890
On high; who into glory him received,
Where now he sits at the right hand of bliss.
    "Thus measuring things in Heaven by things on Earth,
At thy request, and that thou may'st beware
By what is past, to thee I have revealed
What might have else to human race been hid:
The discord which befell, and war in Heaven
Among the angelic powers, and the deep fall
Of those too high aspiring, who rebelled
With Satan, he who envies now thy state,   900
Who now is plotting how he may seduce
Thee also from obedience, that with him
Bereaved of happiness, thou may'st partake
His punishment, eternal misery;
Which would be all his solace and revenge,
As a despite done against the Most High,
Thee once to gain companion of his woe.
But listen not to his temptations; warn
Thy weaker; let it profit thee to have heard
By terrible example, the reward   910
Of disobedience. Firm they might have stood,
Yet fell; remember, and fear to transgress."

BOOK VII

THE ARGUMENT

    Raphael, at the request of Adam, relates how and wherefore
this World was first created: that God, after the expelling of
Satan and his angels out of Heaven, declared his pleasure to
create another World, and other creatures to dwell therein; sends
his Son with glory, and attendance of angels, to perform the work
of creation in six days: the angels celebrate with hymns the performance thereof, and his reascension into Heaven.

    901. **who now is plotting.** The story has been told in pursuance of the
angel's mission to warn Adam.
    909. **Thy weaker,** Eve, "the weaker vessel."

Descend from Heaven Urania, by that name   *Urania*
If rightly thou art called, whose voice divine
Following, above the Olympian hill I soar,
Above the flight of Pegasean wing.
The meaning, not the name I call; for thou
Nor of the Muses nine, nor on the top
Of old Olympus dwell'st, but heavenly born,
Before the hills appeared or fountain flowed,
Thou with eternal Wisdom didst converse,
Wisdom thy sister, and with her didst play   10
In presence of the Almighty Father, pleased
With thy celestial song. Up led by thee
Into the Heaven of Heavens I have presumed,
An earthly guest, and drawn empyreal air,
Thy tempering; with like safety guided down,
Return me to my native element,
Lest from this flying steed unreined (as once
Bellerophon, though from a lower clime)
Dismounted, on the Aleian field I fall,
Erroneous there to wander and forlorn.   20
Half yet remains unsung, but narrower bound
Within the visible diurnal sphere;
Standing on Earth, not rapt above the pole,
More safe I sing with mortal voice, unchanged
To hoarse or mute, though fallen on evil days,
On evil days though fallen, and evil tongues;
In darkness, and with dangers compassed round,
And solitude; yet not alone, while thou
Visit'st my slumbers nightly, or when morn
Purples the east. Still govern thou my song,   30
Urania, and fit audience find, though few.

1. Milton again invokes the Heavenly Muse (Cf. I, 1 ff.), greatly en-
riching the conception out of biblical and neo-Platonic tradition. In calling
her sister Wisdom, he reminds the reader of Prov. 8:29-30: "When he
gave the sea his decree, that the waters should not pass his commandment:
when he appointed the foundations of the earth: Then was I Wisdom by
him: and I was daily his delight, rejoicing always before him." The poet
identifies his own inspiration with that of the great bards of antiquity,
according to the analysis in Plato's dialogue, Ion, but particularly with that
of Moses and the Prophets, who wrote under the direct guidance of the
Holy Spirit.

4. Higher than the flight of Pegasus.

18. **Bellerophon**, the Greek hero who attempted to fly to Olympus on
the winged horse but was thrown down by Jupiter onto the Aleian marshes
in Lycia.

25. A clear reference to Milton's position after the Restoration. His
name was invariably referred to with execration, and the danger for a time
was real.

But drive far off the barbarous dissonance
Of Bacchus and his revellers, the race
Of that wild rout that tore the Thracian bard
In Rhodope, where woods and rocks had ears
To rapture, till the savage clamor drowned
Both harp and voice; nor could the Muse defend
Her son. So fail not thou who thee implores;
For thou art heavenly, she an empty dream.
    Say Goddess, what ensued when Raphael,   40
The affable Archangel, had forewarned
Adam by dire example to beware
Apostasy, by what befell in Heaven
To those apostates, lest the like befall
In Paradise to Adam or his race,
Charged not to touch the interdicted tree,
If they transgress, and slight that sole command,
So easily obeyed amid the choice
Of all tastes else to please their appetite,
Though wandering. He with his consorted Eve   50
The story heard attentive, and was filled
With admiration and deep muse to hear
Of things so high and strange, things to their thought
So unimaginable as hate in Heaven,
And war so near the peace of God in bliss,
With such confusion; but the evil soon
Driven back redounded as a flood on those
From whom it sprung, impossible to mix
With blessedness. Whence Adam soon repealed
The doubts that in his heart arose; and now   60
Led on, yet sinless, with desire to know
What nearer might concern him, how this World
Of Heaven and Earth conspicuous first began;
When, and whereof created, for what cause,
What within Eden or without was done
Before his memory, as one whose drouth
Yet scarce allayed still eyes the current stream,

    34 ff. Milton had already in "Lycidas" used the myth of Orpheus, torn
to pieces by the followers of Bacchus, as a symbol of the poet in a hostile
world. The "barbarous dissonance" may refer more specifically to the
crowds of rioters who were a menace in the London streets in the reign of
Charles II. Orpheus' mother was the muse Calliope.
    59. repealed, as one repeals a law. The doubts which have arisen in
his mind concern the moral structure of the universe. With the reflection
that the evil in Heaven has promptly recoiled on its originators, leaving
God untouched by it, these doubts are canceled and he goes on to ask about
things which concern him more immediately than such speculation.
    63. conspicuous, visible, as distinguished from the celestial realm.

Whose liquid murmur heard new thirst excites,
Proceeded thus to ask his heavenly guest.
   "Great things, and full of wonder in our ears,   70
Far differing from this World, thou hast revealed
Divine interpreter, by favor sent
Down from the Empyrean to forewarn
Us timely of what might else have been our loss,
Unknown, which human knowledge could not reach;
For which to the infinitely Good we owe
Immortal thanks, and his admonishment
Receive with solemn purpose to observe
Immutably his sovran will, the end
Of what we are. But since thou hast vouchsafed   80
Gently for our instruction to impart
Things above earthly thought, which yet concerned
Our knowing, as to highest Wisdom seemed,
Deign to descend now lower, and relate
What may no less perhaps avail us known:
How first began this heaven which we behold
Distant so high, with moving fires adorned
Innumerable, and this which yields or fills
All space, the ambient air wide interfused
Embracing round this florid Earth; what cause   90
Moved the Creator in his holy rest
Through all eternity so late to build
In Chaos, and the work begun, how soon
Absolved, if unforbid thou may'st unfold
What we, not to explore the secrets ask
Of his eternal empire, but the more
To magnify his works, the more we know.
And the great light of day yet wants to run
Much of his race though steep; suspense in heaven
Held by thy voice, thy potent voice he hears,   100
And longer will delay to hear thee tell
His generation, and the rising birth
Of Nature from the unapparent Deep.
Or if the star of evening and the moon
Haste to thy audience, Night with her will bring
Silence, and Sleep listening to thee will watch,
Or we can bid his absence, till thy song
End, and dismiss thee ere the morning shine."
   Thus Adam his illustrious guest besought;
And thus the godlike angel answered mild.   110

99. **suspense,** suspended.
106. **watch,** stay awake.

Raphael

"This also thy request with caution asked
Obtain; though to recount almighty works
What words or tongue of Seraph can suffice,
Or heart of man suffice to comprehend?
Yet what thou canst attain, which best may serve
To glorify the Maker, and infer
Thee also happier, shall not be withheld
Thy hearing, such commission from above
I have received, to answer thy desire
Of knowledge within bounds; beyond abstain   120
To ask, nor let thine own inventions hope
Things not revealed, which the invisible King,
Only omniscient, hath suppressed in night,
To none communicable in Earth or Heaven:
Enough is left besides to search and know.
But knowledge is as food, and needs no less
Her temperance over appetite, to know
In measure what the mind may well contain,
Oppresses else with surfeit, and soon turns
Wisdom to folly, as nourishment to wind.   130
    "Know then, that after Lucifer from Heaven
(So call him, brighter once amidst the host
Of angels than that star the stars among)
Fell with his flaming legions through the Deep
Into his place, and the great Son returned
Victorious with his saints, the omnipotent
Eternal Father from his throne beheld
Their multitude, and to his Son thus spake.
    " 'At least our envious foe hath failed, who thought
All like himself rebellious, by whose aid   140
This inaccessible high strength, the seat
Of Deity supreme, us dispossessed,
He trusted to have seized, and into fraud
Drew many, whom their place knows here no more.

God

    111. Milton takes pains to mark the exact boundary of laudable curios-
ity, remembering that Adam is to fall by eating the fruit of forbidden
knowledge.
    116. **infer**, imply, prove. Adam's request is made in a spirit of accept-
ance and its gratification will further confirm his faith. The angel takes
occasion to elaborate the distinction between useful and dangerous knowledge, which is relevant to the central event of the story. His reiteration of
the warning and Adam's repeated tendency to slip are ominous, since we
know the outcome. There is irony, too, in Adam's easy acceptance of the
principle, as there was in his ready acknowledgment of his duty of main-
taining superiority over Eve.
    131. **Lucifer**, the morning planet, literally the light-bringer. Satan is so
named in Isa. 14:12, "How art thou fallen from Heaven, O Lucifer, son of
the morning!"

Yet far the greater part have kept, I see,
Their station; Heaven, yet populous, retains
Number sufficient to possess her realms
Though wide, and this high temple to frequent
With ministeries due and solemn rites.
But lest his heart exalt him in the harm   150
Already done, to have dispeopled Heaven,
My damage fondly deemed, I can repair
That detriment, if such it be to lose
Self-lost, and in a moment will create
Another world, out of one man a race
Of men innumerable, there to dwell,
Not here, till by degrees of merit raised,
They open to themselves at length the way
Up hither, under long obedience tried,
And Earth be changed to Heaven, and Heaven to Earth,   160
One kingdom, joy and union without end.
Meanwhile inhabit lax, ye Powers of Heaven;
And thou my Word, begotten Son, by thee
This I perform; speak thou, and be it done.
My overshadowing Spirit and might with thee
I send along; ride forth, and bid the Deep
Within appointed bounds be Heaven and Earth;
Boundless the Deep, because I am who fill
Infinitude, nor vacuous the space.
Though I uncircumscribed myself retire,   170
And put not forth my goodness, which is free
To act or not, Necessity and Chance
Approach not me, and what I will is Fate.'
  "So spake the Almighty, and to what he spake
His Word, the Filial Godhead, gave effect.
Immediate are the acts of God, more swift

154. **Self-lost,** that which has lost itself, i.e., the rebel angels, who are responsible for their own loss of Heaven.
160. Though this program for humanity is frustrated by the fall, it remains possible for the individual to follow it within limits, as Adam was to learn after his repentance.
162. **inhabit lax,** take dwellings far apart to fill the vacant room of Heaven.
168 ff. God declares that the undifferentiated matter of Chaos is part of his own substance, but a part into which he has not chosen to project his spirit. The blind chance which seems to dominate it exists only by his permission. He himself is uncircumscribed by any power other than himself. What we see as fate is only a manifestation of his will.
176 ff. As in the case of the war in Heaven Raphael explains that his narrative of the creation of the world is to be regarded as a translation of unknowable reality into human terms. This is the doctrine of accommodation set forth in *Of Christian Doctrine* I. i. Milton there says that the Bible

Than time or motion, but to human ears
Cannot without process of speech be told,
So told as earthly notion can receive.
Great triumph and rejoicing was in Heaven   180
When such was heard declared the Almighty's will;
Glory they sung to the Most High, good will
To future men, and in their dwellings peace;
Glory to him whose just avenging ire
Had driven out the ungodly from his sight
And the habitations of the just; to Him
Glory and praise, whose wisdom had ordained
Good out of evil to create; instead
Of spirits malign a better race to bring
Into their vacant room, and thence diffuse   190
His good to worlds and ages infinite.
"So sang the Hierarchies. Meanwhile the Son
On his great expedition now appeared,
Girt with omnipotence, with radiance crowned
Of majesty divine, sapience and love
Immense, and all his Father in him shone.
About his chariot numberless were poured
Cherub and Seraph, Potentates and Thrones,
And Virtues, winged spirits, and chariots winged
From the armory of God, where stand of old   200
Myriads between two brazen mountains lodged
Against a solemn day, harnessed at hand,
Celestial equipage; and now came forth
Spontaneous, for within them spirit lived,
Attendant on their Lord. Heaven opened wide
Her ever-during gates, harmonious sound
On golden hinges moving, to let forth
The King of Glory in his powerful Word
And Spirit coming to create new worlds.
On heavenly ground they stood, and from the shore   210
They viewed the vast immeasurable Abyss
Outrageous as a sea, dark, wasteful, wild,
Up from the bottom turned by furious winds
And surging waves, as mountains to assault
Heaven's height, and with the center mix the pole.
   " 'Silence, ye troubled waves, and thou Deep, peace,'

is to be taken literally because God chose to reveal himself that way, but we
should remember that the real meaning is something which surpasses human
understanding. This attitude is no unsophisticated Fundamentalism.
   206 ff. There is a deliberate parallel between Christ's going forth into
Chaos to create and Satan's going forth to destroy in Book II. The reader
remembers that the gates of Hell grated harsh thunder as they opened.
   216. and thou Deep, peace. The eighteenth-century commentator,

Said then the omnific Word, 'your discord end.'
Nor stayed, but on the wings of Cherubim
Uplifted, in paternal glory rode
Far into Chaos and the World unborn;   220
For Chaos heard his voice. Him all his train
Followed in bright procession to behold
Creation, and the wonders of his might.
Then stayed the fervid wheels, and in his hand
He took the golden compasses, prepared
In God's eternal store, to circumscribe
This Universe, and all created things.
One foot he centered, and the other turned
Round through the vast profundity obscure,
And said, 'Thus far extend, thus far thy bounds,   230
This be thy just circumference, O World!'
Thus God the Heaven created, thus the Earth,
Matter unformed and void. Darkness profound
Covered the Abyss; but on the watery calm
His brooding wings the Spirit of God outspread,
And vital virtue infused, and vital warmth
Throughout the fluid mass, but downward purged
The black tartareous cold infernal dregs,
Adverse to life; then founded, then conglobed
Like things to like, the rest to several place   240
Disparted, and between spun out the air,
And Earth self-balanced on her center hung.
   " 'Let there be light,' said God; and forthwith light
Ethereal, first of things, quintessence pure,
Sprung from the Deep, and from her native east
To journey through the airy gloom began,
Sphered in a radiant cloud, for yet the sun
Was not; she in a cloudy tabernacle
Sojourned the while. God saw the light was good;

Bentley, assuming that Milton's text was tampered with, emended these
words to "and Peace, thou Deep," thereby reducing the dramatic utterance
to something ordinary.
   225. Cf. Prov. 8:27: "He set a compass upon the face of the deep."
   234–35. Cf. I, 20–21. Milton derived the image of God's spirit as a
bird from the original Hebrew of Gen. 1:2, translated in the King James
version as "moved upon the face of the waters."
   239. then founded, then conglobed. The process is that of ordering
the elements, solidifying them, and shaping the whole into a globe. The
coldest and heaviest elements go to the center of the earth, the lightest
become the starry fires of the encircling spheres.
   242. self-balanced. Cf. Job 26:7, "and hangeth the earth upon
nothing."
   243 ff. The account in Gen. 1 is scrupulously followed, with use of the
scriptural phrases wherever possible.

And light from darkness by the hemisphere   250
Divided: light the Day, and darkness Night
He named. Thus was the first day even and morn;
Nor passed uncelebrated, nor unsung
By the celestial choirs, when orient light
Exhaling first from darkness they beheld,
Birth-day of Heaven and Earth; with joy and shout
The hollow universal orb they filled,
And touched their golden harps, and hymning praised
God and his works; Creator him they sung,
Both when first evening was, and when first morn.   260
    "Again God said, 'Let there be firmament
Amid the waters, and let it divide
The waters from the waters.' And God made
The firmament, expanse of liquid, pure,
Transparent, elemental air, diffused
In circuit to the uttermost convex
Of this great round: partition firm and sure,
The waters underneath from those above
Dividing; for as Earth, so he the World
Built on circumfluous waters calm, in wide   270
Crystalline ocean, and the loud misrule
Of Chaos far removed, lest fierce extremes
Contiguous might distemper the whole frame.
And Heaven he named the firmament. So even
And morning chorus sung the second day.
    "The Earth was formed, but in the womb as yet
Of waters, embryon immature involved,
Appeared not; over all the face of Earth
Main ocean flowed, not idle, but with warm
Prolific humor softening all her globe,   280
Fermented the great mother to conceive,
Satiate with genial moisture; when God said,
'Be gathered now ye waters under heaven
Into one place, and let dry land appear.'
Immediately the mountains huge appear
Emergent, and their broad bare backs upheave

261 ff. The "waters above" are ambiguously located with reference to
the outer shell of the universe. This *primum mobile* should, one would
think, be the firmament separating the created world from Chaos; but the air
is the firmament in Milton's interpretaion, extending from earth to the visible
heavens and diffused throughout the spheres to the outer shell. The "waters
above" would, then, lie outside the shell, but Milton seems to identify them
with the crystalline sphere inside it. The difficulties come from trying to
adapt the language of Genesis to the concepts of the Ptolemaic astronomy.

281-82. The image of the earth-mother becoming pregnant is classical
rather than scriptural.

282. genial, fertilizing.

Into the clouds; their tops ascend the sky.
So high as heaved the tumid hills, so low
Down sunk a hollow bottom broad and deep,
Capacious bed of waters. Thither they   290
Hasted with glad precipitance, uprolled
As drops on dust conglobing from the dry;
Part rise in crystal wall, or ridge direct,
For haste; such flight the great command impressed
On the swift floods. As armies at the call
Of trumpet (for of armies thou hast heard)
Troop to their standard, so the watery throng,
Wave rolling after wave, where way they found,
If steep, with torrent rapture, if through plain,
Soft-ebbing; nor withstood them rock or hill;   300
But they, or under ground, or circuit wide
With serpent error wandering, found their way,
And on the washy ooze deep channels wore;
Easy, ere God had bid the ground be dry,
All but within those banks where rivers now
Stream, and perpetual draw their humid train.
The dry land, Earth, and the great receptacle
Of congregated waters he called seas;
And saw that it was good, and said, 'Let the Earth
Put forth the verdant grass, herb yielding seed,   310
And fruit-tree yielding fruit after her kind,
Whose seed is in herself upon the Earth.'
He scarce had said, when the bare Earth, till then
Desert and bare, unsightly, unadorned,
Brought forth the tender grass, whose verdure clad
Her universal face with pleasant green;
Then herbs of every leaf, that sudden flowered
Opening their various colors, and made gay
Her bosom, smelling sweet; and these scarce blown,
Forth flourished thick the clustering vine, forth crept   320
The swelling gourd, up stood the corny reed
Embattled in her field. Add the humble shrub,
And bush with frizzled hair implicit. Last
Rose as in dance the stately trees, and spread
Their branches hung with copious fruit, or gemmed

290 ff. Milton elaborates this highly rhetorical movement of the waters
from Ps. 104:8.
321. corny reed, grain.
323. implicit, folded in. Milton is thinking of leaves not yet unfolded.
But it is hard to distinguish observation in all this from traditional verbali-
zation such as the poet found in earlier accounts of the creation, notably in
Sylvester's translation of Du Bartas. He is mainly interested in impressing
the reader with the wonder and variety of nature.

Their blossoms. With high woods the hills were crowned,
With tufts the valleys and each fountain side,
With borders long the rivers; that Earth now
Seemed like to Heaven, a seat where gods might dwell,
Or wander with delight, and love to haunt   330
Her sacred shades; though God had yet not rained
Upon the Earth, and man to till the ground
None was, but from the Earth a dewy mist
Went up and watered all the ground, and each
Plant of the field, which ere it was in the Earth
God made, and every herb, before it grew
On the green stem. God saw that it was good.
So even and morn recorded the third day.
    "Again the Almighty spake, 'Let there be lights
High in the expanse of heaven to divide   340
The day from night; and let them be for signs,
For seasons, and for days, and circling years,
And let them be for lights as I ordain
Their office in the firmament of heaven,
To give light on the Earth;' and it was so.
And God made two great lights, great for their use
To Man, the greater to have rule by day,
The less by night altern; and made the stars,
And set them in the firmament of heaven
To illuminate the Earth, and rule the day   350
In their vicissitude, and rule the night,
And light from darkness to divide. God saw,
Surveying his great work, that it was good.
For of celestial bodies first the sun
A mighty sphere he framed, unlightsome first,
Though of ethereal mould; then formed the moon
Globose, and every magnitude of stars,
And sowed with stars the heaven thick as a field.
Of light by far the greater part he took,
Transplanted from her cloudy shrine, and placed   360
In the sun's orb, made porous to receive
And drink the liquid light, firm to retain
Her gathered beams, great palace now of light.
Hither, as to their fountain, other stars
Repairing, in their golden urns draw light,
And hence the morning planet gilds her horns;

335. ere it was in the earth. God created first the ideas or patterns of
the herbs, as in Platonic philosophy.
    351. vicissitude, alternation.
    366. gilds her horns. The expression shows that Milton knew Venus
has phases like the moon, a fact revealed by Galileo's telescope.

By tincture or reflection they augment
Their small peculiar, though from human sight
So far remote, with diminution seen.
First in his east the glorious lamp was seen,   370
Regent of day, and all the horizon round
Invested with bright rays, jocund to run
His longitude through heaven's high road; the grey
Dawn and the Pleiades before him danced,
Shedding sweet influence. Less bright the moon,
But opposite in levelled west was set
His mirror, with full face borrowing her light
From him, for other light she needed none
In that aspect, and still that distance keeps
Till night, then in the east her turn she shines,   380
Revolved on heaven's great axle, and her reign
With thousand lesser lights dividual holds,
With thousand thousand stars, that then appeared
Spangling the hemisphere. Then first adorned
With their bright luminaries that set and rose,
Glad evening and glad morn crowned the fourth day.
   "And God said, 'Let the waters generate
Reptile with spawn abundant, living soul;
And let fowl fly above the Earth, with wings
Displayed on the open firmament of heaven.'   390
And God created the great whales, and each
Soul living, each that crept, which plenteously
The waters generated by their kinds,
And every bird of wing after his kind;
And saw that it was good, and blessed them, saying,
'Be fruitful, multiply, and in the seas
And lakes and running streams the waters fill;
And let the fowl be multiplied on the Earth.'
Forthwith the sounds and seas, each creek and bay,
With fry innumerable swarm, and shoals   400
Of fish that with their fins and shining scales
Glide under the green wave, in sculls that oft
Bank the mid sea. Part single or with mate
Graze the sea weed their pasture, and through groves
Of coral stray, or sporting with quick glance

367. The planets have some brightness of their own ("their small peculiar"), but increase it by absorption (tincture) or reflection from the sun.
   373. longitude, used here and elsewhere as synonymous with latitude.
   375. "Canst thou bind the sweet influences of the Pleiades?" Job 38:31.
   382. dividual, divided.
   402. sculls, shoals; schools of fish.
   403. Bank, make a bank in.

Show to the sun their waved coats dropped with gold,
Or in their pearly shells at ease, attend
Moist nutriment, or under rocks their food
In jointed armor watch; on smooth the seal
And bended dolphins play; part huge of bulk,   410
Wallowing unwieldy, enormous in their gait,
Tempest the ocean. There leviathan *whale*
Hugest of living creatures, on the deep
Stretched like a promontory sleeps or swims,
And seems a moving land, and at his gills
Draws in, and at his trunk spouts out a sea.
Meanwhile the tepid caves and fens and shores
Their brood as numerous hatch, from the egg that soon
Bursting with kindly rupture forth disclosed
Their callow young, but feathered soon and fledge   420
They summed their pens, and soaring the air sublime
With clang despised the ground, under a cloud
In prospect; there the eagle and the stork
On cliffs and cedar tops their eyries build.
Part loosely wing the region, part more wise
In common, ranged in figure wedge their way,
Intelligent of seasons, and set forth
Their airy caravan high over seas
Flying, and over lands with mutual wing
Easing their flight; so steers the prudent crane   430
Her annual voyage, borne on winds; the air
Floats as they pass, fanned with unnumbered plumes.
From branch to branch the smaller birds with song
Solaced the woods, and spread their painted wings
Till even, nor then the solemn nightingale
Ceased warbling, but all night tuned her soft lays.
Others on silver lakes and rivers bathed
Their downy breast; the swan, with archëd neck
Between her white wings mantling proudly, rows
Her state with oary feet; yet oft they quit   440
The dank, and rising on stiff pennons, tower
The mid aerial sky. Others on ground
Walked firm: the crested cock whose clarion sounds

409. smooth, the smooth sea.
412. leviathan. Note that Milton does not identify the sea monster of
Job with the whale, already mentioned. Cf. I, 200–5.
419. kindly, natural.
421. summed their pens, completed the growth of their feathers.
422–23. under a cloud modifies ground; in prospect, to the view.
425. region, sky.
425–26. more wise in common, more intelligent in a group, in contrast to those that fly singly.

The silent hours, and the other whose gay train
Adorns him, colored with the florid hue
Of rainbows and starry eyes. The waters thus
With fish replenished, and the air with fowl,
Evening and morn solemnized the fifth day.
   "The sixth, and of Creation last, arose
With evening harps and matin, when God said,   450
'Let the Earth bring forth soul living in her kind,
Cattle and creeping things, and beast of the Earth,
Each in their kind.' The Earth obeyed, and straight
Opening her fertile womb teemed at a birth
Innumerous living creatures, perfect forms,
Limbed and full grown. Out of the ground up rose
As from his lair the wild beast where he wons
In forest wild, in thicket, brake, or den;
Among the trees in pairs they rose, they walked;
The cattle in the fields and meadows green: 460
Those rare and solitary, these in flocks
Pasturing at once, and in broad herds upsprung.
The grassy clods now calved, now half appeared
The tawny lion, pawing to get free
His hinder parts, then springs as broke from bonds,
And rampant shakes his brinded mane; the ounce,
The libbard, and the tiger, as the mole
Rising, the crumbled earth above them threw
In hillocks; the swift stag from under ground
Bore up his branching head; scarce from his mould   470
Behemoth, biggest born of earth, upheaved
His vastness; fleeced the flocks and bleating rose,
As plants; ambiguous between sea and land,
The river-horse and scaly crocodile.
At once came forth whatever creeps the ground,
Insect or worm: those waved their limber fans
For wings, and smallest lineaments exact
In all the liveries decked of summer's pride
With spots of gold and purple, azure and green;
These as a line their long dimension drew,   480
Streaking the ground with sinuous trace; not all
Minims of nature; some of serpent kind,
Wondrous in length and corpulence, involved
Their snaky folds, and added wings. First crept

444. **the other,** the peacock.
457. **wons,** dwells.
466. **brinded,** brindled; **ounce,** lynx.
471. **Behemoth;** Job 40:15.
474. **river horse,** hippopotamus. Milton translates the Greek word.

The parsimonious emmet, provident
Of future, in small room large heart enclosed,
Pattern of just equality perhaps
Hereafter, joined in her popular tribes
Of commonalty; swarming next appeared
The female bee that feeds her husband drone   490
Deliciously, and builds her waxen cells
With honey stored. The rest are numberless,
And thou their natures know'st, and gav'st them names,
Needless to thee repeated; nor unknown
The serpent, subtlest beast of all the field,
Of huge extent sometimes, with brazen eyes
And hairy mane terrific, though to thee
Not noxious, but obedient at thy call.
  "Now Heaven in all her glory shone, and rolled
Her motions, as the great First Mover's hand   500
First wheeled their course; Earth in her rich attire
Consummate lovely smiled; air, water, earth,
By fowl, fish, beast, was flown, was swum, was walked
Frequent; and of the sixth day yet remained.
There wanted yet the master work, the end
Of all yet done: a creature who not prone
And brute as other creatures, but endued
With sanctity of reason, might erect
His stature, and upright with front serene
Govern the rest, self-knowing, and from thence   510
Magnanimous to correspond with Heaven,
But grateful to acknowledge whence his good
Descends; thither with heart, and voice, and eyes,
Directed in devotion, to adore
And worship God supreme, who made him chief
Of all his works. Therefore the omnipotent
Eternal Father (for where is not he
Present) thus to his Son audibly spake.
  " 'Let us make now Man in our image, Man
In our similitude, and let them rule   520
Over the fish and fowl of sea and air,
Beast of the field, and over all the Earth,
And every creeping thing that creeps the ground.'
This said, he formed thee, Adam, thee O Man,
Dust of the ground, and in thy nostrils breathed
The breath of life; in his own image he
Created thee, in the image of God
Express, and thou becamest a living soul.

    497. Milton adds a mythical touch in the "hairy mane."
    511. magnanimous to correspond, great enough to communicate.

Male he created thee, but thy consort
Female for race; then bless'd mankind, and said,   530
'Be fruitful, multiply, and fill the Earth,
Subdue it, and throughout dominion hold
Over fish of the sea, and fowl of the air,
And every living thing that moves on the Earth.'
Wherever thus created, for no place
Is yet distinct by name, thence, as thou know'st,
He brought thee into this delicious grove,
This garden, planted with the trees of God,
Delectable both to behold and taste;
And freely all their pleasant fruit for food   540
Gave thee—all sorts are here that all the Earth yields,
Variety without end; but of the Tree
Which tasted works knowledge of good and evil,
Thou may'st not; in the day thou eat'st, thou diest;
Death is the penalty imposed, beware,
And govern well thy appetite, lest Sin
Surprise thee, and her black attendant Death.
    "Here finished he, and all that he had made
Viewed, and behold all was entirely good.
So even and morn accomplished the sixth day;   550
Yet not till the Creator from his work
Desisting, though unwearied, up returned,
Up to the Heaven of Heavens his high abode,
Thence to behold this new-created World
The addition of his empire, how it showed
In prospect from his throne, how good, how fair,
Answering his great idea. Up he rode
Followed with acclamation and the sound
Symphonious of ten thousand harps that tuned
Angelic harmonies. The Earth, the air   560
Resounded (thou remember'st, for thou heard'st),
The Heavens and all the constellations rung,
The planets in their stations listening stood,
While the bright pomp ascended jubilant.
'Open, ye everlasting gates,' they sung,
'Open, ye Heavens, your living doors; let in
The great Creator from his work returned
Magnificent, his six days' work, a World;
Open, and henceforth oft; for God will deign   570
To visit oft the dwellings of just men

557. **his great idea.** So in Plato's *Timaeus* the creator surveys his work
and compares it with the idea.
    565 ff. Cf. Ps. 24:7: "Lift up your heads, O ye gates; and be ye lift up,
ye everlasting doors."

Delighted, and with frequent intercourse
Thither will send his wingèd messengers
On errands of supernal grace.' So sung
The glorious train ascending. He through Heaven,
That opened wide her blazing portals, led
To God's eternal house direct the way,
A broad and ample road, whose dust is gold
And pavement stars, as stars to thee appear,
Seen in the Galaxy, that milky way
Which nightly as a circling zone thou seest   580
Powdered with stars. And now on Earth the seventh
Evening arose in Eden, for the sun
Was set, and twilight from the east came on,
Forerunning night; when at the holy mount
Of Heaven's high-seated top, the imperial throne
Of Godhead, fixed for ever firm and sure,
The Filial Power arrived, and sat him down
With his great Father; for he also went
Invisible, yet stayed (such privilege
Hath Omnipresence), and the work ordained,   590
Author and end of all things, and from work
Now resting, blessed and hallowed the seventh day,
As resting on that day from all his work;
But not in silence holy kept: the harp
Had work and rested not, the solemn pipe,
And dulcimer, all organs of sweet stop,
All sounds on fret by string or golden wire
Tempered soft tunings, intermixed with voice
Choral or unison; of incense clouds
Fuming from golden censers hid the mount.   600
Creation and the six days' acts they sung:
'Great are thy works, Jehovah, infinite
Thy power; what thought can measure thee or tongue
Relate thee; greater now in thy return
Than from the giant angels: thee that day
Thy thunders magnified; but to create
Is greater than created to destroy.
Who can impair thee, mighty King, or bound
Thy empire? Easily the proud attempt
Of spirits apostate and their counsels vain   610
Thou hast repelled, while impiously they thought
Thee to diminish, and from thee withdraw
The number of thy worshippers. Who seeks

605. **giant angels.** Here as elsewhere Milton is conscious of the parallel between the revolt of Satan and the gigantomachia, the war of the
Titans against Jupiter.

To lessen thee, against his purpose serves
To manifest the more thy might: his evil
Thou usest, and from thence creat'st more good.
Witness this new-made World, another Heaven
From Heaven gate not far, founded in view
On the clear hyaline, the glassy sea;
Of amplitude almost immense, with stars   620
Numerous, and every star perhaps a world
Of destined habitation; but thou know'st
Their seasons; among these the seat of men,
Earth with her nether ocean circumfused,
Their pleasant dwelling-place. Thrice happy men,
And sons of men, whom God hath thus advanced,
Created in his image, there to dwell
And worship him, and in reward to rule
Over his works, on earth, in sea, or air,
And multiply a race of worshippers   630
Holy and just; thrice happy if they know
Their happiness, and persevere upright.'
    "So sung they, and the Empyrean rung
With halleluiahs. Thus was Sabbath kept.
And thy request think now fulfilled, that asked
How first this world and face of things began,
And what before thy memory was done
From the beginning, that posterity
Informed by thee might know; if else thou seek'st
Aught, not surpassing human measure, say."   640

BOOK VIII

THE ARGUMENT

Adam inquires concerning celestial motions; is doubtfully answered, and exhorted to search rather things more worthy of knowledge. Adam assents, and still desirous to detain Raphael, relates to him what he remembered since his own creation: his placing in Paradise, his talk with God concerning solitude and fit society, his first meeting and nuptials with Eve. His discourse with the angel thereupon; who, after admonitions repeated, departs.

The angel ended, and in Adam's ear
So charming left his voice, that he a while

621. The plurality of habitable worlds was a much discussed idea in the seventeenth century. Cf. VIII, 153–58.
631. **happy if they know.** A famous phrase from Virgil's *Georgics* ii. 158–59.

Thought him still speaking, still stood fixed to hear;
Then as new-waked thus gratefully replied.

"What thanks sufficient, or what recompense
Equal have I to render thee, divine
Historian, who thus largely hast allayed
The thirst I had of knowledge, and vouchsafed
This friendly condescension to relate
Things else by me unsearchable, now heard   10
With wonder, but delight, and, as is due,
With glory attributed to the high
Creator; something yet of doubt remains,
Which only thy solution can resolve.
When I behold this goodly frame, this World
Of Heaven and Earth consisting, and compute
Their magnitudes, this Earth a spot, a grain,
An atom, with the firmament compared
And all her numbered stars, that seem to roll
Spaces incomprehensible (for such   20
Their distance argues and their swift return
Diurnal) merely to officiate light
Round this opacous Earth, this punctual spot,
One day and night, in all their vast survey
Useless besides; reasoning I oft admire
How Nature wise and frugal could commit
Such disproportions, with superfluous hand
So many nobler bodies to create,
Greater so manifold, to this one use,
For aught appears, and on their orbs impose   30
Such restless revolution day by day
Repeated, while the sedentary Earth,
That better might with far less compass move,
Served by more noble than herself, attains
Her end without least motion, and receives,
As tribute, such a sumless journey brought
Of incorporeal speed, her warmth and light;
Speed, to describe whose swiftness number fails."

   So spake our sire, and by his countenance seemed
Entering on studious thoughts abstruse, which Eve 40
Perceiving where she sat retired in sight,
With lowliness majestic from her seat,
And grace that won who saw to wish her stay,

----

25. admire, wonder.
25 ff. The fault in Adam's questionings lies in their implication of an
attitude. He suggests a disproportion in nature, something not quite right
with the divine idea. The deviation from reverent and grateful acceptance
is a slight one and the angel rebukes him very mildly.

Rose, and went forth among her fruits and flowers,
To visit how they prospered, bud and bloom,
Her nursery; they at her coming sprung,
And touched by her fair tendance gladlier grew.
Yet went she not as not with such discourse
Delighted, or not capable her ear
Of what was high: such pleasure she reserved,   50
Adam relating, she sole auditress;
Her husband the relater she preferred
Before the angel, and of him to ask
Chose rather; he she knew would intermix
Grateful digressions, and solve high dispute
With conjugal caresses, from his lip
Not words alone pleased her. Oh when meet now
Such pairs, in love and mutual honor joined?
With goddess-like demeanor forth she went;
Not unattended, for on her as queen   60
A pomp of winning Graces waited still,
And from about her shot darts of desire
Into all eyes to wish her still in sight.
And Raphael now to Adam's doubt proposed
Benevolent and facile thus replied.
    "To ask or search I blame thee not, for Heaven
Is as the Book of God before thee set,
Wherein to read his wondrous works, and learn
His seasons, hours, or days, or months, or years:
This to attain, whether Heaven move or Earth,   70
Imports not, if thou reckon right; the rest
From man or angel the great Architect
Did wisely to conceal, and not divulge
His secrets to be scanned by them who ought
Rather admire; or if they list to try
Conjecture, he his fabric of the heavens
Hath left to their disputes, perhaps to move
His laughter at their quaint opinions wide

46. her nursery, of her nursing.
    61. pomp, procession. It is only in describing Eve that Milton indulges
in just this kind of mythological invention.
    66 ff. The angel's answer shows that Milton was familiar with the argu-
ments for and against the Ptolemaic system. It really tells us nothing of his
own scientific belief. A point is being made about human speculation generally and about the tendencies of Adam's mind in particular. Man has a
natural pride of intellect which finds exercise in skepticism. Adam, though
technically sinless in this regard, is unaware of his weakness and needs a
warning. The angel emphasizes rather the foolishness than the evil of undis-
ciplined inquiry. Part of the background here is Socrates' refusal to interest
himself in the cosmological speculations of his predecessors and his primary
concern with the nature of man.

Hereafter, when they come to model Heaven
And calculate the stars, how they will wield   80
The mighty frame, how build, unbuild, contrive,
To save appearances, how gird the sphere
With centric and eccentric scribbled o'er,
Cycle and epicycle, orb in orb.
Already by thy reasoning this I guess,
Who art to lead thy offspring, and supposest
That bodies bright and greater should not serve
The less not bright, nor Heaven such journeys run,
Earth sitting still, when she alone receives
The benefit. Consider first, that great   90
Or bright infers not excellence: the Earth,
Though in comparison of Heaven so small,
Nor glistering, may of solid good contain
More plenty than the sun that barren shines,
Whose virtue on itself works no effect,
But in the fruitful Earth; there first received,
His beams, unactive else, their vigor find.
Yet not to Earth are those bright luminaries
Officious, but to thee, Earth's habitant.
And for the Heaven's wide circuit, let it speak   100
The Maker's high magnificence, who built
So spacious, and his line stretched out so far,
That Man may know he dwells not in his own;
An edifice too large for him to fill,
Lodged in a small partition, and the rest
Ordained for uses to his Lord best known.
The swiftness of those circles attribute,
Though numberless, to his omnipotence,
That to corporeal substances could add
Speed almost spiritual; me thou think'st not slow,   110
Who since the morning hour set out from Heaven
Where God resides, and ere mid-day arrived
In Eden, distance inexpressible
By numbers that have name. But this I urge,
Admitting motion in the heavens, to show

82. **to save appearances,** to account for the phenomena.
83. **centric and eccentric,** circles around the earth as center combined
with circles around some other center.
84. **epicycle,** a circle on a circle. The planets were supposed to revolve
in epicycles, the center of which moved along the greater circle around the
earth.
90 ff. The introduction of considerations of moral value into the discussion of scientific fact was something that even Galileo did not escape.
99. **officious,** of service, functional.
108. **numberless,** beyond calculation.

Invalid that which thee to doubt it moved;
Not that I so affirm, though so it seem
To thee who hast thy dwelling here on Earth.
God to remove his ways from human sense,
Placed Heaven from Earth so far, that earthly sight, 120
If it presume, might err in things too high,
And no advantage gain. What if the sun
Be center to the World, and other stars
By his attractive virtue and their own
Incited, dance about him various rounds?
Their wandering course, now high, now low, then hid,
Progressive, retrograde, or standing still,
In six thou seest, and what if seventh to these
The planet Earth, so steadfast though she seem,
Insensibly three different motions move? 130
Which else to several spheres thou must ascribe,
Moved contrary with thwart obliquities,
Or save the sun his labor, and that swift
Nocturnal and diurnal rhomb supposed,
Invisible else above all stars, the wheel
Of day and night; which needs not thy belief,
If Earth industrious of herself fetch day
Travelling east, and with her part averse
From the sun's beam meet night, her other part
Still luminous by his ray. What if that light 140
Sent from her through the wide transpicuous air,
To the terrestrial moon be as a star
Enlightening her by day, as she by night
This Earth? reciprocal, if land be there,
Fields and inhabitants. Her spots thou seest
As clouds, and clouds may rain, and rain produce
Fruits in her softened soil, for some to eat
Allotted there; and other suns perhaps

130. The third motion is that which causes the precession of the equinoxes.

132. thwart obliquities, thwart and oblique movements.

134. rhomb supposed, the assumed wheel or turning sphere, i.e., the *primum mobile*. Rhombus in Greek is a spinning top.

144–45. The inference that the moon and planets are like the earth was a natural consequence of the Copernican hypothesis. Under the Ptolemaic they would be essentially different and could hardly be the abode of men. Similarly, the conclusion that the fixed stars were suns and might be the centers of other systems was quickly drawn. There is no indication that Milton shrinks from this disruption of traditional modes of cosmological thinking. Indeed, he makes the angel wax rather eloquent about it. But the point remains that such matters are not a primary human concern and that interest in them represents a special danger for Adam, about to confront the tree of interdicted knowledge.

With their attendant moons thou wilt descry,
Communicating male and female light,   150
Which two great sexes animate the World,
Stored in each orb perhaps with some that live.
For such vast room in Nature unpossessed
By living soul, desert and desolate,
Only to shine, yet scarce to contribute
Each orb a glimpse of light, conveyed so far
Down to this habitable, which returns
Light back to them, is obvious to dispute.
But whether thus these things, or whether not,
Whether the sun predominant in Heaven   160
Rise on the Earth, or Earth rise on the sun,
He from the east his flaming road begin,
Or she from west her silent course advance
With inoffensive pace that spinning sleeps
On her soft axle, while she paces even,
And bears thee soft with the smooth air along,
Solicit not thy thoughts with matters hid:
Leave them to God above, him serve and fear;
Of other creatures, as him pleases best,
Wherever placed, let him dispose; joy thou   170
In what he gives to thee, this Paradise
And thy fair Eve; Heaven is for thee too high
To know what passes there; be lowly wise:
Think only what concerns thee and thy being;
Dream not of other worlds, what creatures there
Live, in what state, condition, or degree,
Contented that thus far hath been revealed
Not of Earth only but of highest Heaven."
    To whom thus Adam cleared of doubt replied.
"How fully hast thou satisfied me, pure   180
Intelligence of Heaven, Angel serene,
And freed from intricacies, taught to live
The easiest way, nor with perplexing thoughts
To interrupt the sweet of life, from which
God hath bid dwell far off all anxious cares,
And not molest us, unless we ourselves
Seek them with wandering thoughts and notions vain.
But apt the mind or fancy is to rove
Unchecked, and of her roving is no end;
Till warned, or by experience taught, she learn   190
That not to know at large of things remote
From use, obscure and subtle, but to know
That which before us lies in daily life,
Is the prime wisdom; what is more, is fume,

Or emptiness, or fond impertinence,
And renders us in things that most concern
Unpractised, unprepared, and still to seek.
Therefore from this high pitch let us descend
A lower flight, and speak of things at hand
Useful, whence haply mention may arise   200
Of something not unseasonable to ask,
By sufferance, and thy wonted favor, deigned.
Thee I have heard relating what was done
Ere my remembrance: now hear me relate
My story, which perhaps thou hast not heard;
And day is yet not spent; till then thou seest
How subtly to detain thee I devise,
Inviting thee to hear while I relate,
Fond, were it not in hope of thy reply.
For while I sit with thee, I seem in Heaven,   210
And sweeter thy discourse is to my ear
Than fruits of palm-tree, pleasantest to thirst
And hunger both, from labor, at the hour
Of sweet repast; they satiate, and soon fill,
Though pleasant, but thy words, with grace divine
Imbued, bring to their sweetness no satiety."
      To whom thus Raphael answered heavenly meek.
"Nor are thy lips ungraceful, Sire of Men,
Nor tongue ineloquent; for God on thee
Abundantly his gifts hath also poured   220
Inward and outward both, his image fair:
Speaking or mute all comeliness and grace
Attends thee, and each word, each motion, forms.
Nor less think we in Heaven of thee on Earth
Than of our fellow-servant, and inquire
Gladly into the ways of God with Man;
For God we see hath honored thee, and set
On Man his equal love. Say therefore on;
For I that day was absent, as befell,
Bound on a voyage uncouth and obscure,   230
Far on excursion toward the gates of Hell,
Squared in full legion (such command we had),
To see that none thence issued forth a spy
Or enemy, while God was in his work,
Lest he incensed at such eruption bold,
Destruction with Creation might have mixed.

      195. **fond impertinence**, foolish and irrelevant.
      198 ff. Adam, his lesson learned, turns the conversation to his own
experience, hoping that his understanding may be deepened by the angel's
comment.

Not that they durst without his leave attempt,
But us he sends upon his high behests
For state, as sovran King, and to inure
Our prompt obedience. Fast we found, fast shut   240
The dismal gates, and barricadoed strong;
But long ere our approaching heard within
Noise, other than the sound of dance or song,
Torment, and loud lament, and furious rage.
Glad we returned up to the coasts of light
Ere Sabbath evening; so we had in charge.
But thy relation now; for I attend,
Pleased with thy words no less than thou with mine."
    So spake the godlike Power, and thus our sire.
"For Man to tell how human life began   250
Is hard; for who himself beginning knew?
Desire with thee still longer to converse
Induced me. As new-waked from soundest sleep
Soft on the flowery herb I found me laid
In balmy sweat, which with his beams the sun
Soon dried, and on the reeking moisture fed.
Straight toward Heaven my wondering eyes I turned,
And gazed a while the ample sky, till raised
By quick instinctive motion up I sprung,
As thitherward endeavoring, and upright   260
Stood on my feet; about me round I saw
Hill, dale, and shady woods, and sunny plains,
And liquid lapse of murmuring streams; by these,
Creatures that lived and moved, and walked or flew,
Birds on the branches warbling; all things smiled;
With fragrance and with joy my heart o'erflowed.
Myself I then perused, and limb by limb
Surveyed, and sometimes went, and sometimes ran
With supple joints, as lively vigor led;
But who I was, or where, or from what cause,   270
Knew not. To speak I tried, and forthwith spake;
My tongue obeyed, and readily could name
Whate'er I saw. 'Thou Sun,' said I, 'fair light,
And thou enlightened Earth, so fresh and gay,
Ye hills and dales, ye rivers, woods, and plains,
And ye that live and move, fair creatures, tell,
Tell, if ye saw, how came I thus, how here?

239. for state, as a matter of ceremony; inure, make habitual.
    253 ff. Adam's account of his own creation is vastly more interesting
and poetic than the angel's labored description of the six days' works of God.
It is an essential part of the human story, as the other was not, and Milton
is writing with a very different inspiration.

Not of myself; by some great Maker then,
In goodness and in power pre-eminent.
Tell me, how may I know him, how adore,   280
From whom I have that thus I move and live,
And feel that I am happier than I know.'
While thus I called, and strayed I knew not whither,
From where I first drew air, and first beheld
This happy light, when answer none returned,
On a green shady bank profuse of flowers,
Pensive I sat me down; there gentle sleep
First found me, and with soft oppression seized
My drowsëd sense, untroubled, though I thought
I then was passing to my former state   290
Insensible, and forthwith to dissolve;
When suddenly stood at my head a dream,
Whose inward apparition gently moved
My fancy to believe I yet had being,
And lived. One came, methought, of shape divine,
And said, 'Thy mansion wants thee, Adam, rise,
First Man, of men innumerable ordained
First father, called by thee I come thy guide
To the garden of bliss, thy seat prepared.'
So saying, by the hand he took me raised,   300
And over fields and waters, as in air
Smooth-sliding without step, last led me up
A woody mountain; whose high top was plain,
A circuit wide, enclosed, with goodliest trees
Planted, with walks and bowers, that what I saw
Of Earth before scarce pleasant seemed. Each tree
Loaden with fairest fruit, that hung to the eye
Tempting, stirred in me sudden appetite
To pluck and eat; whereat I waked, and found
Before mine eyes all real, as the dream   310
Had lively shadowed. Here had new begun
My wandering, had not He who was my guide
Up hither, from among the trees appeared
Presence Divine. Rejoicing, but with awe,
In adoration at his feet I fell
Submiss; he reared me, and 'Whom thou sought'st I am,'
Said mildly, 'Author of all this thou seest
Above, or round about thee, or beneath.
This Paradise I give thee, count it thine

278. by some great Maker then. Adam's natural reason gives him the
idea of a Creator. His instinct cries out, with the psalmist, "O that I knew
where I might find him!" Revelation comes in answer to his human
yearning.

To till and keep, and of the fruit to eat;   320
Of every tree that in the garden grows
Eat freely with glad heart; fear here no dearth.
But of the tree whose operation brings
Knowledge of good and ill, which I have set
The pledge of thy obedience and thy faith,
Amid the garden by the Tree of Life,
Remember what I warn thee, shun to taste,
And shun the bitter consequence. For know,
The day thou eat'st thereof, my sole command
Transgressed, inevitably thou shalt die,   330
From that day mortal, and this happy state
Shalt lose, expelled from hence into a world
Of woe and sorrow.' Sternly he pronounced
The rigid interdiction, which resounds
Yet dreadful in mine ear, though in my choice
Not to incur; but soon his clear aspect
Returned, and gracious purpose thus renewed.
'Not only these fair bounds, but all the Earth
To thee and to thy race I give; as lords
Possess it, and all things that therein live,   340
Or live in sea or air, beast, fish, and fowl.
In sign whereof each bird and beast behold
After their kinds; I bring them to receive
From thee their names, and pay thee fealty
With low subjection; understand the same
Of fish within their watery residence,
Not hither summoned, since they cannot change
Their element to draw the thinner air.'
As thus he spake, each bird and beast behold
Approaching two and two, these cowering low   350
With blandishment, each bird stooped on his wing.
I named them as they passed, and understood
Their nature; with such knowledge God endued
My sudden apprehension. But in these
I found not what methought I wanted still
And to the Heavenly Vision thus presumed.
    " 'O by what name, for thou above all these,
Above mankind, or aught than mankind higher,
Surpassest far my naming, how may I

321 ff. Gen. 2:16–17: "And the Lord God commanded the man, saying, Of every tree of the garden thou mayest freely eat: but of the tree of
the knowledge of good and evil, thou shalt not eat of it: for in the day that
thou eatest thereof thou shalt surely die."
    353. endued, endowed.
    356. presumed, made bold to speak.

Adore thee, Author of this Universe,   360
And all this good to man, for whose well-being
So amply, and with hands so liberal
Thou hast provided all things? But with me
I see not who partakes. In solitude
What happiness? who can enjoy alone,
Or all enjoying, what contentment find?'
Thus I presumptuous; and the Vision bright,
As with a smile more brightened, thus replied.
   " 'What call'st thou solitude? Is not the Earth
With various living creatures, and the air   370
Replenished, and all these at thy command
To come and play before thee? Know'st thou not
Their language and their ways? They also know,
And reason not contemptibly; with these
Find pastime, and bear rule; thy realm is large.'
So spake the universal Lord, and seemed
So ordering. I with leave of speech implored,
And humble deprecation, thus replied.
   " 'Let not my words offend thee, Heavenly Power,
My Maker, be propitious while I speak.   380
Hast thou not made me here thy substitute,
And these inferior far beneath me set?
Among unequals what society
Can sort, what harmony or true delight?
Which must be mutual, in proportion due
Given and received; but in disparity,
The one intense, the other still remiss
Cannot well suit with either, but soon prove
Tedious alike. Of fellowship I speak
Such as I seek, fit to participate   390
All rational delight, wherein the brute
Cannot be human consort; they rejoice
Each with their kind, lion with lioness;
So fitly them in pairs thou hast combined;
Much less can bird with beast, or fish with fowl
So well converse, nor with the ox the ape;
Worse then can man with beast, and least of all.'
   "Whereto the Almighty answered, not displeased.
'A nice and subtle happiness I see
Thou to thyself proposest, in the choice   400
Of thy associates, Adam, and wilt taste
No pleasure, though in pleasure, solitary.

   386–89. When there is disparity between the partners, one being of
high, the other of low intelligence, neither can suit the other.
   399. nice, fastidious, refined.

What thinkest thou then of me, and this my state?
Seem I to thee sufficiently possessed
Of happiness, or not? who am alone
From all eternity; for none I know
Second to me or like, equal much less.
How have I then with whom to hold converse
Save with the creatures which I made, and those
To me inferior infinite descents   410
Beneath what other creatures are to thee?'
  "He ceased; I lowly answered: 'To attain
The height and depth of thy eternal ways
All human thoughts come short, Supreme of things;
Thou in thyself art perfect, and in thee
Is no deficience found; not so is Man,
But in degree, the cause of his desire
By conversation with his like to help
Or solace his defects. No need that thou
Shouldst propagate, already infinite,   420
And through all numbers absolute, though One;
But Man by number is to manifest
His single imperfection, and beget
Like of his like, his image multiplied,
In unity defective, which requires
Collateral love, and dearest amity.
Thou in thy secrecy although alone,
Best with thyself accompanied, seek'st not
Social communication, yet so pleased,
Canst raise thy creature to what height thou wilt   430
Of union or communion, deified;
I by conversing cannot these erect
From prone, nor in their ways complacence find.'
Thus I emboldened spake, and freedom used
Permissive, and acceptance found, which gained
This answer from the gracious Voice Divine.
  " 'Thus far to try thee, Adam, I was pleased,
And find thee knowing not of beasts alone,
Which thou hast rightly named, but of thyself,
Expressing well the spirit within thee free,   440
My image, not imparted to the brute,
Whose fellowship therefore unmeet for thee
Good reason was thou freely shouldst dislike,
And be so minded still. I, ere thou spakest,
Knew it not good for Man to be alone,
And no such company as then thou saw'st
Intended thee, for trial only brought,
To see how thou couldst judge of fit and meet.

What next I bring shall please thee, be assured,
Thy likeness, thy fit help, thy other self,   450
Thy wish exactly to thy heart's desire.'
    "He ended, or I heard no more; for now
My earthly by his heavenly overpowered,
Which it had long stood under, strained to the height
In that celestial colloquy sublime,
As with an object that excels the sense,
Dazzled and spent, sunk down and sought repair
Of sleep, which instantly fell on me, called
By Nature as in aid, and closed mine eyes.
Mine eyes he closed, but open left the cell   _Woman_   460
Of fancy, my internal sight, by which
Abstract as in a trance methought I saw,
Though sleeping, where I lay, and saw the Shape
Still glorious before whom awake I stood;
Who stooping opened my left side, and took
From thence a rib, with cordial spirits warm,
And life-blood streaming fresh; wide was the wound,
But suddenly with flesh filled up and healed.
The rib he formed and fashioned with his hands;
Under his forming hands a creature grew,   470
Man-like, but different sex, so lovely fair
That what seemed fair in all the world seemed now
Mean, or in her summed up, in her contained
And in her looks, which from that time infused
Sweetness into my heart, unfelt before,
And into all things from her air inspired
The spirit of love and amorous delight.
She disappeared, and left me dark; I waked
To find her, or for ever to deplore
Her loss, and other pleasures all abjure: 480
When out of hope, behold her, not far off,
Such as I saw her in my dream, adorned
With what all Earth or Heaven could bestow
To make her amiable. On she came,
Led by her Heavenly Maker, though unseen,
And guided by his voice, nor uninformed
Of nuptial sanctity and marriage rites.
Grace was in all her steps, Heaven in her eye,
In every gesture dignity and love.   490
I overjoyed could not forbear aloud:
    "'This turn hath made amends; thou hast fulfilled
Thy words, Creator bounteous and benign,

452–56. There is something of the quality of Dante in these lines, more
perhaps than anywhere else in *Paradise Lost*.

Giver of all things fair, but fairest this
Of all thy gifts, nor enviest. I now see
Bone of my bone, flesh of my flesh, my self
Before me; Woman is her name, of Man
Extracted; for this cause he shall forgo
Father and mother, and to his wife adhere;
And they shall be one flesh, one heart, one soul.'
   "She heard me thus; and though divinely brought,   500
Yet innocence and virgin modesty,
Her virtue and the conscience of her worth,
That would be wooed, and not unsought be won,
Not obvious, not obtrusive, but retired,
The more desirable; or to say all,
Nature herself, though pure of sinful thought,
Wrought in her so, that seeing me, she turned;
I followed her; she what was honor knew,
And with obsequious majesty approved
My pleaded reason. To the nuptial bower   510
I led her blushing like the Morn; all Heaven
And happy constellations on that hour
Shed their selectest influence; the Earth
Gave sign of gratulation, and each hill;
Joyous the birds; fresh gales and gentle airs
Whispered it to the woods, and from their wings
Flung rose, flung odors from the spicy shrub,
Disporting, till the amorous bird of night
Sung spousal, and bid haste the evening star
On his hill top, to light the bridal lamp.   520
   "Thus I have told thee all my state, and brought
My story to the sum of earthly bliss
Which I enjoy, and must confess to find
In all things else delight indeed, but such
As used or not, works in the mind no change,
Nor vehement desire, these delicacies
I mean of taste, sight, smell, herbs, fruits, and flowers,
Walks, and the melody of birds; but here
Far otherwise, transported I behold,
Transported touch; here passion first I felt,   530
Commotion strange, in all enjoyments else
Superior and unmoved, here only weak

   494 ff. Milton is beautifully paraphrasing Gen. 23-24: "And Adam said This is now bone of my bones, and flesh of my flesh: she shall be called woman, because she was taken out of man. Therefore shall a man leave his father and his mother, and shall cleave unto his wife: and they shall be one flesh."
   508. honor. She recognized honor in me. Marriage is an "honorable estate."

Against the charm of beauty's powerful glance.
Or Nature failed in me, and left some part
Not proof enough such object to sustain,
Or from my side subducting, took perhaps
More than enough; at least on her bestowed
Too much of ornament, in outward show
Elaborate, of inward less exact.
For well I understand in the prime end   540
Of Nature her the inferior, in the mind
And inward faculties, which most excel;
In outward also her resembling less
His image who made both, and less expressing
The character of that dominion given
O'er other creatures; yet when I approach
Her loveliness, so absolute she seems
And in herself complete, so well to know
Her own, that what she wills to do or say
Seems wisest, virtuousest, discreetest, best;   550
All higher knowledge in her presence falls
Degraded, Wisdom in discourse with her
Loses discountenanced, and like Folly shows;
Authority and Reason on her wait,
As one intended first, not after made
Occasionally; and to consummate all,
Greatness of mind and nobleness their seat
Build in her loveliest, and create an awe
About her, as a guard angelic placed."
    To whom the angel with contracted brow.   560
"Accuse not Nature, she hath done her part;
Do thou but thine, and be not diffident
Of Wisdom; she deserts thee not, if thou
Dismiss not her, when most thou need'st her nigh,
By attributing overmuch to things
Less excellent, as thou thyself perceivest.
For what admirest thou, what transports thee so,
An outside? fair no doubt, and worthy well
Thy cherishing, thy honoring, and thy love,
Not thy subjection. Weigh with her thyself;   570
Then value. Oft-times nothing profits more
Than self-esteem, grounded on just and right,
Well managed; of that skill the more thou know'st,

---

560. **with contracted brow.** The angel's severity is directed against a
dangerous flaw in Adam's thought. Passion leads him to exalt Eve above
her place in the scale of nature. He has tried to justify his sense of weakness by deterministic thinking. This is the great heresy which *Paradise Lost*
was written to combat. Man is "by nature free."

The more she will acknowledge thee her head,
And to realities yield all her shows:
Made so adorn for thy delight the more,
So awful, that with honor thou may'st love
Thy mate, who sees when thou art seen least wise.
But if the sense of touch whereby mankind
Is propagated seem such dear delight   580
Beyond all other, think the same vouchsafed
To cattle and each beast; which would not be
To them made common and divulged, if aught
Therein enjoyed were worthy to subdue
The soul of Man, or passion in him move.
What higher in her society thou find'st
Attractive, human, rational, love still;
In loving thou dost well, in passion not,
Wherein true love consists not; love refines
The thoughts, and heart enlarges, hath his seat   590
In Reason, and is judicious, is the scale
By which to heavenly love thou may'st ascend,
Not sunk in carnal pleasure, for which cause
Among the beasts no mate for thee was found."
To whom thus half abashed Adam replied.
"Neither her outside formed so fair, nor aught
In procreation common to all kinds
(Though higher of the genial bed by far,
And with mysterious reverence I deem),
So much delights me as those graceful acts,   600
Those thousand decencies that daily flow
From all her words and actions, mixed with love
And sweet compliance, which declare unfeigned
Union of mind, or in us both one soul;
Harmony to behold in wedded pair
More grateful than harmonious sound to the ear.
Yet these subject not; I to thee disclose
What inward thence I feel, not therefore foiled,
Who meet with various objects, from the sense
Variously representing; yet still free,   610
Approve the best, and follow what I approve.
To love thou blamest me not, for love thou say'st
Leads up to Heaven, is both the way and guide;
Bear with me then, if lawful what I ask:
Love not the heavenly spirits, and how their love

595 ff. Adam is only "half abashed." His thinking is nevertheless cor-
rected, and he succeeds in restating himself without offense.

615-17. Adam does not quite know what he is asking. Hence the ob-
scurity. Do they express their love only by looks? Do they intermingle

Express they, by looks only, or do they mix
Irradiance, virtual or immediate touch?"
　To whom the angel, with a smile that glowed
Celestial rosy red, love's proper hue,
Answered. "Let it suffice thee that thou know'st   620
Us happy, and without love no happiness.
Whatever pure thou in the body enjoy'st
(And pure thou wert created) we enjoy
In eminence, and obstacle find none
Of membrane, joint, or limb, exclusive bars;
Easier than air with air, if spirits embrace,
Total they mix, union of pure with pure
Desiring; nor restrained conveyance need
As flesh to mix with flesh, or soul with soul.
But I can now no more; the parting sun   630
Beyond the Earth's green Cape and verdant Isles
Hesperean sets, my signal to depart.
Be strong, live happy, and love, but first of all
Him whom to love is to obey, and keep
His great command; take heed lest passion sway
Thy judgment to do aught which else free will
Would not admit; thine and of all thy sons
The weal or woe in thee is placed; beware.
I in thy persevering shall rejoice,
And all the Blest. Stand fast; to stand or fall   640
Free in thine own arbitrement it lies.
Perfect within, no outward aid require;
And all temptation to transgress repel."
　So saying, he arose; whom Adam thus
Followed with benediction: "Since to part,
Go heavenly guest, ethereal messenger,
Sent from whose sovran goodness I adore.
Gentle to me and affable hath been
Thy condescension, and shall be honored ever
With grateful memory; thou to Mankind   650
Be good and friendly still, and oft return."
　So parted they, the angel up to Heaven
From the thick shade, and Adam to his bower.

their radiance and thereby virtually touch each other? Or do they actually touch? The angel's answer is inevitably as vague as the question.
With angels the distinction between spiritual and physical love does
not exist. The act of union is single and complete. Milton's underlying metaphysics is apparent here, as elsewhere. There is gradation of
substance but no absolute break between matter and spirit throughout the
universe.
　647. from whose, from him whose.

BOOK IX

THE ARGUMENT

Satan, having compassed the Earth, with meditated guile returns as a mist by night into Paradise; enters into the serpent sleeping. Adam and Eve in the morning go forth to their labors, which Eve proposes to divide in several places, each laboring apart: Adam consents not, alleging the danger, lest that enemy, of whom they were forewarned, should attempt her found alone. Eve, loth to be thought not circumspect or firm enough, urges her going apart, the rather desirous to make trial of her strength; Adam at last yields. The Serpent finds her alone: his subtle approach, first gazing, then speaking, with much flattery extolling Eve above all other creatures. Eve, wondering to hear the Serpent speak, asks how he attained to human speech and such understanding, not till now; the Serpent answers, that by tasting of a certain tree in the garden he attained both to speech and reason, till then void of both. Eve requires him to bring her to that tree, and finds it to be the Tree of Knowledge forbidden. The Serpent, now grown bolder, with many wiles and arguments induces her at length to eat; she, pleased with the taste, deliberates a while whether to impart thereof to Adam or not; at last brings him of the fruit; relates what persuaded her to eat thereof. Adam, at first amazed, but perceiving her lost, resolves through vehemence of love to perish with her, and, extenuating the trespass, eats also of the fruit. The effects thereof in them both; they seek to cover their nakedness; then fall to variance and accusation of one another.

No more of talk where God or angel guest
With Man, as with his friend, familiar used
To sit indulgent, and with him partake
Rural repast, permitting him the while
Venial discourse unblamed. I now must change
Those notes to tragic; foul distrust and breach
Disloyal on the part of man, revolt
And disobedience; on the part of Heaven
Now alienated, distance and distaste,

1 ff. The long conversation between Raphael and Adam, forming the substance of Books V–VIII, has introduced the antecedent action and illuminated more fully the existing situation. Now before entering upon the climax of his narrative, Milton pauses for a brief meditative interlude. The personal allusions in the opening lines of this book are of exceptional interest.

2. as with his friend. Cf. Exod. 33:11.

6–12. Cf. I, 3. The theme announced at the beginning of the poem is repeated in expanded form.

Anger and just rebuke, and judgment given,   10
That brought into this World a world of woe,
Sin and her shadow Death, and Misery
Death's harbinger. Sad task, yet argument
Not less but more heroic than the wrath
Of stern Achilles on his foe pursued
Thrice fugitive about Troy wall; or rage
Of Turnus for Lavinia disespoused;
Or Neptune's ire or Juno's, that so long
Perplexed the Greek and Cytherea's son;
If answerable style I can obtain   20
Of my celestial patroness, who deigns
Her nightly visitation unimplored,
And dictates to me slumbering, or inspires
Easy my unpremeditated verse,
Since first this subject for heroic song
Pleased me long choosing and beginning late;
Not sedulous by nature to indite
Wars, hitherto the only argument
Heroic deemed, chief mastery to dissect
With long and tedious havoc fabled knights   30
In battles feigned; the better fortitude
Of patience and heroic martyrdom
Unsung; or to describe races and games,
Or tilting furniture, imblazoned shields,

13 ff. Having restated his theme, Milton here asserts its superiority to
the themes of the three great classical epics: (1) the *Iliad*, which deals with
the wrath of stern Achilles; (2) the *Odyssey*, which relates the outcome
of Neptune's ire against the Greek Odysseus; (3) the *Aeneid*, the first part
of which is motivated by the hostility of Juno toward Aeneas (Cytherea's
son), and the second part by the anger of Turnus at the loss of Lavinia.
20. answerable style, i.e., a style commensurate with the dignity of the
theme.
21–23. Cf. III, 29–40. The implication is that with Milton composition
was a spontaneous process, based on a passive reception of impressions and
ideas.
25 ff. From the Cambridge MS. it is evident that the subject of *Paradise
Lost* (together with various other subjects drawn from biblical and British
history) was in Milton's mind by 1640 or soon after. The actual composition of the epic could not have been begun much before 1658.
28. the only argument. These lines reveal a definite critical point of
view. Cf. *The Reason of Church Government*, II, Preface, where Milton
communes with himself regarding the worthiest themes of poetry. The test
of value in both the subject matter and the intent of art is the literature of
the Old and New Testaments.
33. races and games. Milton is thinking of the detailed accounts in
Iliad xxiii, and *Aeneid* v. His own references to such games (II, 528–38;
IV, 551, 552) are brief.
34. tilting furniture, etc., i.e., the trappings of chivalry, as set forth by
Ariosto, Tasso, and Spenser.

Impresses quaint, caparisons and steeds,
Bases and tinsel trappings, gorgeous knights
At joust and tournament; then marshalled feast
Served up in hall with sewers and seneshals,
The skill of artifice or office mean,
Not that which justly gives heroic name   40
To person or to poem. Me of these
Nor skilled nor studious, higher argument
Remains, sufficient of itself to raise
That name, unless an age too late, or cold
Climate, or years damp my intended wing
Depressed, and much they may, if all be mine,
Not hers who brings it nightly to my ear.
     The sun was sunk, and after him the star
Of Hesperus, whose office is to bring
Twilight upon the Earth, short arbiter   50
'Twixt day and night, and now from end to end
Night's hemisphere had veiled the horizon round;
When Satan who late fled before the threats
Of Gabriel out of Eden, now improved
In meditated fraud and malice, bent
On Man's destruction, maugre what might hap
Of heavier on himself, fearless returned.
By night he fled, and at midnight returned
From compassing the Earth, cautious of day,
Since Uriel, regent of the sun, descried   60
His entrance, and forewarned the Cherubim
That kept their watch; thence full of anguish driven,
The space of seven continued nights he rode
With darkness, thrice the equinoctial line
He circled, four times crossed the car of Night
From pole to pole, traversing each colure;

   35. impresses, devices on shields (Italian *impresa*).
   36. bases, kilt-like garments worn by knights on horseback.
   41-43. Me ... remains. To me, who am, etc., there remains.
   44-45. an age too late, i.e., too late a period in the world's history. The
notion of universal retrogression was fairly common in the seventeenth century. Though Milton had argued against the theory, he here shows that
he is not unaffected by fear that it may be true. or cold Climate. In
Areopagitica Milton speaks of his "natural endowments haply not the worst
for two and fifty degrees of northern latitude." Cf. also the *Reason of
Church Government* passage noted above. The idea that a northern climate
is unfavorable to works of the mind goes back to Aristotle.
   56. maugre, in spite of (French *malgré*).
   59. from compassing the Earth. Cf. Job 1:7.
   66. traversing each colure. The colures are two great circles intersect-
ing at the poles, one passing through the equinoxes, the other (at right
angles to it) through the solstices. Satan follows each of these lines from
south to north and back, keeping always within the earth's shadow.

On the eighth returned, and on the coast averse
From entrance or cherubic watch, by stealth
Found unsuspected way. There was a place,
Now not, though sin, not time, first wrought the change,   70
Where Tigris at the foot of Paradise
Into a gulf shot under ground, till part
Rose up a fountain by the Tree of Life;
In with the river sunk, and with it rose
Satan involved in rising mist, then sought
Where to lie hid; sea he had searched and land
From Eden over Pontus, and the pool
Mæotis, up beyond the river Ob;
Downward as far antarctic; and in length
West from Orontes to the ocean barred   80
At Darien, thence to the land where flows
Ganges and Indus. Thus the orb he roamed
With narrow search, and with inspection deep
Considered every creature, which of all
Most opportune might serve his wiles, and found
The serpent subtlest beast of all the field.
Him after long debate, irresolute
Of thoughts revolved, his final sentence chose
Fit vessel, fittest imp of fraud, in whom
To enter, and his dark suggestions hide   90
From sharpest sight; for in the wily snake,
Whatever sleights none would suspicious mark,
As from his wit and native subtlety
Proceeding, which in other beasts observed,
Doubt might beget of diabolic power
Active within beyond the sense of brute.
Thus he resolved, but first from inward grief
His bursting passion into plaints thus poured.
"O Earth, how like to Heaven, if not preferred

69 ff. Cf. IV, 223–30. Satan makes his entrance from the north side. Satan's wanderings, first described astronomically, are here described geographically. Northward he had gone over the Black Sea (**Pontus**) and the Sea of Azof (**the pool Mæotis**), beyond the Siberian river **Ob** to the pole; thence southward to the Antarctic. Westward he had gone along the Syrian river **Orontes**, over the Mediterranean and Atlantic to the Isthmus of Panama (**Darien**), and from there across the Pacific to India (**the land of Ganges and Indus**).

82. **orb**, the world (*orbis terrarum*).
86. **The serpent**, etc. Cf. Gen. 3:1.
87. **sentence**, decision (Latin *sententia*).
88. **imp**, offspring.
99 ff. "**O Earth**," etc. Cf. Satan's soliloquy on first gaining sight of Eden, IV, 32 ff. As then, he is torn by passion, but now there is less of remorse, more of bitterness and despair.

More justly, seat worthier of Gods, as built   100
With second thoughts, reforming what was old!
For what God after better worse would build?
Terrestrial Heaven, danced round by other Heavens
That shine, yet bear their bright officious lamps,
Light above light, for thee alone, as seems,
In thee concentring all their precious beams
Of sacred influence. As God in Heaven
Is center, yet extends to all, so thou
Centring receivest from all those orbs; in thee,
Not in themselves, all their known virtue appears   110
Productive in herb, plant, and nobler birth
Of creatures animate with gradual life
Of growth, sense, reason, all summed up in Man.
With what delight could I have walked thee round,
If I could joy in aught, sweet interchange
Of hill and valley, rivers, woods, and plains,
Now land, now sea, and shores with forest crowned,
Rocks, dens, and caves; but I in none of these
Find place or refuge; and the more I see
Pleasures about me, so much more I feel   120
Torment within me, as from the hateful siege
Of contraries; all good to me becomes
Bane, and in Heaven much worse would be my state.
But neither here seek I, no nor in Heaven
To dwell, unless by mastering Heaven's Supreme;
Nor hope to be myself less miserable
By what I seek, but others to make such
As I, though thereby worse to me redound:
For only in destroying I find ease
To my relentless thoughts; and him destroyed,   130
Or won to what may work his utter loss,
For whom all this was made, all this will soon
Follow, as to him linked in weal or woe;
In woe then, that destruction wide may range.
To me shall be the glory sole among
The infernal Powers, in one day to have marred
What he Almighty styled, six nights and days
Continued making, and who knows how long
Before had been contriving, though perhaps
Not longer than since I in one night freed   140

103. **danced round by other Heavens.** Milton frequently compares the motion of the heavenly bodies to a dance (e.g., V, 175–79, 620–24; VIII, 122–25). The probable source of the figure is Plato *Timaeus* 40.

130. **him destroyed.** The construction is evidently used in imitation of the Latin ablative absolute. Cf. VII, 142.

From servitude inglorious well nigh half
The angelic name, and thinner left the throng
Of his adorers. He to be avenged,
And to repair his numbers thus impaired,
Whether such virtue spent of old now failed
More angels to create, if they at least
Are his created, or to spite us more,
Determined to advance into our room
A creature formed of earth, and him endow,
Exalted from so base original,   150
With heavenly spoils, our spoils. What he decreed
He effected; Man he made, and for him built
Magnificent this World, and Earth his seat,
Him lord pronounced, and, O indignity!
Subjected to his service angel wings,
And flaming ministers to watch and tend
Their earthy charge. Of these the vigilance
I dread, and to elude, thus wrapped in mist
Of midnight vapor glide obscure, and pry
In every bush and brake, where hap may find   160
The serpent sleeping, in whose mazy folds
To hide me, and the dark intent I bring.
O foul descent! that I who erst contended
With Gods to sit the highest, am now constrained
Into a beast, and, mixed with bestial slime,
This essence to incarnate and imbrute,
That to the height of deity aspired;
But what will not ambition and revenge
Descend to? Who aspires must down as low
As high he soared, obnoxious first or last   170
To basest things. Revenge, at first though sweet,
Bitter ere long back on itself recoils;
Let it; I reck not, so it light well aimed,
Since higher I fall short, on him who next
Provokes my envy, this new favorite
Of Heaven, this man of clay, son of despite,
Whom us the more to spite his Maker raised
From dust: spite then with spite is best repaid."

142. name, race, stock. Latin *nomen*, occasionally used in the same sense.
163 ff. Cf. IV, 835–40, and note. Satan's imbruting himself within the serpent is the final step in his progressive degeneration. His own words explain the symbolism.
170. obnoxious, liable, subject (Latin *obnoxius*).
176. son of despite. The expression is a Hebraism. Cf. "son of wickedness" (Ps. 89:22), "children of pride" (Job 41:34), etc.
178. spite then with spite is best repaid. Cf. Aeschylus *Prometheus Bound* 944.

So saying, through each thicket dank or dry,
Like a black mist low creeping, he held on   180
His midnight search, where soonest he might find
The serpent. Him fast sleeping soon he found
In labyrinth of many a round self-rolled,
His head the midst, well stored with subtle wiles;
Not yet in horrid shade or dismal den,
Nor nocent yet, but on the grassy herb
Fearless unfeared he slept. In at his mouth
The Devil entered, and his brutal sense,
In heart or head, possessing soon inspired
With act intelligential, but his sleep   190
Disturbed not, waiting close the approach of morn.
Now whenas sacred light began to dawn
In Eden on the humid flowers, that breathed
Their morning incense, when all things that breathe,
From the Earth's great altar send up silent praise
To the Creator, and his nostrils fill
With grateful smell, forth came the human pair
And joined their vocal worship to the choir
Of creatures wanting voice; that done, partake
The season, prime for sweetest scents and airs;   200
Then commune how that day they best may ply
Their growing work; for much their work outgrew
The hands' dispatch of two gardening so wide.
And Eve first to her husband thus began.
"Adam, well may we labor still to dress
This garden, still to tend plant, herb, and flower,
Our pleasant task enjoined, but till more hands
Aid us, the work under our labor grows,
Luxurious by restraint; what we by day
Lop overgrown, or prune, or prop, or bind,   210
One night or two with wanton growth derides
Tending to wild. Thou therefore now advise
Or hear what to my mind first thoughts present:
Let us divide our labors, thou where choice
Leads thee, or where most needs, whether to wind
The woodbine round this arbor, or direct
The clasping ivy where to climb, while I
In yonder spring of roses intermixed
With myrtle, find what to redress till noon.
For while so near each other thus all day   220

192. sacred light. Cf. III, 1–6; also I John 1:5.
199–200. partake the season, i.e., share the beauties of the morning.
As in IV, 640, season refers to the time of day.
218. spring, clump, thicket.

Our task we choose, what wonder if so near
Looks intervene and smiles, or object new
Casual discourse draw on, which intermits
Our day's work, brought to little, though begun
Early, and the hour of supper comes unearned."
    To whom mild answer Adam thus returned.
"Sole Eve, associate sole, to me beyond
Compare above all living creatures dear,
Well hast thou motioned, well thy thoughts employed
How we might best fulfil the work which here   230
God hath assigned us, nor of me shalt pass
Unpraised; for nothing lovelier can be found
In woman, than to study household good,
And good works in her husband to promote.
Yet not so strictly hath our Lord imposed
Labor, as to debar us when we need
Refreshment, whether food, or talk between,
Food of the mind, or this sweet intercourse
Of looks and smiles, for smiles from reason flow,
To brute denied, and are of love the food,   240
Love not the lowest end of human life.
For not to irksome toil, but to delight
He made us, and delight to reason joined.
These paths and bowers doubt not but our joint hands
Will keep from wilderness with ease, as wide
As we need walk, till younger hands ere long
Assist us. But if much converse perhaps
Thee satiate, to short absence I could yield;
For solitude sometimes is best society,
And short retirement urges sweet return.   250
But other doubt possesses me, lest harm
Befall thee severed from me; for thou know'st
What hath been warned us, what malicious foe
Envying our happiness, and of his own
Despairing, seeks to work us woe and shame
By sly assault; and somewhere nigh at hand

    229. **motioned**, proposed.
    232-34. Cf. *Samson Agonistes*, 1046–49; also Prov. 31:10–30.
    235 ff. Adam's view of pleasure in relation to labor follows logically
from the principles laid down by Raphael in Book VIII. The view, moreover, is one which Milton himself shared. Cf. the exposition in *Tetrachordon* of Gen. 2–18, "No mortal nature can endure . . . without sometimes
slackening the cords of intense thought and labor," etc.
    241. **Love not the lowest end.** Cf. Raphael's assertion that there is
"without love no happiness" (VIII, 621).
    245. **wilderness**, wildness (i.e., too luxuriant growth of vegetation).
    247. **converse.** Pronounce convérse.

Watches, no doubt, with greedy hope to find
His wish and best advantage, us asunder,
Hopeless to circumvent us joined, where each
To other speedy aid might lend at need;   260
Whether his first design be to withdraw
Our fealty from God, or to disturb
Conjugal love, than which perhaps no bliss
Enjoyed by us excites his envy more;
Or this, or worse, leave not the faithful side
That gave thee being, still shades thee and protects.
The wife, where danger or dishonor lurks,
Safest and seemliest by her husband stays,
Who guards her, or with her the worst endures."
    To whom the virgin majesty of Eve,   270
As one who loves, and some unkindness meets,
With sweet austere composure thus replied.
    "Offspring of Heaven and Earth, and all Earth's lord,
That such an enemy we have, who seeks
Our ruin, both by thee informed I learn,
And from the parting angel overheard
As in a shady nook I stood behind,
Just then returned at shut of evening flowers.
But that thou shouldst my firmness therefore doubt
To God or thee, because we have a foe   280
May tempt it, I expected not to hear.
His violence thou fear'st not, being such,
As we, not capable of death or pain,
Can either not receive, or can repel.
His fraud is then thy fear, which plain infers
Thy equal fear that my firm faith and love
Can by his fraud be shaken or seduced;
Thoughts, which how found they harbor in thy breast,
Adam, misthought of her to thee so dear?"
    To whom with healing words Adam replied.   290
"Daughter of God and Man, immortal Eve,
For such thou art, from sin and blame entire;
Not diffident of thee do I dissuade
Thy absence from my sight, but to avoid
The attempt itself, intended by our foe.
For he who tempts, though in vain, at least asperses

265. **Or this, or worse,** i.e., whether his design (621) be this or worse.
    276. **from the parting angel,** i.e., from Raphael as he was parting from Adam. Cf. VIII, 633-43.
    285 ff. The sharpness of Eve's logic argues well for the future success of her daughters in masculine debate.
    292. **entire,** untouched (Latin *integer*).

The tempted with dishonor foul, supposed
Not incorruptible of faith, not proof
Against temptation. Thou thyself with scorn
And anger wouldst resent the offered wrong,   300
Though ineffectual found. Misdeem not then,
If such affront I labor to avert
From thee alone, which on us both at once
The enemy, though bold, will hardly dare,
Or daring, first on me the assault shall light.
Nor thou his malice and false guile contemn;
Subtle he needs must be, who could seduce
Angels, nor think superfluous others' aid.
I from the influence of thy looks receive
Access in every virtue, in thy sight   310
More wise, more watchful, stronger, if need were
Of outward strength; while shame, thou looking on,
Shame to be overcome or overreached,
Would utmost vigor raise, and raised unite.
Why shouldst not thou like sense within thee feel
When I am present, and thy trial choose
With me, best witness of thy virtue tried."
So spake domestic Adam in his care
And matrimonial love; but Eve, who thought
Less attributed to her faith sincere,   320
Thus her reply with accent sweet renewed.
  "If this be our condition, thus to dwell
In narrow circuit straitened by a foe,
Subtle or violent, we not endued
Single with like defence, wherever met,
How are we happy, still in fear of harm?
But harm precedes not sin: only our foe
Tempting affronts us with his foul esteem
Of our integrity; his foul esteem
Sticks no dishonor on our front, but turns   330
Foul on himself; then wherefore shunned or feared
By us? who rather double honor gain
From his surmise proved false, find peace within,
Favor from Heaven, our witness, from the event.

309 ff. This statement of Adam's as to the ennobling effect of love and
of the loved one's presence is essentially Platonic. Cf. *Symposium* 178, 179.
  310. access, growth, increase.
  318. domestic, devoted to home life and its duties.
  320. less, too little. The Latin comparative frequently has the same
force.
  328. affronts. The literal meaning "strikes on the forehead" is implied
(Latin *ad* + *frons*). Note how the image is expanded in the two lines following.

And what is faith, love, virtue, unassayed
Alone, without exterior help sustained?
Let us not then suspect our happy state
Left so imperfect by the Maker wise,
As not secure to single or combined.
Frail is our happiness, if this be so,   340
And Eden were no Eden thus exposed."
    To whom thus Adam fervently replied.
"O Woman, best are all things as the will
Of God ordained them; his creating hand
Nothing imperfect or deficient left
Of all that he created, much less Man,
Or aught that might his happy state secure,
Secure from outward force: within himself
The danger lies, yet lies within his power;
Against his will he can receive no harm.   350
But God left free the will, for what obeys
Reason is free, and Reason he made right,
But bid her well be ware, and still erect,
Lest by some fair appearing good surprised
She dictate false, and misinform the will
To do what God expressly hath forbid.
Not then mistrust, but tender love enjoins,
That I should mind thee oft, and mind thou me.
Firm we subsist, yet possible to swerve,
Since Reason not impossibly may meet   360
Some specious object by the foe suborned,
And fall into deception unaware,
Not keeping strictest watch, as she was warned.
Seek not temptation then, which to avoid
Were better, and most likely if from me
Thou sever not; trial will come unsought.
Wouldst thou approve thy constancy, approve
First thy obedience; the other who can know,
Not seeing thee attempted, who attest?

    335. **And what is faith, love, virtue,** etc., i.e., what value have these
qualities unless they have been tested and found able to stand by their own
merits. Milton here puts in the mouth of Eve an argument which he himself used in *Areopagitica.* Cf. the famous passage: "I cannot praise a fugitive and cloistered virtue," etc.
    339. **to single or combined,** i.e., to us singly or together.
    341. **no Eden,** no place of delight. Cf. note on IV, 27, 28.
    348 ff. **within himself . . . no harm.** The principle of human respon-
sibility is fundamental to Milton's whole philosophy. Cf. the numerous
other references to it in *Paradise Lost* (e.g., III, 96–128; V, 524–40, and the
detailed discussion in *Christian Doctrine,* I, 3, 4).
    353. **still erect,** ever alert.
    367. **approve,** give proof of, confirm.

But if thou think trial unsought may find   370
Us both securer than thus warned thou seem'st,
Go; for thy stay, not free, absents thee more;
Go in thy native innocence, rely
On what thou hast of virtue, summon all,
For God towards thee hath done his part, do thine."
    So spake the patriarch of mankind but Eve
Persisted; yet submiss, though last, replied.
    "With thy permission then, and thus forewarned,
Chiefly by what thy own last reasoning words
Touched only, that our trial, when least sought,   380
May find us both perhaps far less prepared,
The willinger I go, nor much expect
A foe so proud will first the weaker seek;
So bent, the more shall shame him his repulse."
    Thus saying, from her husband's hand her hand
Soft she withdrew, and like a wood-nymph light,
Oread or Dryad, or of Delia's train,
Betook her to the groves, but Delia's self
In gait surpassed and goddess-like deport,
Though not as she with bow and quiver armed,   390
But with such gardening tools as art yet rude,
Guiltless of fire had formed, or angels brought.
To Pales, or Pomona, thus adorned,
Likest she seemed, Pomona when she fled
Vertumnus, or to Ceres in her prime,
Yet virgin of Proserpina from Jove.
Her long with ardent look his eye pursued
Delighted, but desiring more her stay.
Oft he to her his charge of quick return
Repeated, she to him as oft engaged   400
To be returned by noon amid the bower,
And all things in best order to invite
Noontide repast, or afternoon's repose.

    371. **securer**, i.e., "less prepared" (381).
    378 ff. The incongruity between Eve's conduct and her professed regard for Adam's advice is most effectively brought out. Milton's handling of the whole episode shows a profound knowledge of human nature.
    387. **Oread or Dryad**, a nymph of the mountains or of the trees. **Delia**, the goddess Diana, born on the island of Delos.
    392. **Guiltless of fire.** The uses of fire are not discovered until after the fall. Cf. X, 1070 ff.
    393 ff. **Pales** was a Roman goddess of flocks, **Pomona** of fruits, **Ceres** of agriculture. The mention of Eve's gardening tools suggests the comparisons. For the allusion to Pomona's being wooed by **Vertumnus**, god of the changing seasons, cf. Ovid *Metamorphoses* xiv. 623 ff.
    396. **yet virgin of**, not yet the mother of.
    402. **And all things in best order**, i.e., to have all things in best order.

O much deceived, much failing, hapless Eve,
Of thy presumed return! event perverse!
Thou never from that hour in Paradise
Found'st either sweet repast or sound repose;
Such ambush, hid among sweet flowers and shades,
Waited with hellish rancor imminent
To intercept thy way, or send thee back   410
Despoiled of innocence, of faith, of bliss.
    For now, and since first break of dawn the Fiend,
Mere serpent in appearance, forth was come,
And on his quest, where likeliest he might find
The only two of mankind, but in them
The whole included race, his purposed prey.
In bower and field he sought, where any tuft
Of grove or garden-plot more pleasant lay,
Their tendance or plantation for delight,
By fountain or by shady rivulet   420
He sought them both, but wished his hap might find
Eve separate; he wished, but not with hope
Of what so seldom chanced; when to his wish,
Beyond his hope, Eve separate he spies,
Veiled in a cloud of fragrance, where she stood,
Half spied, so thick the roses bushing round
About her glowed, oft stooping to support
Each flower of slender stalk, whose head though gay
Carnation, purple, azure, or specked with gold,
Hung drooping unsustained; them she upstays   430
Gently with myrtle band, mindless the while
Herself, though fairest unsupported flower,
From her best prop so far, and storm so nigh.
Nearer he drew, and many a walk traversed
Of stateliest covert, cedar, pine, or palm,
Then voluble and bold, now hid, now seen
Among thick-woven arborets and flowers
Imbordered on each bank, the hand of Eve:
Spot more delicious than those gardens feigned

404. **O much deceived**, etc. Cf. *Iliad* xvii. 497; *Aeneid* x. 501.
432. **Herself . . . flower.** The metaphor is repeated from IV, 270.
436. **voluble**, rolling (Latin *volubilis*).
437. **arborets**, small trees, shrubs.
438. **hand**, handiwork.
439 ff. For the allusion to the gardens of Adonis, see note on *Comus*,
999–1002. The gardens of Alcinous, the Phaeacian ruler who entertained
Odysseus (**old Laertes' son**), are described in *Odyssey* vii. The garden
of Solomon (**the sapient king**) is mentioned in Scripture; hence, from
Milton's point of view, it is not **feigned** or **mystic** (i.e., mythical) like the
others. Cf. Song of Sol. 7:2, and I Kings 3:1.

Or of revived Adonis, or renowned   440
Alcinous, host of old Laertes' son,
Or that, not mystic, where the sapient king
Held dalliance with his fair Egyptian spouse.
Much he the place admired, the person more.
As one who long in populous city pent,
Where houses thick and sewers annoy the air,
Forth issuing on a summer's morn to breathe
Among the pleasant villages and farms
Adjoined, from each thing met conceives delight,
The smell of grain, or tedded grass, or kine,   450
Or dairy, each rural sight, each rural sound;
If chance with nymph-like step fair virgin pass,
What pleasing seemed, for her now pleases more,
She most, and in her look sums all delight.
Such pleasure took the Serpent to behold
This flowery plat, the sweet recess of Eve
Thus early, thus alone; her heavenly form
Angelic, but more soft and feminine,
Her graceful innocence, her every air
Of gesture or least action overawed   460
His malice, and with rapine sweet bereaved
His fierceness of the fierce intent it brought.
That space the Evil One abstracted stood
From his own evil, and for the time remained
Stupidly good, of enmity disarmed,
Of guile, of hate, of envy, of revenge;
But the hot hell that always in him burns,
Though in mid Heaven, soon ended his delight,
And tortures him now more, the more he sees
Of pleasure not for him ordained; then soon   470
Fierce hate he recollects, and all his thoughts
Of mischief, gratulating, thus excites.
    "Thoughts, whither have ye led me, with what sweet
Compulsion thus transported to forget
What hither brought us, hate, not love, nor hope

440, 442. Or . . . or, either . . . or.
445 ff. The attitude toward nature revealed in this simile anticipates
Wordsworth's. Note especially the idea that natural objects, lovely in
themselves, are enhanced in meaning by their human associations. Milton's
treatment is ordinarily more impersonal.
    446. annoy, pollute, render noisome.
    450. tedded grass, grass just mown and spread out for drying.
    465. stupidly good, i.e., stupefied into goodness. This may seem like a
more derogatory comment on Satan's impulses than line 389 in Book IV,
but the underlying theory of Satan's nature is the same.
    467. But the hot . . . burns. Cf. I, 254, 255; IV, 20-23.

Of Paradise for Hell, hope here to taste
Of pleasure, but all pleasure to destroy,
Save what is in destroying; other joy
To me is lost. Then let me not let pass
Occasion which now smiles, behold alone   480
The woman, opportune to all attempts,
Her husband, for I view far round, not nigh,
Whose higher intellectual more I shun,
And strength, of courage haughty, and of limb
Heroic built, though of terrestrial mould,
Foe not informidable, exempt from wound,
I not; so much hath Hell debased, and pain
Enfeebled me, to what I was in Heaven.
She fair, divinely fair, fit love for Gods,
Not terrible, though terror be in love   490
And beauty, not approached by stronger hate,
Hate stronger, under shew of love well feigned,
The way which to her ruin now I tend."
  So spake the Enemy of mankind, enclosed
In serpent, inmate bad, and toward Eve
Addressed his way, not with indented wave,
Prone on the ground as since, but on his rear,
Circular base of rising folds, that towered
Fold above fold a surging maze; his head
Crested aloft, and carbuncle his eyes;   500
With burnished neck of verdant gold, erect
Amidst his circling spires, that on the grass
Floated redundant. Pleasing was his shape,
And lovely, never since of serpent kind
Lovelier; not those that in Illyria changed
Hermione and Cadmus, or the god
In Epidaurus; nor to which transformed
Ammonian Jove, or Capitoline was seen,

485. **of terrestrial mould,** of earthly substance. Cf. 149 and 176.
  496. **with indented wave.** Shakespeare (*As You Like It,* IV, iii, 113)
describes the movement of a snake in similar terms.
  500. **carbuncle,** i.e., deep red, suggesting passion.
  502. **spires,** coils (Latin *spira*).
  505. **changed,** took the place of.
  506. **Hermione** and her husband **Cadmus,** king of Thebes, were
changed into serpents at their own request, in order to escape the miseries of
human life. The god of medicine, Aesculapius, took the form of a serpent
when going from **Epidaurus** to Rome for the purpose of staying a pestilence. Both stories are told by Ovid (*Metamorphoses* iv. 562-602; xv.
622-744).
  507. **nor to which transformed,** etc., i.e., nor those serpents into which
Jove was seen transformed. According to a myth told by Plutarch, Jupiter
Ammon (**Ammonian Jove**) was the father of Alexander the Great, having

He with Olympias, this with her who bore
Scipio the height of Rome. With tract oblique   510
At first, as one who sought access, but feared
To interrupt, sidelong he works his way.
As when a ship by skilful steersman wrought
Nigh river's mouth or foreland, where the wind
Veers oft, as oft so steers, and shifts her sail;
So varied he, and of his tortuous train
Curled many a wanton wreath in sight of Eve,
To lure her eye; she busied heard the sound
Of rustling leaves, but minded not, as used
To such disport before her through the field,   520
From every beast, more duteous at her call,
Than at Circean call the herd disguised.
He bolder now, uncalled before her stood,
But as in gaze admiring. Oft he bowed
His turret crest, and sleek enamelled neck,
Fawning, and licked the ground whereon she trod.
His gentle dumb expression turned at length
The eye of Eve to mark his play; he glad
Of her attention gained, with serpent tongue
Organic, or impulse of vocal air,   530
His fraudulent temptation thus began: *serpent*
     "Wonder not, sovran mistress, if perhaps
Thou canst, who art sole wonder, much less arm
Thy looks, the heaven of mildness, with disdain,
Displeased that I approach thee thus, and gaze
Insatiate, I thus single, nor have feared
Thy awful brow, more awful thus retired.   *flattery*
Fairest resemblance of thy Maker fair,
Thee all things living gaze on, all things thine
By gift, and thy celestial beauty adore,   540
With ravishment beheld, there best beheld
Where universally admired; but here
In this enclosure wild, these beasts among,

been observed in the shape of a serpent with **Olympias**, Alexander's mother.
A similar myth portrayed Jupiter Capitolinus as the father of Scipio
Africanus.
      517. wanton, playful. Here the word has much the same connotation
as in "L'Allegro," 27.
      522. Circean call. The allusion is to the well-known myth of Circe, an
enchantress who changed men into beasts and kept them in complete subjection to her will.
      529. with serpent tongue, etc. Satan either uses the serpent's vocal
organs directly or causes his words seemingly to come from them.
      532 ff. "Wonder not, etc. Cf. the enchanter's approach to the Lady
in *Comus* (264 ff.).

Beholders rude, and shallow to discern
Half what in thee is fair, one man except,
Who sees thee? (and what is one?) who shouldst be seen
A Goddess among Gods, adored and served
By angels numberless, thy daily train."
So glozed the Tempter, and his proem tuned;   550
Into the heart of Eve his words made way,
Though at the voice much marvelling; at length
Not unamazed she thus in answer spake.
"What may this mean? Language of man pronounced
By tongue of brute, and human sense expressed?
The first at least of these I thought denied
To beasts, whom God on their creation-day
Created mute to all articulate sound;
The latter I demur, for in their looks
Much reason, and in their actions, oft appears.
Thee, Serpent, subtlest beast of all the field   560
I knew, but not with human voice endued;
Redouble then this miracle, and say,
How cam'st thou speakable of mute, and how
To me so friendly grown above the rest
Of brutal kind, that daily are in sight?
Say, for such wonder claims attention due."
To whom the guileful Tempter thus replied.
"Empress of this fair World, resplendent Eve,
Easy to me it is to tell thee all
What thou command'st, and right thou shouldst be obeyed.   570
I was at first as other beasts that graze
The trodden herb, of abject thoughts and low,
As was my food, nor aught but food discerned
Or sex, and apprehended nothing high:
Till on a day roving the field, I chanced
A goodly tree far distant to behold
Loaden with fruit of fairest colors mixed,
Ruddy and gold. I nearer drew to gaze;
When from the boughs a savory odor blown,
Grateful to appetite, more pleased my sense   580
Than smell of sweetest fennel or the teats

544. shallow, i.e., too shallow.
549. glozed, smoothed over his real motive with flattery.
558. demur, remain in doubt about. In VIII, 373, 374, Adam is told that the beasts "also know, and reason not contemptibly."
563. How cam'st thou speakable of mute, i.e., how did you, being mute, become capable of speech. The idiom of mute is classical.
581. According to popular belief, serpents were especially fond of fennel and were in the habit of sucking milk from sheep and goats.

Of ewe or goat dropping with milk at even,
Unsucked of lamb or kid, that tend their play.
To satisfy the sharp desire I had
Of tasting those fair apples, I resolved
Not to defer; hunger and thirst at once,
Powerful persuaders, quickened at the scent
Of that alluring fruit, urged me so keen.
About the mossy trunk I wound me soon,
For high from ground the branches would require   590
Thy utmost reach or Adam's: round the tree
All other beasts that saw, with like desire
Longing and envying stood, but could not reach.
Amid the tree now got, where plenty hung
Tempting so nigh, to pluck and eat my fill
I spared not, for such pleasure till that hour
At feed or fountain never had I found.
Sated at length, ere long I might perceive
Strange alteration in me, to degree
Of reason in my inward powers, and speech   600
Wanted not long, though to this shape retained.
Thenceforth to speculations high or deep
I turned my thoughts, and with capacious mind
Considered all things visible in Heaven,
Or Earth, or middle, all things fair and good;
But all that fair and good in thy divine
Semblance, and in thy beauty's heavenly ray
United I beheld; no fair to thine
Equivalent or second, which compelled
Me thus, though importune perhaps, to come   610
And gaze, and worship thee of right declared
Sovran of creatures, universal Dame."
   So talked the spirited sly Snake; and Eve
Yet more amazed unwary thus replied.
   "Serpent, thy overpraising leaves in doubt
The virtue of that fruit, in thee first proved.
But say, where grows the tree, from hence how far?
For many are the trees of God that grow
In Paradise, and various, yet unknown
To us; in such abundance lies our choice,   620
As leaves a greater store of fruit untouched,
Still hanging incorruptible, till men

605. middle, i.e., the air.
   612. universal Dame, mistress of the universe. Dame is here equivalent to Latin *domina*.
   613. spirited, i.e., inspired by Satan.
   622. incorruptible, incapable of decay.

Grow up to their provision, and more hands
Help to disburden Nature of her birth."
    To whom the wily Adder, blithe and glad.
"Empress, the way is ready, and not long;
Beyond a row of myrtles, on a flat,
Fast by a fountain, one small thicket past
Of blowing myrrh and balm; if thou accept
My conduct, I can bring thee thither soon."   630
    "Lead then," said Eve. He leading swiftly rolled
In tangles, and made intricate seem straight,
To mischief swift. Hope elevates, and joy
Brightens his crest, as when a wandering fire,
Compact of unctuous vapor, which the night
Condenses, and the cold environs round;
Kindled through agitation to a flame,
Which oft, they say, some evil spirit attends,
Hovering and blazing with delusive light,
Misleads the amazed night-wanderer from his way   640
To bogs and mires, and oft through pond or pool,
There swallowed up and lost, from succor far.
So glistered the dire Snake, and into fraud
Led Eve our credulous mother, to the tree
Of prohibition, root of all our woe;
Which when she saw, thus to her guide she spake.
    "Serpent, we might have spared our coming hither,
Fruitless to me, though fruit be here to excess,
The credit of whose virtue rest with thee,
Wondrous indeed, if cause of such effects.   650
But of this tree we may not taste nor touch;
God so commanded, and left that command
Sole daughter of his voice; the rest, we live
Law to ourselves, our reason is our law."
    To whom the Tempter guilefully replied.
"Indeed? Hath God then said that of the fruit
Of all these garden trees ye shall not eat,
Yet lords declared of all in Earth or air?"

624. birth, i.e., the products to which she has given birth.
629. blowing, blossoming.
634 ff. This description of the ignis fatuus combines a semiscientific
explanation with a popular superstition. Whether Milton actually believed
the phenomenon the work of an evil spirit he does not say. Cf. his other
references to it: "L'Allegro," 104; Comus, 432.
640. Misleads . . . night-wanderer. Cf. A Midsummer Night's Dream,
II, i, 39.
643. fraud, offense, harm (Latin fraus).
653. sole daughter of his voice. Cf. Wordsworth's adaptation ("Ode
to Duty"): "Stern daughter of the Voice of God." the rest, as for the rest.

To whom thus Eve yet sinless. "Of the fruit
Of each tree in the garden we may eat,   660
But of the fruit of this fair tree amidst
The garden, God hath said, 'Ye shall not eat
Thereof, nor shall ye touch it, lest ye die.'"
    She scarce had said, though brief, when now more bold
The Tempter, but with show of zeal and love
To Man, and indignation at his wrong,
New part puts on, and as to passion moved,
Fluctuates disturbed, yet comely and in act
Raised, as of some great matter to begin.
As when of old some orator renowned   670
In Athens or free Rome, where eloquence
Flourished, since mute, to some great cause addressed,
Stood in himself collected, while each part,
Motion, each act won audience ere the tongue,
Sometimes in height began, as no delay
Of preface brooking through his zeal of right.
So standing, moving, or to height upgrown,
The Tempter all impassioned thus began.
    "O sacred, wise, and wisdom-giving Plant,
Mother of science now I feel thy power   680
Within me clear, not only to discern
Things in their causes, but to trace the ways
Of highest agents, deemed however wise.
Queen of this Universe, do not believe
Those rigid threats of death; ye shall not die:
How should ye? by the fruit? it gives you life
To knowledge; by the threatener? look on me,
Me who have touched and tasted, yet both live,
And life more perfect have attained than fate
Meant me, by venturing higher than my lot.   690
Shall that be shut to Man, which to the beast

661–63. Milton here follows very closely the phraseology of Gen. 3:1–3.
    668. fluctuates. The word is used literally. Milton means that the
serpent moves his body to and fro, in order to give visible expression to his
assumed emotion.
    670 ff. Note Milton's disparagement of modern oratory. When he
thinks of true eloquence, he thinks of Demosthenes and Cicero.
    675. Sometimes in height. The description suggests Cicero's first
oration against Catiline.
    679 ff. "O sacred, wise . . ." The serpent's speech is a masterpiece of
persuasion, uniting intense emotional fervor with closely packed and seemingly irrefutable arguments. Milton does not wish to make Eve too easy a
victim.
    680. science, knowledge (Latin scientia).
    685. ye shall not die. Cf. Gen. 3:4.
    687. To, in addition to.

Is open? or will God incense his ire
For such a petty trespass, and not praise
Rather your dauntless virtue, whom the pain
Of death denounced, whatever thing death be,
Deterred not from achieving what might lead
To happier life, knowledge of good and evil;
Of good, how just? of evil, if what is evil
Be real, why not known, since easier shunned?
God therefore cannot hurt ye, and be just;   700
Not just, not God; not feared then, nor obeyed:
Your fear itself of death removes the fear.
Why then was this forbid? Why but to awe,
Why but to keep ye low and ignorant,
His worshippers; he knows that in the day
Ye eat thereof, your eyes that seem so clear,
Yet are but dim, shall perfectly be then
Opened and cleared, and ye shall be as Gods,
Knowing both good and evil as they know.
That ye should be as Gods, since I as Man,   710
Internal Man, is but proportion meet,
I of brute human, ye of human Gods.
So ye shall die perhaps, by putting off
Human, to put on Gods, death to be wished,
Though threatened, which no worse than this can bring.
And what are Gods, that Man may not become
As they, participating godlike food?
The Gods are first, and that advantage use
On our belief, that all from them proceeds;
I question it, for this fair Earth I see,   720
Warmed by the sun, producing every kind,
Them nothing. If they all things, who enclosed
Knowledge of good and evil in this tree,
That whoso eats thereof, forthwith attains
Wisdom without their leave? and wherein lies
The offence, that Man should thus attain to know?
What can your knowledge hurt him, or this tree
Impart against his will, if all be his?
Or is it envy, and can envy dwell
In heavenly breasts? These, these and many more   730
Causes import your need of this fair fruit.
Goddess humane, reach then, and freely taste!"
    He ended, and his words replete with guile
Into her heart too easy entrance won.

714. to put on Gods, i.e., to "put on immortality" I Cor. 15:53.
729. can envy dwell, etc. Cf. IV, 118, 119, and note.
732. humane, gracious, gentle in demeanor.

Fixed on the fruit she gazed, which to behold
Might tempt alone, and in her ears the sound
Yet rung of his persuasive words, impregned
With reason, to her seeming, and with truth;
Meanwhile the hour of noon drew on, and waked
An eager appetite, raised by the smell   740
So savory of that fruit, which with desire,
Inclinable now grown to touch or taste,
Solicited her longing eye; yet first
Pausing a while, thus to herself she mused.
    "Great are thy virtues, doubtless, best of fruits,
Though kept from Man, and worthy to be admired,
Whose taste, too long forborne, at first assay
Gave elocution to the mute, and taught
The tongue not made for speech to speak thy praise.
Thy praise he also who forbids thy use   750
Conceals not from us, naming thee the Tree
Of Knowledge, knowledge both of good and evil;
Forbids us then to taste, but his forbidding
Commends thee more, while it infers the good
By thee communicated, and our want;
For good unknown sure is not had, or had
And yet unknown, is as not had at all.
In plain then, what forbids he but to know,
Forbids us good, forbids us to be wise?
Such prohibitions bind not. But if Death   760
Bind us with after-bands, what profits then
Our inward freedom? In the day we eat
Of this fair fruit, our doom is, we shall die.
How dies the Serpent? He hath eaten and lives,
And knows, and speaks, and reasons, and discerns,
Irrational till then. For us alone
Was death invented? or to us denied
This intellectual food, for beasts reserved?
For beasts it seems; yet that one beast which first
Hath tasted, envies not, but brings with joy   770
That good befallen him, author unsuspect,
Friendly to man, far from deceit or guile.

737. **impregned**, impregnated. Cf. IV, 500.
    739-43. Physical appetite is an important factor in Eve's decision, but
she does not admit it to herself. In having her rationalize her instinctive
desire, Milton is having her act in a very human manner. Her mental
operations are keen and logical, as Adam's were when he discoursed on
celestial motion, and her own when she argued for working separately from
her husband. But it is not by such processes that wise decision is arrived at.
    758. **In plain**, frankly (i.e., in plain terms).
    771. **author unsuspect**, informant not to be suspected.

What fear I then, rather what know to fear
Under this ignorance of good and evil,
Of God or death, of law or penalty?
Here grows the cure of all, this fruit divine,
Fair to the eye, inviting to the taste,
Of virtue to make wise; what hinders then
To reach, and feed at once both body and mind?"
    So saying, her rash hand in evil hour   780
Forth reaching to the fruit, she plucked, she eat.
Earth felt the wound, and Nature from her seat
Sighing through all her works gave signs of woe,
That all was lost. Back to the thicket slunk
The guilty Serpent, and well might, for Eve
Intent now only on her taste, nought else
Regarded; such delight till then, as seemed,
In fruit she never tasted, whether true
Or fancied so, through expectation high
Of knowledge, nor was Godhead from her thought.   790
Greedily she ingorged without restraint,
And knew not eating death. Satiate at length,
And heightened as with wine, jocund and boon,
Thus to herself she pleasingly began.
    "O sovran, virtuous, precious of all trees
In Paradise, of operation blest
To sapience, hitherto obscured, infamed,
And thy fair fruit let hang, as to no end
Created; but henceforth my early care,
Not without song, each morning, and due praise,   800
Shall tend thee, and the fertile burden ease

    778. Of virtue, i.e., having the power.
    781. eat. Milton regularly uses this form of the preterite. Since the
pronunciation corresponds to the spelling (cf. "L'Allegro," 101, 102), lines
781 and 782 form a rhymed couplet, giving effective emphasis to a crucial
point in the action.
    791. Greedily she ingorged without restraint. In terms of human
ethics as opposed to theology, Milton interprets the sin of Adam and Eve as
a sin of excess, a violation of temperance. Eve's initial greed is therefore
a symbol of all the other forms of excess in which she and Adam afterwards
indulge.
    792. knew not eating, i.e., knew not that she was eating. This use of
the participle after a verb of knowing is common to both Greek and Latin.
Cf. *Aeneid* ii. 377.
    793. boon, gay.
    795. virtuous, precious of all trees, i.e., most virtuous, most precious,
etc. The idiom is classical.
    796–97. of operation blest To sapience, i.e., so blest as to have the
power of conferring wisdom.
    797. infamed, not known.
    800. Not without song. Cf. Horace *Odes* iii. 13. 2: *non sine floribus.*

Of thy full branches offered free to all;
Till dieted by thee I grow mature
In knowledge, as the Gods who all things know;
Though others envy what they cannot give;
For had the gift been theirs, it had not here
Thus grown. Experience, next to thee I owe,
Best guide; not following thee, I had remained
In ignorance, thou open'st Wisdom's way,
And givest access, though secret she retire.   810
And I perhaps am secret; Heaven is high,
High and remote to see from thence distinct
Each thing on Earth; and other care perhaps
May have diverted from continual watch
Our great Forbidder, safe with all his spies
About him. But to Adam in what sort
Shall I appear? Shall I to him make known
As yet my change, and give him to partake
Full happiness with me, or rather not,
But keep the odds of knowledge in my power   820
Without copartner? so to add what wants
In female sex, the more to draw his love,
And render me more equal, and perhaps,
A thing not undesirable, sometime
Superior; for inferior who is free?
This may be well. But what if God have seen
And death ensue? then I shall be no more,
And Adam wedded to another Eve,
Shall live with her enjoying, I extinct;
A death to think. Confirmed then I resolve   830
Adam shall share with me in bliss or woe.
So dear I love him, that with him all deaths
I could endure, without him live no life."
  So saying, from the tree her step she turned,
But first low reverence done, as to the power
That dwelt within, whose presence had infused
Into the plant sciential sap, derived
From nectar, drink of Gods. Adam the while

815. **safe,** not likely to do harm. The word frequently has a similar meaning in Shakespeare: e.g., in *The Tempest,* III, i, 21.
  817 ff. **Shall I to him,** etc. The first fruits of Eve's sin are selfishness and jealousy—the negation of her original qualities.
  835–36. Eve's perverted conception of God quickly manifests itself in idolatry.
  837. **sciential,** capable of bestowing knowledge.
  838–44. **Adam the while . . . delayed.** The situation closely parallels that in *Iliad* xxii. 440 ff., where Andromache is described making preparations for Hector's return, not knowing that he is already slain.

Waiting desirous her return, had wove
Of choicest flowers a garland to adorn   840
Her tresses, and her rural labors crown,
As reapers oft are wont their harvest queen.
Great joy he promised to his thoughts, and new
Solace in her return, so long delayed;
Yet oft his heart, divine of something ill,
Misgave him; he the faltering measure felt;
And forth to meet her went, the way she took
That morn when first they parted. By the Tree
Of Knowledge he must pass; there he her met,
Scarce from the tree returning; in her hand   850
A bough of fairest fruit that downy smiled,
New gathered, and ambrosial smell diffused.
To him she hasted; in her face excuse
Came prologue, and apology to prompt,
Which with bland words at will she thus addressed.
    "Hast thou not wondered, Adam, at my stay?
Thee I have missed, and thought it long, deprived
Thy presence, agony of love till now
Not felt, nor shall be twice, for never more
Mean I to try what rash untried I sought,   860
The pain of absence from thy sight. But strange
Hath been the cause, and wonderful to hear:
This tree is not as we are told, a tree
Of danger tasted, nor to evil unknown
Opening the way, but of divine effect
To open eyes, and make them Gods who taste;
And hath been tasted such. The Serpent wise,
Or not restrained as we, or not obeying,
Hath eaten of the fruit, and is become
Not dead as we are threatened, but thenceforth   870
Endued with human voice and human sense,
Reasoning to admiration, and with me
Persuasively hath so prevailed, that I
Have also tasted, and have also found
The effects to correspond, opener mine eyes,
Dim erst, dilated spirits, ampler heart,

845. **divine of**, foreboding.
846. **faltering measure**, i.e., the uneven beating of his heart.
852. **ambrosial smell diffused.** Cf. Virgil *Georgics* iv. 415.
853–54. **in her face . . . prompt.** Milton means that the appearance of
Eve's face served as a fitting introduction to her verbal apology. The stage
imagery is perhaps intended to suggest her insincerity; she approaches Adam
in an assumed character.
872. **to admiration**, in a way to be admired.

And growing up to Godhead; which for thee
Chiefly I sought, without thee can despise.
For bliss, as thou hast part, to me is bliss;
Tedious, unshared with thee, and odious soon.   880
Thou therefore also taste, that equal lot
May join us, equal joy, as equal love;
Lest thou not tasting, different degree
Disjoin us, and I then too late renounce
Deity for thee, when fate will not permit."
   Thus Eve with countenance blithe her story told;
But in her cheek distemper flushing glowed.
On the other side, Adam, soon as he heard
The fatal trespass done by Eve, amazed,
Astonied stood and blank, while horror chill   890
Ran through his veins, and all his joints relaxed;
From his slack hand the garland wreathed for Eve
Down dropped, and all the faded roses shed.
Speechless he stood and pale, till thus at length
First to himself he inward silence broke.
   "O fairest of creation, last and best
Of all God's works, creature in whom excelled
Whatever can to sight or thought be formed,
Holy, divine, good, amiable, or sweet!
How art thou lost, how on a sudden lost,   900
Defaced, deflowered, and now to death devote!
Rather how hast thou yielded to transgress
The strict forbiddance, how to violate
The sacred fruit forbidden! Some cursèd fraud
Of enemy hath beguiled thee, yet unknown,
And me with thee hath ruined, for with thee
Certain my resolution is to die;
How can I live without thee, how forgo
Thy sweet converse and love so dearly joined,
To live again in these wild woods forlorn?   910
Should God create another Eve, and I
Another rib afford, yet loss of thee
Would never from my heart; no, no! I feel

   877–78. **which for . . . chiefly I sought.** Eve ends her plea with an
open falsehood. Cf. 816–25.
   890–91. **astonied . . . veins.** Cf. *Aeneid* ii. 120, 121.
   901. **devote,** doomed, accursed. The phrase **to death devote** is an echo
of Horace's *devota morti* (*Odes* iv. 14, 18).
   906 ff. **for with thee,** etc. Adam's determination to die with Eve, heroic
as it is from a chivalric point of view, is not a reasoned determination. Its
motive is passion, which sways his judgment to do what "else free will
would not admit" (VIII, 635–37).

The link of nature draw me: flesh of flesh,
Bone of my bone thou art, and from thy state
Mine never shall be parted, bliss or woe."
    So having said, as one from sad dismay
Recomforted, and after thoughts disturbed
Submitting to what seemed remediless,
Thus in calm mood his words to Eve he turned.   920
    "Bold deed thou hast presumed, adventurous Eve,
And peril great provoked, who thus hast dared,
Had it been only coveting to eye
That sacred fruit, sacred to abstinence,
Much more to taste it under ban to touch.
But past who can recall, or done undo?
Not God Omnipotent, nor Fate. Yet so
Perhaps thou shalt not die; perhaps the fact
Is not so heinous now, foretasted fruit,
Profaned first by the Serpent, by him first   930
Made common and unhallowed ere our taste,
Nor yet on him found deadly; he yet lives,
Lives, as thou saidst, and gains to live as Man
Higher degree of life, inducement strong
To us, as likely tasting to attain
Proportional ascent, which cannot be
But to be Gods, or angels, demi-gods.
Nor can I think that God, Creator wise,
Though threatening, will in earnest so destroy
Us his prime creatures, dignified so high,   940
Set over all his works, which in our fall,
For us created, needs with us must fail,
Dependent made; so God shall uncreate,
Be frustrate, do, undo, and labor lose,
Not well conceived of God, who though his power
Creation could repeat, yet would be loth
Us to abolish, lest the Adversary
Triumph and say: 'Fickle their state whom God
Most favors, who can please him long? Me first
He ruined, now mankind; whom will he next?'   950
Matter of scorn not to be given the Foe;
However, I with thee have fixed my lot,

    914 ff. flesh of flesh, etc. Cf. Gen. 2:23. Cf. also VIII, 494–99, where
Milton represents Adam as making a significant addition: "one heart, one
soul."
    928. fact, deed (Latin *factum*).
    932. He yet lives, etc. Having determined his course on nonrational
grounds, Adam proceeds to rationalize just as Eve had done. His arguments,
moreover, are just as specious as hers.
    947. lest the Adversary, etc. Cf. Deut. 32:27.

Certain to undergo like doom: if death
Consort with thee, death is to me as life;
So forcible within my heart I feel
The bond of nature draw me to my own,
My own in thee, for what thou art is mine;
Our state cannot be severed; we are one,
One flesh; to lose thee were to lose myself."
   So Adam, and thus Eve to him replied.   960
"O glorious trial of exceeding love,
Illustrious evidence, example high!
Engaging me to emulate, but short
Of thy perfection, how shall I attain,
Adam, from whose dear side I boast me sprung,
And gladly of our union hear thee speak,
One heart, one soul in both; whereof good proof
This day affords, declaring thee resolved,
Rather than death or aught than death more dread
Shall separate us, linked in love so dear,   970
To undergo with me one guilt, one crime,
If any be, of tasting this fair fruit,
Whose virtue (for of good still good proceeds,
Direct, or by occasion) hath presented
This happy trial of thy love, which else
So eminently never had been known.
Were it I thought death menaced would ensue
This my attempt, I would sustain alone
The worst, and not persuade thee, rather die
Deserted, than oblige thee with a fact   980
Pernicious to thy peace, chiefly assured
Remarkably so late of thy so true,
So faithful love unequalled; but I feel
Far otherwise the event, not death, but life
Augmented, opened eyes, new hopes, new joys,
Taste so divine, that what of sweet before
Hath touched my sense, flat seems to this and harsh.
On my experience, Adam, freely taste,
And fear of death deliver to the winds."
   So saying, she embraced him, and for joy   990
Tenderly wept, much won that he his love
Had so ennobled, as of choice to incur
Divine displeasure for her sake, or death.

    953. **certain,** resolved (Latin *certus*).
    967. **one heart, one soul.** Eve recalls Adam's earlier words. Cf. 914,
915, and note.
    977–83. **Were it I thought . . . unequalled.** Cf. 826–33. **oblige,**
render liable to punishment (Latin *obligare*).

In recompense (for such compliance bad
Such recompense best merits) from the bough
She gave him of that fair enticing fruit
With liberal hand; he scrupled not to eat
Against his better knowledge, not deceived,
But fondly overcome with female charm.
Earth trembled from her entrails, as again   1000
In pangs, and Nature gave a second groan;
Sky loured, and muttering thunder, some sad drops
Wept at completing of the mortal sin
Original; while Adam took no thought,
Eating his fill, nor Eve to iterate
Her former trespass feared, the more to soothe
Him with her loved society that now
As with new wine intoxicated both
They swim in mirth, and fancy that they feel
Divinity within them breeding wings   1010
Wherewith to scorn the Earth. But that false fruit
Far other operation first displayed,
Carnal desire inflaming: he on Eve
Began to cast lascivious eyes, she him
As wantonly repaid; in lust they burn,
Till Adam thus 'gan Eve to dalliance move.
    "Eve, now I see thou art exact of taste,
And elegant, of sapience no small part;
Since to each meaning savor we apply,
And palate call judicious; I the praise   1020
Yield thee, so well this day thou hast purveyed.
Much pleasure we have lost, while we abstained
From this delightful fruit, nor known till now
True relish, tasting; if such pleasure be

999. not deceived. Cf. I Tim. 2:14.
    1000 ff. Earth trembled, etc. The idea that the fall was marked by
convulsions of the earth and other signs of nature's grief is a literary and
theological tradition. While it has no direct scriptural authority, it may
have been suggested by the analogous portents accompanying the crucifixion
of Christ (Matt. 27:51).
    1003–4. the mortal sin Original. This is Milton's only use in the
poem of the theological term "original sin." He expounds it fully in Christian Doctrine, I, 11.
    1009. swim in mirth. Cf. Spenser's line "Yet swimming in that sea of
blissful joy" (Faerie Queene, I, xii, 41). Milton makes a play on the word
in XI, 625, 626.
    1011. to scorn the Earth. Cf. Horace Odes iii. 2, 24.
    1019. The word savor is derived from Latin sapere, which means both
"to taste" and "to be wise." Milton represents Adam as playing on this
double meaning in explaining why Eve's taste can properly be called judicious. The same quibble, much more effective in Latin than in English, is
used by Cicero (De Finibus ii. 8).

In things to us forbidden, it might be wished
For this one tree had been forbidden ten.
But come; so well refreshed, now let us play,
As meet is, after such delicious fare;
For never did thy beauty since the day
I saw thee first and wedded thee, adorned   1030
With all perfections, so inflame my sense
With ardor to enjoy thee, fairer now
Than ever, bounty of this virtuous tree."
     So said he, and forbore not glance or toy
Of amorous intent, well understood   *lust*
Of Eve, whose eye darted contagious fire.
Her hand he seized, and to a shady bank,   *hand in*
Thick overhead with verdant roof embowered,   *hand*
He led her nothing loth; flowers were the couch,   *not united*
Pansies, and violets, and asphodel,   1040
And hyacinth, Earth's freshest softest lap.
There they their fill of love and love's disport
Took largely, of their mutual guilt the seal,
The solace of their sin, till dewy sleep
Oppressed them, wearied with their amorous play.
     Soon as the force of that fallacious fruit,
That with exhilarating vapor bland
About their spirits had played, and inmost powers
Made err, was now exhaled, and grosser sleep,
Bred of unkindly fumes, with conscious dreams   1050
Encumbered, now had left them, up they rose
As from unrest, and each the other viewing,
Soon found their eyes how opened, and their minds
How darkened; innocence, that as a veil
Had shadowed them from knowing ill, was gone;
Just confidence, and native righteousness,
And honor from about them, naked left
To guilty Shame. He covered, but his robe
Uncovered more. So rose the Danite strong,
Herculean Samson, from the harlot-lap   1060

     1029 ff. never did thy beauty, etc. Similar invitations to love are given
by Paris to Helen (*Iliad* iii. 442 ff.) and Zeus to Hera (*Iliad* xiv. 292 ff.).
     1034. toy, caress.
     1037. shady bank . . . lap. Cf. the description of the first nuptial
bower, IV, 690 ff.
     1042. their fill of love. Cf. Prov. 7:18.
     1050. unkindly, contrary to nature.
     1058. He covered, etc., i.e., shame covered them with his robe, but in
so doing revealed to them their nakedness. There is an obvious allusion to
Ps. 109:29.
     1060. So rose the Danite strong, etc. Cf. Judg. 16:4-20, and *Samson
Agonistes.* That Milton was early impressed by the story of Samson is

Of Philistean Delilah, and waked
Shorn of his strength, they destitute and bare
Of all their virtue. Silent, and in face
Confounded, long they sat, as strucken mute,
Till Adam, though not less than Eve abashed,
At length gave utterance to these words constrained,
　　"O Eve, in evil hour thou didst give ear
To that false worm, of whomsoever taught
To counterfeit Man's voice, true in our fall,
False in our promised rising; since our eyes　　　　1070
Opened we find indeed, and find we know
Both good and evil, good lost and evil got,
Bad fruit of knowledge, if this be to know,
Which leaves us naked thus, of honor void,
Of innocence, of faith, of purity,
Our wonted ornaments now soiled and stained,
And in our faces evident the signs
Of foul concupiscence; whence evil store,
Even shame, the last of evils; of the first
Be sure then. How shall I behold the face　　　　1080
Henceforth of God or angel, erst with joy
And rapture so oft beheld? those heavenly shapes
Will dazzle now this earthly, with their blaze
Insufferably bright. Oh might I here
In solitude live savage, in some glade
Obscured, where highest woods impenetrable
To star or sunlight, spread their umbrage broad
And brown as evening! Cover me ye pines,
Ye cedars, with innumerable boughs
Hide me, where I may never see them more.　　　　1090
But let us now, as in bad plight, devise
What best may for the present serve to hide
The parts of each from other that seem most
To shame obnoxious, and unseemliest seen,
Some tree whose broad smooth leaves together sewed,
And girded on our loins, may cover round
Those middle parts, that this new comer, Shame,
There sit not, and reproach us as unclean."

shown by his use of it in the conclusion of *The Reason of Church Government*.
　　1064. **strucken.** The same form of the past participle occurs in Shakespeare (*Comedy of Errors,* I, ii. 45).
　　1068. **worm,** serpent.
　　1079. **the last of evils,** i.e., the greatest (Latin *extremus*). **the first,** i.e., the lesser.
　　1088. **Cover me,** etc. Cf. Rev. 6:16.
　　1094. **obnoxious.** Cf. note on 170.

So counselled he, and both together went
Into the thickest wood; there soon they chose   1100
The fig-tree, not that kind for fruit renowned,   *fig-tree*
But such at this day to Indians known
In Malabar or Decan spreads her arms
Branching so broad and long, that in the ground
The bended twigs take root, and daughters grow
About the mother tree, a pillared shade
High overarched, and echoing walks between;
There oft the Indian herdsman shunning heat
Shelters in cool, and tends his pasturing herds
At loop-holes cut through thickest shade. Those leaves   1110
They gathered, broad as Amazonian targe,
And with what skill they had, together sewed,
To gird their waist, vain covering if to hide
Their guilt and dreaded shame; Oh how unlike
To that first naked glory. Such of late
Columbus found the American so girt
With feathered cincture, naked else and wild
Among the trees on isles and woody shores.
Thus fenced, and as they thought, their shame in part
Covered, but not at rest or ease of mind,   1120
They sat them down to weep, nor only tears
Rained at their eyes, but high winds worse within
Began to rise, high passions, anger, hate,
Mistrust, suspicion, discord, and shook sore
Their inward state of mind, calm region once
And full of peace, now tossed and turbulent;
For Understanding ruled not, and the Will   *Understanding*
Heard not her lore, both in subjection now   *Will*
To sensual Appetite, who from beneath
Usurping over sovran Reason claimed   1130
Superior sway. From thus distempered breast,
Adam, estranged in look and altered style,
Speech intermitted thus to Eve renewed.

1101 ff. The fig tree, etc. This description of the Indian fig or banyan tree follows that given in the standard Elizabethan work on botany, Gerard's *Herball*. Gerard was in error as to the size of the tree's leaves, having apparently relied on an inaccurate statement by Pliny (*Natural History* xii. 5). The leaves of the banyan are actually small.

1103. Malabar refers to the western coast of Hindustan, especially the southern part. Decan or Deccan, is a name applied to the entire peninsula.

1111. Amazonian targe, shield of the Amazons. Virgil (*Aeneid* i. 490) describes these shields as crescent-shaped.

1127 ff. For Understanding . . . sway. The tripartite division of the soul, which underlies this passage, is Platonic. Cf. 351–56, and XII, 82–101. Plato's fullest exposition of the idea is in the *Republic* 439–42.

"Would thou hadst hearkened to my words, and stayed
With me, as I besought thee, when that strange
Desire of wandering this unhappy morn,
I know not whence possessed thee; we had then
Remained still happy, not as now, despoiled
Of all our good, shamed, naked, miserable.
Let none henceforth seek needless cause to approve   1140
The faith they owe; when earnestly they seek
Such proof, conclude, they then begin to fail."
  To whom soon moved with touch of blame thus Eve.
"What words have passed thy lips, Adam severe!
Imputest thou that to my default, or will
Of wandering, as thou call'st it, which who knows
But might as ill have happened thou being by,
Or to thyself perhaps? Hadst thou been there,
Or here the attempt, thou couldst not have discerned
Fraud in the Serpent, speaking as he spake;   1150
No ground of enmity between us known,
Why he should mean me ill, or seek to harm.
Was I to have never parted from thy side?
As good have grown there still a lifeless rib.
Being as I am, why didst not thou the head
Command me absolutely not to go,
Going into such danger as thou saidst?
Too facile then, thou didst not much gainsay,
Nay didst permit, approve, and fair dismiss.
Hadst thou been firm and fixed in thy dissent,   1160
Neither had I transgressed, nor thou with me."
  To whom then first incensed Adam replied.
"Is this the love, is this the recompense
Of mine to thee, ingrateful Eve, expressed
Immutable when thou wert lost, not I,
Who might have lived and joyed immortal bliss,
Yet willingly chose rather death with thee?
And am I now upbraided, as the cause

1141. owe, possess.
1144. What words have passed thy lips. Cf. *Iliad* xiv. 83.
1155. the head. Cf. I Cor. 11:3.
1163 ff. Adam's statement is a fascinating mixture of right and wrong
judgment, self-knowledge, and self-deception. In Milton's theory he is the
superior being, but his reasoning is flawed by passion: "Understanding
ruled not." Lines 1166–67 are certainly not a fair representation of the
facts, being inconsistent with what he said in lines 908–10, above: "How
can I live without thee?" On the other hand, he has come to the point of
partly recognizing his own weakness: "And perhaps I also erred." How
detached Milton himself is in all this it is really very difficult to say.
1164. expressed, demonstrated.

Of thy transgressing? not enough severe,
It seems, in thy restraint. What could I more?   1170
I warned thee, I admonished thee, foretold
The danger, and the lurking enemy
That lay in wait; beyond this had been force,   *free will*
And force upon free will hath here no place.
But confidence then bore thee on, secure
Either to meet no danger or to find
Matter of glorious trial; and perhaps
I also erred in overmuch admiring
What seemed in thee so perfect, that I thought
No evil durst attempt thee, but I rue   1180
That error now, which is become my crime,
And thou the accuser. Thus it shall befall   *women*
Him who to worth in women overtrusting
Lets her will rule; restraint she will not brook,
And left to herself, if evil thence ensue,
She first his weak indulgence will accuse."
Thus they in mutual accusation spent
The fruitless hours, but neither self-condemning,
And of their vain contest appeared no end.

BOOK X

THE ARGUMENT

Man's transgression known, the guardian angels forsake Paradise, and return up to Heaven to approve their vigilance, and are
approved; God declaring that the entrance of Satan could not be
by them prevented. He sends his Son to judge the transgressors;
who descends, and gives sentence accordingly; then in pity clothes
them both, and reascends. Sin and Death, sitting till then at the
gates of Hell, by wondrous sympathy feeling the success of Satan
in this new world, and the sin by Man there committed, resolve
to sit no longer confined in Hell, but to follow Satan, their sire,
up to the place of Man. To make the way easier from Hell to this
world to and fro, they pave a broad highway or bridge over Chaos,
according to the track that Satan first made; then, preparing for
Earth, they meet him, proud of his success, returning to Hell;
their mutual gratulation. Satan arrives at Pandemonium; in full
assembly relates, with boasting, his success against Man; instead
of applause is entertained with a general hiss by all his audience,
transformed, with himself also, suddenly into serpents, according
to his doom given in Paradise; then, deluded with a show of the
Forbidden Tree springing up before them, they greedily reaching
to take of the fruit chew dust and bitter ashes. The proceedings

of Sin and Death; God foretells the final victory of his Son over
them, and the renewing of all things; but for the present commands his angels to make several alterations in the heavens and
elements. Adam, more and more perceiving his fallen condition,
heavily bewails, rejects the condolement of Eve; she persists, and
at length appeases him: then, to evade the curse likely to fall on
their offspring, proposes to Adam violent ways, which he approves
not, but, conceiving better hope, puts her in mind of the late
promise made them, that her seed should be revenged on the
Serpent, and exhorts her with him to seek peace of the offended
Deity by repentance and supplication.

Meanwhile the heinous and despiteful act
Of Satan done in Paradise, and how
He in the Serpent had perverted Eve,
Her husband she, to taste the fatal fruit,
Was known in Heaven; for what can scape the eye
Of God all-seeing, or deceive his heart
Omniscient? who in all things wise and just,
Hindered not Satan to attempt the mind
Of Man, with strength entire, and free will armed,
Complete to have discovered and repulsed   10
Whatever wiles of foe or seeming friend.
For still they knew, and ought to have still remembered
The high injunction not to taste that fruit,
Whoever tempted; which they not obeying,
Incurred (what could they less?) the penalty,
And manifold in sin, deserved to fall.
    Up into Heaven from Paradise in haste
The angelic guards ascended, mute and sad
For Man; for of his state by this they knew,
Much wondering how the subtle Fiend had stolen   20
Entrance unseen. Soon as the unwelcome news
From Earth arrived at Heaven gate, displeased
All were who heard; dim sadness did not spare
That time celestial visages, yet mixed
With pity, violated not their bliss.
About the new-arrived, in multitudes
The ethereal people ran, to hear and know
How all befell. They towards the throne supreme

    28–32. There is an ambiguity in the grammar of this sentence which
has given the commentators trouble. They made haste to the throne to render their account, but also, to justify their vigilance by a plea of righteousness. **And easily approved** may be read "and they were easily approved,
easily won approval." But it may also be taken as parallel to **accountable**
and modifying **vigilance.** They went to the throne to win approval for
their vigilance.

Accountable made haste to make appear
With righteous plea, their utmost vigilance,   30
And easily approved; when the Most High
Eternal Father, from his secret cloud
Amidst, in thunder uttered thus his voice.   *God*
    "Assembled Angels, and ye Powers returned
From unsuccessful charge, be not dismayed,
Nor troubled at these tidings from the Earth,
Which your sincerest care could not prevent,
Foretold so lately what would come to pass,
When first this Tempter crossed the gulf from Hell.
I told ye then he should prevail and speed   40
On his bad errand; Man should be seduced
And flattered out of all, believing lies
Against his Maker; no decree of mine
Concurring to necessitate his fall,
Or touch with lightest moment of impulse
His free will, to her own inclining left   *free will*
In even scale. But fallen he is; and now
What rests but that the mortal sentence pass
On his transgression, death denounced that day,
Which he presumes already vain and void,   50
Because not yet inflicted, as he feared,
By some immediate stroke; but soon shall find
Forbearance no acquittance ere day end.
Justice shall not return as bounty scorned.
But whom send I to judge them? whom but thee,
Vicegerent Son? to thee I have transferred
All judgment, whether in Heaven, or Earth, or Hell.
Easy it may be seen that I intend
Mercy colleague with justice, sending thee
Man's friend, his Mediator, his designed   60
Both ransom and Redeemer voluntary,
And destined Man himself to judge Man fallen."
    So spake the Father; and unfolding bright
Toward the right hand his glory, on the Son
Blazed forth unclouded deity; he full
Resplendent all his Father manifest
Expressed, and thus divinely answered mild.   *Son*
    "Father Eternal, thine is to decree,
Mine both in Heaven and Earth to do thy will
Supreme, that thou in me thy Son beloved,   70

    54. Justice shall not be returned in the form of a bounty which has been
and will be scorned.
    58 ff. Man is to be judged by Christ, who is destined himself to become
man. This is evidence that God intends mercy as well as justice.

May'st ever rest well pleased. I go to judge
On Earth these thy transgressors; but thou knowst,
Whoever judged, the worst on me must light,
When time shall be; for so I undertook
Before thee, and not repenting, this obtain
Of right, that I may mitigate their doom
On me derived; yet I shall temper so
Justice with mercy, as may illustrate most
Them fully satisfied, and thee appease.
Attendance none shall need, nor train, where none   80
Are to behold the judgment but the judged,
Those two; the third best absent is condemned,
Convict by flight, and rebel to all law
Conviction to the Serpent none belongs."
      Thus saying, from his radiant seat he rose
Of high collateral glory; Him Thrones and Powers,
Princedoms, and Dominations ministrant
Accompanied to Heaven gate, from whence
Eden and all the coast in prospect lay.
Down he descended straight; the speed of Gods   90
Time counts not, though with swiftest minutes winged.
      Now was the sun in western cadence low
From noon, and gentle airs due at their hour
To fan the Earth now waked, and usher in
The evening cool, when he from wrath more cool,
Came the mild Judge and intercessor both
To sentence Man. The voice of God they heard
Now walking in the garden, by soft winds
Brought to their ears, while day declined; they heard,
And from his presence hid themselves among   100
The thickest trees, both man and wife, till God
Approaching, thus to Adam called aloud.
      "Where art thou Adam, wont with joy to meet
My coming seen far off? I miss thee here,
Not pleased, thus entertained with solitude,
Where obvious duty erewhile appeared unsought.
Or come I less conspicuous, or what change
Absents thee, or what chance detains? Come forth."
      He came, and with him Eve, more loth, though first
To offend, discountenanced both, and discomposed;   110
Love was not in their looks, either to God
Or to each other, but apparent guilt,
And shame, and perturbation, and despair,

78–79. illustrate most them fully satisfied; i.e., in such a way as shall
best show both justice and mercy to have been fulfilled.

Anger, and obstinacy, and hate, and guile.
Whence Adam, faltering long, thus answered brief.
  "I heard thee in the garden, and of thy voice
Afraid, being naked, hid myself." To whom
The gracious Judge without revile replied.
  "My voice thou oft hast heard, and hast not feared,
But still rejoiced; how is it now become   120
So dreadful to thee? That thou art naked, who
Hath told thee? Hast thou eaten of the tree
Whereof I gave thee charge thou shouldst not eat?"
To whom thus Adam sore beset replied.
  "Oh Heaven! in evil strait this day I stand
Before my Judge, either to undergo
Myself the total crime, or to accuse
My other self, the partner of my life;
Whose failing, while her faith to me remains,
I should conceal, and not expose to blame   130
By my complaint; but strict necessity
Subdues me, and calamitous constraint,
Lest on my head both sin and punishment,
However insupportable, be all
Devolved; though should I hold my peace, yet thou
Wouldst easily detect what I conceal.
This woman whom thou mad'st to be my help,
And gav'st me as thy perfect gift, so good,
So fit, so acceptable, so divine,
That from her hand I could suspect no ill,   140
And what she did, whatever in itself,
Her doing seemed to justify the deed;
She gave me of the tree, and I did eat."
  To whom the Sovran Presence thus replied.
  "Was she thy God, that her thou didst obey
Before his voice, or was she made thy guide,
Superior, or but equal, that to her
Thou didst resign thy manhood, and the place
Wherein God set thee above her made of thee,
And for thee, whose perfection far excelled   150
Hers in all real dignity. Adorned
She was indeed, and lovely to attract
Thy love, not thy subjection, and her gifts

125 ff. Milton follows the biblical account (Gen. 3:8-21) phrase by
phrase but interprets it to fit his own meaning. Thus he gives the rational
and noble Adam some worthy reasons for incriminating Eve. Lines 138-40
carry us back to the discussion with the angel and his confession of weakness in Eve's presence, and God's reply echoes the terms of Raphael's
warning.

Were such as under government well seemed,
Unseemly to bear rule, which was thy part
And person, hadst thou known thyself aright."
  So having said, he thus to Eve in few:
"Say Woman, what is this which thou hast done?"
  To whom sad Eve with shame nigh overwhelmed,
Confessing soon, yet not before her Judge   160
Bold or loquacious, thus abashed replied.
"The Serpent me beguiled and I did eat."
  Which when the Lord God heard, without delay
To judgment he proceeded on the accused
Serpent, though brute, unable to transfer
The guilt on him who made him instrument
Of mischief, and polluted from the end
Of his creation; justly then accurst,
As vitiated in nature. More to know
Concerned not Man (since he no further knew)   170
Nor altered his offence; yet God at last
To Satan first in sin his doom applied,
Though in mysterious terms, judged as then best;
And on the Serpent thus his curse let fall.
  "Because thou hast done this, thou art accurst
Above all cattle, each beast of the field;
Upon thy belly grovelling thou shalt go,
And dust shalt eat all the days of thy life.
Between thee and the Woman I will put
Enmity, and between thine and her seed;   180
Her seed shall bruise thy head, thou bruise his heel."
  So spake this oracle, then verified
When Jesus, son of Mary, second Eve,
Saw Satan fall like lightning down from Heaven,
Prince of the air; then rising from his grave
Spoiled Principalities and Powers, triumphed
In open show, and with ascension bright
Captivity led captive through the air,
The realm itself of Satan long usurped,
Whom he shall tread at last under our feet;   190
Even he who now foretold his fatal bruise,
And to the woman thus his sentence turned.
  "Thy sorrow I will greatly multiply
By thy conception; children thou shalt bring

184. In Luke 10:17–18 the disciples say to Jesus, "Even the devils are
subject to us through thy name" and he replies: "I beheld Satan as lightning fall from Heaven." This is the fulfillment of the prophecy that the
woman's seed shall bruise the serpent's head. Christ is "the last Adam"
(I Cor. 15:45).

In sorrow forth, and to thy husband's will
Thine shall submit, he over thee shall rule."
   On Adam last thus judgment he pronounced.
"Because thou hast hearkened to the voice of thy wife,
And eaten of the tree concerning which
I charged thee, saying, 'Thou shalt not eat thereof,'   200
Cursed is the ground for thy sake, thou in sorrow
Shalt eat thereof all the days of thy life;
Thorns also and thistles it shall bring thee forth
Unbid, and thou shalt eat the herb of the field,
In the sweat of thy face shalt thou eat bread,
Till thou return unto the ground, for thou
Out of the ground wast taken, know thy birth,
For dust thou art, and shalt to dust return."
   So judged he Man, both Judge and Savior sent,
And the instant stroke of death, denounced that day,   210
Removed far off; then pitying how they stood
Before him naked to the air, that now
Must suffer change, disdained not to begin
Thenceforth the form of servant to assume;
As when he washed his servants' feet, so now
As father of his family he clad
Their nakedness with skins of beasts, or slain,
Or as the snake with youthful coat repaid;
And thought not much to clothe his enemies.
Nor he their outward only with the skins   220
Of beasts, but inward nakedness, much more
Opprobrious, with his robe of righteousness
Arraying, covered from his Father's sight.
To him with swift ascent he up returned,
Into his blissful bosom reassumed
In glory as of old; to him appeased,
All, though all-knowing, what had passed with Man
Recounted, mixing intercession sweet.
   Meanwhile ere thus was sinned and judged on Earth,
Within the gates of Hell sat Sin and Death,   230
In counterview within the gates, that now
Stood open wide, belching outrageous flame
Far into Chaos, since the Fiend passed through,
Sin opening, who thus now to Death began.
   "O Son, why sit we here each other viewing
Idly, while Satan our great author thrives
In other worlds, and happier seat provides
For us his offspring dear? It cannot be
But that success attends him; if mishap,
Ere this he had returned, with fury driven   240

By his avengers, since no place like this
Can fit his punishment, or their revenge.
Methinks I feel new strength within me rise,
Wings growing, and dominion given me large
Beyond this Deep; whatever draws me on,
Or sympathy or some connatural force
Powerful at greatest distance to unite
With secret amity things of like kind
By secretest conveyance. Thou my shade
Inseparable must with me along;   250
For Death from Sin no power can separate.
But lest the difficulty of passing back
Stay his return perhaps over this gulf
Impassable, impervious, let us try
Adventurous work, yet to thy power and mine
Not unagreeable, to found a path
Over this main from Hell to that new World
Where Satan now prevails, a monument
Of merit high to all the infernal host,
Easing their passage hence, for intercourse   260
Or transmigration, as their lot shall lead.
Nor can I miss the way, so strongly drawn
By this new-felt attraction and instinct."
        Whom thus the meager Shadow answered soon.
"Go whither fate and inclination strong
Leads thee, I shall not lag behind, nor err
The way, thou leading, such a scent I draw
Of carnage, prey innumerable, and taste
The savor of death from all things there that live;
Nor shall I to the work thou enterprisest   270
Be wanting, but afford thee equal aid."
        So saying, with delight he snuffed the smell
Of mortal change on Earth. As when a flock
Of ravenous fowl, though many a league remote,
Against the day of battle, to a field
Where armies lie encamped, come flying, lured
With scent of living carcasses designed
For death the following day in bloody fight.
So scented the grim Feature, and upturned
His nostril wide into the murky air,   280
Sagacious of his quarry from so far.
Then both from out Hell gates into the waste
Wide anarchy of Chaos damp and dark
Flew diverse, and with power (their power was great)
Hovering upon the waters, what they met
Solid or slimy, as in raging sea

Tossed up and down, together crowded drove
From each side shoaling towards the mouth of Hell.
As when two polar winds blowing adverse
Upon the Cronian Sea, together drive   290
Mountains of ice, that stop the imagined way
Beyond Petsora eastward, to the rich
Cathaian coast. The aggregated soil
Death with his mace petrific, cold and dry,
As with a trident smote, and fixed as firm
As Delos floating once; the rest his look
Bound with Gorgonian rigor not to move,
And with asphaltic slime; broad as the gate,
Deep to the roots of Hell the gathered beach
They fastened, and the mole immense wrought on   300
Over the foaming Deep high-arched, a bridge
Of length prodigious joining to the wall
Immovable of this now fenceless World
Forfeit to Death; from hence a passage broad,
Smooth, easy, inoffensive, down to Hell.
So, if great things to small may be compared,
Xerxes, the liberty of Greece to yoke,
From Susa his Memnonian palace high
Came to the sea, and over Hellespont
Bridging his way, Europe with Asia joined,   310
And scourged with many a stroke the indignant waves.
Now had they brought the work by wondrous art
Pontifical, a ridge of pendent rock
Over the vexed Abyss, following the track
Of Satan, to the self-same place where he
First lighted from his wing, and landed safe
From out of Chaos to the outside bare
Of this round World. With pins of adamant
And chains they made all fast, too fast they made
And durable; and now in little space   320
The confines met of empyrean Heaven
And of this World, and on the left hand Hell

288. shoaling, forming a shoal or bank.
290. Cronian Sea, the Arctic Ocean.
292. Petsora, the gulf of Petchora in the Arctic. The imagined way
is the northeast passage which explorers made repeated efforts to go through.
294. petrific, capable of turning things to stone.
296. Delos in the Aegean was said to have been a floating island till
Zeus fastened it to the bottom of the sea.
297. The look of the Gorgon turned the beholder to stone.
305. "Easy is the descent to Hell."
313. Pontifical, bridge-building (pontem + facere), but one suspects
a pun on Pontiff (pontifex).

With long reach interposed; three several ways
In sight, to each of these three places led.
And now their way to Earth they had descried,
To Paradise first tending, when behold
Satan in likeness of an angel bright
Betwixt the Centaur and the Scorpion steering
His zenith, while the sun in Aries rose.
Disguised he came, but those his children dear   330
Their parent soon discerned, though in disguise.
He after Eve seduced, unminded slunk
Into the wood fast by, and changing shape
To observe the sequel, saw his guileful act
By Eve, though all unweeting, seconded
Upon her husband, saw their shame that sought
Vain covertures; but when he saw descend
The Son of God to judge them, terrified
He fled, not hoping to escape, but shun
The present, fearing guilty what his wrath   340
Might suddenly inflict; that past, returned
By night, and listening where the hapless pair
Sat in their sad discourse and various plaint,
Thence gathered his own doom; which understood
Not instant, but of future time, with joy
And tidings fraught, to Hell he now returned,
And at the brink of Chaos, near the foot
Of this new wondrous pontifice, unhoped
Met who to meet him came, his offspring dear.
Great joy was at their meeting, and at sight   350
Of that stupendous bridge his joy increased.
Long he admiring stood, till Sin, his fair
Enchanting daughter, thus the silence broke.
    "O Parent, these are thy magnific deeds,
Thy trophies, which thou view'st as not thine own,
Thou art their author and prime architect;
For I no sooner in my heart divined
(My heart, which by a secret harmony
Still moves with thine, joined in connexion sweet)
That thou on Earth hadst prospered, which thy looks   360
Now also evidence, but straight I felt,
Though distant from thee worlds between, yet felt
That I must after thee with this thy son;
Such fatal consequence unites us three.
Hell could no longer hold us in her bounds,
Nor this unvoyageable gulf obscure

    344. which understood, i.e., when he understood that their doom was
not immediate.

Detain from following thy illustrious track.
Thou hast achieved our liberty, confined
Within Hell gates till now, thou us empowered
To fortify thus far, and overlay   370
With this portentous bridge the dark Abyss.
Thine now is all this World, thy virtue hath won
What thy hands builded not, thy wisdom gained
With odds what war hath lost, and fully avenged
Our foil in Heaven; here thou shalt monarch reign,
There didst not; there let him still victor sway,
As battle hath adjudged, from this new World
Retiring, by his own doom alienated,
And henceforth monarchy with thee divide
Of all things, parted by the empyreal bounds,   380
His quadrature, from thy orbicular World,
Or try thee now more dangerous to his throne."
     Whom thus the Prince of Darkness answered glad.
"Fair daughter, and thou son and grandchild both,
High proof ye now have given to be the race
Of Satan (for I glory in the name,
Antagonist of Heaven's Almighty King),
Amply have merited of me, of all
The infernal empire, that so near Heaven's door
Triumphal with triumphal act have met,   390
Mine with this glorious work, and made one realm
Hell and this World, one realm, one continent
Of easy thoroughfare. Therefore while I
Descend through darkness, on your road with ease
To my associate Powers, them to acquaint
With these successes, and with them rejoice,
You two this way, among those numerous orbs
All yours, right down to Paradise descend;
There dwell and reign in bliss; thence on the Earth
Dominion exercise and in the air,   400
Chiefly on Man, sole lord of all declared,
Him first make sure your thrall, and lastly kill.
My substitutes I send ye, and create
Plenipotent on Earth, of matchless might
Issuing from me: on your joint vigor now
My hold of this new kingdom all depends,
Through Sin to Death exposed by my exploit.
If your joint power prevail, the affairs of Hell
No detriment need fear, go and be strong."

372. **virtue,** power, ability.
381. **quadrature,** square territory, i.e., Heaven.
386. The Hebrew meaning of Satan is "adversary."

So saying he dismissed them, they with speed   410
Their course through thickest constellations held
Spreading their bane; the blasted stars looked wan,
And planets, planet-struck, real eclipse
Then suffered. The other way Satan went down
The causey to Hell gate; on either side
Disparted Chaos over-built exclaimed,
And with rebounding surge the bars assailed,
That scorned his indignation. Through the gate,
Wide open and unguarded, Satan passed,
And all about found desolate; for those   420
Appointed to sit there, had left their charge,
Flown to the upper World; the rest were all
Far to the inland retired, about the walls
Of Pandemonium, city and proud seat
Of Lucifer, so by allusion called
Of that bright star to Satan paragoned.
There kept their watch the legions, while the Grand
In council sat, solicitous what chance
Might intercept their Emperor sent; so he
Departing gave command, and they observed.   430
As when the Tartar from his Russian foe
By Astracan over the snowy plains
Retires, or Bactrian Sophi, from the horns
Of Turkish crescent, leaves all waste beyond
The realm of Aladule, in his retreat
To Tauris or Casbeen. So these the late
Heaven-banishd host, left desert utmost Hell
Many a dark league, reduced in careful watch
Round their metropolis, and now expecting
Each hour their great adventurer from the search   440
Of foreign worlds. He through the midst unmarked,
In show plebeian angel militant
Of lowest order, passed; and from the door
Of that Plutonian hall, invisible
Ascended his high throne, which under state
Of richest texture spread, at the upper end
Was placed in regal luster. Down a while
He sat, and round about him saw unseen.
At last as from a cloud his fulgent head

413. **planet-struck,** blasted with a malign influence, as the planets
were in turn to blast things on earth.
426. **paragoned,** likened.
433. **Bactrian Sophi,** Persian Shah.
435. **Aladule,** Greater Armenia; **Casbeen,** Kazvin, north of Teheran.
Milton is looking at or remembering an Atlas.

And shape star-bright appeared, or brighter, clad   450
With what permissive glory since his fall
Was left him, or false glitter. All-amazed
At that so sudden blaze the Stygian throng
Bent their aspect, and whom they wished beheld,
Their mighty Chief returned: loud was the acclaim;
Forth rushed in haste the great consulting peers,
Raised from their dark divan, and with like joy
Congratulant approached him, who with hand
Silence, and with these words attention won.
    "Thrones, Dominations, Princedoms, Virtues, Powers,   460
For in possession such, not only of right,
I call ye and declare ye now, returned
Successful beyond hope, to lead ye forth
Triumphant out of this infernal pit
Abominable, accursed, the house of woe,
And dungeon of our tyrant. Now possess,
As lords, a spacious World, to our native Heaven
Little inferior, by my adventure hard
With peril great achieved. Long were to tell
What I have done, what suffered, with what pain   470
Voyaged the unreal, vast, unbounded Deep
Of horrible confusion, over which
By Sin and Death a broad way now is paved
To expedite your glorious march; but I
Toiled out my uncouth passage, forced to ride
The untractable Abyss, plunged in the womb
Of unoriginal Night and Chaos wild,
That jealous of their secrets fiercely opposed
My journey strange, with clamorous uproar
Protesting Fate supreme; thence how I found   480
The new-created World, which fame in Heaven
Long had foretold, a fabric wonderful
Of absolute perfection, therein Man
Placed in a Paradise, by our exile
Made happy; him by fraud I have seduced
From his Creator, and the more to increase
Your wonder, with an apple; he thereat
Offended, worth your laughter, hath given up
Both his beloved Man and all his World,
To Sin and Death a prey, and so to us,   490
Without our hazard, labor, or alarm,
To range in, and to dwell, and over Man
To rule, as over all he should have ruled.
True is, me also he hath judged, or rather
Me not, but the brute serpent in whose shape

Man I deceived; that which to me belongs
Is enmity, which he will put between
Me and mankind; I am to bruise his heel;
His seed, when is not set, shall bruise my head.
A world who would not purchase with a bruise,   500
Or much more grievous pain? Ye have the account
Of my performance; what remains, ye Gods,
But up and enter now into full bliss."
  So having said, a while he stood, expecting
Their universal shout and high applause
To fill his ear, when contrary he hears
On all sides, from innumerable tongues
A dismal universal hiss, the sound
Of public scorn; he wondered, but not long
Had leisure, wondering at himself now more;   510
His visage drawn he felt to sharp and spare,
His arms clung to his ribs, his legs entwining
Each other, till supplanted down he fell
A monstrous serpent on his belly prone,
Reluctant, but in vain: a greater power
Now ruled him, punished in the shape he sinned,
According to his doom. He would have spoke,
But hiss for hiss returned with forkèd tongue
To forkèd tongue, for now were all transformed
Alike, to serpents all, as accessories   520
To his bold riot. Dreadful was the din
Of hissing through the hall, thick swarming now
With complicated monsters, head and tail,
Scorpion and asp, and amphisbæna dire,
Cerastes horned, hydrus, and ellops drear,
And dipsas (not so thick swarmed once the soil

  504 ff. This transformation of Satan to a serpent is the final stage of the progressive deterioration of his outward form toward correspondence with the evil of his inner being. It is an exemplification of the Platonic philosophy of the relation of the spiritual and the material world, as expressed by Milton's poet-teacher, Spenser:

> For of the soul the body form doth take;
> For soul is form and doth the body make.

  511–18. It is well worth while to compare Milton's metaphorsis with the classical originals in Ovid and Lucan and with the fantastically horrible scene in Dante, *Inferno*, xxix, 46 ff. See Ovid, *Met.* 4 and Lucan, *Pharsalia* 10:700 ff.

  524 ff. Milton has accumulated the serpent lore and terminology of the ancients: **amphisbœna,** a serpent with a head at either end; **cerastes,** a horned snake; **hydrus,** a water snake; **dipsas,** a snake whose bite produced thirst; **Ophiusa,** the isle of serpents in the Belearic group; **python,** a serpent born of the earth's slime after the flood of Deucalion; **Megæra,** one of the Furies, who had snakes in their hair.

Bedropt with blood of Gorgon, or the isle
Ophiusa); but still greatest he the midst,
Now dragon grown, larger than whom the sun
Engendered in the Pythian vale on slime,   530
Huge Python, and his power no less he seemed
Above the rest still to retain. They all
Him followed issuing forth to the open field,
Where all yet left of that revolted rout
Heaven-fallen, in station stood or just array,
Sublime with expectation when to see
In triumph issuing forth their glorious Chief;
They saw, but other sight instead, a crowd
Of ugly serpents; horror on them fell,
And horrid sympathy; for what they saw,   540
They felt themselves now changing; down their arms,
Down fell both spear and shield, down they as fast,
And the dire hiss renewed, and the dire form
Catched by contagion, like in punishment,
As in their crime. Thus was the applause they meant,
Turned to exploding hiss, triumph to shame
Cast on themselves from their own mouths. There stood
A grove hard by, sprung up with this their change,
His will who reigns above, to aggravate
Their penance, laden with fair fruit like that   550
Which grew in Paradise, the bait of Eve
Used by the Tempter. On that prospect strange
Their earnest eyes they fixed, imagining
For one forbidden tree a multitude
Now risen, to work them further woe or shame;
Yet parched with scalding thirst and hunger fierce,
Though to delude them sent, could not abstain,
But on they rolled in heaps, and up the trees
Climbing, sat thicker than the snaky locks
That curled Megæra. Greedily they plucked   560
The fruitage fair to sight, like that which grew
Near that bituminous lake where Sodom flamed;
This more delusive, not the touch, but taste
Deceived; they fondly thinking to allay
Their appetite with gust, instead of fruit
Chewed bitter ashes, which the offended taste
With spattering noise rejected. Oft they assayed,
Hunger and thirst constraining, drugged as oft,
With hatefulest disrelish writhed their jaws
With soot and cinders filled; so oft they fell   570

570–72. They fell repeatedly and did not, like man, over whom they
were triumphing, fall once only.

Into the same illusion, not as Man
Whom they triumphed once lapsed. Thus were they plagued
And worn with famine long, and ceaseless hiss,
Till their lost shape, permitted, they resumed,
Yearly enjoined, some say, to undergo
This annual humbling certain numbered days,
To dash their pride, and joy for Man seduced.
However, some tradition they dispersed
Among the heathen of their purchase got,
And fabled how the Serpent, whom they called   580
Ophion, with Eurynome, the wide-
Encroaching Eve perhaps, had first the rule
Of high Olympus, thence by Saturn driven
And Ops, ere yet Dictæan Jove was born.
    Meanwhile in Paradise the hellish pair
Too soon arrived, Sin there in power before,
Once actual, now in body, and to dwell
Habitual habitant; behind her Death
Close following pace for pace, not mounted yet
On his pale horse; to whom Sin thus began.   590
    "Second of Satan sprung, all-conquering Death,
What think'st thou of our empire now, though earned
With travail difficult? not better far
Than still at Hell's dark threshold to have sat watch,
Unnamed, undreaded, and thyself half-starved?"
    Whom thus the Sin-born Monster answered soon.
"To me, who with eternal famine pine,
Alike is Hell, or Paradise, or Heaven,
There best, where most with ravin I may meet;
Which here, though plenteous, all too little seems   600
To stuff this maw, this vast unhide-bound corpse."
    To whom the incestuous mother thus replied.
"Thou therefore on these herbs, and fruits, and flowers
Feed first; on each beast next, and fish, and fowl,
No homely morsels; and whatever thing
The scythe of Time mows down, devour unspared;
Till I in Man residing through the race,
His thoughts, his looks, words, actions all infect,
And season him thy last and sweetest prey."
    This said, they both betook them several ways,   610
Both to destroy, or unimmortal make
All kinds, and for destruction to mature

580–84. Ophion and his wife, Eurynome, were Titans and the first
rulers of Olympus. Ops was the wife of Saturn. It is the etymological
meaning of Ophion, serpent, which suggests the identification. **Eurynome**
means "wide ruling."

Sooner or later; which the Almighty seeing,
From his transcendent seat the Saints among,
To those bright Orders uttered thus his voice.
"See with what heat these dogs of Hell advance
To waste and havoc yonder World, which I
So fair and good created, and had still
Kept in that state, had not the folly of Man
Let in these wasteful furies, who impute   620
Folly to me (so doth the Prince of Hell
And his adherents), that with so much ease
I suffer them to enter and possess
A place so heavenly, and conniving seem
To gratify my scornful enemies,
That laugh, as if transported with some fit
Of passion, I to them had quitted all,
At random yielded up to their misrule;
And know not that I called and drew them thither
My Hell-hounds, to lick up the draff and filth   630
Which Man's polluting sin with taint hath shed
On what was pure, till crammed and gorged, nigh burst
With sucked and glutted offal, at one sling
Of thy victorious arm, well-pleasing Son,
Both Sin, and Death, and yawning Grave at last
Through Chaos hurled, obstruct the mouth of Hell
For ever, and seal up his ravenous jaws.
Then Heaven and Earth renewed shall be made pure
To sanctity that shall receive no stain;
Till then the curse pronounced on both precedes."   640
   He ended, and the heavenly audience loud
Sung Halleluiah, as the sound of seas,
Through multitude that sung: "Just are thy ways,
Righteous are thy decrees on all thy works;
Who can extenuate thee? Next, to the Son,
Destined restorer of mankind, by whom
New Heaven and Earth shall to the ages rise,
Or down from Heaven descend." Such was their song,
While the Creator calling forth by name
His mighty angels gave them several charge,   650
As sorted best with present things. The sun
Had first his precept so to move, so shine,
As might affect the Earth with cold and heat
Scarce tolerable, and from the north to call
Decrepit winter, from the south to bring
Solstitial summer's heat. To the blanc moon

---

640. precedes. The curse, for the time being, takes precedence.

Her office they prescribed, to the other five
Their planetary motions and aspects
In sextile, square, and trine, and opposite,
Of noxious efficacy, and when to join   660
In synod unbenign, and taught the fixed
Their influence malignant when to shower,
Which of them rising with the sun, or falling,
Should prove tempestuous. To the winds they set
Their corners, when with bluster to confound
Sea, air, and shore, the thunder when to roll
With terror through the dark aerial hall.
Some say he bid his angels turn askance
The poles of Earth twice ten degrees and more
From the sun's axle; they with labor pushed   670
Oblique the centric globe: some say the sun
Was bid turn reins from the equinoctial road
Like distant breadth to Taurus with the seven
Atlantic Sisters, and the Spartan Twins,
Up to the Tropic Crab; thence down amain
By Leo and the Virgin and the Scales,
As deep as Capricorn, to bring in change
Of seasons to each clime; else had the spring
Perpetual smiled on Earth with vernant flowers,
Equal in days and nights, except to those   680
Beyond the polar circles; to them day
Had unbenighted shone, while the low sun
To recompense his distance, in their sight
Had rounded still the horizon, and not known
Or east or west, which had forbid the snow
From cold Estotiland, and south as far
Beneath Magellan. At that tasted fruit
The sun, as from Thyestean banquet, turned

658–62. Hitherto the stars in whatever position have been favorable to man; henceforth some of their aspects are malign. Opposition and conjunction (**synod**, the technical term in Greek) were the most unfavorable planetary relationships. **Sextile**, **square**, and **trine** [aspects] refer to the angle made by the rays of two planets when they are sixty, ninety, and 120 degrees apart in the Zodiac respectively.

668 ff. The idea is that before the earth was cursed it moved in the same plane as the sun's equator, in which case there would be no seasons. The angels either incline the earth's axis 23½ degrees or set the sun to moving north and south of the plane of the earth's equator to the limits of the zodiac, north through Taurus in the spring, south through Libra, etc., in the fall and winter.

686. Estotiland, the name vaguely used for the region north of Hudson's Bay.

688. Thyestes unwittingly ate the bodies of his own children served by his enemy Atreus. The sun was said to have turned from witnessing the horrible spectacle.

His course intended; else how had the World
Inhabited, though sinless, more than now   690
Avoided pinching cold and scorching heat?
These changes in the heavens, though slow, produced
Like change on sea and land, sideral blast,
Vapor, and mist, and exhalation hot,
Corrupt and pestilent. Now from the north
Of Norumbega, and the Samoed shore,
Bursting their brazen dungeon, armed with ice
And snow and hail and stormy gust and flaw,
Boreas and Cæcias and Argestes loud
And Thrascias rend the woods and seas upturn;   700
With adverse blast upturns them from the south
Notus and Afer black with thunderous clouds
From Serraliona; thwart of these as fierce
Forth rush the Levant and the Ponent winds
Eurus and Zephyr with their lateral noise,
Sirocco and Libecchio. Thus began
Outrage from lifeless things; but Discord first,
Daughter of Sin, among the irrational,
Death introduced through fierce antipathy.
Beast now with beast 'gan war, and fowl with fowl,   710
And fish with fish; to graze the herb all leaving,
Devoured each other; nor stood much in awe
Of Man, but fled him, or with countenance grim
Glared on him passing. These were from without
The growing miseries, which Adam saw
Already in part, though hid in gloomiest shade,
To sorrow abandoned, but worse felt within,
And in a troubled sea of passion tossed,
Thus to disburden sought with sad complaint.
    "O miserable of happy! is this the end   720
Of this new glorious World, and me so late
The glory of that glory, who now, become
Accurst of blessed, hide me from the face
Of God, whom to behold was then my height
Of happiness. Yet well, if here would end
The misery; I deserved it, and would bear
My own deservings; but this will not serve:
All that I eat or drink, or shall beget,

696. **Norumbega,** the name given in old maps to New England and
part of Canada; **Samoed shore,** northeastern Siberia.
    699–700. **Cæcias, Argestes, Thracias,** the northeast, northwest, and
north-northwest winds.
    703. **Serraliona,** Sierra Leone.
    704-6. **Ponent,** wind from the setting sun; **Sirocco, Libecchio,** sea-
sonal winds in the Mediterranean region.

Is propagated curse. O voice once heard
Delightfully, 'Increase and multiply,'   730
Now death to hear! for what can I increase
Or multiply, but curses on my head?
Who of all ages to succeed, but feeling
The evil on him brought by me, will curse
My head: 'Ill fare our Ancestor impure,
For this we may thank Adam'; but his thanks
Shall be the execration; so besides
Mine own that bide upon me, all from me
Shall with a fierce reflux on me redound,
On me as on their natural center light   740
Heavy, though in their place. O fleeting joys
Of Paradise, dear bought with lasting woes!
Did I request thee, Maker, from my clay
To mould me Man, did I solicit thee
From darkness to promote me, or here place
In this delicious garden? As my will
Concurred not to my being, it were but right
And equal to reduce me to my dust,
Desirous to resign and render back
All I received, unable to perform   750
Thy terms too hard, by which I was to hold
The good I sought not. To the loss of that,
Sufficient penalty, why hast thou added
The sense of endless woes? inexplicable
Thy justice seems; yet to say truth, too late
I thus contest; then should have been refused
Those terms whatever, when they were proposed.
Thou didst accept them; wilt thou enjoy the good,
Then cavil the conditions? And though God
Made thee without thy leave, what if thy son   760
Prove disobedient, and reproved, retort,
'Wherefore didst thou beget me? I sought it not.'
Wouldst thou admit for his contempt of thee
That proud excuse? yet him not thy election,
But natural necessity begot.
God made thee of choice his own, and of his own
To serve him, thy reward was of his grace,
Thy punishment then justly is at his will.
Be it so, for I submit, his doom is fair,
That dust I am, and shall to dust return.   770
O welcome hour whenever! Why delays
His hand to execute what his decree

759 ff. Cf. Isa. 45:9: "Shall the clay say to him that fashioneth it,
What makest thou?"

Fixed on this day? Why do I overlive,
Why am I mocked with death, and lengthened out
To deathless pain? How gladly would I meet
Mortality my sentence, and be earth
Insensible, how glad would lay me down
As in my mother's lap! There I should rest
And sleep secure; his dreadful voice no more
Would thunder in my ears, no fear of worse   780
To me and to my offspring would torment me
With cruel expectation. Yet one doubt
Pursues me still, lest all I cannot die,
Lest that pure breath of life, the spirit of Man
Which God inspired, cannot together perish
With this corporeal clod; then in the grave
Or in some other dismal place, who knows
But I shall die a living death? O thought
Horrid, if true! Yet why? It was but breath
Of life that sinned; what dies but what had life   790
And sin? the body properly hath neither.
All of me then shall die: let this appease
The doubt, since human reach no further knows.
For though the Lord of all be infinite,
Is his wrath also? Be it, Man is not so,
But mortal doomed. How can he exercise
Wrath without end on Man whom death must end?
Can he make deathless death? That were to make
Strange contradiction, which to God himself
Impossible is held, as argument   800
Of weakness, not of power. Will he draw out,
For anger's sake, finite to infinite
In punished Man, to satisfy his rigor
Satisfied never? That were to extend
His sentence beyond dust and Nature's law,
By which all causes else according still
To the reception of their matter act,
Not to the extent of their own sphere. But say
That death be not one stroke, as I supposed,
Bereaving sense, but endless misery   810
From this day onward, which I feel begun
Both in me and without me, and so last

773. **overlive**, survive.
775 ff. Adam's lament is like Job's: "Wherefore then hast thou brought me forth out of the womb? Oh that I had given up the ghost, and no eye had seen me! I should then have been as though I had not been."
805–8. Causes are limited in their effect by the capacity of the matter on which they are exercised.

To perpetuity: Ay me, that fear
Comes thundering back with dreadful revolution
On my defenceless head; both Death and I
Am found eternal, and incorporate both,
Nor I on my part single, in me all
Posterity stands cursed. Fair patrimony
That I must leave ye, sons; oh were I able
To waste it all myself, and leave ye none!   820
So disinherited how would ye bless
Me now your curse! Ah, why should all mankind
For one man's fault thus guiltless be condemned,
If guiltless? But from me what can proceed
But all corrupt, both mind and will depraved,
Not to do only, but to will the same
With me? How can they then acquitted stand
In sight of God? Him after all disputes
Forced I absolve; all my evasions vain
And reasonings, though through mazes, lead me still   830
But to my own conviction: first and last
On me, me only, as the source and spring
Of all corruption, all the blame lights due;
So might the wrath. Fond wish! couldst thou support
That burden heavier than the Earth to bear,
Than all the World much heavier, though divided
With that bad woman? Thus what thou desirest
And what thou fearst, alike destroys all hope
Of refuge, and concludes thee miserable
Beyond all past example and future,   840
To Satan only like, both crime and doom.
O Conscience, into what abyss of fears
And horrors hast thou driven me; out of which
I find no way, from deep to deeper plunged!"
    Thus Adam to himself lamented loud
Through the still night, not now, as ere Man fell,
Wholesome and cool and mild, but with black air
Accompanied, with damps and dreadful gloom,
Which to his evil conscience represented
All things with double terror. On the ground   850
Outstretched he lay, on the cold ground, and oft
Cursed his creation, Death as oft accused
Of tardy execution, since denounced
The day of his offence. "Why comes not Death,"
Said he, "with one thrice-acceptable stroke
To end me? Shall Truth fail to keep her word,

852. Cf. Job 3:1: "After this opened Job his mouth and cursed his day."

Justice divine not hasten to be just?
But Death comes not at call, Justice divine
Mends not her slowest pace for prayers or cries.
O woods, O fountains, hillocks, dales, and bowers,   860
With other echo late I taught your shades
To answer, and resound far other song."
Whom thus afflicted when sad Eve beheld,
Desolate where she sat, approaching nigh,
Soft words to his fierce passion she assayed;
But her with stern regard he thus repelled.
    "Out of my sight, thou serpent, that name best
Befits thee with him leagued, thyself as false
And hateful; nothing wants, but that thy shape,
Like his, and color serpentine, may show   870
Thy inward fraud, to warn all creatures from thee
Henceforth; lest that too heavenly form, pretended
To hellish falsehood, snare them. But for thee
I had persisted happy, had not thy pride
And wandering vanity, when least was safe,
Rejected my forewarning, and disdained
Not to be trusted, longing to be seen
Though by the Devil himself, him overweening
To overreach, but with the Serpent meeting
Fooled and beguiled, by him thou, I by thee,   880
To trust thee from my side, imagined wise,
Constant, mature, proof against all assaults,
And understood not all was but a show
Rather than solid virtue, all but a rib
Crooked by nature, bent, as now appears,
More to the part sinister from me drawn;
Well if thrown out, as supernumerary
To my just number found. Oh why did God,
Creator wise, that peopled highest Heaven
With spirits masculine, create at last   890
This novelty on Earth, this fair defect
Of Nature, and not fill the World at once
With men as angels without feminine,
Or find some other way to generate
Mankind? This mischief had not then befallen,
And more that shall befall, innumerable
Disturbances on Earth through female snares,
And strait conjunction with this sex. For either
He never shall find out fit mate, but such
As some misfortune brings him, or mistake,   900

888. The passage is an elaboration of Euripides, *Hypolytus*, 616–18.

Or whom he wishes most shall seldom gain,
Through her perverseness, but shall see her gained
By a far worse, or if she love, withheld
By parents, or his happiest choice too late
Shall meet, already linked and wedlock-bound
To a fell adversary, his hate or shame;
Which infinite calamity shall cause
To human life, and household peace confound."

    He added not, and from her turned, but Eve
Not so repulsed, with tears that ceased not flowing,   910
And tresses all disordered, at his feet
Fell humble, and embracing them, besought
His peace, and thus proceeded in her plaint:
    "Forsake me not thus, Adam, witness Heaven
What love sincere and reverence in my heart
I bear thee, and unweeting have offended,
Unhappily deceived; thy suppliant
I beg, and clasp thy knees; bereave me not,
Whereon I live, thy gentle looks, thy aid,
Thy counsel in this uttermost distress,   920
My only strength and stay. Forlorn of thee,
Whither shall I betake me, where subsist?
While yet we live, scarce one short hour perhaps,
Between us two let there be peace, both joining,
As joined in injuries, one enmity
Against a foe by doom express assigned us,
That cruel Serpent. On me exercise not
Thy hatred for this misery befallen,
On me already lost, me than thyself
More miserable. Both have sinned, but thou   930
Against God only, I against God and thee,
And to the place of judgment will return,
There with my cries importune Heaven, that all
The sentence from thy head removed may light
On me, sole cause to thee of all this woe,
Me, me only, just object of his ire."
    She ended weeping, and her lowly plight,
Immovable till peace obtained from fault
Acknowledged and deplored, in Adam wrought
Commiseration; soon his heart relented   940
Towards her, his life so late and sole delight,
Now at his feet submissive in distress,
Creature so fair his reconcilement seeking,
His counsel whom she had displeased, his aid;

    938. It is Eve who is immovable till Adam pardons her.

As one disarmed, his anger all he lost,
And thus with peaceful words upraised her soon:
    "Unwary, and too desirous, as before,
So now, of what thou knowst not, who desirest
The punishment all on thyself; alas,
Bear thine own first, ill able to sustain   950
His full wrath whose thou feel'st as yet least part,
And my displeasure bear'st so ill. If prayers
Could alter high decrees, I to that place
Would speed before thee, and be louder heard,
That on my head all might be visited,
Thy frailty and infirmer sex forgiven,
To me committed and by me exposed.
But rise, let us no more contend, nor blame
Each other, blamed enough elsewhere, but strive
In offices of love, how we may lighten   960
Each other's burden in our share of woe;
Since this day's death denounced, if aught I see,
Will prove no sudden, but a slow-paced evil,
A long day's dying to augment our pain,
And to our seed (O hapless seed!) derived."
    To whom thus Eve, recovering heart, replied.
"Adam, by sad experiment I know
How little weight my words with thee can find,
Found so erroneous, thence by just event
Found so unfortunate; nevertheless,   970
Restored by thee, vile as I am, to place
Of new acceptance, hopeful to regain
Thy love, the sole contentment of my heart
Living or dying, from thee I will not hide
What thoughts in my unquiet breast are risen,
Tending to some relief of our extremes,
Or end, though sharp and sad, yet tolerable,
As in our evils, and of easier choice.
If care of our descent perplex us most,
Which must be born to certain woe, devoured   980
By Death at last, (and miserable it is
To be to others cause of misery,
Our own begotten, and of our loins to bring
Into this cursèd World a woeful race,
That after wretched life must be at last
Food for so foul a monster), in thy power
It lies, yet ere conception, to prevent

    958–61. Adam takes the lead in seeing a constructive use of their rela-
tionship. The restoration of a broken home is an important part of Milton's
theme.

The race unblest, to being yet unbegot.
Childless thou art, childless remain; so Death
Shall be deceived his glut, and with us two   990
Be forced to satisfy his ravenous maw.
But if thou judge it hard and difficult,
Conversing, looking, loving, to abstain
From love's due rites, nuptial embraces sweet,
And with desire to languish without hope,
Before the present object languishing
With like desire, which would be misery
And torment less than none of what we dread,
Then both our selves and seed at once to free
From what we fear for both, let us make short,   1000
Let us seek Death, or he not found, supply
With our own hands his office on ourselves;
Why stand we longer shivering under fears
That show no end but death, and have the power,
Of many ways to die the shortest choosing,
Destruction with destruction to destroy."
    She ended here, or vehement despair
Broke off the rest; so much of death her thoughts
Had entertained as dyed her cheeks with pale.
But Adam with such counsel nothing swayed,   1010
To better hopes his more attentive mind
Laboring had raised, and thus to Eve replied.
    "Eve, thy contempt of life and pleasure seems
To argue in thee something more sublime
And excellent than what thy mind contemns;
But self-destruction therefore sought, refutes
That excellence thought in thee, and implies,
Not thy contempt, but anguish and regret
For loss of life and pleasure overloved.
Or if thou covet death, as utmost end   1020
Of misery, so thinking to evade
The penalty pronounced, doubt not but God
Hath wiselier armed his vengeful ire than so
To be forestalled; much more I fear lest death
So snatched will not exempt us from the pain
We are by doom to pay; rather such acts
Of contumacy will provoke the Highest
To make death in us live. Then let us seek
Some safer resolution, which methinks

    1000. make short, i.e., make short work. There is a touch of defiance
as well as of desperation in Eve's language.
    1013-15. Eve's stoical proposal proves that there is in her nature a prin-
ciple higher than pleasure and the love of life.

I have in view, calling to mind with heed
Part of our sentence, that thy seed shall bruise
The Serpent's head; piteous amends, unless
Be meant, whom I conjecture, our grand foe
Satan, who in the serpent hath contrived
Against us this deceit. To crush his head
Would be revenge indeed; which will be lost
By death brought on ourselves, or childless days
Resolved, as thou proposest; so our foe
Shall scape his punishment ordained, and we
Instead shall double ours upon our heads.   1040
No more be mentioned then of violence
Against ourselves, and wilful barrenness,
That cuts us off from hope, and savors only
Rancor and pride, impatience and despite,
Reluctance against God and his just yoke
Laid on our necks. Remember with what mild
And gracious temper he both heard and judged,
Without wrath or reviling; we expected
Immediate dissolution, which we thought
Was meant by death that day, when lo, to thee   1050
Pains only in child-bearing were foretold,
And bringing forth, soon recompensed with joy,
Fruit of thy womb; on me the curse aslope
Glanced on the ground: with labor I must earn
My bread; what harm? Idleness had been worse;
My labor will sustain me; and lest cold
Or heat should injure us, his timely care
Hath unbesought provided, and his hands
Clothed us unworthy, pitying while he judged;
How much more, if we pray him, will his ear   1060
Be open, and his heart to pity incline,
And teach us further by what means to shun
The inclement seasons, rain, ice, hail, and snow,
Which now the sky with various face begins
To show us in this mountain, while the winds
Blow moist and keen, shattering the graceful locks
Of these fair spreading trees; which bids us seek
Some better shroud, some better warmth to cherish
Our limbs benumbed, ere this diurnal star
Leave cold the night, how we his gathered beams   1070
Reflected, may with matter sere foment,
Or by collision of two bodies grind
The air attrite to fire, as late the clouds

1073. attrite, rubbed.

Justling or pushed with winds rude in their shock
Tine the slant lightning, whose thwart flame driven down
Kindles the gummy bark of fir or pine,
And sends a comfortable heat from far,
Which might supply the sun. Such fire to use,
And what may else be remedy or cure
To evils which our own misdeeds have wrought,   1080
He will instruct us praying, and of grace
Beseeching him, so as we need not fear
To pass commodiously this life, sustained
By him with many comforts, till we end
In dust, our final rest and native home.
What better can we do, than to the place
Repairing where he judged us, prostrate fall
Before him reverent, and there confess
Humbly our faults, and pardon beg, with tears
Watering the ground, and with our sighs the air   1090
Frequenting, sent from hearts contrite, in sign
Of sorrow unfeigned, and humiliation meek.
Undoubtedly he will relent and turn
From his displeasure; in whose look serene,
When angry most he seemed and most severe,
What else but favor, grace, and mercy shone?"
    So spake our father penitent, nor Eve
Felt less remorse. They forthwith to the place
Repairing where he judged them, prostrate fell
Before him reverent, and both confessed   1100
Humbly their faults, and pardon begged, with tears
Watering the ground, and with their sighs the air
Frequenting, sent from hearts contrite, in sign
Of sorrow unfeigned, and humiliation meek.

BOOK XI

THE ARGUMENT

The Son of God presents to his Father the prayers of our first
parents now repenting, and intercedes for them. God accepts
them, but declares that they must no longer abide in Paradise;
sends Michael with a band of Cherubim to dispossess them, but

1075. tine, kindle. Adam suggests first some kind of burning glass,
then something like flint and steel, in imitation of what he supposes to be a
process of nature, i.e., the production of fire by clouds striking against each
other.
    1086–92. The verbal repetition of these lines below is a Homeric prac-
tice not often used by Milton.

first to reveal to Adam future things; Michael's coming down.
Adam shows to Eve certain ominous signs; he discerns Michael's
approach; goes out to meet him; the Angel denounces their departure. Eve's lamentation. Adam pleads, but submits; the Angel
leads him up to a high hill; sets before him in vision what shall
happen till the Flood.

Thus they in lowliest plight repentant stood
Praying, for from the mercy-seat above
Prevenient grace descending had removed
The stony from their hearts, and made new flesh
Regenerate grow instead, that sighs now breathed
Unutterable which the spirit of prayer
Inspired, and winged for Heaven with speedier flight
Than loudest oratory. Yet their port
Not of mean suitors, nor important less
Seemed their petition, than when the ancient pair   10
In fables old, less ancient yet than these,
Deucalion and chaste Pyrrha to restore
The race of mankind drowned, before the shrine
Of Themis stood devout. To Heaven their prayers
Flew up, nor missed the way, by envious winds
Blown vagabond or frustrate: in they passed
Dimensionless through heavenly doors; then clad
With incense, where the golden altar fumed
By their great Intercessor, came in sight
Before the Father's throne. Then the glad Son   20
Presenting, thus to intercede began.
    "See Father, what first-fruits on Earth are sprung
From thy implanted grace in Man, these sighs
And prayers, which in this golden censer, mixed
With incense, I thy priest before thee bring,
Fruits of more pleasing savor from thy seed
Sown with contrition in his heart, than those
Which his own hand manuring, all the trees
Of Paradise could have produced, ere fallen
From innocence. Now therefore bend thine ear   30
To supplication, hear his sighs though mute;
Unskilful with what words to pray, let me
Interpret for him, me his advocate

    3. **Prevenient grace,** grace which comes to man before the act of re-
pentance and makes such an act possible.
    10-14. These two were the only survivors of the flood in classical
mythology. They inquired of the goddess Themis how mankind might be
restored.
    16. **Blown vagabond,** i.e., in the Limbo of vanities described in III,
444 ff.

And propitiation, all his works on me,
Good or not good ingraft, my merit those
Shall perfect, and for these my death shall pay.
Accept me, and in me from these receive
The smell of peace toward mankind, let him live
Before thee reconciled, at least his days
Numbered, though sad, till death, his doom (which I   40
To mitigate thus plead, not to reverse)
To better life shall yield him, where with me
All my redeemed may dwell in joy and bliss,
Made one with me as I with thee am one."
    To whom the Father, without cloud, serene.
"All thy request for Man, accepted Son,
Obtain, all thy request was my decree.
But longer in that Paradise to dwell
The law I gave to Nature him forbids;
Those pure immortal elements that know   50
No gross, no unharmonious mixture foul,
Eject him tainted now, and purge him off
As a distemper, gross to air as gross,
And mortal food, as may dispose him best
For dissolution wrought by sin, that first
Distempered all things, and of incorrupt
Corrupted. I at first with two fair gifts
Created him endowed, with happiness
And immortality: that fondly lost,
This other served but to eternize woe;   60
Till I provided death; so death becomes
His final remedy, and after life
Tried in sharp tribulation, and refined
By faith and faithful works, to second life,
Waked in the renovation of the just,
Resigns him up with Heaven and Earth renewed.
But let us call to synod all the blest
Through Heaven's wide bounds; from them I will not hide
My judgments, how with mankind I proceed,
As how with peccant angels late they saw;   70
And in their state, though firm, stood more confirmed."
    He ended, and the Son gave signal high
To the bright minister that watched, he blew
His trumpet, heard in Oreb since perhaps
When God descended, and perhaps once more
To sound at general doom. The angelic blast
Filled all the regions; from their blissful bowers

    35–36. Christ's merits, engrafted on man's good deeds, perfect them; his
death atones for man's sin.

Of amarantine shade, fountain or spring,
By the waters of life, where'er they sat
In fellowships of joy, the Sons of Light   80
Hasted, resorting to the summons high,
And took their seats; till from his throne supreme
The Almighty thus pronounced his sovran will.
    "O Sons, like one of us Man is become
To know both good and evil, since his taste
Of that defended fruit; but let him boast
His knowledge of good lost, and evil got,
Happier, had it sufficed him to have known
Good by itself, and evil not at all.
He sorrows now, repents, and prays contrite,   90
My motions in him; longer than they move,
His heart I know, how variable and vain
Self-left. Lest therefore his now bolder hand
Reach also of the Tree of Life, and eat,
And live for ever, dream at least to live
For ever, to remove him I decree,
And send him from the garden forth to till
The ground whence he was taken, fitter soil.
Michael, this my behest have thou in charge,
Take to thee from among the Cherubim   100
Thy choice of flaming warriors, lest the Fiend,
Or in behalf of Man, or to invade
Vacant possession some new trouble raise;
Haste thee, and from the Paradise of God
Without remorse drive out the sinful pair,
From hallowed ground the unholy, and denounce
To them and to their progeny from thence
Perpetual banishment. Yet lest they faint
At the sad sentence rigorously urged,
For I behold them softened and with tears   110
Bewailing their excess, all terror hide.
If patiently thy bidding they obey,
Dismiss them not disconsolate; reveal
To Adam what shall come in future days,
As I shall thee enlighten, intermix
My covenant in the Woman's seed renewed;
So send them forth, though sorrowing, yet in peace;
And on the east side of the garden place,
Where entrance up from Eden easiest climbs,
Cherubic watch, and of a sword the flame   120

    93. **self-left,** left to itself, no longer immediately moved by God.
    95. **dream at least to live.** By thus interpreting Gen. 3:22 Milton
avoids the primitive magical implications of the original.

Wide-waving, all approach far off to fright,
And guard all passage to the Tree of Life;
Lest Paradise a receptacle prove
To spirits foul, and all my trees their prey,
With whose stolen fruit Man once more to delude."
    He ceased; and the Archangelic Power prepared
For swift descent, with him the cohort bright
Of watchful Cherubim; four faces each
Had, like a double Janus, all their shape
Spangled with eyes more numerous than those   130
Of Argus, and more wakeful than to drowse,
Charmed with Arcadian pipe, the pastoral reed
Of Hermes, or his opiate rod. Meanwhile
To resalute the world with sacred light
Leucothea waked, and with fresh dews embalmed
The Earth, when Adam and first matron Eve
Had ended now their orisons, and found
Strength added from above, new hope to spring
Out of despair, joy, but with fear yet linked;
Which thus to Eve his welcome words renewed.   140
    "Eve, easily may faith admit that all
The good which we enjoy from Heaven descends;
But that from us aught should ascend to Heaven
So prevalent as to concern the mind
Of God high-blest, or to incline his will,
Hard to belief may seem; yet this will prayer,
Or one short sigh of human breath, upborne
Even to the seat of God. For since I sought
By prayer the offended Deity to appease,
Kneeled and before him humbled all my heart,   150
Methought I saw him placable and mild,
Bending his ear; persuasion in me grew
That I was heard with favor; peace returned
Home to my breast, and to my memory
His promise that thy seed shall bruise our foe;
Which then not minded in dismay, yet now
Assures me that the bitterness of death
Is past, and we shall live. Whence hail to thee,
Eve rightly called, Mother of all Mankind,
Mother of all things living, since by thee   160
Man is to live, and all things live for Man."
    To whom thus Eve with sad demeanor meek.

    128-30. The description is again from Ezek. 1, but it is the wheels that
are full of eyes.
    131. The hundred-eyed Argus was set by Juno to watch her rival Io, but
Mercury charmed them all asleep.

"Ill-worthy I such title should belong
To me transgressor, who for thee ordained
A help, became thy snare; to me reproach
Rather belongs, distrust and all dispraise.
But infinite in pardon was my Judge,
That I who first brought death on all, am graced
The source of life; next favorable thou,
Who highly thus to entitle me vouchsafest,   170
Far other name deserving. But the field
To labor calls us now with sweat imposed,
Though after sleepless night; for see the Morn,
All unconcerned with our unrest, begins
Her rosy progress smiling, let us forth,
I never from thy side henceforth to stray,
Where'er our day's work lies, though now enjoined
Laborious, till day droop; while here we dwell,
What can be toilsome in these pleasant walks?
Here let us live, though in fallen state, content."   180
    So spake, so wished, much-humbled Eve, but Fate
Subscribed not; Nature first gave signs, impressed
On bird, beast, air, air suddenly eclipsed
After short blush of morn; nigh in her sight
The bird of Jove, stooped from his airy tour,
Two birds of gayest plume before him drove;
Down from a hill the beast that reigns in woods,
First hunter then, pursued a gentle brace,
Goodliest of all the forest, hart and hind;
Direct to the eastern gate was bent their flight.   190
Adam observed, and with his eye the chase
Pursuing, not unmoved to Eve thus spake.
    "O Eve, some further change awaits us nigh,
Which Heaven by these mute signs in Nature shows
Forerunners of his purpose, or to warn
Us haply too secure of our discharge
From penalty, because from death released
Some days; how long, and what till then our life,
Who knows or more than this, that we are dust,
And thither must return and be no more.   200
Why else this double object in our sight
Of flight pursued in the air and o'er the ground
One way the self-same hour? why in the east
Darkness ere day's mid-course, and morning-light
More orient in yon western cloud that draws

190. The incident portends their own later flight from Paradise, Jove's
eagle representing the angel.

O'er the blue firmament a radiant white,
And slow descends, with something heavenly fraught."
    He erred not, for by this the heavenly bands
Down from a sky of jasper lighted now
In Paradise, and on a hill made halt,   210
A glorious apparition, had not doubt
And carnal fear that day dimmed Adam's eye.
Not that more glorious, when the angels met
Jacob in Mahanaim, where he saw
The field pavilioned with his guardians bright;
Nor that which on the flaming mount appeared
In Dothan, covered with a camp of fire,
Against the Syrian king, who to surprise
One man, assassin-like had levied war,
War unproclaimed. The princely Hierarch   220
In their bright stand, there left his Powers to seize
Possession of the garden; he alone,
To find where Adam sheltered, took his way,
Not unperceived of Adam, who to Eve,
While the great visitant approached, thus spake.
    "Eve, now expect great tidings, which perhaps
Of us will soon determine, or impose
New laws to be observed; for I descry
From yonder blazing cloud that veils the hill
One of the heavenly host, and by his gait   230
None of the meanest, some great Potentate
Or of the Thrones above, such majesty
Invests him coming; yet not terrible,
That I should fear, nor sociably mild,
As Raphael, that I should much confide,
But solemn and sublime, whom not to offend,
With reverence I must meet, and thou retire."
    He ended; and the Archangel soon drew nigh,
Not in his shape celestial, but as man
Clad to meet man; over his lucid arms   240
A military vest of purple flowed,
Livelier than Melibœan, or the grain
Of Sarra, worn by kings and heroes old
In time of truce; Iris had dipt the woof;
His starry helm unbuckled showed him prime
In manhood where youth ended; by his side
As in a glistening zodiac hung the sword,
Satan's dire dread, and in his hand the spear.

213–14. Gen. 32:1, 2.
215–20. II Kings 6:17.
242–43. Melibœa and Sarra (Tyre) were places famous for purple dye.

Adam bowed low, he kingly from his state
Inclined not, but his coming thus declared.   250
    "Adam, Heaven's high behest no preface needs:
Sufficient that thy prayers are heard, and Death,
Then due by sentence when thou didst transgress,
Defeated of his seisure many days
Given thee of grace, wherein thou may'st repent,
And one bad act with many deeds well done
May'st cover; well may then thy Lord appeased
Redeem thee quite from Death's rapacious claim;
But longer in this Paradise to dwell
Permits not; to remove thee I am come,   260
And send thee from the garden forth to till
The ground whence thou wast taken, fitter soil."
    He added not, for Adam at the news
Heart-struck with chilling gripe of sorrow stood,
That all his senses bound; Eve, who unseen
Yet all had heard, with audible lament
Discovered soon the place of her retire.
    "O unexpected stroke, worse than of Death!
Must I thus leave thee Paradise? thus leave
Thee native soil, these happy walks and shades,   270
Fit haunt of Gods? where I had hope to spend,
Quiet though sad, the respite of that day
That must be mortal to us both. O flowers,
That never will in other climate grow,
My early visitation, and my last
At even, which I bred up with tender hand
From the first opening bud, and gave ye names,
Who now shall rear ye to the sun, or rank
Your tribes, and water from the ambrosial fount?
Thee lastly nuptial bower, by me adorned   280
With what to sight or smell was sweet; from thee
How shall I part, and whither wander down
Into a lower world, to this obscure
And wild, how shall we breathe in other air
Less pure, accustomed to immortal fruits?"
    Whom thus the Angel interrupted mild.
"Lament not Eve, but patiently resign
What justly thou has lost; nor set thy heart,
Thus over-fond, on that which is not thine;
Thy going is not lonely, with thee goes   290
Thy husband, him to follow thou art bound;
Where he abides, think there thy native soil."

    283. to this, in comparison to this.

Adam by this from the cold sudden damp
Recovering, and his scattered spirits returned,
To Michael thus his humble words addressed.
"Celestial, whether among the Thrones, or named
Of them the highest, for such of shape may seem
Prince above princes, gently hast thou told
Thy message, which might else in telling wound,
And in performing end us; what besides   300
Of sorrow and dejection and despair
Our frailty can sustain, thy tidings bring,
Departure from this happy place, our sweet
Recess, and only consolation left
Familiar to our eyes; all places else
Inhospitable appear and desolate,
Nor knowing us nor known. And if by prayer
Incessant I could hope to change the will
Of him who all things can, I would not cease
To weary him with my assiduous cries;   310
But prayer against his absolute decree
No more avails than breath against the wind,
Blown stifling back on him that breathes it forth:
Therefore to his great bidding I submit.
This most afflicts me, that departing hence,
As from his face I shall be hid, deprived
His blessed countenance; here I could frequent,
With worship, place by place where he vouchsafed
Presence Divine, and to my sons relate;
'On this mount he appeared, under this tree   320
Stood visible, among these pines his voice
I heard, here with him at this fountain talked.'
So many grateful altars I would rear
Of grassy turf, and pile up every stone
Of luster from the brook, in memory,
Or monument to ages, and thereon
Offer sweet-smelling gums and fruits and flowers.
In yonder nether world where shall I seek
His bright appearances or footstep trace?
For though I fled him angry, yet recalled   330
To life prolonged and promised race, I now
Gladly behold though but his utmost skirts
Of glory, and far off his steps adore."
To whom thus Michael with regard benign.
"Adam, thou know'st Heaven his, and all the Earth,
Not this rock only; his omnipresence fills

297. the highest, i.e., the seraphim.

Land, sea, and air, and every kind that lives,
Fomented by his virtual power and warmed.
All the Earth he gave thee to possess and rule,
No despicable gift; surmise not then   340
His presence to these narrow bounds confined
Of Paradise or Eden: this had been
Perhaps thy capital seat, from whence had spread
All generations, and had hither come
From all the ends of the Earth, to celebrate
And reverence thee their great progenitor.
But this pre-eminence thou has lost, brought down
To dwell on even ground now with thy sons.
Yet doubt not but in valley and in plain
God is as here, and will be found alike   350
Present, and of his presence many a sign
Still following thee, still compassing thee round
With goodness and paternal love, his face
Express, and of his steps the track divine.
Which that thou may'st believe, and be confirmed,
Ere thou from hence depart, know I am sent
To show thee what shall come in future days
To thee and to thy offspring; good with bad
Expect to hear, supernal grace contending
With sinfulness of men; thereby to learn   360
True patience, and to temper joy with fear
And pious sorrow, equally inured
By moderation either state to bear,
Prosperous or adverse: so shalt thou lead
Safest thy life, and best prepared endure
Thy mortal passage when it comes. Ascend
This hill; let Eve (for I have drenched her eyes)   *Eve sleeps*
Here sleep below while thou to foresight wakest,
As once thou slept'st, while she to life was formed."
    To whom thus Adam gratefully replied.   *adam*   370
"Ascend, I follow thee, safe guide, the path
Thou lead'st me, and to the hand of Heaven submit,
However chastening, to the evil turn
My obvious breast, arming to overcome
By suffering, and earn rest from labor won,
If so I may attain." So both ascend
In the visions of God. It was a hill   *hill*
Of Paradise the highest, from whose top
The hemisphere of Earth in clearest ken

377. The phrase is from Ezek. 10:2. This line represents about the
widest divergence from the regular metrical pattern that Milton permits
himself.

Stretched out to amplest reach of prospect lay.   380
Not higher that hill nor wider looking round,
Whereon for different cause the Tempter set
Our second Adam in the wilderness,
To show him all Earth's kingdoms and their glory.
His eye might there command wherever stood
City of old or modern fame, the seat
Of mightiest empire, from the destined walls
Of Cambalu, seat of Cathaian Can
And Samarchand by Oxus, Temir's throne,
To Paquin of Sinæan kings, and thence   390
To Agra and Lahor of Great Mogul
Down to the golden Chersonese, or where
The Persian in Ecbatan sat, or since
In Hispahan, or where the Russian Ksar
In Mosco, or the Sultan in Bizance,
Turchestan-born; nor could his eye not ken
The empire of Negus to his utmost port
Ercoco and the less maritime kings
Mombaza, and Quiloa, and Melind,
And Sofala thought Ophir, to the realm   400
Of Congo, and Angola farthest south;
Or thence from Niger flood to Atlas mount
The kingdoms of Almansor, Fez and Sus,
Marocco and Algiers, and Tremisen;
On Europe thence, and where Rome was to sway
The world. In spirit perhaps he also saw
Rich Mexico the seat of Motezume,
And Cusco in Peru, the richer seat
Of Atabalipa, and yet unspoiled
Guiana, whose great city Geryon's sons   410
Call El Dorado. But to nobler sights
Michael from Adam's eyes the film removed
Which that false fruit that promised clearer sight
Had bred; then purged with euphrasy and rue
The visual nerve, for he had much to see;

383. **second Adam,** i.e., Christ. The allusion is to the temptation in
the wilderness, which Milton was to make the theme of *Paradise Regained*.
    386 ff. The geographical survey moves from China to India and Malaya,
to Persia, to Russia, to Turkey, to Abyssinia (empire of Negus), to east
Africa (Ercoco, Sofala, etc.), to North Africa, to Europe, to America.
Paquin is Pekin; the Golden Chersonese, Siam; Bizance, Byzantium (Con-
stantinople). Geryon's sons are the Spanish. A similar incantation with
exotic names will be found in the parallel vision of the Savior in *Paradise
Regained*, III, 250 ff.
    414. **euphrasy and rue,** two of the innumerable eye remedies in use by
such physicians as Milton himself consulted.

And from the well of life three drops instilled.
So deep the power of these ingredients pierced,
Even to the inmost seat of mental sight,
That Adam now enforced to close his eyes,
Sunk down and all his spirits became entranced;   420
But him the gentle Angel by the hand
Soon raised, and his attention thus recalled.
    "Adam, now ope thine eyes, and first behold
The effects which thy original crime hath wrought
In some to spring from thee, who never touched
The excepted tree, nor with the Snake conspired,
Nor sinned thy sin, yet from that sin derive
Corruption to bring forth more violent deeds."
    His eyes he opened, and beheld a field,
Part arable and tilth, whereon were sheaves   430
New-reaped, the other part sheep-walks and folds;
I' the midst an altar as the landmark stood
Rustic, of grassy sward; thither anon
A sweaty reaper from his tillage brought
First-fruits, the green ear and the yellow sheaf,
Unculled, as came to hand; a shepherd next
More meek came with the firstlings of his flock
Choicest and best; then sacrificing laid
The inwards and their fat, with incense strewed,
On the cleft wood, and all due rites performed.   440
His offering soon propitious fire from heaven
Consumed with nimble glance and grateful steam;
The other's not, for his was not sincere;
Whereat he inly raged, and as they talked,
Smote him into the midriff with a stone
That beat out life; he fell, and deadly pale
Groaned out his soul with gushing blood effused.
Much at that sight was Adam in his heart
Dismayed, and thus in haste to the angel cried.
    "O Teacher, some great mischief hath befallen   450
To that meek man, who well had sacrificed;
Is piety thus and pure devotion paid?"
    To whom Michael thus, he also moved, replied.
"These two are brethren, Adam, and to come
Out of thy loins; the unjust the just hath slain,

429 ff. The vision serves the purpose of an epic prophecy like that of
the future of the Roman empire in Virgil; dramatically and ideologically it
is part of Adam's punishment, "the fruit of that forbidden tree." Finally, it
is a didactic exposition of the gist of biblical and church history from the
viewpoint of Milton as a son of the Reformation and of English Puritanism.
The detail is naturally greater for the earlier events. The spiritual elevation
rises with the coming of Christ to a great climax at the end of the poem.

For envy that his brother's offering found
From Heaven acceptance; but the bloody fact
Will be avenged, and the other's faith approved
Lose no reward, though here thou see him die,
Rolling in dust and gore. To which our Sire.   460
    "Alas, both for the deed and for the cause!
But have I now seen Death? Is this the way
I must return to native dust? O sight
Of terror, foul and ugly to behold,
Horrid to think, how horrible to feel!"
To whom thus Michael. "Death thou has seen
In his first shape on Man; but many shapes
Of Death, and many are the ways that lead
To his grim cave, all dismal; yet to sense
More terrible at the entrance than within.   470
Some, as thou saw'st, by violent stroke shall die,
By fire, flood, famine, by intemperance more
In meats and drinks which on the Earth shall bring
Diseases dire, of which a monstrous crew
Before thee shall appear, that thou may'st know
What misery th' inabstinence of Eve
Shall bring on men." Immediately a place
Before his eyes appeared, sad, noisome, dark,
A lazar-house it seemed, wherein were laid
Numbers of all diseased, all maladies   480
Of ghastly spasm, or racking torture, qualms
Of heart-sick agony, all feverous kinds,
Convulsions, epilepsies, fierce catarrhs,
Intestine stone and ulcer, colic pangs,
Demoniac frenzy, moping melancholy
And moon-struck madness, pining atrophy,
Marasmus, and wide-wasting pestilence,
Dropsies and asthmas, and joint-racking rheums.
Dire was the tossing, deep the groans, despair
Tended the sick busiest from couch to couch;   490
And over them triumphant Death his dart
Shook, but delayed to strike, though oft invoked
With vows, as their chief good, and final hope.
Sight so deform what heart of rock could long
Dry-eyed behold? Adam could not, but wept,
Though not of woman born; compassion quelled
His best of man, and gave him up to tears
A space, till firmer thoughts restrained excess,
And scarce recovering words his plaint renewed.

    497. His best of man, a recollection of Macbeth: "for it hath cowed
my better part of man," i.e., the better part of my manhood.

"O miserable Mankind, to what fall
Degraded, to what wretched state reserved!
Better end here unborn. Why is life given
To be thus wrested from us? rather why
Obtruded on us thus? who if we knew
What we receive, would either not accept
Life offered, or soon beg to lay it down,
Glad to be so dismissed in peace. Can thus
Th' image of God in Man, created once
So goodly and erect, though faulty since,
To such unsightly sufferings be debased   510
Under inhuman pains? Why should not man,
Retaining still divine similitude
In part, from such deformities be free,
And for his Maker's image sake exempt?"
    "Their Maker's image," answered Michael, "then
Forsook them, when themselves they vilified
To serve ungoverned appetite, and took
His image whom they served, a brutish vice,
Inductive mainly to the sin of Eve.
Therefore so abject is their punishment,   520
Disfiguring not God's likeness, but their own
Or if his likeness, by themselves defaced
While they pervert pure Nature's healthful rules
To loathsome sickness; worthily, since they
God's image did not reverence in themselves."
    "I yield it just," said Adam, "and submit.
But is there yet no other way, besides
These painful passages, how we may come
To death, and mix with our connatural dust?"
    "There is," said Michael, "if thou well observe   530
The rule of *Not too much*, by temperance taught
In what thou eat'st and drink'st, seeking from thence
Due nourishment, not gluttonous delight,
Till many years over thy head return.
So may'st thou live, till like ripe fruit thou drop
Into thy mother's lap, or be with ease
Gathered, not harshly plucked, for death mature:
This is old age; but then thou must outlive
Thy youth, thy strength, thy beauty, which will change
To withered weak and gray; thy senses then   540
Obtuse, all taste of pleasure must forgo
To what thou hast, and for the air of youth
Hopeful and cheerful, in thy blood will reign

    519. inductive, leading to, i.e., Ungoverned appetite was a main cause
of her sin, and is a main cause of sin like hers.

A melancholy damp of cold and dry
To weigh thy spirits down, and last consume
The balm of life." To whom our Ancestor.
    "Henceforth I fly not death, nor would prolong
Life much, bent rather how I may be quit
Fairest and easiest of this cumbrous charge,
Which I must keep till my appointed day   550
Of rendering up, and patiently attend
My dissolution." Michael replied.
    "Nor love thy life, nor hate; but what thou livest
Live well, how long or short permit to Heaven:
And now prepare thee for another sight."
    He looked and saw a spacious plain, whereon
Were tents of various hue; by some were herds
Of cattle grazing; others, whence the sound
Of instruments that made melodious chime
Was heard, of harp and organ; and who moved   560
Their stops and chords was seen: his volant touch
Instinct through all proportions low and high
Fled and pursued transverse the resonant fugue.
In other part stood one who at the forge
Laboring, two massy clods of iron and brass
Had melted (whether found where casual fire
Had wasted woods on mountain or in vale,
Down to the veins of earth, thence gliding hot
To some cave's mouth, or whether washed by stream
From underground) the liquid ore he drained   570
Into fit moulds prepared; from which he formed
First his own tools; then, what might else be wrought
Fusil or graven in metal. After these,
But on the hither side a different sort
From the high neighboring hills, which was their seat,
Down to the plain descended: by their guise
Just men they seemed, and all their study bent
To worship God aright, and know his works
Not hid, nor those things last which might preserve
Freedom and peace to men. They on the plain   580
Long had not walked, when from the tents behold

    553 ff. Here, as elsewhere, Michael is rectifying Adam's natural reac-
tions to what he sees and giving him sound moral attitudes.
    561. volant, flying, rapid.
    562. instinct through all proportions, inspired to move through all
degrees of pitch.
    563. transverse, across the keys.
    574 ff. The descendants of Seth were traditionally located west of Eden
("on the hither side"). Milton identifies them with the sons of God in
Gen. 6:2.

A bevy of fair women, richly gay
In gems and wanton dress; to the harp they sung
Soft amorous ditties, and in dance came on:
The men though grave, eyed them, and let their eyes
Rove without rein, till in the amorous net
Fast caught, they liked, and each his liking chose;
And now of love they treat till the evening star
Love's harbinger appeared; then all in heat
They light the nuptial torch, and bid invoke   590
Hymen, then first to marriage rites invoked;
With feast and music all the tents resound.
Such happy interview and fair event
Of love and youth not lost, songs, garlands, flowers,
And charming symphonies attached the heart
Of Adam, soon inclined to admit delight,
The bent of Nature; which he thus expressed.
  "True opener of mine eyes, prime Angel blest,
Much better seems this vision, and more hope
Of peaceful days portends, than those two past;   600
Those were of hate and death, or pain much worse,
Here Nature seems fulfilled in all her ends."
  To whom thus Michael. "Judge not what is best
By pleasure, though to Nature seeming meet,
Created, as thou art, to nobler end
Holy and pure, conformity divine.
Those tents thou saw'st so pleasant, were the tents
Of wickedness, wherein shall dwell his race
Who slew his brother; studious they appear
Of arts that polish life, inventors rare,   610
Unmindful of their Maker, though his Spirit
Taught them, but they his gifts acknowledged none.
Yet they a beauteous offspring shall beget;
For that fair female troop thou saw'st, that seemed
Of goddesses, so blithe, so smooth, so gay,
Yet empty of all good wherein consists
Woman's domestic honor and chief praise;
Bred only and completed to the taste
Of lustful appetence, to sing, to dance,
To dress, and troll the tongue, and roll the eye.   620
To these that sober race of men, whose lives
Religious titled them the Sons of God,
Shall yield up all their virtue, all their fame
Ignobly, to the trains and to the smiles
Of these fair atheists, and now swim in joy

624. trains, wiles.

(Erelong to swim at large) and laugh; for which
The world erelong a world of tears must weep."
　　To whom thus Adam of short joy bereft.
"O pity and shame, that they who to live well
Entered so fair should turn aside to tread   630
Paths indirect, or in the mid way faint!
But still I see the tenor of Man's woe
Holds on the same, from Woman to begin."
　　"From Man's effeminate slackness it begins,"
Said the Angel, "who should better hold his place
By wisdom, and superior gifts received.
But now prepare thee for another scene."
　　He looked and saw wide territory spread
Before him, towns, and rural works between,
Cities of men with lofty gates and towers,   640
Concourse in arms, fierce faces threatening war,
Giants of mighty bone and bold emprise;
Part wield their arms, part curb the foaming steed,
Single or in array of battle ranged
Both horse and foot, nor idly mustering stood;
One way a band select from forage drives
A herd of beeves, fair oxen and fair kine
From a fat meadow ground; or fleecy flock,
Ewes and their bleating lambs over the plain,
Their booty; scarce with life the shepherds fly,   650
But call in aid, which makes a bloody fray;
With cruel tournament the squadrons join;
Where cattle pastured late, now scattered lies
With carcasses and arms the ensanguined field
Deserted. Others to a city strong
Lay siege, encamped; by battery, scale, and mine,
Assaulting; others from the wall defend
With dart and javelin, stones and sulphurous fire;
On each hand slaughter and gigantic deeds.
In other part the sceptred heralds call   660
To council in the city gates: anon
Grey-headed men and grave, with warriors mixed,
Assemble, and harangues are heard, but soon
In factious opposition, till at last
Of middle age one rising, eminent
In wise deport, spake much of right and wrong,
Of justice, of religion, truth and peace,
And judgment from above: him old and young
Exploded and had seized with violent hands,

　　665 ff. Enoch. See Gen. 5:24.　　　669. exploded, hooted away.

prophet

Had not a cloud descending snatched him thence   670
Unseen amid the throng: so violence
Proceeded, and oppression, and sword-law
Through all the plain, and refuge none was found.
Adam was all in tears, and to his guide
Lamenting turned full sad. "O what are these,
Death's ministers, not men, who thus deal death
Inhumanly to men, and multiply
Ten thousandfold the sin of him who slew
His brother; for of whom such massacre
Make they but of their brethren, men of men?   680
But who was that just man, whom had not Heaven
Rescued, had in his righteousness been lost?"
    To whom thus Michael. "These are the product   *michael*
Of those ill-mated marriages thou saw'st;
Where good with bad were matched, who of themselves
Abhor to join, and by imprudence mixed,
Produce prodigious births of body or mind.
Such were these giants, men of high renown;
For in those days might only shall be admired,
And valor and heroic virtue called;   *might*   690
To overcome in battle, and subdue
Nations, and bring home spoils with infinite
Man-slaughter, shall be held the highest pitch   *man-slaughter*
Of human glory, and for glory done
Of triumph, to be styled great conquerors,
Patrons of mankind, gods, and sons of gods,
Destroyers rightlier called and plagues of men.
Thus fame shall be achieved, renown on Earth,
And what most merits fame in silence hid.
But he the seventh from thee, whom thou beheld'st   700
The only righteous in a world perverse,
And therefore hated, therefore so beset
With foes for daring single to be just,
And utter odious truth, that God would come
To judge them with his saints: Him the Most High
Rapt in a balmy cloud with wingèd steeds,
Did, as thou saw'st, receive, to walk with God
High in salvation and the climes of bliss,
Exempt from death; to show thee what reward
Awaits the good, the rest what punishment;   710
Which now direct thine eyes and soon behold."
    He looked and saw the face of things quite changed,
The brazen throat of war had ceased to roar,
All now was turned to jollity and game,
To luxury and riot, feast and dance,   *luxury*

Marrying or prostituting, as befell,
Rape or adultery, where passing fair
Allured them; thence from cups to civil broils.
At length a reverend sire among them came,
And of their doings great dislike declared,   720
And testified against their ways; he oft
Frequented their assemblies, whereso met,
Triumphs or festivals, and to them preached
Conversion and repentance, as to souls
In prison under judgments imminent;
But all in vain; which when he saw, he ceased
Contending, and removed his tents far off;
Then from the mountain hewing timber tall,
Began to build a vessel of huge bulk,
Measured by cubit, length, and breadth, and height,   730
Smeared round with pitch, and in the side a door
Contrived, and of provisions laid in large
For man and beast: when lo a wonder strange!
Of every beast, and bird, and insect small
Came sevens and pairs, and entered in, as taught
Their order; last the sire and his three sons
With their four wives; and God made fast the door.
Meanwhile the southwind rose, and with black wings
Wide hovering, all the clouds together drove
From under heaven; the hills, to their supply,   740
Vapor, and exhalation dusk and moist,
Sent up amain; and now the thickened sky
Like a dark ceiling stood: down rushed the rain
Impetuous, and continued till the earth
No more was seen; the floating vessel swum
Uplifted; and secure with beakèd prow
Rode tilting o'er the waves, all dwellings else
Flood overwhelmed, and them with all their pomp
Deep under water rolled; sea covered sea,
Sea without shore; and in their palaces   750
Where luxury late reigned, sea-monsters whelped
And stabled; of mankind, so numerous late,
All left, in one small bottom swum embarked.
How didst thou grieve then, Adam, to behold
The end of all thy offspring, end so sad,
Depopulation; thee another flood,
Of tears and sorrow a flood thee also drowned,

719. a reverend sire, Noah. See Gen. 6 ff.
733. a wonder. The wonder is that they could all get in. Milton sur-
mises a miracle like the transformation of Satan's councilors to pigmies in
Book I.

And sunk thee as thy sons; till gently reared
By the Angel, on thy feet thou stood'st at last,
Though comfortless, as when a father mourns   760
His children, all in view destroyed at once;
And scarce to the Angel utter'dst thus thy plaint.
    "O visions ill foreseen! better had I
Lived ignorant of future, so had borne
My part of evil only, each day's lot
Enough to bear; those now, that were dispensed
The burden of many ages, on me light
At once, by my foreknowledge gaining birth
Abortive, to torment me ere their being,
With thought that they must be. Let no man seek   770
Henceforth to be foretold what shall befall
Him or his children, evil he may be sure,
Which neither his foreknowing can prevent,
And he the future evil shall no less
In apprehension than in substance feel
Grievous to bear. But that care now is past,
Man is not whom to warn; those few escaped
Famine and anguish will at last consume,
Wandering that watery desert. I had hope
When violence was ceased and war on Earth,   780
All would have then gone well, peace would have crowned
With length of happy days the race of Man;
But I was far deceived; for now I see
Peace to corrupt no less than war to waste.
How comes it thus? unfold, Celestial Guide,
And whether here the race of Man will end."
    To whom thus Michael. "Those whom last thou saw'st
In triumph and luxurious wealth, are they
First seen in acts of prowess eminent
And great exploits, but of true virtue void;   790
Who having spilt much blood, and done much waste
Subduing nations, and achieved thereby
Fame in the world, high titles, and rich prey,
Shall change their course to pleasure, ease, and sloth,
Surfeit, and lust, till wantonness and pride
Raise out of friendship hostile deeds in peace.
The conquered also, and enslaved by war
Shall with their freedom lost all virtue lose

773-74. A Latin idiom; neither can prevent the future evil nor feel it
less than as if it were actually present.
    796. raise out of friendship, etc. A morally corrupt nation, though
prosperous and at peace, starts wars of aggression.

And fear of God, from whom their piety feigned
In sharp contest of battle found no aid   800
Against invaders; therefore cooled in zeal
Thenceforth shall practise how to live secure,
Worldly or dissolute, on what their lords
Shall leave them to enjoy; for the Earth shall bear
More than enough, that temperance may be tried:
So all shall turn degenerate, all depraved,
Justice and temperance, truth and faith forgot;
One man except, the only son of light
In a dark age, against example good,
Against allurement, custom, and a world   810
Offended; fearless of reproach and scorn,
Or violence, he of their wicked ways
Shall them admonish, and before them set
The paths of righteousness, how much more safe
And full of peace, denouncing wrath to come
On their impenitence; and shall return
Of them derided, but of God observed
The one just man alive; by his command
Shall build a wondrous ark, as thou beheld'st,
To save himself and household from amidst   820
A world devote to universal wrack.
No sooner he with them of man and beast
Select for life shall in the ark be lodged,
And sheltered round, but all the cataracts
Of Heaven set open on the Earth shall pour
Rain day and night, all fountains of the Deep
Broke up, shall heave the ocean to usurp
Beyond all bounds, till inundation rise
Above the highest hills: then shall this mount
Of Paradise by might of waves be moved   830
Out of his place, pushed by the hornèd flood,
With all his verdure spoiled, and trees adrift
Down the great river to the opening gulf,
And there take root an island salt and bare,
The haunt of seals and orcs, and sea-mews' clang.
To teach thee that God attributes to place
No sanctity, if none be thither brought

799–800. Milton's wide historical reading would have given him many
examples of peoples who, though unjustly attacked, found no aid in God
despite their pretense of piety, and who, when their liberty was lost, gave
up the effort to resist in favor of easy living. This, in his thought, was the
case with the English after the restoration of the Stuarts.

808. **One man except.** This is Milton's favorite moral image. See the
portrait of Abdiel, III, 896 ff.

By men who there frequent or therein dwell.
And now what further shall ensue, behold."
   He looked, and saw the ark hull on the flood,   840
Which now abated, for the clouds were fled,
Driven by a keen north-wind, that blowing dry
Wrinkled the face of deluge, as decayed;
And the clear sun on his wide watery glass
Gazed hot, and of the fresh wave largely drew,
As after thirst, which made their flowing shrink
From standing lake to tripping ebb, that stole
With soft foot towards the Deep, who now had stopped
His sluices, as the heaven his windows shut.
The ark no more now floats, but seems on ground   850
Fast on the top of some high mountain fixed.
And now the tops of hills as rocks appear;
With clamor thence the rapid currents drive
Towards the retreating sea their furious tide.
Forthwith from out the ark a raven flies,
And after him, the surer messenger,
A dove sent forth once and again to spy
Green tree or ground whereon his foot may light;
The second time returning, in his bill
An olive leaf he brings, pacific sign: 860
Anon dry ground appears, and from his ark
The ancient sire descends with all his train;
Then with uplifted hands and eyes devout,
Grateful to Heaven, over his head beholds
A dewy cloud, and in the cloud a bow
Conspicuous with three listed colors gay,
Betokening peace from God, and covenant new.
Whereat the heart of Adam erst so sad
Greatly rejoiced, and thus his joy broke forth.
   "O thou who future things canst represent   870
As present, Heavenly Instructor, I revive
At this last sight, assured that Man shall live
With all the creatures, and their seed preserve.
Far less I now lament for one whole world
Of wicked sons destroyed, than I rejoice
For one man found so perfect and so just,
That God vouchsafes to raise another world
From him, and all his anger to forget.
But say, what mean those colored streaks in Heaven,

874–78. Adam's rejoicing in the good as outweighing a world of evil
anticipates his attitude at the conclusion of the poem. This is the paradox
of man's fallen state. Without sin there could be illustration of the spiritual
triumph of the "one just man."

Distended as the brow of God appeased,   880
Or serve they as a flowery verge to bind
The fluid skirts of that same watery cloud,
Lest it again dissolve and shower the Earth?"
    To whom the Archangel. "Dextrously thou aim'st;
So willingly doth God remit his ire,
Though late repenting him of Man depraved,
Grieved at his heart, when looking down he saw
The whole Earth filled with violence, and all flesh
Corrupting each their way; yet those removed,
Such grace shall one just man find in his sight,   890
That he relents, not to blot out mankind,
And makes a covenant never to destroy
The Earth again by flood, nor let the sea
Surpass his bounds, nor rain to drown the world
With man therein or beast; but when he brings
Over the Earth a cloud, will therein set
His triple-colored bow, whereon to look
And call to mind his covenant. Day and night,
Seed-time and harvest, heat and hoary frost
Shall hold their course, till fire purge all things new,   900
Both Heaven and Earth, wherein the just shall dwell."

BOOK XII

THE ARGUMENT

The Angel Michael continues from the Flood to relate what
shall succeed; then, in the mention of Abraham, comes by degrees
to explain, who that Seed of the Woman shall be which was promised Adam and Eve in the Fall; his incarnation, death, resurrection, and ascension; the state of the Church till his second coming.
Adam greatly satisfied and recomforted by these relations and
promises descends the hill with Michael; wakens Eve, who all this
while had slept, but with gentle dreams composed to quietness of
mind and submission. Michael in either hand leads them out of
Paradise, the fiery sword waving behind them, and the Cherubim
taking their stations to guard the place.

As one who in his journey bates at noon,
Though bent on speed, so here the Archangel paused
Betwixt the world destroyed and the world restored,
If Adam aught perhaps might interpose;
Then with transition sweet new speech resumes.

    881 ff. Adam's poetic fancy that the rainbow binds the clouds against
producing another flood is praised as a shrewd guess at the truth: "Dex-
trously thou aim'st."

"Thus thou hast seen one world begin and end;
And Man as from a second stock proceed.
Much thou hast yet to see, but I perceive
Thy mortal sight to fail; objects divine
Must needs impair and weary human sense: 10
Henceforth what is to come I will relate,
Thou therefore give due audience, and attend.
   "This second source of men, while yet but few,
And while the dread of judgment past remains
Fresh in their minds, fearing the Deity,
With some regard to what is just and right
Shall lead their lives, and multiply apace,
Laboring the soil, and reaping plenteous crop,
Corn, wine and oil; and from the herd or flock,
Oft sacrificing bullock, lamb, or kid,   20
With large wine-offerings poured, and sacred feast
Shall spend their days in joy unblamed, and dwell
Long time in peace by families and tribes
Under paternal rule; till one shall rise
Of proud ambitious heart, who not content
With fair equality, fraternal state,
Will arrogate dominion undeserved
Over his brethren, and quite dispossess
Concord and law of Nature from the Earth;
Hunting (and men not beasts, shall be his game)   30
With war and hostile snare such as refuse
Subjection to his empire tyrannous.
A mighty hunter thence he shall be styled
Before the Lord, as in despite of Heaven,
Or from Heaven claiming second sovranty;
And from rebellion shall derive his name,
Though of rebellion others he accuse.
He with a crew whom like ambition joins
With him or under him to tyrannize,

   24 ff. Scripture says of Nimrod that he "began to be a mighty one in
the earth" and that the "beginning of his kingdom was Babel." It was natural, therefore, to make him the symbol of empire-building power and arrogant defiance of God's will. Milton's language reveals him as interpreting
the experience of his own times in the light of these ideas. The idea that
Nimrod was the builder of the Tower of Babel was traditional. Cf. Dante,
Inferno, XXXI, 76–77: "Nimrod, to whose evil thought we owe it that
there is more than one language in the world."
   33–38. The tyrant who, by falsely claiming divine authority, becomes a
rebel against God and at the same time accuses others of rebellion is obviously the image of Charles I. This identification shows how easy it was for
Milton to equate rebel Satan with tyrant Charles, in contradiction to the
other association which must have forced itself on him, of the revolting
angels with the leaders of the Puritan revolution.

Marching from Eden towards the west, shall find   40
The plain, wherein a black bituminous gurge
Boils out from under ground, the mouth of Hell;
Of brick, and of that stuff, they cast to build
A city and tower, whose top may reach to Heaven;
And get themselves a name, lest far dispersed
In foreign lands their memory be lost,
Regardless whether good or evil fame.
But God who oft descends to visit men
Unseen, and through their habitations walks
To mark their doings, them beholding soon,   50
Comes down to see their city, ere the tower
Obstruct Heaven towers, and in derision sets
Upon their tongues a various spirit to rase
Quite out their native language, and instead
To sow a jangling noise of words unknown:
Forthwith a hideous gabble rises loud
Among the builders; each to other calls
Not understood, till hoarse, and all in rage,
As mocked they storm; great laughter was in Heaven
And looking down, to see the hubbub strange   60
And hear the din; thus was the building left
Ridiculous, and the work Confusion named."
      Whereto thus Adam fatherly displeased.
"O execrable son so to aspire
Above his brethren, to himself assuming
Authority usurped, from God not given;
He gave us only over beast, fish, fowl
Dominion absolute; that right we hold
By his donation; but man over men
He made not lord; such title to himself   70
Reserving, human left from human free.
But this usurper his encroachment proud
Stays not on Man; to God his tower intends
Siege and defiance. Wretched man! what food
Will he convey up thither to sustain
Himself and his rash army, where thin air
Above the clouds will pine his entrails gross,
And famish him of breath, if not of bread?"
      To whom thus Michael. "Justly thou abhorr'st
That son, who on the quiet state of men   80

79 ff. These lines contain the gist of Milton's interpretation of what
had happened in England, read in the light of Plato's political philosophy in
the Republic. Reason rules in the state when the best and wisest men are in
authority. Abrogation of reason, in the state as in the individual soul, leads
to chaos, with tyranny as its inevitable consequence. To Plato, aristocracy is
the best form of government and democracy the worst.

Such trouble brought, affecting to subdue
Rational liberty; yet know withal,
Since thy original lapse, true liberty
Is lost, which always with right reason dwells
Twinned, and from her hath no dividual being;
Reason in Man obscured, or not obeyed,
Immediately inordinate desires
And upstart passions catch the government
From reason, and to servitude reduce
Man till then free. Therefore since he permits   90
Within himself unworthy powers to reign
Over free reason, God in judgment just
Subjects him from without to violent lords;
Who oft as undeservedly enthral
His outward freedom: tyranny must be,
Though to the tyrant thereby no excuse.
Yet sometimes nations will decline so low
From virtue, which is reason, that no wrong,
But justice, and some fatal curse annexed
Deprives them of their outward liberty,   100
Their inward lost: witness the irreverent son
Of him who built the ark, who for the shame
Done to his father, heard this heavy curse,
Servant of servants, on his vicious race.
Thus will this latter, as the former world,
Still tend from bad to worse, till God at last
Wearied with their iniquities, withdraw
His presence from among them, and avert
His holy eyes; resolving from thenceforth
To leave them to their own polluted ways;   110
And one peculiar nation to select
From all the rest, of whom to be invoked,
A nation from one faithful man to spring.
Him on this side Euphrates yet residing,
Bred up in idol-worship; O that men
(Canst thou believe?) should be so stupid grown,
While yet the patriarch lived who scaped the Flood,
As to forsake the living God, and fall
To worship their own work in wood and stone
For gods! yet him God the Most High vouchsafes   120
To call by vision from his father's house,
His kindred and false gods, into a land
Which he will shew him, and from him will raise
A mighty nation, and upon him shower
His benediction so, that in his seed
All nations shall be blest; he straight obeys,

Not knowing to what land, yet firm believes.
I see him, but thou canst not, with what faith
He leaves his gods, his friends, and native soil
Ur of Chaldæa, passing now the ford   130
To Haran, after him a cumbrous train
Of herds and flocks, and numerous servitude;
Not wandering poor, but trusting all his wealth
With God, who called him, in a land unknown.
Canaan he now attains; I see his tents
Pitched about Sechem, and the neighboring plain
Of Moreh; there by promise he receives
Gift to his progeny of all that land;
From Hamath northward to the Desert south
(Things by their names I call, though yet unnamed)   140
From Hermon east to the great western sea,
Mount Hermon, yonder sea, each place behold
In prospect, as I point them; on the shore
Mount Carmel; here the double-founted stream
Jordan, true limit eastward; but his sons
Shall dwell to Senir, that long ridge of hills.
This ponder, that all nations of the Earth
Shall in his seed be blessed; by that seed
Is meant thy great Deliverer, who shall bruise
The Serpent's head; whereof to thee anon   150
Plainlier shall be revealed. This patriarch blest,
Whom *faithful Abraham* due time shall call,
A son, and of his son a grandchild leaves,
Like him in faith, in wisdom, and renown;
The grandchild with twelve sons increased, departs
From Canaan, to a land hereafter called
Egypt, divided by the river Nile;
See where it flows, disgorging at seven mouths
Into the sea. To sojourn in that land
He comes invited by a younger son   160
In time of dearth, a son whose worthy deeds
Raise him to be the second in that realm
Of Pharaoh. There he dies, and leaves his race
Growing into a nation, and now grown
Suspected to a sequent king, who seeks
To stop their overgrowth, as inmate guests
Too numerous; whence of guests he makes them slaves
Inhospitably, and kills their infant males:
Till by two brethren (those two brethren call
Moses and Aaron) sent from God to claim   170
His people from enthralment, they return
With glory and spoil back to their promised land.

But first the lawless tyrant, who denies
To know their God, or message to regard,
Must be compelled by signs and judgments dire;
To blood unshed the rivers must be turned,
Frogs, lice and flies must all his palace fill
With loathed intrusion, and fill all the land;
His cattle must of rot and murrain die,
Botches and blains must all his flesh emboss,   180
And all his people; thunder mixed with hail,
Hail mixed with fire must rend the Egyptian sky
And wheel on the earth, devouring where it rolls;
What it devours not, herb, or fruit, or grain,
A darksome cloud of locusts swarming down
Must eat, and on the ground leave nothing green;
Darkness must overshadow all his bounds,
Palpable darkness, and blot out three days;
Last with one midnight stroke all the first-born
Of Egypt must lie dead. Thus with ten wounds   190
The river-dragon tamed at length submits
To let his sojourners depart, and oft
Humbles his stubborn heart, but still as ice
More hardened after thaw, till in his rage
Pursuing whom he late dismissed, the sea
Swallows him with his host, but them lets pass
As on dry land between two crystal walls,
Awed by the rod of Moses so to stand
Divided, till his rescued gain their shore:
Such wondrous power God to his saint will lend,   200
Though present in his angel, who shall go
Before them in a cloud, and pillar of fire,
By day a cloud, by night a pillar of fire,
To guide them in their journey, and remove
Behind them, while the obdurate king pursues.
All night he will pursue, but his approach
Darkness defends between till morning watch;
Then through the fiery pillar and the cloud
God looking forth will trouble all his host
And craze their chariot wheels: when by command   210
Moses once more his potent rod extends
Over the sea; the sea his rod obeys;
On their embattled ranks the waves return,
And overwhelm their war. The race elect
Safe toward Canaan from the shore advance
Through the wild desert, not the readiest way,
Lest entering on the Canaanite alarmed
War terrify them inexpert, and fear

Return them back to Egypt, choosing rather
Inglorious life with servitude; for life   220
To noble and ignoble is more sweet
Untrained in arms, where rashness leads not on.
This also shall they gain by their delay
In the wide wilderness, there they shall found
Their government, and their great senate choose
Through the twelve tribes, to rule by laws ordained:
God from the mount of Sinai, whose grey top
Shall tremble, he descending, will himself
In thunder, lightning and loud trumpet's sound
Ordain them laws; part such as appertain   230
To civil justice, part religious rites
Of sacrifice, informing them, by types
And shadows, of that destined Seed to bruise
The Serpent, by what means he shall achieve
Mankind's deliverance. But the voice of God
To mortal ear is dreadful; they beseech
That Moses might report to them his will,
And terror cease; he grants what they besought
Instructed that to God is no access
Without Mediator, whose high office now   240
Moses in figure bears, to introduce
One greater, of whose day he shall foretell,
And all the Prophets in their age the times
Of great Messiah shall sing. Thus laws and rites
Established, such delight hath God in men
Obedient to his will, that he vouchsafes
Among them to set up his tabernacle,
The Holy One with mortal men to dwell:
By his prescript a sanctuary is framed
Of cedar, overlaid with gold, therein   250
An ark, and in the ark his testimony,
The records of his covenant; over these
A mercy-seat of gold between the wings
Of two bright Cherubim; before him burn
Seven lamps, as in a zodiac representing
The heavenly fires; over the tent a cloud
Shall rest by day, a fiery gleam by night,
Save when they journey, and at length they come,
Conducted by his angel to the land
Promised to Abraham and his seed. The rest   260
Were long to tell, how many battles fought,
How many kings destroyed, and kingdoms won,
Or how the sun shall in mid heaven stand still
A day entire, and night's due course adjourn,

Man's voice commanding, 'Sun, in Gibeon stand,
And thou Moon in the vale of Aialon,
Till Israel overcome'; so call the third
From Abraham, son of Isaac, and from him
His whole descent, who thus shall Canaan win."
   Here Adam interposed. "O sent from Heaven,   *Adam*   270
Enlightener of my darkness, gracious things
Thou hast revealed, those chiefly which concern
Just Abraham and his seed. Now first I find
Mine eyes true opening, and my heart much eased,
Erewhile perplexed with thoughts what would become
Of me and all mankind; but now I see
His day, in whom all nations shall be blest,
Favor unmerited by me, who sought
Forbidden knowledge by forbidden means.
This yet I apprehend not, why to those   280
Among whom God will deign to dwell on Earth
So many and so various laws are given;
So many laws argue so many sins
Among them; how can God with such reside?"
   To whom thus Michael. "Doubt not but that sin   *Michael*
Will reign among them, as of thee begot;
And therefore was law given them to evince
Their natural pravity, by stirring up
Sin against law to fight; that when they see
Law can discover sin, but not remove,   290
Save by those shadowy expiations weak,
The blood of bulls and goats, they may conclude
Some blood more precious must be paid for Man,
Just for unjust, that in such righteousness
To them by faith imputed, they may find
Justification towards God, and peace
Of conscience, which the law by ceremonies
Cannot appease, nor man the moral part
Perform, and not performing cannot live.
So law appears imperfect, and but given   300
With purpose to resign them in full time
Up to a better covenant, disciplined
From shadowy types to truth, from flesh to spirit,
From imposition of strict laws, to free
Acceptance of large grace, from servile fear

---

287. evince, to demonstrate. In Milton's theology the Mosaic law was
given "for the hardness of men's hearts." It was abrogated by the new testament of love in Christ, the "better covenant" of line 302.

   303. shadowy types. Christian interpretation found allegorical illus-
trations of the truth everywhere in Old Testament history. Thus the burnt

To filial, works of law to works of faith.
And therefore shall not Moses, though of God
Highly beloved, being but the minister
Of law, his people into Canaan lead;
But Joshua whom the Gentiles Jesus call,   310
His name and office bearing, who shall quell
The adversary Serpent, and bring back
Through the world's wilderness long-wandered Man
Safe to eternal Paradise of rest.
Meanwhile they in their earthly Canaan placed
Long time shall dwell and prosper, but when sins
National interrupt their public peace,
Provoking God to raise them enemies,
From whom as oft he saves them penitent
By judges first, then under kings; of whom   320
The second, both for piety renowned
And puissant deeds, a promise shall receive
Irrevocable, that his regal throne
For ever shall endure; the like shall sing
All prophecy: that of the royal stock
Of David (so I name this king) shall rise
A Son, the Woman's Seed to thee foretold,
Foretold to Abraham, as in whom shall trust
All nations, and to kings foretold, of kings
The last, for of his reign shall be no end.   330
But first a long succession must ensue,
And his next son for wealth and wisdom famed,
The clouded ark of God till then in tents
Wandering, shall in a glorious temple enshrine.
Such follow him, as shall be registered
Part good, part bad, of bad the longer scroll,
Whose foul idolatries and other faults
Heaped to the popular sum, will so incense
God, as to leave them, and expose their land,
Their city, his temple, and his holy ark   340
With all his sacred things, a scorn and prey
To that proud city, whose high walls thou saw'st
Left in confusion, Babylon thence called.
There in captivity he lets them dwell
The space of seventy years, then brings them back,
Remembering mercy, and his covenant sworn

offerings are a symbol of the true sacrifice of a contrite heart; Moses is a
mediator and foreshadows the office of the Redeemer; Joshua, leading his
people into the promised land, is again Christ making possible salvation for
the elect.
    332. his next son, Solomon. See I Kings 6–7 and II Chron. 3–4.

To David, stablished as the days of Heaven.
Returned from Babylon by leave of kings
Their lords, whom God disposed, the house of God
They first re-edify, and for a while   350
In mean estate live moderate, till grown
In wealth and multitude, factious they grow;
But first among the priests dissension springs,
Men who attend the altar, and should most
Endeavor peace; their strife pollution brings
Upon the temple itself; at last they seize
The scepter and regard not David's sons,
Then lose it to a stranger, that the true
Anointed King Messiah might be born
Barred of his right; yet at his birth a star   360
Unseen before in Heaven proclaims him come,
And guides the eastern sages, who inquire
His place, to offer incense, myrrh, and gold;
His place of birth a solemn angel tells
To simple shepherds, keeping watch by night;
They gladly thither haste, and by a choir
Of squadroned angels hear his carol sung.
A Virgin is his mother, but his Sire
The Power of the Most High; he shall ascend
The throne hereditary, and bound his reign   370
With Earth's wide bounds, his glory with the Heavens."
　　He ceased, discerning Adam with such joy
Surcharged, as had like grief been dewed in tears,
Without the vent of words, which these he breathed.
　　"O prophet of glad tidings, finisher
Of utmost hope! now clear I understand
What oft my steadiest thoughts have searched in vain,
Why our great Expectation should be called
The Seed of Woman: Virgin Mother, hail,
High in the love of Heaven, yet from my loins   380
Thou shalt proceed, and from thy womb the Son
Of God Most High; so God with Man unites.
Needs must the Serpent now his capital bruise
Expect with mortal pain: say where and when
Their fight, what stroke shall bruise the Victor's heel."
　　To whom thus Michael. "Dream not of their fight
As of a duel, or the local wounds
Of head or heel: not therefore joins the Son
Manhood to Godhead, with more strength to foil
Thy enemy; nor so is overcome   390

　　373. **had**, would have.
　　383. **capital**, of the head, but with the idea also of "chief."

Satan, whose fall from Heaven, a deadlier bruise,
Disabled not to give thee thy death's wound;
Which he, who comes thy Savior, shall recure,
Not by destroying Satan, but his works
In thee and in thy seed. Nor can this be,
But by fulfilling that which thou didst want,
Obedience to the law of God, imposed
On penalty of death, and suffering death,
The penalty to thy transgression due,
And due to theirs which out of thine will grow: 400
So only can high justice rest appaid.
The law of God exact he shall fulfil
Both by obedience and by love, though love
Alone fulfil the law; thy punishment
He shall endure by coming in the flesh
To a reproachful life and cursèd death,
Proclaiming life to all who shall believe
In his redemption, and that his obedience
Imputed becomes theirs by faith, his merits
To save them, not their own, though legal works.   410
For this he shall live hated, be blasphemed,
Seized on by force, judged, and to death condemned
A shameful and accursed, nailed to the cross
By his own nation, slain for bringing life;
But to the cross he nails thy enemies,
The law that is against thee, and the sins
Of all mankind, with him there crucified,
Never to hurt them more who rightly trust
In this his satisfaction; so he dies,
But soon revives, Death over him no power   420
Shall long usurp; ere the third dawning light
Return, the stars of morn shall see him rise
Out of his grave, fresh as the dawning light,
Thy ransom paid, which Man from Death redeems,
His death for Man, as many as offered life
Neglect not, and the benefit embrace
By faith not void of works. This godlike act
Annuls thy doom, the death thou shouldst have died,
In sin for ever lost from life; this act
Shall bruise the head of Satan, crush his strength   430
Defeating Sin and Death, his two main arms,
And fix far deeper in his head their stings
Than temporal death shall bruise the Victor's heel,
Or theirs whom he redeems, a death like sleep,
A gentle wafting to immortal life.
Nor after resurrection shall he stay

Longer on Earth than certain times to appear
To his disciples, men who in his life
Still followed him; to them shall leave in charge
To teach all nations what of him they learned   440
And his salvation, them who shall believe
Baptizing in the profluent stream, the sign
Of washing them from guilt of sin to life
Pure, and in mind prepared, if so befall,
For death, like that which the Redeemer died.
All nations they shall teach; for from that day
Not only to the sons of Abraham's loins
Salvation shall be preached, but to the sons
Of Abraham's faith wherever through the world;
So in his seed all nations shall be blest.   450
Then to the Heaven of Heavens he shall ascend
With victory, triumphing through the air
Over his foes and thine; there shall surprise
The Serpent, Prince of air, and drag in chains
Through all his realm, and there confounded leave;
Then enter into glory, and resume
His seat at God's right hand, exalted high
Above all names in Heaven; and thence shall come,
When this world's dissolution shall be ripe,
With glory and power to judge both quick and dead,   460
To judge the unfaithful dead, but to reward
His faithful, and receive them into bliss,
Whether in Heaven or Earth, for then the Earth
Shall all be Paradise, far happier place
Than this of Eden, and far happier days."
    So spake the Archangel Michael, then paused,
As at the world's great period; and our Sire
Replete with joy and wonder thus replied.
    "O goodness infinite, goodness immense!
That all this good of evil shall produce,   470
And evil turn to good; more wonderful
Than that which by creation first brought forth
Light out of darkness! full of doubt I stand,
Whether I should repent me now of sin
By me done and occasioned, or rejoice
Much more, that much more good thereof shall spring,
To God more glory, more good will to men
From God, and over wrath grace shall abound.
But say, if our Deliverer up to Heaven

    473 ff. The paradox which makes the Fall of Man at once the greatest
of human calamities and the occasion of man's highest experience of good is
a commonplace of Christian thinking.

Must reascend, what will betide the few
His faithful, left among the unfaithful herd,
The enemies of truth; who then shall guide
His people, who defend? will they not deal
Worse with his followers than with him they dealt?"
"Be sure they will," said the Angel; "but from Heaven
He to his own a Comforter will send,
The promise of the Father, who shall dwell
His Spirit within them, and the law of faith
Working through love, upon their hearts shall write,
To guide them in all truth, and also arm   490
With spiritual armor, able to resist
Satan's assaults, and quench his fiery darts,
What man can do against them, not afraid,
Though to the death, against such cruelties
With inward consolations recompensed,
And oft supported so as shall amaze
Their proudest persecutors. For the Spirit
Poured first on his Apostles, whom he sends
To evangelize the nations, then on all
Baptized, shall them with wondrous gifts endue   500
To speak all tongues, and do all miracles,
As did their Lord before them. Thus they win
Great numbers of each nation to receive
With joy the tidings brought from Heaven: at length
Their ministry performed, and race well run,
Their doctrine and their story written left,
They die; but in their room, as they forewarn,
Wolves shall succeed for teachers, grievous wolves,
Who all the sacred mysteries of Heaven
To their own vile advantages shall turn   510
Of lucre and ambition, and the truth
With superstitions and traditions taint,
Left only in those written records pure,
Though not but by the Spirit understood.
Then shall they seek to avail themselves of names,
Places and titles, and with these to join

508 ff. Wolves shall succeed for teachers. In this review of the per-
version of the Church Milton touches on every essential point in the attack
of Protestant against Catholic, of Puritan against Anglican. The clergy have
substituted "man-made tradition" for the "plain truth of Scripture"; they
have sought rank and title instead of imitating the simplicity of the early
church; they have invoked secular power for the suppression of dissent; they
have taught that authority and not inner conviction should rule the individual in matters of belief, and that salvation may be obtained by ritualistic
observance rather than by repentance. Milton had been saying these things
more or less all his life.

Secular power, though feigning still to act
By spiritual, to themselves appropriating
The Spirit of God, promised alike and given
To all believers; and from that pretence,   520
Spiritual laws by carnal power shall force
On every conscience; laws which none shall find
Left them enrolled, or what the Spirit within
Shall on the heart engrave. What will they then
But force the Spirit of Grace itself, and bind
His consort Liberty; what but unbuild
His living temples, built by faith to stand,
Their own faith, not another's: for on earth
Who against faith and conscience can be heard
Infallible? yet many will presume: 530
Whence heavy persecution shall arise
On all who in the worship persevere
Of Spirit and Truth; the rest, far greater part,
Will deem in outward rites and specious forms
Religion satisfied; Truth shall retire
Bestuck with slanderous darts, and works of faith
Rarely be found. So shall the world go on,
To good malignant, to bad men benign,
Under her own weight groaning till the day
Appear of respiration to the just,   540
And vengeance to the wicked, at return
Of Him so lately promised to thy aid,
The Woman's Seed, obscurely then foretold,
Now amplier known thy Savior and thy Lord,
Last in the clouds from Heaven to be revealed
In glory of the Father, to dissolve
Satan with his perverted world, then raise
From the conflagrant mass, purged and refined
New Heavens, new Earth, ages of endless date
Founded in righteousness and peace and love,   550
To bring forth fruits joy and eternal bliss."
    He ended; and thus Adam last replied.
"How soon hath thy prediction, Seer blest,
Measured this transient world, the race of time,
Till time stand fixed: beyond is all abyss,
Eternity, whose end no eye can reach.
Greatly instructed I shall hence depart,
Greatly in peace of thought, and have my fill
Of knowledge, what this vessel can contain;
Beyond which was my folly to aspire.   560

    540. respiration, "when the times of refreshing shall come from the
presence of the Lord." Acts 3:19. Milton retranslates the Greek word.

Henceforth I learn, that to obey is best,
And love with fear the only God, to walk
As in his presence, ever to observe
His providence, and on him sole depend,
Merciful over all his works, with good
Still overcoming evil, and by small
Accomplishing great things, by things deemed weak
Subverting worldly strong, and worldly wise
By simply meek; that suffering for truth's sake
Is fortitude to highest victory,   570
And to the faithful death the gate of life;
Taught this by his example whom I now
Acknowledge my Redeemer ever blest."
    To whom thus also the Angel last replied.
"This having learned, thou hast attained the sum
Of wisdom; hope no higher, though all the stars
Thou knew'st by name, and all the ethereal powers,
All secrets of the deep, all Nature's works,
Or works of God in heaven, air, earth, or sea,
And all the riches of this world enjoy'dst,   580
And all the rule, one empire; only add
Deeds to thy knowledge answerable, add faith,
Add virtue, patience, temperance, add love,
By name to come called charity, the soul
Of all the rest: then wilt thou not be loth
To leave this Paradise, but shalt possess
A Paradise within thee, happier far.
Let us descend now therefore from this top
Of speculation; for the hour precise
Exacts our parting hence; and see the guards,   590
By me encamped on yonder hill, expect
Their motion, at whose front a flaming sword,
In signal of remove, waves fiercely round;
We may no longer stay: go, waken Eve;
Her also I with gentle dreams have calmed
Portending good, and all her spirits composed
To meek submission: thou at season fit
Let her with thee partake what thou hast heard,
Chiefly what may concern her faith to know,
The great deliverance by her seed to come   600
(For by the Woman's Seed) on all mankind.
That ye may live, which will be many days,
Both in one faith unanimous though sad,
With cause for evils past, yet much more cheered
With meditation on the happy end."

    591–92. expect their motion, await the moment of moving.

He ended, and they both descend the hill;
Descended, Adam to the bower where Eve
Lay sleeping ran before, but found her waked;
And thus with words not sad she him received.
   "Whence thou return'st, and whither went'st, I know;   610
For God is also in sleep, and dreams advise,
Which he hath sent propitious, some great good
Presaging, since with sorrow and heart's distress
Wearied I fell asleep. But now lead on;
In me is no delay; with thee to go,
Is to stay here; without thee here to stay,
Is to go hence unwilling; thou to me
Art all things under Heaven, all places thou,
Who for my wilful crime art banished hence.
This further consolation yet secure   620
I carry hence; though all by me is lost,
Such favor I unworthy am vouchsafed,
By me the Promised Seed shall all restore."
   So spake our mother Eve, and Adam heard
Well pleased, but answered not; for now too nigh
The Archangel stood, and from the other hill
To their fixed station, all in bright array
The Cherubim descended; on the ground
Gliding meteorous, as evening mist
Risen from a river o'er the marish glides,   630
And gathers ground fast at the laborer's heel
Homeward returning. High in front advanced,
The brandished sword of God before them blazed
Fierce as a comet; which with torrid heat,
And vapor as the Libyan air adust,
Began to parch that temperate clime; whereat
In either hand the hastening angel caught
Our lingering parents, and to the eastern gate
Led them direct, and down the cliff as fast
To the subjected plain; then disappeared.   640
They looking back, all the eastern side beheld
Of Paradise, so late their happy seat,
Waved over by that flaming brand, the gate
With dreadful faces thronged and fiery arms.
Some natural tears they dropped, but wiped them soon;
The world was all before them, where to choose
Their place of rest, and Providence their guide.
They hand in hand with wandering steps and slow,
Through Eden took their solitary way.

   614 ff. Eve's words suggest those of Ruth, "Whither thou goest I will
go," but also Andromache's to Hector in the *Iliad*.

PARADISE REGAINED

A Poem
in Four Books

INTRODUCTION TO
PARADISE REGAINED

Milton's second epic was, according to Edward Phillips, "begun, finished and printed after the publication of its predecessor." This would put the period of its composition between 1667 and 1671. Thomas Ellwood, the Quaker, visited the poet at Chalfont St. Giles and, if his own report is to be trusted, suggested the subject: "Thou hast said much of *Paradise Lost*, but what hast thou to say of Paradise found?" The theme is, to be sure, in a sense included in *Paradise Lost* itself, where Michael predicts the sacrifice of Christ and points out to Adam the way of man's salvation by works and faith. But Ellwood's naïve remark showed Milton that one reader, at least, did not feel the story of God's ways with man to be complete, and justified the writing of a companion poem in which Christ should be represented dramatically in the rôle of a new Adam.

In selecting the temptation rather than the crucifixion of Christ as his subject Milton was consulting his own deepest interest and convictions. The ethical struggle is central in his thought. Christ meets the moral issues of life, not in the simple form that tempted Eve, but as a developed civilization presents them to the most sophisticated of men. Milton gives himself in this epic the opportunity, lacking in the other, to elaborate and analyze both the lure of evil and the reasoned program by which the highest wisdom will reject its baits.

The three temptations are taken up in the order given in Luke: "Command this stone that it be made bread"; "All this power will I give thee and the glory of them"; "If thou be the Son of God cast thyself down." Milton has interpreted the first victory as a simple act of obedience and faith. Christ rejects the proposal without argument because he recognizes its source. His decision contains the whole triumph over evil and is the exact counterpart of Eve's act when Satan offers her

491

the apple. What follows is for the instruction of mankind and the further humiliation of his enemy.

The second temptation is treated at great length. Milton interprets the phrase "the kingdoms of the world and the glory of them," in a series of graded enticements, presented with eloquence by Satan, examined and rejected by Christ with Socratic insight. Foiled in his first trial of strength, the Tempter has realized the difficulty of his task. He accordingly summons an Infernal Council, but rejects Belial's suggestion, "Set women in his eye," as inappropriate, and proposes to try Christ's constancy "with manlier objects." The incident is made the occasion of a diatribe of Satan's against the weakness of those who fall a prey to women and a repetition of Raphael's teaching in *Paradise Lost* that

> Beauty stands
> In the admiration only of weak minds
> Led captive.

It is not difficult to see why Milton, who aspired to such assured self-control but knew his weakness, should have ruled out female charm from among the objects which might plausibly have been supposed to have tempted the Saviour of mankind.

The first glory of the kingdoms of the earth is set before Christ in the form of a luxurious banquet, designed, not only to satisfy his hunger, but to do so exquisitely and with all the stimulation to sensual enjoyment that the arts of civilization can provide. Satan advances the old arguments of Comus in favor of self-indulgence:

> These are not fruits forbidden; no interdict
> Defends the touching of these viands pure.
> Their taste no knowledge works, at least of evil,
> But life preserves, destroys life's enemy.

Christ rejects the offer as a wile of Satan without the usual debate. His ability to endure hunger is supernatural; his invincibility needs therefore no reasons to support it. With the following offer the case is different. Christ has set his heart on high designs. Wealth, glory, military power, majesty, knowledge are proposed as instruments for achieving them. Christ's insight teaches him that the spiritual kingdom is not to be won by material means; in rejecting them as useless to his own purposes he exposes their hollowness as ends in themselves. Riches are "the toil of fools, the wise man's cumbrance, if not snare"; glory is but the praise of a miscellaneous rabble who extol "things vulgar and, well weighed, scarce worth the praise"; power of arms is "argument of weakness not of strength"; grandeur, symbolized by imperial Rome, is false and transitory; human wisdom, embodied in the literature and philosophy of Greece, fails to provide the key of truth. Into this long dialogue Milton has put the fruits of a life-time of meditation on values human and divine. The speeches are packed with thought and knowledge. If the color and emotion of *Paradise Lost* are lacking, mature and sobered wisdom, "distilled into an essence", have come to take their place. *Paradise Regained* is didactic poetry at its best and highest.

The last temptation is spectacular and dramatic. Christ's faith has already been tried, his wisdom proved. It remains only that God should put the seal on his spiritual triumph. Satan, confessing defeat, resorts to violence, as Comus had done when the Lady had resisted all his wiles. He carries Christ to the pinnacle of the temple, where it requires a miracle for him to stand upright. The miracle is performed; Christ stands, and Satan, smitten with amazement,

> Fell where he thought to see his victor fall.

Angels bear Christ to a valley and minister to him.

This third temptation, as treated by Milton, is parallel to the first in suddenness and significance. Placed before and after the main body of the poem, the two balance each other and give symmetry to the whole. In general *Paradise Regained* is a work of the most consummate art. Transitions are skilfully handled. There is steady progress toward a climax. The expository material, though predominant, is skilfully broken by narrative and description. The characterization, though in no sense so striking as in *Paradise Lost*, is appropriate, and not without human insight. Both Satan and Christ appear in very different rôles from those which they assumed in the earlier poem. Satan has lost his dynamic energy. He does not expect to win. He proceeds with no knowledge of his adversary's nature. His self-pity, once affecting, has become hypocrisy, and nothing he says or does commands the reader's admiration. Christ is serene and god-like. Milton elaborates the perspective of his early career, the concern of Mary, the devotion of the apostles; and there is something touching in the portraiture. But the human element is largely lost sight of in the idea. Christ represents the life of reason as Milton himself would have liked to live it. His victory is the victory of truth. He has no moment of indecision, his arguments have the finality and completeness of one who has arrived at an absolute understanding of the world and of the part which he himself has been assigned to play in it.

In elaborating the biblical materials of *Paradise Regained* Milton is dependent on no specific earlier treatment of the subject. His conception of the central figure is, however, as Professor Hughes has shown, deeply influenced by the cultural tradition of the Renaissance, in which Christ was a heroic, more than an ascetic, figure. It is in this spirit that Milton likens him to Hercules. The heroes of ancient epic, particularly Aeneas, were interpreted as patterns of human excellence. Christ is a divine fulfilment of their strength and righteousness. Spenser's Sir Guyon in the second book of *The Faerie Queene* is another kind of parallel to Milton's Christ. Giles Fletcher's poem, *Christ's Victory and Triumph*, furnishes a few hints for both Christ and Satan.

The form of Milton's poem owes something to the Book of Job, which he mentions as a type of the "short epic" in a passage in *The Reason of Church Government*. Both are mainly dialogue, with long philosophical speeches on opposing points of view. In both there is a narrative introduction and conclusion and brief linking passages throughout the debate. Both poems, finally, deal with a trial of faith. In the detail Milton has drawn on the whole stock of his reading in literature, history, and philosophy. Many of the ideas are recorded in the quotations set down by him in his Commonplace Book. There is a remarkable historical grasp displayed in the accounts of the Parthian and Roman empires; the passages on Greek and Hebrew literature show a scholar's and a poet's knowledge of the subjects.

The style of *Paradise Regained* is much more even and much less highly colored than that of *Paradise Lost*. The one passage in which Milton gives full rein to his sensuous imagination is the description of the banquet. There is, however, great vividness and imaginative beauty in the picture of imperial Rome and elsewhere. But the chief merit of Milton's expression is to be sought in its precision, its condensation, its uniform dignity. There is a classic fitness in the phrasing

which commands an admiration. Milton evidently composed
the poem in a mood of calm serenity. That his old passions
were still smoldering is apparent from their later outburst in
Samson Agonistes but for the moment the poet is as he wished
to be, the spokesman of that unimpassioned truth "which came
once into the world with her divine Master and was a perfect
shape, most glorious to look on."

PARADISE REGAINED

BOOK I

I who erewhile the happy garden sung,
By one man's disobedience lost, now sing
Recovered Paradise to all mankind,
By one man's firm obedience fully tried
Through all temptation, and the Tempter foiled
In all his wiles, defeated and repulsed,
And Eden raised in the waste wilderness.
   Thou Spirit who led'st this glorious Eremite
Into the desert, his victorious field
Against the spiritual foe, and brought'st him thence   10
By proof the undoubted Son of God, inspire,
As thou art wont, my prompted song else mute,
And bear through height or depth of Nature's bounds
With prosperous wing full summed to tell of deeds
Above heroic, though in secret done,
And unrecorded left through many an age,
Worthy to have not remained so long unsung.
   Now had the great Proclaimer with a voice
More awful than the sound of trumpet, cried
Repentance, and Heaven's kingdom nigh at hand   20
To all baptized. To his great baptism flocked
With awe the regions round, and with them came
From Nazareth the son of Joseph deemed
To the flood Jordan, came as then obscure,
Unmarked, unknown; but him the Baptist soon
Descried, divinely warned, and witness bore
As to his worthier, and would have resigned

   8 ff. In *Paradise Lost* Milton invoked, first, the Heavenly Muse, then
the divine spirit which was the source of Mosaic inspiration; here there is
no such suggestion of the Pagan-Christian analogy.
   14 ff. full summed, having feathers fully developed; a term from fal-
conry.
   18 ff. The action of the poem is based on Luke 4:1-13, with some use
of the parallel account in Matt. 4:1-11.

To him his heavenly office, nor was long
His witness unconfirmed: on him baptized
Heaven opened, and in likeness of a dove   30
The Spirit descended, while the Father's voice
From Heaven pronounced him his beloved Son.
That heard the Adversary, who roving still
About the world, at that assembly famed
Would not be last, and with the voice divine
Nigh thunder-struck, the exalted man to whom
Such high attest was given, a while surveyed
With wonder, then with envy fraught and rage
Flies to his place, nor rests, but in mid air
To council summons all his mighty peers,   40
Within thick clouds and dark tenfold involved,
A gloomy consistory; and then amidst,
With looks aghast and sad, he thus bespake.
     "O ancient Powers of Air and this wide World
For much more willingly I mention Air,
This our old conquest, than remember Hell
Our hated habitation, well ye know
How many ages, as the years of men,
This Universe we have possessed and ruled
In manner at our will the affairs of Earth,   50
Since Adam and his facile consort Eve
Lost Paradise, deceived by me, though since
With dread attending when that fatal wound
Shall be inflicted by the seed of Eve
Upon my head; long the decrees of Heaven
Delay, for longest time to him is short;
And now too soon for us the circling hours
This dreaded time have compassed, wherein we
Must bide the stroke of that long-threatened wound,
At least if so we can, and by the head   60
Broken be not intended all our power
To be infringed, our freedom and our being
In this fair empire won of Earth and Air
For this ill news I bring, the Woman's Seed
Destined to this, is late of woman born.
His birth to our just fear gave no small cause,
But his growth now to youth's full flower, displaying
All virtue, grace and wisdom to achieve
Things highest, greatest, multiplies my fear.
Before him a great Prophet, to proclaim   70
His coming, is sent harbinger, who all
Invites, and in the consecrated stream
     34. that assembly, i.e., the baptism.

Pretends to wash off sin, and fit them so
Purified to receive him pure, or rather
To do him honor as their King. All come,
And he himself among them was baptized,
Not thence to be more pure, but to receive
The testimony of Heaven, that who he is
Thenceforth the nations may not doubt; I saw
The Prophet do him reverence, on him rising   80
Out of the water, Heaven above the clouds
Unfold her crystal doors, thence on his head
A perfect dove descend, whate'er it meant,
And out of Heaven the sovran voice I heard,
'This is my Son beloved, in him am pleased.'
His mother then is mortal, but his Sire,
He who obtains the monarchy of Heaven,
And what will he not do to advance his Son?
His first-begot we know, and sore have felt
When his fierce thunder drove us to the Deep;   90
Who this is we must learn, for Man he seems
In all his lineaments, though in his face
The glimpses of his Father's glory shine.
Ye see our danger on the utmost edge
Of hazard, which admits no long debate,
But must with something sudden be opposed,
Not force, but well-couched fraud, well-woven snares,
Ere in the head of nations he appear
Their king, their leader, and supreme on Earth.
I, when no other durst, sole undertook   100
The dismal expedition to find out
And ruin Adam, and the exploit performed
Successfully; a calmer voyage now
Will waft me; and the way found prosperous once
Induces best to hope of like success."
    He ended, and his words impression left
Of much amazement to the infernal crew,
Distracted and surprised with deep dismay
At these sad tidings; but no time was then
For long indulgence to their fears or grief: 110
Unanimous they all commit the care
And management of this main enterprise
To him their great Dictator, whose attempt
At first against mankind so well had thrived
In Adam's overthrow, and led their march
From Hell's deep-vaulted den to dwell in light,
Regents, and potentates, and kings, yea gods

89. Satan does not know that Jesus and the "first-begot" are the same.

Of many a pleasant realm and province wide.
So to the coast of Jordan he directs
His easy steps, girded with snaky wiles,   120
Where he might likeliest find this new-declared,
This man of men, attested Son of God,
Temptation and all guile on him to try,
So to subvert whom he suspected raised
To end his reign on Earth so long enjoyed.
But contrary unweeting he fulfilled
The purposed counsel pre-ordained and fixed
Of the Most High, who in full frequence bright
Of Angels, thus to Gabriel smiling spake.
    "Gabriel, this day by proof thou shalt behold,   130
Thou and all angels conversant on Earth
With man or men's affairs, how I begin
To verify that solemn message late,
On which I sent thee to the Virgin pure
In Galilee, that she should bear a son
Great in renown, and called the Son of God.
Then told'st her doubting how these things could be
To her a virgin, that on her should come
The Holy Ghost, and the Power of the Highest
O'ershadow her. This man, born and now upgrown,   140
To show him worthy of his birth divine
And high prediction, henceforth I expose
To Satan; let him tempt and now assay
His utmost subtlety, because he boasts
And vaunts of his great cunning to the throng
Of his apostasy. He might have learnt
Less overweening, since he failed in Job,
Whose constant perseverance overcame
Whate'er his cruel malice could invent.
He now shall know I can produce a man   150
Of female seed far abler to resist
All his solicitations, and at length
All his vast force, and drive him back to Hell,
Winning by conquest what the first man lost
By fallacy surprised. But first I mean
To exercise him in the wilderness;
There he shall first lay down the rudiments
Of his great warfare, ere I send him forth
To conquer Sin and Death the two grand foes,
By humiliation and strong sufferance.   160
His weakness shall o'ercome Satanic strength
And all the world, and mass of sinful flesh;
That all the angels and ethereal Powers,

They now, and men hereafter may discern
From what consummate virtue I have chose
This perfect man, by merit called my Son,
To earn salvation for the sons of men."
  So spake the Eternal Father, and all Heaven
Admiring stood a space, then into hymns
Burst forth, and in celestial measures moved,   170
Circling the throne and singing, while the hand
Sung with the voice, and this the argument.
  "Victory and triumph to the Son of God
Now entering his great duel, not of arms,
But to vanquish by wisdom hellish wiles.
The Father knows the Son; therefore secure
Ventures his filial virtue, though untried,
Against whate'er may tempt, whate'er seduce,
Allure, or terrify, or undermine.
Be frustrate all ye stratagems of Hell,   180
And devilish machinations come to nought."
  So they in Heaven their odes and vigils tuned.
Meanwhile the Son of God, who yet some days
Lodged in Bethabara, where John baptized,
Musing and much revolving in his breast,
How best the mighty work he might begin
Of Savior to mankind, and which way first
Publish his godlike office now mature,
One day forth walked alone, the Spirit leading,
And his deep thoughts, the better to converse   190
With solitude, till far from track of men,
Thought following thought, and step by step led on,
He entered now the bordering desert wild,
And with dark shades and rocks environed round,
His holy meditations thus pursued.
  "O what a multitude of thoughts at once
Awakened in me swarm, while I consider
What from within I feel myself, and hear
What from without comes often to my ears,
Ill sorting with my present state compared.   200
When I was yet a child, no childish play
To me was pleasing, all my mind was set
Serious to learn and know, and thence to do
What might be public good; myself I thought
Born to that end, born to promote all truth,
All righteous things. Therefore above my years,
The Law of God I read, and found it sweet,
Made it my whole delight, and in it grew
To such perfection, that ere yet my age

Had measured twice six years, at our great Feast
I went into the Temple, there to hear
The teachers of our Law, and to propose
What might improve my knowledge or their own,
And was admired by all. Yet this not all
To which my spirit aspired. Victorious deeds
Flamed in my heart, heroic acts; one while
To rescue Israel from the Roman yoke,
Then to subdue and quell o'er all the earth
Brute violence and proud tyrannic power,
Till truth were freed, and equity restored;   220
Yet held it more humane, more heavenly, first
By winning words to conquer willing hearts,
And make persuasion do the work of fear;
At least to try, and teach the erring soul
Not wilfully misdoing, but unaware
Misled; the stubborn only to subdue.
These growing thoughts my mother soon perceiving
By words at times cast forth, only rejoiced,
And said to me apart, 'High are thy thoughts
O Son, but nourish them and let them soar   230
To what height sacred virtue and true worth
Can raise them, though above example high;
By matchless deeds express thy matchless Sire.
For know, thou art no son of mortal man,
Though men esteem thee low of parentage,
Thy Father is the Eternal King, who rules
All Heaven and Earth, angels and sons of men;
A messenger from God foretold thy birth
Conceived in me a virgin, he foretold
Thou should'st be great and sit on David's throne,   240
And of thy kingdom there should be no end.
At thy nativity a glorious choir
Of angels in the fields of Bethlehem sung
To shepherds watching at their folds by night,
And told them the Messiah now was born,
Where they might see him, and to thee they came,
Directed to the manger where thou lay'st,
For in the inn was left no better room.
A star, not seen before in heaven appearing
Guided the wise men thither from the East,   250
To honor thee with incense, myrrh, and gold,
By whose bright course led on they found the place,
Affirming it thy star new-graven in heaven,
By which they knew thee King of Israel born.
Just Simeon and prophetic Anna, warned

By vision, found thee in the Temple, and spake
Before the altar and the vested priest
Like things of thee to all that present stood.'
This having heard, straight I again revolved
The Law and Prophets, searching what was writ   260
Concerning the Messiah, to our scribes
Known partly, and soon found of whom they spake
I am; this chiefly, that my way must lie
Through many a hard assay even to the death,
Ere I the promised kingdom can attain,
Or work redemption for mankind, whose sins
Full weight must be transferred upon my head.
Yet neither thus disheartened or dismayed,
The time prefixed I waited, when behold
The Baptist, (of whose birth I oft had heard,   270
Not knew by sight) now come, who was to come
Before Messiah and his way prepare.
I as all others to his baptism came,
Which I believed was from above; but he
Straight knew me, and with loudest voice proclaimed
Me him (for it was shown him so from Heaven)
Me him whose harbinger he was; and first
Refused on me his baptism to confer,
As much his greater, and was hardly won.
But as I rose out of the laving stream,   280
Heaven opened her eternal doors, from whence
The Spirit descended on me like a dove,
And last, the sum of all, my Father's voice,
Audibly heard from Heaven, pronounced me his,
Me his beloved Son, in whom alone
He was well pleased; by which I knew the time
Now full, that I no more should live obscure,
But openly begin, as best becomes
The authority which I derived from Heaven.
And now by some strong motion I am led   290
Into this wilderness, to what intent
I learn not yet, perhaps I need not know;
For what concerns my knowledge God reveals."
    So spake our Morning Star then in his rise,
And looking round on every side beheld
A pathless desert, dusk with horrid shades.
The way he came not having marked, return
Was difficult, by human steps untrod;
And he still on was led, but with such thoughts
Accompanied of things past and to come   300
Lodged in his breast, as well might recommend

Such solitude before choicest society.
　　Full forty days he passed, whether on hill
Sometimes, anon in shady vale, each night
Under the covert of some ancient oak
Or cedar to defend him from the dew,
Or harbored in one cave, is not revealed;
Nor tasted human food, nor hunger felt
Till those days ended, hungered then at last
Among wild beasts; they at his sight grew mild,   310
Nor sleeping him nor waking harmed; his walk
The fiery serpent fled and noxious worm;
The lion and fierce tiger glared aloof.
But now on aged man in rural weeds,
Following, as seemed, the quest of some stray ewe,
Or withered sticks to gather, which might serve
Against a winter's day when winds blow keen
To warm him wet returned from field at eve,
He saw approach, who first with curious eye
Perused him, then with words thus uttered spake.   320
　　"Sir, what ill chance hath brought thee to this place
So far from path or road of men, who pass
In troop or caravan? for single none
Durst ever, who returned, and drop not here
His carcass, pined with hunger and with drouth.
I ask thee rather, and the more admire,
For that to me thou seemest the man whom late
Our new baptizing Prophet at the ford
Of Jordan honored so, and called thee Son
Of God. I saw and heard, for we sometimes   330
Who dwell this wild, constrained by want, come forth
To town or village nigh (nighest is far)
Where aught we hear, and curious are to hear,
What happens new; fame also find us out."
　　To whom the Son of God. "Who brought me hither
Will bring me hence; no other guide I seek."
　　"By miracle he may," replied the swain,
"What other way I see not; for we here
Live on tough roots and stubs, to thirst inured
More than the camel, and to drink go far,   340
Men to much misery and hardship born.
But if thou be the Son of God, command
That out of these hard stones be made thee bread;

　　343. Milton treats the first and third temptations very briefly and greatly
elaborates the second. It is not here the stress of hunger that Satan is rely-
ing on so much as the danger of the situation Christ is in. The next attack
begins with an appeal to appetite. See II, 229 ff.

So shalt thou save thyself and us relieve
With food, whereof we wretched seldom taste."
   He ended, and the Son of God replied.
"Thinkest thou such force in bread? Is it not written
(For I discern thee other than thou seemest)
Man lives not by bread only, but each word
Proceeding from the mouth of God, who fed   350
Our fathers here with manna; in the Mount
Moses was forty days, nor eat nor drank,
And forty days Elijah without food
Wandered this barren waste; the same I now.
Why dost thou then suggest to me distrust,
Knowing who I am, as I know who thou art?"
   Whom thus answered the Arch-Fiend now undisguised.
" 'Tis true, I am that spirit unfortunate,
Who leagued with millions more in rash revolt
Kept not my happy station, but was driven   360
With them from bliss to the bottomless Deep,
Yet to that hideous place not so confined
By rigor unconniving but that oft
Leaving my dolorous prison I enjoy
Large liberty to round this globe of Earth,
Or range in the air, nor from the Heaven of Heavens
Hath he excluded my resort sometimes.
I came among the Sons of God when he
Gave up into my hands Uzzean Job
To prove him, and illustrate his high worth;   370
And when to all his angels he proposed
To draw the proud king Ahab into fraud
That he might fall in Ramoth, they demurring,
I undertook that office, and the tongues
Of all his flattering prophets glibbed with lies
To his destruction, as I had in charge.
For what he bids I do; though I have lost
Much luster of my native brightness, lost
To be beloved of God, I have not lost
To love, at least contemplate and admire   380
What I see excellent in good, or fair,
Or virtuous; I should so have lost all sense.
What can be then less in me than desire
To see thee and approach thee, whom I know
Declared the Son of God, to hear attent
Thy wisdom, and behold thy godlike deeds?
Men generally think me much a foe

   363. unconniving, not shutting the eyes, never relaxing.
   371 ff. See I Kings 22:19-23.

To all mankind. Why should I? they to me
Never did wrong or violence. By them
I lost not what I lost; rather by them   390
I gained what I have gained, and with them dwell
Copartner in these regions of the world,
If not disposer; lend them oft my aid,
Oft my advice by presages and signs,
And answers, oracles, portents and dreams,
Whereby they may direct their future life.
Envy they say excites me, thus to gain
Companions of my misery and woe.
At first it may be; but long since with woe
Nearer acquainted, now I feel by proof   400
That fellowship in pain divides not smart,
Nor lightens aught each man's peculiar load;
Small consolation then were Man adjoined.
This wounds me most (what can it less?) that Man,
Man fallen, shall be restored, I never more."
    To whom our Savior sternly thus replied.
"Deservedly thou griev'st, composed of lies
From the beginning, and in lies wilt end,
Who boast'st release from Hell, and leave to come
Into the Heaven of Heavens. Thou com'st indeed,   410
As a poor miserable captive thrall
Comes to the place where he before had sat
Among the prime in splendor, now deposed,
Ejected, emptied, gazed, unpitied, shunned,
A spectacle of ruin or of scorn
To all the host of Heaven; the happy place
Imparts to thee no happiness, no joy,
Rather inflames thy torment, representing
Lost bliss, to thee no more communicable;
So never more in Hell than when in Heaven.   420
But thou art serviceable to Heaven's King.
Wilt thou impute to obedience what thy fear
Extorts, or pleasure to do ill excites?
What but thy malice moved thee to misdeem
Of righteous Job, then cruelly to afflict him
With all afflictions? but his patience won.
The other service was thy chosen task,
To be a liar in four hundred mouths;
For lying is thy sustenance, thy food.
Yet thou pretend'st to truth; all oracles   430
By thee are given, and what confessed more true
Among the nations? That hath been thy craft,
By mixing somewhat true to vent more lies.

But what have been thy answers? what but dark,
Ambiguous, and with double sense deluding,
Which they who asked have seldom understood,
And not well understood, as good not known?
Who ever by consulting at thy shrine
Returned the wiser, or the more instruct
To fly or follow what concerned him most,   440
And run not sooner to his fatal snare?
For God hath justly given the nations up
To thy delusions; justly, since they fell
Idolatrous, but when his purpose is
Among them to declare his providence,
To thee not known, whence hast thou then thy truth
But from him or his angels president
In every province, who themselves disdaining
To approach thy temples, give thee in command
What to the smallest tittle thou shalt say   450
To thy adorers? Thou with trembling fear,
Or like a fawning parasite obey'st;
Then to thyself ascrib'st the truth foretold.
But this thy glory shall be soon retrenched;
No more shalt thou by oracling abuse
The Gentiles; henceforth oracles are ceased,
And thou no more with pomp and sacrifice
Shall be inquired at Delphos or elsewhere,
At least in vain, for they shall find thee mute.
God hath now sent his living Oracle   460
Into the world to teach his final will,
And sends his Spirit of truth henceforth to dwell
In pious hearts, an inward oracle
To all truth requisite for men to know."
    So spake our Savior; but the subtle Fiend,
Though inly stung with anger and disdain,
Dissembled, and this answer smooth returned.
    "Sharply thou hast insisted on rebuke,
And urged me hard with doings, which not will
But misery hath wrested from me; where   470
Easily canst thou find one miserable,
And not enforced oft-times to part from truth,
If it may stand him more in stead to lie,
Say and unsay, feign, flatter, or abjure?
But thou art placed above me, thou art Lord;
From thee I can and must submiss endure
Check or reproof, and glad to scape so quit.
Hard are the ways of truth, and rough to walk,
Smooth on the tongue discoursed, pleasing to the ear,

And tunable as sylvan pipe or song;   480
What wonder then if I delight to hear
Her dictates from thy mouth? most men admire
Virtue who follow not her lore. Permit me
To hear thee when I come (since no man comes),
And talk at least, though I despair to attain.
Thy Father, who is holy, wise and pure,
Suffers the hypocrite or atheous priest
To tread his sacred courts, and minister
About his altar, handling holy things,
Praying or vowing, and vouchsafed his voice   490
To Balaam reprobate, a prophet yet
Inspired; disdain not such access to me."
     To whom our Savior, with unaltered brow.
"Thy coming hither, though I know thy scope,
I bid not or forbid; do as thou find'st
Permission from above; thou canst not more."
     He added not; and Satan bowing low
His gray dissimulation, disappeared
Into thin air diffused: for now began
Night with her sullen wing to double-shade   500
The desert, fowls in their clay nests were couched;
And now wild beasts came forth the woods to roam.

BOOK II

Meanwhile the new-baptized, who yet remained
At Jordan with the Baptist, and had seen
Him whom they heard so late expressly called
Jesus Messiah, Son of God declared,
And on that high authority had believed,
And with him talked, and with him lodged, I mean
Andrew and Simon, famous after known
With others though in Holy Writ not named,
Now missing him their joy so lately found,
So lately found, and so abruptly gone,   10
Began to doubt, and doubted many days,
And as the days increased, increased their doubt.
Sometimes they thought he might be only shown,
And for a time caught up to God, as once
Moses was in the Mount and missing long,
And the great Thisbite who on fiery wheels
Rode up to Heaven, yet once again to come.
Therefore as those young prophets then with care
Sought lost Elijah, so in each place these
     16 ff. See II Kings 2:16–17.

Nigh to Bethabara; in Jericho 20
The city of palms, Ænon, and Salem old,
Machærus, and each town or city walled
On this side the broad lake Genezaret,
Or in Peræa, but returned in vain.
Then on the bank of Jordan, by a creek
Where winds with reeds, and osiers whispering play,
Plain fishermen, no greater men them call,
Close in a cottage low together got,
Their unexpected loss and plaints outbreathed.
"Alas, from what high hope to what relapse 30
Unlooked-for are we fallen! Our eyes beheld
Messiah certainly now come, so long
Expected of our fathers; we have heard
His words, his wisdom full of grace and truth;
Now, now, for sure, deliverance is at hand,
The kingdom shall to Israel be restored:
Thus we rejoiced, but soon our joy is turned
Into perplexity and new amaze;
For whither is he gone? what accident
Hath rapt him from us? will he now retire 40
After appearance and again prolong
Our expectation? God of Israel,
Send thy Messiah forth, the time is come;
Behold the kings of the earth, how they oppress
Thy Chosen, to what height their power unjust
They have exalted, and behind them cast
All fear of thee; arise and vindicate
Thy glory, free thy people from their yoke!
But let us wait; thus far he hath performed,
Sent his Anointed, and to us revealed him, 50
By his great Prophet, pointed at and shown,
In public, and with him we have conversed.
Let us be glad of this, and all our fears
Lay on his providence; he will not fail
Nor will withdraw him now, nor will recall,
Mock us with his blest sight, then snatch him hence;
Soon we shall see our hope, our joy return."
Thus they out of their plaints new hope resume
To find whom at the first they found unsought.
But to his mother Mary, when she saw 60
Others returned from baptism, not her Son,
Nor left at Jordan, tidings of him none,
Within her breast, though calm, her breast though pure,
Motherly cares and fears got head, and raised
Some troubled thoughts, which she in sighs thus clad.

"Oh what avails me now that honor high
To have conceived of God, or that salute,
'Hail highly favored, among women blest!'
While I to sorrows am no less advanced,
And fears as eminent, above the lot   70
Of other women, by the birth I bore,
In such a season born when scare a shed
Could be obtained to shelter him or me
From the bleak air? A stable was our warmth,
A manger his, yet soon enforced to fly
Thence into Egypt, till the murderous king
Were dead, who sought his life, and missing filled
With infant blood the streets of Bethlehem;
From Egypt home returned, in Nazareth
Hath been our dwelling many years, his life   80
Private, unactive, calm, contemplative,
Little suspicious to any king. But now
Full grown to man, acknowledged, as I hear,
By John the Baptist, and in public shown,
Son owned from Heaven by his Father's voice,
I looked for some great change. To honor? no;
But trouble, as old Simeon plain foretold,
That to the fall and rising he should be
Of many in Israel, and to a sign
Spoken against, that through my very soul   90
A sword shall pierce. This is my favored lot,
My exaltation to afflictions high;
Afflicted I may be, it seems, and blest;
I will not argue that, nor will repine.
But where delays he now? Some great intent
Conceals him. When twelve years he scarce had seen,
I lost him, but so found, as well I saw
He could not lose himself, but went about
His Father's business; what he meant I mused,
Since understand; much more his absence now   100
Thus long to some great purpose he obscures.
But I to wait with patience am inured;
My heart hath been a storehouse long of things
And sayings laid up, portending strange events."
    Thus Mary pondering oft, and oft to mind
Recalling what remarkably had passed
Since first her salutation heard, with thoughts
Meekly composed awaited the fulfilling;
The while her Son tracing the desert wild,
Sole but with holiest meditations fed,   110

87. See Luke 2:34-35.

Into himself descended, and at once
All his great work to come before him set;
How to begin, how to accomplish best
His end of being on Earth, and mission high.
For Satan with sly preface to return
Had left him vacant, and with speed was gone
Up to the middle region of thick air,
Where all his Potentates in council sat;
There without sign of boast, or sign of joy,
Solicitous and blank he thus began.   120
    "Princes, Heaven's ancient Sons, Ethereal Thrones,
Demonian Spirits now, from the element
Each of his reign allotted, rightlier called,
Powers of Fire, Air, Water, and Earth beneath,
So may we hold our place and these mild seats
Without new trouble, such an enemy
Is risen to invade us, who no less
Threatens than our expulsion down to Hell.
I, as I undertook, and with the vote
Consenting in full frequence was empowered,   130
Have found him, viewed him, tasted him, but find
Far other labor to be undergone
Than when I dealt with Adam first of men,
Though Adam by his wife's allurement fell,
However to this Man inferior far,
If he be Man by mother's side at least,
With more than human gifts from Heaven adorned,
Perfections absolute, graces divine,
And amplitude of mind to greatest deeds.
Therefore I am returned, lest confidence   140
Of my success with Eve in Paradise
Deceive ye to persuasion over-sure
Of like succeeding here; I summon all
Rather to be in readiness with hand
Or counsel to assist, lest I who erst
Thought none my equal, now be overmatched."
    So spake the old Serpent doubting, and from all
With clamor was assured their utmost aid
At his command; when from amidst them rose
Belial, the dissolutest spirit that fell,   150
The sensualest, and after Asmodai
The fleshliest Incubus, and thus advised.
    "Set women in his eye and in his walk,

121 ff. The tortured grammar of this sentence, rare in *Paradise Regained*, may be compared with that of Satan's speech in *Paradise Lost*, I,
84 ff.

Among daughters of men the fairest found;
Many are in each region passing fair
As the noon sky, more like to goddesses
Than mortal creatures, graceful and discreet,
Expert in amorous arts, enchanting tongues
Persuasive, virgin majesty with mild
And sweet allayed, yet terrible to approach,   160
Skilled to retire, and in retiring draw
Hearts after them tangled in amorous nets.
Such object hath the power to soften and tame
Severest temper, smooth the ruggedest brow,
Enerve, and with voluptuous hope dissolve,
Draw out with credulous desire, and lead
At will the manliest, resolutest breast,
As the magnetic hardest iron draws.
Women, when nothing else, beguiled the heart
Of wisest Solomon, and made him build,   170
And made him bow to the gods of his wives."
    To whom quick answer Satan thus returned.
"Belial, in much uneven scale thou weigh'st
All others by thyself; because of old
Thou thyself doat'st on womankind, admiring
Their shape, their color, and attractive grace,
None are, thou think'st, but taken with such toys.
Before the Flood thou with thy lusty crew,
False-titled Sons of God, roaming the Earth
Cast wanton eyes on the daughters of men,   180
And coupled with them, and begot a race.
Have we not seen, or by relation heard,
In courts and regal chambers how thou lurk'st,
In wood or grove by mossy fountain side,
In valley or green meadow, to waylay
Some beauty rare, Callisto, Clymene,
Daphne, or Semele, Antiopa,
Or Amymone, Syrinx, many more
Too long, then lay'st thy scapes on names adored,
Apollo, Neptune, Jupiter, or Pan,   190
Satyr, or Faun, or Silvan? But these haunts
Delight not all; among the sons of men,
How many have with a smile made small account
Of beauty and her lures, easily scorned
All her assaults, on worthier things intent?
Remember that Pellean conqueror,
A youth, how all the beauties of the East

189. scapes, escapades.
196. Pellean conqueror, i.e., Alexander the Great, born at Pella.

He slightly viewed, and slightly overpassed;
How he surnamed of Africa dismissed
In his prime youth the fair Iberian maid.   200
For Solomon he lived at ease, and full
Of honor, wealth, high fare, aimed not beyond
Higher design than to enjoy his state;
Thence to the bait of women lay exposed.
But he whom we attempt is wiser far
Than Solomon, of more exalted mind,
Made and set wholly on the accomplishment
Of greatest things. What woman will you find,
Though of this age the wonder and the fame,
On whom his leisure will vouchsafe an eye   210
Of fond desire? Or should she confident,
As sitting queen adored on Beauty's throne,
Descend with all her winning charms begirt
To enamor, as the zone of Venus once
Wrought that effect on Jove, so fables tell;
How would one look from his majestic brow
Seated as on the top of Virtue's hill,
Discountenance her despised, and put to rout
All her array, her female pride deject,
Or turn to reverent awe? for Beauty stands   220
In the admiration only of weak minds
Led captive; cease to admire, and all her plumes
Fall flat and shrink into a trivial toy,
At every sudden slighting quite abashed.
Therefore with manlier objects we must try
His constancy, with such as have more show
Of worth, of honor, glory, and popular praise;
Rocks whereon greatest men have oftest wrecked;
Or that which only seems to satisfy
Lawful desires of nature, not beyond;   230
And now I know he hungers where no food
Is to be found, in the wide wilderness;
The rest commit to me; I shall let pass
No advantage, and his strength as oft assay."
    He ceased, and heard their grant in loud acclaim;
Then forthwith to him takes a chosen band
Of spirits likest to himself in guile
To be at hand, and at his beck appear,

199. he surnamed of Africa, i.e., Scipio, who received the title Africanus after his victory over Carthage. Livy tells of his respectful treatment
of a beautiful Spanish prisoner.
    216–17. I.e., the majestic brow of Christ seated· etc.
    219. deject, cast down (transitive).

If cause were to unfold some active scene
Of various persons, each to know his part;   240
Then to the desert takes with these his flight,
Where still from shade to shade the Son of God
After forty days' fasting had remained,
Now hungering first, and to himself thus said.
    "Where will this end? Four times ten days I have passed
Wandering this woody maze, and human food
Not tasted, nor had appetite. That fast
To virtue I impute not, or count part
Of what I suffer here; if nature need not,
Or God support nature without repast   250
Though needing, what praise is it to endure?
But now I feel hunger, which declares
Nature hath need of what she asks; yet God
Can satisfy that need some other way,
Though hunger still remain. So it remain
Without this body's wasting, I content me,
And from the sting of famine fear no harm,
Nor mind it, fed with better thoughts that feed
Me hungering more to do my Father's will."
    It was the hour of night, when thus the Son   260
Communed in silent walk, then laid him down
Under the hospitable covert nigh
Of trees thick interwoven; there he slept,
And dreamed, as appetite is wont to dream,
Of meats and drinks, nature's refreshment sweet.
Him thought, he by the brook of Cherith stood
And saw the ravens with their horny beaks
Food to Elijah bringing even and morn,
Though ravenous, taught to abstain from what they brought.
He saw the Prophet also how he fled   270
Into the desert, and how there he slept
Under a juniper, then how, awaked,

245 ff. Milton has so interpreted the first temptation (see note on I.
343.) as to leave room for including another offer of food in the second
(the kingdoms of the world and the glory of them). That this is in the form
of a luxurious Roman banquet makes the transition easy to more serious
objects of appeal—money, empire, military power, pagan learning—all of
which Milton (following Plato, and Spenser in *Faerie Queene,* Book II)
would classify as involving the nonrational part of the soul. But there are
complications in the adjustment of Milton's humanistic ethics to the scriptural incident.
    264 ff. We are reminded of Eve's dream (*Paradise Lost,* V, 28 ff.), but
that was a dream of succumbing to appetite against conscience, whereas this
is of the reward of virtue. And Eve's sleep is restless but Christ rises lightly
from his couch. There is much observation here, if no analysis in modern
terms.

He found his supper on the coals prepared,
And by the angel was bid rise and eat,
And eat the second time after repose,
The strength whereof sufficed him forty days;
Sometimes that with Elijah he partook,
Or as a guest with Daniel at his pulse.
Thus wore out night, and now the herald lark
Left his ground-nest, high towering to descry   280
The Morn's approach, and greet her with his song;
As lightly from his grassy couch up rose
Our Savior, and found all was but a dream;
Fasting he went to sleep, and fasting waked.
Up to a hill anon his steps he reared,
From whose high top to ken the prospect round,
If cottage were in view, sheep-cote or herd;
But cottage, herd or sheep-cote none he saw,
Only in a bottom saw a pleasant grove,
With chant of tuneful birds resounding loud;   290
Thither he bent his way, determined there
To rest at noon, and entered soon the shade
High-roofed, and walks beneath, and alleys brown
That opened in the midst a woody scene;
Nature's own work, it seemed (Nature taught Art),
And to a superstitious eye the haunt
Of wood-gods and wood-nymphs. He viewed it round,
When suddenly a man before him stood,
Not rustic as before, but seemlier clad,
As one in city or court or palace bred,   300
And with fair speech these words to him addressed.
  "With granted leave officious I return,
But much more wonder that the Son of God
In this wild solitude so long should bide
Of all things destitute, and well I know,
Not without hunger. Others of some note,
As story tells, have trod this wilderness;
The fugitive bond-woman with her son
Outcast Nebaioth, yet found he relief
By a providing angel; all the race   310
Of Israel here had famished, had not God
Rained from heaven manna; and that Prophet bold
Native of Thebez wandering here was fed

308. The fugitive bond-woman is Hagar; her son was Ishmael, his son
was Nabaioth. See Gen. 21 and 25.

312. Prophet bold, i.e., Elijah. This prophet was a particular favorite
of Milton's and doubtless served him as a model in courageous utterance of
God's word.

Twice by a voice inviting him to eat.
Of thee these forty days none hath regard,
Forty and more deserted here indeed."
    To whom thus Jesus. "What concludest thou hence?
They all had need, I as thou seest have none."
    "How hast thou hunger then?" Satan replied.
"Tell me, if food were now before thee set,   320
Would'st thou not eat?" "Thereafter as I like
The giver," answered Jesus. "Why should that
Cause thy refusal," said the subtle Fiend,
"Hast thou not right to all created things,
Owe not all creatures by just right to thee
Duty and service, nor to stay till bid,
But tender all their power? Nor mention I
Meats by the law unclean, or offered first
To idols, those young Daniel could refuse;
Nor proffered by an enemy, though who   330
Would scruple that, with want oppressed? Behold
Nature ashamed, or better to express,
Troubled that thou shouldst hunger, hath purveyed
From all the elements her choicest store
To treat thee as beseems, and as her Lord
With honor; only deign to sit and eat."
    He spake no dream, for as his words had end,
Our Savior lifting up his eyes beheld
In ample space under the broadest shade
A table richly spread, in regal mode,   340
With dishes piled, and meats of noblest sort
And savor, beasts of chase, or fowl of game,
In pastry built, or from the spit, or boiled,
Gris-ambered-steamed, all fish from sea or shore,
Freshet, or purling brook, of shell or fin,
And exquisitest name, for which was drained
Pontus and Lucrine bay, and Afric coast.
Alas how simple, to these cates compared,
Was that crude apple that diverted Eve!
And at a stately sideboard by the wine   350
That fragrant smell diffused, in order stood
Tall stripling youths rich-clad, of fairer hue
Than Ganymed or Hylas; distant more
Under the trees now tripped, now solemn stood
Nymphs of Diana's train, and Naiades
With fruits and flowers from Amalthea's horn,
And ladies of the Hesperides, that seemed

    356. Amalthea's horn, the mythical horn of the goat which suckled
Zeus; the horn of plenty.

Fairer than feigned of old, or fabled since
Of faery damsels met in forest wide
By knights of Logres, or of Lyones,   360
Lancelot or Pelleas, or Pellenore;
And all the while harmonious airs were heard
Of chiming strings or charming pipes, and winds
Of gentlest gale Arabian odors fanned
From their soft wings, and Flora's earliest smells.
Such was the splendor, and the Tempter now
His invitation earnestly renewed.
　　"What doubts the Son of God to sit and eat?
These are not fruits forbidden, no interdict
Defends the touching of these viands pure,   370
Their taste no knowledge works, at least of evil,
But life preserves, destroys life's enemy,
Hunger, with sweet restorative delight.
All these are spirits of air, and woods, and springs,
Thy gentle ministers, who come to pay
Thee homage, and acknowledge thee their Lord.
What doubt'st thou, Son of God? Sit down and eat."
　　To whom thus Jesus temperately replied.
"Said'st thou not that to all things I had right?
And who withholds my power that right to use?   380
Shall I receive by gift what of my own,
When and where likes me best, I can command?
I can at will, doubt not, as soon as thou,
Command a table in this wilderness,
And call swift flights of angels ministrant,
Arrayed in glory on my cup to attend.
Why shouldst thou then obtrude this diligence
In vain, where no acceptance it can find?
And with my hunger what hast thou to do?
Thy pompous delicacies I contemn,   390
And count thy specious gifts no gifts but guiles."
　　To whom thus answered Satan malecontent.
"That I have also power to give thou seest;
If of that power I bring thee voluntary
What I might have bestowed on whom I pleased,
And rather opportunely in this place

360. The wandering maiden found by a knight in the woods in numerous romances was sometimes a demon. At Satan's banquet all the parts are
taken by members of his own unholy crew, the "spirits likest himself in
guile" whom he had taken along to be at hand (line 236 above). En-
chanters like Archimago in *Faerie Queene* Book I are good at putting on
this kind of devil-show.
368. **What doubts**, why hesitates, or why fears.
369 ff. The terms in which Christ rejects Satan's offer should be com-

Chose to impart to thy apparent need,
Why shouldst thou not accept it? But I see
What I can do or offer is suspect;
Of these things others quickly will dispose   400
Whose pains have earned the far-fet spoil." With that
Both table and provision vanished quite
With sound of harpies' wings and talons heard;
Only the importune Tempter still remained,
And with these words his temptation pursued.
    "By hunger, that each other creature tames,
Thou art not to be harmed, therefore not moved;
Thy temperance invincible besides,
For no allurement yields to appetite,
And all thy heart is set on high designs,   410
High actions. But wherewith to be achieved?
Great acts require great means of enterprise;
Thou art unknown, unfriended, low of birth,
A carpenter thy father known, thyself
Bred up in poverty and straits at home,
Lost in a desert here and hunger-bit.
Which way or from what hope dost thou aspire
To greatness? whence authority deriv'st?
What followers, what retinue canst thou gain,
Or at thy heels the dizzy multitude,   420
Longer than thou canst feed them on thy cost?
Money brings honor, friends, conquest, and realms.
What raised Antipater the Edomite,
And his son Herod placed on Judah's throne
(Thy throne), but gold that got him puissant friends?
Therefore, if at great things thou wouldst arrive,
Get riches first, get wealth, and treasure heap,
Not difficult, if thou hearken to me;
Riches are mine, fortune is in my hand;
They whom I favor thrive in wealth amain,   430
While virtue, valor, wisdom, sit in want."
    To whom thus Jesus patiently replied.
"Yet wealth without these three is impotent

pared with the Lady's "None but good men can give good gifts" in *Comus*,
and with Christ's rejection of pagan learning in Book IV. In *Paradise Lost*
and elsewhere Milton argues against asceticism as such. The problem of the
use of God's gifts to man (food, sex, beauty, intellect) is one that the poet
evidently pondered over. His theory about it is perfectly clear and consistent, however the case may be with his emotions.
    423. Antipater used his wealth to gain political power in Judea. He
aided Caesar against Pompey and was made Procurator in 47 B.C. His son,
Herod the Great, ruled Judea as king from 37 B.C. to 4 B.C. Other Herods
followed.

To gain dominion or to keep it gained.
Witness those ancient empires of the earth,
In height of all their flowing wealth dissolved;
But men endued with these have oft attained
In lowest poverty to highest deeds;
Gideon and Jephtha, and the shepherd lad,
Whose offspring on the throne of Judah sat   440
So many ages, and shall yet regain
That seat, and reign in Israel without end.
Among the Heathen (for throughout the world
To me is not unknown what hath been done
Worthy of memorial) canst thou not remember
Quintius, Fabricius, Curius, Regulus?
For I esteem those names of men so poor
Who could do mighty things, and could contemn
Riches though offered from the hand of kings.
And what in me seems wanting, but that I   450
May also in this poverty as soon
Accomplish what they did, perhaps and more?
Extol not riches then, the toil of fools,
The wise man's cumbrance if not snare, more apt
To slacken virtue and abate her edge
Than prompt her to do aught may merit praise.
What if with like aversion I reject
Riches and realms; yet not for that a crown,
Golden in show, is but a wreath of thorns,
Brings dangers, troubles, cares, and sleepless nights   460
To him who wears the regal diadem,
When on his shoulders each man's burden lies;
For therein stands the office of a king,
His honor, virtue, merit, and chief praise,
That for the public all this weight he bears.
Yet he who reigns within himself, and rules
Passions, desires, and fears, is more a king;
Which every wise and virtuous man attains;
And who attains not, ill aspires to rule
Cities of men, or headstrong multitudes,   470
Subject himself to anarchy within,
Or lawless passions in him, which he serves.
But to guide nations in the way of truth
By saving doctrine, and from error lead
To know, and knowing worship God aright,
Is yet more kingly; this attracts the soul,

439. **shepherd lad**, David.
460 ff. Milton's *locus classicus* for the cares of sovereignty was doubtless
Shakespeare. See II *Henry IV*, III, i. and *Henry V*, IV, i.

Governs the inner man, the nobler part,
That other o'er the body only reigns,
And oft by force, which to a generous mind
So reigning can be no sincere delight.   480
Besides, to give a kingdom hath been thought
Greater and nobler done, and to lay down
Far more magnanimous, than to assume.
Riches are needless then, both for themselves,
And for thy reason why they should be sought,
To gain a scepter, oftest better missed."

BOOK III

So spake the Son of God, and Satan stood
A while as mute confounded what to say,
What to reply, confuted and convinced
Of his weak arguing and fallacious drift;
At length collecting all his serpent wiles,
With soothing words renewed, him thus accosts.
    "I see thou know'st what is of use to know,
What best to say canst say, to do canst do;
Thy actions to thy words accord, thy words
To thy large heart give utterance due, thy heart   10
Contains of good, wise, just, the perfect shape.
Should kings and nations from thy mouth consult,
Thy counsel would be as the oracle
Urim and Thummim, those oraculous gems
On Aaron's breast, or tongue of seers old
Infallible; or wert thou sought to deeds
That might require the array of war, thy skill
Of conduct would be such, that all the world
Could not sustain thy prowess, or subsist
In battle, though against thy few in arms.   20
These godlike virtues wherefore dost thou hide?
Affecting private life, or more obscure
In savage wilderness, wherefore deprive
All Earth her wonder at thy acts, thyself
The fame and glory, glory the reward
That sole excites to high attempts the flame
Of most erected spirits, most tempered pure
Ethereal, who all pleasures else despise,
All treasures and all gain esteem as dross,
And dignities and powers, all but the highest?   30
Thy years are ripe, and over-ripe; the son
Of Macedonian Philip had ere these
Won Asia and the throne of Cyrus held

At his dispose, young Scipio had brought down
The Carthaginian pride, young Pompey quelled
The Pontic king and in triumph had rode.
Yet years, and to ripe years judgment mature,
Quench not the thirst of glory, but augment.
Great Julius, whom now all the world admires,
The more he grew in years, the more inflamed   40
With glory, wept that he had lived so long
Inglorious. But thou yet art not too late."
  To whom our Savior calmly thus replied.
"Thou neither dost persuade me to seek wealth
For empire's sake, nor empire to affect
For glory's sake by all thy argument.
For what is glory but the blaze of fame,
The people's praise, if always praise unmixed?
And what the people but a herd confused,
A miscellaneous rabble, who extol   50
Things vulgar, and well weighed, scarce worth the praise?
They praise and they admire they know not what,
And know not whom, but as one leads the other;
And what delight to be by such extolled,
To live upon their tongues and be their talk,
Of whom to be dispraised were no small praise?
His lot who dares be singularly good.
The intelligent among them and the wise
Are few, and glory scarce of few is raised.
This is true glory and renown, when God   60
Looking on the Earth, with approbation marks
The just man, and divulges him through Heaven
To all his angels, who with true applause
Recount his praises. Thus he did to Job,
When to extend his fame through Heaven and Earth,
As thou to thy reproach may'st well remember,
He asked thee, 'Hast thou seen my servant Job?'
Famous he was in Heaven; on Earth less known,
Where glory is false glory, attributed
To things not glorious, men not worthy of fame.   70
They err who count it glorious to subdue
By conquest far and wide, to overrun
Large countries, and in field great battles win,
Great cities by assault. What do these worthies,
But rob and spoil, burn, slaughter, and enslave
Peaceable nations, neighboring or remote,
Made captive, yet deserving freedom more
Than those their conquerors, who leave behind
Nothing but ruin wheresoe'er they rove,

And all the flourishing works of peace destroy,   80
Then swell with pride, and must be titled Gods,
Great Benefactors of mankind, Deliverers,
Worshipped with temple, priest, and sacrifice;
One is the son of Jove, of Mars the other,
Till conqueror Death discover them scarce men,
Rolling in brutish vices, and deformed,
Violent or shameful death their due reward.
But if there be in glory aught of good,
It may by means far different be attained
Without ambition, war, or violence;   90
By deeds of peace, by wisdom eminent,
By patience, temperance. I mention still
Him whom thy wrongs with saintly patience borne,
Made famous in a land and times obscure;
Who names not now with honor patient Job?
Poor Socrates (who next more memorable?)
By what he taught and suffered for so doing,
For truth's sake suffering death unjust, lives now
Equal in fame to proudest conquerors.
Yet if for fame and glory aught be done,   100
Aught suffered, if young African for fame
His wasted country freed from Punic rage,
The deed becomes unpraised, the man at least,
And loses, though but verbal, his reward.
Shall I seek glory then, as vain men seek,
Oft not deserved? I seek not mine, but His
Who sent me, and thereby witness whence I am."
  To whom the Tempter murmuring thus replied.
"Think not so slight of glory, therein least
Resembling thy great Father: he seeks glory,   110
And for his glory all things made, all things
Orders and governs, nor content in Heaven
By all his angels glorified, requires
Glory from men, from all men good or bad,
Wise or unwise, no difference, no exemption;
Above all sacrifice or hallowed gift
Glory he requires, and glory he receives
Promiscuous from all nations, Jew, or Greek,
Or Barbarous, nor exception hath declared;
From us his foes pronounced, glory he exacts."   120
  To whom our Savior fervently replied.
"And reason; since his word all things produced,
Though chiefly not for glory as prime end,
But to show forth his goodness, and impart
His good communicable to every soul

Freely; of whom what could he less expect
Than glory and benediction, that is thanks,
The slightest, easiest, readiest recompense
From them who could return him nothing else,
And not returning that would likeliest render   130
Contempt instead, dishonor, obloquy?
Hard recompense, unsuitable return
For so much good, so much beneficence.
But why should man seek glory, who of his own
Hath nothing, and to whom nothing belongs
But condemnation, ignominy, and shame?
Who for so many benefits received
Turned recreant to God, ingrate and false,
And so of all true good himself despoiled,
Yet, sacrilegious, to himself would take   140
That which to God alone of right belongs;
Yet so much bounty is in God, such grace,
That who advance his glory, not their own,
Them he himself to glory will advance."
     So spake the Son of God; and here again
Satan had not to answer, but stood struck
With guilt of his own sin, for he himself
Insatiable of glory had lost all.
Yet of another plea bethought him soon.
     "Of glory as thou wilt," said he, "so deem,   150
Worth or not worth the seeking, let it pass.
But to a kingdom thou art born, ordained
To sit upon thy father David's throne,
By mother's side thy father, though thy right
Be now in powerful hands, that will not part
Easily from possession won with arms;
Judæa now and all the Promised Land,
Reduced a province under Roman yoke,
Obeys Tiberius; nor is always ruled
With temperate sway; oft have they violated   160
The Temple, oft the Law with foul affronts,
Abominations rather, as did once
Antiochus. And think'st thou to regain
Thy right by sitting still or thus retiring?
So did not Machabeus: he indeed
Retired unto the desert, but with arms;
And o'er a mighty king so oft prevailed,
That by strong hand his family obtained,
Though priests, the crown, and David's throne usurped,
With Modin and her suburbs once content.   170
If kingdom move thee not, let move thee zeal

And duty; zeal and duty are not slow,
But on occasion's forelock watchful wait.
They themselves rather are occasion best—
Zeal of thy Father's house, duty to free
Thy country from her heathen servitude;
So shalt thou best fulfil, best verify
The Prophets old, who sung thy endless reign,
The happier reign the sooner it begins.
Reign then; what canst thou better do the while?"   180
   To whom our Savior answer thus returned.
"All things are best fulfilled in their due time,
And time there is for all things, Truth hath said.
If of my reign prophetic Writ hath told
That it shall never end, so when begin
The Father in his purpose hath decreed,
He in whose hand all times and seasons roll.
What if he hath decreed that I shall first
Be tried in humble state, and things adverse,
By tribulations, injuries, insults,   190
Contempts, and scorns, and snares, and violence,
Suffering, abstaining, quietly expecting
Without distrust or doubt, that he may know
What I can suffer, how obey? Who best
Can suffer best can do; best reign who first
Well hath obeyed; just trial ere I merit
My exaltation without change or end.
But what concerns it thee when I begin
My everlasting kingdom? Why art thou
Solicitous? What moves thy inquisition?   200
Know'st thou not that my rising is thy fall,
And my promotion will be thy destruction?"
   To whom the Tempter inly racked replied.
"Let that come when it comes; all hope is lost
Of my reception into grace; what worse?
For where no hope is left, is left no fear.
If there be worse, the expectation more
Of worse torments me than the feeling can.
I would be at the worst; worst is my port,
My harbor and my ultimate repose,   210
The end I would attain, my final good.
My error was my error, and my crime

212–15. The meaning is: my crime will be condemned for what it was,
and my punishment will be the same whether you rule or not. The punctuation is that of the original text, but logic would seem to require a comma
after "crime" ("my crime, whatever it may have been") and no mark after
"punished."

My crime; whatever, for itself condemned,
And will alike be punished; whether thou
Reign or reign not; though to that gentle brow
Willingly I could fly, and hope thy reign,
From that placid aspect and meek regard,
Rather than aggravate my evil state,
Would stand between me and thy Father's ire
(Whose ire I dread more than the fire of Hell)   220
A shelter and a kind of shading cool
Interposition, as a summer's cloud.
If I then to the worst that can be haste,
Why move thy feet so slow to what is best,
Happiest both to thyself and all the world,
That thou who worthiest art shouldst be their king?
Perhaps thou linger'st in deep thoughts detained
Of the enterprise so hazardous and high;
No wonder, for though in thee be united
What of perfection can in man be found,   230
Or human nature can receive, consider
Thy life hath yet been private, most part spent
At home, scarce viewed the Galilean towns,
And once a year Jerusalem, few days'
Short sojourn; and what thence couldst thou observe?
The world thou hast not seen, much less her glory,
Empires, and monarchs, and their radiant courts,
Best school of best experience, quickest insight
In all things that to greatest actions lead.
The wisest, unexperienced, will be ever   240
Timorous and loth, with novice modesty
(As he who seeking asses found a kingdom)
Irresolute, unhardy, unadventurous.
But I will bring thee where thou soon shalt quit
Those rudiments, and see before thine eyes
The monarchies of the Earth, their pomp and state,
Sufficient introduction to inform
Thee, of thyself so apt, in regal arts,
And regal mysteries; that thou may'st know
How best their opposition to withstand."   250
  With that (such power was given him then) he took
The Son of God up to a mountain high.
It was a mountain at whose verdant feet
A spacious plain outstretched in circuit wide

242. Saul, who, seeking his father's asses, met the prophet Samuel and
was anointed by him (I Sam. 9).
  251 ff. Christ is now shown the kingdoms of earth "in a moment of
time" (Luke 4:5).

Lay pleasant; from his side two rivers flowed,
The one winding, the other straight, and left between
Fair champaign with less rivers interveined,
Then meeting joined their tribute to the sea.
Fertile of corn the glebe, of oil, and wine;
With herds the pastures thronged, with flocks the hills;   260
Huge cities and high-towered, that well might seem
The seats of mightiest monarchs; and so large
The prospect was, that here and there was room
For barren desert, fountainless and dry.
To this high mountain top the Tempter brought
Our Savior, and new train of words began.
    "Well have we speeded, and o'er hill and dale,
Forest and field, and flood, temples and towers,
Cut shorter many a league. Here thou behold'st
Assyria and her empire's ancient bounds,   270
Araxes and the Caspian lake, thence on
As far as Indus east, Euphrates west,
And oft beyond; to south the Persian bay,
And inaccessible the Arabian drouth.
Here Nineveh, of length within her wall
Several days' journey, built by Ninus old,
Of that first golden monarchy the seat,
And seat of Salmanassar, whose success
Israel in long captivity still mourns;
There Babylon, the wonder of all tongues,   280
As ancient, but rebuilt by him who twice
Judah and all thy father David's house
Led captive and Jerusalem laid waste,
Till Cyrus set them free; Persepolis
His city there thou seest, and Bactra there;
Ecbatana her structure vast there shows,
And Hecatompylos her hundred gates;
There Susa by Choaspes, amber stream,
The drink of none but kings; of later fame
Built by Emathian, or by Parthian hands,   290

278. Shalmaneser IV conquered Israel, the northern kingdom of the Hebrews, in 726 B.C.

281 ff. Nebuchadnezzar II captured Jerusalem in 597 and carried the king and others to Babylon. In 586 B.C. he destroyed the city after a revolt and led many more Jews into exile.

290. Emathian, Macedonian. The kingdom of Seleucia was founded after the death of Alexander by one of his Macedonian generals. The dynasty was overthrown by Arsaces, king of Parthia, in 250 B.C. Sogdiana (line 302) was the Parthian province bordering Scythia. Satan's survey of the eastern empires has led up to the present political situation in which Christ is invited to play the ancient game of power and conquest.

The great Seleucia, Nisibis, and there
Artaxata, Teredon, Ctesiphon,
Turning with easy eye thou may'st behold.
All these the Parthian, now some ages past
By great Arsaces led, who founded first
That empire, under his dominion holds,
From the luxurious kings of Antioch won.
And just in time thou com'st to have a view
Of his great power; for now the Parthian king
In Ctesiphon hath gathered all his host   300
Against the Scythian, whose incursions wild
Have wasted Sogdiana; to her aid
He marches now in haste. See, though from far,
His thousands, in what martial equipage
They issue forth, steel bows and shafts their arms,
Of equal dread in flight or in pursuit,
All horsemen, in which fight they most excel;
See how in warlike muster they appear,
In rhombs and wedges, and half-moons, and wings."
    He looked and saw what numbers numberless   310
The city gates outpoured, light-armëd troops
In coats of mail and military pride;
In mail their horses clad, yet fleet and strong,
Prancing their riders bore, the flower and choice
Of many provinces from bound to bound,
From Arachosia, from Candaor east,
And Margiana to the Hyrcanian cliffs
Of Caucasus, and dark Iberian dales,
From Atropatia and the neighboring plains
Of Adiabene, Media, and the south   320
Of Susiana, to Balsara's haven.
He saw them in their forms of battle ranged,
How quick they wheeled, and flying behind them shot
Sharp sleet of arrowy showers against the face
Of their pursuers, and overcame by flight;
The field all iron cast a gleaming brown,
Nor wanted clouds of foot, nor on each horn
Cuirassiers all in steel for standing fight,
Chariots or elephants indorsed with towers
Of archers, nor of laboring pioners   330

318. **Iberian.** The reference is not to Spain but to a region near the
Caspian. Milton is constructing this passage from a map.
    329. Elephants were a feature of the Persian as well as the Carthaginian
armies. Milton was a student of the art of war and this representation may
be set beside the account of the military organization of Satan in *Paradise
Lost.* which is its prototype.

A multitude with spades and axes armed
To lay hills plain, fell woods, or valleys fill,
Or where plain was raise hill, or overlay
With bridges rivers proud, as with a yoke;
Mules after these, camel and dromedaries,
And wagons fraught with útensils of war.
Such forces met not, nor so wide a camp,
When Agrican with all his northern powers
Besieged Albracca, as romances tell,
The city of Gallaphrone, from thence to win   340
The fairest of her sex Angelica
His daughter, sought by many prowest knights,
Both Paynim and the peers of Charlemain.
Such and so numerous was their chivalry;
At sight whereof the Fiend yet more presumed,
And to our Savior thus his words renewed.
    "That thou may'st know I seek not to engage
Thy virtue, and not every way secure
On no slight grounds thy safety, hear, and mark
To what end I have brought thee hither and shown   350
All this fair sight. Thy kingdom though foretold
By prophet or by angel, unless thou
Endeavor, as thy father David did,
Thou never shalt obtain; prediction still
In all things, and all men, supposes means;
Without means used, what it predicts revokes.
But say thou wert possessed of David's throne
By free consent of all, none opposite,
Samaritan or Jew; how couldst thou hope
Long to enjoy it quiet and secure   360
Between two such enclosing enemies,
Roman and Parthian? Therefore one of these
Thou must make sure thy own; the Parthian first
By my advice, as nearer and of late
Found able by invasion to annoy
Thy country, and captive lead away her kings
Antigonus and old Hyrcanus bound,
Maugre the Roman. It shall be my task

339. The reference is to Boiardo's *Orlando Inamorato,* which tells of the exploits of the twelve peers of Charlemagne against the paynims. Agrican was king of Tartary, Gallaphrone of Cathay. Roland and other Christians were enlisted in the siege.
367. Antigonus, king of Judea, had been supported by the Parthians against Hyrcanus in spite of Roman friendship for the latter. He was replaced in turn by Herod I in 37 b.c. A new revolution led by a Jewish messiah using Parthian arms against Roman interference seems logical enough.

To render thee the Parthian at dispose;
Choose which thou wilt, by conquest or by league; 370
By him thou shalt regain, without him not,
That which alone can truly reinstall thee
In David's royal seat, his true successor;
Deliverance of thy brethren, those ten tribes
Whose offspring in his territory yet serve
In Habor, and among the Medes dispersed;
Ten sons of Jacob, two of Joseph lost
Thus long from Israel, serving as of old
Their fathers in the land of Egypt served,
This offer sets before thee to deliver. 380
These if from servitude thou shalt restore
To their inheritance, then, nor till then,
Thou on the throne of David in full glory,
From Egypt to Euphrates and beyond
Shalt reign, and Rome or Cæsar not need fear."
　　To whom our Savior answered thus, unmoved.
"Much ostentation vain of fleshly arm,
And fragile arms, much instrument of war
Long in preparing, soon to nothing brought,
Before mine eyes thou hast set; and in my ear 390
Vented much policy, and projects deep
Of enemies, of aids, battles and leagues,
Plausible to the world, to me worth nought.
Means I must use thou say'st, prediction else
Will unpredict and fail me of the throne:
My time I told thee (and that time for thee
Were better farthest off), is not yet come.
When that comes think not thou to find me slack
On my part aught endeavoring, or to need
Thy politic maxims, or that cumbersome 400
Luggage of war there shown me, argument
Of human weakness rather than of strength.
My brethren, as thou call'st them, those Ten Tribes
I must deliver, if I mean to reign
David's true heir, and his full scepter sway
To just extent over all Israel's sons;
But whence to thee this zeal? Where was it then
For Israel, or for David, or his throne,
When thou stood'st up his tempter to the pride
Of numbering Israel, which cost the lives 410

375-76. See line 278 and note; the biblical text is II Kings 17:6: "and
placed them in Halah and in Habor by the river of Gozan, and in the cities
of the Medes."
409-12. See I Chron. 21:1-15.

Of threescore and ten thousand Israelites
By three days' pestilence? Such was thy zeal
To Israel then, the same that now to me.
As for those captive tribes, themselves were they
Who wrought their own captivity, fell off
From God to worship calves, the deities
Of Egypt, Baal next and Ashtaroth,
And all the idolatries of heathen round,
Besides their other worse than heathenish crimes;
Nor in the land of their captivity   420
Humbled themselves, or penitent besought
The God of their forefathers, but so died
Impenitent, and left a race behind
Like to themselves, distinguishable scarce
From Gentiles but by circumcision vain,
And God with idols in their worship joined.
Should I of these the liberty regard,
Who freed, as to their ancient patrimony,
Unhumbled, unrepentant, unreformed,
Headlong would follow, and to their gods perhaps   430
Of Bethel and of Dan? No, let them serve
Their enemies, who serve idols with God.
Yet he at length, time to himself best known,
Remembering Abraham, by some wondrous call
May bring them back repentant and sincere,
And at their passing cleave the Assyrian flood,
While to their native land with joy they haste,
As the Red Sea and Jordan once he cleft,
When to the Promised Land their fathers passed.
To his due time and providence I leave them."   440
    So spake Israel's true King, and to the Fiend
Made answer meet, that made void all his wiles.
So fares it when with truth falsehood contends.

BOOK IV

Perplexed and troubled at his bad success
The Tempter stood, nor had what to reply,
Discovered in his fraud, thrown from his hope,
So oft, and the persuasive rhetoric
That sleeked his tongue, and won so much on Eve,
So little here, nay lost. But Eve was Eve;
This far his over-match, who self-deceived

434. For God's promise to Abraham see Gen. 15:18: "Unto thy seed
have I given this land from the river of Egypt unto the great river, the river
Euphrates."

And rash, beforehand had no better weighed
The strength he was to cope with, or his own.
But as a man who had been matchless held   10
In cunning, over-reached where least he thought,
To salve his credit, and for very spite
Still will be tempting him who foils him still,
And never cease, though to his shame the more;
Or as a swarm of flies in vintage time,
About the wine-press where sweet must is poured,
Beat off, returns as oft with humming sound;
Or surging waves against a solid rock,
Though all to shivers dashed, the assault renew,
Vain battery, and in froth or bubbles end;   20
So Satan, whom repulse upon repulse
Met ever; and to shameful silence brought,
Yet gives not o'er though desperate of success,
And his vain importunity pursues.
He brought our Savior to the western side
Of that high mountain, whence he might behold
Another plain, long but in breadth not wide;
Washed by the southern sea, and on the north
To equal length backed with a ridge of hills
That screened the fruits of the earth and seats of men   30
From cold Septentrion blasts; thence in the midst
Divided by a river, of whose banks
On each side an imperial city stood,
With towers and temples proudly elevate
On seven small hills, with palaces adorned,
Porches and theaters, baths, aqueducts,
Statues and trophies, and triumphal arcs,
Gardens and groves presented to his eyes,
Above the height of mountains interposed.
By what strange parallax or optic skill   40
Of vision multiplied through air, or glass
Of telescope, were curious to inquire.
And now the Tempter thus his silence broke.
"The city which thou seest no other deem
Than great and glorious Rome, Queen of the Earth
So far renowned, and with the spoils enriched
Of nations; there the Capitol thou seest
Above the rest lifting his stately head
On the Tarpeian rock, her citadel

---

40. Milton means that Satan must have engineered a change in the
angle of vision, as in a periscope.
41. To multiply the vision through air might be to double the image, as
above; but Milton is thinking also of its magnification.

Impregnable; and there Mount Palatine 50
The imperial palace, compass huge, and high
The structure, skill of noblest architects,
With gilded battlements, conspicuous far,
Turrets and terraces, and glittering spires;
Many a fair edifice besides, more like
Houses of gods (so well I have disposed
My airy microscope) thou may'st behold
Outside and inside both, pillars and roofs
Carved work, the hand of famed artificers
In cedar, marble, ivory or gold. 60
Thence to the gates cast round thine eye, and see
What conflux issuing forth or entering in:
Prætors, proconsuls to their provinces
Hasting or on return, in robes of state;
Lictors and rods the ensigns of their power;
Legions and cohorts, turms of horse and wings;
Or embassies from regions far remote
In various habits on the Appian road,
Or on the Æmilian, some from farthest south,
Syene, and where the shadow both way falls, 70
Meroë, Nilotic isle, and more to west,
The realm of Bocchus to the Blackmoor sea,
From the Asian kings and Parthian among these,
From India and the Golden Chersonese,
And utmost Indian isle Taprobane,
Dusk faces with white silken turbans wreathed,
From Gallia, Gades, and the British west,
Germans, and Scythians, and Sarmatians north
Beyond Danubius to the Tauric pool.
All nations now to Rome obedience pay, 80
To Rome's great Emperor, whose wide domain
In ample territory, wealth and power,
Civility of manners, arts, and arms,
And long renown thou justly may'st prefer
Before the Parthian. These two thrones except,
The rest are barbarous, and scarce worth the sight,
Shared among petty kings too far removed;
These having shown thee, I have shown thee all

70. **Syene,** modern Aswan in southern Egypt.
71. **Meroë,** in the Sudan, anciently capital of Ethiopia. **Nilotic,** of the Nile.
72. Milton is marking the southern boundary of the empire in Mauretania.
73-75. Among the representatives of Roman tributaries are visitors from farther east, Malaya and Ceylon (**Taprobane**).
79. **Tauric pool,** the sea of Azov.

The kingdoms of the world, and all their glory.
This Emperor hath no son, and now is old,   90
Old and lascivious, and from Rome retired
To Capreæ, an island small but strong
On the Campanian shore, with purpose there
His horrid lusts in private to enjoy,
Committing to a wicked favorite
All public cares, and yet of him suspicious,
Hated of all, and hating. With what ease,
Endued with regal virtues as thou art,
Appearing, and beginning noble deeds,
Might'st thou expel this monster from his throne   100
Now made a sty, and in his place ascending
A victor people free from servile yoke?
And with my help thou may'st; to me the power
Is given, and by that right I give it thee.
Aim therefore at no less than all the world,
Aim at the highest; without the highest attained
Will be for thee no sitting, or not long,
On David's throne, be prophesied what will."
    To whom the Son of God unmoved replied.
"Nor doth this grandeur and majestic show   110
Of luxury, though called magnificence,
More than of arms before, allure mine eye,
Much less my mind; though thou should'st add to tell
Their sumptuous gluttonies, and gorgeous feasts
On citron tables or Atlantic stone;
(For I have also heard, perhaps have read)
Their wines of Setia, Cales, and Falerne,
Chios and Crete, and how they quaff in gold,
Crystal and myrrhine cups embossed with gems
And studs of pearl, to me should'st tell who thirst   120
And hunger still. Then embassies thou show'st
From nations far and nigh; what honor that,
But tedious waste of time to sit and hear
So many hollow compliments and lies,
Outlandish flatteries? Then proceed'st to talk
Of the emperor, how easily subdued,
How gloriously; I shall, thou say'st, expel
A brutish monster; what if I withal
Expel a devil who first made him such?

90. **This emperor**, Tiberius, who resigned his power to Sejanus.
115. citrus wood and stone from Mount Atlas.
    116. **perhaps have read.** While it is possible to take expressions like
this as dramatic they find their real explanation in Milton's scholarly unwill-
ingness to commit himself on Christ's learning. Cf. 286–87, below.

Let his tormentor Conscience find him out;   130
For him I was not sent, nor yet to free
That people victor once, now vile and base,
Deservedly made vassal; who once just,
Frugal, and mild, and temperate, conquered well,
But govern ill the nations under yoke,
Peeling their provinces, exhausted all
By lust and rapine; first ambitious grown
Of triumph, that insulting vanity;
Then cruel, by their sports to blood inured
Of fighting beasts, and men to beasts exposed,   140
Luxurious by their wealth, and greedier still,
And from the daily scene effeminate.
What wise and valiant man would seek to free
These thus degenerate, by themselves enslaved,
Or could of inward slaves make outward free?
Know therefore when my season comes to sit
On David's throne, it shall be like a tree
Spreading and overshadowing all the earth,
Or as a stone that shall to pieces dash
All monarchies besides throughout the world,   150
And of my kingdom there shall be no end.
Means there shall be to this, but what the means,
Is not for thee to know, nor me to tell."
　　To whom the Tempter impudent replied.
"I see all offers made by me how slight
Thou valuest, because offered, and reject'st.
Nothing will please the difficult and nice,
Or nothing more than still to contradict.
On the other side know also thou, that I
On what I offer set as high esteem,   160
Nor what I part with mean to give for nought.
All these which in a moment thou behold'st,
The kingdoms of the world to thee I give;
For given to me, I give to whom I please,
No trifle; yet with this reserve, not else,
On this condition, if thou wilt fall down,
And worship me as thy superior lord,
Easily done, and hold them all of me;
For what can less so great a gift deserve?"
　　Whom thus our Savior answered with disdain.   170

　　145. Milton had applied this principle to the Romanized Britons in his
History of Britain and to the English of his own time. The lesson that
spiritual and moral degradation led to political downfall was enforced by
the history of the Hebrews (see above, III, 427 ff., and *Samson Agonistes*,
240 ff.).
　　156. *nice*, overparticular.

"I never liked thy talk, thy offers less;
Now both abhor, since thou hast dared to utter
The abominable terms, impious condition.
But I endure the time, till which expired,
Thou hast permission on me. It is written
The first of all commandments, 'Thou shalt worship
The Lord thy God, and only him shalt serve';
And darest thou to the Son of God propound
To worship thee accurst, now more accurst
For this attempt bolder than that on Eve,   180
And more blasphemous? which expect to rue.
The kingdoms of the world to thee were given,
Permitted rather, and by thee usurped;
Other donation none thou canst produce.
If given, by whom but by the King of kings,
God over all supreme? If given to thee,
By thee how fairly is the Giver now
Repaid? But gratitude in thee is lost
Long since. Wert thou so void of fear or shame
As offer them to me the Son of God,   190
To me my own, on such abhorred pact,
That I fall down and worship thee as God?
Get thee behind me; plain thou now appear'st
That Evil One, Satan for ever damned."
    To whom the Fiend with fear abashed replied.
"Be not so sore offended, Son of God,
Though Sons of God both angels are and men,
If I to try whether in higher sort
Than these thou bear'st that title, have proposed
What both from men and angels I receive,   200
Tetrarchs of Fire, Air, Flood, and on the Earth
Nations besides from all the quartered winds,
God of this world invoked and world beneath;
Who then thou art, whose coming is foretold
To me so fatal, me it most concerns.
The trial hath indamaged thee no way,
Rather more honor left and more esteem;
Me nought advantaged, missing what I aimed.
Therefore let pass, as they are transitory,
The kingdoms of this world; I shall no more   210

193–94. It is interesting that Milton puts Christ's scriptural reply to
Satan's offer of the kingdoms of earth and the glory of them at just this
point. What follows is still a part of the second temptation logically but the
object of enticement is on a higher level, really different in kind, and the
reasons for its rejection less obvious. It is as if Milton were introducing a
more personal and modern problem into the hitherto dramatic representation.

Advise thee; gain them as thou canst, or not.
And thou thyself seem'st otherwise inclined
Than to a worldly crown, addicted more
To contemplation and profound dispute,
As by that early action may be judged,
When slipping from thy mother's eye thou went'st
Alone into the Temple; there wast found
Among the gravest Rabbis disputant
On points and questions fitting Moses' chair,
Teaching not taught; the childhood shows the man,   220
As morning shows the day. Be famous then
By wisdom; as thy empire must extend,
So let extend thy mind o'er all the world,
In knowledge, all things in it comprehend.
All knowledge is not couched in Moses' law,
The Pentateuch or what the Prophets wrote;
The Gentiles also know, and write, and teach
To admiration, led by Nature's light;
And with the Gentiles much thou must converse,
Ruling them by persuasion as thou mean'st,   230
Without their learning, how wilt thou with them,
Or they with thee hold conversation meet?
How wilt thou reason with them, how refute
Their idolisms, traditions, paradoxes?
Error by his own arms is best evinced.
Look once more ere we leave this specular mount
Westward, much nearer by south-west, behold
Where on the Ægean shore a city stands
Built nobly, pure the air, and light the soil,
Athens, the eye of Greece, mother of arts   240
And eloquence, native to famous wits
Or hospitable, in her sweet recess,
City or suburban, studious walks and shades;
See there the olive-grove of Academe,
Plato's retirement, where the Attic bird
Trills her thick-warbled notes the summer long,

235. The early Christians had to decide whether they would or would
not become masters of pagan culture in order to refute the arguments
against the new religion; the problem of resisting the lure of classical studies
for their own sakes, instead as of a means of understanding revealed truth,
continued to present itself even to the humanist. We have seen Milton
troubled by it in *Paradise Lost*, where the claims of pure inquiry are disparaged by the Angel. In *Areopagitica* Milton is an advocate of free intellectual exploration and says that only by studying heresies can heresies be
refuted, exactly Satan's proposition here. It is an open question how much
his attitude has really changed. He never states the issue in a balanced way.

245. **Attic bird,** the nightingale. Milton is recalling a famous chorus in
Sophocles.

There flowery hill Hymettus with the sound
Of bees' industrious murmur oft invites
To studious musing; there Ilissus rolls
His whispering stream; within the walls then view   250
The schools of ancient sages; his who bred
Great Alexander to subdue the world,
Lyceum there, and painted Stoa next.
There thou shalt hear and learn the secret power
Of harmony in tones and numbers hit
By voice or hand, and various-measured verse,
Æolian charms and Dorian lyric odes,
And his who gave them breath, but higher sung,
Blind Melesigenes thence Homer called,
Whose poem Phoebus challenged for his own.   260
Thence what the lofty grave Tragedians taught
In chorus or iambic, teachers best
Of moral prudence, with delight received
In brief sententious precepts, while they treat
Of fate, and chance, and change in human life,
High actions and high passions best describing.
Thence to the famous Orators repair,
Those ancient, whose resistless eloquence
Wielded at will that fierce democraty,
Shook the Arsenal and fulmined over Greece,   270
To Macedon, and Artaxerxes' throne;
To sage Philosophy next lend thine ear,
From heaven descended to the low-roofed house
Of Socrates, see there his tenement,
Whom well inspired the oracle pronounced
Wisest of men; from whose mouth issued forth
Mellifluous streams that watered all the schools
Of Academics old and new, with those
Surnamed Peripatetics, and the sect
Epicurean, and the Stoic severe;   280
These here revolve, or, as thou likest, at home,
Till time mature thee to a kingdom's weight;
These rules will render thee a king complete
Within thyself, much more with empire joined."
    To whom our Savior sagely thus replied.
"Think not but that I know these things, or think
I know them not; not therefore am I short
Of knowing what I ought. He who receives
Light from above, from the Fountain of Light,

276. **wisest of men.** Satan (or Milton) says exactly the right things
about Socrates. The best commentary on this whole passage is a good history of Greek literature and philosophy, or better still the books themselves.

No other doctrine needs, though granted true; 290
But these are false, or little else but dreams,
Conjectures, fancies, built on nothing firm.
The first and wisest of them all professed
To know this only, that he nothing knew;
The next to fabling fell and smooth conceits;
A third sort doubted all things, though plain sense;
Others in virtue placed felicity,
But virtue joined with riches and long life;
In corporal pleasure he, and careless ease;
The Stoic last in philosophic pride, 300
By him called virtue; and his virtuous man,
Wise, perfect in himself, and all possessing
Equal to God, oft shames not to prefer,
As fearing God nor man, contemning all
Wealth, pleasure, pain or torment, death and life,
Which when he lists, he leaves, or boasts he can,
For all his tedious talk is but vain boast,
Or subtle shifts conviction to evade.
Alas what can they teach, and not mislead,
Ignorant of themselves, of God much more, 310
And how the world began, and how Man fell
Degraded by himself, on grace depending?
Much of the Soul they talk, but all awry,
And in themselves seek virtue, and to themselves
All glory arrogate, to God give none,
Rather accuse him under usual names,
Fortune and Fate, as one regardless quite
Of mortal things. Who therefore seeks in these
True wisdom, finds her not, or by delusion
Far worse, her false resemblance only meets, 320
An empty cloud. However, many books
Wise men have said are wearisome; who reads
Incessantly, and to his reading brings not
A spirit and judgment equal or superior,
(And what he brings, what needs he elsewhere seek)
Uncertain and unsettled still remains,

295. **The next**, Plato. Elsewhere Milton shows himself capable of admiring and using the Platonic myths.

296–99. The Pyrrhonists, the Peripatetics (followers of Aristotle), the Epicureans; or perhaps the "he" of 299 is Aristippus, founder of the Cyrenaic school.

310. **ignorant**, etc. Cf. the philosophic speculations of the recreating devils in *Paradise Lost* II, who, while inventing the noblest of moral philosophies to sustain them in their suffering, were without the key of faith and "found no end in wandering mazes lost." Milton's final meditation on this subject is in *Samson Agonistes*, 653 ff.

Deep versed in books and shallow in himself,
Crude or intoxicate, collecting toys,
And trifles for choice matters, worth a sponge,
As children gathering pebbles on the shore.   330
Or if I would delight my private hours
With music or with poem, where so soon
As in our native language can I find
That solace? All our law and story strewed
With hymns, our Psalms with artful terms inscribed,
Our Hebrew songs and harps in Babylon,
That pleased so well our victors' ear, declare
That rather Greece from us these arts derived;
Ill imitated, while they loudest sing
The vices of their deities, and their own,   340
In fable, hymn, or song, so personating
Their gods ridiculous, and themselves past shame.
Remove their swelling epithets thick laid
As varnish on a harlot's cheek, the rest,
Thin sown with aught of profit or delight,
Will far be found unworthy to compare
With Sion's songs, to all true tastes excelling,
Where God is praised aright, and godlike men,
The Holiest of Holies, and his saints;
Such are from God inspired, not such from thee;   350
Unless where moral virtue is expressed
By light of Nature, not in all quite lost.
Their Orators thou then extoll'st, as those
The top of eloquence, statists indeed,
And lovers of their country, as may seem;
But herein to our prophets far beneath,
As men divinely taught, and better teaching
The solid rules of civil government
In their majestic unaffected style
Than all the oratory of Greece and Rome.   360
In them is plainest taught, and easiest learnt,
What makes a nation happy, and keeps it so,
What ruins kingdoms, and lays cities flat;
These only with our Law best form a king."
  So spake the Son of God; but Satan now
Quite at a loss, for all his darts were spent,
Thus to our Savior with stern brow replied.
  "Since neither wealth, nor honor, arms nor arts,
Kingdom nor empire pleases thee, nor aught
By me proposed in life contemplative,   370
Or active, tended on by glory, or fame,
What dost thou in this world? The wilderness

For thee is fittest place; I found thee there,
And thither will return thee. Yet remember
What I foretell thee; soon thou shalt have cause
To wish thou never hadst rejected thus
Nicely or cautiously my offered aid,
Which would have set thee in short time with ease
On David's throne, or throne of all the world,
Now at full age, fulness of time, thy season,　　　　　380
When prophecies of thee are best fulfilled.
Now contrary, if I read aught in heaven,
Or heaven write aught of fate, by what the stars
Voluminous, or single characters
In their conjunction met, give me to spell,
Sorrows, and labors, opposition, hate,
Attends thee, scorns, reproaches, injuries,
Violence and stripes, and lastly cruel death;
A kingdom they portend thee, but what kingdom,
Real or allegoric, I discern not,　　　　　390
Nor when; eternal sure, as without end,
Without beginning; for no date prefixed
Directs me in the starry rubric set."
　So saying he took (for still he knew his power
Not yet expired) and to the wilderness
Brought back the Son of God, and left him there,
Feigning to disappear. Darkness now rose,
As daylight sunk, and brought in louring Night,
Her shadowy offspring, unsubstantial both,
Privation mere of light and absent day.　　　　　400
Our Saviour meek and with untroubled mind
After his airy jaunt, though hurried sore,
Hungry and cold betook him to his rest,
Wherever, under some concourse of shades
Whose branching arms thick intertwined might shield
From dews and damps of night his sheltered head,
But sheltered slept in vain, for at his head
The Tempter watched, and soon with ugly dreams
Disturbed his sleep. And either tropic now
'Gan thunder, and both ends of heaven; the clouds　　　　　410
From many a horrid rift abortive poured
Fierce rain with lightning mixed, water with fire
In ruin reconciled; nor slept the winds

　　393. rubric, words written in red in medieval manuscripts, here specifically title page. Satan reads no date in the prophecy spelled out by the stars.
　　408 ff. Again a dream, but Christ's sleep is disturbed by terrors, not
temptations. The disturbances of nature which fill the night remind us of
those described as following Adam's fall.

Within their stony caves, but rushed abroad
From the four hinges of the world, and fell
On the vexed wilderness, whose tallest pines,
Though rooted deep as high, and sturdiest oaks
Bowed their stiff necks, loaden with stormy blasts,
Or torn up sheer. Ill wast thou shrouded then,
O patient Son of God, yet only stood'st   420
Unshaken; nor yet staid the terror there.
Infernal ghosts, and hellish furies, round
Environed thee; some howled, some yelled, some shrieked,
Some bent at thee their fiery darts, while thou
Sat'st unappalled in calm and sinless peace.
Thus passed the night so foul till Morning fair
Came forth with pilgrim steps in amice gray,
Who with her radiant finger stilled the roar
Of thunder, chased the clouds, and laid the winds
And grisly specters, which the Fiend had raised   430
To tempt the Son of God with terrors dire.
And now the sun with more effectual beams
Had cheered the face of earth, and dried the wet
From drooping plant, or dropping tree; the birds,
Who all things now behold more fresh and green,
After a night of storm so ruinous,
Cleared up their choicest notes in bush and spray
To gratulate the sweet return of morn.
Nor yet amidst this joy and brightest morn
Was absent, after all his mischief done,   440
The Prince of Darkness; glad would also seem
Of this fair change, and to our Saviour came,
Yet with no new device, they all were spent,
Rather by this his last affront resolved,
Desperate of better course, to vent his rage
And mad despite to be so oft repelled.
Him walking on a sunny hill he found,
Backed on the north and west by a thick wood;
Out of the wood he starts in wonted shape,
And in a careless mood thus to him said.   450
    "Fair morning yet betides thee Son of God,
After a dismal night; I heard the wrack
As earth and sky would mingle, but myself
Was distant; and these flaws, though mortals fear them
As dangerous to the pillared frame of Heaven,
Or to the earth's dark basis underneath,
Are to the main as inconsiderable,
And harmless, if not wholesome, as a sneeze
To man's less universe, and soon are gone.

Yet as being oft-times noxious where they light   460
On man, beast, plant, wasteful and turbulent,
Like turbulencies in the affairs of men,
Over whose heads they roar, and seem to point,
They oft fore-signify and threaten ill.
This tempest at this desert most was bent;
Of men at thee, for only thou here dwell'st.
Did I not tell thee, if thou didst reject
The perfect season offered with my aid
To win thy destined seat, but wilt prolong
All to the push of fate, pursue thy way   470
Of gaining David's throne no man knows when,
For both the when and how is nowhere told,
Thou shalt be what thou art ordained, no doubt;
For angels have proclaimed it, but concealing
The time and means: each act is rightliest done,
Not when it must, but when it may be best.
If thou observe not this, be sure to find,
What I foretold thee, many a hard assay
Of dangers, and adversities and pains,
Ere thou of Israel's scepter get fast hold;   480
Whereof this ominous night that closed thee round,
So many terrors, voices, prodigies
May warn thee, as a sure foregoing sign."
    So talked he, while the Son of God went on
And staid not, but in brief him answered thus.
    "Me worse than wet thou find'st not; other harm
Those terrors which thou speak'st of did me none.
I never feared they could, though noising loud
And threatening nigh; what they can do as signs
Betokening or ill-boding I contemn   490
As false portents, not sent from God, but thee;
Who knowing I shall reign past thy preventing,
Obtrudest thy offered aid, that I accepting
At least might seem to hold all power of thee,
Ambitious Spirit, and would'st be thought my God,
And storm'st refused, thinking to terrify
Me to thy will; desist, thou art discerned
And toil'st in vain, nor me in vain molest."
    To whom the Fiend now swollen with rage replied.
"Then hear, O Son of David, virgin-born,   500
For Son of God to me is yet in doubt;
Of the Messiah I have heard foretold

    467 ff. **Did I not tell thee,** etc. Milton loses the thread of the grammar
here. A new sentence beginning in line 477 takes the place of an object
clause.

By all the prophets; of thy birth, at length
Announced by Gabriel, with the first I knew,
And of the angelic song in Bethlehem field,
On thy birth-night, that sung thee Savior born.
From that time seldom have I ceased to eye
Thy infancy, thy childhood, and thy youth,
Thy manhood last, though yet in private bred;
Till at the ford of Jordan whither all   510
Flocked to the Baptist, I among the rest,
Though not to be baptized, by voice from Heaven
Heard thee pronounced the Son of God beloved.
Thenceforth I thought thee worth my nearer view
And narrower scrutiny, that I might learn
In what degree or meaning thou art called
The Son of God, which bears no single sense;
The Son of God I also am, or was,
And if I was, I am; relation stands;
All men are Sons of God; yet thee I thought   520
In some respect far higher so declared.
Therefore I watched thy footsteps from that hour,
And followed thee still on to this waste wild,
Where by all best conjectures I collect
Thou art to be my fatal enemy.
Good reason then, if I beforehand seek
To understand my adversary, who
And what he is; his wisdom, power, intent;
By parle, or composition, truce, or league
To win him, or win from him what I can.   530
And opportunity I here have had
To try thee, sift thee, and confess have found thee
Proof against all temptation as a rock
Of adamant, and as a center, firm
To the utmost of mere man both wise and good,
Not more; for honors, riches, kingdoms, glory
Have been before contemned, and may again;
Therefore to know what more thou art than man,
Worth naming Son of God by voice from Heaven,
Another method I must now begin."   540
    So saying he caught him up, and without wing
Of hippogrif bore through the air sublime
Over the wilderness and o'er the plain,
'Till underneath them fair Jerusalem,
The Holy City lifted high her towers,

538–40. In the first temptation Satan invited Christ to perform a miracle
which might be interpreted as revealing his divinity. Now the test is made
by violence, and the miracle is performed.

And higher yet the glorious Temple reared
Her pile, far off appearing like a mount
Of alabaster, topped with golden spires:
There on the highest pinnacle he set
The Son of God, and added thus in scorn.   550
    "There stand, if thou wilt stand; to stand upright
Will ask thee skill. I to thy Father's house
Have brought thee, and highest placed, highest is best,
Now show thy progeny; if not to stand,
Cast thyself down; safely if Son of God;
For it is written, 'He will give command
Concerning thee to his angels; in their hands
They shall uplift thee, lest at any time
Thou chance to dash thy foot against a stone.'"
    To whom thus Jesus. "Also it is written,   560
'Tempt not the Lord thy God.'" He said, and stood.
But Satan smitten with amazement fell
As when Earth's son Antæus (to compare
Small things with greatest) in Irassa strove
With Jove's Alcides, and oft foiled still rose,
Receiving from his mother Earth new strength,
Fresh from his fall, and fiercer grapple joined,
Throttled at length in the air, expired and fell;
So after many a foil the Tempter proud,
Renewing fresh assaults, amidst his pride   570
Fell whence he stood to see his victor fall.
And as that Theban monster that proposed
Her riddle, and him who solved it, not devoured,
That once found out and solved, for grief and spite
Cast herself headlong from the Ismenian steep,
So strook with dread and anguish fell the Fiend,
And to his crew, that sat consulting, brought
Joyless triumphals of his hoped success,
Ruin, and desperation, and dismay,
Who durst so proudly tempt the Son of God.   580
So Satan fell and straight a fiery globe
Of angels on full sail of wing flew nigh,
Who on their plumy vans received Him soft
From his uneasy station, and upbore

551-52. Milton's interpretation of the scriptural text, making the "pinnacle" a pointed spire, gives a brilliantly dramatic ending. Satan is blind
enough to think that he must either actually fall or invoke his magic power.
Christ makes no effort, and God approves his faith by sustaining him on his
uneasy station till the angels bear him down. Satan's own fall is a final
spiritual defeat, corresponding to his original fall from Heaven. The two
classical similes which follow are a unique instance of this device in *Paradise Regained* and are the more effective for being so.

As on a floating couch through the blithe air,
Then in a flowery valley set him down
On a green bank, and set before him spread
A table of celestial food, divine,
Ambrosial, fruits fetched from the Tree of Life,   590
And from the Fount of Life ambrosial drink,
That soon refreshed him wearied, and repaired
What hunger, if aught hunger had impaired,
Or thirst, and as he fed, angelic choirs
Sung heavenly anthems of his victory
Over temptation and the Tempter proud.
     "True Image of the Father, whether throned
In the bosom of bliss, and light of light
Conceiving, or remote from Heaven, enshrined
In fleshly tabernacle, and human form,   600
Wandering the wilderness, whatever place,
Habit, or state, or motion, still expressing
The Son of God, with Godlike force endued
Against the attempter of thy Father's throne,
And thief of Paradise; him long of old
Thou didst debel, and down from Heaven cast
With all his army; now thou hast avenged
Supplanted Adam, and by vanquishing
Temptation, hast regained lost Paradise,
And frustrated the conquest fraudulent.
He never more henceforth will dare set foot   610
In Paradise to tempt; his snares are broke.
For though that seat of earthly bliss be failed,
A fairer Paradise is founded now
For Adam and his chosen sons, whom thou
A Savior art come down to reinstall;
Where they shall dwell secure, when time shall be
Of tempter and temptation without fear.
But thou, Infernal Serpent, shalt not long
Rule in the clouds; like an autumnal star
Or lightning thou shalt fall from Heaven trod down   620
Under his feet. For proof, ere this thou feel'st
Thy wound, yet not thy last and deadliest wound
By this repulse received, and hold'st in Hell
No triumph; in all her gates Abaddon rues
Thy bold attempt. Hereafter learn with awe
To dread the Son of God: He all unarmed

613. **A fairer Paradise.** This is the Kingdom of Heaven which is in
the heart of the believer, but also the "New Heavens, new earth, ages of
endless date" after Christ's second coming, when Satan shall receive his
"deadliest wound."

Shall chase thee with the terror of his voice
From thy demoniac holds, possession foul,
Thee and thy legions, yelling they shall fly,
And beg to hide them in a herd of swine,   630
Lest he command them down into the Deep,
Bound, and to torment sent before their time.
Hail Son of the Most High, heir of both Worlds,
Queller of Satan, on thy glorious work
Now enter, and begin to save mankind."
     Thus they the Son of God our Saviour meek
Sung victor, and from heavenly feast refreshed
Brought on his way with joy; he unobserved
Home to his mother's house private returned.

SAMSON AGONISTES

INTRODUCTION TO
SAMSON AGONISTES

Milton's first and only tragedy appeared with *Paradise Regained* in 1671. It was the fulfilment of a purpose formed soon after his return from Italy, at which time he set down a list of dramatic subjects in the Cambridge Manuscript. Among these occur the titles "Samson Marrying, or Ramath-Lechi," "Samson Pyrsophorus or Hybristes," "Dagonalia." The last, embodying as it did in retrospect the whole life of the hero, was naturally his final choice. That the figure of Israel's champion continued in his thoughts and began to take on a more than common significance, is shown by allusions in the prose works. In *Areopagitica*, for example, England, filled with energy and righteous zeal, is pictured as "rousing herself like a strong man after sleep and shaking her invincible locks." It was but a step from the identification of his nation with Samson to the identification of himself. The drama thus became an instrument for the expression of old purposes and desires which were now frustrate, and a safe outlet for the residuum of anger, rebelliousness, self-pity, and doubt which were still in him.

The personal parallel is too obvious to be missed even by one only slightly acquainted with Milton's life. Samson had been appointed by God to scourge his enemies and free Israel from the heathen yoke. He had accomplished great deeds which his supine countrymen had failed to turn to their advantage. He had made an unwise marriage. He suffered from the affliction of blindness. His cause was lost, and he himself, deprived of power, was a captive and an object of daily insult by his foes. In all this Milton could easily read his own career and fate. But there is more to it than this. Milton had reacted sharply against the suggestion that his own blindness was a punishment for sin.[1] In reply he had declared it to be a mark

[1] Milton insisted in *The Second Defense* that such a suggestion had been made by the author of *The Cry of the Royal Blood* in 1652, the only

547

of consecration, carrying with it a special gift of insight and giving him the sense of enjoying God's favor in an unusual degree. In these respects Samson's experience, after his fall, is the exact opposite of Milton's and the poet makes the point explicitly. The drama becomes, therefore, an additional commentary on his own case. It is as if he were saying, "How horrible would my blindness be if inner light put forth no visual beam." One wonders, however, whether Milton's security was quite all that his words imply. It is hard to believe that he was never a prey to fear or to the sense of guilt. The soul-searchings and the protestations themselves tell another story. It is no wonder that *Samson Agonistes* should seem to bring us closer to the real Milton than any of the preceding works. The mighty struggle of the spirit which is the heart of the poet's experience of life is the dominating motive of the drama.

The narrative source of Milton's drama is the biblical account of Samson in Judg. 13–16. Milton has embodied in one way or another pretty much the whole story, but he has transformed the main character from a half comic, folklore type to a tragic hero and has made his career a new and memorable illustration of God's ways with man. Samson appears first before us in extreme lassitude and depression. His mind runs bitterly over the contrast between the promise of his birth and the melancholy state into which he has fallen. He stifles a murmur against Providence and lets his attention dwell upon his blindness until his utterance becomes a cry of woe. The Chorus of timid Hebrews echoes his lament and blames him for Israel's misfortune. Samson resists the imputation of sole responsibility for the failure of his nation to seize the deliverance which his deeds had offered. The visit of Manoa awakes another inward grief, but Samson clear-sightedly reviews the past and, while admitting that his weakness has brought honor to Dagon and renewed distrust to Israel, voices the conviction that God will yet assert himself in triumph over those who have dared to enter the lists against him. To all proposals for his own relief he turns a deaf ear. The will to action is not yet roused in him. The third episode carries further the testing of Samson's mind and will. Dalila's repentant blandishments are met with implacable hostility, and Samson

ground for this idea being the chance application to Milton of Virgil's description of Polyphemus, *"monstrum, horrendum, informe, ingens, cui lumen ademptum,"* together with the general abuse.

proves to himself that he is free from her influence forever. He is now ready to defy Harapha, the giant sent to threaten him. The conflict of words produces a new consciousness of returning force, and the order of the Philistines to be present at their festival is accepted as an opportunity provided by God for the fulfilment of a purpose as yet dark. Samson has been brought from passivity to resolution. By confronting his own sin and proving firm against the suggestions of sensuality and fear, he has won again God's favor and has only to entrust himself to the inspiration of the hour. Manoa is misguided in his endeavor to procure his ransom. Samson knows that the preservation of his life is not a part of the divine plan. When his final act is accomplished, Manoa and the Hebrews see that all is best, and the drama ends in the combined emotions of tragic pity and religious exaltation.

So interpreted, *Samson Agonistes* marches steadily toward its goal. It is hardly true, as Johnson said, that it has a beginning and an end but no middle. There is both an inner and an outward conflict. Samson's first antagonist is represented by the Hebrews, Manoa and Dalila, who, whether by design or not, endeavor to weaken his self-confidence and induce him to choose the path of personal escape. The less dangerous opposition is the external one of the Philistines. The judgment has been made that *Samson Agonistes* is not genuine tragedy because Providence and not Fate dominates the action. This is true, yet there remains the unresolved sense of human waste in Samson's suffering and death. Though we see and assent to the operation of the divine will, we cannot understand why it should crush the individual in the working out of its design. The spectacle that lives with us is that of Samson or of Milton, pitted against visible and invisible foes, and manifesting by indomitable energy the greatness of the human spirit.

In dramatic method *Samson Agonistes* is Greek, and Milton proudly invites comparisons with ancient tragedy. The work is, first of all, he implies, effective in producing the Aristotelian catharsis. His own experience in writing it, as already analyzed, must have supported him in this conviction. Samson's thoughts are described as an inner ulcer. He is relieved through utterance and action. The "calm of mind all passion spent" of the close is the fruit of the experience for actors, audience, and author alike.

In the interpretation of tragic character Milton is again guided by classic precept and example. Samson is Aristotle's great man, essentially good, but possessed of a weakness which explains his downfall. The poet even represents his error as *hybris*, the pride and self-will which provokes the anger of the gods.

> But I *God's* counsel have not kept, his holy secret
> Presumptuously have published, impiously,
> Weakly at least and shamefully—a sin.
> That Gentiles in their parables condemn
> To their Abyss and horrid pains confined.
>
> Fearless of danger, like a petty god
> I walked about.

The sacred unities are consistently maintained. The action is confined to a single day and place, the Chorus remaining on the stage throughout. Samson leaves the scene to perform his final feat of strength and the catastrophe is reported by a messenger. It is possible to divide the drama into five acts. The first would include lines 1–331, the dialogue between Samson and the Chorus; the second, lines 331–724, the visit of Manoa; the third, lines 724–1061, the visit of Dalila; the fourth, lines 1061–1308, the visit of Harapha, and as scene ii, lines 1308–1444, the coming of the officer and the departure of Samson; the fifth, lines 1444–1758, Manoa's return and the messenger's narrative. Milton himself would have preferred to use in the analysis of his tragedy the terms employed by the Greeks themselves. Thus we have (1) prologue, consisting of the opening speech of Samson, (2) a parodos, or entering song of the Chorus, (3) four episodes, marked off by stasima or chants by the Chorus when stationary, (4) an exode, including the final episode and chorus. We may also recognize the so-called lyric dialogues between the protagonist and the Chorus, and lyric songs by the protagonist.

The Chorus is employed by Milton in the Greek fashion, to comment on the action and to enrich its background by references to the past. Its utterances reflect the changing emotion of the drama, passing from despondency and disappointment, through agonized sympathy and philosophic contemplation of the state of man, to hopefulness and triumph. It also, as we have seen, plays the part of an actor. Milton's success in thus vitalizing an ancient device is unique in the history of classical imitation and marks the completeness with which he had assimilated the spirit of Greek drama. There was no need for him to adopt the artificial divisions of strophe, antistrophe, and epode, "a kind of stanza framed only for music," and he wisely left himself free to suit the lyric form to the variations of idea and mood.

What Milton says in the preface about the plot is not very definite. The qualities which he aimed at and achieved are simplicity, dignity, proportion, naturalness, coherence. The characters are fewer than in modern dramas. There is no sub-plot and no "intermixing of comic stuff with tragic." The two individual Greek dramas which come closest to *Samson Agonistes* in idea and plan are the *Deianira* and the *Oedipus at Colonus* of Sophocles. Heracles in the first of these is, like Samson, a strong man, performer of incredible labors, en-thralled by a woman. Oedipus is desolated by blindness and catastrophe and obliged to endure the blandishments and threats of his enemy. The development of the plot by a suc-cession of visits perhaps suggested this method to Milton, for there is nothing of the kind in Scripture.

The style of *Samson Agonistes* in the dialogue portions is even plainer than that of *Paradise Regained*, but it is always dignified and impressive. Milton never breaks into the natural dramatic expression of the Elizabethans, as he sometimes does in *Comus*. The more exciting passages, as for example the an-nouncement of Samson's death, lines 1539–70, are phrased in the artificial Greek manner. The long speeches are not, however, mere philosophic recitations but direct expressions of personality and emotion. It is not appropriate to say that Milton is without the power of dramatic utterance, but rather that he deliberately adopts the classic manner as appropriate to the lofty artistic effect at which he aims. The lyric passages, whether in the mouth of Samson or the Chorus, are truly marvellous both in style and rhythm. No English poet has risen to such heights in the expression of that tragic sense of life in which the individual becomes a type of humanity wrestling with an inexplicable and overwhelming fate. As the emotion rises, the rhythm becomes turbulent and irregular. Milton never quite writes free verse, but he goes as far as it is possible to go without wholly losing the iambic pattern:

> O dark, dark, dark, amid the blaze of noon,
> Irrecoverably dark, total eclipse,
> Without all hope of day.

The suggestions of Greek lyric measures are present in his mind, though not slavishly imitated. We may note, as an example of the effectiveness with which he employs his freedom, the first part of the opening chorus, lines 115–134. The trochaic measures of the first two short lines yield to long sweeping iambics, quickened here and there by trochees, anapests, and dactyls, or slowed down by spondees. Equally remarkable is the paragraph beginning with line 652, where there is no such sensational manipulation of sound, but an even flow of rhythm as the philosophic reflection is carried steadily through a single complicated sentence. Greek and Hebrew elements unite in the language of *Samson Agonistes* as in the content and feeling. The combination may perhaps best be illustrated by the antiphonal choric song beginning in line 1669.

Milton probably had no expectation that *Samson Agonistes* would ever be performed. He says in the Preface that it was not intended for the stage, yet it represents exactly what he had in his first enthusiasm for service hoped to substitute for the artistically and morally inferior public entertainment of his own time.

SAMSON AGONISTES [2]

OF THAT SORT OF DRAMATIC POEM WHICH

IS CALLED TRAGEDY

Tragedy, as it was anciently composed, hath been ever held the gravest, moralest, and most profitable of all other poems; therefore said by Aristotle to be of power, by raising pity and fear, or terror, to purge the mind [3] of those and such-like passions; that is, to tem-

---

[2] **Samson Agonistes.** Literally, the adjective means "contestant in athletic games," the reference being to Samson's final role as performer of feats of strength at the public festival of the Philistines. In the context of the drama itself the term has a multiple suggestiveness. Samson's wrestling, his agony of effort, is not with the pillars of the temple alone; and he is "champion" in a larger sense than that of being able to outdo the rival strong man: "All the contest is now twixt God and Dagon."

[3] **to purge the mind.** This is the classic statement in English of Aristotle's psychological formula for the effect of tragedy. The homeopathic analogy, in which Milton was anticipated by the Italian critic Minturno,

per and reduce them to just measure with a kind of delight, stirred up by reading or seeing those passions well imitated. Nor is Nature wanting in her own effects to make good his assertion; for so in physic things of melancholic hue and quality are used against melancholy, sour against sour, salt to remove salt humours. Hence philosophers and other gravest writers, as Cicero, Plutarch, and others, frequently cite out of tragic poets, both to adorn and illustrate their discourse. The Apostle Paul himself thought it not unworthy to insert a verse of Euripides into the text of Holy Scripture, I Cor. xv. 33; and Paræus, commenting on the Revelation, divides the whole book as a tragedy, into acts, distinguished each by a Chorus of heavenly harpings and song between. Heretofore men in highest dignity have labored not a little to be thought able to compose a tragedy. Of that honor Dionysius the elder was no less ambitious than before of his attaining to the tyranny. Augustus Cæsar also had begun his *Ajax,* but unable to please his own judgment with what he had begun, left it unfinished. Seneca the philosopher is by some thought the author of those tragedies (at least the best of them) that go under that name. Gregory Nazianzen, a Father of the Church, thought it not unbeseeming the sanctity of his person to write a tragedy, which he entitled *Christ Suffering.* This is mentioned to vindicate Tragedy from the small esteem, or rather infamy, which in the account of many it undergoes at this day, with other common interludes; happening through the poet's error of intermixing comic stuff with tragic sadness and gravity; or introducing trivial and vulgar persons: which by all judicious hath been counted absurd, and brought in without discretion, corruptly to gratify the people. And though ancient Tragedy use no Prologue, yet using sometimes, in case of self-defence, or explanation, that which Martial calls an Epistle; in behalf of this tragedy, coming forth after the ancient manner,[4] much different from what among us passes for best, thus much beforehand may be epistled: that Chorus is here introduced after the Greek

almost certainly points the way to what Aristotle meant, or ought to have meant. The difficulty of incorporating such a principle in the general theory of tragedy, as expressed in this Preface, is obvious. How is the delight of seeing the passions well imitated related to the emotional identification demanded by the theory of like curing like? Milton raises basic aesthetic questions but by no means solves them. As he proceeds he seems to be content to accept "gravest, moralest and most profitable" in the conventional sense of Satan's characterization of the tragedians in *Paradise Regained* as "teachers best of moral prudence, with delight received."

[4] *after the ancient manner.* Milton touches on the essential points of superiority claimed by Renaissance criticism of classical as opposed to modern drama: (1) purity of genre, violated by the mixture of comic and tragic; (2) decorum in the dramatis personae, violated by the portrayal of common men; (3) concentration of action and unity of time; (4) the use of chorus.

manner, not ancient only but modern, and still in use among the Italians. In the modelling therefore of this poem, with good reason, the Ancients and Italians are rather followed, as of much more authority and fame. The measure of verse used in the Chorus is of all sorts, called by the Greeks *Monostrophic*,[5] or rather *Apolelymenon*, without regard had to Strophe, Antistrophe, or Epode, which were a kind of stanzas framed only for the music, then used with the Chorus that sung; not essential to the poem, and therefore not material; or, being divided into stanzas or pauses, they may be called *Allæostropha*. Division into act and scene, referring chiefly to the stage (to which this work never was intended), is here omitted.

It suffices if the whole drama be found not produced beyond the fifth act. Of the style and uniformity, and that commonly called the plot, whether intricate or explicit, which is nothing indeed but such economy, or disposition of the fable, as may stand best with verisimilitude and decorum; they only will best judge who are not unacquainted with Æschylus, Sophocles, and Euripides, the three tragic poets unequalled yet by any, and the best rule to all who endeavor to write Tragedy. The circumscription of time wherein the whole drama begins and ends, is, according to ancient rule, and best example, within the space of twenty-four hours.

THE ARGUMENT [6]

Samson, made captive, blind, and now in the prison at Gaza, there to labor as in a common workhouse, on a festival day, in the general cessation from labor, comes forth into the open air, to a place nigh, somewhat retired, there to sit a while and bemoan his condition. Where he happens at length to be visited by certain friends and equals of his tribe, which make the Chorus, who seek to comfort him what they can; then by his old father, Manoa, who endeavors the like, and withal tells him his purpose to procure his liberty by ransom; lastly, that this feast was proclaimed by the Philistines as a day of thanksgiving for their deliverance from the hands of Samson, which yet more troubles him. Manoa then

---

[5] **Monostrophic, apolelymenon, allæostropha.** Milton is apologizing for not following the usual pattern of a tragic chorus, with its strophe, antistrophe, and epode, repeated three times in an identical pattern. He says we can consider each chorus as one long stanza or divide it into a succession of stanzas without recurrence. *Apolelymenon* means "loosened," i.e., not confined to a regular form.

[6] **The Argument.** The crucial steps in the action are clearly indicated: Manoa "tells him his purpose to secure his liberty"; Samson first refuses the officer who summons him, "at length persuaded inwardly he yields to go with him"; Manoa returns full of joyful hope; a Hebrew relates what Samson has done.

departs to prosecute his endeavor with the Philistian lords for Samson's redemption; who in the meanwhile is visited by other persons; and lastly by a public officer to require his coming to the feast before the lords and people, to play or show his strength in their presence. He at first refuses, dismissing the public officer with absolute denial to come; at length persuaded inwardly that this was from God, he yields to go along with him, who came now the second time with great threatenings to fetch him. The Chorus yet remaining on the place, Manoa returns full of joyful hope to procure ere long his son's deliverance; in the midst of which discourse an Ebrew comes in haste, confusedly at first, and afterward more distinctly relating the catastrophe, what Samson had done to the Philistines, and by accident to himself; wherewith the tragedy ends.

THE PERSONS

SAMSON.
MANOA, the father of Samson.
DALILA, his wife.
HARAPHA of Gath.
PUBLIC OFFICER.
MESSENGER.
CHORUS OF DANITES.

The Scene, before the Prison in Gaza.

Samson. A little onward lend thy guiding hand
To these dark steps, a little further on;
For yonder bank hath choice of sun or shade;
There I am wont to sit, when any chance
Relieves me from my task of servile toil,
Daily in the common prison else enjoined me,
Where I a prisoner chained, scarce freely draw
The air imprisoned also, close and damp,
Unwholesome draught. But here I feel amends,
The breath of heaven fresh-blowing, pure and sweet,   10
With day-spring born; here leave me to respire.
This day a solemn feast the people hold
To Dagon their sea-idol, and forbid
Laborious works, unwillingly this rest
Their superstition yields me; hence with leave

13. **a solemn feast.** Judg. 16:23. Since Milton uses or refers to almost every incident in the life of Samson as narrated in Judges specific biblical references will not hereafter be given in the notes. See Introduction p. 548 for a general discussion of Milton's treatment of the material.

Retiring from the popular noise, I seek
This unfrequented place to find some ease,
Ease to the body some, none to the mind
From restless thoughts, that like a deadly swarm
Of hornets armed, no sooner found alone,   20
But rush upon me thronging, and present
Times past, what once I was, and what am now.
Oh wherefore was my birth from Heaven foretold
Twice by an angel, who at last in sight
Of both my parents all in flames ascended
From off the altar, where an offering burned,
As in a fiery column charioting
His godlike presence, and from some great act
Or benefit revealed to Abraham's race?
Why was my breeding ordered and prescribed   30
As of a person separate to God,
Designed for great exploits; if I must die
Betrayed, captived, and both my eyes put out,
Made of my enemies the scorn and gaze;
To grind in brazen fetters under task
With this heaven-gifted strength? O glorious strength
Put to the labor of a beast, debased
Lower than bond-slave! Promise was that I
Should Israel from Philistian yoke deliver;
Ask for this great deliverer now, and find him   40
Eyeless in Gaza at the mill with slaves,
Himself in bonds under Philistian yoke;
Yet stay, let me not rashly call in doubt
Divine prediction; what if all foretold
Had been fulfilled but through mine own default,
Whom have I to complain of but myself?
Who this high gift of strength committed to me,
In what part lodged, how easily bereft me,
Under the seal of silence could not keep,
But weakly to a woman must reveal it,   50
O'ercome with importunity and tears.
O impotence of mind, in body strong!
But what is strength without a double share
Of wisdom, vast, unwieldy, burdensome,
Proudly secure, yet liable to fall
By weakest subtleties, not made to rule,
But to subserve where wisdom bears command.

33. **captived.** Here, as in Milton's only other use of captive as a verb
(*Samson Agonistes*, 684), the accent is on the second syllable.
47-49. The sense is "who could not keep the secret of where this gift
was lodged and how easily it could be taken away."

God, when he gave me strength, to show withal
How slight the gift was, hung it in my hair.
But peace, I must not quarrel with the will   60
Of highest dispensation, which herein
Haply had ends above my reach to know:
Suffices that to me strength is my bane,
And proves the source of all my miseries;
So many, and so huge, that each apart
Would ask a life to wail, but chief of all,
O loss of sight, of thee I most complain!
Blind among enemies, O worse than chains,
Dungeon, or beggary, or decrepit age!
Light, the prime work of God, to me is extinct,   70
And all her various objects of delight
Annulled, which might in part my grief have eased,
Inferior to the vilest now become
Of man or worm; the vilest here excel me,
They creep, yet see, I dark in light exposed
To daily fraud, contempt, abuse and wrong,
Within doors, or without, still as a fool,
In power of others, never in my own;
Scarce half I seem to live, dead more than half.
O dark, dark, dark, amid the blaze of noon,   80
Irrecoverably dark, total eclipse
Without all hope of day!
O first-created beam, and thou great Word,
"Let there be light, and light was over all;"
Why am I thus bereaved thy prime decree
The Sun to me is dark
And silent as the Moon,
When she deserts the night
Hid in her vacant interlunar cave.
Since light so necessary is to life,   90
And almost life itself, if it be true
That light is in the soul,
She all in every part, why was the sight
To such a tender ball as the eye confined?
So obvious and so easy to be quenched,
And not as feeling through all parts diffused,
That she might look at will through every pore?
Then had I not been thus exiled from light;
As in the land of darkness yet in light,

74–79. The grammar is fluid and Milton's punctuation makes it more so.
81. The line may be scanned with five accents: "Írrecóverably dárk, tótal eclípse." However, we soon meet lines which obviously exceed this number, e.g., 145, 157, etc.

To live a life half dead, a living death,   100
And buried; but O yet more miserable!
Myself, my sepulchre, a moving grave,
Buried, yet not exempt
By privilege of death and burial
From worst of other evils, pains and wrongs,
But made hereby obnoxious more
To all the miseries of life,
Life in captivity
Among inhuman foes.
But who are these? for with joint pace I hear   110
The tread of many feet steering this way;
Perhaps my enemies who come to stare
At my affliction, and perhaps to insult,
Their daily practice to afflict me more.
      Chorus. This, this is he; softly a while,
Let us not break in upon him;
O change beyond report, thought, or belief!
See how he lies at random, carelessly diffused,
With languished head unpropt,
As one past hope, abandoned,   120
And by himself given over:
In slavish habit, ill-fitted weeds
O'er-worn and soiled;
Or do my eyes misrepresent? Can this be he,
That heroic, that renowned,
Irresistible Samson? whom unarmed
No strength of man, or fiercest wild beast could withstand;
Who tore the lion, as the lion tears the kid,
Ran on embattled armies clad in iron,
And weaponless himself,   130
Made arms ridiculous, useless the forgery
Of brazen shield and spear, the hammered cuirass,
Chalybean-tempered steel, and frock of mail
Adamantean proof;
But safest he who stood aloof,
When insupportably his foot advanced,
In scorn of their proud arms and warlike tools,

      106. **obnoxious,** exposed to injury.
      116. This line is trochaic throughout. No other chorus goes to the lengths of this one in illustration of Milton's statement in his preface that the verse is "of all sorts." But even here the prevailing pattern is iambic.
      134-35. Rhyme occurs occasionally in short lines, as here. Note that these short lines are usually either trimeter or tetrameter. Line 123 has only two accents. The irregularity is made somewhat less than it appears to be to the eye by the fact that successive lines of 3 or 4 beats often go together to make a longer rhythmic unit.

Spurned them to death by troops. The bold Ascalonite
Fled from his lion ramp, old warriors turned
Their plated backs under his heel;   140
Or groveling soiled their crested helmets in the dust.
Then with what trivial weapon came to hand,
The jaw of a dead ass, his sword of bone,
A thousand foreskins fell, the flower of Palestine,
In Ramath-lechi famous to this day;
Then by main force pulled up, and on his shoulders bore
The gates of Azza, post and massy bar
Up to the hill by Hebron, seat of giants old,
No journey of a sabbath-day, and loaded so;
Like whom the Gentiles feign to bear up Heaven.   150
Which shall I first bewail,
Thy bondage or lost sight,
Prison within prison
Inseparably dark?
Thou art become (O worst imprisonment!)
The dungeon of thyself; thy soul
(Which men enjoying sight oft without cause complain)
Imprisoned now indeed,
In real darkness of the body dwells,
Shut up from outward light   160
To incorporate with gloomy night;
For inward light alas
Puts forth no visual beam.
O mirror of our fickle state,
Since man on earth unparalleled!
The rarer thy example stands,
By how much from the top of wondrous glory,
Strongest of mortal men,
To lowest pitch of abject fortune thou art fallen.
For him I reckon not in high estate   170
Whom long descent of birth
Or the sphere of fortune raises;
But thee whose strength, while virtue was her mate
Might have subdued the Earth,
Universally crowned with highest praises.
    Sams. I hear the sound of words, their sense the air
Dissolves unjointed ere it reach my ear.
    Chor. He speaks, let us draw nigh. Matchless in might,
The glory late of Israel, now the grief;
We come thy friends and neighbors not unknown   180
From Eshtaol and Zora's fruitful vale
To visit or bewail thee, or if better,
Counsel or consolation we may bring,

Salve to thy sores, apt words have power to swage
The tumors of a troubled mind,
And are as balm to festered wounds.
   Sams. Your coming, friends, revives me, for I learn
Now of my own experience, not by talk,
How counterfeit a coin they are who "friends"
Bear in their superscription (of the most   190
I would be understood). In prosperous days
They swarm, but in adverse withdraw their head
Not to be found, though sought. Ye see, O friends,
How many evils have enclosed me round;
Yet that which was the worst now least afflicts me,
Blindness, for had I sight, confused with shame,
How could I once look up, or heave the head,
Who like a foolish pilot have shipwrecked
My vessel trusted to me from above,
Gloriously rigged; and for a word, a tear,   200
Fool, have divulged the secret gift of God
To a deceitful woman. Tell me friends,
Am I not sung and proverbed for a fool
In every street, do they not say, "How well
Are come upon him his deserts"? Yet why?
Immeasurable strength they might behold
In me, of wisdom nothing more than mean;
This with the other should, at least, have paired,
These two proportioned ill drove me transverse.
   Chor. Tax not divine disposal, wisest men   210
Have erred, and by bad women been deceived;
And shall again, pretend they ne'er so wise.
Deject not then so overmuch thyself,
Who hast of sorrow thy full load besides;
Yet truth to say, I oft have heard men wonder
Why thou shouldst wed Philistian women rather
Than of thine own tribe fairer, or as fair,
At least of thy own nation, and as noble.
   Sams. The first I saw at Timna, and she pleased
Me, not my parents, that I sought to wed,   220
The daughter of an infidel: they knew not
That what I motioned was of God; I knew
From intimate impulse, and therefore urged

209 ff. Samson is rebuked by the Chorus, as Adam was by Raphael (*Paradise Lost* VIII, 561), for blaming his weakness on an ill proportion in his nature. But they themselves find it difficult to reconcile the idea of his God-appointed championship with his deviations in marriage. Samson himself is very sure that he once enjoyed God's special favor. The problem of the drama is whether, after experiencing God's chastisement and fully acknowledging his own guilt, he will recover it.

The marriage on; that by occasion hence
I might begin Israel's deliverance,
The work to which I was divinely called;
She proving false, the next I took to wife
(O that I never had; fond wish too late!)
Was in the vale of Sorec, Dalila,
That specious monster, my accomplished snare.   230
I thought it lawful from my former act,
And the same end; still watching to oppress
Israel's oppressors. Of what now I suffer
She was not the prime cause, but I myself,
Who vanquished with a peal of words (O weakness!)
Gave up my fort of silence to a woman.
    Chor. In seeking just occasion to provoke
The Philistine, thy country's enemy,
Thou never wast remiss, I bear thee witness:
Yet Israel still serves with all his sons.   240
    Sams. That fault I take not on me, but transfer
On Israel's governors and heads of tribes,
Who seeing those great acts which God had done
Singly by me against their conquerors
Acknowledged not, or not at all considered
Deliverance offered; I on the other side
Used no ambition to commend my deeds,
The deeds themselves, though mute, spoke loud the doer;
But they persisted deaf, and would not seem
To count them things worth notice, till at length   250
Their lords the Philistines with gathered powers
Entered Judea seeking me, who then
Safe to the rock of Etham was retired,
Not flying, but forecasting in what place
To set upon them, what advantage best;
Meanwhile the men of Judah to prevent
The harass of their land, beset me round;
I willingly on some conditions came
Into their hands, and they as gladly yield me
To the uncircumcised a welcome prey,   260
Bound with two cords; but cords to me were threads
Touched with the flame: on their whole host I flew
Unarmed, and with a trivial weapon felled
Their choicest youth; they only lived who fled.
Had Judah that day joined, or one whole tribe,
They had by this possessed the towers of Gath,
And lorded over them whom now they serve;
But what more oft in nations grown corrupt,
And by their vices brought to servitude,

Than to love bondage more than liberty,   270
Bondage with ease than strenuous liberty;
And to despise, or envy, or suspect
Whom God hath of his special favor raised
As their deliverer; if he aught begin,
How frequent to desert him, and at last
To heap ingratitude on worthiest deeds?
    Chor. Thy words to my remembrance bring
How Succoth and the fort of Penuel
Their great deliverer contemned,
The matchless Gideon in pursuit   280
Of Madian and her vanquished kings:
And how ingrateful Ephraim
Had dealt with Jephtha, who by argument,
Not worse than by his shield and spear,
Defended Israel from the Ammonite,
Had not his prowess quelled their pride
In that sore battle when so many died
Without reprieve adjudged to death,
For want of well pronouncing *Shibboleth.*
    Sams. Of such examples add me to the roll;   290
Me easily indeed mine may neglect,
But God's proposed deliverance not so.
    Chor. Just are the ways of God,
And justifiable to men;
Unless there be who think not God at all:
If any be, they walk obscure;
For of such doctrine never was there school,
But the heart of the fool,
And no man therein doctor but himself.
    Yet more there be who doubt his ways not just,   300
As to his own edicts, found contradicting,
Then give the reins to wandering thought,
Regardless of his glory's diminution;
Till by their own perplexities involved
They ravel more, still less resolved,
But never find self-satisfying solution.

278 ff. For these incidents see Judg. 8, 11.
298. "The fool hath said in his heart, There is no God." Ps. 14:1.
300. doubt, fear. The Arminian modification of Calvinistic theology
was designed to preserve God's justice, which seemed imperiled by the strict
doctrine of predestination. Calvinists, on the other hand, feared the diminution of God's glory in any limitation of his power by man's free will. Milton
tended to treat these problems simply and was impatient with the more
intricate speculations on either side, taking his stand on the Bible texts. It
was the devils in Hell who first perplexed themselves and "found no end in
wandering mazes lost."

As if they would confine the interminable,
And tie him to his own prescript,
Who made our laws to bind us, not himself,
And hath full right to exempt   310
Whomso it pleases him by choice
From national obstriction, without taint
Of sin, or legal debt;
For with his own laws he can best dispense.
　　He would not else who never wanted means,
Nor in respect of the enemy just cause
To set his people free,
Have prompted this heroic Nazarite,
Against his vow of strictest purity,
To seek in marriage that fallacious bride,   320
Unclean, unchaste.
　　Down Reason then, at least vain reasoning down,
Though Reason here aver
That moral verdict quits her of unclean:
Unchaste was subsequent, her stain not his.
　　But see here comes thy revered sire
With careful step, locks white as down,
Old Manoa: advise
Forthwith how thou ought'st to receive him.
　　Sams. Ay me, another inward grief awaked,   330
With mention of that name renews the assault.
　　Manoa. Brethren and men of Dan, for such ye seem,
Though in this uncouth place; if old respect,
As I suppose, towards your once gloried friend,
My son now captive, hither hath informed
Your younger feet, while mine cast back with age
Came lagging after; say if he be here.
　　Chor. As signal now in low dejected state,
As erst in highest, behold him where he lies.
　　Man. O miserable change! is this the man,   340
That invincible Samson, far renowned,
The dread of Israel's foes, who with a strength
Equivalent to angels' walked their streets,
None offering fight; who single combatant
Duelled their armies ranked in proud array,
Himself an army, now unequal match
To save himself against a coward armed
At one spear's length? O ever-failing trust

314. It was a congenial thought with Milton that God might grant a
dispensation from the letter of the law to an individual who came to know
his will "by intimate impulse," and this, in Samson's case, even before the
great abrogation of the law under Christ.

In mortal strength! and oh what not in man
Deceivable and vain! Nay what thing good   350
Prayed for, but often proves our woe, our bane?
I prayed for children, and thought barrenness
In wedlock a reproach; I gained a son,
And such a son as all men hailed me happy:
Who would be now a father in my stead?
O wherefore did God grant me my request,
And as a blessing with such pomp adorned?
Why are his gifts desirable, to tempt
Our earnest prayers, then given with solemn hand
As graces, draw a scorpion's tail behind?   360
For this did the angel twice descend? for this
Ordained thy nurture holy, as of a plant;
Select and sacred, glorious for a while,
The miracle of men: then in an hour
Ensnared, assaulted, overcome, led bound,
Thy foes' derision, captive, poor, and blind,
Into a dungeon thrust, to work with slaves?
Alas, methinks whom God hath chosen once
To worthiest deeds, if he through frailty err,
He should not so o'erwhelm, and as a thrall   370
Subject him to so foul indignities,
Be it but for honor's sake of former deeds.
   Sams. Appoint not heavenly disposition, father,
Nothing of all these evils hath befallen me
But justly; I myself have brought them on,
Sole author I, sole cause: if aught seem vile,
As vile hath been my folly, who have profaned
The mystery of God given me under pledge
Of vow, and have betrayed it to a woman,
A Canaanite, my faithless enemy.   380
This well I knew, nor was at all surprised,
But warned by oft experience: did not she
Of Timna first betray me, and reveal
The secret wrested from me in her height
Of nuptial love professed, carrying it straight
To them who had corrupted her, my spies,

373. **appoint not,** do not attempt to prescribe, do not quarrel with. It is now Samson who rebukes a murmur against the apparent injustice of God's ways to man. Manoa's doubts and fears are a heavy burden on Samson's faith, including, as they do, skepticism as to the rightness of choices which his son feels to have been made under divine guidance. He is motivated to seek release for Samson by the thought that Samson may destroy himself and by a scruple as to his serving the Philistines with the strength that was given him to annoy them (lines 577 ff.), as well as by natural pity for his son's distress.

And rivals? In this other was there found
More faith? who also in her prime of love,
Spousal embraces, vitiated with gold,
Though offered only, by the scent conceived   390
Her spurious first-born; treason against me?
Thrice she assayed with flattering prayers and sighs,
And amorous reproaches to win from me
My capital secret, in what part my strength
Lay stored, in what part summed, that she might know:
Thrice I deluded her, and turned to sport
Her importunity, each time perceiving
How openly, and with what impudence
She purposed to betray me, and (which was worse
Than undissembled hate) with what contempt   400
She sought to make me traitor to myself;
Yet the fourth time, when mustering all her wiles,
With blandished parleys, feminine assaults,
Tongue-batteries, she surceased not day nor night
To storm me over-watched, and wearied out
At times when men seek most repose and rest,
I yielded, and unlocked her all my heart,
Who with a grain of manhood well resolved
Might easily have shook off all her snares;
But foul effeminacy held me yoked   410
Her bond-slave; O indignity, O blot
To honor and religion! servile mind
Rewarded well with servile punishment!
The base degree to which I now am fallen,
These rags, this grinding, is not yet so base
As was my former servitude, ignoble,
Unmanly, ignominious, infamous,
True slavery, and that blindness worse than this,
That saw not how degenerately I served.
  Man. I cannot praise thy marriage choices, son,   420
Rather approved them not; but thou didst plead
Divine impulsion prompting how thou might'st
Find some occasion to infest our foes.
I state not that; this I am sure; our foes
Found soon occasion thereby to make thee
Their captive, and their triumph; thou the sooner
Temptation found'st, or over-potent charms
To violate the sacred trust of silence
Deposited within thee; which to have kept
Tacit, was in thy power; true; and thou bear'st   430
Enough, and more, the burden of that fault;

     424. **state not**, make no statement about.

Bitterly hast thou paid, and still art paying
That rigid score. A worse thing yet remains,
This day the Philistines a popular feast
Here celebrate in Gaza; and proclaim
Great pomp, and sacrifice, and praises loud
To Dagon, as their god who hath delivered
Thee Samson bound and blind into their hands,
Them out of thine, who slew'st them many a slain.
So Dagon shall be magnified, and God,   440
Besides whom is no god, compared with idols,
Disglorified, blasphemed, and had in scorn
By the idolatrous rout amidst their wine;
Which to have come to pass by means of thee,
Samson, of all thy sufferings think the heaviest,
Of all reproach the most with shame that ever
Could have befallen thee and thy father's house.
    Sams. Father, I do acknowledge and confess
That I this honor, I this pomp have brought
To Dagon, and advanced his praises high   450
Among the heathen round; to God have brought
Dishonor, obloquy, and oped the mouths
Of idolists and atheists; have brought scandal
To Israel, diffidence of God, and doubt
In feeble hearts, propense enough before
To waver, or fall off and join with idols;
Which is my chief affliction, shame and sorrow,
The anguish of my soul, that suffers not
Mine eye to harbor sleep, or thoughts to rest.
This only hope relieves me, that the strife   460
With me hath end; all the contest is now
'Twixt God and Dagon; Dagon hath presumed,
Me overthrown, to enter lists with God,
His deity comparing and preferring
Before the God of Abraham. He, be sure,
Will not connive, or linger, thus provoked,
But will arise and his great name assert:
Dagon must stoop, and shall ere long receive
Such a discomfit, as shall quite despoil him
Of all these boasted trophies won on me,   470
And with confusion blank his worshippers.
    Man. With cause this hope relieves thee, and these words
I as a prophecy receive; for God,
Nothing more certain, will not long defer
To vindicate the glory of his name
Against all competition, nor will long

    455. propense, having a propensity, inclined.

Endure it, doubtful whether God be Lord,
Or Dagon. But for thee what shall be done?
Thou must not in the mean while here forgot
Lie in this miserable loathsome plight   480
Neglected. I already have made way
To some Philistian lords, with whom to treat
About thy ransom: well they may by this
Have satisfied their utmost of revenge;
By pains and slaveries, worse than death inflicted
On thee, who now no more canst do them harm.

   Sams. Spare that proposal, father, spare the trouble
Of that solicitation; let me here,
As I deserve, pay on my punishment;
And expiate, if possible, my crime,   490
Shameful garrulity. To have revealed
Secrets of men, the secrets of a friend,
How heinous had the fact been, how deserving
Contempt and scorn of all, to be excluded
All friendship, and avoided as a blab,
The mark of fool set on his front! But I
God's counsel have not kept, his holy secret
Presumptuously have published, impiously,
Weakly at least, and shamefully: a sin
That Gentiles in their parables condemn   500
To their Abyss and horrid pains confined.

   Man. Be penitent, and for thy fault contrite,
But act not in thy own affliction, son,
Repent the sin, but if the punishment
Thou canst avoid, self-preservation bids;
Or the execution leave to high disposal,
And let another hand, not thine, exact
Thy penal forfeit from thyself; perhaps
God will relent, and quit thee all his debt;
Who ever more approves and more accepts   510
(Best pleased with humble and filial submission)
Him who imploring mercy sues for life,
Than who self-rigorous chooses death as due;
Which argues over-just, and self-displeased
For self-offence, more than for God offended.
Reject not then what offered means, who knows
But God hath set before us, to return thee
Home to thy country and his sacred house,
Where thou may'st bring thy offerings, to avert

    500. Tantalus, son of Jupiter, was punished for betraying the secrets of
the gods and otherwise abusing their trust. The impiety and presumption
of his acts do not exactly fit Samson, hence the "weakly at least."

His further ire, with prayers and vows renewed.   520
  Sams. His pardon I implore; but as for life,
To what end should I seek it? When in strength
All mortals I excelled, and great in hopes
With youthful courage and magnanimous thoughts
Of birth from Heaven foretold and high exploits,
Full of divine instinct, after some proof
Of acts indeed heroic, far beyond
The sons of Anak, famous now and blazed,
Fearless of danger, like a petty god
I walked about admired of all and dreaded   530
On hostile ground, none daring my affront.
Then swollen with pride into the snare I fell
Of fair fallacious looks, venereal trains,
Softened with pleasure and voluptuous life
At length to lay my head and hallowed pledge
Of all my strength in the lascivious lap
Of a deceitful concubine who shore me
Like a tame wether, all my precious fleece,
Then turned me out ridiculous, despoiled,
Shaven, and disarmed among my enemies.   540
  Chor. Desire of wine and all delicious drinks,
Which many a famous warrior overturns,
Thou could'st repress, nor did the dancing ruby
Sparkling out-poured, the flavor, or the smell,
Or taste that cheers the heart of gods and men,
Allure thee from the cool crystalline stream.
  Sams. Wherever fountain or fresh current flowed
Against the eastern ray, translucent, pure
With touch ethereal of Heaven's fiery rod,
I drank, from the clear milky juice allaying   550
Thirst, and refreshed; nor envied them the grape
Whose heads that turbulent liquor fills with fumes.
  Chor. O madness, to think use of strongest wines
And strongest drinks our chief support of health,
When God with these forbidden made choice to rear
His mighty champion, strong above compare,
Whose drink was only from the liquid brook.
  Sams. But what availed this temperance, not complete
Against another object more enticing?
What boots it at one gate to make defence,   560

  528. sons of Anak, the giants mentioned in Num. 13:33, alluded to in
line 148 above.
  529. like a petty God. Samson describes his behavior in terms of the
Greek *hybris,* the arrogant pride of mortals who have forgotten their true
position with relation to the gods.
  533. trains, allurements.

And at another to let in the foe
Effeminately vanquished? by which means,
Now blind, disheartened, shamed, dishonored, quelled,
To what can I be useful, wherein serve
My nation, and the work from Heaven imposed,
But to sit idle on the household hearth,
A burdenous drone; to visitants a gaze,
Or pitied object; these redundant locks
Robustious to no purpose, clustering down,
Vain monument of strength; till length of years   570
And sedentary numbness craze my limbs
To a contemptible old age obscure.
Here rather let me drudge and earn my bread,
Till vermin or the draff of servile food
Consume me, and oft-invocated death
Hasten the welcome end of all my pains.
  Man. Wilt thou then serve the Philistines with that gift
Which was expressly given thee to annoy them?
Better at home lie bed-rid, not only idle,
Inglorious, unemployed, with age outworn.   580
But God who caused a fountain at thy prayer
From the dry ground to spring, thy thirst to allay
After the brunt of battle, can as easy
Cause light again within thy eyes to spring,
Wherewith to serve him better than thou hast;
And I persuade me so; why else this strength
Miraculous yet remaining in those locks?
His might continues in thee not for nought,
Nor shall his wondrous gifts be frustrate thus.
  Sams. All otherwise to me my thoughts portend,   590
That these dark orbs no more shall treat with light,
Nor the other light of life continue long,
But yield to double darkness nigh at hand:
So much I feel my genial spirits droop,
My hopes all flat; Nature within me seems
In all her functions weary of herself;
My race of glory run, and race of shame,
And I shall shortly be with them that rest.
  Man. Believe not these suggestions which proceed
From anguish of the mind and humors black,   600

594. **genial**, innate, natural.
600. **humors black**, i.e., melancholy, literally black bile, one of the four humors the unbalance of which was supposed to produce disease. Manoa's reference to the physical cause of Samson's mental distress gives rise to the imagery of his next speech. From this analysis of painful and injurious emotion we understand more fully what Milton meant by his interpretation of Aristotle's catharsis in the Preface.

That mingle with thy fancy. I however
Must not omit a father's timely care
To prosecute the means of thy deliverance
By ransom or how else: meanwhile be calm,
And healing words from these thy friends admit.

   Sams. O that torment should not be confined
To the body's wounds and sores
With maladies innumerable
In heart, head, breast, and reins;
But must secret passage find   610
To the inmost mind,
There exercise all his fierce accidents,
And on her purest spirits prey,
As on entrails, joints, and limbs,
With answerable pains, but more intense,
Though void of corporal sense.
   My griefs not only pain me
As a lingering disease,
But finding no redress, ferment and rage,
Nor less than wounds immedicable   620
Rankle, and fester, and gangrene,
To black mortification.
Thoughts my tormentors armed with deadly stings
Mangle my apprehensive tenderest parts,
Exasperate, exulcerate, and raise
Dire inflammation which no cooling herb
Or medicinal liquor can asswage,
Nor breath of vernal air from snowy Alp.
Sleep hath forsook and given me o'er
To death's benumbing opium as my only cure.   630
Thence faintings, swoonings of despair,
And sense of Heaven's desertion.
   I was his nursling once and choice delight,
His destined from the womb,
Promised by heavenly message twice descending.
Under his special eye
Abstemious I grew up and thrived amain;
He led me on to mightiest deeds
Above the nerve of mortal arm
Against the uncircumcised, our enemies.   640
But now hath cast me off as never known,
And to those cruel enemies,
Whom I by his appointment had provoked,
Left me all helpless with the irreparable loss

   612. his fierce accidents. The antecedent of **his** is torment. **accidents** means properties or concomitants.

Of sight, reserved alive to be repeated
The subject of their cruelty or scorn.
Nor am I in the list of them that hope;
Hopeless are all my evils, all remediless;
This one prayer yet remains, might I be heard,
No long petition, speedy death,   650
The close of all my miseries, and the balm.
   Chor. Many are the sayings of the wise
In ancient and in modern books enrolled;
Extolling patience as the truest fortitude;
And to the bearing well of all calamities,
All chances incident to man's frail life
Consolatories writ
With studied argument, and much persuasion sought,
Lenient of grief and anxious thought,
But with the afflicted in his pangs their sound   660
Little prevails, or rather seems a tune,
Harsh, and of dissonant mood from his complaint
Unless he feel within
Some source of consolation from above;
Secret refreshings that repair his strength,
And fainting spirits uphold.
   God of our fathers, what is man!
That thou towards him with hand so various,
Or might I say contrarious,
Temperest thy providence through his short course,   670
Not evenly, as thou rulest
The angelic orders and inferior creatures mute,
Irrational and brute.
Nor do I name of men the common rout,
That wandering loose about
Grow up and perish, as the summer fly,
Heads without name, no more remembered,
But such as thou hast solemnly elected,
With gifts and graces eminently adorned
To some great work, thy glory,   680
And people's safety, which in part they effect;
Yet toward these thus dignified, thou oft
Amidst their height of noon,

678. **solemnly elected.** Here and elsewhere Milton uses the term
"elect," not in the Calvinistic sense of those predestined to salvation but of
those whom God has chosen as special recipients of his favor. He tells us in
Christian Doctrine (I, iv) that grace, which is given to all men sufficiently
for salvation, is not given to all in equal measure. And see *Paradise Lost,*
III, 183-4:

                Some have I chosen of peculiar grace
                Elect above the rest; so is my will.

Changest thy countenance and thy hand, with no regard
Of highest favors past
From thee on them, or them to thee of service.
   Nor only dost degrade them, or remit
To life obscured, which were a fair dismission,
But throw'st them lower than thou didst exalt them high,
Unseemly falls in human eye,   690
Too grievous for the trespass or omission,
Oft leavest them to the hostile sword
Of heathen and profane, their carcasses
To dogs and fowls a prey, or else captived,
Or to the unjust tribunals, under change of times,
And condemnation of the ingrateful multitude.
If these they scape, perhaps in poverty
With sickness and disease thou bow'st them down,
Painful diseases and deformed,
In crude old age;   700
Though not disordinate, yet causeless suffering
The punishment of dissolute days, in fine,
Just or unjust, alike seem miserable,
For oft alike, both come to evil end.
   So deal not with this once thy glorious champion,
The image of thy strength, and mightier minister.
What do I beg? how hast thou dealt already?
Behold him in this state calamitous, and turn
His labors, for thou canst, to peaceful end.
   But who is this? what thing of sea or land?   710
Female of sex it seems,
That so bedecked, ornate, and gay,
Comes this way sailing
Like a stately ship
Of Tarsus, bound for the isles
Of Javan or Gadire

691. Milton has in mind Aristotle's description of the tragic hero as a
good great man who has some flaw of character which leads to his downfall.
The sense of tragedy arises from the disproportion between the error and its
consequences. It is inevitable that we should be reminded that Milton himself had witnessed reversals of fortune of a tragic magnitude at the Restoration of the Stuarts. The following lines suggest the execution of men like
Sir Henry Vane, the indignities suffered by the bodies of Cromwell and
other leaders of the Commonwealth, and finally his own lapse into comparative poverty and deforming gout.
   701-2. **disordinate**, intemperate. **the punishment of dissolute days,**
i.e., the sicknesses which are ordinarily the result of dissipation.
   703. Note that it is the Chorus and not Samson who says this. In spite
of the unrelieved misery of his preceding speech no such expression escapes
him. We have reached the darkest point in the drama, but Samson is spir-
itually prepared for the external trials which follow.

With all her bravery on, and tackle trim,
Sails filled, and streamers waving,
Courted by all the winds that hold them play,
An amber scent of odorous perfume   720
Her harbinger, a damsel train behind;
Some rich Philistian matron she may seem,
And now at nearer view, no other certain
Than Dalila thy wife.
    Sams. My wife, my traitress, let her not come near me.
    Chor. Yet on she moves, now stands and eyes thee fixed,
About to have spoke, but now, with head declined
Like a fair flower surcharged with dew, she weeps,
And words addressed seem into tears dissolved,
Wetting the borders of her silken veil;   730
But now again she makes address to speak.
    Dal. With doubtful feet and wavering resolution
I came, still dreading thy displeasure, Samson,
Which to have merited, without excuse,
I cannot but acknowledge; yet if tears
May expiate (though the fact more evil drew
In the perverse event than I foresaw)
My penance hath not slackened, though my pardon
No way assured. But conjugal affection
Prevailing over fear and timorous doubt   740
Hath led me on desirous to behold
Once more thy face, and know of thy estate.
If aught in my ability may serve
To lighten what thou suffer'st, and appease
Thy mind with what amends is in my power,
Though late, yet in some part to recompense
My rash but more unfortunate misdeed.
    Sams. Out, out, hyæna; these are thy wonted arts,
And arts of every woman false like thee,
To break all faith, all vows, deceive, betray,   750
Then as repentant to submit, beseech,
And reconcilement move with feigned remorse,
Confess, and promise wonders in her change,
Not truly penitent, but chief to try
Her husband, how far urged his patience bears,
His virtue or weakness which way to assail;
Then with more cautious and instructed skill
Again transgresses, and again submits;
That wisest and best men, full oft beguiled,
With goodness principled not to reject   760
The penitent, but ever to forgive,
Are drawn to wear out miserable days,

Entangled with a poisonous bosom snake,
If not by quick destruction soon cut off
As I by thee, to ages an example.
    Dal. Yet hear me Samson; not that I endeavor
To lessen or extenuate my offence,
But that on the other side if it be weighed
By itself, with aggravations not surcharged,
Or else with just allowance counterpoised,   770
I may, if possible, thy pardon find
The easier towards me, or thy hatred less.
First, granting, as I do, it was a weakness
In me, but incident to all our sex,
Curiosity, inquisitive, importune
Of secrets, then with like infirmity
To publish them, both common female faults;
Was it not weakness also to make known
For importunity, that is for nought,
Wherein consisted all thy strength and safety?   780
To what I did thou show'dst me first the way.
But I to enemies revealed, and should not.
Nor should'st thou have trusted that to woman's frailty:
Ere I to thee, thou to thyself wast cruel.
Let weakness then with weakness come to parle,
So near related, or the same of kind,
Thine forgive mine that men may censure thine
The gentler, if severely thou exact not
More strength from me, than in thyself was found.
And what if love, which thou interpret'st hate,   790
The jealousy of love, powerful of sway
In human hearts, nor less in mine towards thee,
Caused what I did? I saw thee mutable
Of fancy, feared lest one day thou would'st leave me
As her at Timna, sought by all means therefore
How to endear, and hold thee to me firmest:
No better way I saw than by importuning
To learn thy secrets, get into my power
Thy key of strength and safety. Thou wilt say,
'Why then revealed?' I was assured by those   800
Who tempted me, that nothing was designed
Against thee but safe custody and hold:
That made for me; I knew that liberty
Would draw thee forth to perilous enterprises,
While I at home sat full of cares and fears,
Wailing thy absence in my widowed bed;
Here I should still enjoy thee day and night
Mine and love's prisoner, not the Philistines',

Whole to myself, unhazarded abroad,
Fearless at home of partners in my love.   810
These reasons in love's law have passed for good,
Though fond and reasonless to some perhaps;
And love hath oft, well meaning, wrought much woe,
Yet always pity or pardon hath obtained.
Be not unlike all others, not austere
As thou art strong, inflexible as steel.
If thou in strength all mortals dost exceed,
In uncompassionate anger do not so.
 Sams. How cunningly the sorceress displays
Her own transgressions, to upbraid me mine!   820
That malice not repentance brought thee hither,
By this appears: I gave, thou say'st, the example,
I led the way; bitter reproach, but true,
I to myself was false ere thou to me,
Such pardon therefore as I give my folly,
Take to thy wicked deed; which when thou seest
Impartial, self-severe, inexorable,
Thou wilt renounce thy seeking, and much rather
Confess it feigned; weakness is thy excuse,
And I believe it, weakness to resist   830
Philistian gold; if weakness may excuse,
What murderer, what traitor, parricide,
Incestuous, sacrilegious, but may plead it?
All wickedness is weakness: that plea therefore
With God or man will gain thee no remission.
But love constrained thee; call it furious rage
To satisfy thy lust: love seeks to have love;
My love how could'st thou hope, who took'st the way
To raise in me inexpiable hate,
Knowing, as needs I must, by thee betrayed?   840
In vain thou strivest to cover shame with shame,
Or by evasions thy crime uncover'st more.
 Dal. Since thou determin'st weakness for no plea
In man or woman, though to thy own condemning,
Hear what assaults I had, what snares besides,
What sieges girt me round, ere I consented;
Which might have awed the best-resolved of men,
The constantest, to have yielded without blame.
It was not gold, as to my charge thou lay'st,
'That wrought with me: thou know'st the magistrates   850
And princes of my country came in person,
Solicited, commanded, threatened, urged,
Adjured by all the bonds of civil duty
And of religion, pressed how just it was,

How honorable, how glorious to entrap
A common enemy, who had destroyed
Such numbers of our nation: and the priest
Was not behind, but ever at my ear,
Preaching how meritorious with the gods
It would be to ensnare an irreligious   860
Dishonorer of Dagon. What had I
To oppose against such powerful arguments?
Only my love of thee held long debate;
And combated in silence all these reasons
With hard contest. At length, that grounded maxim
So rife and celebrated in the mouths
Of wisest men, that to the public good
Private respects must yield, with grave authority
Took full possession of me and prevailed;
Virtue, as I thought, truth, duty so enjoining.   870
  Sams. I thought where all thy circling wiles would end;
In feigned religion, smooth hypocrisy.
But had thy love, still odiously pretended,
Been, as it ought, sincere, it would have taught thee
Far other reasonings, brought forth other deeds.
I before all the daughters of my tribe
And of my nation chose thee from among
My enemies, loved thee, as too well thou knew'st,
Too well, unbosomed all my secrets to thee,
Not out of levity, but overpowered   880
By thy request, who could deny thee nothing;
Yet now am judged an enemy. Why then
Didst thou at first receive me for thy husband?
Then, as since then, my country's foe professed?
Being once a wife, for me thou wast to leave
Parents and country; nor was I their subject,
Nor under their protection, but my own,
Thou mine, not theirs. If aught against my life
Thy country sought of thee, it sought unjustly,
Against the law of nature, law of nations,   890
No more thy country, but an impious crew
Of men conspiring to uphold their state
By worse than hostile deeds, violating the ends
For which our country is a name so dear;
Not therefore to be obeyed. But zeal moved thee;
To please thy gods thou didst it; gods unable
To acquit themselves and prosecute their foes
But by ungodly deeds, the contradiction
Of their own deity, gods cannot be:
Less therefore to be pleased, obeyed, or feared.   900

These false pretexts and varnished colors failing,
Bare in thy guilt how foul must thou appear?
   Dal. In argument with men a woman ever
Goes by the worse, whatever be her cause.
   Sams. For want of words, no doubt, or lack of breath,
Witness when I was worried with thy peals.
   Dal. I was a fool, too rash, and quite mistaken
In what I thought would have succeeded best.
Let me obtain forgiveness of thee, Samson;
Afford me place to show what recompense   910
Towards thee I intend for what I have misdone,
Misguided; only what remains past cure
Bear not too sensibly, nor still insist
To afflict thyself in vain. Though sight be lost,
Life yet hath many solaces, enjoyed
Where other senses want not their delights
At home in leisure and domestic ease,
Exempt from many a care and chance to which
Eyesight exposes daily men abroad.
I to the lords will intercede, not doubting   920
Their favorable ear, that I may fetch thee
From forth this loathsome prison-house, to abide
With me, where my redoubled love and care
With nursing diligence, to me glad office,
May ever tend about thee to old age
With all things grateful cheered, and so supplied,
That what by me thou hast lost thou least shall miss.
   Sams. No, no, of my condition take no care;
It fits not; thou and I long since are twain;
Nor think me so unwary or accurst   930
To bring my feet again into the snare
Where once I have been caught; I know thy trains
Though dearly to my cost, thy gins, and toils;
Thy fair enchanted cup, and warbling charms
No more on me have power, their force is nulled,
So much of adder's wisdom I have learned
To fence my ear against thy sorceries.
If in my flower of youth and strength, when all men
Loved, honored, feared me, thou alone could hate me
Thy husband, slight me, sell me, and forgo me;   940

   928 ff. The momentary softening of Samson's tone as he rejects Dalila's
kindly proposal is as subtle as it is moving. His quick reaction against her
physical approach (line 952) and his forgiveness of her "at distance" show
Milton at his dramatic best. In the whole dialogue Dalila's psychology
seems less intelligible than Samson's. The portrayal is remarkably in contrast to that of Eve in *Paradise Lost,* where we seem to have no difficulty in
following all the complications of thought and feeling.

How would'st thou use me now, blind, and thereby
Deceivable, in most things as a child
Helpless, hence easily contemned, and scorned,
And last neglected! How would'st thou insult
When I must live uxorious to thy will
In perfect thraldom, how again betray me,
Bearing my words and doings to the lords
To gloss upon, and censuring, frown or smile!
This jail I count the house of liberty
To thine whose doors my feet shall never enter.   950
    Dal. Let me approach at least, and touch thy hand.
    Sams. Not for thy life, lest fierce remembrance wake
My sudden rage to tear thee joint by joint.
At distance I forgive thee, go with that;
Bewail thy falsehood, and the pious works
It hath brought forth to make thee memorable
Among illustrious women, faithful wives;
Cherish thy hastened widowhood with the gold
Of matrimonial treason: so farewell.
    Dal. I see thou art implacable, more deaf   960
To prayers than winds and seas, yet winds to seas
Are reconciled at length, and sea to shore:
Thy anger, unappeasable, still rages,
Eternal tempest never to be calmed.
Why do I humble thus myself, and suing
For peace, reap nothing but repulse and hate?
Bid go with evil omen and the brand
Of infamy upon my name denounced?
To mix with thy concernments I desist
Henceforth, nor too much disapprove my own.   970
Fame if not double-faced is double-mouthed,
And with contrary blast proclaims most deeds,
On both his wings, one black, the other white,
Bears greatest names in his wild airy flight.
My name perhaps among the circumcised
In Dan, in Judah, and the bordering tribes,
To all posterity may stand defamed,
With malediction mentioned, and the blot
Of falsehood most unconjugal traduced.
But in my country where I most desire,   980
In Ecron, Gaza, Asdod, and in Gath
I shall be named among the famousest
Of women, sung at solemn festivals,
Living and dead recorded, who to save
Her country from a fierce destroyer, chose
Above the faith of wedlock bands, my tomb

With odors visited and annual flowers.
Not less renowned than in Mount Ephraim,
Jael, who with inhospitable guile
Smote Sisera sleeping through the temples nailed.   990
Nor shall I count it heinous to enjoy
The public marks of honor and reward
Conferred upon me, for the piety
Which to my country I was judged to have shown.
At this whoever envies or repines
I leave him to his lot, and like my own.
    Chor. She's gone, a manifest serpent by her sting
Discovered in the end, till now concealed.
    Sams. So let her go, God sent her to debase me,
And aggravate my folly who committed   1000
To such a viper his most sacred trust
Of secrecy, my safety, and my life.
    Chor. Yet beauty, though injurious, hath strange power,
After offence returning, to regain
Love once possessed, nor can be easily
Repulsed, without much inward passion felt
And secret sting of amorous remorse.
    Sams. Love quarrels oft in pleasing concord end,
Not wedlock treachery endangering life.
    Chor. It is not virtue, wisdom, valor, wit,   1010
Strength, comeliness of shape, or amplest merit
That woman's love can win or long inherit;
But what it is, hard is to say,
Harder to hit,
(Which way soever men refer it)
Much like thy riddle, Samson, in one day
Or seven, though one should musing sit;
    If any of these or all, the Timnian bride
Had not so soon preferred
Thy paranymph, worthless to thee compared,   1020

989. Jael. See Judg. 4:15–21.
    1000. **aggravate my folly,** etc., i.e., to show my folly in a worse light
by making Dalila reveal her worthlessness. Her motivation in coming to
visit Samson would therefore be, like his own in going to the Philistine
feast, "of God." But this formula does not prevent speculation as to why,
in human terms, she did come to him.
    1003. The choric comment suggests that Samson's firmness has been
undergoing a kind of trial. Has he really at last learned his lesson, as he
had not learned it from the faithlessness of the woman of Timnath?
    1010 ff. Milton is too fond of giving voice to such sentiments for us to
believe, as some critics would have us, that they are purely conventional or
dramatic.
    1020. **paranymph,** groomsman, the friend to whom Samson's first wife
was given.

Successor in thy bed,
Nor both so loosely disallied
Their nuptials, nor this last so treacherously
Had shorn the fatal harvest of thy head.
Is it for that such outward ornament
Was lavished on their sex, that inward gifts
Were left for haste unfinished, judgment scant,
Capacity not raised to apprehend
Or value what is best
In choice, but oftest to affect the wrong?   1030
Or was too much of self-love mixed,
Of constancy no root infixed,
That either they love nothing, or not long?
   Whate'er it be, to wisest men and best
Seeming at first all heavenly under virgin veil,
Soft, modest, meek, demure,
Once joined, the contrary she proves, a thorn
Intestine, far within defensive arms
A cleaving mischief, in his way to virtue
Adverse and turbulent, or by her charms   1040
Draws him awry, enslaved
With dotage, and his sense depraved
To folly and shameful deeds which ruin ends.
What pilot so expert but needs must wreck
Embarked with such a steers-mate at the helm?
   Favored of Heaven who finds
One virtuous, rarely found,
That in domestic good combines!
Happy that house! his way to peace is smooth;
But virtue which breaks through all opposition,   1050
And all temptation can remove,
Most shines and most is acceptable above.
   Therefore God's universal law
Gave to the man despotic power
Over his female in due awe,
Nor from that right to part an hour,
Smile she or lour:
So shall he least confusion draw
On his whole life, not swayed
By female usurpation, nor dismayed.   1060
   But had we best retire? I see a storm.
   Sams. Fair days have oft contracted wind and rain.
   Chor. But this another kind of tempest brings.

1022. **both,** both the Timnian bride and Dalila.
1053 ff. The biblical texts for man's authority over woman in St. Paul
(I Tim. 2:12 and Eph. 5:22–23) lack the harshness of this utterance.

Sams. Be less abstruse, my riddling days are past.
Chor. Look now for no enchanting voice, nor fear
The bait of honeyed words; a rougher tongue
Draws hitherward, I know him by his stride,
The giant Harapha of Gath, his look
Haughty, as is his pile high-built and proud.
Comes he in peace? What wind hath blown him hither   1070
I less conjecture than when first I saw
The sumptuous Dalila floating this way;
His habit carries peace, his brow defiance.
Sams. Or peace or not, alike to me he comes.
Chor. His fraught we soon shall know, he now arrives.
Harapha. I come not Samson, to condole thy chance,
As these perhaps, yet wish it had not been,
Though for no friendly intent. I am of Gath,
Men call me Harapha, of stock renowned
As Og or Anak and the Emims old   1080
That Kiriathaim held, thou knowest me now
If thou at all art known. Much I have heard
Of thy prodigious might and feats performed
Incredible to me, in this displeased,
That I was never present on the place
Of those encounters where we might have tried
Each other's force in camp or listed field:
And now am come to see of whom such noise
Hath walked about, and each limb to survey,
If thy appearance answer loud report.   1090
Sams. The way to know were not to see, but taste.
Har. Dost thou already single me; I thought
Gyves and the mill had tamed thee; O that fortune
Had brought me to the field where thou art famed
To have wrought such wonders with an ass's jaw;
I should have forced thee soon wish other arms,
Or left thy carcass where the ass lay thrown:
So had the glory of prowess been recovered
To Palestine, won by a Philistine
From the unforeskinned race, of whom thou bear'st   1100
The highest name for valiant acts, that honor
Certain to have won by mortal duel from thee,
I lose, prevented by thy eyes put out.
Sams. Boast not of what thou would'st have done, but do
What then thou would'st, thou seest it in thy hand.
Har. To combat with a blind man I disdain,
And thou hast need much washing to be touched.
Sams. Such usage as your honorable lords
Afford me assassinated and betrayed,

Who durst not with their whole united powers   1110
In fight withstand me single and unarmed,
Nor in the house with chamber ambushes
Close-banded durst attack me, no not sleeping,
Till they had hired a woman with their gold
Breaking her marriage faith, to circumvent me.
Therefore without feigned shifts let be assigned
Some narrow place enclosed, where sight may give thee,
Or rather flight, no great advantage on me;
Then put on all thy gorgeous arms, thy helmet
And brigandine of brass, thy broad habergeon,   1120
Vant-brace and greaves, and gauntlet, add thy spear
A weaver's beam, and seven-times-folded shield,
I only with an oaken staff will meet thee,
And raise such outcries on thy clattered iron,
Which long shall not withhold me from thy head,
That in a little time while breath remains thee,
Thou oft shalt wish thyself at Gath to boast
Again in safety what thou would'st have done
To Samson, but shalt never see Gath more.
    Har. Thou durst not thus disparage glorious arms   1130
Which greatest heroes have in battle worn,
Their ornament and safety, had not spells
And black enchantments, some magician's art
Armed thee or charmed thee strong, which thou from Heaven
Feignedst at thy birth was given thee in thy hair,
Where strength can least abide, though all thy hairs
Were bristles ranged like those that ridge the back
Of chafed wild boars, or ruffled porcupines.
    Sams. I know no spells, use no forbidden arts;
My trust is in the living God who gave me   1140
At my nativity this strength, diffused
No less through all my sinews, joints and bones,
Than thine, while I preserved these locks unshorn,
The pledge of my unviolated vow.
For proof hereof, if Dagon be thy god,
Go to his temple, invoke his aid
With solemnest devotion, spread before him
How highly it concerns his glory now
To frustrate and dissolve these magic spells,
Which I to be the power of Israel's God   1150
Avow, and challenge Dagon to the test,
Offering to combat thee, his champion bold,
With the utmost of his godhead seconded:
Then thou shalt see, or rather to thy sorrow
Soon feel, whose God is strongest, thine or mine.

Har. Presume not on thy God, whate'er he be;
Thee he regards not, owns not, hath cut off
Quite from his people, and delivered up
Into thy enemies' hand, permitted them
To put out both thine eyes, and fettered send thee   1160
Into the common prison, there to grind
Among the slaves and asses thy comrades,
As good for nothing else, no better service
With those thy boisterous locks, no worthy match
For valor to assail, nor by the sword
Of noble warrior, so to stain his honor,
But by the barber's razor best subdued.
   Sams. All these indignities, for such they are
From thine, these evils I deserve and more,
Acknowledge them from God inflicted on me   1170
Justly, yet despair not of his final pardon
Whose ear is ever open and his eye
Gracious to re-admit the suppliant;
In confidence whereof I once again
Defy thee to the trial of mortal fight,
By combat to decide whose god is God,
Thine or whom I with Israel's sons adore.
   Har. Fair honor that thou dost thy god, in trusting
He will accept thee to defend his cause,
A murderer, a revolter, and a robber.   1180
   Sams. Tongue-doughty giant, how dost thou prove me these?
   Har. Is not thy nation subject to our lords?
Their magistrates confessed it, when they took thee
As a league-breaker and delivered bound
Into our hands: for hadst thou not committed
Notorious murder on those thirty men
At Ascalon, who never did thee harm,
Then like a robber, stripp'dst them of their robes?
The Philistines, when thou hadst broke the league,
Went up with armëd powers thee only seeking,   1190
To others did no violence nor spoil.
   Sams. Among the daughters of the Philistines
I chose a wife, which argued me no foe;
And in your city held my nuptial feast;
But your ill-meaning politician lords,
Under pretence of bridal friends and guests,
Appointed to await me thirty spies,
Who threatening cruel death constrained the bride
To wring from me and tell to them my secret,
That solved the riddle which I had proposed.   1200
When I perceived all set on enmity,

As on my enemies, wherever chanced,
I used hostility, and took their spoil
To pay my underminers in their coin.
My nation was subjected to your lords.
It was the force of conquest; force with force
Is well ejected when the conquered can.
But I a private person, whom my country
As a league-breaker gave up bound, presumed
Single rebellion and did hostile acts.   1210
I was no private but a person raised
With strength sufficient and command from Heaven
To free my country; if their servile minds
Me their deliverer sent would not receive,
But to their masters gave me up for nought,
The unworthier they; whence to this day they serve.
I was to do my part from Heaven assigned,
And had performed it if my known offence
Had not disabled me, not all your force.
These shifts refuted, answer thy appellant   1220
Though by his blindness maimed for high attempts,
Who now defies thee thrice to single fight,
As a petty enterprise of small enforce.
    Har. With thee a man condemned, a slave enrolled,
Due by the law to capital punishment?
To fight with thee no man of arms will deign.
    Sams. Cam'st thou for this, vain boaster, to survey me,
To descant on my strength, and give thy verdict?
Come nearer, part not hence so slight informed;
But take good heed my hand survey not thee.   1230
    Har. O Baal-zebub! can my ears unused
Hear these dishonors, and not render death?
    Sams. No man withholds thee, nothing from thy hand
Fear I incurable; bring up thy van,
My heels are fettered, but my fist is free.
    Har. This insolence other kind of answer fits.
    Sams. Go baffled coward, lest I run upon thee,
Though in these chains, bulk without spirit vast,
And with one buffet lay thy structure low,
Or swing thee in the air, then dash thee down   1240
To the hazard of thy brains and shattered sides.

1207-10. Samson is phrasing the indictment against him. No question is
raised in the biblical account of the lawfulness of Samson's violent deeds.
Anything done against the Philistines was right. The substance of his
justification is clearly enough suggested: "Thou hast given this great deliverance into the hand of thy servant." But nothing is said of the failure
of the Hebrews to take advantage of his deeds.

Har. By Astaroth ere long thou shalt lament
These braveries in irons loaden on thee.
  Chor. His giantship is gone somewhat crest-fallen,
Stalking with less unconscionable strides,
And lower looks, but in a sultry chafe.
  Sams. I dread him not, nor all his giant brood,
Though fame divulge him father of five sons,
All of gigantic size, Goliah chief.
  Chor. He will directly to the lords, I fear,   1250
And with malicious counsel stir them up
Some way or other yet further to afflict thee.
  Sams. He must allege some cause, and offered fight
Will not dare mention, lest a question rise
Whether he durst accept the offer or not,
And that he durst not plain enough appeared.
Much more affliction than already felt
They cannot well impose, nor I sustain;
If they intend advantage of my labors
The work of many hands, which earns my keeping   1260
With no small profit daily to my owners.
But come what will, my deadliest foe will prove
My speediest friend, by death to rid me hence,
The worst that he can give, to me the best.
Yet so it may fall out, because their end
Is hate, not help to me, it may with mine
Draw their own ruin who attempt the deed.
  Chor. Oh how comely it is and how reviving
To the spirits of just men long oppressed!
When God into the hands of their deliverer   1270
Puts invincible might
To quell the mighty of the earth, the oppressor,
The brute and boisterous force of violent men,
Hardy and industrious to support
Tyrannic power, but raging to pursue
The righteous and all such as honor truth;
He all their ammunition
And feats of war defeats
With plain heroic magnitude of mind
And celestial vigor armed,   1280
Their armories and magazines contemns,
Renders them useless, while

1265–67. Samson is given an intimation of what actually will happen.
A forward movement of the inner action of the drama is markedly felt at
this point. Samson is clear-headed and calm. The Chorus has been roused
to confidence by his defiance to Harapha. They are, however, still blind
to the possibility of a new triumph of Samson's strength.

With winged expedition
Swift as the lightning glance he executes
His errand on the wicked, who surprised
Lose their defence distracted and amazed.
    But patience is more oft the exercise
Of saints, the trial of their fortitude,
Making them each his own deliverer,
And victor over all   1290
That tyranny or fortune can inflict,
Either of these is in thy lot,
Samson, with might endued
Above the sons of men; but sight bereaved
May chance to number thee with those
Whom patience finally must crown.
    This Idol's day hath been to thee no day of rest,
Laboring thy mind
More than the working day thy hands,
And yet perhaps more trouble is behind.   1300
For I descry this way
Some other tending, in his hand
A scepter or quaint staff he bears,
Comes on amain, speed in his look.
By his habit I discern him now
A public officer, and now at hand.
His message will be short and voluble.
    Off. Ebrews, the prisoner Samson here I seek.
    Chor. His manacles remark him, there he sits.
    Off. Samson, to thee our lords thus bid me say;   1310
This day to Dagon is a solemn feast,
With sacrifices, triumph, pomp, and games;
Thy strength they know surpassing human rate,
And now some public proof thereof require
To honor this great feast, and great assembly;
Rise therefore with all speed and come along,
Where I will see thee heartened and fresh clad
To appear as fits before the illustrious lords.
    Sams. Thou know'st I am an Ebrew, therefore tell them,
Our law forbids at their religious rites   1320
My presence; for that cause I cannot come.
    Off. This answer, be assured, will not content them.
    Sams. Have they not sword-players, and every sort
Of gymnic artists, wrestlers, riders, runners,

1319 ff. Suspense is well managed in the following passage and a problem presented which heightens interest in the outcome, the mere facts of which are well known to the reader in advance. The quickness of the action in this crisis has been thoroughly prepared for.

Jugglers and dancers, antics, mummers, mimics,
But they must pick me out with shackles tired,
And over-labored at their public mill,
To make them sport with blind activity?
Do they not seek occasion of new quarrels
On my refusal to distress me more,   1330
Or make a game of my calamities?
Return the way thou camest, I will not come.
    Off. Regard thyself, this will offend them highly.
    Sams. Myself? my conscience, and internal peace.
Can they think me so broken, so debased
With corporal servitude, that my mind ever
Will condescend to such absurd commands?
Although their drudge, to be their fool or jester,
And in my midst of sorrow and heart-grief
To shew them feats and play before their god,   1340
The worst of all indignities, ye on me
Joined with extreme contempt? I will not come.
    Off. My message was imposed on me with speed,
Brooks no delay; is this thy resolution?
    Sams. So take it with what speed thy message needs.
    Off. I am sorry what this stoutness will produce.
    Sams. Perhaps thou shalt have cause to sorrow indeed.
    Chor. Consider, Samson; matters now are strained
Up to the height, whether to hold or break;
He's gone, and who knows how he may report   1350
Thy words by adding fuel to the flame?
Expect another message, more imperious,
More lordly thundering than thou well wilt bear.
    Sams. Shall I abuse this consecrated gift
Of strength, again returning with my hair
After my great transgressions, so requite
Favor renewed, and add a greater sin
By prostituting holy things to idols;
A Nazarite in place abominable
Vaunting my strength in honor to their Dagon?   1360
Besides, how vile, contemptible, ridiculous,
What act more execrably unclean, profane?
    Chor. Yet with this strength thou servest the Philistines,
Idolatrous, uncircumcised, unclean.
    Sams. Not in their idol-worship, but by labor
Honest and lawful to deserve my food
Of those who have me in their civil power.
    Chor. Where the heart joins not, outward acts defile not.
    Sams. Where outward force constrains, the sentence holds;
But who constrains me to the temple of Dagon,   1370

Not dragging? The Philistian lords command.
Commands are no constraints. If I obey them,
I do it freely; venturing to displease
God for the fear of man, and man prefer,
Set God behind; which in his jealousy
Shall never, unrepented, find forgiveness.
Yet that he may dispense with me or thee
Present in temples at idolatrous rites
For some important cause, thou need'st not doubt.
  Chor. How thou wilt here come off surmounts my reach. 1380
  Sams. Be of good courage, I begin to feel
Some rousing motions in me which dispose
To something extraordinary my thoughts.
I with this messenger will go along,
Nothing to do, be sure, that may dishonor
Our law, or stain my vow of Nazarite.
If there be aught of presage in the mind,
This day will be remarkable in my life
By some great act, or of my days the last.
  Chor. In time thou hast resolved, the man returns. 1390
  Off. Samson, this second message from our lords
To thee I am bid to say. Art thou our slave,
Our captive, at the public mill our drudge,
And darest thou at our sending and command
Dispute thy coming? Come without delay;
Or we shall find such engines to assail
And hamper thee, as thou shalt come of force,
Though thou wert firmlier fastened than a rock.
  Sams. I could be well content to try their art,
Which to no few of them would prove pernicious. 1400
Yet knowing their advantages too many,
Because they shall not trail me through their streets
Like a wild beast, I am content to go.
Masters' commands come with a power resistless
To such as owe them absolute subjection;
And for a life who will not change his purpose?
(So mutable are all the ways of men)
Yet this be sure, in nothing to comply
Scandalous or forbidden in our law.
  Off. I praise thy resolution, doff these links; 1410
By this compliance thou wilt win the lords
To favor, and perhaps to set thee free.
  Sams. Brethren farewell, your company along
I will not wish, lest it perhaps offend them
To see me girt with friends; and how the sight
Of me as of a common enemy,

So dreaded once, may now exasperate them
I know not. Lords are lordliest in their wine;
And the well-feasted priest then soonest fired
With zeal, if aught religion seem concerned; 1420
No less the people on their holy-days
Impetuous, insolent, unquenchable;
Happen what may, of me expect to hear
Nothing dishonorable, impure, unworthy
Our God, our law, my nation, or myself,
The last of me or no I cannot warrant.
   Chor. Go, and the Holy One
Of Israel be thy guide
To what may serve his glory best, and spread his name
Great among the heathen round; 1430
Send thee the Angel of thy birth, to stand
Fast by thy side, who from thy father's field
Rode up in flames after his message told
Of thy conception, and be now a shield
Of fire; that spirit that first rushed on thee
In the camp of Dan
Be efficacious in thee now at need.
For never was from Heaven imparted
Measure of strength so great to mortal seed,
As in thy wondrous actions hath been seen. 1440
But wherefore comes old Manoa in such haste
With youthful steps? Much livelier than erewhile
He seems: supposing here to find his son,
Or of him bringing to us some glad news?
   Man. Peace with you brethren; my inducement hither
Was not at present here to find my son,
By order of the lords new-parted hence
To come and play before them at their feast.
I heard all as I came, the city rings
And numbers thither flock, I had no will, 1450
Lest I should see him forced to things unseemly.
But that which moved my coming now, was chiefly
To give ye part with me what hope I have
With good success to work his liberty.

1441 ff. This unexpected interlude is a piece of dramatic invention
necessitated by the Greek convention of Milton's plot which requires the
catastrophe to take place off stage. We are waiting for news but our minds
are engaged by Manoa's false hopes. The first shout startles us with the
thought that Samson has done his deed and tension remains at a high
point until the great outcry which announces the massacre. That Manoa
and the Chorus go on building up their expectation of another outcome
produces an effect of irony as elaborate as anything in Greek drama.

Chor. That hope would much rejoice us to partake
With thee; say reverend sire, we thirst to hear.

Man. I have attempted one by one the lords
Either at home, or through the high street passing,
With supplication prone and father's tears
To accept of ransom for my son their prisoner.   1460
Some much averse I found and wondrous harsh,
Contemptuous, proud, set on revenge and spite;
That part most reverenced Dagon and his priests,
Others more moderate seeming, but their aim
Private reward, for which both God and State
They easily would set to sale, a third
More generous far and civil, who confessed
They had enough revenged, having reduced
Their foe to misery beneath their fears,
The rest was magnanimity to remit,   1470
If some convenient ransom were proposed.
What noise or shout was that? It tore the sky.

Chor. Doubtless the people shouting to behold
Their once great dread, captive, and blind before them,
Or at some proof of strength before them shewn.

Man. His ransom, if my whole inheritance
May compass it, shall willingly be paid
And numbered down; much rather I shall choose
To live the poorest in my tribe, than richest,
And he in that calamitous prison left.   1480
No, I am fixed not to part hence without him.
For his redemption all my patrimony,
If need be, I am ready to forgo
And quit; not wanting him, I shall want nothing.

Chor. Fathers are wont to lay up for their sons,
Thou for thy son art bent to lay out all;
Sons wont to nurse their parents in old age,
Thou in old age car'st how to nurse thy son
Made older than thy age through eye-sight lost.

Man. It shall be my delight to tend his eyes,   1490
And view him sitting in his house, ennobled
With all those high exploits by him achieved,
And on his shoulders waving down those locks
That of a nation armed the strength contained.
And I persuade me God had not permitted
His strength again to grow up with his hair
Garrisoned round about him like a camp
Of faithful soldiery, were not his purpose

1470. **The rest,** etc. What remained of punishment due him it would
be magnanimous to remit.

To use him further yet in some great service,
Not to sit idle with so great a gift 1500
Useless, and thence ridiculous about him.
And since his strength with eye-sight was not lost,
God will restore him eye-sight to his strength.
  Chor. Thy hopes are not ill-founded nor seem vain
Of his delivery, and thy joy thereon
Conceived, agreeable to a father's love,
In both which we, as next participate.
  Man. I know your friendly minds and—O what noise!
Mercy of Heaven what hideous noise was that!
Horribly loud unlike the former shout. 1510
  Chor. Noise call you it or universal groan
As if the whole inhabitation perished,
Blood, death, and deathful deeds are in that noise,
Ruin, destruction at the utmost point.
  Man. Of ruin indeed methought I heard the noise,
Oh it continues, they have slain my son.
  Chor. Thy son is rather slaying them, that outcry
From slaughter of one foe could not ascend.
  Man. Some dismal accident it needs must be;
What shall we do, stay here or run and see? 1520
  Chor. Best keep together here, lest running thither
We unawares run into danger's mouth.
This evil on the Philistines is fallen,
From whom could else a general cry be heard?
The sufferers then will scarce molest us here,
From other hands we need not much to fear.
What if his eye-sight (for to Israel's God
Nothing is hard) by miracle restored,
He now be dealing dole among his foes,
And over heaps of slaughtered walk his way? 1530
  Man. That were a joy presumptuous to be thought.
  Chor. Yet God hath wrought things as incredible
For his people of old; what hinders now?
  Man. He can I know, but doubt to think he will;
Yet hope would fain subscribe, and tempts belief.
A little stay will bring some notice hither.
  Chor. Of good or bad so great, of bad the sooner;

1530. The Chorus is still in error as to what has happened. Dramatic
attention is centered on the reversal of Manoa's hope. With the assurance
given him that his son's death is not to be construed as suicide (lines 1584–
89) the tension ends and we are ready to hear the messenger's circumstan-
tial narrative. This in turn rises to a climax and occasions a choric song of
triumph (lines 1660 ff.). The father gives the "fair dismission" of Samson
and pronounces on the values of his career. The final Chorus generalizes
the spiritual effect of this great event on those who have been its witnesses.

For evil news rides post, while good news baits.
And to our wish I see one hither speeding,
An Ebrew, as I guess, and of our tribe.   1540
    Messenger. O whither shall I run, or which way fly
The sight of this so horrid spectacle
Which erst my eyes beheld and yet behold;
For dire imagination still pursues me.
But providence or instinct of nature seems,
Or reason though disturbed, and scarce consulted
To have guided me aright, I know not how,
To thee first, reverend Manoa, and to these
My countrymen, whom here I knew remaining,
As at some distance from the place of horror,   1550
So in the sad event too much concerned.
    Man. The accident was loud, and here before thee
With rueful cry, yet what it was we hear not,
No preface needs, thou seest we long to know.
    Mess. It would burst forth, but I recover breath
And sense distract, to know well what I utter.
    Man. Tell us the sum, the circumstance defer.
    Mess. Gaza yet stands, but all her sons are fallen,
All in a moment overwhelmed and fallen.
    Man. Sad, but thou know'st to Israelites not saddest   1560
The desolation of a hostile city.
    Mess. Feed on that first, there may in grief be surfeit.
    Man. Relate by whom.
    Mess.   By Samson.
    Man.   That still lessens
The sorrow, and converts it nigh to joy.
    Mess. Ah, Manoa I refrain, too suddenly
To utter what will come at last too soon;
Lest evil tidings with too rude irruption
Hitting thy aged ear, should pierce too deep.
    Man. Suspense in news is torture, speak them out.
    Mess. Then take the worst in brief, Samson is dead.   1570
    Man. The worst indeed, O all my hope's defeated
To free him hence! but Death who sets all free
Hath paid his ransom now and full discharge.
What windy joy this day had I conceived
Hopeful of his delivery, which now proves
Abortive as the first-born bloom of spring
Nipt with the lagging rear of winter's frost.
Yet ere I give the reins to grief, say first,
How died he? death to life is crown or shame.
All by him fell thou say'st, by whom fell he,   1580
What glorious hand gave Samson his death's wound?

Mess. Unwounded of his enemies he fell.
Man. Wearied with slaughter then or how? explain.
Mess. By his own hands.
Man.   Self-violence? What cause
Brought him so soon at variance with himself
Among his foes?
Mess.   Inevitable cause
At once both to destroy and be destroyed;
The edifice where all were met to see him
Upon their heads and on his own he pulled.
Man. O lastly over-strong against thyself!   1590
A dreadful way thou took'st to thy revenge.
More than enough we know; but while things yet
Are in confusion, give us if thou canst,
Eye-witness of what first or last was done,
Relation more particular and distinct.
Mess. Occasions drew me early to this city,
And as the gates I entered with sun-rise,
The morning trumpets festival proclaimed
Through each high street. Little I had despatched
When all abroad was rumored that this day   1600
Samson should be brought forth to shew the people
Proof of his mighty strength in feats and games;
I sorrowed at his captive state, but minded
Not to be absent at that spectacle.
The building was a spacious theater
Half round on two main pillars vaulted high,
With seats where all the lords and each degree
Of sort, might sit in order to behold,
The other side was open, where the throng
On banks and scaffolds under sky might stand;   1610
I among these aloof obscurely stood.
The feast and noon grew high, and sacrifice
Had filled their hearts with mirth, high cheer, and wine,
When to their sports they turned. Immediately
Was Samson as a public servant brought,
In their state livery clad; before him pipes
And timbrels, on each side went armèd guards,
Both horse and foot before him and behind
Archers, and slingers, cataphracts and spears.
At sight of him the people with a shout   1620
Rifted the air clamoring their god with praise,
Who had made their dreadful enemy their thrall.
He patient but undaunted where they led him,
Came to the place, and what was set before him
Which without help of eye, might be assayed,

To heave, pull, draw, or break, he still performed
All with incredible, stupendous force,
None daring to appear antagonist.
At length for intermission sake they led him
Between the pillars; he his guide requested   1630
(For so from such as nearer stood we heard)
As over-tired to let him lean a while
With both his arms on those two massy pillars
That to the arched roof gave main support.
He unsuspicious led him; which when Samson
Felt in his arms, with head a while inclined,
And eyes fast fixed he stood, as one who prayed,
Or some great matter in his mind revolved.
At last with head erect thus cried aloud,
"Hitherto, Lords, what your commands imposed   1640
I have performed, as reason was, obeying,
Not without wonder or delight beheld.
Now of my own accord such other trial
I mean to show you of my strength, yet greater;
As with amaze shall strike all who behold."
This uttered, straining all his nerves he bowed;
As with the force of winds and waters pent
When mountains tremble, those two massy pillars
With horrible convulsion to and fro
He tugged, he shook, till down they came and drew   1650
The whole roof after them, with burst of thunder
Upon the heads of all who sat beneath,
Lords, ladies, captains, counsellors, or priests,
Their choice nobility and flower, not only
Of this but each Philistian city round
Met from all parts to solemnize this feast.
Samson with these immixed, inevitably
Pulled down the same destruction on himself;
The vulgar only scaped, who stood without.

    Chor. O dearly-bought revenge, yet glorious!   1660
Living or dying thou hast fulfilled
The work for which thou wast foretold
To Israel, and now liest victorious
Among thy slain self-killed
Not willingly, but tangled in the fold,
Of dire necessity, whose law in death conjoined
Thee with thy slaughtered foes, in number more
Than all thy life had slain before.

    Semichor. While their hearts were jocund and sublime,
Drunk with idolatry, drunk with wine,   1670
And fat regorged of bulls and goats,

Chanting their idol, and preferring
Before our living Dread who dwells
In Silo his bright sanctuary,
Among them he a spirit of phrenzy sent,
Who hurt their minds,
And urged them on with mad desire
To call in haste for their destroyer;
They only set on sport and play
Unweetingly importuned   1680
Their own destruction to come speedy upon them.
So fond are mortal men
Fallen into wrath divine,
As their own ruin on themselves to invite,
Insensate left, or to sense reprobate,
And with blindness internal struck.
    Semichor. But he though blind of sight,
Despised and thought extinguished quite,
With inward eyes illuminated
His fiery virtue roused   1690
From under ashes into sudden flame,
And as an evening dragon came,
Assailant on the perchèd roosts,
And nests in order ranged
Of tame villatic fowl; but as an eagle
His cloudless thunder bolted on their heads.
So virtue, given for lost,
Depressed, and overthrown, as seemed,
Like that self-begotten bird
In the Arabian woods embost,   1700
That no second knows nor third,
And lay erewhile a holocaust,
From out her ashy womb now teemed,
Revives, reflourishes, then vigorous most
When most unactive deemed,

    1675. a spirit of phrenzy. This is an application of the ancient formula of the "madness of the gods." Impious pride incenses the gods to punish men by making them authors of their own destruction. Shakespeare in *Julius Caesar* and in *Antony and Cleopatra* illustrates the impairment of judgment which precedes the hero's fall but without Milton's technically accurate use of terms. The thesis was earlier applied to Samson himself.
    1692 ff. The outburst of similes, occurring uniquely here to enhance the climactic episode, reminds us of the similar indulgence in the relatively bare text of *Paradise Regained* at the moment of Satan's downfall (lines 568 ff. in Book IV).
    1699. that self-begotten bird, the phoenix, which renewed itself out of its own funeral pyre once every five hundred years.
    1700. embost, imbosked, concealed in a wood.

And though her body die, her fame survives,
A secular bird, ages of lives.
    Man. Come, come, no time for lamentation now,
Nor much more cause, Samson hath quit himself
Like Samson, and heroicly hath finished   1710
A life heroic, on his enemies
Fully revenged, hath left them years of mourning,
And lamentation to the sons of Caphtor
Through all Philistian bounds. To Israel
Honor hath left, and freedom, let but them
Find courage to lay hold on this occasion,
To himself and father's house eternal fame;
And which is best and happiest yet, all this
With God not parted from him, as was feared,
But favoring and assisting to the end.   1720
Nothing is here for tears, nothing to wail
Or knock the breast, no weakness, no contempt,
Dispraise, or blame, nothing but well and fair,
And what may quiet us in a death so noble.
Let us go find the body where it lies
Soaked in his enemies' blood, and from the stream
With lavers pure and cleansing herbs wash off
The clotted gore. I with what speed the while
(Gaza is not in plight to say us nay)
Will send for all my kindred, all my friends   1730
To fetch him hence and solemnly attend
With silent obsequy and funeral train
Home to his father's house: there will I build him
A monument, and plant it round with shade
Of laurel ever green, and branching palm,
With all his trophies hung, and acts enrolled
In copious legend, or sweet lyric song.
Thither shall all the valiant youth resort,
And from his memory inflame their breasts
To matchless valor and adventures high;   1740
The virgins also shall on feastful days
Visit his tomb with flowers, only bewailing
His lot unfortunate in nuptial choice,
From whence captivity and loss of eyes.

    1719. With God not parted from him as was feared. This doubt and
its resolution are evidently important in the meaning of the drama. It has
lingered in Manoa's mind after Samson's recovery from his "sense of
Heaven's desertion," and underlies his distress at the thought of suicide, a
mortal sin. He does not at once accept the messenger's comment in lines
1586–89, but when the explanation is repeated (lines 1657–58) and the
Chorus amplifies it he finds in the manner of his son's death "no weakness,
no contempt."

Chor. All is best, though we oft doubt,
What the unsearchable dispose
Of highest wisdom brings about,
And ever best found in the close.
Oft he seems to hide his face,
But unexpectedly returns   1750
And to his faithful champion hath in place
Bore witness gloriously; whence Gaza mourns
And all that band them to resist
His uncontrollable intent,
His servants he with new acquist
Of true experience from this great event
With peace and consolation hath dismissed,
And calm of mind all passion spent.

1745-50. These lines are reminiscent of the sentiment expressed at the close of several Euripidean plays: "The gods bring many unhoped for things to pass, and what men expect they do not fulfill. So it is with this marvellous event." But Milton's God is Providence and his disposition of the fates of men is always just.

APPENDIX

APPENDIX

STUDY TOPICS

The Psalm Paraphrases. Compare these verses with the translations in the Authorized Version. Why do they seem inferior?

The Latin and Italian Poems. The merits of Cowper's translations may be tested by comparison with any of the prose versions. The best is perhaps that of William Vaughn Moody, as revised by Rand, in the Cambridge Edition (edited by Fletcher). Read a few of Ovid's elegies in the *Amores*, of Virgil's Eclogues, and of Horace's Epistles as representing Milton's classical models. Also read some of Petrarch's sonnets. Is there anything individual in Milton's imitations? What is his attitude toward love and women in these poems?

"At a Vacation Exercise." Who are the "late fantastics," some group locally known at Cambridge or one of the London coteries? Read some of George Herbert's poems and say what characteristics of style Milton might have been resolving not to imitate. Read the song of Demodocus in Book VIII of the *Odyssey*.

"On the Death of a Fair Infant." Study the stanza form of Phineas Fletcher's *Eliza* as a possible model for this poem. What expressions suggest the imagery of the Jacobean masque? Compare Milton's use of metaphor and poetical wit with that of the metaphysicals. See Brooks, "Milton and the New Criticism," *Sewanee Review*, LIX (1951), 1 ff.

"On the Morning of Christ's Nativity." Compare the spirit of the poem with that of the Christmas carols and the mystery plays. Why does Milton introduce the passage about the pagan deities? Study Elegy VI as evidence of the spirit in which Milton undertook the writing of the ode. Read for comparison the nativity odes by Crashaw and Jonson; how does Milton's ode differ? What significance is there in the conception of Christ as Pan and as Hercules? Professor Tillyard describes this ode as of wholly un-Miltonic inspiration; even though you may not as yet have read Milton's later works in detail, can you select passages and stanzas which seem "un-Miltonic"? The present editor believes that some passages are truly "Miltonic." Can you find such passages?

"The Passion." What are the evidences of Milton's difficulty with this poem?

"Upon the Circumcision." Read the service for the Circumcision of Christ in the Episcopal Prayer Book (January 1). What is meant by "true circumcision of the spirit"? Is this the theme of Milton's poem? Why is the subject more manageable than that of "The Passion"? "In this case, because God is more nearly alive, still on the stage of Earth and Air, the poet need not resort to the pathetic fallacy" (Brooks).

"On Time, At a Solemn Music." What is the effect of the short lines, of the complex rhyme? Compare the metrical scheme of "Lycidas." The "individual kiss," the "undisturbed song," are regularly present in Milton's descriptions of the heavenly ecstasy in his early poems. Compare the various examples. "Happy-making sight" is English for "vision beatific," which suggests Dante's *Paradiso*. Light and music are united in the last line of "At a Solemn Music." Trace this imagery also through the early poems, Latin and English.

"An Epitaph on the Marchioness of Winchester." William Browne, Ben Jonson, and others use this meter, sometimes for elegy. What is its effect and what kind of style goes with it, as compared with "The Nativity," etc.? The scene from line 60 on should be compared with Dante's celestial rose. Read *Paradiso* XXXIII.

"On Shakespeare." Compare the allusion to Shakespeare in "L'Allegro." What does Milton most value in Shakespeare? Is there any implied reservation in his praise? Compare his point of view with that of Ben Jonson.

"L'Allegro" and "Il Penseroso." Draw up schemes for the two poems to show their parallelism in detail. What do you think of the idea that "Il Penseroso" more truly represents Milton himself than "L'Allegro"? Compare the record of Milton's interests and occupations in these poems with that in *Elegy I*. What characteristic Miltonic interests are omitted? Comment on Johnson's statement: "No mirth can, indeed, be found in his melancholy; but I am afraid I always meet some melancholy in his mirth." On Tillyard's idea that the poems imply an academic audience and are to be looked at as a rhetorical debate. On Brooks's thesis that the sense of unity in variety would have been lost if Milton had been content with a mere contrast in the two poems, and that the "Mountain Nymph, sweet Liberty," and the "Cherub Contemplation" tend to merge into the same figure.

Arcades. How successful is Milton in striking a balance between adaptation to the requirements of the social situation and his own artistic purposes? Compare *Comus* in this respect. Read the vision of Er in Plato's *Republic*, Book X. How direct is Milton's use of the passage? Are there any figures in Shakespeare kindred to the Genius of the Wood? Compare the lyrics with those in the Elizabethan song books, e.g. Campion.

Comus. Compare *Comus* with the Jonsonian masque it most resembles, *Pleasure Reconciled to Virtue*, and with Fletcher's pastoral drama, *The Faithful Shepherdess*. Which model is Milton following more closely? What are the essential points of difference from either? Lines 779–806 and lines 999–1011 were added by Milton to the original version when *Comus* was printed in 1637. What is the significance of these additions? After trying to figure this out for yourself read Tillyard's explanation (*The Miltonic Setting*, pp. 82 ff.). What is there to support the supposition that the Elder Brother is Milton's spokesman in the play? Is the Platonic doctrine of love (in the *Symposium*), as interpreted, for example, in Spenser's "Four hymns," relevant to Milton's doctrine? What part is played in his meaning by the Christian idea of Grace? (See the elaborate discussion by Woodhouse, "The Argument of *Comus*," *The University of Toronto Quarterly*, XI (1941), 46–71.)

"Lycidas." This poem is a happy hunting ground for speculation on the relation of the poet personally to the work of his imagination. Is Milton's grief real or assumed? To what extent does Milton identify himself with Edward King and express in the poem his own ideals, aspirations, fears, and hopes? Is the pastoral singer, the "uncouth swain," Milton or a dramatic *persona*? Are Shelley's "Adonais" and Arnold's "Thyrsis" more "detached" than "Lycidas." (See Ransom, "A Poem Nearly Anonymous" in *The World's Body* for acute discussion of these problems.) Study the pastoral tradition which Milton used: in Theocritus *Idyl* 2; Moschus "Lament for Bion; Virgil Eclogues 5 and 10; Spenser, *Shephearde's Calender,* November. Does Milton use the stock devices more completely in this poem or in his own "Lament for Damon"? Study the metrical pattern of "Lycidas" in comparison with that of Spenser's "Epithalamium." What is the effect of the greater license in stanza form and of the unrhymed lines? Read Ruskin's comment on "Lycidas" in *Of King's Gardens* and try to carry the analysis of Milton's language and imagery further. Describe the progression of idea. What preparation is there for the change from grief to joy? What do you think of Ranson's comment that "Peter sounds like another Puritan zealot, and less than apostolic." Compare *Paradiso* XXVII, 10–27.

The Sonnets. Read Wordsworth's early sonnets and compare them in substance and form with Milton's. Look for Elizabethan sonnets on themes other than love and compare them with Milton's. Milton's close relation to the Italian tradition of sonnet writing may be studied in John Smart, *The Sonnets of Milton*, 1921. What use is made in the sonnets of literary and historical allusion? What ranges of interest, mood, and temperament do the Sonnets represent? What do you think of Samuel Johnson's judgment of the Sonnets in his *Life of Milton*: "of the best it can only be said that they are not bad." Which are the best? Johnson says the eighth ("Captain or Colonel") and the twenty-first ("Cyriack, whose grandsire"), a strange choice.

Paradise Lost. What is the theme of the poem? Who is the hero? What makes the poem an epic? What are the dramatic elements? In what structural features does it follow classical epic?

MILTON'S SATAN. What material did Milton find in the Bible for his representation of Satan? (Use a concordance and locate all the texts referring to "Satan," the Devil, Lucifer, etc.) Compare Milton's

Satan with Goethe's in the first part of *Faust*. Compare him with popular representations of the Devil, as for example in Robert Burns's "Address to the Deil." Compare him with the figure of Lucifer in Byron's *Cain*. Compare him with Shakespeare's Iago in *Othello*.

What is Satan's motive for rebellion? What does he expect to gain by corrupting Adam? Consider Satan and Christ as opposites. What does each represent philosophically? How is the contrast between their natures and acts worked out in the poem? Trace the degeneration of Satan in personal appearance and in character from his first state as a rebel leader to his metamorphosis into a snake.

MILTON'S ADAM. Does Adam play a merely passive role in the poem? Is he an individual as well as a prototype of man? What are his strengths and weaknesses? Does Milton convince us that he is a free agent? Does Milton seem to view him with detachment? Where does he lose and where gain our sympathy?

MILTON'S EVE. What is Eve's attitude toward Adam in her state of innocence? Does she exhibit any of the weaknesses which lead to her fall? Is she in the right in insisting on working apart from Adam? By appealing to what elements in her make-up does Satan succeed in getting her to eat the apple? What are the immediate effects of sin on her personality and reasoning powers? Does she anywhere command our sympathy and admiration after the Fall? Compare the arguments of Eve in Book IX, especially lines 321–40, with the ideas expressed by Milton in *Areopagitica*. Milton's attitude toward Eve is an open revelation of his own hopes and fears; what is the detailed autobiographic background which helps to explain, for instance, lines 867–908 in Book X?

MILTON'S ANGELS. What is their nature and function? What angelic traits do the fallen spirits retain? What do they lose? How do Raphael and Michael differ? Comment on Abdiel as a symbol of Milton's personal ideal of loyalty. Where else in the poetry and prose and in Milton's life record is this ideal expressed?

MILTON'S PARADISE. A fairly exact diagram can be made of Eden and Paradise from the description in Book IV. Try both a map and a cross-section. What features in Milton's account are conventional? (Look up the names of gardens mentioned by Milton in Osgood's *Classical Dictionary of Milton* and in Gilbert's *Geographical Dictionary*.) Compare in detail the garden of Adonis in Spenser's *Faerie Queene*, Book III.

MILTON'S SYSTEM OF THE UNIVERSE. Make a diagram showing the relative positions of the earth, sun, moon, planets, and fixed stars in Milton's scheme. Where is Heaven? Hell? (Data can be found in Books II, III, V, VI of *Paradise Lost*.) What precisely does Milton say of the relative merits of the Copernican and the Ptolemaic hypotheses at the beginning of Book VIII? Why do you think he used the Ptolemaic in the poem?

MILTON'S BLANK VERSE. Select from the first hundred lines of *Paradise Lost* the five which seem most regular and mark the accents and pauses. Compare with these the lines which seem most irregular. Wherein do the "irregularities" seem to lie? Find passages in which the sound seems particularly appropriate to the sense. Masson speaks of Milton's "blank verse paragraphs." What does this mean? Compare his verse with Marlowe's, Shakespeare's in both his earlier and later periods, and Wordsworth's. Are the choruses of *Samson Agonistes* "free verse"? Confining yourself to Book I of *Paradise Lost* select passages to illustrate the various characteristics of Milton's style.

Paradise Regained. Would you say that *Paradise Regained* is the sequel of *Paradise Lost?* in what way? What triumphs in *Paradise Lost?* in *Paradise Regained?* Are there any echoes here of attitude or philosophy expressed in his earlier poems, *Comus*, for example? What experiences of Milton help to explain lines 50–59, Book III? Refer to lines 321–34, Book IV; then read *Of Education.* Do you think Milton's system of education would have prevented such errors as he mentions?

SATAN. How does the Satan of *Paradise Regained* differ from the Satan of *Paradise Lost?* To what extent does Milton put his own thoughts in the mouth of Satan; that is, are the objects which he presents as temptations such as actually tempted Milton?

CHRIST. Compare the moral Christ of *Paradise Regained* with the theological Christ of *Paradise Lost.* Is either one the Christ of scripture? Is the Christ the same symbol here as in the Nativity ode? To what extent does Milton identify himself with Christ?

Samson Agonistes. How does the play differ structurally from a Shakespearean drama? Is it deficient in incident? ("Nothing passes between the first act and the last that either hastens or delays the death of Samson." Johnson) What is the function of each of the episodes? Toward what goal is the drama moving? Find all the points of similarity you can between *Samson* and Sophocles' *Oedipus at Colonus*, the Greek play which most resembles it. In what ways does Milton make the biblical Samson over into a Greek tragic hero? What is the function of the Chorus? Is the use of the messenger effective? Are Dalila's motives in going to Samson clear? What use does Milton make of irony? of hybris? of the idea of catharsis? Are there comic elements in the drama? Does it come short of Shakespeare in tragic effect? Does *Samson Agonistes*, like *Paradise Lost*, "justify the ways of God to man"? What is the degree of Milton's personal detachment from this poem? Point out all the parallels between Milton's situation after the Restoration and Samson's in bondage to the Philistines. Compare the passages in which Milton seems to be expressing his own emotions in *Samson* with similar passages in the sonnets and *Paradise Lost.* What differences are there between the personal and the dramatic utterances? Students who care to explore the full relationship between *Samson Agonistes* and Greek drama will find a detailed guide in W. R. Parker's *Milton's Debt to Greek Tragedy in Samson Agonistes.*

THE IDEA OF FAME. Locate all the passages in the poetry and prose which speak of fame, ambition, renown, etc., and define Milton's attitude. Compare Shakespeare's Sonnets and read the chapter on the Renaissance love of fame in Burckhardt's *Civilization in Italy in the Renaissance.*

MILTON'S HERESIES. Read the statements about predestination in Book III of *Paradise Lost* and compare the discussion in Milton's prose work *Of Christian Doctrine.* Then read the article on the same subject in the *Cyclopedia of Religious Knowledge.* The ambitious student will carry the investigation to Calvin's *Institutes* and perhaps consult some minister interested in theological subtleties. Study also the problem of the nature of Christ. *Of Christian Doctrine* contains a clear statement of Milton's non-trinitarian position. Is this in harmony with the teaching of *Paradise Lost?* Find passages to illustrate Milton's view. Is Milton's statement on free will in *Paradise Lost,* Book V, lines 235–37, a heresy? In what way? Is his idea of the relation of matter and spirit a heresy? Is it proper to call him a pantheist?

MILTON'S INTEREST IN NATURE. Compare Milton's representation of Nature with Wordsworth's or Shelley's or Tennyson's. What classes of objects is he most interested in? Do his descriptions show minute observation or are they bookish? How far does scientific interest enter into his account of the physical world?

MILTON'S USE OF CLASSICAL MYTHOLOGY. Take a standard book on mythology like Bullfinch's *Age of Fable* and see how many of the major myths can be illustrated by allusions in Milton's poems. For what artistic purposes does Milton allude to these stories? Has he any favorite myths? What comparisons does he draw between pagan and biblical stories?

MILTON'S BLINDNESS. Locate all the references in the poems, including Samson's laments for his loss of sight, which are, in a sense, Milton's own. What are the deprivations and what the compensations of his affliction? Can you suggest any possible effects of blindness on the quality of his imagination in *Paradise Lost?*

SOME CRITICAL DICTA. What are the meaning and validity of each of the following pronouncements?
In studying *Paradise Lost* we come to perceive that the verse is continuously animated by the departure from, and return to, the regular measure (Eliot).
Milton is the great standard in the use of counterpoint. . . . The choruses in *Samson Agonistes* are counterpointed throughout; that is, each line (or nearly so) has two different coexisting scansions (Hopkins).
If this host of readers [those who know no Greek or Latin] are to gain any sense of the power and charm of the great poets of antiquity,

their way to gain it is not through translations of the ancients but through the original poetry of Milton (Arnold).

We must, then, in reading *Paradise Lost* not expect to see clearly; our sense of sight must be blurred, so that our hearing may become more acute. . . . The emphasis is on the sound, not the vision, upon the word, not the idea (Eliot).

He did not think into the human heart, as Wordsworth has done (Keats).

The whole poem of *Paradise Lost* is vitiated by a kind of antinomy, by the conjoint necessity and impossibility of taking its contents literally (Sherer).

Are not all men fortified by the bravery, the purity, the temperance, the toil, the independence, and the angelic devotion of this man, who, in a revolutionary age, taking counsel only of himself, endeavored, in his writing and his life, to carry out the life of man to new heights of spiritual grace and dignity, without any abatement of its strength (Emerson).

He was not a Puritan. He was not a free thinker. He was not a Royalist. In his character the noblest qualities of every party were combined in harmonious union (Macaulay).

Milton may be called the last great exponent of Christian humanism in its historical continuity, the tradition of classical reason fused with Christian faith which had been the main line of European development (Bush).

BIBLIOGRAPHY

(For a fuller list see David H. Stevens, *A Reference Guide to Milton from 1800 to the Present Day*, Chicago, 1930; the bibliographies in the most recent editions; studies and biographies noted below.)

EDITIONS

TODD, H. J. *The Poetical Works of Milton.* 2d ed. 7 vols. London, 1809.

VERITY, A. W. *Arcades* and *Comus, Ode on the Morning of Christ's Nativity*, etc.; *L'Allegro, Il Penseroso, Lycidas, Paradise Lost, Samson Agonistes.* Edited by A. W. Verity. Cambridge, 11 vols. "Pitt Press Series." 1891–1912. Revised edition of *Paradise Lost* in one volume, 1910.

HUGHES, M. Y. *Paradise Lost.* New York, 1935.

HUGHES, M. Y. *Paradise Regained, the Minor Poems and Samson Agonistes.* New York, 1937.

PATTERSON, F. A. *The Works of Milton.* 23 vols. (The Columbia Edition.) New York, 1931–40.

FLETCHER, H. F. *John Milton's Complete Poetical Works Reproduced in Photographic Facsimile.* Cambridge, 1943.

WOLFE, DON M. and others. *Milton's Prose Works* (The Yale Edition.) In preparation.

BROOKS, CLEANTH, and HARDY, JOHN E. *Poems of Mr. John Milton. The 1645 Edition with Essays in Analysis.* New York, 1951.

LEXICONS, HANDBOOKS, ETC.

BRADSHAW, JOHN. *A Concordance to the Poetical Works of John Milton.* London, 1894.

COOPER, LANE. *A Concordance to the Greek, Latin, and Italian Poems of John Milton.* Halle, 1923.

GILBERT, ALLAN H. *A Geographical Dictionary of Milton* (Cornell Studies in English.) New Haven, Yale Press, 1919.

HANFORD, J. H. *A Milton Handbook.* Fourth Edition. New York, Crofts, 1946.

LOCKWOOD, LAURA. *Lexicon to the English Poetical Works of John Milton.* New York, 1907.

OSGOOD, C. G. *The Classical Mythology of Milton's English Poems.* New York, 1900. Reprinted, Oxford, 1925.

BIOGRAPHIES

DARBISHIRE, HELEN. *The Early Lives of Milton.* London, 1932.
BELLOC, HILAIRE. *Milton.* Philadelphia, 1935.
FRENCH, J. M. *Life Records of John Milton.* 2 vols., others in preparation. New Brunswick, 1949–   .
HANFORD, J. H. *John Milton, Englishman.* New York, 1949.
MASSON, DAVID. *The Life of Milton.* London. 6 vols., Index, 1859–94.
PATTISON, MARK. *Milton.* ("English Men of Letters"). London, 1879.
RALEIGH, W. A. *Milton.* London, 1900.
SAURAT, DENIS. *Milton, Man and Thinker.* New York, 1925.
TILLYARD, E. M. W. *Milton.* New York, 1930.

OTHER BOOKS PUBLISHED SINCE 1940

(No attempt is here made to select from the vast scholarly literature about Milton which has appeared recently in periodical form. The following complete volumes will serve to represent the direction of study and to guide the reader to the entire corpus both of older and of current investigation.)

BANKS, T. H. *Milton's Imagery.* New York, 1950.
BARKER, ARTHUR. *Milton and the Puritan Dilemma.* Toronto, 1942.
BUSH, DOUGLAS. *Paradise Lost in Our Time.* Ithaca, 1945.
CAWLEY, ROBERT R. *Milton's Literary Craftsmanship. A Study of a Brief History of Muscovia.* Princeton, 1941.
CAWLEY, ROBERT R. *Milton and the Literature of Travel.* Princeton, 1951.
CLARK, D. L. *John Milton at St. Paul's School. A Study of the Ancient Rhetoric in English Literature.* New York, 1948.
CONKLIN, G. H. *Biblical Criticism and Heresy in Milton.* New York, 1949.
CORCORAN, SISTER MARY I. *Milton's Paradise with Reference to the Hexameral Background.* Washington, 1945.
DIEKHOFF, JOHN S. *Milton's Paradise Lost. A Commentary on the Argument.* New York, 1946.
DORIAN, DONALD C. *The English Diodatis.* New Brunswick, 1950.
GILBERT, ALLAN H. *On the Composition of Paradise Lost.* Chapel Hill, 1947.
HAMILTON, G. R. *Hero or Fool? A Study of Milton's Satan.* London, 1944.
HARDING, DAVIS P. *Milton and the Renaissance Ovid.* Urbana, 1946.
JOCHUMS, M. C., ed. *An Apology, etc.* Urbana, 1951.
KELLEY, MAURICE. *This Great Argument. A Study of Milton's De Doctrina Christiana.* Princeton, 1941.
KNIGHT, G. WILSON. *Chariot of Wrath: the Message of John Milton to Democracy at War.* London, 1942.
KROUSE, MICHAEL. *Milton's Samson and the Christian Tradition.* Princeton, 1949.

LEWIS, C. S. *A Preface to Paradise Lost.* Oxford, 1942.

McCOLLEY, GRANT. *Paradise Lost. An Account of Its Growth and Major Origins.* Chicago, 1940.

MOHL, RUTH. *Studies in Spenser, Milton and the Theory of Monarchy.* New York, 1950.

PARKER, W. R. *Milton's Contemporary Reputation.* Columbus, 1940.

POMMER, H. F. *Milton and Melville.* Pittsburgh, 1950.

RAJAN, B. *Paradise Lost and the Seventeenth Century Reader.* London, 1947.

ROSS, MALCOLM M. *Milton's Royalism. A Study of the Conflict of Symbol and Idea in the Poems.* Ithaca, 1943.

SAMUEL, IRENE. *Plato and Milton.* Ithaca, 1947.

SENSABAUGH, GEORGE F. *That Grand Whig Milton.* Stanford, 1952.

SMITH, LOGAN P. *Milton and His Modern Critics.* Boston, 1941.

THORPE, JAMES, ed. *Milton Criticism. Selections from Four Centuries.* New York, 1950.

TILLYARD, E. M. W. *Studies in Milton.* New York, 1951.

WALDOCK, A. J. A. *Paradise Lost and Its Critics.* New York, 1947.

WERBLOWSKY, R. J. Z. *Lucifer and Prometheus: a Study of Milton's Satan.* London, 1952.

WOLFE, D. M. *Milton in the Puritan Revolution.* New York, 1941.

INDEX OF TITLES AND FIRST LINES